THE NATIONAL
GEOGRAPHIC TRAVELER
CANADA

THE NATIONAL
GEOGRAPHIC TRAVELER

CANADA

Michael Ivory

Contents

How to use this guide 6–7 About the author 8
The Regions 53–338 Travelwise 339–89
Index 390–97 Credits 398–99

**Page 1: Totem, Museum of
Anthropology, Vancouver,
British Columbia
Pages 2–3: Canoeing on
Lake Louise, Alberta
Left: Polar bear, Churchill,
Manitoba**

How to use this guide

See back flap for keys to text and map symbols

The *National Geographic Traveler* brings you the best of Canada in text, pictures, and maps. Divided into three main sections, the guide begins with an overview of history and culture. Following are eight regional chapters with sites selected by the author for their particular interest and treated in depth. Each chapter opens with its own contents list for easy reference.

The regions and sites within the regions are arranged geographically, by province and by proximity. A map introduces each region, highlighting the featured sites. Walks and drives, all plotted on their own

maps, suggest routes for discovering an area. Features and sidebars offer detail on history, culture, or contemporary life. A More Places to Visit page rounds off the regional chapters.

The final section, Travelwise, lists essential information for the traveler—pre-trip planning, getting around, communications, money matters, and emergencies—plus a selection of hotels, restaurants, shops, entertainment, and activities.

To the best of our knowledge, site information is accurate as of the press date. However, it's always advisable to call ahead.

National Historic Sites Many of the attractions in this guide are National Historic Sites. Due to space restrictions this has sometimes been abbreviated to NHS.

Color coding

Each region is color coded for easy reference. Find the region you want on the map on the front flap, and look for the color flash at the top of the pages of the relevant chapter. Information in **Travelwise** is also color coded to each region.

SkyDome

- 281G3
- 1 Blue Jays Way
- 416/341-3663
- $$$
- Closed off-season
- Union, then C.N. Skywalk

Visitor information

Practical information is given in the side column by each major site (see key to symbols on back flap). The map reference gives the page number where the site is mapped, followed by the grid reference. Further details include the site's address, telephone number, days closed, entrance fee in a range from $ (under $4) to $$$$$ (over $25), and the nearest metro or subway stop for Montreal and Toronto sites. Visitor information for smaller sites is provided within the text.

TRAVELWISE

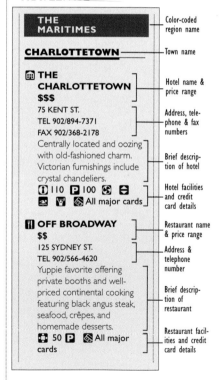

Color-coded region name
Town name
Hotel name & price range
Address, telephone & fax numbers
Brief description of hotel
Hotel facilities and credit card details
Restaurant name & price range
Address & telephone number
Brief description of restaurant
Restaurant facilities and credit card details

Hotel & restaurant prices

An explanation of the price ranges used in entries is given in the Hotels & Restaurants section beginning on p. 348.

REGIONAL MAPS

Province

Point of interest

Important point
of interest

Important
featured
town

Map reference

- A locator map accompanies each regional map and shows the location of that region in the country.
- Adjacent regions are shown, together with a page reference.

WALKING TOURS

Featured site (in bold) on walk route

Direction of route

Walk route

Building outline

Point of interest not on walk route

Red numbered bullet links site on map to description in the text

Start point

- An information box gives the starting and ending points, time and length of walk, and places not to be missed along the route.
- Where two walks are marked on the map, the second route is shown in orange.

DRIVING TOURS

Red numbered bullet links site on map to description in the text

Line of route

Point of interest on route

- An information box provides details including starting and finishing points, and places not to be missed along the route, time and length of drive, or tips on terrain.

THE NATIONAL
GEOGRAPHIC TRAVELER
CANADA

About the author

After studying modern langauages at Oxford University, Michael Ivory qualified as a landscape architect and town planner. A former Canadian resident, Ivory is now based in the United Kingdom and currently works as a freelance lecturer and travel writer. His many books have included guides to Australia, the Czech Republic, and Hungary.

With contributions by:
Richard Sale, Arctic ecology specialist and travel writer
Mitchell Davis, director of the James Beard Foundation, New York
Fiona Malins, journalist, travel writer, and specialist tour guide
Sean Connolly, travel writer and editor

History & Culture

**Maple leaf clipped
into a Mounty's horse**

Canada today

ASK MOST PEOPLE TO THINK OF CANADA AND A STRING OF FAMILIAR images appears: the peaks and ice fields of the Rockies, the vast expanse of the Prairies, endless forests of dark conifers, the austere and icy North…a world of untouched nature, a wilderness of almost infinite extent. Then there is another side, almost cozy by contrast, which might include the silhouette of Quebec City on its rock above the broad St. Lawrence, or the Gothic towers of Ottawa's Parliament Hill guarded by smiling Mounties.

Like most clichés, these images are true, and you could spend your time in Canada confirming them. A ten-day Highlights of Canada tour could whisk you across the country from one three-star sight to another, starting perhaps with a whale-watching trip off the Newfoundland coast, going on to where Anne of Green Gables lived on Prince Edward Island, to Old Montreal, Niagara Falls, Banff National Park, and ending up with afternoon tea in Victoria's Empress Hotel. What a marathon! What marvelous pictures you would have to show family and friends! You would have enjoyed contact with wildlife, dipped into childhood memories, visited a fascinating city, marveled at a great natural wonder, had a taste of the wilderness, and rounded off the trip in Edwardian comfort.

But most—if not all—of these ingredients of a memorable journey could be enjoyed in Canada without having to travel 3,000 miles or more. Every region of the country has something of this rich mixture. Far apart from one another, provincial capitals and other cities have developed strong identities of their own. Each is proud of its history, which in the east may go back four centuries, and presents it with verve and flair in carefully restored heritage buildings and in museums that include some of the world's finest works of art.

The Frenchness of Montreal and Quebec gives them a special savor, but all Canadian cities have become more vibrant in recent years, in part because of the multicultural transformation many of them have undergone. Toronto "The Good" has metamorphosed into something far more exciting, a world city of enormous ethnic variety and endless fascination.

Each city is within easy reach of countryside that may have been lived in for hundreds of years, like rural Quebec, which still breathes the atmosphere of New France. There is a strong sense of the past in other rural areas too, in the outports of Newfoundland, the fishing villages of the Maritimes, and the Loyalist towns of Ontario. Equally compelling are places settled almost within living memory, like Ukrainian villages of the Prairies or mining towns in British Columbia.

Wilderness or the ocean is near at hand, too. Halifax is backed by vast forests and looks out across its Atlantic harbor, one of the finest in the world. Quebec, Montreal, Ottawa, Toronto…all are within a short distance of the forests, lakes, and uplands of the Canadian Shield. The Rockies can be seen from Calgary, while incomparable Vancouver is blessed by both sea and mountains.

Areas within easy reach of cities are understandably more popular. Farther afield, you will find places shared only with others who have made the same effort to escape as you. It could be aboard ship among the icebergs off the Labrador coast, on the tundra of polar bear country around Hudson Bay, at a deserted Haida village in the far-off Queen Charlotte Islands, or at the very end of the highway at Yellowknife on the northern shore of Great Slave Lake.

CANADIANS

What is a real Canadian? The question troubles many citizens of this prosperous and decent-minded country, ranked high, even top in most surveys of people's preferences of where they would like to live in the world. A glance along the shelves of any big bookstore in Canada will reveal a clutch of titles attempting an answer, usually with the word

Spectacular views abound in Canada's Rockies, such as this one over Moraine Lake near Banff National Park.

"identity" featuring prominently.

Canada's original inhabitants were, of course, the Inuit and the several hundred thousand members of the First Nations, but the first Canadians as such were the "Canadiens"—the French-speaking subjects of the King of France, who settled in the St. Lawrence Valley in the 17th and 18th centuries. Abandoned by France after 1763, they then shared their name with their new, English-speaking fellow citizens—English, Irish, Scots, and Welsh from across the Atlantic, or Loyalists from the United States. In the 20th century, "Canadien" has given way to "Québécois" as French speakers in Quebec (or Francophones, to use another new term) have felt the need to affirm their own particular identity. Alongside English speakers (Anglophones), French-speakers form one of the country's founding nations. In the province of Quebec they are the majority of the population, but there are important French-speaking minorities in other provinces, particularly Manitoba (around 50,000, about five percent of the population), New Brunswick (around 240,000, about 32 percent), and Ontario (more than 550,000, about five percent).

Canadian "mosaic"
From the early 19th century until quite recently, people of British or Irish descent formed the majority of the country's population, and for many years Canada had a distinctly "British" identity, the weakening of which was symbolized by the replacement of the Union flag with the maple leaf in 1965. Without even thinking about it, nearly all migrants to Canada adopted English as their language and the key to opportunity in North America as a whole. These newcomers came from all over the world, but the most important sources of new Canadians were Germany, the Ukraine, Italy, the Netherlands, and Poland. More recently there has been an upsurge in migrants from Asia, the Indian subcontinent, and the Caribbean. Canada is officially a multicultural country; the word "mosaic" appeared early in the 20th century to describe a pattern of population in which newcomers were not thrown into a "melting pot" but maintained many of the traditions of

their countries of origin. This is most obvious in the prairie provinces, which were settled from the outset by cohesive ethnic communities, particularly from the Ukraine, and in Toronto with its distinctive ethnic "villages" and public services in an extraordinary array of languages.

At the federal level, Canada is officially a bilingual country, committed to serving its citizens in either English or French across the country and even outside it. Thus your phone call to a Canadian embassy will be answered by a friendly *bonjour* as well as "hello," and the ranger in the Rockies will have a badge showing "Parc Banff." Among the provinces, New Brunswick is bilingual, but Quebec, despite its large anglophone population, is officially monolingual. For many French-speaking Québécois, this is a vital question of identity. They fear that failure to assert the primacy of French would eventually result in its dilution and the loss of the francophone culture of 6 million people isolated among the nearly 300 million English-speaking North Americans.

GIANT TO THE SOUTH
But what about the distinctive culture of English-speaking Canadians? Far from being isolated, many such Canadians feel themselves to be very much, perhaps too much involved with what goes on south of the 49th parallel. American culture is everywhere, in books, magazines, on radio, and on TV. Every agreement on trade has increased American participation in the Canadian economy. American vacation destinations draw millions of Canadians southward every year, most famously the "snowbirds" who migrate to Florida every winter. American job opportunities and higher salaries exert a similar pull on the career-minded. And American speech patterns exercise an increasing influence on the way Canadians express themselves. Some Canadians feel closer to their near neighbors just across the border than to their fellow citizens in provinces thousands of miles away.

That Canadians were not Americans once seemed guaranteed by the British connection,

A walk through the Galleria of Toronto's BCE building is a must for all modern architecture enthusiasts.

but as ties with the United Kingdom weakened, this no longer applied. Nevertheless, Canada has so far not followed the example of Australia in moving toward republicanism, and the image of the British monarch still appears on the coinage. Canadians like to think of themselves as good partners of the United States, but take great care to point out

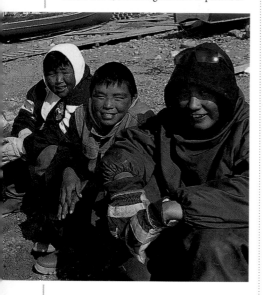

Three occupants of the village of Povungnituk in the newly formed territory of Nunavut

the ways in which the two countries' views of the world differ. Early recognition of communism in Cuba and China is a case in point, a detached attitude to the United States predicament in Vietnam another—between 1965 and 1974 as many as 125,000 young Americans found sanctuary from the draft in Canada. Canadian forces fought in Korea and in the Persian Gulf, and were stationed for many years in Germany, but otherwise their service abroad has been as United Nations peacekeepers. The country has enjoyed an enviable international reputation for mediation and compromise and for support of the United Nations generally. Way down the international league in terms of wealth and population, the country makes the fourth largest contribution to the UN budget.

Canadian compromises

The ability to make creative compromises is perhaps one of the qualities that characterize the Canadian way of doing things. The Confederation of 1867 was essentially a compromise between the potentially conflicting interests of the provinces which it united, and over recent years much effort has gone into formulating a resolution that would keep Quebec in Canada. Canadians are more ready to mock themselves than most, and this desire for moderation has not escaped the attention of humorists:

> Question: Why did the Canadian cross the road?
> Answer: To get to the middle.

GOVERNMENT & POLITICS

Canada's ten provinces and three territories are part of a federation, a parliamentary democracy that is a member of the British Commonwealth and whose head of state is the British monarch. The monarch's functions, almost entirely ceremonial, are carried out by a governor general, appointed by the monarch but chosen by the prime minister and cabinet. Legislative power rests with the lower chamber of parliament, the Commons, with 295 elected M.P.s (members of parliament) representing ridings (constituencies) across the country. The timing of elections is the responsibility of the prime minister, but the maximum term between elections is five years. The upper chamber of parliament is the Senate, with 104 members appointed by the governor general on the advice of the prime minister. The Senate's right to block legislation is little used in practice, its main role being to give bills a second hearing and clarify their content. Parliament sits in the handsome Gothic Revival buildings in Ottawa, chosen as capital in 1867.

Political roots

Political parties are organized on provincial and federal levels. For many years the balance of power in Ottawa swung between two great rivals, the Tories (Progressive Conservatives) and the Liberals ("Grits"). Both parties are centrist, with Tories inclining more toward maintaining the British connection and supporting Canadian business, and the Liberals concerned with the rights of the individual and promotion of free trade. Both were traditionally able to draw support from across the nation, but in the 1993 election the Conservatives, who had previously ruled the country under Brian Mulroney, were reduced to a bare minimum, with only two seats in parliament. The role of official opposition to the Liberal government formed by Prime Minister Jean Chrétien fell to the Bloc Québécois, whose priorities, as its name implies, were less national than provincial. Another party operating at a national level is the New Democratic Party. A member of the Socialist International, it represents the interests of organized labor and is social-democratic in character. The Reform Party has grown out of an early 20th-century populist movement known as Social Credit, and is almost as closely identified with the regional interests of western Canada as the Bloc Québécois is with Quebec.

Provincial matters

In the provinces, political parties may or may not have a strong link with their counterpart at federal level, and it is common for voters to support one party in provincial elections and another in Ottawa. Leading politicians have been known to switch their allegiance, too. In the mid-1990s, Quebec's separatist party, the Parti Québécois, had as its leader Lucien Bouchard, a former member of the Progressive Conservative party. The chief opponents of separatism in Quebec are the provincial Liberals. In 1998 they offered their leadership to Jean Charest, who resigned as chief of the federal Conservatives in order to accept.

Confronting Canada's concerns

Canada faces most of the problems that confront any Western democracy. The financing of a large public sector is a constant concern and in Ontario, for example, this issue has led to confrontation between a heavily unionized teaching profession and a provincial government intent on reducing public expenditures. The country is proud of having established universal health care, but the performance of the system docs not always measure up to expectations. Increasing crime is a worry, but in comparison with the United States, levels of criminal activity are very low.

Many issues in Canadian politics concern the relationship between national and provincial interests, inevitably so in such a vast country where the individual provinces differ so much from one another. The position of Quebec within the federation is the greatest of these issues, but by no means the only one. With their resource-based industrial structure,

Young and old Quebecers came out to help campaign for the Parti Québécois in the referendum of 1995.

the western provinces in particular often feel that their priorities are taken little notice of by a federal government far away in central Canada with its much greater population and its dynamic, diversified economy. Also, the fundamental reasons for the disastrous decline of the vital Atlantic cod fishery may never be discovered, but many in the Maritimes and Newfoundland point to the federal Department of Fisheries and Oceans as the chief culprit.

The attempts made in recent years to renew the fabric of the Canadian state have so far come to nothing, but have given a new twist to the perennial debate about the nature of Canadian identity. High-profile Prime Minister Pierre Elliott Trudeau put all his passion into promoting an all-Canadian

identity encompassing the two founding
nations (French and British), as well as native
peoples and migrants from whatever
background. The keystone of his policy was
the repatriation of the Constitution; in 1982
the British North America Act of 1867 was
replaced by a Constitution Act and by a
Canadian Charter of Rights and Freedoms.
But Quebec failed to endorse the new
arrangements. After several years of debate,
Prime Minister Brian Mulroney and all ten

**The ceremonial dress of the Royal 22nd
Regiment band illustrates the strong
British influence in Canada.**

provincial premiers assembled in 1987 at
Meech Lake just outside Ottawa and managed
to agree on a form of words that, among other
things, recognized Quebec's special status as a
"distinct society." When some of the provinces
had second thoughts, the agreement faltered.
It was finally killed in 1990 by the "No" of a

Cree member of the Manitoba Parliament. Undaunted, Mulroney tried again. In 1992 a deal was signed at Prince Edward Island's Charlottetown, the place where the Confederation had been agreed to in 1867. As well as satisfying the ten provincial premiers, it pleased the leaders of the two territories, the First Nations, the Inuit, and the Métis. The population at large, however, was not persuaded: In the referendum that followed, the Charlottetown Accord was rejected by the electorate.

An massive upsurge of Quebec separatist feeling followed the failure of the Charlottetown agreement but when in 1995 the Parti Québécois government put the question of secession to Quebec voters in another referendum, they were defeated, albeit by the narrowest of margins. These events of the 1990s seemed to show that however unhappy Canadians might be with their living arrangements, it is very difficult to find a real alternative to staying together. ∎

Native peoples today

CANADA'S ORIGINAL INHABITANTS BELONG TO MANY DIFFERENT GROUPS who followed different ways of life, the vestiges of which remain to this day.

The people of the Arctic are perhaps the most distinctive of Canada's native people. Until recently, they were referred to as Eskimos, although the term used today is Inuit (singular, Inuk), which in their own language of Inuktitut means simply "the people." Inuit depended traditionally on the resources of the sea, especially sea mammals such as whale, seal, and walrus, all of which they exploited using advanced hunting techniques. They traveled over vast areas of tundra to maximize their use of these resources. The big change in their lives came during World War II and the Cold War, when the Arctic took on new strategic significance, and the building of airfields and radar sites across the area brought to the Inuit the full impact of outside culture, including wage employment.

Today, almost all Inuit live in settlements, many of which had their origins either in wartime or postwar military sites, or in the fur-trading posts or mission stations that preceded them. Although many Inuit still enjoy being on the land and will go on extended hunting, sealing or fishing trips, their home base is now in the villages. Thanks to satellites, television, telephone service, and other forms of telecommunications, they enjoy most of the amenities of modern life, even though their community may be thousands of miles from the commercial hubs. Larger towns are served by frequent jet service to outside centers. To a visitor, an Arctic Canadian community presents an odd mixture of the traditional and the modern, perhaps best exemplified by an Inuk grandmother dressed in traditional clothes hurtling across the snow on her snowmobile.

The First Nations

Canada's other original inhabitants, the First Nations, as they are now called, consist of the people who used to be called Indians and are still, to their growing dissatisfaction, administered under the Federal Indian Act. Although they belong to many different nations, each with its own language and culture, they have

This caribou-clad Inuk hunter and his dog sled present a classic image of the frozen Canadian north.

now found common cause in reasserting their identity. Political action has often focused on wresting control of their educational systems from the federal government and establishing locally controlled schools that reflect their own languages and cultures. Reserves that were first established to segregate First Nations peoples from nonnatives have now become the basis for extensive land claims. For many First Nations people, political action is seen as the best way of redressing some of the injustices of the past, especially those created by a system of residential schools that forcibly removed children from what was then seen as the corrupting influence of their parents and their home community.

Constitutional issues

The Assembly of First Nations, with its elected Grand Chief, seeks to speak for all First Nations people in Canada, and its views are increasingly heard in constitutional debate. The high rates of alcoholism and substance abuse, of diseases such as diabetes, and of violence, which prevail on many of Canada's 2,400 reserves, and which many First Nations spokespeople attribute directly to the abuses of the residential school system, have often acted as the lightning rod for political action by the assembly and other groups. Nevertheless, many First Nations communities can also show a record of gradual success, with many more young people than in the past going on to secondary school and to university.

Although First Nations people often speak with a common voice on political matters, they come from widely differing cultures, many of them based on the resources of the land they occupied. These cultures are reflected in the more than 50 languages they speak and in the ways they express themselves through the arts. Inuit soapstone carvings have developed to the point where fine pieces by well-known carvers command very high prices in the best galleries. From the totem poles and other wood carvings of the West Coast Salish, Haida, Kwakiutl, and other nations, to the basketwork of the East Coast Mi'kmaq, First Nations communities are using art not only as a means of expressing their distinctive cultures, but as an important base for commercial development. ■

Land & landscape

COMPLAINING ABOUT THE SHEER SIZE OF THE YOUNG COUNTRY, PRIME Minister W. L. Mackenzie King once remarked, "If some countries have too much history, we have too much geography." Covering 3.9 million square miles, Canada is second only to Russia in area. Point Pelee on Lake Erie shares the same latitude as central Italy, while the country's northernmost point is a mere 500 miles from the North Pole. A journey from Cape Spear in the east to the Alaskan border in the west covers about 3,500 miles and crosses six time zones. Such vastness encompasses great extremes of climate, landscape, and human settlement. Canadian winters are famous, but proximity to the ocean or to the Great Lakes tempers their harshness, as well as making summers cooler. The barren land above the Arctic Circle is virtually uninhabited, the Canadian Shield covering almost half the country hardly less so. The overwhelming majority of the population of about 30 million lives along the U.S. border, most of them in towns and cities. The people of the Maritimes are closer to Europe than to their fellow-countrymen in British Columbia, and most Canadians have more neighbors along the U.S. border than in the adjoining provinces to the east or west.

CANADIAN SHIELD

This two-million-square-mile mass of ancient rock planed by glaciers is the dominant feature on the map of Canada, sweeping in a great arc around Hudson Bay from far northwest to far northeast. In the south it fringes the Great Lakes and extends to city suburbs in Ontario and Quebec. Between southern Ontario and Manitoba it forms a formidable thousand-mile-wide barrier that had to be overcome before these long-settled eastern provinces could be united with the newer Canada of the west.

The rocks of the shield are among the most ancient on earth, mainly granites and gneisses formed nearly four billion years ago. During the ice ages glaciers advanced and retreated over the area, scraping the surface down to its present level, hollowing out the countless lakes, and removing most of the existing soil. Along its southern rim, the shield forms uplands like the Laurentian Mountains, which reach a maximum height of 3,175 feet at Mont Tremblant. It then slopes gradually down to sea level along the shore of Hudson Bay, though in the east the Torngat range overlooks the Labrador Sea from a height of more than 5,000 feet. North of the timberline stretches the tundra, a bleak landscape of dwarf birch and willow, mosses, lichens, and a burst of small flowering plants in the short summer. This merges southward with the boreal forest or taiga, with conifers like black and white spruce and jack pine together with willow and poplar, and extensive areas of muskeg, basins filled with peat moss.

Clay soils exist in a few areas on the southern fringe of the shield, but attempts to bring them into agricultural use have met with little success. Wildlife was the great resource of the shield, supporting the native population and supplying the fur trade with much of its material. Since the end of the 19th century, the area's mineral wealth has sustained both temporary and permanent settlements, and, more recently, some of its vast potential for hydroelectric power has been tapped, notably by the giant Hyrdo-Québec corporation. Logging has also occurred over much of the area, making full use of the many rivers and streams as rafting routes.

APPALACHIAN REGION

The northernmost parts of the Appalachian range reach into eastern Quebec and the Maritimes, then appear again in Newfoundland. They consist of complex folded mountains, eroded by the ice that once covered them, and smaller areas of lowland along river valleys or coastlines.

A lone rower savors the spectacular setting of Dougans Lake in British Columbia.

The mountains and uplands are generally rounded, reaching heights of more than 4,000 feet in the Gaspé Peninsula, and more than 2,500 feet in Newfoundland, but only 1,750 feet on Cape Breton Island.

The central feature of the region is the Gulf of St. Lawrence, an inland sea with outlets via the Cabot Strait between Cape Breton Island and Newfoundland, and through the Strait of Belle Isle separating Newfoundland from the Labrador mainland. The scattered human settlements of the region used to be linked to each other and to the outside world by the sea rather than by land routes. It was the sea's produce that until recently provided a living for many of its inhabitants. The extension of the continental shelf called the Grand Banks was one of the world's richest fishing grounds (see pp. 92–93). The cod may have disappeared, but the sea, with its mixing of cold and warm currents and its highly indented coastline, still forms a rich habitat for marine life, including several species of whale. Here, offshore oil has become an important resource.

Inland, most of the area is covered with mixed woodlands, once ruthlessly exploited for timber used in the shipyards that existed all along the coast.

ATLANTIC REGION

This area overlaps the Appalachian region in parts, but is largely defined by Nova Scotia, New Brunswick, and Prince Edward Island. Moderately fertile soils support agriculture in a number of areas including the St. John River Valley and Sussex country in New Brunswick; on Prince Edward Island where a famous crop of potatoes is produced; and in the Annapolis Valley of Nova Scotia, equally well known for its orchards. Halifax is the largest city, but there is no regional metropolis; Moncton, Saint John, and Fredericton all have their own hinterland in New Brunswick, while St. John's, despite its location on the far eastern coast of Newfoundland, is the island's undisputed capital.

GREAT LAKES

More than half the population of Canada lives in the relatively benign environment along the shores of the Great Lakes and in the St. Lawrence Valley. Between Detroit's neighbor,

Storm clouds gather over this canola field and settlement near Edmonton in Alberta.

Windsor, and Quebec City, about 700 miles to the northeast, the chain of urban settlements includes Canada's two greatest metropolitan cities, Toronto and Montreal.

Much of the country's earliest human history was played out in this region, leaving a visible heritage in the form of fine old towns like Ontario's Niagara-on-the-Lake and mature rural landscapes like Quebec's Richelieu Valley.

Although winters are cold and summers hot, the climate is less extreme than in most of the rest of the country, allowing a wide range of crops to be grown. The vast quantities of water held in the Great Lakes have a balancing effect on local climates, tempering both winter cold and summer heat. Many areas have fertile soils that have formed on the sedimentary rocks overlying the far older rocks of the Canadian Shield. The diversity of crops grown even includes vines, most importantly in the Niagara area but also in other parts of Ontario and even in southern Quebec. In places such as Point Pelee on Lake Erie, luxuriant remnants of natural woodland represent the northernmost extension of the Carolinian forest with southern species like tulip trees and hackberries. Elsewhere, although 90 percent of the mixed forest was cleared by pioneer farmers or logged by lumbermen, enough remains

to justify the use of the maple leaf for the national flag, delight visitors with the spectacle of autumn leaves, and provide abundant sap for maple syrup.

INTERIOR PLAINS

The interior plains are the extension of the lowlands that run northward from the Rio Grande through the United States. In Canada they stretch more than 1,500 miles between the shield and the Rocky Mountains to where the Mackenzie River discharges through its delta into the Arctic Ocean. The plains include the southern parts of Manitoba and Saskatchewan, most of Alberta and the southwestern part of the Northwest Territories. Along the boundary with the shield are great

Untracked Rockies wilderness is known as "shin tangle"—a phrase that contributed to the naming of Tangle Falls.

bodies of water such as Lake Winnipeg, Lake Athabasca, and Great Slave Lake. Boreal forest and tundra dominate the north, but in the south the fertile soils that once supported an ocean of grassland are now farmed, producing the bulk of the country's grain. Along with the prairie grasses, the countless bison that once roamed the plains have been virtually exterminated.

Cattle ranching as well as grain brought settlers to the plains, but it is the oil and gas resources beneath the surface that have determined the recent economic pace of the prairie provinces, particularly Alberta, where Edmonton and Calgary have outpaced Winnipeg, Manitoba, the original capital of the region.

CANADIAN CORDILLERA

Part of the 9,000-mile chain of mountains stretching from the Tierra del Fuego to Alaska, a series of ranges and plateaus 500 miles across, makes up all the Yukon and most of British Columbia, while the crest of the Rocky Mountains forms much of the border with Alberta. Here are the highest peaks and most dramatic landscapes in Canada, a challenge to explorers until late in the country's history. The highest point in the Canadian Rockies is Mount Robson (12,972 feet). Several peaks in the Yukon's Mackenzie Mountains exceed 8,000 feet, but the highest mountain in Canada and the second highest in all of North America is Mount Logan (19,850 feet) in the St. Elias Mountains of the northwest.

NUNAVUT
On April 1, 1999, Canada established the new territory of Nunavut—meaning "our land."

Queen Elizabeth Islands

Baffin Bay

Banks Island

Victoria Island

Baffin Island

Davis Strait

NUNAVUT

Foxe Basin

Iqaluit ★

Yellowknife

Great Slave Lake

Lake Athabasca

CANADA

Back

Thelon

Hudson Strait

Torngat Mts.

Labrador Sea

Hudson Bay

NEWFOUNDLAND

SASKATCHEWAN

Churchill

Nelson

MANITOBA

Saskatchewan

Lake Winnipeg

James Bay

Koksoak

La Grande Rivière

Churchill

Island of Newfoundland

★ St. John's

QUÉBEC

Regina ★

Winnipeg ★

ONTARIO

Albany

R. de Rupert

Shield

St. Lawrence River

Appalachian Mts.

PRINCE EDWARD ISLAND

★ Charlottetown

NEW BRUNSWICK   **NOVA SCOTIA**

Québec ★

Fredericton ★

★ Halifax

Lake Superior

Ottawa

MONTRÉAL ●

Ottawa ⊛

Lake Michigan

L. Huron

TORONTO ★

L. Ontario

Windsor ●

L. Erie

ATLANTIC OCEAN

| 0 | 400 miles |
| 0 | 400 kilometers |

The mountains were formed in a complex folding process that began some 70 million years ago, but their present outline is due to the action of ice, and glaciers are still at work today, as in the great Columbia Icefield. The alpine climate yields some of the country's highest snowfall, up to 370 inches a year in Glacier National Park. By contrast, the area around the Strait of Georgia on the Pacific coast has an almost balmy local climate, with frequent rain but relatively rare frosts.

The wildlife that brought fur traders into the region is still abundant in many places. Brown and grizzly bears still inhabit the alpine forests of the east and the cool rain forest of the west, but the once plentiful salmon have experienced a severe decline in numbers. Logging remains a vitally important industry, though its operations are often contested by environmentalists.

Settlement is thinly distributed over the cordillera, mainly in old mining towns or in the fertile valleys along the U.S. border, where warm summers favor fruit and wine production. The majority of the region's population lives in an emerging, outward-looking metropolitan region based on the Strait of Georgia with Vancouver as its focal point. ■

Canadian history

THE VAST LAND THAT LAY UNKNOWINGLY IN WAIT FOR EUROPEAN SUBJUG-
ation was already a complex cultural mosaic, the home of peoples as varied and distinctive as those of the continent on the far shore of the eastern Atlantic. Population densities
were low; there may have been a total of some 300,000 inhabitants just before the period
of European contact, but all parts of the country were occupied by people extremely well
adapted to the very diverse resources of the different regions.

FIRST PEOPLES

Perhaps up to 20,000 years ago, when sea levels
were much lower than today, the first human
beings to live in Canada were Siberian hunters
who had pursued their prey of giant bison,
wooly mammoth, and hairy rhino over the
Bering Strait. As they and their descendants
spread throughout North and South America,
they were followed by successive waves of
migrants. Among them, about 5,000 years ago,

were the first Inuit people, identified as the
Dorset. They were displaced by people of the
Thule culture, the direct ancestors of today's
Inuit. Living between the Arctic shore and the
northern limit of the boreal forest, they were
hunters, following the seasonal movements of
the creatures (whales, seals, fish, caribou) on
which they depended not only for food, but for
clothing and every kind of implement, including expertly fashioned bone harpoons. In drier

areas like southern Labrador, a winter shelter might have consisted of a shallow pit and wood-frame structure with a sod roof. But the archetypal dwelling was the snowhouse or igloo, whose geometrical perfection caused one European explorer to compare it with a "Grecian temple…both are triumphs of art, inimitable in their kinds."

Woodland tribes

Within the forests to the south lived other hunters, speaking dialects of the Athapaskan and Algonquian languages, members of what have come to be called the Woodland tribes. Their mobility depended on use of that supremely functional artifact, the birchbark canoe, highly maneuverable and light enough

Paul Kane's 19th-century painting depicts First Nations' life on Lake Huron.

to carry over long portages. Where cultivable soil occurred and the climate was milder, as in the St. Lawrence Valley, the Iroquois lived a more settled life, building villages and long-houses, and growing maize, beans, and squash. Sophisticated political structures were able to develop, of which the most famous was the League of the Iroquois—comprising the Seneca, Cayuga, Oneida, Onondaga, and Mohawk. This high degree of organization enabled the Iroquois to trade with their Algonquian neighbors to the north, exchanging surplus corn for furs and game. It also seems to have encouraged their warlike tendencies. They were implacable foes of the Huron, whose society they destroyed, and came into constant conflict with the French.

People of the plains

In the endless grasslands between the Canadian Shield and the Rocky Mountains lived the Plains tribes—Cree, Assiniboine, Blackfoot, and others—often in mutual hostility despite their shared way of life. Much more than any other animal, the favorite quarry of these hunters was the bison, which roamed the plains in huge herds and which supplied them with meat from its flesh, tools from its bones, garments and tepee coverings from its hide, glue from its hooves, and even kettles from its paunch. Bison were slaughtered in large numbers, in winter by being decoyed into pounds, in summer by being driven over the cliffs known as buffalo jumps, some of which (like Alberta's famous Head-Smashed-In) were in use for thousands of years. Women were responsible for the butchering and for making pemmican, a concentrated and highly nutritious mixture of powdered meat and grease, often flavored with Saskatoon berries.

Pacific coast

In what is now British Columbia, West Coast natives such as the Gitksan and Haida did not need to go to such lengths to feed themselves. The abundance of fish, fur, and game and a benign climate created a high standard of material life. Cedar trees supplied the planks with which substantial houses were built as well as the material for superb canoes, some of them up to 70 feet long and capable of ocean journeys of several hundred miles. Trading networks were well developed: Even the fat extracted from the eulachon or candlefish was carried far inland along routes that came to be known as "grease trails." Perhaps the most remarkable achievement of West Coast people lay in the powerful art that graced and gave meaning to everyday life and to ritual. Tools, baskets, and clothing were all elaborately decorated, but the most impressive works of art were the great totem poles with their bold carvings of men and beasts.

FIRST EUROPEANS

Commissioned by royalty and required to report fully on their findings, John Cabot (1450–1498) and Jacques Cartier (1491–1557) have gone down in the history books as the "discoverers" of Canada. The look-out aboard Cabot's *Matthew* sighted land on June 24, 1497, although it is still a matter of speculation whether it was Newfoundland or Cape Breton Island. Cartier sailed through the Strait of Belle Isle between Newfoundland and Labrador 37 years later, in May 1534. But Europeans had been crossing the Atlantic long before these well-documented voyages.

Medieval Norse sagas told of adventurers such as Leif Eriksson (10th–11th centuries) bound from Greenland finding a land of vines and plentiful timber, and archaeologists have found evidence at L'Anse aux Meadows in northern Newfoundland of a Viking settlement dating from around the year A.D. 1000 (see pp. 100–101). In the years that followed, Viking interest diminished, but it is possible that Basque and British fishermen had discovered the cod-rich waters around Newfoundland in the years preceding Cabot's venture.

Trading contact

Neither Cabot nor Cartier had crossed the Atlantic in search of codfish, but to look for a more direct route to the silks, spices, and other riches of the Orient. Nothing of this kind could be found on the bleak coasts of eastern Canada. Nevertheless, on Cabot's return to England, Henry VII (R. 1485–1509) was sufficiently impressed to reward him with a princely £10 and to finance a second voyage, in 1498. This time Cabot did not return, and no trace of him or his ships has been found (see pp. 334-5).

Cartier's contact with the new continent was more prolonged. After passing through the Strait of Belle Isle, he sailed past the Magdalen Islands, landed on Prince Edward Island, and looked into the Baie des Chaleurs, where he was greeted by Mi'kmaq wanting to trade furs with him. At Gaspé he encountered Iroquois on a fishing expedition from their settlement at Stadacona, near present-day Quebec City. Pleasantries were exchanged, but when Cartier erected a huge cross on shore bearing the emblem of the king of France, his hosts declared that the land was their domain and definitely not for the taking. Cartier returned the following year, sailing up the St. Lawrence as far as the Iroquois village of Hochelaga, the future site of Montreal, where he was

Massive quantities of furs were shipped to Europe from the desolate shores of Hudson Bay.

welcomed with great ceremony. Wintering close to Stadacona, he began to lose his men to scurvy until the Iroquois showed him how to treat it with a brew of cedar leaves and bark, but relations between the French and natives had already become strained. Cartier kidnapped several Iroquois and took them back to France, where they died, probably of a European disease to which they had no immunity, a harbinger of the fate many more were to suffer in the years to come. When Cartier returned once again in 1541, the Iroquois put to siege his winter encampment. He left for France for the last time, hoping that his cargo of glittering rocks contained gold. It turned out to be iron pyrites.

Fish and furs

For the next half century, European interest in Canada was confined to cod. British, French, Basque, and Portuguese fished the Grand Banks (see pp. 92–3). They made no real attempt to found permanent settlements on the coast of Newfoundland, though annoyed the Beothuk natives by cluttering up their best fishing sites with gear and destroying the forest for firewood.

At the beginning of the 17th century, French interest in the new land gained a fresh impulse—from fur. Beaver felt was the ideal material—easily shaped, durable, and waterproof—for hats. While European beavers were on the point of extinction, the Canadian forests teemed with them. Once more, royal encouragement was given to an expedition. In 1603 the man subsequently regarded as the Father of New France, Samuel de Champlain (1567–1635), was instructed to survey the St. Lawrence. In 1605 he founded a fortified post known as the Habitation, at Port Royal on the Annapolis Basin in what is now Nova Scotia. This Habitation was soon abandoned, but in 1608 Champlain founded another. Beneath a great rock overlooking the St. Lawrence, at a place the Iroquois called Kebek, or "the narrowing of the waters," this Habitation was destined to endure and to become the capital of New France.

COLONIZATION & CONFLICT

Cartier claimed Canada for France in 1534, and in 1583 Sir Humphrey Gilbert (1539–1583) claimed Newfoundland for England. For two centuries, the English and French led an uneasy coexistence that often developed into harassment, piracy, and warfare.

French control

At the beginning, the French grip on the new land was far firmer. Towns were founded and colonists brought in to settle them and the nearby countryside. The church was a major player, establishing monasteries and sending missions far into the interior, as at Sainte-Marie among the Hurons on Georgian Bay. The basis of the fur trade was established, with natives using their traditional expertise to supply French traders with the beaver pelts and other furs. From the earliest days, French strategy favored the Huron, long-standing enemies of the Iroquois who often blocked the routes leading into the interior from the colony. As early as 1609, Champlain fought an Iroquois army near the lake subsequently named after him. Caught in the open and subjected to fire from the Europeans' harquebuses, the Iroquois were routed, but remained formidable foes. In the late 1640s their attacks on Huronia led to martyrdom of missionaries, the abandonment of Sainte-Marie among the Hurons, and the destruction of the Huron nation. In the early 1660s, the Iroquois terrorized New France, besieging Montreal and pillaging the countryside. Their attack led directly to the fall of

The Father of New France—Samuel de Champlain (1567–1635)

the Cent-Associés, the trading association that had hitherto run the affairs of New France, and to the placing of the colony under royal control.

Far away, other Frenchmen were settling the shores of the Bay of Fundy, where Champlain had located his first two Habitations. Raiders from Virginia destroyed the Habitation at Port Royal. The Acadians developed stronger trading ties to New England than their fellow countrymen in the St. Lawrence Valley though they, too, were harrassed by the Colonies to the south. In the 1620s a British attempt was made to found a colony in their midst by Sir William Alexander. His venture failed but the name he gave to the land stuck—Nova Scotia.

British inroads

English fishermen had already settled along the coasts of Newfoundland, despite official prohibition. St. John's, on its wonderful sheltered harbor, was the largest settlement. Attempts were made to found organized colonies, by John Guy of Bristol at Conception Bay in 1610, then a decade later by Lord Baltimore at Ferryland on the Avalon Peninsula. Guy's party stayed, but after one winter Lord Baltimore left for the much milder shores of Maryland.

Despite the development of New France

Champlain's arrival in New France stimulated conflict with the Hurons.

under the royal regime, the "French fact" in North America was very vulnerable. British sea power was constantly growing and the population along the St. Lawrence Valley was a fraction of that in the 13 Colonies. In 1670 the Hudson's Bay Company had been founded, a northern rival to the French fur trade and a portent of things to come in the west. Intermittent fighting broke out again toward the end of the 17th century. The Iroquois had been armed by the English; in 1689 they made a famous attack on Lachine near Montreal, and in 1692 another at Vercheres in which they were beaten off by the 15-year-old daughter of the local seigneur. In 1690 the English adventurer Sir William Phips, fresh from attacking Port Royal, sailed up the St. Lawrence to Quebec City and commanded Governor Frontenac to surrender. "I have no reply to make to your general other than from the mouths of my cannon," was Frontenac's immortal response to Phips's emissary, and Phips retired, discouraged by this show of resistance but also wary of the ice threatening to imprison his ships. In 1711 another British plan to attack Quebec failed when the ships of Admiral Walker's fleet came to grief on the coast of Anticosti Island in the Gulf of St. Lawrence. The Quebec church which had been renamed Notre-Dame de la Victoire in 1690 now added an "s" to its name.

Atlantic possessions

The turn-of-the-century conflict between Britain and a now bankrupt France was brought to an end by the Treaty of Utrecht of 1713, in which France ceded Acadia/Nova Scotia, gave up claims to parts of Newfoundland, and renounced interest in Hudson Bay. But France kept Cape Breton Island, and, to protect the vulnerable approach to the St. Lawrence through the Cabot Strait, began to build the huge fortress of Louisbourg looking out over the Atlantic. This was not to New England's liking, and, when Britain and France went to war again in 1744, a force of militia supported by the British Caribbean fleet stormed the fortress and after a six-week siege deported its population to France. But in the diplomatic maneuvers that ended what had been a war partly about issues in Europe, Louisbourg was returned to France and rapidly regarrisoned. The end of the war turned out to be no more than a truce. Anglo-French rivalry in North America intensified. As a counterweight to Louisbourg, Halifax was founded in 1749, its citadel and magnificent harbor destined to watch over Britain's Atlantic interests for the next two centuries. At this time Britain preferred not to send emigrants overseas, and when the town of Lunenburg was established down the Nova Scotia coast from Halifax, it was populated by foreign Protestants. Mostly from Germany and Switzerland, these people were thought to be more reliable subjects of His Majesty than the Catholic Acadians, whose calvary was soon to begin. As the war clouds gathered, British officialdom felt unable to trust these French speakers to maintain their neutrality in the coming conflict. The Acadians were rounded up, deported, and dispersed around the American Colonies, which were often unwilling to receive them. The rich pastures that their ancestors had laboriously reclaimed from the marshlands around the Bay of Fundy mostly fell into the hands of migrants from New England, and the Acadians who doggedly made their way back home had to resettle elsewhere, usually on far less favorable land.

"First World War"

The year 1756 saw the outbreak of what has been called the first war fought on a global scale, the Seven Years' War. In North America there was fighting on the western frontier and on the invasion corridor between New York

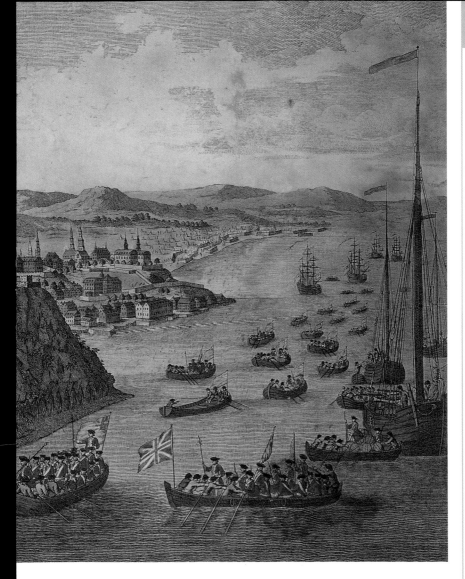

The elevated Plains of Abraham near Quebec City saw Canada's defining battle in 1759, as shown in this engraving by Bowles.

and Montreal around Lake Champlain. But the decisive battle was fought in Quebec. Louisbourg had been taken again, and its garrison and inhabitants sent permanently packing. It could now serve as a base for the invasion of Quebec. By 1759 New France had lost all its forts on the Great Lakes and Lake Champlain. Its survival depended on French naval power, but France was preoccupied in Europe. In June the British commander, Gen. James Wolfe (1727–1759), sailed unopposed up the St. Lawrence to confront his adversary, the Marquis de Montcalm (1712–1759). The

residents had rallied to the flag, and Montcalm had more men at his command than the Englishman, but, wrote Wolfe, "Montcalm is at the head of a great number of bad soldiers and I am at the head of a small number of good ones." The preliminary skirmishes at Montmorency Falls, however, showed the French militiamen and their native allies as more than a match for the British. Wolfe

The capture of the H.M. *Cyane* **and** *Levant* **by the U.S.** *Constitution* **during the War of 1812**

ranged up and down the St. Lawrence, destroying crops and property in a scorched earth campaign, and subjected Quebec to a more or less continuous bombardment. As autumn approached, Wolfe sought a decisive encounter before the river began to freeze and immobilize his ships. On the night of September 12, he sent his men up a dry streambed to the heights of the Plains of Abraham, taking the French by surprise and defeating them in a 15-minute battle.

The war was not over. The French forces retreated to Montreal, and by the following spring sallied forth and gave the British a bloody nose at Sainte-Foy, only a mile or so southwest of the Plains of Abraham. Hoping for naval help from France, they subjected Quebec to a second siege, but the first ships to come up the St. Lawrence were British. In the summer, three British armies advancing from Quebec, Lake Champlain, and Lake Ontario delivered the coup de grâce, and Montreal surrendered.

The defeat of New France was a great bargaining chip for the British when peace negotiations began in 1763, but it was by no means inevitable that Britain would hold on to its conquest in the St. Lawrence Valley. Strong arguments were made in favor of trading Quebec for warmer and more fertile French possessions in the Caribbean, but in the end it was decided that henceforth Canada was to be British. Tears were shed in France over this, but many agreed with cynical Voltaire that these *quelques arpents de neige* (few acres of snow) had already cost the mother country far too dearly and that she was well rid of them.

French exodus

Military men and high officials in Quebec had to leave for France; the citizens and habitants who had nowhere else to go were more preoccupied with putting their lives back together again after the disruption of a long war that had killed up to a tenth of the population.

There were too many of them—around 80,000—to be dealt with as the British had dealt with their cousins the Acadians, by scattering them around the Colonies. The French fact in Canada would have to stay, and even be courted, to prevent the spread of the growing restlessness in the American Colonies. In 1774 the Quebec Act was passed, reassuring Canadiens that their Catholic religion and civil law would not be tampered with by their new Protestant masters. The outrage felt by many New Englanders that their old foes should be so favored added to American unrest, and the feeling was shared by the Boston merchants who had flocked to Canada in the wake of victory.

American advances
In 1775 the Americans advanced along the Lake Champlain invasion route toward Montreal, while another force struggled through the forests of Maine toward Quebec City. Their hope that the Canadiens would join them in defeating the British was not fulfilled, and local militiamen helped defeat the American attack. There was fierce fighting when Quebec City was besieged and Montreal was occupied for several months, but in 1776 naval defeat on Lake Champlain spelled the end of the American invasion. In the east, despite the close connections many of its inhabitants had with New England, Nova Scotia resisted American blandishments and fought off raids by privateers to remain in what came to be known as British North America.

The American Revolution helped solve Britain's problem of how to colonize Canada with people of British stock. Numerous Americans who resisted independence and wished to remain British migrated northward. By 1783 some 45,000 Loyalists had crossed into Canada, most settling in Nova Scotia, others in the Eastern Townships of Quebec, and some in what was to become Ontario. They set a pattern of migration that other Americans were soon to follow, less for political reasons than in search of cheap land. The balance of population in what was still called Quebec began to turn against French speakers, and in 1791, in an attempt to reconcile differences, two provinces came into being: Upper Canada (present-day Ontario), mostly English speaking, and Lower Canada (today's Quebec), mostly French speaking.

PRESSING NORTH & WEST
During this time, the native population of what was to become Canada still outnumbered Europeans, though in the east Caucasians now predominated. Here, native numbers had declined because of disease and other pressures on traditional ways of life. In the west, European explorers pressed onward in search of alternative outlets for the fur trade. In 1789 Alexander Mackenzie (1755–1820) reached the

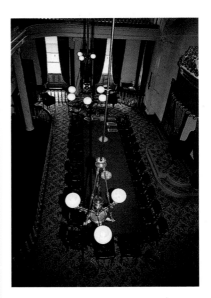

The confederation chamber in Charlottetown, Prince Edward Island, was the scene of Canada's creation in 1864.

Arctic and in 1793 the Pacific, the first European to cross the continent north of Mexico. He narrowly missed encountering Captain George Vancouver aboard H.M.S. *Discovery*, who was surveying the Pacific coast. In 1808 Simon Fraser made the journey down the river to be named after him and reached the Pacific near present-day Vancouver. Both he and Mackenzie were in the employ of the North West Company, soon to be merged with the Hudson's Bay Company, which still held sway over all the vast territory west and north of Lake Superior.

TOWARD A UNITED CANADA
The War of 1812 between the United States and Britain saw plenty of fighting in Canada. Many Americans assumed that their overwhelming superiority in numbers meant the end of British North America, that Canada's conquest would be, in President Thomas Jefferson's words, "a mere matter of marching." But resistance to American attack was stiffer than expected. A famous victory was won at Queenston Heights above the Niagara River. And though U.S. forces occupied and burned York (the future Toronto), British naval power

was decisive in the end, assuring the political independence of Canada from its great neighbor. Britain then built great forts such as Quebec's Citadel, just in case.

Internal problems now became the main concern. Britain had initially hoped that Canada might resemble the old country, with a local aristocracy to keep the lower orders in place and to discourage contamination by democratic ideas from the south. In practice, this led to rule by an oligarchy, nicknamed "the family compact" in Upper Canada and the *château clique* in Lower Canada.

Resentment grew, fanned in York by a firebrand journalist, William Lyon Mackenzie (1795–1861), and given an extra edge in Lower Canada by French–British antagonism. In 1837–38, resentment turned to rebellion. In York, the uprising led by Mackenzie (see p. 171) almost degenerated into farce, as his motley army of toughs was quickly routed by the local militia. In Lower Canada, the *Patriote* followers of Louis-Joseph Papineau fought valiantly against British troops, but the issue was never really in doubt, especially after nearly a hundred of them were killed at Sainte-

Whether in agreement or not, it is difficult to ignore this assertion from the Parti Québécois.

Eustache near Montreal.

Canada needed attention. It got it from a new governor-general, John George Lambton, Earl of Durham, who soon earned his nickname "Radical Jack" by his ruthless anatomy of the Canadian problem and his willingness to think of innovative solutions. His description of French–British relations as "two nations warring in the bosom of a single state" still resonates today. But his promotion of a union of all Britain's North American colonies came a little too early, and in 1841 he had to content himself with reuniting Upper and Lower Canada in a system of "responsible government" where unelected cliques would no longer be dominant.

The country was developing rapidly as immigrants poured in from Great Britain and Ireland, though a proportion of them subsequently moved on to the even more rapidly developing United States. The Pacific coast experienced sudden growth from 1858, when tens of thousands of mostly American prospectors used Victoria on Vancouver Island as a staging post on the way to the gold strikes on the mainland. Fearful of a U.S. takeover (as had happened in California), the mainland and Vancouver Island were joined together as the new colony of British Columbia. Meanwhile, around the Red River in what was to

The monument to fallen Canadian soldiers at Vimy Ridge, France

become Manitoba, land-hungry farmers moving west from Ontario were disturbing the way of life of the Métis, people of French and native descent, who lived by bison-hunting and providing the Hudson's Bay Company with pemmican and other supplies.

Dawn of the Confederation

The passions unleashed by the Civil War in the United States disturbed the inhabitants of British North America. Perhaps it was time to get together after all. In 1864 representatives from the province of Canada gate-crashed a meeting at Charlottetown that politicians from Nova Scotia, Prince Edward Island, New Brunswick, and Newfoundland had called to discuss a possible union of the Maritime colonies. In a remarkable display of synergy, a few days of debate, drinks, and dances sufficed for the idea of a confederation of all the colonies to be accepted. The Canadian Confederation was established by the British North America Act of 1867. A strong federal government was to rule from Ottawa, but the provinces retained many powers.

In 1868 the new Confederation gave notice of its serious interest in the west by buying most of the Hudson's Bay domain, at the bargain price of $1.5 million. British Columbia joined the Confederation in 1871, having been promised a railroad linking it with its new partners thousands of miles to the east. Prince Edward Island remained outside until 1873, when it persuaded Ottawa to take over its debts and provide a ferry service in perpetuity (replaced in 1997 by the aptly named Confederation Bridge). But Newfoundland resisted and stayed a colony of Great Britain until 1949.

Resistance to the smooth completion of Confederation came from the Prairies, where the Métis' grievances led to the Red River Rebellion of 1869–1870 led by Louis Riel (see pp. 228–9). Though Riel himself was forced into exile, many of the issues he raised were dealt with when the province of Manitoba was created in 1870. The Métis' way of life was doomed to disappear, whatever government guarantees were given; the bison had almost been exterminated, and the Prairies were soon to be put under the plow or converted into grazing grounds for cattle. In 1885 the Métis, together with some natives, rebelled again, but were swiftly put down by troops. Probably the most famous photograph in Canadian history was taken later that year, as Donald Smith, a director of the Canadian Pacific Railway, hammered home the last spike at Craigellachie in the Columbia Mountains (see pp. 262-3). In June the following year, the first scheduled train made its six-day, 2,891-mile journey across the continent from Montreal to Port Moody on the Pacific, a potent demonstration of the new country stretching *A mari usque ad mare* (from sea to sea)—Canada's motto.

MODERN TIMES

In the late 19th and early 20th centuries, the Prairies filled up with settlers from many parts of Europe, and the open grasslands that had stretched for a thousand miles gave way to fields, farms, and grain elevators. The provinces of Alberta and Saskatchewan were carved out of the Northwest Territories in 1905. In the years before 1914, the country boomed economically, and continued to prosper during World War I. Canada had loyally entered the war at Great Britain's side, but the pledge to raise a force of half a million men by voluntary enlistment proved impossible to fulfill. Conscription was eventually introduced, against the opposition of most French Canadians, who saw the war as a far-off struggle between European powers. British Canadians took great pride in the fighting prowess of the army in France; the fall of Vimy Ridge to Canadian troops after the failure of British and French attacks became a symbol of national valor. More than 60,000 Canadians were killed in the conflict. In gratitude, France gave Canada a square kilometer of land on Vimy Ridge, and one of the greatest memorials of the war was erected there in 1936.

Comradeship in arms could not conceal the waning of British influence in Canada. In 1922 American investment in the country surpassed the British total for the first time. Like the rest of the industrial world, Canada suffered the Great Depression that followed the Wall Street crash of 1929. The promise of the Prairies seemed negated by the dust-bowl conditions of the 1930s. Canada tried to stand aside from the worsening world crisis of the '30s, but in 1939 was once more obliged to go to war at Britain's side. Canada's war effort was immense; by 1945 a million people had put on uniform. Once again conscription threatened natonal unity, which was nevertheless held together by the excellent political skills of Prime Minister Mackenzie King (1874–1950).

Postwar prosperity brought a new stream of immigrants to Canada. Britons came, but were outnumbered by waves of displaced people from Central Europe, then by southern Europeans. Resistance to non-European immigration crumbled, adding Asians and Caribbean Islanders to the mosaic.

In the 1950s and 1960s the British Commonwealth was a focus of interest, but this declined as Britain turned to Europe. As a member of NATO, Canada kept troops in Europe, and sent others in support of UN missions around the world. A friendly but sometimes critical view was taken of American foreign policy.

The Quebec issue

At home, Quebec found a new voice and confidence as a result of the Révolution Tranquille (Quiet Revolution) of the 1960s. A cultural flowering accompanied a rejection of the Catholic Church's lead in education and social welfare and the growth of a new middle class, mainly employed in a vastly expanded public sector. The issue of Quebec's role in the country had never gone away; now it steadily intensified.

The most dramatic episode came in 1970,

Canada's armed forces have served as UN peacekeepers repeatedly since World War II.

when a terrorist group called the Front de Libération du Québec, kidnapped and subsequently murdered a British diplomat, then a provincial government minister. Prime Minister Pierre Trudeau declared martial law. Canadians across the country were shocked by scenes of armed troops on Montreal streets. Québécois were shocked, too, though many resented Trudeau's action, seeing it as a heavy-handed military occupation of their province.

More significant were federal attempts to give French speakers (including the hundreds of thousands outside Quebec) the same status as English speakers. Canada became officially bilingual, and, the government made great efforts to increase the number of Francophones in the public service. But Quebec refused to be placated. The nationalist Parti Québécois came to power in 1976 and pushed, if not for outright independence for the province, then for a form of "sovereignty association." Put to referendum, however, such aspirations have been defeated, roundly in 1980 and by a very narrow margin in 1995. Canada, for the time being, remains united, however shakily. ■

Building Canada

THE GROWTH AND DEVELOPMENT OF CANADA—AND THE EVER EVOLVING idea of what it means to be Canadian—can be observed through the country's architecture. From the first dwellings erected by native peoples to the imperial edifices of French and British culture, and onward to the futuristic skyscrapers in most Canadian cities, architecture has been an accurate barometer of national identity and aspiration.

EARLIEST STRUCTURES

No examples remain of buildings erected in Canada before the arrival of the Europeans, but numerous reconstructions and copies give an excellent idea of the variety of ways First Nations provided shelter for themselves. People who lived a migratory existence needed portable structures, and Europeans have long marveled at the superb functionality of the tepee used by Plains people. The tepee was made of bison hides stretched over a conical framework of wooden poles, and could easily be taken apart, transported, and re-erected. The wigwam used by the Algonquian groups in eastern Canada was also transportable. Its shape could be domed as well as conical, while its covering could be of bark, mats of reeds, or hides.

Leading a more settled existence, various Iroquois groups built permanent longhouses of timber, often grouped together in a palisaded village. Up to 180 feet in length, longhouses could accommodate several families and a number of separate hearths. An example of a Huron longhouse has been rebuilt at the settlement of Sainte-Marie among the Hurons in Ontario. The most impressive First Nations architecture, however, belongs to the Pacific coast, where groups like the Haida or Gitksan took advantage of the availability of fine timber to construct longhouses of imposing dimensions and great durability. Even in ruin, the Haida villages of the Queen Charlotte Islands are a magnificent sight.

EUROPEAN INFLUENCES

The first Europeans to build in Canada were the Vikings, who ranged along the Atlantic coast around A.D. 1000. One of the most fascinating sites in the country is the reconstructed Viking settlement at L'Anse aux Meadows (see p. 99) in Newfoundland, close to the northern end of the Strait of Belle Isle. Substantial longhouses with walls and roofs of sod must have been built with permanent residence in mind, but it seems that the occupants made only a short stay before abandoning what might have become the continent's first European colony.

As whaling and fishing developed in the 16th century, Basque whalers built tryworks and simple dwellings on the coast of Labrador,

Ice skating in Nathan Philips Square is a popular pastime for many Torontonians during the long winter.

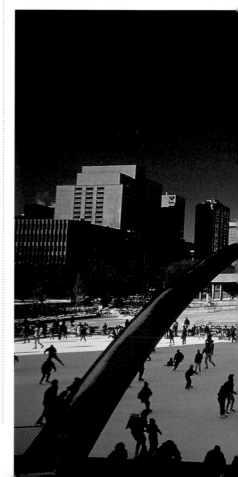

while English and French fishermen erected various structures, including the primitive shelters known as tilts, along the rugged coast of Newfoundland.

FORTIFICATION

Far more sophisticated were the Habitations, a series of compact fortified settlements built by Samuel de Champlain and his associates as they attempted to establish a French presence in the New World. While the Habitation of 1604 on Île Sainte-Croix in Passamaquoddy Bay lasted only a year, the Habitation established in 1608 at the foot of Cap Diamant grew into the city of Quebec. The Habitation of 1605 at Port Royal in Nova Scotia was destroyed, but was meticulously reconstructed in the 1930s. The other Habitations were protected by a palisade, but at Port Royal the solid timber buildings are grouped around a quad-rangle and are defended by their almost windowless outer walls as well as by the cannon mounted on a protruding bastion.

Champlain's Habitations introduce a persistent theme of fortification in Canadian building. The French and British needed protection from wild beasts, and natives, but most of all from each other and later from Americans. The fur trade was conducted from fortified posts, usually consisting of a timber palisade enclosing an array of structures. A fort of the Hudson's Bay Company, like Lower Fort Garry near Winnipeg, achieved a degree of grandeur. Begun in 1830, it is surrounded by a rectangle of substantial stone walls with circular bastions at the corners. Its centerpiece, the splendid governor's residence, called the Big House, was protected by a picket fence intended to exclude all but company officers and their families.

Defensive designs

Franco-British rivalry in the early 18th century led to the strengthening of Quebec City's defenses and from 1713 onward the construction of the remarkable fortified town of Louisbourg on Cape Breton Island. Louisbourg covered an area of 60 acres, and

Because it could be transported with ease, the functional tepee was the preferred dwelling of the Plains people.

for several decades flourished as a port and trading center. It was protected from the sea by a series of batteries and landward by a curtain wall with bastions that failed to save it from British attacks. This whole complex has been magnificently rebuilt from ruin.

Where Louisbourg failed, Halifax prospered. Begun in 1749 as a counterweight to the French fortress, Halifax was protected by a palisade and by a citadel. The palisade was soon absorbed into the growth of the town, but the citadel, much extended over the years, is still a dominating presence. With its star-shaped plan, bastions, ditch, and outworks, it reflects the principles on which European fortresses had been built a century before, and was obsolete before it was completed. This was true, too, of the great citadel at Quebec City, built between 1820 and 1832 and complemented by a wonderful circuit of city walls unique in North America.

The layout of Quebec City, and of Montreal as well, is attractively irregular. Some streets are straight, others reflect the lie of the land or, like Montreal's Rue Saint-Paul, follow the meandering alignment of old footpaths. The townscape that results recalls the ancient towns of Europe. By contrast, most towns laid out by the British conform to the gridiron plan so familiar in the rest of North America, imposed on the land with scant regard to natural features. Halifax is one example where the grid of streets has survived two and a half centuries of building and rebuilding, and there are many others, including Charlottetown and York, the ancestor of Toronto. In Nova Scotia's Lunenburg, little seems to have changed since 1753, when the surveyors traced out the rectangular street pattern stepping up the slopes overlooking the harbor. Like Quebec City, this wonderfully preserved example of urban design has been designated by UNESCO as a world heritage site.

CABINS, CHURCHES, & GOVERNMENT BUILDINGS

Early settlers built themselves cabins and modest houses of timber, practically none of which have survived. By the start of the 18th century in the Quebec countryside, the inhabitants of Quebec began to live in fieldstone houses with steep roofs of timber or thatch, whose designs owed at least something to the vernacular building in France's Normandy, Maine, and Anjou provinces. A century later, a characteristically French-Canadian house had developed, again of fieldstone, with a more gently sloping roof with overhanging eaves and perhaps dormer windows. A seigneur's manor might be indistinguishable from the houses of his former neighbors, or simply be a larger, more ornamental version. In Quebec, Montreal, and Trois-Rivières, a number of houses from the time of the French Regime survive. A distinguishing feature where buildings adjoin one another is the firewall extending above the roofline, a response to the terrible fires that periodically devastated towns built of timber.

Churches and other religious buildings dominated the countryside as well as the townscape of French Canada. Country churches were usually built in a prominent position, on a bluff overlooking a river or at a bend in a road. Many are overly simple, others elaborate, sometimes with exquisite interiors.

The central role of the Roman Catholic

Church in Quebec's history is expressed by such great religious institutions as the Couvent des Ursulines in Quebec City, begun in 1641, or the Vieux Séminaire de Saint-Sulpice in Montreal, begun in 1685. Montreal also has two superb 19th-century basilicas: Notre-Dame, with its twin towers and mystically lit interior, and Marie-Reine-du-Monde, modeled on St. Peter's in the Vatican. Pilgrimages played—and still play—an important part in the religious life of Quebec; their setting could be simple, like the hillside Stations of the Cross at Oka outside Montreal, or truly monumental, like the great shrines of Montreal's Saint-Joseph (begun in 1924) or Sainte-Anne-de-Beaupré (completed in 1934). Saint-Joseph was partly the work of architect-monk Dom Bellot, who in the 1930s created a brilliantly successful fusion of the traditional and the modern at the monastery of Saint-Benoit-du-Lac in Quebec's Eastern Townships.

British contributions

French Canadian architectural traditions persisted in Quebec long after the British Conquest, but they were soon complemented by styles that had their origin in Britain, and later New England. Like other churches in the New World, the Anglican Christ Church Cathedral in Quebec City (begun in 1800) is closely modeled on London's St. Martin-in-the-Fields of three-quarters of a century earlier. These Georgian churches were followed in the mid-19th century by edifices in the Gothic Revival style, among them the Anglican cathedrals in Montreal and Fredericton and Toronto's tall-spired St. James's. But the greatest Gothic structure in Canada is a secular one, the government complex gracing Ottawa's Parliament Hill, built in a direct line of descent from London's Houses of Parliament and in a magnificent setting overlooking the Ottawa River.

PROGRESS IN THE PROVINCES

Almost matching the grandeur of the buildings housing the federal government are some of the provincial parliaments. Ontario's parliament in Toronto (1893) is in the neo-Romanesque style developed by the U.S. architect Henry Hobson Richardson, quite distinct from the beaux arts style favored for the capi-

tals of the Prairie Provinces. Winnipeg, Regina, and Edmonton all have early 20th-century legislative buildings that perfectly express the high aspirations of the more recent provincial capitals.

The railroad stations of this era were equally grandiose. Montreal's Windsor Station is an exercise in Richardsonian Romanesque,

Toronto's downtown includes a wealth of outstanding contemporary office buildings.

while the beaux arts magnificence of the Great Hall of Toronto's Union Station is unmatched elsewhere in North America. Intimately associated with the railroads were the great hotels of the era. Beginning with the Banff Springs Hotel in 1888, a "Canadian château" architectural style was developed with which luxury trans-Canada travel will always be associated. The finest of these gloriously picturesque structures is perhaps the Château Frontenac in Quebec City, followed closely by Victoria's waterfront Empress Hotel.

Individuals could not hope to match the scale of these institutional buildings, but Canada has many distinguished houses. They range from the elegant Grange (1817) in Toronto, a Palladian mansion that could have come straight from the countryside of Georgian England, to Victoria's ostentatious mock-castle of Craigdarroch (1890) or the delightfully Italianate Bellevue (1841) at Kingston, early home of future Prime Minister John A. Macdonald (1815–1891). A world removed from the luxury of such edifices was housing for the masses. In Montreal, the developers of row houses in working-class suburbs saved on construction costs by putting the staircases outside. Often attractively curved and with balconies to match, they were a real menace in icy winter weather, but have become a much loved feature of the townscape.

International themes

In the course of the 20th century, international architectural influences have tended to outweigh any specifically Canadian characteristics. There are fine examples of art deco skyscrapers in Quebec City (Price Building, 1930) and in Vancouver (Marine Building, 1930).

The country even has examples of the work of that most international of all architects, Mies van der Rohe. Austere towers in black steel and glass designed by him or by his followers form the Toronto Dominion Centre (begun in 1964) and rise over Westmount Square in Montreal (1966). Since the 1970s, Canadian architects have cast aside such severity and attempted to design structures with more individuality, and occasionally with

Cabins on the shoreline of Lake O'Hara, British Columbia

greater sensitivity to their surroundings. Among recent high buildings in Toronto is the Royal Bank Plaza (1976), whose glittering gilt skin reflects every change in the light. Vancouver's Cathedral Place (1991) pays tribute to its château-style hotel neighbor in much the same way as Montreal's Place de la Cathédrale (1988) makes friendly gestures to the adjacent Christ Church Cathedral.

But perhaps the most characteristically Canadian developments have been those that respond to the country's long winter by creating an interior, weather-proof world. Montreal has its Underground City, fully integrated with its marvelous modern Metro, while Toronto has its PATH system of pedestrian spaces threading through the city center. Winnipeg, Calgary, and Edmonton have all striven to give pedestrians the same sort of shelter in their city centers, while suburban Edmonton boasts the biggest shopping center in the world, the internationally famous West Edmonton Mall. ■

The cultural scene

CANADIAN CULTURE SINCE THE 18TH CENTURY HAS REFLECTED A GROWING sense of place, which in turn has evolved into a notion of nationhood. The two main strands—French and English—began by trying to match the standards of the "home country." Confederation in 1867 brought this sense of nationhood into focus.

A Confederation school of poetry, dealing with specifically Canadian concerns, gave it a voice and visually, this pride of place culminated in the paintings of the Group of Seven—unsentimental studies of Canada in all its diversity. This regional awareness was, in turn, reflected in novels like *Anne of Green Gables*, Lucy Maud Montgomery's tender account of life on Prince Edward Island.

In recent years Canada has earned a distinctive reputation in the arts, achieving a high profile worldwide. Perhaps its modern population is the clue to this success, as the often cited Canadian mosaic has encouraged individuality and distinctive cultural pursuits among the many peoples who now make up the Canadian nation. One of the striking aspects of culture today is not its division into British and French camps but its multiethnic face. Ballet stars with Chinese roots or writers with origins in Sri Lanka and Brazil, are becoming as representative of Canada as the Stratford Festival has been for English culture and the Festival d'été for French culture.

Visual Arts

For Canadian artists imbued with the sense of the modern, the Group of Seven's representational landscapes presented a stylistic straighjacket. Quebec artists, their eyes fixed on Paris, were quick to pick up on movements such as cubism and surrealism. The major Québécois artist in the 1940s was Paul Emile Borduas, whose abstract paintings inspired the group known as the Automatistes. These painters saw spontaneous creation as the way forward. At the same time, the Toronto-based Painters Eleven were producing works that were at the forefront of abstract expressionism.

Since the 1970s, Canada's artistic community has exhibited an incredible richness and diversity. Michael Snow broke new ground in

Film shoots are common occurrences in Toronto.

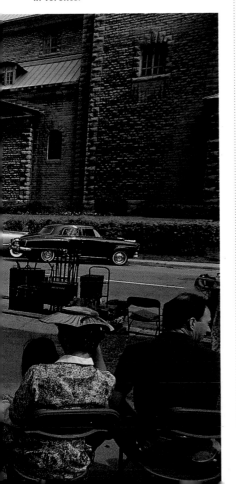

abstract painting while Inuit artists have benefited from cultural reappraisals. In the midst of these developments is the mainstay of Canadian art—the landscape—although now it is often given a new twist from Canada'a foreign-born artists such as Samir Ghanem, Elena Khomoutova, and Robert Milner.

Literature

Outstanding among recent Canadian novelists who have made their mark internationally is Robertson Davies, who died in 1995. His final work, *The Cunning Man* (1994) was acclaimed worldwide. In 1992, Michael Ondaatjee was a joint Booker Prize winner with his novel *The English Patient*, which has also been made into a successful film. Toronto's Margaret Atwood (*Alias Grace,* 1997) has an international profile, as have literary curmudgeon, Mordecai Richler of Montreal (*Barney's Version,* 1997) and Carol Shields (*Larry's Party,* 1997).

Among writers of historical narrative, few can rival Pierre Berton with his more than 40 books on different aspects of Canada's history. Up-and-coming writers include Joy Nozomi Kogawa, Ruby Wiebe, Rohinton Mistry, Neil Bissoondath, and Thomson Highway.

Among numerous first-rate writers in French, Anne Hébert's name stands out with many titles to her credit. Her *Kamouraska* is considered a classic and was made into a film of the same name by Claude Jutra.

Theater

The granddaddy of Canadian theater in both age and influence is the Shakespeare festival founded in 1953 in Stratford, Ontario. Featuring musicals and contemporary classics as well as Shakespeare, it is the largest classical theater company in Canada and is an important training ground for actors, directors, and stage technicians. Another important theater company performs at the Shaw Festival in Niagara-on-the-Lake, Ontario, and there are more than 90 other regional theaters across the country.

French-language theater flourishes with the works of well-established playwrights such as Michel Tremblay, who has revolutionized the scene in Quebec with his works in "joual" (slang), such as *Les Belles Soeurs* and more recently *Un geste de beauté,* and Michel-Marc

Oscar Peterson's dazzling skills have thrilled jazz fans since the late forties.

Joni Mitchell's soul baring lyrics have inspired songwriters worldwide.

Bouchard, whose works such as *Les Muses Orphelines* are similarly popular. There are also avant-garde companies such as Gilles-Maheu's Carbon 14 dance theater, whose recent work, *l'Hiver*, was first performed in early 1998.

In a category all of its own is the Montreal-based Cirque du Soleil, a nontraditional circus with no animal acts, where trapeze artists, jugglers, and acrobats of all kinds create a fast-moving, almost magical festival of francophone culture in North America.

Music
In the world of classical music, the Orchestre Symphonique de Montréal, with its conductor Charles Dutoit, is world renowned. Famous Canadian performers included the late virtuoso pianist, Glenn Gould. The country boasts several opera companies, notably the Toronto, with such opera singers as Maureen Forrester, Jon Vickers, and Teresa Stratas.

In the world of jazz, Montreal has a highly respected festival (Festival international de jazz), and the city was home to the brilliant and popular pianist Oscar Peterson.

Turning to popular music, the fame of several very different women has transcended Canadian borders. Singer-songwriter Joni

Mitchell is from Macleod, Alberta, pop diva Céline Dion from Montreal, and rocker Alanis Morrissette from Ottawa. The popularity of these very talented women has reached phenomenal proportions, each scoring huge record sales worldwide.

Dance
Canada boasts several world-class classical ballet companies, such as the Royal Winnipeg, with prima ballerina Evelyn Hart; Les Grands Ballets Canadiens, based in Montreal; and the National Ballet of Canada, with their long-time prima ballerina, Karen Kain, known as Canada's sweetheart until her 1997 retirement.

Montreal has become the Canadian capital of contemporary choreography both in dance and theater, thanks to some very avant-garde troupes, among them the Marie Chouinard Company, Ginette Laurin's company, O Vertigo Danse, and Edouard Lock's incredibly energetic and acrobatic Lalala Human Steps.

Broadcasting & film
Television in Canada is dominated by the Canadian Broadcasting Corporation, which has existed since 1936. Today, it is a continent-wide network of television and radio stations

Novelist Margaret Atwood dissects Canadian life in her unflinching prose.

Screen actor Donald Sutherland hails from Saint John, New Brunswick.

broadcasting in English, French, and a number of First Nations and Inuit languages, and is a major producer of shows and series of all types.

In the realm of film, the National Film Board of Canada trains and develops filmmakers. It also produces its own features for theatrical and nontheatrical release, as well as its famous film shorts that have won a number of Oscars, notably works by, Frédéric Back ("The Man who Planted Trees and Crack").

Important film festivals are held every year in Toronto, Vancouver, and Montreal. Among Canadian directors with an international reputation are David Cronenberg, whose horror movie *Crash* caused a sensation in 1997, Atom Egoyan (*Sweet Hereafter*, 1997), Bruce Beresford (*Black Robe*, 1991), and James Cameron, director of the enormously successful *Titanic* (1997).

Famous Canadian actors include Michael J. Fox, Donald Sutherland, Christopher Plummer, Genevieve Bujold, and Carole Laure; First Nations stars Graham Greene (*Dances with Wolves*) and Tina Keeper and Tom Jackson of CBC's popular series *North of '60* also have an international profile.

In French, Claude Jutra's coming-of-age classic, *Mon oncle Antoine* (1971), is considered by many to be Canada's best ever film. Other notable directors include Gilles Carle (whose *Maria Chapdelaine* starred Genevieve Bujold), Denys Arcand (*The Decline and Fall of the American Empire* and *Jesus of Montreal*), and Jean-Claude Lauzon (*Léolo*, 1992).

In a category of his own is Quebec City's Robert Lepage, an immensely talented actor, director, producer, and most recently filmmaker (*Le Confessional*, 1995) who was catapulted to fame with his *Plaques tectoniques,* which had worldwide success for its unusual visual effects and music.

Comedy

From Wayne and Schuster to Rich Little, Canadians have a distinctive, rather self-deprecatory wit. Celebrating 25 years of existence in 1998, the *Royal Canadian Air Farce,* which started life on CBC Radio, is now a Friday night television tradition in most Canadian homes, closely followed by a brash young crowd from Newfoundland who produce *22 Minutes Live*—a satirical look at the news, also on CBC Television.

Finally, Montreal's Festival Juste pour Rire ("Just for Laughs Festival") has created a solid reputation for humor in its 15-year existence and is the world's largest comedy fest. ∎

What to see & how to go about it

INTIMIDATED BY THE SHEER SCALE OF THE COUNTRY, MANY VISITORS TO Canada find themselves at a loss to decide just what they will do. Should they try to get an "all-over" look at Canada, touching base in the Atlantic provinces and moving west through the shield, plains, Rockies, and then to the northern wilderness—or would it be more sensible to single out a city or a region? Either choice is feasible, and many visitors manage to combine bits of both approaches.

TOURING

Some Canadians consider it a rite of passage to have crossed their vast country by car, but you don't have to follow them! However, it is perfectly possible to base a car tour on part of a province or region. Provincial tourist departments have helped by naming routes, some of which have become classics, like Nova Scotia's Cabot Trail. Find out also about ferry crossings, particularly in the east, where ferries may help you devise an interesting circular route. In the west, four ferry routes link the B.C. mainland with Vancouver Island, making a number of permutations possible. This gives a taste of the Pacific coast, enough perhaps to whet the appetite for the Inside Passage, the stunning journey linking Port Hardy with Prince Rupert and Alaska's Skagway.

Canada is, of course, the home of the bush plane, which has a much more exciting relationship with the earth's surface than any airliner. Some places are only accessible by this form of transport, but even the short trip from Vancouver across the Georgia Strait is a lot of fun in a little floatplane, and far quicker than the ferry.

VIEW FROM THE TRAIN

The all-time classic train route is, of course, the crossing of the Rocky Mountains. There are in fact three routes from the Prairies to the Pacific; the first, the original line of the Canadian Pacific, links Calgary with Vancouver via Banff, while the second also has Vancouver as its destination but starts at Edmonton and enters the mountains near Jasper, converging with the C.P.R. at Kamloops. The third route connects Edmonton with the far-off port of Prince Rupert via the spectacular Skeena Valley. VIA Rail has abandoned the C.P.R. line, but both this and the Edmonton–Jasper–Vancouver route have been revived by a private company. You can start out from either end of the route. An overnight stop in Kamloops means that you don't miss any of the scenery. You may find it worth the extra cost to sit in one of the panorama cars as you glide effortlessly through some of the world's finest mountain landscapes. Less well-known is another route in British Columbia, run by B.C. Rail, which takes its passengers north from Vancouver through the grand scenery of the Cariboo.

A rail trip is perhaps the easiest way to get the measure of the vastness of the Canadian Shield. The lonely port of Churchill on Hudson Bay has become a visitor destination because of its wildlife, particularly the polar bears. You can fly there, of course, but why not take the two-night train from Winnipeg, at least one way?

In central and eastern Canada, the train is more of an everyday means of transport, but the line that curls around the Gaspé Peninsula is an effortless way of getting to know this remote part of eastern Quebec.

SEEING THE CITIES

Most of Canada's large cities are extremely visitor friendly and easily explored on foot. The main attractions are often close together, and when they're not, a well-developed and efficient public transportation system will usually be the best way of reaching them. Traveling underground on Montreal's immaculate rubber-tired Metro is an experience in itself.

Canada's landscapes and resources are so diverse as to accommodate even the most daring hobbies.

You should have little difficulty in finding your way to places where locals and visitors hang out and which seem to encapsulate the spirit of the city. Halifax has its waterfront Historic Properties, Quebec its Place Royale, Winnipeg its new meeting-place around The Forks. City authorities usually position their information bureaus in these locations.

Canada's many miles of highway make touring by car an easy option for exploring the country.

GETTING OUT OF TOWN
In a country with a tourist industry as well developed as Canada's, you'll find plenty of organized bus tours, and choosing between them may be difficult. Most operations are seasonal, with less choice of destination and timing at the beginning and end of the season.

Renting a car, of course, will give you more flexibility, and is possible throughout the country.

GREAT OUTDOORS
One of the best ways of finding out about nature in Canada is by visiting the national parks. The country has a total of 168 national parks and national historic sites. Parks Canada is set up on broadly similar lines to the U.S. National Park Service, and protects the finest and most representative landscapes and habitats across the country, as well as providing high quality information and appropriate access for the public. A national park visitor center will often be the best place to start your exploration, whether it is of the Saguenay Marine Park, with its whales and other wildlife, or Banff National Park, where you may pick up useful hints on how to avoid the crowds.

There are also many provincial parks, where the scenery is often no less spectacular, and where there may be more campgrounds and other facilities.

WHEN TO GO
Canada welcomes visitors at all times of the year, and it might be simpler to ask when not to go. The least attractive times of the year are the brief transition periods between fall and winter, when it is cold but winter sports haven't begun, and between winter and spring, when conditions can be wet and slushy. Otherwise, every season has its attraction, though heat and humidity might be a problem for some in high summer in the east. Canadians have long known that winter is the season for fun. It is fun in town, when the bright lights and warmth of indoors contrast with the chill outside, city streets become hockey rinks, parks are laced with cross-country ski trails, and civil servants skate to work along Ottawa's Rideau Canal. Nothing could be more fun than Quebec City's winter carnival, when the populace goes wild in the streets at the sight of the Bonhomme (giant snowman), and ice castles sprout from the snow. It is fun in the countryside, too, when Canadians mix with Americans and the rest of the world in world-class ski resorts such as B.C.'s Whistler or at Mont Tremblant and Mont Sainte-Anne in Quebec. ∎

Steeped in sea air, Canada's three Maritime Provinces preserve an old-fashioned atmosphere, with pretty fishing villages, towns with a Loyalist imprint, and plenty of evocative reminders of the French Acadia of long ago.

The Maritimes

**Lobster traps
at North Rustic Harbour**

The Maritimes

THE MOSAIC OF DIVERSE LANDSCAPES that make up this sparsely populated region have one thing in common—the sea. The Maritime Provinces—New Brunswick, Prince Edward Island, and Nova Scotia—were settled from the sea, and most of their two million or so inhabitants live in coastal settlements of one kind or another. It is the timeless-seeming fishing villages and little ports that draw many of today's visitors to this long and deeply indented coastline, with its bays and coves, inlets and estuaries, cliffs and islands, and awe-inspiring Fundy tides.

The interior of the Maritimes, by contrast, seems deserted, blanketed by forest growing on the thin and hungry soils of uplands whose rocks are related to those of the Appalachians. The fertile intervals that do occur seem all the more welcoming, as in New Brunswick's Saint John River Valley, and the Annapolis Valley in Nova Scotia. Prince Edward Island (P.E.I.) is an exception: The neatly ordered farming pattern in which cultivation of the potato prevails has earned the province the name of "Million Acre Farm," or, less politely, "Spud Island."

The Maritimes have no natural focus; the sea divides and brings together. Halifax may be the biggest city, but its destiny has always been an oceanic one, with strong ties to Europe and the United States as well as with its hinterland. Well inland, genteel Fredericton, the capital of New Brunswick, shares the province's urban functions with the port city of Saint John and with Moncton, which still serves as the regional rail hub and in a newer role as a center for the Acadian population. Prince Edward Island, reluctant to join the rest of Canada at the time of Confederation, is still immersed in dreams of a separate identity, despite the recent construction of a great bridge linking it to its neighbors across the Northumberland Strait. Cape Breton Island, too, is quite distinct—its rust-belt industries lie cheek by jowl with the wild scenery of its Gaelic coast and Cape Breton Highlands National Park. Cape Breton is also the site of the greatest of the Maritimes' many historic monuments—the vast, reconstructed French fortress of Louisbourg.

The Maritimes are the most ethnically homogenous of Canada's regions. The French are still present in all three provinces, despite the rigors of the Acadian deportation carried out by the British in the mid-18th century. Though their numbers are small in P.E.I. and only slightly larger in Nova Scotia, they form about a third of the population in New Brunswick, the nation's only officially bilingual province. Otherwise the vast majority of the population claim descent from

Baie des Chaleurs
Miscou Island
Gulf of St. Lawrence
Îles de la Madeleine (Quebec)
St. Paul Island
Petit-Rocher
Caraquet
Shippagan
Village Historique Acadien
Bathurst
Cape North
Bay St. Lawrence
CAPE BRETON HIGHLANDS NATIONAL PARK
532m
Miramichi Bay
Pleasant Bay
Chéticamp
Ingonish
North Point
Tignish
Chatham
Newcastle
KOUCHIBOUGAC NATIONAL PARK
West Point
PRINCE EDWARD ISLAND
Cape Breton Island
Renous
Richibucto
Harcourt
Bouctouche
Miscouche
Cavendish
PRINCE EDWARD ISLAND NATIONAL PARK
New London
Souris
Elmira
Basin Head Fisheries Museum
Margaree Harbour
North Sydney
Summerside
Charlottetown
South Gut
St. Ann's
Inverness
Baddeck
Glace Bay
Sydney
Shediac
Borden
Port Elgin
Fort Amherst
Orwell
Port Hood
PARLEE BEACH PROV. PARK
Moncton
Cape Tormentine
Wood Islands
St. George's Bay
Bras d'Or Lake
Louisbourg
Hopewell Cape
Amherst
Pugwash
Caribou
Antigonish
Port Hastings
St. Peter's
Isle Madame
FUNDY NATIONAL PARK
Fort Beauséjour
Wentworth
Pictou
Port Hawkesbury
Canso
Sussex
Springhill
New Glasgow
Mulgrave
Hampton
Parrsboro
Glenholme
Truro
St. Martins
Minas Basin
St. Mary's
Wolfville
Stewiacke
Sherbrooke
Kentville
GRANDE PRÉ NAT. HIST. PARK
Sheet Harbour
Liscomb
Windsor
Port Dufferin
Fort Anne
Middleton
Bridgetown
Dartmouth
Bedford
Musquodoboit Harbour
Annapolis Royal
Port Royal Nat. Hist. Park - The Habitation
Mahone Bay
Chester
Peggys Cove
HALIFAX
Digby
KEJIMKUJIK NAT. PARK
South Brookfield
Lunenburg
Bridgewater
Church Point
Lake Rossignol
Liverpool
Shelburne
Lockeport
Barrington
Shag Harbour
Cape Sable

0   100 kilometers
0   50 miles

Area of map detail
Ottawa

British or Irish stock. Scots live all over Nova Scotia, with Highlanders and Islanders concentrated on Cape Breton Island; Irish inhabit the cities as do American Loyalists, for whom New Brunswick in particular became a second home. Among the Loyalists were freed slaves, ancestors of Halifax's contemporary black community. Earlier, the British had settled "foreign Protestants," mostly German in origin, in the planned port town of Lunenburg, part of the strategy for consolidating their hold on a region whose colonial population was almost entirely French. It took many years, the expulsion of the Acadians (1755),

and two sieges of Louisbourg (1745 and 1758) before the Maritimes finally passed wholly into British hands, and Ile St.-Jean became St. John's Island, and, later, Prince Edward Island.

In the 19th century, the economy of the Maritimes boomed on "wood, wind, and water." Local timber was exported or used in building the region's famed sailing ships. With the advent of steel ships after 1880, a long slump began, relieved temporarily by two world wars, and, more recently, by determined modernization and encouragement of such enterprises as salmon, agriculture, and—increasingly—tourism. ■

New Brunswick's
Fundy Shore

THE BAY OF FUNDY IS A REMARKABLE BODY OF TIDAL water. Nothing else quite like it exists in the marine world. Some of the world's highest tides—as much as 50 feet—have been recorded here. Their height is caused by the bay's funnel shape—wide and deep at the entrance, narrow and shallow at the head. These impressive tides carry about 100 billion tons of water in and out of the bay every day, providing a magnificent display in the process.

Tourism New Brunswick
☎ 800/561-0123

St. Andrews
⛰ 54A3

Visitor Information
✉ 46 Reed Ave.
☎ 506/529-3000
🕐 Closed Nov.–April

Fundy National Park's Bennett Lake guarantees beautiful scenery both on and off the water.

The incessant movement of the waters help create an array of fascinating phenomena such as the sculptured rocks at Hopewell Cape, the Reversing Falls at Saint John, and the Old Sow whirlpool among the Islands of Passamaquoddy Bay. It also acts as a nutrient pump to support an extraordinary variety of marine life in the broad intertidal zone and offshore. For example, off the Fundy Islands, swarms of krill attract fin and humpback whales, along with large flocks of maritime birds such as phalaropes, shearwaters, and gulls.

Visitors should be warned that the great difference between the high and low tides and the speed of the incoming tide make it essential to consult the tide table carefully before taking a walk along the beach. (Tide timetables are available from tourist offices throughout the region.) Bear in mind that the Bay of Fundy is also renowned for its fogs.

ST. ANDREWS & THE FUNDY ISLANDS

In 1604 a tiny island in the St. Croix River dividing New Brunswick from Maine was chosen by Sieur des Monts and Samuel de Champlain as their first Habitation, though their first winter caused them to abandon the site in favor of Port Royal on the Nova Scotia shore. Today, St. Croix Island, visible from the riverside roads on both sides of the U.S./Canada border, is an international historic site. You will, however, need your own boat if you wish to visit it.

Passamaquoddy Bay essentially remains a summer place, a

favored vacation spot for well-to-do Americans and Canadians. Its focal point is **St. Andrews** (*Welcome Centre, 506/529-3556*), now primarily a fishing harbor and resort, but once a flourishing trading port. The town was founded in 1783 by Loyalists who had fled north and settled in Castine, Maine, only to discover a few years later that a redrawing of the frontier had left them stranded in the United States. Undaunted, they dismantled their newly built houses and shipped them north again, reerecting them in St. Andrews, where some of them still stand today and help to give the town its particular charm. Named for the 15 children of King George III, its tree-lined streets are fringed with elegant houses and churches. Among the most distinguished of these buildings are **Sheriff Andrews House Provincial Historic Site** (*63 King St., Tel 506/529-5080*) of 1820 and the exquisitely furnished 1824 **Ross Memorial Museum.**

DEER ISLAND & CAMPOBELLO

If you have half a day to spare, an island-hopping excursion in Passamaquoddy Bay is fun. From Letete take the free ferry to **Deer Island** (*Bay ferries, Tel 888/249-7245*); it offers lots of spray and bracing sea air. Then continue to **Campobello Island** by the rather primitive ferry, which gives you a close-up view of the **Old Sow Whirlpool**—but not too close. Take the Roosevelt International Suspension Bridge (a very long name for a short bridge) to Lubec, Maine, and then US 1 and Maine 189 to the Canadian border. If time permits, you won't regret making a stop at the **Ganong Chocolatier Plant** in St. Stephen (*73 Milltown Blvd., Tel 506/465-5611*).

SAINT JOHN

New Brunswick's biggest city straddles the rocky ground astride the mouth of the Saint John River.

Ross Memorial Museum
- ⊠ King & Montague Sts.
- ☎ 506/529-5124
- 🕘 Closed Sun.–Mon. late June–Oct., Sun. rest of year
- 💲 $

Saint John
- 🅰 54A3

Visitor Information
- ⊠ City Hall Annexe Building, New Gower St.
- ☎ 506/576-8106
- 🕘 Closed Sat.–Sun.

Franklin D. Roosevelt & Campobello

In 1883, a land development company promoted the soft yet bracing air and fog of Campobello Island as "gentle restoratives for an overstrung race." Among those enticed were James and Sara Delano Roosevelt, parents of one-year-old Franklin D. Roosevelt (1882–1945).

In 1904, Franklin and his young wife, Eleanor, acquired their own home here. Many years later, in 1921, after fighting a forest fire for hours, he took a dip in the frigid Bay of Fundy waters and contracted the polio

An early photograph of Franklin D. Roosevelt

virus that was to cripple him for the rest of his life. Twelve years passed before he felt able to return to his "beloved island," and by that time he was President of the United States.

A visit to Campobello is a poignant return in time. Franklin and Eleanor's 34-room abode is impeccably maintained as a historic site by the governments of Canada and the U.S. as Roosevelt Campobello International Park (*see map pp. 54–5, Tel 506/752-2922, closed mid-Oct.–early May*). ∎

Loyalist House

- 120 Union St.
- 506/652-3590
- Closed Labor Day—mid-May
- $

Barbour's General Store

- The Market Slip
- 506/658-2939
- Closed mid-Oct.—mid-May

Salt spray has not prevented the vigorous growth of vegetation on the sandstone sea stacks at Hopewell Cape.

Home to the wealthy and powerful Irving family, who control many of the city's interests, Saint John is an important port, with a huge oil refinery (the biggest in Canada) and a mighty pulp mill. Fondly known as Fog City throughout New Brunswick, it is laid out on a series of dead-end streets that can cause frustrations for visitors.

The waterfront at Market Slip makes a good starting point for exploring the city's attractions. The centerpiece is **Barbour's General Store,** an authentic 19th-century emporium stocked with goods of the period. Old warehouses have been incorporated into Market Square, completed in 1983 as a multipurpose development. Its main feature is the **New Brunswick Museum** (*Market Square, Tel 506/643-2300*) opening off the central atrium. Its rich collections cover much of the province's human and natural history.

Every July the waterfront is the site of an annual reenactment of the Loyalist landing, and the city center has several reminders of this period in Saint John's history. The **Loyalist House** of 1817 escaped a great fire in 1877 and has a beautifully furnished interior. King Square is laid out in the form of a British Union flag, and is bounded

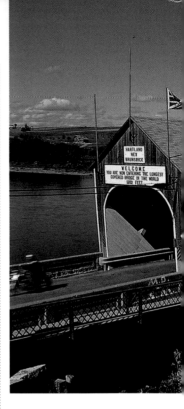

by the **Loyalist Burial Ground** with many original tombstones.

The city's biggest tourist draw is just outside the city's center. A trip to see **Reversing Falls Rapids** (*lookout point off Hwy. 100, Tel 506/658-2937*) is a memorable part of a visit to Saint John. At low tide the river current carries water downstream to the Bay of Fundy. At high tide the force of the Fundy tides carries water upstream. From the viewpoint you can see the water flow as it reverses over the rapids. Be warned that the smell of the pulp mill upstream can be rather strong.

THE FUNDY SHORE

Eastward from the attractive little lobster port of St. Martins stretch 25 miles of rugged coastline, one of the least accessible shorelines in eastern North America.

The coast can also be reached at the **Fundy National Park,** with its tracts of mixed hardwood and evergreen forest as well as cliffs, coves, rock pools, and intertidal flats. **St. Mary's Point,** an important resting and feeding site for countless migratory seabirds, marks the division between Chignecto and Shepody Bays. At **Hopewell Cape** (*south of Moncton by Rte. 114*), the scouring Fundy tides have carved the cliffs of red standstone into improbable flowerpot shapes, capped by vigorous tree growth. The trees are all that show at high tide and the flowerpots have become a scatter of little islands.

MONCTON

Originally called The Bend because of its location on a curve of the Petitcodiac River, Moncton then became The Hub, the focus of the Maritimes' railroad network and the site of Canadian National (CN) huge maintenance depot. CN closed the depot in 1989, but the town has partly recovered by becoming the telecommunications center of Canada. Moncton's bilingualism helped here; the town is also the informal capital of Acadia, with about 30 percent of its population descended from returning Acadians (see pp. 62–3).

The Fundy tides have a final fling as they meet the Petitcodiac. The wave that precedes the incoming tide (known as the Tidal Bore) can be viewed from **Boreview Park** (*Main & King Sts.*) in the center of town. The bore can vary from a ripple to nearly two feet in height (but is commonly a ripple), depending on the phase of the moon. What is generally much more impressive is the tremendous inrush of water that follows the bore and the rapid rise in the water level. From a small stream crossing mudflats a mile wide, the Petitcodiac River becomes a wide channel with no mud in sight.

The longest of New Brunswick's covered bridges spans the Saint John River at Hartland.

Fundy National Park

- 🅰 55B3
- ✉ Box 40, Alma
- ☎ 506/887-6000
- 💲 $ vehicle fee, free in winter

Moncton visitor information

- 🅰 55B3
- ✉ City Hall, 655 Main St.
- ☎ 506/853-3590

Fort Beauséjour
 55B3

Visitor information
Off Hwy. 114
506/536-0720
Closed mid-Oct.–May

Acadian Shore
55B5

A solitary walker savors the sandy shoreline of Kouchibouguac National Park.

FORT BEAUSÉJOUR

Overlooking the marshlands at the head of the Cumberland Basin is **Fort Beauséjour,** which commands the Chignecto isthmus, the neck of land separating New Brunswick from Nova Scotia. Four years after its completion by the French in 1751, it was attacked by a party of British regulars and Massachusetts volunteers led by Col. Robert Monckton, and fell after a siege of two weeks. The French commandant, De Vergor, who was allowed to march his men out with banners flying and band playing, was fated to meet the British once again, in 1759, below the Plains of Abraham at Quebec. As for Monckton, his name, misspelled, was given to the nearby settlement previously known as The Bend; his action, carried out in time of peace, helped precipitate the Seven Years' War.

In 1776, refortified, renamed Fort Cumberland, and commanded by Col. Joseph Goreham of the Royal Fencible Americans, the stronghold successfully beat off an attack by rebel New Englanders. Strengthened again against a possible U.S. attack in the War of 1812, it was finally abandoned in 1835.

The fort's star-shaped hilltop earthworks are still an imposing sight, and cannon and mortar evoke its days of action. The visitor center has excellent displays, not only on military history, but on the deportation of the Acadians and on the surrounding landscape, which still bears the imprint of the Acadians' extensive dike and drainage systems.

THE ACADIAN SHORE

Appreciated for its sandy beaches, warm water, and abundant seafood, the eastern coast of New Brunswick facing the Northumberland Strait and the Gulf of St. Lawrence is the heartland of the Maritimes' Acadian population. The Acadian tricolor flies from many a residence, there are Acadian festivals and blessings of the fishing fleet, and numerous attractions have distinctive Acadian flavor.

The province makes much of the coast, enjoying some of the warmest saltwater swimming north of Virginia. Because of the shallowness of the sea, water temperatures can indeed reach 70°F or more in summer. From Moncton it is a short drive to the resort of **Shediac** and the fine sand of the extremely popular **Parlee Beach Provincial Park** (*Tel 506/533-3363*). Farther north is **Kouchibouguac National Park** (*Tel 506/876-2443, visitor center closed mid-Oct.–mid-May*),

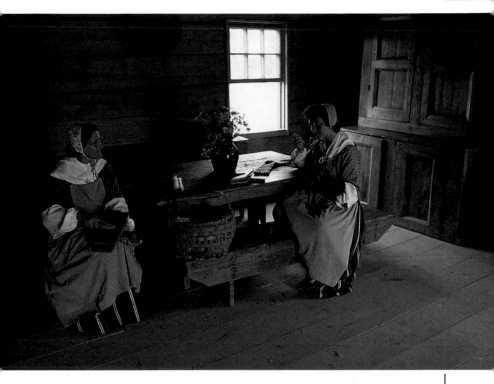

with a landscape of forest, bog, marsh, and meadowland, and a shoreline of sandy beaches and warm water lagoons, protected by barrier islands and sand dunes.

There are plenty of accessible beaches along the shores of the Acadian Peninsula, whose north coast faces the long inlet of the sea named Baie des Chaleurs (Warm Bay) by Jacques Cartier. Lovers of solitary walks by the sea will head for remote Miscou Island at the very tip of the peninsula, reached by free ferry *(bridge under construction at press time)*.

It is easy for visitors to make contact with some aspect of Acadian life, past or present. At **Bouctouche,** the **Musée de Kent** realistically re-creates the regime endured by girls at a 19th-century Roman Catholic boarding school, while the **Pays de la Sagouine** *(Tel 506/743-1400, closed winter)* is a theme park devoted to the doings of the colorful characters created by the popular novelist Antonine Maillet. On the Acadian Peninsula, **Caraquet** has a rambunctious Festival Acadien on the Feast of the Assumption (August 15), as well as the fascinating **Acadian Museum** (*15 blvd. Saint-Pierre East, Tel 506/727-1713, closed Sept.–June*) and the nearby **Village Historique Acadien** (*6 miles west of Caraquet on Rte. 11, Tel 506/726-2600, closed mid-Oct.–May*). This excellent counterpart to Kings Landing Historical Settlement (see p. 64) in the southwest offers an array of traditional buildings from all over New Brunswick, all set in a re-created landscape and "populated" by 19th-century folk who help bring alive the Acadia of yesteryear. ∎

The Village Historique Acadien evokes the simple life of Acadian countryfolk.

Musée de Kent
- ✉ 150 rue du Couvent
- ☎ 506/743-5005
- ◷ Closed Oct.–May

Acadie & after

Acadia (Acadie in French) was the name given to the Atlantic region of New France to distinguish it from Canada, which in those days consisted only of the settled area of the St. Lawrence Valley. At the beginning of the 17th century, Acadia was the site of the first permanent European settlement north of Florida. Although its population was subjected to massive deportation by the British in the mid-18th century, the name and a distinctive francophone culture lives on in the Maritime Provinces.

Acadia's origins

The word "Acadia" is derived from Arcadia, the province that the ancient Greeks thought of as an earthly paradise. The term was used in 1524 by Giovanni da Verrazano (1485–1528) to describe the coastline well to the south of present-day Acadia—the "r" in the name was lost by mapmakers long ago. French colonization of the area began in 1604, with the establishment by explorers Sieur des Monts and Samuel de Champlain of the short-lived Habitation on Île Sainte Croix, followed by the

more permanent fortified settlement at Port Royal the following year. More colonists arrived in the 1630s, mostly from the western regions of France, but disputes between its leaders held back the colony's development. Franco-British rivalry was present from the earliest days; Port Royal was sacked in 1613 by raiders from Virginia, and parts of the colony passed between the French and British several times before the definitive establishment of British rule in 1763.

The Acadians concentrated on making a living by farming the marshlands they expertly reclaimed from the sea around the Bay of Fundy. Trading relations were closer with New England, the home of *nos amis l'ennemi* (our friends the enemy), than with far-off France. The British rulers of Nova Scotia attempted to extract an oath of unconditional loyalty from their Acadians, but they refused, preferring to remain neutral in what to them seemed irrelevant struggles between imperial powers. As tensions rose in the build-up to the Seven Years' War (1756–1763), the British felt unable to tolerate the threat from what they saw as a potentially hostile population. In 1755 the majority of the Acadians were rounded up and deported, some to France, some to Britain, some to the American Colonies. A significant number escaped into the forests or made their way to Quebec. Many ended up in Louisiana, where their name metamorphosed into "cajun." Their homes were destroyed to discourage any thoughts of returning.

Despite the rigors of the *Grand Dérangement* (the Deportation), in which many perished of hunger and disease, the Acadians proved tenacious. Many made the journey back to their lands, only to find them in the hands of New England colonists encouraged to move north by the British. Joined by released prisoners and others emerging from the shelter of the forests, the returnees settled on far less fertile lands and found new livelihoods in fishing and lumbering—important occupations to this day.

For decades, the Acadians accepted their lot as second-class citizens in a conquered land, unable to vote, exploited economically, and

The expulsion depicted at the Museum of the Acadians in Bonaventure

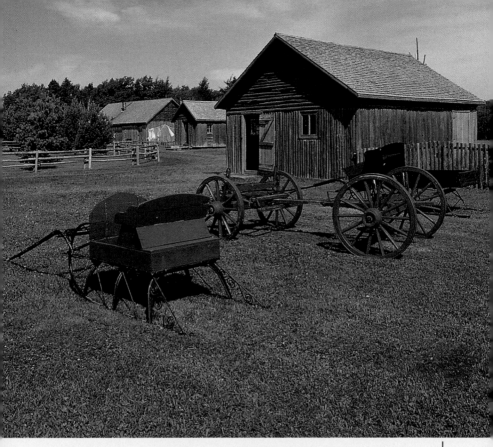

The Acadian Village at Mount Carmel on Prince Edward Island is an evocative and informative reminder of the Acadian presence in the Maritimes.

with no institutions of their own other than the Roman Catholic Church, which itself was largely staffed by clergy from Quebec.

But revival began in the 19th century. A wider world became aware of Acadian identity through the 1847 sentimental epic *Evangeline* by Henry Wadsworth Longfellow (1807–1882), which dramatized the Deportation. Acadians won the right to vote, and by the end of the century they had adopted a flag (a French tricolor with the Marian star), a national holiday (August 15, the Feast of the Assumption), and a national anthem ("Ave Maria Stella"). As in Quebec, population increased rapidly, from about 8,500 at the start of the 19th century to around 300,000 today. During the 20th century, economic underprivilege was reduced by the establishment of cooperatives, political representation improved, and language rights were legislated.

A vigorous middle class came into being as Acadians moved away from farming, fishing, and forestry into administrative and professional work. Their vital folk culture continued to thrive, supplemented by new initiatives in theater, literature, film, radio, and television.

Today's Acadians live all over the Maritime Provinces. The greatest concentration (one-third of the province's total population) is in New Brunswick, particularly in the Saint John River Valley and along the "Acadian shore." The city of Moncton serves as a focus of francophone culture, with its university and TV and radio stations. Smaller numbers of Acadians also live on the west side of Prince Edward Island and on Cape Breton Island and the "French shore" of Nova Scotia.

To understand the Acadians and their eventful history, it is worth a visit to Grand-Pré National Historic Site (see p. 80). ■

Saint John River Valley drive

Between the headwaters of its several branches in the wooded wildernesses of Maine and Quebec and its mouth on the Bay of Fundy, the Saint John River drains a basin of some 25,000 square miles, passing through some of the most attractive and agriculturally rich countryside in New Brunswick. This driving route covers about 175 miles, following Trans-Canada 2 and linking Edmundston, near the Quebec border, with Fredericton.

QUEBEC START
Edmundston
St.-Basile
Rivière-Verte
Ste.-Anne-de-Madawaska
Saint John
Siegas
St.-Léonard
① Grand Falls
MAINE
Drummond
Aroostock
Tobique
Perth-Andover
Kilburn
Bath
Florenceville   Bristol
U.S.A.   CANADA
② Hartland
Grafton
Woodstock
Nackawic
Saint John
Meductic
Pokiok

Hartland covered bridge

Starting from French-accented Edmundston, follow Trans-Canada 2 and admire the views of the Saint John, as it sweeps peacefully through farming landscapes and forms the boundary between the United States and Canada. Much of the valley's farmland is devoted to potato growing, second only in importance to the Prince Edward Island crop. At **Grand Falls ①** (*access from Malabeam reception center on Madawaska Rd. Tel 506/473-6013, closed mid-Oct.–mid-May*), the river's character changes dramatically, it plunges over 80-foot falls and rushes down a rocky chasm in whose bed great potholes can be seen when water levels are low.

More pastoral landscapes follow the park, backed by rounded, forested hills. At **Hartland ②** (*visitor center at bridge, closed Oct.–May*), the river is crossed by a particularly fine covered bridge, at 1,282 feet the world's longest. Dams along the river's course have flooded farmland and disturbed salmon runs, but the linear lakes formed are a haven for other wildlife, and the flooding stimulated the establishment of the valley's greatest visitor attraction, **Kings Landing Historical Settlement ③** (*Tel 506/363-5805, closed mid-Oct.–May*). In the early 1960s, some 50 structures were uprooted from their original sites in the valley bottom and reerected on higher land. With carefully re-created surroundings of fields and meadows, fences, and gardens, the 300-acre site of Kings Landing evokes life in the valley from the arrival of the Loyalists in

1784 to the end of the 19th century. As well as a variety of houses, there is a sawmill, gristmill, forge, store, church, pub, and theater with live performances. Attention to detail and costumed villagers going about their everyday tasks help make this one of the best re-creations of traditional rural life in North America.

From Kings Landing the highway follows the river northeast until it reaches the genteel capital of New Brunswick. With its population of academics and civil servants **Fredericton** ❹ (*Visitor center, City Hall, 397 Queen St., Tel 506/452-9616*) stands on a bend of the Saint John River close to the river's tidal limit. Well inland, and thus relatively safe from American incursions, it seemed to the Loyalists who established it in 1784 a better choice as provincial capital than coastal Saint John. A grandiose **Provincial Legislative Assembly Building** (*Queen & John Sts., Tel 506/453-2527*) in Second Empire style, the stately stone-built **Christ Church Cathedral** (*Church & Brunswick Sts., Tel 506/450-8500*) with a tall spire, and remnants of the British garrison's presence in the **Military Compound Provincial Historic Site** (*Tel 506/452-9508*) set the tone of the place, as do elm-lined streets and a number of Regency houses. To complete the neocolonial picture there is a ceremonial **Changing of the Guard** (*twice a day,*

Tues.–Sat.) during the summer season. The British garrison departed following the Confederation in 1867, but Fredericton retained its military importance; Canadian forces trained here in both world wars, and in the 1950s nearby Camp Gagetown became the country's largest army base.

In the **York-Sunbury Historical Society Museum** (*Queen St., Tel 506/455-6041, closed Jan.–Feb.*) the town possesses an intriguing local museum, crammed with curiosities. The exhibit everyone comes to see, however, is Fred Coleman's giant frog, fed lovingly until it attained a weight of 44 pounds, then stuffed.

Fredericton's art collection is equally compelling. The city benefited greatly from favors bestowed by politician and newspaper magnate Lord Beaverbrook (1879–1964), a resident of New Brunswick. Along with university buildings and a theater, Beaverbrook gave Fredericton its **Beaverbrook Art Gallery** (*703 Queen St., Tel 506/458-8545, closed Mon. Sept.–May*). The gallery has old masters, the country's largest collection of British art, and an array of Canadian pictures. ■

🔲 See area map pp. 54–5
➤ Edmundston
↔ 175 miles
◎ Allow 2–3 days
➤ Fredericton

NOT TO BE MISSED

- Grand Falls
- Hartland covered bridge
- Kings Landing Historical Settlement
- Beaverbrook Art Gallery

Fredericton City Hall

Prince Edward Island

PHYSICALLY LINKED TO THE REST OF CANADA BY THE
Confederation Bridge since 1997, Prince Edward Island strives to
maintain the offshore identity of which it is so proud and which kept
it aloof from Confederation until there seemed no alternative to join-
ing. That identity is partly the land, partly human.

P.E.I. has been an island since about
5,000 years ago, when the sea level
rose to create the Northumberland
Strait, Its glaciated surface is flat or
gently rolling. Beneath the distinctive red soil, in which the famous
potatos flourish, are layers of soft
red sedimentary rock, exposed in
crumbling cliffs at many places
along the shore. Though some
woodland remains, it is agriculture
that has determined the patchwork
pattern of fields and farms, so
much in contrast to the inter-
minable forest blanketing much of
the Maritimes.

P.E.I.'s first European settlers
came directly from France, brought
here in 1720 to secure the island
for the mother country after it
had lost Acadia and Newfoundland to Britain in 1713. Like the
rest of the francophone population
of the Maritimes, this community
was deported in mid-century as
tensions rose between Britain and
France. But many later returned,
and today some 12 percent of the
population is of French or Acadian
descent, though only a fraction still
have French as their mother
tongue. Otherwise it is the British
Isles that have supplied the island
with its European inhabitants. The
English mainly arrived after the
Acadian deportation in 1755, when
it was decided to replace the French
with a more docile population.
When Charlottetown was founded
as the island's capital in 1768, the
English were followed by Scots, the
majority of them Gaelic-speaking
Highlanders, then later by Irish,

both Protestant and Catholic.
This settlement and the maintenance of cultural tradition has
made the island one of the most
Anglo-Celtic areas of Canada.

CONFEDERATION BRIDGE

It is still possible to travel to
P.E.I. by ferry (*Tel 902/566-3838*)
but since 1997 most visitors' introduction to the Island has been via
the **Confederation Bridge**
(*$35 toll payable on leaving only;
pedestrians and cyclists must take
bus*), which leaps 8 miles across
the Northumberland Strait between
Cape Tourmentine, New Brunswick,
and Borden-Carleton, P.E.I. The
longest continuous marine span
bridge in the world, it has a two-lane
highway supported on 65 piers and
rises to a height of nearly 200 feet to
allow shipping to pass.

One of the terms of entry into
the Confederation insisted on in
1873 by the island's leadership was
that the federal government should
provide "continuous communication" between the island and the
mainland. The merits of a "fixed
link" were the subject of endless
debate, some people favoring a rail
tunnel, others a bridge. In the
meantime, ferries maintained a
link which, given winter ice floes,
was far from reliable. Nevertheless,
the 1993 decision to build the link
in the form of a bridge was not
greeted with universal acclaim.
There were deep fears about the
possible effects of the bridge
on the strait's environment, in

🅰 55C4

**Visitor
information
for P.E.I. &
Charlottetown**

✉ Hillsborough St.,
   Charlottetown

☎ 902/368-444

**Above: Prince
Edward Island's
coat of arms
mixes oak trees
and the British
lion.**

**Right: Since the
opening of the
Confederation
Bridge in 1997, ice
floes in the
Northumberland
Strait no longer
cut off links with
the mainland.**

Charlottetown

🅰 55C3

Province House National Historic Site

✉ Richmond St.

☎ 902/566-7626

🕐 Closed weekends mid-Oct.–May

Province House is one of Charlottetown's fine public buildings designed by P.E.I's leading early 19th-century architect, Isaac Smith.

particular on its potential to prolong the presence of ice in the strait and thus shorten the island's growing season. Its impact on the equally crucial lobster fishery was also a source of worry, while some islanders feared the effect of unrestrained tourism on a relatively protected way of life.

The **Gateway Village Complex** *(Tel 902/437-8539)* by the Borden-Carleton toll plaza has an exhibition entitled "Our Island Home," whose displays and artworks make an excellent introduction to the island and its links to the mainland.

CHARLOTTETOWN

Prince Edward Island's miniature capital was founded in 1768, the successor to the nearby French settlement of Port La Joye, abandoned at the time of the Acadian deportation. Well sited on the natural harbor formed by the confluence of the Hillsborough River and its north and west tributaries, Charlottetown has preserved its original layout. A typical example of the British colonial gridiron plan, it has refinements in the shape

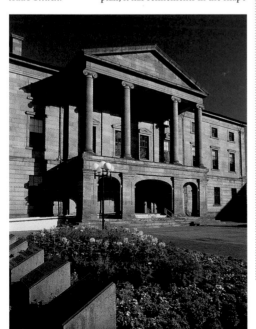

of a central square for civic edifices and four smaller squares symmetrically placed. From the town's **Victoria Park** (*Lower Kent St.*) there is a fine view across the water to the site of **Fort Amherst** (*off Rte. 19, 25 miles west of Charlottetown, Tel 902/672-6350*), built by the British over the remains of Port la Joye to guard the approaches to the harbor. Only the earthworks of the fort remain, but there is a panorama of Charlottetown and an interpretive center with displays on the history of the site.

The dignified white neoclassic edifice of **Government House,** one of a number of prestige buildings in Charlottetown designed by the local architect Isaac Smith (ca 1795–1871), stands among the trees of Victoria Park. Close by is **Beaconsfield** (*2 Kent St., Tel 902/368-6603*), a handsome villa from 1877, now the headquarters of P.E.I.'s Museum Service. There are more well-preserved 19th-century structures around early 20th-century Gothic **St. Dunstan's Basilica** and along Great George Street, the route linking the harbor to the central square. But the building everyone is urged to see in Charlottetown is **Province House National Historic Site,** considered to be one of the most elegant examples of Georgian architecture in the Maritimes. Completed in 1848 by Isaac Smith, it still houses the provincial legislature and was the site in 1864 of the first of the meetings held to discuss the Confederation. The island may have hesitated to join with the other provinces to form a united Canada, but it is proud of its role as the "Cradle of Confederation", and of the hospitality offered to the provincial premiers when they met here. On the upper floor of

Province House is the Confederation Chamber, where they held their deliberations, as well as other rooms (Library, Secretariat) with exhibits recalling these stirrings of Canadian unity. Close by is the bunker-like **Confederation Centre of the Arts** (*Queen St., Tel 800/565-0278, closed Mon. Oct.–May*), built in 1964 to commemorate the centenary of the Charlottetown Conference. With its library, theater, art gallery, and museum arranged around a memorial hall, it is as representative of its time as was Province House. The musical version of *Anne of Green Gables* (*Tel 800/565-0278 for ticket information*) plays every summer to packed audiences in its theater.

ANNE'S ISLAND

Lucy Maud Montgomery (see p. 71) described her beloved Prince Edward Island as an "Emerald, Ruby and Sapphire land," and the island repays the compliment with an array of attractions which should satisfy even the most devoted follower of the cult of *Anne of Green Gables.*

In addition to summer performances of a musical version of Anne's adventures and an annual Lucy Maud Montgomery festival in the Cavendish area, there are several sites with Montgomery and Anne associations. They include: the **Lucy Maud Montgomery Birthplace** (*Jct. of Rtes. 6 & 20, Tel 902/886-2099, closed mid-Oct.–early May*) in New London, which houses many of the author's personal effects including her wedding dress; the **Lucy Maud Montgomery Heritage Museum** (*east of Jct. of Rtes. 6 & 13, Tel 902/963-2231*), a farmhouse in Cavendish where she was brought up by her grandparents; and her uncle and aunt's house at Park Corner, "the big white beautiful house which was the wonder castle of my childhood," now the **Anne of Green Gables Museum** at Silverbush filled with much memorabilia.

Pilgrims will find their way to these and other sites, while those ignorant of Montgomery and her fictional offspring would do well to

Attractive and productive farmland makes up much of the landscape of Prince Edward Island.

Anne of Green Gables Museum

✉ Silverbush, P.E.I. National Park

☎ 902/436-7329

🕐 Closed Nov.–May

💲 $

The ocean eats away steadily at the soft sandstone cliffs of P.E.I. National Park.

visit **Green Gables House** in Cavendish. The centerpiece of the extensive site managed by Parks Canada is the white house (with green gables) once lived in by the cousins with whom Lucy Maud spent many happy times, and which she used as the setting of her novel. Originally built in 1830, their residence has been restored and refurbished to suggest scenes from the novel. Extensive restoration work has been carried on around the house to complete the picture of an Edwardian childhood, and the imposing farm buildings have been saved from dereliction. The visitor center has displays which give an excellent introduction to the whole Anne phenomenon. Those who wish to immerse themselves further into her world will take a stroll along nearby Lovers' Lane or venture into the Haunted Wood.

PRINCE EDWARD ISLAND NATIONAL PARK

One of the smallest of Canada's National Parks is also one of the most popular, its dunes and beaches drawing thousands of visitors. The park is a long and narrow strip, stretching along the island's northern coast for some 25 miles between Cavendish Beach and Stanhope Beach. The Gulf of St. Lawrence is shallow here, no more than 50 feet deep 12 miles out from the shore, and its waters warm up quickly in summer. Most of the park's beaches are backed by dunes, which you can reach on board-walks, but in places there are low cliffs. These make fine viewpoints, but be warned—their red sand-stone is being continually undercut by the sea and crumbles easily. The cliffs are liable to sudden collapse, and visitors should keep away from the edge. Behind the cliffs and dunes is a wooded strip of spruce forest, interspersed with meadows, salt marsh, and freshwater ponds, all connected by interpretive trails.

The popularity of this coastline has led to intensive development of its hinterland, in particular along Rte. 6, where multiple attractions compete for the visitor's attention.

ISLAND EXTREMITIES

Both Prince County in the west of the island and Kings County in the east have their share of man-made attractions. Between the Nova Scotia ferry terminal at Wood

Green Gables House

- ✉ off Rte. 6 just west of Rte. 13
- ☎ 902/672-6350
- 🕐 Closed Nov.–mid-May
- 💲 $

Prince Edward Island National Park

- 🅰 53C4
- ✉ 15 miles north of Charlottetown on Rte. 15
- ☎ 902/672-6350

Islands and Charlottetown is **Orwell Corner Historic Village** (*Off Trans-Canada 1, Tel 902/651-8510, closed Sat.–Sun. mid-May–late June, Mon. rest of year*), once abandoned but now restored, while farther east, beyond the port of Souris, is the **Basin Head Fisheries Museum** (*Off Rte. 16, Tel 902/357-2966, closed Sat.–Sun. late June–Sept.*), detailing the life and work of inshore fishermen and the **Elmira Railway Museum,** in what was P.E.I.'s easternmost station (*Rte. 16, Tel 902/357-2481, closed Nov.–May*). In the west, as well as **"Canada's only Potato Museum"**

(*O'Leary Centennial Park, Tel 902/859-2039, closed Nov.–May*), there is the modern **Acadian Museum at Miscouche** (*Rte. 2 west of Summerside, Tel 902/432-2880, closed Sept.–early June*), which tells the story of the P.E.I. Acadians, most of whom live on this part of the island. But the real point in moving on from the more crowded center of the island is to meander along quiet side roads, wiggle your toes in the sand of unpeopled beaches, brace yourself on a cliff top against the sea breeze, and set off for the brightly painted beacon of a lighthouse on a distant headland. ■

Lucy Maud, Anne, & their island

Although the latter part of her life was spent in Ontarian exile, Lucy Maud Montgomery (1874–1942) never forgot the island where she was born, and 19 of her 20 novels were set here, most famously those that record the doings of the mettlesome little lass known as Anne of Green Gables.

Born in P.E.I.'s New London (then called Clifton), the young Montgomery was brought up in Cavendish by her elderly and severe maternal grandparents. She found solace and stimulation in the landscape, and in books and writing. Her emotional life was far from untroubled; she had a history of secret loves and broken engagements, and the clergyman she finally did marry fell prey to religious melancholia. But her books, letters, and journals are full of spirit and sensitivity, as well as humor. A prolific writer, she penned 450 poems, 500 short stories, and 5,000 diary pages as well as her novels. *Anne of Green Gables*, published in 1908, was an instant best-seller, and was

followed by several sequels. Described by Mark Twain as "the sweetest creation of child life ever written," the tale of irrepressible orphan Anne has been translated into 20 languages. The little girl herself enjoys cult status, particularly among young Japanese women, who can be seen around P.E.I. wearing her trademark boater and pigtails. ■

An irresistible attraction to all "Anne" fans: the green-gabled farmhouse at Cavendish

Nova Scotia

THE BEST INTRODUCTION TO NOVA SCOTIA—AND IN many ways the ideal way to grasp the significance of the sea to all the Maritime Provinces—is Halifax. Virtually a creation of the sea itself, and with a sometimes explosive history, the provincial capital sets the tone for the rest of this fascinating and attractive province.

The Town Clock has told the time to Haligonians since 1803.

Halifax
🅰 53C2

Visitor information
✉ 1595 Burrington & Sackville
☎ 902/490-5946

HALIFAX

Although possessing many of the attributes of a modern metropolis, Halifax remains deeply marked by its history; after two and a half centuries, warships still shelter in its superb natural harbor, and a grim citadel still commands the city from its hilltop site. Cheek by jowl with glittering downtown office towers are venerable Georgian and Victorian edifices. The waterfront is dominated by the 19th-century warehouses and other immaculately restored buildings known as the Historic Properties. The city's suburban fringe with its malls and freeways may be unremarkable, but just beyond begins the boundless forest that cloaks so much of the Maritimes, and on either side of the city the coastline has a timeless air, with innumerable bays, coves, and fishing villages.

Dominance by the ocean explains Halifax's creation. The city's gaze is still turned resolutely toward the Atlantic, beyond the headlands and islands guarding the deep inlet leading to Bedford Basin. In the mid-18th century, prompted by New Englanders, the British decided to counter continuing French command of the eastern seaboard and move the capital of Nova Scotia from Annapolis Royal. In 1749, H.M.S. *Sphinx* led a convoy of 13 ships into the deep inlet that the native Mi'kmaq had called Chebucto; aboard was a motley crew of would-be settlers, led by a future governor, Col. Edward Cornwallis. They laid out a

ten-acre grid of streets on the slopes leading from the waterfront to the hilltop, where they placed a timber stockade, the predecessor of today's much larger citadel.

From its foundation, the city's fortunes fluctuated with the tides of international and national history. Wartime brought prosperity, from the early days when soldiers and sailors sallied forth to besiege Louisbourg (see p. 84) and capture Quebec to the world wars of the 20th century, when the convoys that kept Britain alive assembled in Bedford Bay before braving the U-boat wolfpacks of the North Atlantic.

Explorations of this salty city are best begun at the waterfront. Here, the **Historic Properties** (*below Upper Water St., north of Maritime Museum*) comprise an array of sturdy stone or timber buildings saved from the threat of a waterside freeway in the late 1960s. One, the **Privateer's Warehouse,** was used in Napoleonic times to store the plundered cargoes of enemy ships, often American, during the War of 1812.

Even more intriguing is the waterfront itself. The famous *Bluenose II* (*Tel 902/634-1963*) is moored here when in Halifax; the chubby ferries linking Halifax to Dartmouth (*leave from George St. every 15 minutes*) bustle to and fro; historic vessels, including the World War II H.M.C.S. *Sackville*, form the outdoor exhibits of the **Maritime Museum of the Atlantic;** and there may even be a visiting warship to be boarded. The rich collections of the museum bring to life much of the eventful story of Halifax's relationship with the sea; as well as any number of superb ship models, actual crafts range from humble vessels like jolly boats, skiffs, and gigs to Queen Victoria's elegant royal barge. Paneling from the *Titanic* is a poignant reminder that the bodies of many of the great

liner's drowned passengers were brought to Halifax for burial in the city's cemeteries. Other displays include shipwrecks and lifesaving, the Age of Steam, the achievements of Halifax-born Samuel Cunard and his shipping line, and Halifax's role as the most important Canadian naval base—its dockyard was founded in 1759 as the home of the Royal Navy's North American Squadron. The Halifax explosion of 1917 (see p. 74) is evoked in a dramatic audiovisual presentation.

Inland from the waterfront is the **Art Gallery of Nova Scotia,** housed in the 19th-century courthouse building. It has a good general selection of Canadian art, from the cheery snowbound scenes of Cornelius Krieghoff (1815–1872) to the Ontario-based Group of Seven (see pp. 186–7), and there are plenty of local works, including early ones that attempted to fit Halifax and its surroundings into the European picturesque tradition; lively etchings of city life by Donald C. MacKay (1906–1979); and some charming examples of folk and naive art.

Maritime Museum of the Atlantic
- ✉ 1675 Lower Water St.
- ☎ 902/424-7490
- ⏱ Closed Sun.–Mon. mid-Oct.–May
- 💲 $

Art Gallery of Nova Scotia
- ✉ 1741 Hollis St. at Cheapside
- ☎ 902/424-7542
- ⏱ Closed Mon.

Contemporary high-rises dominate the skyline above Halifax's historic waterfront.

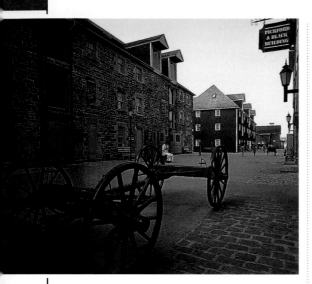

people could see them. The Town Clock has become one of the great emblems of Halifax, even if it has had no noticeable effect on punctuality in this resolutely laid-back city.

The clock stands at the foot of the steep grassy slope below the **Halifax Citadel National Historic Site** (*Tel 902/426-5080*). This formidable-looking star-shaped stronghold, the fourth to be built on the site, was constructed between 1828 and 1856 to defend both the landward approach to the city and its harbor. One of the most visited of Canada's national historic sites, it is full of the atmosphere of the British presence in North America. There are kilted sentries, a ceremonial firing of the noonday cannon, and a number of fascinating displays and exhibits, including an exciting audiovisual show "The Tides of History." The fort's placement is stunning, and there is an incomparable panorama of Halifax in its magnificent setting from the ramparts.

Province House, on Hollis Street, is the home of the Nova Scotia legislature, an institution that has existed since 1758. Built in 1819, the present sandstone structure was once described as a "gem of Georgian architecture" by British novelist Charles Dickens (1812–1870). ∎

Saved from destruction by an expressway, Halifax's Historic Properties are now a magnet for locals and visitors alike.

Province House
✉ Hollis St.
☎ 902/424-8967
🕐 Closed Sat.–Sun. Sept.–June

THE HISTORIC CENTER

The best way to get the feel of the historic center of Halifax city is to stand by St Paul's Anglican Church and City Hall on the **Grand Parade.** From here, walk up George Street to the **Town Clock** bequeathed to the city in 1803 by Edward, Duke of Kent. A punctilious disciplinarian, Edward found Haligonians, or natives of Halifax, very casual about time. The faces on the north and east sides are bigger than the other two, because these were the sides that faced the town, and Edward wanted to make sure

The Halifax Explosion

Before Hiroshima, the world's most devastating man-made explosion occurred in Halifax. On the morning of December 6, 1917, the French ship *Mont Blanc*, fully laden with a cargo of mixed explosives, collided with the Norwegian vessel *Imo* at the entrance to the Narrows. Fire broke out aboard the *Mont Blanc*, and 20 minutes later, abandoned by her crew, she blew up, completely destroying

1,630 houses and instantly killing some 1,400 people, with many more dying in the tidal wave. Buildings 60 miles away lost their windows, and the explosion was heard as far away as Prince Edward Island. Relief efforts came from all over the Maritimes and New England; a Nova Scotia Christmas tree stands every year in central Boston, a symbol of Haligonians' gratitude. ∎

Atlantic Coast drive:
Halifax to Barrington

This 250-mile drive southwest of Halifax takes in some of the finest coastal scenery on Nova Scotia's Atlantic shore and introduces a number of the province's most attractive harbor villages and small towns.

Leave Halifax via Hwy. 3. Join Rte. 333 at the turnoff and head southwest to **Peggys Cove ①**. Elemental harshness and cozy domesticity exist side by side in this tiny fishing port; battered by the ocean, a treeless landscape of monstrous glacier-scraped boulders is humanized by a scattering of colorful cottages and by fishermen's shacks perched precariously over the waters of the tiny harbor. A red-capped, brilliant white lighthouse crowns a granite outcrop made slippery by sea spray, a trap for the unwary scrambler. Fishing tackle on the dockside and boats in the water are evidence that hard work is still carried on here, but Peggys Cove's main role nowadays is to be admired. The village has long attracted the attention of visitors. By the mid-20th century, writers, artists and photographers had made the place famous, and you are unlikely to be able to enjoy it on your own, except perhaps when a sea mist rolls in (as it frequently does) and your fellow tourists seek refuge in the big café on the headland.

From Peggys Cove rejoin Hwy. 3, and follow this road north and gradually east around the shore of St. Margarets Bay and Mahone Bay. Among the charming villages that line this coast is **Chester ②** (*Visitor information: Old Station, Hwy. 3, Tel 902/275-4616, closed Oct.–June*). Its tree-lined streets and elegant residences have been a favorite summer resort for vacationers from America's East Coast for more than a century and a half. With two harbors, Front and Back, and access to the bay with its 365 islands, handsome Chester is a yachtsman's paradise, at its liveliest during mid-August's Race Week.

About 14 miles along the old coast road is the equally distinguished but much smaller town of **Mahone Bay ③** itself, once famous for its shipbuilders, who are celebrated in the annual Wooden Boat Festival in July (*Tel. 902/624-8443*). The best view of the town is from the far side of the fine harbor; rising over the well-treed waterfront in friendly proximity are the towers of the town's three churches, a much photographed scene. A few miles to the south along Hwy. 3, the fishing port of **Lunenburg ④** (*Visitor information: Blockhouse Hill Rd., Tel 902/634-3656, closed*

Filled with colonial buildings, Lunenburg's grid of streets climbs steeply from the waterfront.

Nov.–May) is the undoubted star of the Atlantic coast, its unique character given international recognition by its designation in 1995 as a UNESCO world heritage site. The area had long been frequented by natives and Acadians, before the town itself was founded in 1753. Most of the settlers who built their timber houses along its grid of streets were Germans, intermixed with people from Switzerland and the Montbéliard district of France, all categorized as "foreign Protestants," whom the British regarded as reliable to populate and control the coast.

The layout of old town **Lunenburg,** with its rectangular residential plots and space reserved for public buildings, is a classic example of British colonial town planning, perhaps the best preserved of its kind in the whole of North America. The architecture is equally remarkable. The oldest structure, perhaps built as early as the 1770s, is the gambrel roofed **Romkey House,** but most of Lunenburg's houses are late 19th century. Timber-built, painted in cheerful colors, they rise up the slope overlooking the wharves of the Front Harbour. Many have intriguing details borrowed from the shipwright's craft, but the most characteristic feature is the mildly ostentatious "Lunenburg Bump," a dormer window extended out over the front door. **St. John's Church** has been described as "Carpenter-Gothic style at its finest."

Originally farmers, Lunenburg's settlers soon turned to the sea for their living. In the 1850s they sent the first schooner fleet to the Grand Banks; in the 1870s they introduced double-dory trawl fishing, then in the 1920s pioneered fresh-fish processing. The famous racing schooner *Bluenose* was built here in 1921, and Lunenburgers' shipbuilding and repairing skills are still much in demand, not only for routine tasks. The beautiful *Bluenose II* was built here in 1963 (see p. 79), as was an equally exact reproduction of H.M.S. *Bounty*; in 1997, the copy of Cabot's *Matthew* called in for repairs.

The **Fisheries Museum of the Atlantic** (*Tel 902/634-4794, closed Sat.–Sun. mid-Oct.–mid-May*), housed in the Salt Hall, Ice House, and other waterfront buildings of the former fish processing plant, is one of the most rewarding museums in the Maritimes.

As well as an aquarium, there are fascinating displays on the history of the Grand Banks fishery, rum-running, and the life of the community. The *Bluenose,* the only human artifact to be featured on a Canadian coin (the dime), is celebrated in style, and there are real vessels tied up along the dockside.

Leave Lunenburg via Hwy. 3 and follow it west to Bridgewater. Pick up Rte. 331 and, enjoy the coastal views. If you're interested in natural attractions, this drive south has splendid sandy beaches. A picture of one of them, **Crescent Beach,** once graced the $50 bill.

After 28 miles turn south on Hwy. 103 towards **Liverpool** ❺ (*Visitor information: Henry Hensey Dr., Tel 902/354-5421*). Located at the mouth of the Mersey, like its English counterpart, this port specialized in that licensed system of piracy known as privateering. One of its vessels, the *Liverpool Packet,* captured no fewer than 100 American ships. Yankee patience ran out, and in 1780 the town had to swallow its own medicine when it was sacked by a fleet of American privateers. These stirring times are evoked in the **Queen's County Museum** (*109 Main St., Tel 902/354-4058*) and the adjacent 1766 **Perkin's House** (*105 Main Street, Tel 902/354-4058, closed Sun. mid-Oct.–May*), one of the finest late 18th-century residences in eastern Canada.

As you depart Liverpool keep following Hwy. 103 west to **Shelburne** ⑥ (*Visitor information: north end of Dock St., Tel 902/875-4547, closed winter*). Founded in 1783, this town was built when thousands of New York loyalists arrived and rapidly assembled a town. For a brief moment, it was the largest in British North America. Like Halifax, Shelburne has a superb natural harbor, but this failed to save it from the decline that perhaps preserved its charm. There are fine houses, and among the attractions is the **Dory Shop** (*Dock St., Tel 902/875-3219, closed mid-*

Sept.–mid-June), now a museum, but still producing the sturdy fishing craft that were so vital to the fishery.

Between Shelburne and Yarmouth lies the workaday terminus for the ferries from Maine. It is worth stopping in tiny **Barrington** ⑦, with its historic mill and replica lighthouse as well as the **Old Meeting House** of 1765, the oldest Nonconformist place of worship in Canada. ■

The fisheries museum at Lunenburg

🅜 See area map pp. 54–5
▶ Halifax
↔ 250 miles
🕓 Allow 4 days
▶ Barrington

NOT TO BE MISSED
- Peggys Cove
- Lunenburg
- Crescent Beach
- Liverpool

0   40 kilometers

0   20 miles

Maritime heritage

Not without reason are Canada's eastern provinces called the Maritimes. European colonists came here from across the ocean, and for many years remained dependent on the sea routes from France and Britain. Travel by sea and inland waterway was the principal means of communication within the region, and in the 18th century the combined operations of sea and land forces characterized the Franco-British struggle for supremacy. Settlement in this forested, largely infertile area was concentrated along the long and complex coastlines and to a lesser extent along accessible river valleys. Most towns were ports, and many villages lived from fishing.

From the very earliest days, ships were built here. In 1606, a year after Champlain's establishment of his Habitation (see pp. 80–81), two small crafts were launched into the Annapolis Basin at Port Royal. At first, craftsmen replicated European boat plans, but using local designs and timber harvested from the hinterland. By the late 18th century, shipbuilding was well established, local skills supplemented

by the migration northward of New England shipwrights and carpenters. The glory days of Maritime shipping came in the 19th century, when some 200 shipyards were operating, turning out a huge tonnage of timber vessels and contributing to Canada's position as the world's fourth largest ship-owning nation.

As well as countless small "home-built" fishing vessels, there were sloops and schooners handling coastal commerce. Larger ships traded wherever a cargo was to be found and carried local fish and timber to Britain, the Mediterranean, the Caribbean, and South America. The 1625-ton *Marco Polo*, built at Saint John in 1851, was claimed to be the fastest ship in the world, and in 1858, of the vessels over 500 tons on the Liverpool (England) *Register*, more than three-quarters were Canadian built.

But toward the end of the century, ships of iron and steel began to dominate the shipping scene, and this Canadian preeminence disappeared, though maritime yards continued to build timber sailing vessels well into the 20th century. The most famous ship of all, the elegant schooner *Bluenose*, came off the slip at

The sea has shaped the character of The Maritimes and remains their defining feature. Lighthouses, such as this one (opposite left), line the treacherous rocky coast. A Nova Scotian skipper (opposite right), dressed in traditional Sou'wester, gazes seaward. The elegant schooner Bluenose II (above) enters Halifax harbor.

the Smith and Rhuland yard in Lunenburg in 1921. She repeatedly won the annual Fishermen's Trophy against the stiffest competition New England could muster. Despite being wrecked off Haiti in 1944, the *Bluenose* has joined the immortals, gracing the ten cent coin and reincarnated in *Bluenose II*, an exact replica built at the same yard in 1963, and frequently on show in both Lunenburg and Halifax (see p. 76).

More modest craft command almost as much affection as the thoroughbred *Bluenose*. Archetypal Maritime vessels include the *Cape Islander* with its high bow and cabin well forward, first developed by Ephraim Atkinson on Cape Sable Island, or the ubiquitous flat-bottomed dory. The skills that built such boats

are still practiced today, in places such as the Dory Shop in Shelburne (see p. 77) or alongside the splendid Fisheries Museum of the Atlantic (see p. 76) in Lunenburg. Both the Fisheries Museum of the Atlantic and the Halifax Maritime Museum of the Atlantic have fine collections of historic ships.

Together with Newfoundland, the Maritimes are the closest lands on the North American continent to Europe, and in two world wars their waters have been the scene of intense naval activity. In both conflicts, U-boats sowed mines and sank both merchant vessels and warships; techniques of anti-submarine warfare and convoy management were developed and applied to protect the endless stream of vessels supplying Britain with essential provisions and war material. The focus of much of this activity was the magnificent natural harbor of Halifax, and these tense times are recalled not only in the Maritime Museum (see p. 73) but also in the Maritime Command Museum (*Admiralty House, Gottingen St., Halifax, Tel 902/427-0550, closed weekends*), devoted to the city's naval history. ■

Annapolis Valley & the French shore

▲ 55B2

ITS FLANKS PROTECTED BY THE NORTH AND SOUTH mountain ranges running parallel to the Fundy shore, the Annapolis Valley is the sunniest and most fertile part of Nova Scotia. The valley is famous for its apple orchards, less extensive than they once were, but still a glorious show of blossom in springtime. Many visitors start a tour of the area at Grand-Pré.

Gently rolling hills flank the fertile farmlands of the Annapolis Valley.

Grand-Pré National Historic Site
▲ 55B3
✉ 2½ miles east of Wolfville on Hwy. 101
☎ 902/542-3631
🕐 Closed mid-Oct.–mid-May

Port Royal National Historic Site
▲ 55B2
✉ 8 miles west of Annapolis Royal
☎ 902/532-2898
🕐 Closed mid-Oct.–mid-May
💲 $

GRAND-PRÉ NATIONAL HISTORIC SITE

Once a flourishing Acadian town of 5,000 inhabitants, **Grand-Pré** is now a national historic site, surrounded by the rich agricultural landscape of the Annapolis Valley. It is a tiny yet poignant memorial to one of the most tragic events in the history of the Maritimes, the Deportation of 1755.

There is not a lot to see here, but you will not forget your visit. Few people are unmoved by it. Take a walk to the tiny chapel to see lists of the families deported and maps showing where they went. You can even read a copy of Governor Lawrence's Deportation Order.

Take a look at the marvelous life-size sculpture of Evangeline by Louis-Philippe Hébert, the great Montreal sculptor who was himself of Acadian descent.

Close to Grand-Pré is the refined little town of **Wolfville** (*Visitor information, Tel 902/542-*

7000, *closed Nov.–May*), its elegant streets lined with Victorian villas and shaded by great trees. Home to **Acadia University,** whose origins go back to 1838, Wolfville is also known for the annual Atlantic Theatre Festival.

ANNAPOLIS VALLEY

The many attractive communities that line Highway 1 make a drive to the southwestern end of the valley delightful. The one with the most small town charm is **Bridgetown.** Stop to admire the fine houses built by Loyalists on elm-lined streets.

Farther southwest, where the Annapolis River broadens into a great tidal basin, are two of Nova Scotia's outstanding sights–the superb reconstruction of Port Royal Habitation and the tiny town of Annapolis Royal.

Port Royal Habitation

After passing the disastrous winter of 1604–1605 on Île Sainte-Croix in Passamaquoddy Bay, the party led by Sieur des Monts and Samuel de Champlain crossed the Bay of Fundy and rebuilt their habitation in a more clement location on the bluff looking south over the Annapolis Basin. "Ten fathoms in length and eight in breadth," according to Champlain's account, the Habitation was a survival capsule, containing all that European culture and technology could devise to sustain life in these unexplored surroundings.

While relatively short-lived (de Monts departed in 1607 when his fur-trading license was revoked, and a raiding party from Virginia sacked the place in 1613), the Habitation was the first successful European colony north of St. Augustine, predating the founding of Jamestown, Virginia, by two years.

No trace of the Habitation remained above ground until the meticulous reconstruction of the buildings in 1939. Nowadays at **Port Royal National Historic Site,** visitors can see an almost exact re-creation of the site as it would have looked in the 17th century. Traditional techniques have helped rebuild the central well and courtyard, the palisade guarding the entrance, the accommodation of all ranks and the storehouse and service wing—all of which make this one of the most evocative historical sites in Canada.

Annapolis Royal

On the far side of the Annapolis Basin, just beyond the power station which harnesses the energy of the massive Fundy tides, stands **Annapolis Royal,** the successor to Port Royal, renamed after Britain's Queen Anne when it briefly became the capital of Nova Scotia in 1713. Once a bustling port and garrison town, Annapolis Royal is now a showcase of

heritage restoration.

At its heart, commanding the waters of the basin, are the remaining buildings and earthworks of **Fort Anne National Historic Site** (*295 George St., Tel 902/532-2397*), much fought over by French and British. Nearby are the extensive **Annapolis Royal Historic Gardens** (*441 George St., Tel 902/532-7018, closed mid-Oct.–mid-May*), which were established in 1981 to illustrate the development of horticulture.

The French coast

Of all the areas in Nova Scotia resettled by returning Acadians in the 1760s and later, **Clare County** on the coast between the ports of Digby and Yarmouth has the most distinctively French character and the greatest concentration of Acadian population. The thin soils along the shoreline of St. Marys Bay forced the resettled Acadians to abandon their farming skills and turn to lumbering and fishing. Their villages along the old Highway 1 run into one another, only grandly scaled churches distinguishing one parish from another. At **Pointe de l'Église** (Church Point) is Sainte-Marie, the largest timber church in North America, its 185-foot spire steadied against the coastal gales by 40 tons of ballast, while St. Bernard can shelter a congregation of 1,000, three times the population of the parish. ■

A European outpost in the Canadian wilderness—Port Royal Habitation

Longfellow's poem, *Evangeline,* is honored by a bust at Grand-Pré National Historic Site.

Cape Breton Island & the Cabot Trail

Rugged Cape Breton Island is a rocky finger pointing northward across the Cabot Strait, which links the Gulf of St. Lawrence with the Atlantic. The northwest section of Cape Breton Island has a spectacular circular drive known as the Cabot Trail.

In spite of its name, Cape Breton has not been an island since 1955, when a 2-mile causeway, the deepest in the world (217 feet), was constructed across the Strait of Canso. After crossing it, look back at the cliffs which supplied the ten million tons of rock required for its construction. The signs proclaim "Ciad Mile Failte" ("a hundred thousand welcomes" in Gaelic). You have entered a fiercely independent part of the province where natives, many of whom are descendents of settlers from the Scottish Highlands, often have little time for their fellow "mainland" Nova Scotians.

This memorable drive passes through Cape Breton Highlands National Park and is undoubtedly one of the most beautiful and dramatic drives of eastern North America. With whales offshore, moose inland and bald eagles circling above you, the Cabot Trail is a paradise for nature lovers. The wary drive it in a clockwise direction away from the sometimes precipitous drops to the sea. But it is even more spectacular if taken counterclockwise. Be warned that fog can roll in and obscure views, especially on the eastern side.

The starting point of the trail is the resort of **Baddeck ❶** (*Visitor information, Chebueto St., Tel 902/295-1911*), charmingly sited on the shore of Cape Breton's inland sea, the Bras d'Or. Much cherished by locals for his appreciation of the attractions of his adopted home ("For simple beauty, Cape Breton Island outrivals them all"), Alexander Graham Bell (1847–1922) first came here in 1885, building his home Beinn Bhreag ("Beautiful Mountain" in Gaelic) and conceiving and testing some of his myriad inventions here. The **Alexander**

Graham Bell National Historic Site (*Hwy. 205, Tel 902/295-2069*) is comprehensive in scope; there are, of course, telephones, but much else besides, including a splendid reproduction of the 60-foot long HD-4.

Driving west on Trans-Canada 105 you join the Cabot Trail. Beyond the Margaree River, with its unrivaled salmon fishing, and the Acadian port of **Chéticamp ❷**, the trail enters **Cape Breton Highlands National Park** (*Tel 902/285-2691*). "Where the mountains meet the sea" is the apt description applied to this park, which has hardwood forest, mountain plateau, and a rugged but beautiful coast. The trail winds through the park between Chéticamp and **Pleasant Bay.** Stop at the designated pulloffs to admire the superb views of the dramatic coastline.

A short walk inland takes you to the **Lone Shieling,** an evocative reconstruction of a Highland crofter's cottage. On the inland section between **Cape North** and Neil Harbour, look out for moose by the road.

From Pleasant Bay the trail heads east and inland, following the Park's northern boundary until it reaches Neils Harbour. Here the trail hugs the east coast again. **Black Brook Cove** is splendid, with pink rocks stretching into the sea and views ahead of Ingonish Bay, dominated by the slopes of Cape Smokey.

The resort hotel **Keltic Lodge ❸** (*Visitor information, Tel 902/285-2880*) has a spectacular location on **Middle Head,** which cuts Ingonish Bay in two. Park at the lodge and follow the trail to the end of the peninsula for views of Cape Smokey and Tern Rock, a nesting place for common and arctic tern (*path closed in nesting season, mid-May–July*), as well as other seabirds.

In the summer taking part in one of the popular whale-watching boat tours can be a highlight of your trip (*Ingonish Harbour, Tel 902/285-2714; Chéticamp, Tel 902/224-1088*).

The Cabot Trail and the scenic grandeur of the Cape Breton Highlands National Park

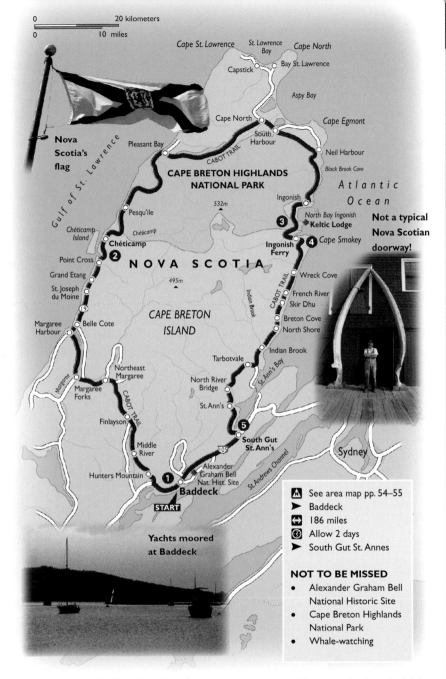

	0	20 kilometers
0		10 miles

Cape St. Lawrence

St. Lawrence Bay

Cape North

Capstick

Bay St. Lawrence

Aspy Bay

Cape North

Cape Egmont

Nova Scotia's flag

Pleasant Bay

South Harbour

Neil Harbour

CABOT TRAIL

Black Brook Cove

CAPE BRETON HIGHLANDS NATIONAL PARK

Gulf of St. Lawrence

532m

Ingonish

Atlantic Ocean

Pesqu'ile

North Bay Ingonish

3 ◆ Keltic Lodge

Not a typical Nova Scotian doorway!

Chéticamp Island

Chéticamp

Chéticamp 2

NOVA SCOTIA

Ingonish Ferry

4 Cape Smokey

Point Cross

Grand Etang

495m

Wreck Cove

St. Joseph du Moine

CAPE BRETON ISLAND

French River

Skir Dhu

19

Indian Brook

Breton Cove

Margaree Harbour

Belle Cote

North Shore

Margaree

CABOT TRAIL

Tarbotvale

Indian Brook

Northeast Margaree

North River Bridge

St. Ann's Bay

Margaree Forks

St. Ann's

Finlayson

CABOT TRAIL

5

Middle River

South Gut St. Ann's

Sydney

105

Hunters Mountain

Alexander Graham Bell Nat. Hist. Site

1

St. Andrews Channel

Baddeck

START

Yachts moored at Baddeck

⓶ See area map pp. 54–55
➤ Baddeck
⬌ 186 miles
🕐 Allow 2 days
➤ South Gut St. Annes

NOT TO BE MISSED
- Alexander Graham Bell National Historic Site
- Cape Breton Highlands National Park
- Whale-watching

After Ingonish, follow the trail south. Over **Cape Smokey 4** (902/285-2778) it passes through a series of Gaelic fishing villages and precariously clings to the sides of St. Anns Bay. At **South Gut St. Anns 5** visit the **Gaelic College of Arts and Crafts** (Tel 902/295-

2441). Founded in 1938, it has been the driving force behind the Gaelic revival. As well as promoting the Gaelic language, virtually extinct here by the early 20th century, it has courses in traditional Highland activities like bagpiping and tartan-weaving. ∎

Louisbourg

**Fortress of
Louisbourg
National Historic
Site**

🅰 55E3

✉ 22 miles south of
Sydney on Rte. 22

☎ 902/733-2280

🕐 Closed Oct.–May

💲 $$$

**Completed in
the early 1730s,
Louisbourg's
Château Saint-
Louis was the
most imposing
building in all of
New France.**

ONCE A PAWN IN THE DEADLY GAME OF CONTINENTAL
domination played by Britain and France, the great coastal fortress
of Louisbourg has been rebuilt in one of the most ambitious histori-
cal reconstruction projects ever undertaken in North America.

Covering more than 12 acres, with
more than 50 restored buildings,
and staffed in season with costumed
townsfolk and soldiers, **Fortress
of Louisbourg National
Historic Site** offers visitors a
compelling experience of the 18th-
century colonial world.

In 1713, driven out of
Newfoundland and faced with the
loss of peninsular Nova Scotia
and its capital, Port Royal, France
tried to safeguard its position in
North America by establishing a
new stronghold on Cape Breton
Island. The site of Louisbourg was
selected in 1715. It had a fine harbor
and was well located in relation to
the Grand Banks fishery and the
Cabot Strait that guarded the sea
route to Quebec. By the 1730s, the
bastion town of Louisbourg had a
thriving population of some 4,000
civilians and the same number of
military personnel.

A BARGAINING CHIP

The strength of Louisbourg
provoked the very reaction it was
intended to deter. In 1745, alarmed
by its menacing presence, a force of
New Englanders, supported by a
British naval squadron, attacked the
fortress—not from the sea as the
French had expected, but from the
land. In the first of two successful
siege actions, Louisbourg surren-
dered, but was returned to France in
1749, having served as a useful bar-
gaining chip in one of the perennial
redrawings of the European politi-
cal map. A second siege, in 1758, in
which James Wolfe played a key
role, led to a more decisive result:
After its surrender, its garrison and
inhabitants were deported to
France, then, in the following year,
Louisbourg served as the base for
Wolfe's victory on Quebec's Plains
of Abraham. Having no further
need of it (Halifax was now estab-
lished as Nova Scotia's capital
and major port), the British razed
the fortifications to the ground.

Allow a whole day to savor fully
this remarkable reconstruction,
with its dockside, its Citadel, its
gateways, walls and bastions, and
numerous residences. ■

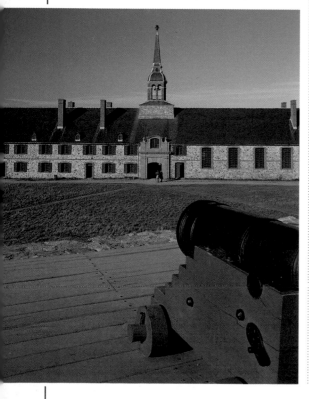

This great island out in the cold waters of the North Atlantic, part of Canada only since 1949, is utterly distinctive. So, too, are its inhabitants, their warmth and humor contrasting with the harshness of their vast and empty land.

Newfoundland

Waves crash on Cape Spear's rocky coast.

Newfoundland

NO NEWFOUNDLANDER WOULD CLAIM THEIR ISLAND TO BE A PRETTY place. "A monstrous mass of rock and gravel… like a strange thing from the bottom of the great deep" is one telling description. Despite its long history of European settlement, Newfoundland bears fewer traces of human occupation than most of the continent. Much of its sparsely scattered population clings to the coast as it always has done, looking to the sea for sustenance and for connections to the outside world.

The outport is the characteristic Newfoundland settlement, a clutch of raggedy fishermen's houses clinging to the water's edge or strewn over the nearby slopes, inhabited because of the once abundant fishery that brought settlers sailing across the Atlantic hundreds of years ago. The only really substantial city is St. John's, with its wonderful sheltered harbor and long-standing dominance of the island's fishing economy. Inland places are few—Gander, with its strategic airport, and Grand Falls, with its pulp mill processing the interior's main crop, coniferous forest. Away from the often spectacularly rugged 6,000-mile coast, much of the landscape of scrub, rock outcrops, ponds, and bogs seems to have only just emerged from the crushing weight of the Ice Age glaciers. With a climate whose harshness can be felt even in the summer months, Newfoundland is a place for those in search of all kinds of outdoor challenges, whether hunting or fishing, canoeing or hiking into the wilderness. The somber mountains of Gros Morne National Park offer a special kind of wilderness experience, while bird-watching or whale-spotting can be enjoyed by every visitor.

The fish-rich waters of the Grand Banks may have been known to fishermen from the northwest coasts of Europe even before John Cabot made his historic voyage in 1497, but it was in the following centuries that the fishery thrived (see pp. 92–93). Despite the disapproval of the English government, what was supposed to be a strictly seasonal activity soon led to permanent settlement, quite apart from the less successful, officially sponsored colonial developments such as Ferryland on the Avalon Peninsula. Early Newfoundlanders were mostly of English West Country origin, followed by Scots, and, in the early 19th century, a flood of Irish, who soon formed the majority of the population in St. John's and along much of the coast. Many migrants moved on elsewhere, establishing a tradition that still sends young Newfoundlanders southward to the northeastern states of the U.S. or westward to Ontario and Alberta. In time a characteristically

In spring and summer, the Labrador Current brings icebergs to the Newfoundland coast, such as this one in Trinity Bay, near Old Bonaventure.

Cape Chidley

Ungava Bay

Torngat Mts.

1729m
Mt. Caubvick

Hebron

Nutak

Nain

QUEBEC
p. 102

Hopedale

Scheffervelle

*Menihek
Lake*

*Smallwood
Reservoir*

Kanairiktok

LABRADOR

Hamilton Inlet

*Labrador
Sea*

Churchill
Falls

North West River

Cartwright

Labrador
City

*Lake
Melville*

Wabush

Goose Bay

Churchill

*Lac
Joseph*

Mealy Mts.

Port Hope Simpson

QUEBEC
p. 102

Red Bay

L'Anse Amour

**L'Anse aux
Meadows**

St. Anthony

St. Barbe

Englee

Port au Choix

Strait of Belle Isle

Notre
Dame
Bay

Long Range Mts.

806m
Gros Morne Mt.

Rocky Harbour

**GROS MORNE
NATIONAL PARK**

Deer Lake

Lewisporte

Gander

Corner Brook

**Grand
Falls**

TERRA NOVA
NATIONAL
PARK

Bonavista

Port-au-Port

Trinity

*St. George's
Bay*

NEWFOUNDLAND

Trinity
Bay

Heart's Content

Harbour Grace

Brigus

St. John's

Cabot Strait

Burgeo

Hermitage

Petty Harbour

Placentia

Bay Bulls

**Channel-Port-
aux-Basques**

Marystown

Argentia

Witless Bay

Burin Pen.

Avalon Pen.

Ferryland

St-Pierre et
Miquelon
(France)

Grand
Bank

Cape
St. Mary's

Cape Race

Area of map detail

Ottawa

0 ——— 200 kilometers
0 ——— 100 miles

Newfoundland speech developed, rich enough to baffle many a visitor as well as to justify the compilation of a lengthy *Dictionary of Newfoundland English*. Newfoundlanders remain one of the main reasons for coming to the "Rock." Quirky, hospitable, old-fashioned in many ways, they welcome visitors in the way that people do who live off the beaten track. The novel *The Shipping News* by American writer Annie Proulx provides a droll introduction to their ways as well as being a sparkling evocation of local land- and seascapes.

"Come near at your peril, Canadian wolf"

chanted 19th-century Newfoundlanders, and it was only by a narrow margin that this erstwhile British colony decided to join the Confederation in 1949. Newfoundland remains defiantly different from the rest of Canada, determined, despite its economic difficulties, to make its way in the world. ∎

St. John's

St. John's
🅰 87D2

Visitor information
✉ City Hall Annexe Building, New Gower St.
☎ 709/576-8106
🕐 Closed Sat.–Sun.

✉ The Old Railcar, Harbour Drive, Ayres Cove
☎ 709/576-8514
🕐 Closed mid-Sept.–June

Whale-watching tours
✉ Adventure Tours on the Scademia
☎ 709/726-5000
🕐 Closed Nov.–May
💲 $$$$$

✉ J & B Schooner Tours
☎ 709/753-7245
🕐 Closed mid-Oct.–mid-May
💲 $$$$$

WELL-SHELTERED FROM THE ATLANTIC GALES IN ITS fjordlike harbor, Newfoundland's atmospheric capital city boasts a history going back to 1583 when Sir Humphrey Gilbert sailed in and took possession of the island in the name of Queen Elizabeth I. Its harborfront site, like those of most other sizable cities along Canada's Atlantic coast, determined its growth and subsequent history. Today the sea remains as all-pervasive to the residents of St. John's, as it does for townsfolk in the most remote coastal Newfoundland settlements.

Fishermen from Normandy, Brittany, and Portugal as well as England had wintered here before Gilbert's arrival, but it was only after Sir Humphrey's visit in 1583 that permanent buildings were erected. A history of attacks by the French, raids by pirate gangs, and a series of devastating fires has left little trace of the early architecture of North America's earliest urban settlement. In any case, much building tended to be of a temporary or makeshift nature, and for centuries, Mother England remained hostile to the idea of permanent settlement. Early houses clustered around Fort William, a compact stronghold built in 1689 on the site of the present **Hotel Newfoundland,** while later development took place along **Water Street.** Here rose the warehouses, offices, and commercial premises that controlled the island's fishing economy and ensured the town's prosperity.

As late as the early 19th century there were virtually no structures built of stone, and Water Street, the principal thoroughfare, remained unpaved, unlighted, and in places no more than six feet wide. Even after the great fires that raged on several occasions in the early part of the 19th century, many residents steadfastly refused to rebuild in anything but timber, preparing the way for the greatest conflagration of all, in 1892, which destroyed two

thirds of the town and left 10,000 homeless.

St. John's may appear a jumble of unregulated building, but its layout is in fact logical. A series of long thoroughfares like Water Street and **Duckworth Street** run along the contours of the steep slope rising from the waterfront, linked by short cross streets or flights of steps. The city's focus remains the harbor, tidied up, with the old finger jetties replaced by a continuous dockside. It may lack the bustle of years past, but the harbor is still full of interest, with a variety of craft including coast guard cutters, fishing boats, tankers, and research vessels as well as conventional freighters and ships serving the offshore oil rigs and the occasional warship. Sailboats lie ready to take visitors iceberg-spotting or whale-watching, perhaps combined with a mildly embarrassing "screech-in," involving the consumption of rum and intimate contact with a codfish.

Just behind the dockside stand the venerable **Murray Premises** *(between Water St. and Harbour Dr.)*, the last of the city's mid-19th-century waterfront mercantile complexes. Housing an informal restaurant, boutiques, and an information point, its solid stone walls and charming cobblestone courtyard make an atmospheric start to an exploration of the city. A block or so inland, beyond **George Street's** pubs and restaurants and next to the brutalist concrete of the modern City Hall, a marker defines Mile 0 of the Trans-Canada Highway, which stretches 4,857 miles west from here to far-off Victoria, B.C. East along Water Street stands the **Courthouse,** a substantial granite structure built in 1901 and once used by the prime minister and cabinet. Steep steps lead up to Duckworth Street and the **Newfoundland Museum,** where a frieze depicts mining,

The summit above Signal Hill National Historic Site provides a dramatic vantage point over St. John's and its harbor.

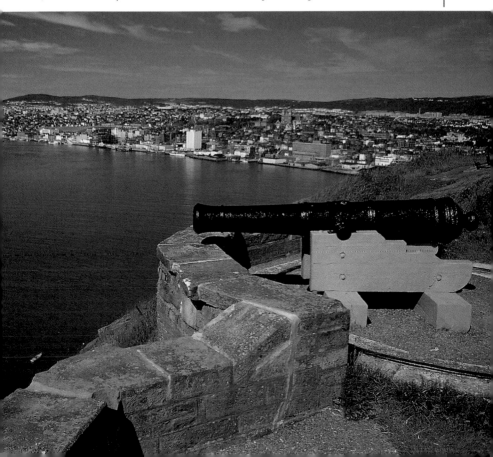

Newfoundland Museum

- ✉ 285 Duckworth Street
- ☎ 709/729-2329
- 🕐 Closed Mon.

Cathedral of St. John the Baptist

- ✉ Church Hill on Gower Street
- ☎ 709/726-5677 or 709/726-2053
- 🕐 By appointment only Sept.—June
- 💲 Donation

Basilica of St. John the Baptist

- ✉ Military Road
- ☎ 709/754-2170
- 💲 Guided tours $$$, Museum $

At St John's Signal Hill, a simple memorial commemorates Marconi's historic achievement in receiving a radio signal from across the Atlantic.

fishing, and forestry, the traditional mainstays of the island's economy. Inside, extensive collections give an excellent overview of Newfoundland's ecology and unique history, including the life of the Labrador Inuit and the island's original inhabitants, the Beothuk.

The streets climbing the slopes above Duckworth Street are lined with charming clapboard houses, reminiscent of a miniature San Francisco. Substantial churches dot the neighborhood, including the Anglican **Cathedral of St. John the Baptist** and the Roman Catholic **Basilica of St. John the Baptist.** Both churches are dedicated to the saint, from whom the city supposedly takes its name. The cathedral is the successor to earlier timber churches, while its parish, established in 1699, is the oldest Anglican parish in North America. The present imposing building was begun in 1846 by the great British architect of the Gothic Revival, George Gilbert Scott (1811–1878). Subsequent work, including extensive reconstruction following the great fire of 1892, was continued by the Scott family firm, who remained cathedral architects into the 1950s.

An even greater landmark, the basilica, commands a position farther up the slope, where its twin towers have served as beacons to seamen since the building's completion in 1892. Within the ornate interior is a figure of Our Lady of Fatima, a gift from the Portuguese fishermen of the White Fleet that once put in regularly at St. John's.

To the north clusters historic structures built to serve official functions. The neoclassic **Colonial Building** of 1850 (*Military Rd., Tel 709/729-3065, closed weekends*) housed Newfoundland's parliament until 1969, when it moved to the modern

Confederation Building on the outskirts of town. Even grander is **Government House** (*Military Rd., Tel 709/729-4494, by appointment only*). The fine red sandstone edifice was the lieutenant governor's residence until 1949. It was begun in 1827 to plans supplied from England by the prospective governor, Sir Thomas Cochrane. Sir Thomas's willful changes in the design of his future residence were the despair of the engineer in charge of the works, who eventually obtained a transfer elsewhere. It still remains unclear why a building in Newfoundland should be surrounded by a moat (seemingly designed to deter poisonous snakes and other undesirable tropical creatures). Both buildings contain ceiling frescoes by Alexander Pindokowski, a convicted forger whose jail sentence was reduced to reward the quality of his work.

Close to the Church of St. Thomas, Newfoundland's oldest surviving church, is another handsome Georgian-style structure, **Commissariat House** (*Kings Bridge Rd., Tel 709/729-2460, closed mid-Oct.–mid-June*). Built in 1820 and used by the British military until their withdrawal from the colony in 1870, it boasts interiors restored to their early 19th-century appearance, a re-created Victorian garden, and a small interpretive center housed in a coach house.

C.A. Pippy Park occupies an elevated position to the west of the center of St. John's. It is the location of the Newfoundland Freshwater Resource Centre, with its main attraction, the **Fluvarium.** This fascinating three-level series of displays provides a detailed introduction to the freshwater ecology of Newfoundland, with informative exhibits on fish, plants, bogs, and streams and even a model iceberg.

Although modern St. John's has acquired extensive suburbs, it is still a small town, at least in capital city terms, and nature is never very far away. Rising some 500 feet over the constricted entrance to the harbor known as the Narrows, windswept **Signal Hill National Historic Site** is a wild landscape on the very edge of town, with the characteristic Newfoundland scrub of partridge-berry and rowan among outcrops of bare rock. The hill is topped by the **Cabot Tower,** erected in 1897 to mark Queen Victoria's Diamond Jubilee as well as the 400th anniversary of Cabot's voyage. From the beginning of the 18th century, look-outs manned the summit, signaling the approach of ships to owners and merchants in the city below. Almost every visitor to St. John's makes it to the hilltop—the more energetic by a spectacular footpath, others by the winding road. Halfway up the road is the modern Parks Canada Interpretive Centre, whose well-presented exhibits make it one of the best places to become acquaint-ed not only with Signal Hill but with the history of Newfoundland in general.

But the real attraction of the site is the stunning panorama from the summit: To the west spreads the harbor and the whole of the city, to the east the infinite Atlantic rimmed by rugged cliffs. An occasional ship threads its way through the rocky Narrows far below.

Perhaps the most epoch-making occurrence on the hill took place on December 12, 1901, when Guglielmo Marconi (1874–1937) launched a kite 400 feet into gale-force winds and received the first-ever transatlantic wireless signal in Morse code from England. Just north of Signal Hill is the pleasant fishing village of **Quidi Vidi.** Tidy cottages and fishing shacks nestle beneath dramatic cliffs and a recon-structed 18th-century gun battery (*Tel 709/729-7977*) guards the coast. To the north, beyond Quidi Vidi Lake, lies the suburb of **Pleasantville,** successor to a big U.S. base established in World War II. Every summer a tattoo (*mid-July–Aug. Wed., Thurs., Sat. & Sun.*) recalls aspects of the long British military presence in St. John's. ∎

Buildings old and new overlook St. John's magnificent natural harbor.

Fluvarium
- ✉ Nagles Pl.
- ☎ 709/754-3474
- 🕐 Closed Jan.–March
- 💲 $

Signal Hill National Historic Site
- ✉ Cabot Tower & Visitor Reception Centre
- ☎ 709/772-5367
- 💲 $

Fish & more fish

"The fisheries of Newfoundland are inexhaustible and are of more value to the Empire than all the silver mines of Peru," declared the English essayist Francis Bacon (1561–1626) in the early 17th century. Even today, despite a disastrous decline in stocks and the much-resented 1991 federal moratorium on fishing for cod, Newfoundland manages to export millions of dollars, worth of seafood annually, although much of the catch consists of crab and other shellfish.

Crab was once despised by Newfoundlanders. The only sea creature worth talking about was cod, to the extent that in local parlance the word "fish" became synonymous with cod. It was cod that filled the basket hoisted from the waters off Newfoundland by Cabot's sailors in the course of his 1497 voyage, and it was cod that drew myriad fishing boats from the ports of northwest Europe to the banks. The cod congregated here for the same reason as the fishermen: the presence of abundant food. The shallow waters of the continental shelf known as the Grand Banks are where the warm waters of the Gulf Stream and the chilly Labrador Current meet and mix, stirring up minerals from the ocean floor and providing nutrients for the plankton, which, in turn, feeds the smaller fish preyed on by the cod.

In its beginnings the fishery was a seasonal one. Flotillas of vessels from Portugal, Brittany, the Basque country of Spain, and the West Country of England would set out for the Grand Banks in early spring and remain until September. (A custom was initiated by which the first sea captain to arrive in harbor was made Fishing Admiral, with full authority for the season over his fellow fishermen.). The French first ran a "wet" fishery, cleaning their catch on board and preserving it in salt. The English fishery, by contrast, was "dry." With less salt at their disposal, they landed their catch on the coast, cleaned it there and cured it by laying it out to dry on the timber "flakes" that are still a feature of some of Newfoundland's outports.

Permanent settlements

Rivalry between English and French characterized the early years of the fishery. As autumn set in and the fleets returned to Europe, the English left behind a small work force to guard and repair installations and tackle. Such supposedly temporary footholds developed over the years into more permanent settlements, consolidating the English presence despite government attempts to maintain the strictly seasonal character of the fishery. The French were pushed aside, though a series of treaties throughout the 18th century and into the 19th allowed them to use parts of the Newfoundland coast for fishing purposes, not permanent settlement. These rights along the "French shore" lasted until 1904, when they were extinguished by the Anglo-French Convention.

By the 19th century the fishery, always the basis of the Newfoundland economy, was largely controlled by merchants based in St. John's. They marketed the catch supplied by the fishermen working out of the 600 or so villages, or outports, around the island's long coastline. In return, the merchants provided goods in kind—fishing equipment, clothing, rum, and all the many foodstuffs that could not be grown on the thin soils of outport small holdings. This system guaranteed good profits for the merchants while keeping the outporters in a more or less permanent state of debt and dependence. But even in the

Despite depleted stocks and moratoriums, fishing is still vital to Newfoundland.

hardest of times, men could always set out in tiny boats they had built themselves and catch enough fish to feed the family on brewis, the Newfoundland national dish of cod, hardtack, and crisp-fried pork fat.

Today's moratorium

Previously, the hard times came when markets had failed. More recently, it is the fish themselves that have failed. Whether this is because of overfishing, particularly by high-tech foreign fleets, or as a result of natural causes, remains a matter of dispute. What is clear is the deep resentment felt by most Newfoundlanders at the fishing moratorium instituted by a federal goverment that in their view has consistently mismanaged Newfoundland's greatest asset, its immensely productive fishery. However much money Ottawa pumps into the provincial economy in the form of income support or retraining schemes, it cannot compensate for the loss of a livelihood that goes to the very root of a Newfoundlander's identity. ∎

While it is a rare sight nowadays, cod laid out to dry on "flakes" (above and below) have been a familiar feature of the Newfoundland fisheries since the 16th century.

Avalon Peninsula

Avalon Wilderness Reserve
⛰ 87D2

Visitor information
✉ Parks Division, Dept. of Tourism, Culture, & Recreation
☎ 709/729-2421

Colony of Avalon Archaeology Site
⛰ 85D2
✉ The Pool, Ferryland
☎ 709/432-3200
⏱ Closed Oct.–June

A puffin, commonly seen along the Avalon coastline

CONNECTED TO THE CENTRAL PART OF THE ISLAND BY A narrow isthmus, the Avalon Peninsula is Newfoundland's most densely settled and history-rich area, while still encompassing wild and spectacular landscapes and lonely places. A number of a fascinating excursions revealing the peninsula's essential character can be undertaken from St. John's.

NORTH & SOUTH OF ST. JOHN'S

A 40-plus-mile trip northward along Marine Drive reveals the Atlantic in all its majesty, bounded by high cliffs and wave-battered beaches. However, the most popular nearby destination is southeast at **Cape Spear National Historic Site** (*Tel 709/772-5367, lighthouse closed late Sept.–mid-June*), the easternmost point in North America. Its lighthouse, built in 1836, has been restored to its original condition, although its warning functions are now undertaken by a modern light station. It is the oldest surviving lighthouse in Newfoundland. The domed light itself is surrounded by the two-story keeper's house, its classical proportions enhanced by false windows.

To the south, Hwys. 11 and 10 reveal more of Newfoundland's coastal scenery. The little outport of **Petty Harbour** with its fish-drying flakes is picturesque enough to have featured in a number of films. The deep harbor of **Bay Bulls** is bigger altogether, proud of having the earliest known English place-name in Newfoundland (the bull bird or dovekie was once common here). Together with Witless Bay and Cape Broyle, this is one of the starting points for a boat trip (*O'Briens Whale & Bird Tours, Tel 709/334–2355; Gatheralls Puffin & Whale Watch, Tel 709/384–2887*) around Great, Green, and Gull Islands, collectively known as the

Witless Bay Ecological Reserve (*Tel 709/729–2431*). The islands are home to countless gulls, razorbills, murres, guillemots, kittiwakes, and above all, puffins, one of the emblems of Newfoundland. Whales, too, are much in evidence from around mid-June to the end of July, devouring the capelin that run at this time.

The interior

Hwy. 10 runs away from the coast, with side roads leading down to such melancholy and half-deserted outports as little **Brigus South.** Inland, the desolate 385-square-mile tract of the **Avalon Wilderness Reserve,** accessible only by permit, offers a haven for wildlife including a large caribou herd. Some 40 miles south of St. John's, an ongoing archaeological dig, **Colony of Avalon Archaeology Site,** continues to reveal fascinating details about the early European colonization of North America. Now the town of **Ferryland,** it was established as the colony of Avalon in 1621 on the orders of Sir George Calvert, later the first Baron Baltimore. A four-acre enclosure, defended by a palisade, contained a mansion house, other dwellings, a forge, saltworks, and a wharf. Other amenities included what was probably North America's first flushing toilet (worked by the action of seawater). Despite his followers' efforts, this environment proved too inhospitable for Calvert's liking.

After the rigorous winter of 1628–29 he took his family to Maryland, whose largest city still bears his name. Some of the more elegant of the half million objects uncovered can be viewed in the attractive visitor center.

WEST OF ST. JOHN'S

Only 10 miles west of St. John's lies the deeply indented far shore of **Conception Bay,** site of some of Newfoundland's earliest and most fascinating settlements. Attractive **Brigus** is associated with the American artist Rockwell Kent (1882–1971), who had a summer studio here, as well as with the indomitable Arctic mariner Captain Bob Bartlett (1875–1946), whose **Hawthorne Cottage National Historic Site** (*South St., Tel 709/528-4004, closed mid-Oct.– May*) is a now open to the public.

Stunning coastal scenery at Bird Rock, Cape St. Mary's Ecological Reserve

Brigus
 87D

St.-Pierre and Miquelon
▲ 87D1

Incipient allies: Roosevelt and Churchill confer aboard the battleship H.M.S. *Prince of Wales* in Placentia Bay.

The nearby town of **Cupids** was site of an even earlier plantation than that at Ferryland. In 1610 the Bristol merchant venturer John Guy landed here with 39 colonists, founding the first formal English colony in Newfoundland. A year later, the "Pirate Admiral," the renegade Royal Navy man Peter Easton, erected a stronghold at **Harbour Grace** to the north. The scale and success of his subsequent operations allowed him to retire and live in splendor in Europe. The site of his fort is now occupied by the **Conception Bay Museum** (*Water St., Tel 709/596-3042, closed Nov.–May*), which among other themes recalls the town's role in transatlantic aviation—many pioneering flights started here, including Amelia Earhart's historic crossing to Ireland in 1932.

A further reminder of Newfoundland's relative closeness to Europe may be found at **Heart's Content,** overlooking Trinity Bay. It was here in 1866, after previous attempts had failed, that the first transatlantic telegraph cable was successfully hauled ashore from the majestic S.S. *Great Eastern*, the largest ship of her day. Only superseded a century later, in 1965, by a modern installation, the **Cable Station** (*Hwy. 80, Tel 709/729-0592, by appointment off-season*) exhibits equipment and displays on the impact the cable had on North America and Europe.

Also connecting Newfoundland and the world beyond is the ferry service to North Sydney, Nova Scotia. Boats dock at **Argentia** on rocky Placentia Bay. This was the center of Allied anti-U boat operations during World War II. Earlier, when Placentia was known as Plaisance, it was central to France's attempts to turn Newfoundland into a French colony. To that end, Castle Hill was fortified in 1692, and served as a base for attacks on the English in St. John's. The **Castle Hill National Historic Site** (*Tel 709/227-2401*), which is built bunkerlike into the hillside, tells the poignant story of this part of the French empire in North America. To the south of Placentia, a switchback road gives plunging views of the gloriously rugged coves of **Cape Shore** far below. The tip of the peninsula holds what is probably Newfoundland's most spectacular bird sanctuary, **Cape St. Mary's Ecological Reserve** (*Hwy. 100, Tel 709/729-2431, closed Nov.–April*). Its Bird Rock, reached by clifftop footpath, hosts one of the largest colonies of gannets in North America.

St.-Pierre & Miquelon

After passing from French to British rule and back several times, these islands off Newfoundland's Burin Peninsula have stayed definitively French since 1814, when the Treaty of Paris recognized their pivotal role in the French Atlantic fishery. A political deputy is sent to Paris, the streets of St. Pierre are lined with archetypal French buildings and patrolled by gendarmes, and gourmet meals are served in atmospheric bistros. This tiny remnant of the once extensive French North American empire can be reached by air from St. John's (*Lakes Travel, Fortune, Tel 709/832-2006*), Halifax, and Montreal (*Air St. Pierre, Tel 709/722-4103*), and by ferry from Grand Bank. Bring a passport (or other means of identification if you are a U.S. or Canadian citizen). ∎

Bonavista Peninsula

"O BUONA VISTA!" WAS JOHN CABOT'S HEARTFELT CRY ON reaching this wild and rocky coastline in 1497. At least that is the generally accepted version of where and how the great navigator first came upon the New World. In 1997 the fifth centennial of his arrival was celebrated in style when a reproduction of his ship *Matthew* sailed into Bonavista harbor after repeating his epic voyage.

Close to the tip of the peninsula dividing Bonavista Bay from Trinity Bay sprawls the village of **Bonavista,** established in the late 16th century, the peninsula's principal settlement. Its long history can be traced by visiting the **Bonavista Museum** (*Church St., Tel 709/468-2575/2880*); the group of old buildings known as the **Mockbeggar Property** (*Off Rte. 230, Tel 709/729-2460, closed late Oct.–mid-June*); and, most evocatively of all, the recently restored **Ryan Premises National Historic Site** (*Ryan's Hill & Old Catalina Rd., Tel 709/772-5364, closed late Oct.–mid-June*), which includes a shop, fish store, and salt shed.

Battered by wind and spray, the cape to the north of the village is graced by the bold, red-and-white-striped **Cape Bonavista Lighthouse** (*Tel 709/729-2460, 468-7444, closed off-season*) dating from 1843. It has become one of the emblems of Newfoundland.

Many of the little villages clinging to this desolate coastline deserve more than a casual visit, but one particularly attractive to visitors is **Trinity.** Set among coves and inlets and backed by low hills, Trinity once rivaled St. John's in importance. Its name may date to when the Portuguese sailor Gaspar Corte-Real sailed into the bay on Trinity Sunday in 1500. By the end of that century it had been fortified by the English, and in 1615 Newfoundland's first Court of Admiralty was held here to adjudicate disputes between migratory fishermen and permanent settlers. Trinity's golden age came in the late 18th and early 19th centuries when prosperous merchants made their fortunes here, but subsequent decline has merely added to the township's charm. Today this backwater of delightful clapboard houses linked by picket fences and winding lanes offers many attractions, including the **Trinity Interpretation Centre** (*Rte. 239, Tel 709/729-2460 or 709/464-2042*), and the **Green Family Forge** (*Church Rd., Tel 709/464-3720 or 709/464-3706*). The **Trinity Historical Society Museum and Archives** (*Church Rd., Tel 709/464-3720 or 709/464-3706, closed mid-Sept.–mid-June*) is crammed full of memorabilia. The Roman Catholic church is the island's oldest, and the Anglican church is a carpentry tour-de-force. ∎

One of Newfoundland's oldest lighthouses warns ships of the dangers posed by Cape Bonavista's rugged coast.

87D2

Bonavista Peninsula visitor information

✉ Trans-Canada 1 near Clarenville

☎ 709/466–3100

🕐 Closed mid-Oct.–May

Trinity

🅰 87D2

Terra Nova National Park & the interior

Terra Nova National Park

⚠ 87D2

✉ 80 miles west of Clarenville on Trans-Canada 1

☎ 709/533-2801

💲 $ mid-May–mid-Oct.

Grand Falls

⚠ 87D2

Gander

⚠ 87D2

Deer Lake

⚠ 87C2

Corner Brook

⚠ 87C2

Lewisporte

⚠ 85D2

Terra Nova National Park presents an array of beautiful and diverse landscapes.

FROM THE BASE OF THE BONAVISTA PENINSULA, TRANS-Canada 1 cuts through the 150-square-mile Terra Nova National Park. With its well-marked trails, campgrounds, and a new visitor center overlooking Newman Sound, the park is one of the best places to explore a variety of Newfoundland landscapes.

The highly indented coastline shelters fjordlike inlets, beaches of sand and pebble, caves, cliffs, and sea stacks, while inland lie the bogs, barrens, and boreal forest, so characteristic of the island's rugged landscape. One of the best places to learn about this environment is the **Marine Interpretation Centre** (*Salton's day-use area, off Trans-Canada 1, Tel 709/533-2801, closed mid-Oct.–early June*), in the heart of the Terra Nova National Park.

Trans-Canada 1 continues to **Gander.** Developed in the 1930s as a relatively fog-free refueling base for transatlantic air traffic, the airport came into its own in wartime, retaining its importance as "Crossroads of the World" until well into the postwar period, when jets developed the range enabling them to fly direct from Europe into the heart of North America. A short distance north off Hwy. 340 is **Lewisporte,** the embarkation point for ferries to the Labrador coast.

Developed in the early 20th century as a company town to supply newsprint to British newspapers, **Grand Falls** (*Tel 709/489–6332*) is one of the few settlements in Newfoundland built away from the sea. It has a reproduction **Beothuk Village** (*St. Catherine St., Tel 709/489-9629, closed Oct.–May*). The **Mary March Regional Museum** (*24 St. Catherine St., Tel 709/292-4523, closed Nov.–April*) recalls the sad fate of one of the last of these unfortunate people, along with displays on regional history. **Deer Lake** (*Visitor information, off Trans-Canada 1, Tel 709/635-2202, closed Nov.–June*), with its airport, is gateway to the great northern peninsula and one of Newfoundland's greatest attractions, Gros Morne National Park, reached via Hwy. 430. Trans-Canada 1 continues to busy **Corner Brook** (*Visitor information, Confederation Dr., Tel 709/634–5831*), the island's second largest city (population about 25,000), past the Port au Port Peninsula, where French can still be heard, and on to Channel-Port aux Basques and its ferry service to Nova Scotia's North Sydney (*Tel 709/435–4100 for schedules*). ■

Gros Morne National Park

87D3

A HIGH POINT OF ANY VISIT TO NEWFOUNDLAND, GROS Morne National Park, on the exposed west coast of the island's great northern peninsula, holds some of eastern Canada's most spectacular scenery as well as an array of unique geological features—all contributing to its designation as a UNESCO world heritage site.

**Rocky Harbour
visitor center**
☎ 709/931-2309
   or 709/726-0015
$ $ mid-May—mid-Oct.

Reached via Hwy. 430 from Deer Lake, this park has a variety of landscapes: a coastline of cliffs, dunes, sea stacks, beaches, and fjords penetrating deep inland. The coast formed part of the French shore, where, in the 19th century, France was granted special fishing rights. Although permanent settlement was forbidden, some of the villages clinging to the shore attest to the defiance of this proscription. Inland, a narrow plain with mixed woodland and bogs blooms with orchids and Newfoundland's provincial flower, the pitcher plant, in season. To the east rise the **Long Range Mountains,** the northernmost extension of the Appalachians, their flat tops forming a vast plateau some 2,000 feet above sea level. Southwest spread the desolate **Tablelands,** a high plateau formed from toxic peridotite, a rock normally only present in the earth's mantle but here forced to the surface when the ancient continents of North America and Eurafrica collided.

The best place to start exploring the park is in **Rocky Harbour,** with its excellent visitor center Nearby is the starting point of the demanding James Callaghan Trail, which brings determined hikers scrambling to the top of Gros Morne Mountain. Its 2,644-foot-high summit, a chaos of frost-shattered rock, offers magnificent views over uplands, coastline, and the pond-filled glacial valleys all around. An equally unforgettable, and less demanding, excursion is to hike the

The sun sets over one of the coast's many lighthouses.

2-mile trail across the wetlands to the tip of Western Brook Pond, then board one of the **Western Brook Pond Boat Tours** (*Bontours, Ocean View Motel, Tel 709/458-2730*). These explore this superb landlocked fjord.

Beyond Gros Morne, Hwy. 430 continues north, hugging the coast much of the way. Important evidence of the presence here nearly 4,000 years ago of Maritime Archaic people and of the Dorset Eskimo community that followed them is displayed at **Port au Choix National Historic Site** (*Off Hwy. 430, Tel 709/864-3522, closed late-Sept.–mid-June*). Farther north, **St. Barbe** is a departure point for the Labrador ferry (*Tel 709/931–2309*), and beyond the township and port of **St. Anthony** is a site resonant with meaning for all North Americans—the Viking settlement excavated at **L'Anse aux Meadows National Historic Site** (see pp. 100–101). ∎

L'Anse aux Meadows National Historic Site
✉ Rte. 436, 27 miles from St. Anthony
☎ 709/623-2608
🕐 Closed Sept.–May

Norsemen in Newfoundland

Near the tip of Newfoundland's great northern peninsula stands a cluster of sod-built structures huddling from the winds blowing off rocky Epaves Bay. L'Anse aux Meadows is one of the most evocative sites in North America, a place touched by the restless questing of European mariners a full 500 years before the voyages of Columbus and Cabot but forgotten for nearly a millennium.

Around A.D. 985–86, the Norsemen who had colonized Iceland ventured even farther from their Scandinavian homeland, founding settlements on the Greenland coast. Blown off course, one of their number, the trader Bjarni Herjolfsson, discovered a well-wooded coastline, almost certainly that of Newfoundland. This, the first recorded sighting by a European of the continent of North America, encouraged a bold spirit by the name of Leif Eriksson to undertake a voyage of southward exploration. Starting out around the turn of the millennium, in the course of his travels he wintered in "Vinland," seemingly a frost-free land of vines, a place evidently far to the south of chilly Newfoundland. Its exact location—not to mention its translation—remains a subject for scholarly dispute to this day.

A year or two later, in 1004, another expedition from Greenland set off southward, evidently with a longer stay in mind, as women and cattle accompanied the warrior-sailors led by Thorfinnr Karlsefni. But the semi-permanent base established at Straumfiord (most likely the Strait of Belle Isle between Newfoundland and Labrador) was abandoned after a few years. Bloody encounters with native groups may have contributed to the decision to discontinue this colonizing endeavor, though it seems certain that Greenlanders continued to make occasional visits to the mainland in the years that followed, using it as a fishing base.

The historical source for all these ventures are the medieval Icelandic sagas, and much skepticism has been expressed about their literal accuracy. Norwegian explorer and writer Helge Ingstad had no such doubts; for years he traveled the coasts of eastern North America looking for evidence of Vinland. Encouraged by an alternative interpretation of "vin" as meaning "meadow" rather than wine, and led to what local people had always thought to be an aboriginal site haunted by ancient ghosts, Ingstad concluded that the humpy grassland overlooking Epaves Bay was, if not Vinland, certainly a Norse site of some kind. The excavations he undertook in the early 1960s with his wife, archaeologist Anne Stine, proved him right; the remains of eight sod-built huts were found, together with artifacts of indisputable Norse origin such as a bronze pin, sewing

Above: At L'Anse aux Meadows, a woven fence defines the enclosure occupied a thousand years ago by the Vikings.
Left: A reproduction Norse boat
Below: Vikings may have sheltered from the storms inside a house like this reconstructed version.

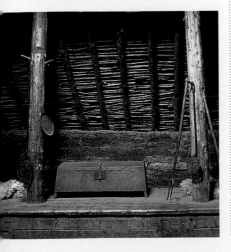

implements, and a soapstone spindle whorl.

This was no temporary camp. Sod walls and sod roofs built over a timber frame indicate buildings substantial enough for permanent occupation. Eight in number, they included three long and narrow dwellings with features similar to those found in Norse buildings in Greenland and Iceland. Other, smaller buildings, used mainly as stores and workshops, include a forge that used iron ore extracted from peat bogs—thrilling evidence of the first iron-working on the North American continent.

Today the site is managed by Parks Canada. Within the enclosure of a woven wood fence, three sod houses have been painstakingly reconstructed using such traditional techniques as wooden "nails" and fastenings made from roots or sealskin. Roofs and walls are of sod, the latter up to 6 feet in thickness. The interiors have been furnished as authentically as possible to convey the living conditions of these pioneers who, a thousand years ago, crossed stormy seas in open boats to seek a foothold in an utterly unknown land. ■

Labrador

Labrador
[M] 87B4

A VAST AREA OF SUBARCTIC WILDERNESS, LABRADOR stretches northward more than 600 miles from the Strait of Belle Isle to Cape Chidley, overlooking the icy waters of Ungava Bay some 500 miles from Greenland. Only a few permanent residents brave the fierce climate to live here, most of them dependent on fishing, forestry, iron-ore extraction, and hydropower generation.

At Battle Harbour, scattered dwellings and rudimentary port facilities typify settlements along the inhospitable Labrador coast.

Much of Labrador is inaccessible except by air, although Rte. 389 (gravel in part) runs 380 miles from Baie Comeau on the St. Lawrence River to Labrador City and Wabush, townships that owe their existence to the iron-ore deposits, which have been exploited commercially since the 1950s.

A gravel road (Rte. 500), the Trans-Labrador Highway, runs eastward from **Labrador City** about 325 miles to **Goose Bay,** the embarkation point for ships serving the rugged north coast or linking with Lewisporte in Newfoundland.

The leisurely ferry trip northward (*Labrador coast ferries, Tel 800/563-6353*) up the coast to **Nain** stops at tiny settlements, some with roots in the fur trade, others established by the Moravian Brethren. Some of their late 18th- and early 19th-century missions have been conserved as national historic sites, including the **Piulimatsivik-Nain Museum** (*Tel 709/922-2327, 709/922-2158*), with its array of fascinating Inuit items. The landscape becomes even more spectacular farther north, where fjords cut deeply into the rocky terrain. Here are the highest Canadian peaks east of the Rockies (Mount Caubvick: 5,671 feet).

Far to the south, and much more accessible, a string of settlements, is linked by a paved highway along the Belle Isle Strait and reached by ferry from **St. Barbe** (*Tel 709/931-2309*) on the Newfoundland shore. In the mid-16th century, this coastline witnessed activity on an almost industrial scale, conducted by whalers from the Basque country. The recently discovered, evocative remains of their main base at Red Bay are part of **Red Bay National Historic Site** (*Off Rte. 510, Tel 709/920-2197, by appointment Oct.–May*).

A feature of far greater antiquity is the burial mound at the **Maritime Archaic Funeral Monument National Historic Site** (*Tel 709/623-2601 or 709/623-2608*). The oldest of its kind in North America, it is a reminder of the presence of the Maritime Archaic people who established coastal settlements here some 7,500 years ago. ■

Goose Bay
[M] 87C3
Nain
[M] 87B5
St. Barbe
[M] 87C3

Canada's most distinct province is evoked by the words that used to grace its license plates, "*La Belle Province.*" The current "*Je me souviens*" (I remember) recalls the history of a land first settled by the French four centuries ago.

Quebec

Statue at Notre-Dame-de-Bonsecours, Montreal

Quebec

QUEBEC EXTENDS FROM THE FER-
tile and populous St. Lawrence lowlands
across miles of forest and tundra to the
desolate coastline of the Hudson Strait.
Still part of Canada despite a quarter century of uncertainty, the province has
become more distinctively French in character since the changes began in the period of the 1960s Quiet Revolution.

Language laws ensure the visual dominance of
French in advertising and signs of all kinds,
while the long-lasting domination of business
life by English speakers has been brought to an
end. This doesn't mean you have to speak
French in order to enjoy a stay in Quebec.
Virtually everyone an English-speaking visitor
is likely to meet will understand English and
probably speak it as well as you do. And despite
rumors to the contrary, the anglophone population of Montreal has not decamped en masse
to Toronto. The signs may be in French in the
city's downtown, but you're just as likely to
hear English spoken as French. Adding to the
charm and diversity of rural Quebec are many
pockets of English-speaking communities
dotted around the countryside, descendants of
Loyalist, Irish, Scottish, or Channel Islands
settlers, and just as proud of their Quebec
identity as any Québécois.

The Quebec countryside is one thing, the
cities another. Montreal and Quebec City
attract international visitors by the million,
and once you've arrived in either of them it
is easy to see why. Montreal is a great metropolis, whose deep-rooted past is reflected in its
claim to the biggest concentration of historic
buildings in North America, but whose future
aspirations are expressed in a skyline of skyscrapers, some of great elegance and beauty.
At its foot swirls a cosmopolitan population,
intent on getting the most out of life, especially where food and drink are concerned; the
city claims the finest array of restaurants outside New York. You can eat well in Quebec
City, too, but the great attraction in the continent's only walled city is a sense of history.
Even in Europe there a few places that match
Quebec City's marvelous fusion of human

handiwork and nature: A great rock commanding the St. Lawrence, a Lower Town
huddling at its foot, and an Upper Town
crowning the heights with steep roofs,
towers, and a great Citadel.

Québécois people are very attached
to their countryside. Although the province
is highly urbanized, rural roots count for
a lot. City dwellers dream of owning an
old *maison québécoise*, built in fieldstone
under a steep-pitched roof. They flock to
weekend homes and chalets in the delightful rural areas on the fringe of the cities:

Area of map detail

Montrealers to the Laurentian Uplands, Richelieu Valley, and Eastern Townships; Quebec City folk to the villages and countryside of Charlevoix. Weekend escapes are fine at any time of year, but perhaps best of all in winter; the many ski resorts may get crowded, but you can always slip away on cross-country skis or snowshoes and find unexplored places and perfect silence.

A second trip to Quebec might take you along the north shore of the St. Lawrence, where some villages can still only be reached by boat, or to the islands of the gulf (Magdalen Islands and Anticosti). A third trip might lead northward, to the great hydroelectric projects of James Bay, or, properly equipped and advised, farther north still, to the Inuit and Cree villages of one of the last frontiers of travel. ■

The administrative center of New France—Quebec City in 1740

New France

Farmhouses strung out along the riverside, their long and narrow lots reaching far inland, gray stone churches with glittering roofs and steeples, fine town houses that would not be out of place in Brittany or Normandy—there is a lot in the landscape of Quebec that still breathes the spirit of the French North America of 300 years ago.

New France was intended to dominate the continent. French settlers lived on the Atlantic coast, traders pushed west to the Great Lakes and beyond, Détroit was a French fort, and the Mississippi a potential link to the southern colony of Louisiane. But the French presence was strongest in the lower valley of the St. Lawrence. Here were large towns: the capital, Quebec, profiting from its position at the head of navigation for oceangoing ships, and, not far behind it in terms of population, Montreal, founded as the City of Mary (Ville–Marie) by the devout De Maisonneuve as a missionary city in the wilderness, but increasingly the capital of the fur trade, which was the single greatest source of the colony's wealth.

In its early years, the life of the colony was dominated by the fur trade and the companies that ran it (see pp. 220–21), particularly the Compagnie des Cent-Associés. In 1663 their failure to attract settlers—by that time the population amounted to a mere 3,000—prompted Louis XIV to take control. From then until the British conquest a century later, New France was ruled as a royal province of the mother country. The king's representative was the governor general, supported (and sometimes undermined) by the intendant, in charge of day-to-day administration. Beneath these high officials, an urban aristocracy of mostly military men formed the top layer of society, pushing the frontier of French control farther into the continent and securing the colony against Iroquois and British attack. They shared the towns with a merchant class and with the Church, which sent missionaries to evangelize the natives and dispatched priests to the countryside to remind the rural population of their religious duties, a frequently unrewarding task.

Because the first priority of New France was trade and not settlement, the countryside was slow to develop, but following the term in office of the vigorous Jean Talon, the first royal intendant, immigrants from France arrived in greater numbers, the birth rate rose, the population increased substantially, and pressure for land grew. The way in which farmland was allocated was semifeudal. The land granted to a seigneur (not necessarily an aristocrat) was parceled out in long lots to tenants in return

A romanticized view of French-Canadian life by Cornelius Krieghoff

for annual, usually not very substantial, tithes, and the obligation to use the mill that the seigneur, in turn, was obliged to build.

Farmhouses were built along the river, close, but not too close, to the neighboring family's dwelling. Government would have preferred the rural population to have lived in villages, where they could be supervised more keenly, but the habitants (as they liked to call themselves) preferred to live in this semi-autonomous way, enjoying their freedoms but able to call on neighbors for help when necessary. Many of them had memories of being the outcasts of French society, as orphans, ex-prisoners, or soldiers, and enjoyed their independence. Urban officialdom worried about habitants having their throats cut by people lurking in the forest, but many Canadians admired those they called *les sauvages* for their pride, bushcraft, and refusal to be bound by routine.

In his homespun coat and moccasins, the typical habitant was quite content if his land yielded sufficient food for his family, and was rarely tempted to try and enrich himself by farming for the market. His sons might well take to the woods, disappearing for a season, or perhaps forever, in search of beaver pelts and other furs. With their adoption of native ways and their willingness to trade with anyone who would pay well (like the otherwise scorned New Englanders), these unlicensed *coureurs de bois* were a constant headache for

the authorities, who wished to keep the fur trade under their control.

After the British conquest, the representatives of French authority were shipped back to France. The habitants stayed, adjusting to the new regime, but continuing their settled ways, living in a landscape that they created and whose patterns persist today. ■

Stalwart French habitants adapted perfectly to their harsh environment.

ST.-ANDRÉ

Aéroport de Dorval

Musée des Beaux-Arts de Montréal

Oratoire St.-Joseph

Université Concordia

Centre Canadien d'Architecture
Lucien-L'Allier

RUE SHERBROOKE OUEST

112

Université McGill

Musée Redpath

Musée McCord

McGill

BOULEVARD DE MAISONNEUVE OUEST

Place Montreal Trust

Centre Eaton

La Baie

Square Dominion
SQUARE-DORCHESTER
PLACE VILLE-MARIE

Cathédrale Marie-Reine-du-Monde

Église St.-Georges

Gare Windsor

1000 de la Gauchetière

SQUARE CHABOILLEZ

Planetarium Dow

RUE NOTRE-DAME OUEST

RUE ST.-JACQUES

136

Mont-Royal

RUE SHERBROOKE OUEST

Salle Wilfrid-Pelletier

U.Q.A.M.

Musée d'Art Contemporain de Montréal

Place des Arts

Cathédrale Christ Church

Sun Life
ST.-GEORGES

La Reine Élizabeth
PLACE DU CANADA
Bonaventure

Gare Central

PLACE BONA-VENTURE

Square-Victoria

AVENUE VIGER OUEST

RUE ST.-ANTOINE OUEST

Banque de Montréal
PLACE D'ARMES

Basilique Notre-Dame

Séminaire de St.-Sulpice

PLACE ROYALE

Centre d'Histoire de Montréal

Immeuble des Douanes

Pointe-à-Callière & Musée d'Archéologie et d'Histoire

Musée Marc-Aurèle Fortin

Bassin Alexandra

Complexe Desjardins

BOULEVARD RENÉ LÉVESQUE EST

Complexe Guy-Favreau

Place d'Armes

Palais des Congrès

QUARTIER LATIN

PARC DES HABITATIONS JEAN-MANCE

BOULEVARD DE MAISONNEUVE EST

RUE STE.-CATHERINE EST

U.Q.A.M.

Saint Laurent

720

AUTOROUTE VILLE-MARIE

VILLE-MARIE
CHAMP-DE-MARS

Hôtel de Ville

VIEUX-MONTRÉAL

Marché Bonsecours

VIEUX-PORT

Quai King Edward

Bassin Jacques-Cartier

Quai Jacques-Cartier

Quai King Edward

Berri-U.Q.A.M.

Termini Voyageur

SQUARE BERRI

Champ-de-Mars

QUARTIER CHINOIS

AVENUE VIGER EST

AUTOROUTE VILLE-MARIE

Lieu hist. Sir G.É.-Cartier

Château Ramezay

Chapelle Notre-Dame-de-Bonsecou

Clock Tow

Bassin Bonsecours

Quai de l'Horloge

St.-Laurent (St. Lawrence)

Parc Olympique, Jardin botanique

Aéroport de Mirabel

0 ——— 400 meters
0 ——— 400 yards

RUE WELLINGTON

10

Montreal

105C1

Visitor information

1001 Square-Dorchester

514/873-2015

Metro: Peel

Vieux-Montreal Visitor information

174 Rue Notre Dame Est

514/873-2015

Metro: Champs-de-Mars

TORONTO MAY HAVE SNATCHED THE BATON FROM Montreal as Canada's biggest city, but Montreal remains the country's most diverse and fascinating metropolis, an extraordinary fusion of rich European tradition and North American modernity. Montreal is on an island, the biggest in an archipelago downstream from the confluence of the Ottawa River and the St. Lawrence.

For a seat-of-the-pants understanding of why there is a city here at all (if you don't mind a bit of a soaking), take the powerboat ride from the Old Port to the Lachine Rapids. The foaming water blocked further navigation upstream by oceangoing vessels, making it necessary to reload, store, and supervise goods going to and from the continent's interior. So the mission of Ville-Marie established in 1642 by Paul de Chomedy Maisonneuve (1612–1676) soon developed as the base for explorers and for the *coureurs de bois* and voyageurs who ran the fur trade (see pp. 220–21).

Though Ville-Marie was soon renamed Montreal, the power of the Catholic Church remained strong. Missionaries had their headquarters here, and the Sulpician Order, which had sponsored Maisonneuve, stayed seigneurs of the city for more than 200 years. Their seminary of 1685 still stands next to their glorious basilica of Notre-Dame in the heart of Old Montreal.

TODAY'S MONTREAL

Once defended by a double line of stone walls, Vieux-Montréal has the biggest collection of historic buildings in the whole of North America. No longer the powerhouse of the Canadian economy—though its Wall Street, Rue Saint-Jacques, is still dominated by banks—it has been rescued from mid-century decay to become a focal point of the city for locals and visitors alike. The resurrection of the adjacent Vieux-Port (Old Port) as a leisure and recreational area has only added to its attraction.

The 19th-century development of Montreal as the nation's commercial and industrial capital and its greatest port saw the bypassing of the rapids on the St. Lawrence by the Lachine Canal (1825) and the extension of the city's influence by the building of railroads, including the Canadian Pacific, which had its headquarters here. Immigrants arrived from Britain and Ireland and for a few decades the city had an anglophone majority. The balance changed as burgeoning industries sucked in a francophone work force from the countryside. French speakers lived east of St. Lawrence Boulevard, English speakers to the west, where the wealthiest of them built the great mansions of the Golden Square Mile at the foot of leafy Mont-Royal, the city's great natural landmark.

In the early 20th century the city's center of gravity shifted to the west, reflecting the realities of anglophone dominance of the economy. But from the late 1950s Montreal was the focus of Quebec's Quiet Revolution, which coincided with the physical transformation of the cityscape. The cross-shaped tower of Place Ville-Marie was among the first of a forest of skyscrapers, some of great architectural beauty. Beneath the streets the Underground City (see p. 116) began to form, connecting stores, stations, places of entertainment, and the sparkling new Metro. An almost completely self-contained subterranean world, insulated from the rigors of the Montreal winter, came into being. This was the era of Mayor Jean Drapeau, flamboyant ruler of the city for 29 years, who not only gave Montreal the Metro, but also presided over Expo 67 and the Summer Olympics of 1976. When, vexed by the promotion of French in public life from the mid-1970s onward, English speakers left the city in large numbers, Drapeau commented "Let Toronto become Milan, Montreal will always be Rome."

Street scene in Old Montreal

Montreal may not have Rome's Eseven hills, but it is home to some 200,000 Italians, the largest of the migrant communities attracted here since World War II. The ethnic diversity of immigrants, who now make up more than a fifth of the city's population, has not only diluted the intensity of the French-English polarity, which was once so dominant, but has added immensely to the richness of the city's cultural scene. Montreal is currently only one step behind New York as North America's capital of gastronomy.

Once you've finished eating, it is time to party. This is truly one of those cities that never sleeps, with an almost infinite choice of bars, cafés, cabarets, night spots, and entertainment. And when you've recovered from partying, there is an array of museums awaiting—some, like the Fine Arts Museum or the Museum of Contemporary Art, in world-class new buildings. ■

Nighttime in downtown Montreal from the heights of Mont-Royal

A Walk in Old Montreal

The historic core of Montreal, with its wonderful array of old buildings, is once more a fashionable place to live and work, and is the best place to begin your exploration of this fascinating, many-sided metropolis. The 18th-century stone walls have long since been pulled down, but Old Montreal, on its low ridge overlooking the St. Lawrence, is still well defined and a pure delight to stroll around.

The main east–west streets, Rue Saint-Jacques, Rue Notre-Dame, and Rue Saint-Paul, still follow the alignment traced out in the 1670s. There are boutiques, bars, restaurants, the occasional bed-and-breakfast in an 18th-century house built from Montreal's hard, gray limestone. Running north–south, the cross streets descend to what was once a busy dockside. Commerce has retreated from the Vieux-Port, giving way to riverside parkland and recreational facilities.

Take Montreal's squeaky clean Metro to **Champ-de-Mars** ❶ and leave the station by the south exit. Walk diagonally across the Champ-de-Mars, the old parade ground that for many years served as a popular space for gatherings of all kinds.

From here there are views westward of the soaring towers of the downtown area, but below and in front of you are the bases of Montreal's old walls, a double line of defense erected early in the 18th century. Resist the temptation to go down Place Jacques-Cartier and instead walk east along Rue Notre-Dame, past bulky **Hôtel de Ville** on the left and modest **Château de Ramezay** ❷ on the right (see p. 112).

Some of the numerous cafés on Rue Crescent in Old Montreal

As you turn right down **Rue Bonsecours,** there is a charming view downhill of the **Chapelle Notre-Dame-de-Bonsecours** (see pp. 112–3) at the foot of the street. Rue Bonsecours has a number of fine old houses, including the 1785 **Maison Papineau** (No. 440) and the **Maison du Calvet** (No. 401) at the corner by the chapel.

Walk west past the 500-foot facade of **Marché Bonsecours**, then turn left and cross the railroad track to get a taste of the **Vieux-Port**. From the upper levels of the **Pavillon Jacques-Cartier** unfolds a panorama of the long, irregular line of mostly 19th-century shipping offices and storehouses that once marked the boundary between city and waterfront.

Recross the railroad tracks and enjoy the lively (summertime) ambience of **Place Jacques-Cartier** ❸. Walk west along narrow Rue Saint-Amable, then down Rue Saint-Vincent and west again on Rue Saint-Paul, perhaps the most picturesque of all the streets in Old Montreal. At Place Royale, turn left to Pointe-à-Callière and the **Musée d'Archéologie et d'Histoire de Montréal** (see p. 113–4). Go west again on **Place d'Youville** ❹, where, as well as the **Centre**

- ⓜ See area map pp. 104–105
- ► Champ-de-Mars
- ⬌ 1.7 miles
- ⏱ 3 hours
- ► Basilique Notre-Dame

NOT TO BE MISSED
- Chapelle Notre-Dame-de-Bonsecours
- Musée d'Archéologie et d'Histoire de Montréal
- Basilique Notre-Dame

A view from the port illustrates the architectural contrasts of Montreal.

d'Histoire de Montréal (see p. 114), there are splendid old stone buildings that once housed the **Écuries d'Youville** (Nos. 298–300) and the **Gray Nuns' Convent** founded in 1693 (Rue Saint-Pierre).

Go north on Rue Saint-Pierre and turn right onto Rue Saint-Jacques, which, under its English name of St. James' Street, was the Wall Street of Canada until well into the 20th century.

Among the ostentatious bank buildings the Banque de Montreal (No. 119) is outstanding, a Roman temple built to house the financing of Canada's imperial expansion. Its neighbors on **Place d'Armes ❺** include the city's first skyscraper, the New York Life Insurance Building of 1889, and the art deco Aldred Building. To the south are the twin towers of the **Basilique Notre-Dame** (see p. 114). ∎

Old Montreal

Château Ramezay
- ✉ 280 Rue Notre-Dame Est
- ☎ 514/861-3708
- ⊕ Closed Mon. Oct.–May
- 💲 $
- 🚇 Metro: Champ-de-Mars

Lieu Historique Sir George Étienne-Cartier
- ✉ 458 Rue Notre-Dame Est
- ☎ 514/283-2282
- 💲 $
- 🚇 Metro: Champ-de-Mars

Chapelle Notre-Dame-de-Bonsecours
- ✉ 400 Rue Saint-Paul Est
- ☎ 514/845-9991
- ⊕ Restricted hours in winter
- 💲 Museum $
- 🚇 Metro: Champ-de-Mars

THE OBVIOUS FIRST CHOICE FOR MANY PEOPLE FINDING their bearings in Old Montreal is Place Jacques-Cartier (*Metro: Champ-de-Mars*). Named after the great French explorer, the square descends from the Nelson statue at the top of the slope to Rue de la Commune along the line of the old dockside. You are unlikely to be alone here; this is where city visitors hop aboard a horse-drawn carriage, watch the street entertainers from an outdoor café, and admire the offerings of the street artists in narrow Rue Saint-Amable just to the west.

But the square is far from being just a tourist trap. Half the city turns out here on summer days, overflowing across Rue de la Commune to the generous spaces of the the Vieux-Port. Before you join them, make sure you have had a good look at some of the fine old buildings lining the square, like No. 410, the restored **Maison Viger** at the corner of Saint-Amable, or No. 404, the **Maison del Vecchio,** also from the early years of the 19th century.

Nearby is the **Hôtel de Ville.** Dating from 1878, this monumental city hall in Second Empire style was faithfully rebuilt after burning down in 1922. The focus of Montreal's often convoluted city politics, it enjoyed a moment of international glory in 1967 when visiting President of France Charles de Gaulle cried "*Vive le Québec libre!*" from its balcony to the huge crowd assembled below. Apparently surprised at their ecstatic reaction, De Gaulle turned to his host, Quebec premier Daniel Johnson, for an explanation. "You've just repeated the slogan of my opponents at the last election!" was the mortified reply.

Château Ramezay is one of the oldest and most evocative buildings in North America. This long, low, farmhouse-like structure in gray fieldstone has had an illustrious history. Completed in 1705

as the home of Claude de Ramezay, the 11th governor of Montreal, it was successively the headquarters of the Compagnie des Indes, the great fur-trading company, then the residence of the British governor-general. Benjamin Franklin lodged here during the 1775 American occupation of Montreal, but failed in his mission to persuade the citizens to sign up as the 14th state. The château has been a museum for over a century. Among its exhibits on domestic and First Nations themes is superb early 18th-century paneling from France.

A more recent chapter in Canadian history is preserved at **Lieu Historique Sir George Étienne-Cartier.** Revered as a Father of Confederation by federalists, denounced as a stooge and collaborator by Quebec nationalists, Sir George Étienne-Cartier (1814–1873) attracts controversy long after his death. The point of this charming museum, set out in the adjacent houses where he lived and worked, is not politics so much as the comfortable upper-middle-class life led in Montreal in the mid-19th century, with a wealth of period furniture and other artifacts.

Chapelle Notre-Dame-de-Bonsecours is also known as the Sailors' Church. This delightful 18th-century chapel is topped by a tall copper statue of the Virgin Mary, her arms outstretched to all those who sail on the St. Lawrence. Grateful seafarers donated the ship models displayed inside. The building is a successor to the wooden chapel built in 1657 on the initiative of Marguerite Bourgeoys. Canonized in 1982, this indomitable lady from Troyes in France made her mark on Ville-Marie in all sorts of ways, not only founding an order of nuns, but establishing schools for both French and local girls and, most famously, shipping in young women (*Les filles du Roy*) as wives for bachelor colonists.

The Old Port
Summer is the time to enjoy the exciting new park laid out on the docksides of the **Vieux-Port,** when thousands of city dwellers congregate to stroll, cycle, Roller-blade, lounge around, see and be seen, and enjoy the cooling breezes. The breezes are a bit too cool in the winter, but hardy souls can still be seen skating and sliding. There is

open-air entertainment, an IMAX cinema, a spectacular modern maze called SOS Labyrinthe, and the Magic and Illusion Houdini Theatre. Of the various boat trips offered, the most exciting dares passengers to brave a soaking on the famous Lachine Rapids (*Tel 514/284-9607*).

POINTE-À-CALLIÈRE
All levels of Montreal's history come together in the fascinating complex of buildings known collectively as the **Musée d'Archéologie et d'Histoire de Montréal,** where there is an intriguing underground display of archaeological excavations. The area known as **Pointe-à-Callière** is the very birthplace of the city, the spot at which Champlain landed in 1611 and where Maisonneuve and his party of settlers landed in 1642. This, and much more, is entertainingly brought to life in a witty audiovisual show which painlessly combines

Montrealers reconstructed their Second Empire-style city hall after a fire in 1922.

Musée d'Archéologie et d'Histoire de Montréal
- ✉ 350 Place Royale
- ☎ 514/872-9150
- 🕐 Closed Sat.–Mon.
- 💲 $$$
- 🚇 Metro: Place-d'Armes

A pronounced maritime flavor pervades the Chapelle Notre-Dame-de-Bonsecours, also known as the Sailors' Church.

English and French and in the space of a few minutes tells you most of what you need to know about Montreal's three-and-a-half centuries of existence. From here, you go beneath the surface to an atmospheric crypt, with evocative remains of walls, water conduits, sewers, even a cemetery. Back up on ground level, you find yourself inside the dignified old **Customs House** overlooking Place Royale, site of Maisonneuve's first residence.

To complete the history lesson begun at Pointe-à-Callière, come inside the splendidly ornate old fire station that now houses the **Centre d'Histoire de Montréal.** Full of displays on all aspects of Montreal's past, its 11 rooms evoke the texture of urban life as you ride a trolley, climb up one of the city's famous outside staircases, or eavesdrop in a 1940s living room.

The **Basilique Notre-Dame** is one of the outstanding architectural achievements in a city that has more than its share of lovely buildings. In 1824 the Sulpician seigneurs who ruled Montreal ordered the building of a great church that would accommodate all the faithful of the parish (which covered the whole city). Their cho-

sen architect was an Irish-American Protestant named James O'Donnell, who was so moved by the magnificence of his achievement that he converted to Catholicism and was eventually buried here. For half a century, the twin-towered, Gothic Revival basilica was the biggest church in North America, and it remains a Montreal landmark despite the proliferation of skyscrapers. Its interior is of the utmost sumptuousness, a fusion of richly detailed carving, stained glass, and subtly controlled natural and artificial lighting. The gilt of woodwork and the mystic blue of vaults and altarpiece create an atmosphere of great serenity. The high pulpit is a masterpiece, carved by the sculptor Louis-Philippe Hébert. The windows, from Limoges in France, tell the tale of early Montreal.

The basilica is flanked by Montreal's oldest building, the **Vieux Séminaire de Saint-Sulpice,** erected by the Sulpician Order in 1685. The seminary is still in use by the order and is not open to the public. Behind its courtyard wall the symmetrical freestone building breathes the spirit of 17th-century New France. Its elegant clock is reputed to be the oldest of its kind in North America. ■

Centre d'Histoire de Montréal
- ✉ 335 Place d'Youville
- ☎ 514/872-3207
- 🕐 Closed Dec.
- 💲 $
- Ⓜ Metro: Place-d'Armes

Basilique Notre-Dame
- ✉ 110 Rue Notre-Dame Ouest
- ☎ 514/842-2925
- 💲 Museum $
- Ⓜ Metro: Place-d'Armes

Square-Dorchester & downtown

TOGETHER WITH PLACE DU CANADA ON THE FAR SIDE OF Boulevard Réné-Lévesque, leafy Square-Dorchester (*Metro: Peel or Bonaventure*) is traditionally held to be the heart of Montreal, though it has to be said that the city's vibrant pulse beats in many places. For visitors, it is a good place to start exploring the downtown area, not least because of the presence of the visitor information center (Center Infotouriste) in the Dominion Square Building on the north side of the square.

A glance at the buildings around the square takes in much of Montreal's recent history. Starting with **Place du Canada,** nothing could be more British than the oldest structure, **St. George's Church,** a fine example of Gothic Revival architecture, with a hammerbeam roof. Next to the church is **Windsor Station,** a splendid Romanesque Revival building of 1889, the grand terminus of the Canadian Pacific Railway.

Despite the presence of several skyscrapers, the most compelling building is still the **Cathédrale Marie-Reine-du-Monde,** consecrated in 1894 and dedicated to Mary, Queen of the World. A scaled-down copy of St. Peter's in Rome, it is an emphatic statement of the power of the Catholic Church here in the western part of the city center, once the stronghold of British Protestantism. Gesticulating from the cornice are the patron saints of the various city parishes that helped finance the construction of the monumental building, while inside is a magnificent reproduction of the baldachino (altar canopy) in St. Peter's.

On the east side of the square, a whole block is occupied by the pale granite **Sun Life Building,** begun in 1914 and progressively added to until it reached its present huge size. It is easy to believe the claim

(made for quite a number of buildings in Canada) that it was once the biggest building in the British Empire. Bigger, but slimmer, is Montreal's tallest (672 feet) structure, 1000 de la Gauchtière, with a quietly sumptuous interior incorporating a skating rink.

OTHER DOWNTOWN SIGHTS

Begun in 1958, I.M. Pei's **Place Ville-Marie** (*corner of Mansfield & Cathcart*) ushered in the modern transformation of Montreal's

St. George's Church
- ✉ Corner of Peel & de la Gauchetière
- ☎ 514/866-7113
- 🕐 Closed Oct.–May

Cathédrale Marie-Reine-du-Monde
- ✉ 1085 Rue de la Cathédrale
- ☎ 514/866-1661
- 🕐 Closed weekdays fall–spring
- 🚇 Metro: Bonaventure

A monument to former Prime Minister Sir Wilfred Laurier (1841–1919) stands in Square-Dorchester.

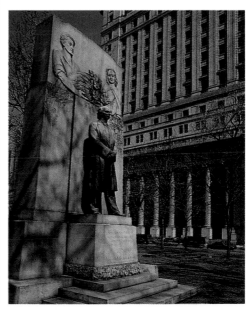

McGill University

✉ Rue Sherbrooke
Ouest
☎ 514/398-6555
🚇 Metro: McGill

Musée McCord

✉ 690 Sherbrooke
Ouest
☎ 514/398-7100
🕐 Closed Mon.
💲 $$$
🚇 Metro: McGill

**Christ Church
Cathedral**

✉ 635 Ste.-Cathérine
Ouest
☎ 514/843-6577
💲 Donation
🚇 Metro: McGill

center. Above the esplanade with its fine vista up **Avenue McGill College** rises the 42-story cruciform tower in glass and aluminum topped by a rotating searchlight. Below the esplanade is a covered shopping center. This was the first of its kind, and now forms the nucleus of the Underground City.

Leading north from Place Ville-Marie is Avenue McGill College, which was widened in 1988 in order to create a visual link between the city center, **McGill University,** and Mont-Royal. The avenue provides a dignified setting for a number of highly individual new buildings. They include **Place Montréal Trust,** with its spectacular five-story atrium, and the crystalline blue glass

BNP/Laurentian Bank Tower, (*corner of Ave. McGill College & Ave. du Président Kennedy*) with its landmark sculpture, "The Illuminated Crowd" by the British-born sculptor Raymond Mason.

Avenue McGill College ends, not surprisingly, at McGill University. You're free to walk through the campus of this world-famous university, although you may stand out among the throng of students. There are about 30,000 of them, most, but not all, English-speaking. The campus is a wonderful oasis of green space in downtown Montreal, with an amazing variety of buildings that somehow blend effectively together to create an archetypal university atmosphere.

The Underground City

*M*on pays c'est l'hiver (Winter is the name of my country) sang *chansonnier* Gilles Vignault in the 1960s, and Quebecers certainly know how to make the best of their fierce climate, what with superlative winter sports and rambunctious carnivals. But you don't want to struggle through snow and slush when you're doing the shopping or going to the theater. Montrealers have solved this problem by going underground. Since the Place Ville-Marie mall was completed in the early 1960s, an 18-mile network of weatherproof passageways has spread all over the city center, linking Metro and train stations, shops and stores (1,700 of them), theaters, hotels, offices, and apartments. In winter it is possible to enjoy city life to the fullest without ever having to venture outside, and the air-conditioned underground is equally welcome during Montreal's humid summer. ∎

Montreal's metro travels quietly alongside a library.

The **Arts Building** tops the rise. Although much modified this is the oldest structure, dating from 1839, not long after the university was founded in 1821 with resources from the estate of prominent Scottish fur-trader James McGill.

Musée McCord is a testament to the inveterate collector David McCord. Despite this museum's modern extension only a fraction of the tens of thousands of objects assembled by him can be shown at any one time. Their richness and variety enables the museum to stage fascinating exhibitions on all kinds of themes, from ice hockey to satirical cartoons, and you should certainly check on what is currently on display. One of the museum's great strengths is its array of First Nations artifacts, symbolized by the magnificent cedar totem pole from far-off Queen Charlotte Islands. Another is the unique **Notman Photographic Archives,** an astonishingly complete record of Canadian life in the 19th and early 20th centuries.

Christ Church Cathedral (Cathédral Christ Church), Montreal's splendid Gothic Revival Anglican cathedral, was built in 1859 and has led a rather precarious existence. The stone spire turned out to be too heavy for the foundations to bear, and an aluminum replacement had to be fitted. A solution to the sinking of the foundations was found in the 1980s, when the whole building, all 9,000 tons of it, was jacked up and a new basement was constructed. This underground addition houses **Les Promenades de la Cathédrale,** a shopping mall, though no stores were permitted to be built directly below the church.

In the days of Quebec's Quiet Revolution, a concerted effort was made to revitalize the eastern, more francophone part of the city center. The **Université du Québec à**

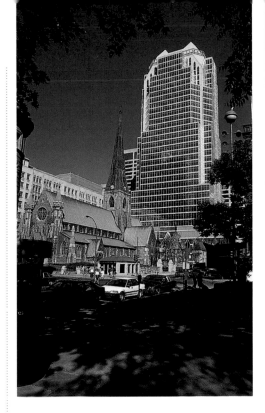

Montréal was established here, as was the **Complexe Desjardins** *(corner of Rue. St.-Urbain & Ste.-Cathérine Ouest),* its huge atrium a forum for popular events and entertainment. Arranged around a public square, which is at its liveliest in summer, the **Place des Arts** *(Tel 514/790-ARTS, Metro: Place des Arts)* comprises several auditoriums and the lavish new **Musée d'Art Contemporain de Montréal.** Opened in 1992, this museum is a spacious home for the province's extensive collection of post-1945 works, mostly but not exclusively by artists from Quebec. Visiting exhibitions are a major feature of its program.

The largest of the auditoriums is the **Salle Wilfrid-Pelletier,** where up to 2,892 spectators can watch performances by the resident ensembles, the Montreal Symphony Orchestra, the Opera, and the Grands Ballets Canadiens.

Christ Church Cathedral is dwarfed by one of Montreal's many contemporary towers.

Musée d'Art Contemporain de Montréal

✉ 185 Rue Ste-Cathérine Ouest

☎ 514/847-6212

🕐 Closed Mon.

💲 $$$

🚇 Metro: Place des Arts

Musée des Beaux-Arts de Montréal

- ✉ 1379–1380 Sherbrooke Ouest
- ☎ 514/285-2000
- ◷ Closed Mon.
- 💲 $$$
- Ⓜ Metro: Guy-Concordia

Musée des Arts Decoratifs

- ✉ 2200 Crescent
- ☎ 514/284-1252
- ◷ Closed Mon.
- Ⓜ Metro: Guy-Concordia

Centre Canadien d'Architecture

- ✉ 1920 Rue Baile
- ☎ 514/939-7026
- ◷ Closed Mon. June–Sept., Mon.–Tues. rest of year
- 💲 $$$
- Ⓜ Metro: Atwater or Guy-Concordia

Oratoire Saint-Joseph

- ✉ 3800 Chemin Queen Mary
- ☎ 514/733-8211
- 💲 Museum donation requested
- Ⓜ Metro: Côte-des-Neiges

WEST OF DOWNTOWN

The **Musée des Beaux-Arts de Montréal** is one of the most distinguished collections in North America, in terms of both the quality of its art and its architectural setting. The pictures, sculptures, drawings, and other art objects are housed in two very different buildings, linked by underground galleries beneath busy Sherbrooke Street. The 1912 North Pavilion is a neoclassic temple to the arts, as grandiose inside as out. Completed in 1991, the striking South Pavilion is the work of Montreal architect Moshe Safdie.

The South Pavilion has space for prestigious temporary exhibitions as well as for its extensive collection of European art, which ranges from superb medieval sculpture to Old Master paintings, including works by Memling, Mantegna, Rembrandt, El Greco, and Gainsborough. In addition there is a fine selection of 19th- and early 20th-century pictures. Contemporary Canadian and international art is represented too. The intimate spaces of the below-ground galleries seem just right for treasures from the ancient world, Asia, and Oceania.

The North Pavilion is devoted to Canadian art. The collection of paintings, drawings, and sculpture is as good as any in the country.

Adjacent to the Musée des Beaux-Arts is the **Musée des Arts Decoratifs,** a structure designed by Canadian-born Frank Gehry specifically to show off a fine collection of 20th-century objects from art nouveau onward.

Concerned at the loss of so much of Montreal's fine architectural heritage, Phyllis Lambert saved the historic **Shaughnessy House** of 1874 from demolition, and incorporated it into the sensitively designed new complex known as the **Centre Canadien d'Architecture.** This fascinating center sees its mission as promoting a humane approach to architecture and its allied disciplines like urban planning and landscape design.

Mont-Royal

Known affectionately as "the mountain" though it only rises 768 feet above sea level, leafy Mont-Royal is a wonderful asset in a city where there is less public open space per head than in any other Canadian metropolis. Responsible for the tree-planting and subtle layout of roads, paths, and viewpoints was North America's greatest landscape architect, Frederick Law Olmsted, designer of New York's Central Park.

From downtown you can climb the mountain via a footpath and steps from the top of Rue Peel, but the easy way up is to take the No. 11 bus (which connects with the Metro at Mont-Royal station), get off at Lac-aux-Castors (Beaver Lake), and walk up the gentle slope to the big, stone-built **Chalet.** The lookout here gives a superb panorama of the city. A further climb brings you to the 120-foot metal cross, a great landmark especially at night, when it is illuminated. It is the 20th-century successor to the cross erected here by Paul de Maisonneuve in 1642 in thanksgiving for Ville-Marie's escaping a Christmas flood.

Popular all year round, the mountain is just as crowded in winter, with skaters on the lake, skiers on the slopes and trails, and visitors in horse-drawn carriages.

Oratoire Saint-Joseph, the massive pilgrimage church on the northern ridge of Westmount Mountain, grew from the humblest of beginnings. In 1904, Brother André, porter at Notre-Dame College opposite the oratory, built a small shrine to St. Joseph to receive the growing number of sick people who benefited from his healing powers. As the crowds of pilgrims increased, work was begun in 1924 on a great oratory to accommodate them. Interruptions and difficulties were triumphantly overcome by Dom Paul Bellot (1876–1944), the architect-monk also responsible for the abbey at St.-Benoît-du-Lac.

The interior is sparsely decorated with artwork and stained glass. Brother André's remains are here, and there is a small museum dedicated to him. The original shrine is outside the main building where there are Stations of the Cross, too. The oratory stands at the top of a flight of 99 steps, which some pilgrims still climb on their knees. There is a view of all of northern Montreal from the terrace; the most prominent feature is the complex of the Université de Montréal, the largest francophone university in the world outside Paris. ■

The massive bulk of Oratoire Saint-Joseph dominates the high ground to the west of Mont-Royal.

Two solitudes

The title of Montreal author Hugh McLennan's 1945 novel has become synonymous with the awkward relationship that has always existed between Canada's two founding nations. Translated into many languages (*Deux Solitudes* in French), the book deals with the identity crisis faced by a young man from the Quebec countryside who, despite his bilingualism, is as ill at ease among his own folk as with the Montreal English speakers with whom he associates.

Montreal has long been the place where the two solitudes have confronted, or more often, failed to confront each other. Canada's economic development in the 19th and early 20th century was directed from here, by a business class almost entirely of British origin, and for many years, it was English-speaking immigrants who provided them with the necessary working-class manpower. For a while, in the middle of the 19th century, the city had an anglophone majority.

Elsewhere, especially in the countryside, French Canadians seemed trapped in a mid-18th-century time warp. After the British conquest, the community had turned in on

Unusually united—the federal maple leaf and the Quebec fleur-de-lys fly from the same flagpole.

itself, protecting its identity by clinging to traditional ways and looking for leadership to the powerful Roman Catholic Church. The Church promoted a high birthrate, not least in order to ensure the survival of the community among the more numerous English speakers of Canada as a whole. But as Montreal grew in the late 19th century, more and more French-speakers were drawn in from the rural hinterland to man the new industries. Once described as "hewers of wood and drawers of water," they now formed the majority of the working class, toiling in enterprises whose bosses and managers were English Canadians, if not British or American.

Language & prestige

Inevitably, it was the English language that gave status. To get on in the dominant world of business, a French speaker would have to become bilingual, but even then career opportunities were limited. Downtown Montreal wore an almost entirely English face: Signs and advertising were in English, anyone a visitor might encounter would be an English speaker, and altogether there was little that distinguished Montreal from any other large North American city.

French Canadians might be at home in the countryside, but their big city was slipping away from them. Whatever their origin, successive waves of immigrants naturally identified with the dominant culture and sent their children to English schools. Securely on top, comfortable folk living in exclusive suburbs like Westmount needed to have little more contact with their French-speaking fellow citizens than their anglophone equivalents in Toronto. The preferred picture of a French Canadian was a patronizing one, that of the habitant with his sash and clay pipe, living with his enormous family in picturesque squalor in an overcrowded farmstead. In town, he was an irritant: "Speak white!" was a not infrequent retort to someone who failed to understand English.

Whether or not French speakers understood English, their language was increasingly influenced by it, much to the chagrin of intel-

Only signs in French may appear on Montreal streets.

lectuals. The vocabulary of work, technology, and material progress generally was English, and French Canada had no equivalent of the Académie Française to police the entry of undesirable words into general use. A real fear arose that French could be swamped by the more powerful and prestigious language.

French resurgence

But with the coming of the Quiet Revolution in the 1960s, the French-speaking community emerged from its solitude. Even before the election of the Parti Québécois in 1976, the process which has been called "the reconquest of Montreal" had begun. A huge expansion of the public sector gave a growing French-speaking middle class jobs in schools, universities, hospitals, and administration generally. Steps were taken to promote the use of French in business, schools, and in signs and advertising. With the P.Q. in power, these processes intensified, finding their most complete expression in the ominously Orwellian-sounding Bill 101. Much to the dismay of many Anglophones, this Charter of the French Language asserted the primacy of French in all spheres of life in Quebec. Some found the situation intolerable, and set off down Highway 401 to Toronto or to other places in the rest of Canada where English solitude could still be enjoyed. Other perhaps braver spirits stuck it out, abandoning that solitude to learn French themselves, seeing advantages for their children in becoming bilingual and accepting, with varying degrees of reluctance, their minority status. This doesn't prevent today's most prominent anglophone writer in Montreal, Mordecai Richler, from firing off frequent salvoes of acid comment on what he sees as overzealous enforcement of language laws. Among his favorite targets are what he refers to as the "tongue-troopers," the officials who ensure that Montreal's townscape is kept free of unauthorized outbreaks of English. ∎

Shanghai Dream Lake Garden in the Jardin Botanique de Montréal

More places to visit in Montreal

OLYMPIC STADIUM

One of the world's most spectacular follies, the huge stadium built for the 1976 Olympic Games is dominated by an extraordinary leaning tower from which a retractable roof is suspended by 26 cables. Endless difficulties attended the building of the stadium, designed by an architect hired from France. The tower and roof, made of a woven synthetic material, were only completed in 1987, more than a decade after the Games, and the city is still burdened with the billion-dollar bill for the complex. Postgames, the stadium is the home ground of the Montreal Expos, and hosts concerts and gatherings of all kinds, including the Pope's visit in 1984. For those with no fear of heights, a strange self-righting vehicle crawls up the spine of the tower to an observation deck giving an unparalleled view of Montreal's east end and far beyond.

✉ 4141 Ave. Pierre-de-Coubertin
☎ 514/252-8687 $ $$$ Metro: Viau

BIODÔME

The elegant concrete shell of the velodrome built for the 1976 Olympic Games now covers an ambitious and very convincing re-creation of four characteristic ecosystems of the Americas. You can step straight from the rigors of the Montreal winter into the warmth and humidity of a tropical forest inhabited by sloths, monkeys, and some 350 bats, or alternatively escape from the city's scorching July to the shores of the polar world, where a blizzard rages and penguins show their paces. Equally fascinating are the Laurentian forest and the ecosystem of the St. Lawrence.

✉ 4777 Ave. Pierre-de-Coubertin
☎ 514/868-3000 $ $ Metro: Viau

JARDIN BOTANIQUE DE MONTRÉAL

This paradise of plants, one of the world's great botanical gardens, extends over 185 acres to the north of the Olympic complex. Even if you go around on board the little sightseeing train, it is not possible to do justice to the whole of the gardens, so begin your exploration at the Reception Centre, where a giant computerized model will help you decide what to see. The conservatories contain an array of plants from all over the world, the biggest Chinese garden outside China, an equally fascinating and authentic Japanese garden, a total of 30 thematic gardens, a forest arboretum with more than 10,000 trees, and the fascinating Insectarium.

✉ 4101 Rue Sherbrooke Est ☎ 514/872-1400 $ $$$$$ Metro: Pie-IX

PARC-DES-ÎLES

Straddled by the Jacques-Cartier Bridge, Île Sainte-Hélène is a natural island, extended when it was chosen as the site for Expo 67.

The hills and trees of Île Sainte-Hélene create an atmosphere far removed from the city's center, visible just across the water. One of the most admired structures at Expo was Buckminster Fuller's great geodesic dome, housing the U.S. pavilion. Now called the **Biosphere** (*160 chemin du Tour-de-l'Île, Tel 514/283-5000*), it contains an elaborate and user-friendly ecowatch facility, devoted to raising the profile of the St. Lawrence ecosystem.

Built on the orders of the Duke of Wellington, a fort houses one of Montreal's most appealing history museums, the intimate **Musée David M. Stewart** (*Tel 514/861-6701*). The museum draws on its extensive collections of maps, weapons, and navigational aids to illustrate aspects of the discovery and exploration of the New World. On the far side of the Pont Jacques-Cartier is the vast amusement park of **La Ronde** (*Tel 514/872-4537*).

Neighboring **Île Notre-Dame** (*Tel 514/872-6211*) is entirely artificial. It has a beach, an open-air theater, Formula One racing, extensive gardens, and the Montreal Casino (*Tel 514/392-2746*), housed in the striking building that was the French pavilion in 1967.

☎ 514/872-4537 🚇 Metro: Île-Sainte-Hélène ■

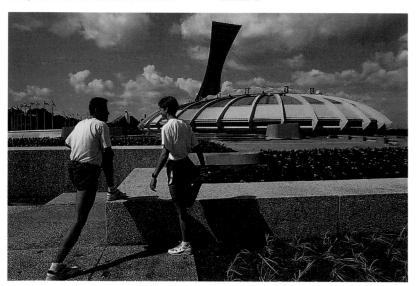

Runners pause for a break outside Montreal's Olympic Stadium.

Terre des hommes—Man & his world

This was the theme of *Expo 67*, the world's fair so triumphantly staged by Canada toward the end of the optimistic 1960s to celebrate the country's hundredth birthday. The construction of Montreal's Metro provided the fill to extend Île Sainte-Hélène and make the completely artificial Île Notre-Dame. The Canadian provinces, private bodies, and dozens of countries sprinkled their often exciting pavilions across the islands, which were lavishly landscaped and linked by futuristic transportation systems. Some 50 million visitors came to the show and apparently enjoyed themselves immensely, spending far more than the fair had cost to put on. But Expo was followed by the October Crisis (see p.39) and by the gross overspending on the 1976 Olympic Games, for which the city is still paying. ■

Montreal streets & suburbs

◢ 105B1

**Abbaye
Cistercienne d'Oka**
✉ 1600 Chemin d'Oka
☎ 450/479-8361
🕐 Closed Sun.

THE DOWNTOWN STRETCH OF RUE SAINTE-CATHÉRINE Ouest still attracts the city crowds with its stores and places of entertainment. Celebrated by Quebec-Irish singers Kate and Anna McGarrigle, it is a bit seedy in places and has lost some of its vitality to indoor malls and the Underground City, but a stroll here is an essential part of the Montreal experience. Between St. Catherine and Sherbrooke is Rue Crescent, which has kept most of its late 19th-century charm. Winter evenings and summer days see it blossom as a focal point of anglophone social life.

Traditionally the dividing line between French east Montreal and the Anglo-dominated west, **Boulevard Saint-Laurent,** or the "Main" as it is known, has been the conduit along which successive waves of new Montrealers have moved inland from the port to found their new communities. Hop aboard a No. 55 bus (*Tel 414/842-2281 for schedule*) near Saint-Laurent Metro station and travel north past vendors of smoked meat and bagels, Greek travel agents, Portuguese restaurants, a branch of the Ukrainian National Bank, and a whole medley of multicultural shop signs. The **Marché Jean-Talon** is at the heart of the Italian quarter.

An island of an independent municipality in the ocean of Montreal, **Westmount** took over the role of the Golden Square Mile as the favored residential area of

English-speaking Montreal and for many years its name was synonymous with anglophone style and power. Leafy streets lined with prosperous-looking villas climb the western slope of Mont-Royal toward Oratoire Saint-Joseph. By contrast, Westmount Square has a metropolitan atmosphere, its exclusive shops and Metro station topped by a trio of elegant black towers by the great modern architect Mies van der Rohe.

Between Sainte-Cathérine and Duluth, **Rue Saint-Denis** runs through Montreal's Latin Quarter, thronged by students from the university. There are cafés, bistros, galleries, bookstores, and restaurants galore, some occupying the charming old town houses built here in the 19th century when this was the fashionable francophone suburb. Carré Saint-Louis is the prettiest square in Montreal, lined with row houses that somehow combine extreme picturesqueness with good manners. Running west from the square, pedestrian-only Prince Arthur Street (Rue Prince-Arthur) offers a bewildering choice of places to eat.

OKA

Oka (30 miles west of Montreal by road) has a wonderful location at the foot of the last outliers of the Laurentian uplands, overlooking the splendid stretch of water known

Oka Beach on the Lac des Deux Montagnes is a popular recreation area.

as **Le Lac des Deux Montagnes.**
The village is famous for its great
Abbaye cistercienne d'Oka,
founded in 1881 by Trappist monks
from France. Individuals can come
here on a retreat, but the public is
also welcome, and you can tour the
gardens, look into the modest
miller's house that was the monks'
first home, and buy home-made
cheese. Two miles away, Stations
of the Cross were laid out on
Calvary Mountain in 1742 by the
Sulpicians as part of their campaign
to convert the natives, and for many
years the hill attracted pilgrims.

The contemplative idyll that
Oka tends to induce in its visitors
was rudely interrupted in 1990
when a dispute erupted over a pro-
posal to build a golf course over a
Mohawk burial ground. The
Mohawks built blockades and a
policeman was killed in an
exchange of gunfire. The army was
sent in, and a photograph of a
masked Mohawk "warrior" eyeball-
to-eyeball with a helmeted soldier

helped the Oka Confrontation
make headlines round the world.
In the end, after two-and-a-half
months of negotiations, the dispute
was defused, but served to galvanize
Canadian opinion about First
Nations issues generally.

MUSÉE FERROVIAIRE CANADIEN

Without railroads the Canada of
today could hardly have come into
being. The **Musée ferroviaire
canadien** is the country's major
railroad museum, with a superb
array of locomotives, rolling stock,
and all kinds of railroad memorabilia. In addition to the giants of
steam that conquered the Rockies
there are engines from abroad,
including the British locomotive
that once hauled the *Flying
Scotsman.* The director's car used by
Sir William Van Horne in the building of the Canadian Pacific Railway
across the continent is also on
show. On weekends there are live
steam train and streetcar rides. ■

**A center of
anglophone
Montreal—Rue
Sainte-Cathérine**

**Musée ferroviaire
canadien**

✉ 120 rue Saint-
Pierre, Saint-
Constant, 12 miles
south of Montreal
☎ 450/632-2410
🕐 Closed Nov.–April
💲 $$$

The Laurentians (Les Laurentides)

PART OF THE CANADIAN SHIELD, THE LAURENTIAN UPLANDS reach right across Quebec from near Ottawa in the west to the Saguenay in the east. But for Montrealers, and for countless winter and summer vacationers from Canada and the United States, the bit of the Laurentians that counts is the hilly country northwest of Montreal, once reached by *l'petit train du Nord* (the little train of the north) and now by Trans-Canada 15.

The region has been developed with lodges, ski resorts, weekend homes, and recreational facilities of all kinds, including water sports on the rivers and many lakes. An elevation of 3,175 feet makes Mont Tremblant, the highest point in the area, a real mountain, but the rolling, humpbacked uplands, delightful though they are, don't quite have the drama of alpine terrain. Their slopes are fine for skiing, though, and the once continuous forest cover is now patched with stripes where trees have given way to pistes.

Vacationers have been the salvation of the region. In the second half of the 19th century Father Antoine Labelle made heroic attempts to stem the flow of young folk away from Quebec to the mills of New England by opening up the area for agriculture. His efforts were largely in vain. Though he brought the railroad here and created many new parishes, the infertile soils resisted cultivation and much cleared land was eventually abandoned. But even in the 1890s, the wealthy had begun to come here for summer vacations. Winter sports developed in the 1920s, and in the 1960s the construction of the Autoroute des Laurentides brought the region within the reach of all.

The substantial town of **Saint-Jérome,** situated 32 miles from Montreal at the point where

the Rivière du Nord leaves the uplands, acts as the gateway to the Laurentians. Father Labelle was its parish priest for many years, and his statue stands in front of the cathedral. The fun really begins at **Saint-Sauveur-des-Monts** (*Visitor information, 100 Rue Guindon, Tel 450/227-2564*), the oldest of the Laurentian resorts, the most fashionable, and one of the best equipped both for skiing and après-ski. The imposing timber ski-lodge called **Pavillon Soixante-Dix** is an acclaimed work by the postmodern Montreal architect Peter Rose.

Sainte-Adele (43 miles from Montreal) is a small and leafy town with a pretty location on its lake. It is famous as the hometown of the writer Claude-Henri Grignon, whose 1933 novel *The Woman and the Miser* inspired the construction of the **Musée-village de Séraphin,** a collection of reconstructed traditional rural buildings of the Quebec countryside.

HEART OF THE LAURENTIANS

The focal point of tourism in the Laurentians is **Sainte-Agathe-des-Monts** (*Visitor information: opposite shopping mall on Hwy. 117*), a bustling little place with a wide range of services and facilities. Its attractive situation on the shores of Lac des Sables has made it a favored location for prestigious second homes, but there are public beaches, too, and a lakeside drive taking in the lovely views.

Mont Tremblant

After the crossroads town of **Saint-Jovite,** Rte. 327 leads past picturesque Lake Ouimet to little **Mont-Tremblant Village** (*Visitor information: 305 Chemin Brébeuf, St.-Jovite*) on its long and narrow lake. Mont Tremblant acquired its name—"shaking mountain"—from the natives, who thought that the wickedness of men would cause the mountain to shake in anger. So far

Mont Tremblant has tolerated the thousands of skiers who frequent its dozens of runs, among them one of the longest in Quebec. Covering 930 square miles of superb forested upland, and at its most glorious when suffused with autumn color, **Mont Tremblant Provincial Park** (*Tel 819/688-2281, some park roads closed in winter*) was the first of its kind (1894) to be designated by the government of Quebec. It is possible to see some of its splendid lakes and waterfalls by car, but for the best of the park and the chance of seeing deer, moose, and bears, take to the trails. ∎

Autumn tints touch the Laurentians, a rural paradise at any time of year.

Mont Tremblant
🄰 105C2

Mont Tremblant Provincial Park
🄰 105C2

Richelieu River Valley

RUNNING NORTHWARD 80 MILES FROM LAKE CHAMPLAIN and the U.S. border to the St. Lawrence at the town of Sorel, the valley of the Richelieu River has long served as a corridor of movement and as a focal point of national rivalries. Its contemporary role is an entirely peaceful one. The agricultural lands of its lower course are some of the most fertile in Quebec, while its waterways and countryside form a popular recreational area for its many visitors.

One of the attractive features of the Richelieu River is the way in which its course is diversified by numerous islands. The first island downstream from Lake Champlain, **Ash Island,** used to bear the grisly name of Île aux Têtes (Island of the Heads). After a bloody battle between Algonquin and Iroquois around 1580, the defeated Iroquois had their heads impaled on stakes here. The movement of Europeans into the area brought other rivalries with it, and led to the construction of so many defense works that this southern part of the Richelieu is known as the "valley of forts."

Nearby, close to the confluence of the Richelieu with its tributary the Lacolle, is the timber-built

Blockhaus de Lacolle, the only one of its kind still standing in Quebec. Constructed in 1781, it formed part of the British defense system against American attack and saw action during the War of 1812, as bullet holes in its walls testify.

The French were the first to fortify the Richelieu Valley, one of their strongholds being **Fort Lennox National Historic Site,** built on this 210-acre island. But the imposing buildings and earthworks that can be seen today are the result of the British refortification of the site after the island had been occupied by the Americans in 1775–76. Protected by a typically baroque star-shaped moat and ramparts, a series of military struc-

A sight to lift the spirits of city dwellers—the famous balloon-fest at Saint-Jean-sur-Richelieu

Quashed rebellion

In 1837 the lower Richelieu Valley was the scene of fighting between French Patriote rebels and British forces. Alarmed by a mass meeting at the village of Saint-Charles at which Patriote leaders pledged to "direct not words, but bullets against our enemies," the British sent out a force from Montreal. Despite their numerical superiority over the Patriotes, who had assembled at Saint-Denis, and some of whom were only armed with pitchforks, the British were forced to retreat. But this was the Patriotes' only victory. Within days they were overwhelmed at Saint-Charles and again in the Deux-Montagnes region, where 70 of them were slaughtered as they tried to escape from the burning parish church at Saint-Eustache. ■

Musée du Fort Saint-Jean
- ✉ Campus du Fort de Saint-Jean
- ☎ 450/358-6500
- ⏱ Closed late Sept.—mid-June
- 💲 $

Chambly
- ⚠ 105C1

Fort Chambly National Historic Site
- ☎ 450/658-1585
- ⏱ Closed late Dec.—March

Mont-Saint-Hilaire
- ✉ Chemin des Moulins
- ☎ 450/467-1755

---

tures in an austere classical style include barracks, officers' quarters, and guardhouse. It is quite a thrill to take the ferry across the Richelieu, cross the moat, enter the fort through its severe stone gateway, and inspect the buildings where the harsh conditions of soldierly life have been convincingly re-created.

Founded by the French in 1666 as a link in their system of defenses against the Iroquois, **Saint-Jean-sur-Richelieu** became an industrial town famous for its pottery and ceramics. In 1775 the British garrison of the fort here withstood 45 days of an American siege before surrendering. This stirring episode, and other aspects of the stronghold's history, are explained in the old guardhouse, known as **Musée du Fort Saint-Jean.**

Cambly is only a short drive via Hwy. 10 from the center of Montreal and attractively located at a point where the Richelieu widens out into a broad basin. This historic center is now a popular residential town for city commuters. It is famous for its fort, first built in 1665, and for the **Chambly Canal,** completed in 1843 to bypass the rapids between here and Saint-Jean, and now restored by Parks Canada. With its nine locks, the canal was an important link on the trade route between Montreal and towns along the Hudson, but nowadays its still substantial traffic consists purely of pleasure craft.

Originally a timber structure, **Fort Chambly National Historic Site** was rebuilt in stone in 1711, and it is to its 18th-century state that the rectangle of walls and corner bastions have been restored.

Mont-Saint-Hilaire imposes a massive presence on the surrounding plain and on the charming village (St.-Hilaire) at its foot—a favorite haunt of artists. The near-pristine state of the forest led to its being designated Canada's first UNESCO biosphere reserve. Part of it is sealed off for scientific research, but you can wander an extensive trail network, climb to little glacial **Lake Hertel** or to the top of **Pain de Sucre** (Sugarloaf), where there are magnificent views over the plains. ■

Long gone cold, a cannonball heater drawn up in the central enclosure of Fort Lennox.

The Eastern Townships
(Cantons de l'Est)

**Regional visitor
information**

✉ Hwy. 10
☎ 800/355-5755

**Musée des Beaux-
Arts de
Sherbrooke**

🅰 103C1
✉ 241 Rue Dufferin
☎ 819/821-2115
🕐 Closed a.m. & Mon.
💲 $

SOME OF THE MOST ATTRACTIVE COUNTRYSIDE IN QUEBEC
can be seen among the Eastern Townships, the rolling wooded
uplands and lake- and river-filled valleys along the Vermont border.
Little more than an hour's drive from Montreal, the area is popular
with weekenders from the city, as well as with visitors enchanted by
the comfortable, well-lived-in landscape with its farmlands, charming villages, clapboard churches, covered bridges, and round barns.

The area owes much of its character
to the Loyalists who settled here
after the American Revolution.
Other Americans, mostly New
Englanders, followed in search of
cheap land when the British government lifted restrictions after the
War of 1812, and well into the
19th century the townships looked
south for economic and cultural
sustenance rather than to Lower
Canada. By the middle of the
century, nearly 100,000 English
speakers lived here, but they were
soon outnumbered by French-
Canadian immigrants who came to
farm or to work in the many small-
scale industries. Today the population of the townships is

overwhelmingly French-speaking,
but there are many places that will
remind New Englanders of home,
like the village of **North Hatley**
12 miles south of Sherbrooke.

The region welcomes guests at
all times of the year. The fall colors
of the forest make a lovely backdrop to the ripening fruit of
orchards and vineyards, best seen
around little **Dunham,** the very
first township to be established in
the region. Winter brings both
downhill and cross-country skiers;
there are popular resorts at
Sutton, Mount Orford (*Visitor
information, off Rte. 141, Tel
819/843-6233*), and a number of
other small resorts.

**Abbaye de
St.-Benoît-du-Lac**

Snowmobile center

If you've ever wondered where Skidoos came from, it is here! Bombardier is one of Quebec's big industrial names, with headquarters in Montreal and a manufacturing plant in the Townships village of Valcourt, the birthplace of its founder, Joseph-Armand Bombardier. In 1937 the inventive Joseph-Armand put together an all-terrain vehicle using skis and a tracked drive, but it was his world-beating Skidoo of 1959 that caught the world's imagination, revolutionizing mobility in the winter countryside. Full tribute is paid to the man and his invention in Musée J.-Armand Bombardier. ■

Sold by the thousands, snowmobiles have transformed life in the winter countryside.

Industrial **Sherbrooke,** located at the meeting-point of the Magog and Saint-Francois Rivers, is the capital of the Eastern Townships. As well as an imposing cathedral, there is the very American-looking **Plymouth Trinity Church**, built in 1848 for a congregation with roots in Massachusetts. Among the attractions of mainly local interest is the **Musée des Beaux-Arts de Sherbrooke,** which has a fascinating collection of international naive art as well as many fine pictures by Quebec artists. In the 19th and early 20th centuries, Sherbrooke's captains of industry built their mansions in a variety of extravagant styles in the **Old Quartier du Vieux-Nord** (North Ward district). The best way to explore this and other historic parts of town is to take an audio tour; inquire at the **Centre d'Interpretation de l'Histoire de Sherbrooke.**

Lake Memphremagog is the largest lake in the Eastern Townships, extending into the United States to Newport, Vermont.

Between the northern end of the lake and Mount Orford is the resort of **Magog**, the main visitor center in the townships. A 12-mile drive down the west bank of the lake brings you to **Abbaiye de Saint-Benoît-du-Lac** (*Tel 819/843-4080*). In an idyllic situation among the woods, the abbey was founded in 1924 and extended in the 1930s by architect-monk Dom Bellot, designer of St. Joseph's Oratory in Montreal. Visitors are can attend some services and the abbey shop sells an excellent cheese made by the monks.

One of several little towns around the shores of Lake Brome, **Knowlton** has kept its strongly Loyalist flavor with a largely anglophone population, fine old 19th-century houses, and a fascinatingly heterogeneous local museum—the **Brome County Historical Museum,** housed in a number of heritage buildings. There is a courthouse, a restocked village store from long ago, and a collection of militaria including a World War I German pursuit plane. ■

Centre d'Interpretation de l'Histoire de Sherbrooke
- ✉ 275 Rue Dufferin
- ☎ 819/821-5406
- 🕐 Closed Mon.
- 💲 $$$

Brome County Historical Museum
- ✉ 130 Lakeside, Knowlton
- ☎ 450/243-6782
- 🕐 Closed mid-Sept.—mid-May

Musée J.-Armand Bombardier
- ✉ 1001 ave. J.-Armand Bombardier
- ☎ 450/532-5300
- 🕐 Closed Mon. mid-Oct.—May
- 💲 $

Trois-Rivières

TROIS-RIVIÈRES OWES ITS NAME AND ITS FORTUNE TO THE
Saint-Maurice River. As the Saint-Maurice joins the far larger St.
Lawrence, it divides into three branches (*trois rivières*) to flow around
a pair of islands, and for many years the town has been the world's
foremost producer of newsprint, made from the timber floated down
the river from the forests to the north.

The origins of Trois-Rivières go
back much further than the timber
industry established in the 19th
century. It is in fact the second oldest settlement in Quebec, founded
as a fur-trading post in 1634 only a
few years after Quebec City. Despite
the ravages of a great fire in 1908,
there remain enough old buildings
in the center to give you a strong
sense of the city's long past.

The historic core of Trois-
Rivières was built on a terrace high
above river level. The site of the
original fort overlooking the St.
Lawrence is known as **Le Platon**
and has a bust of the founder,
Nicolas Goupil, Sieur de la Violette.
Also overlooking the river is the
elaborate terracing of the **Parc
Portuaire** (waterfront park). From
here there is access to the **Centre
d'Exposition sur l'Industrie
des Pâtes et Papiers,** which does
a workmanlike job on all aspects of
the industry that sustains Trois-
Rivières and its region.

One block inland from the
waterfront is venerable Rue des
Ursulines, which runs parallel to
the river. The domed **Monastère
des Ursulines,** founded in 1700,
dominates the street and the
attractive gardens laid out in front
of it. Inside, there is an ornate
chapel and the **Musée des
Ursulines,** a museum with a
wonderful assortment of religious
objects and furniture from the 17th
century forward. Opposite Anglican
St. James' Church are particularly
fine examples of 18th- and early

19th-century houses, and to the
west is **Manoir de Tonnancour**
(*864 Rue Bonaventure, closed a.m. &
Mon.*), a distinguished stone edifice
dating from the early 18th century
but rebuilt in 1795 after a fire. It
now houses an art gallery. There is
another superb manor house a little
farther inland; follow Rue
Bonaventure to the **Manoir
Boucher-de-Niverville,** which
is now the home of the regional
Chamber of Commerce. Built in
1730, and housing a collection of
fine old furniture, it breathes the
atmosphere of New France. Go up
into the attic to marvel at the carpentry of the roof structure.

On the edge of the old quarter
of Trois-Rivières stands the newly
opened **Musée des Arts et
Traditions Populaires du
Québec** (*200 Rue Laviolette,
Tel 819/372-0406, closed late
Sept.–May*). Linked to the city jail of
1822, it tells in an entertaining way
the story of everyday life in Quebec
from the earliest times to the days of
the explorers and habitants.

For nearly a century, the people
of New France paid high prices for
any objects made of metal, all of
which had to be imported from the
mother country. At last, in 1734, a
Canadian ironworks was established
at **Forges-du-Saint-Maurice
National Historic Site.** For its
raw material it used the bog-iron
along the riverbank. For 150 years
the works turned out metal objects
ranging from ax heads to the
engines for the 1809 steamboat

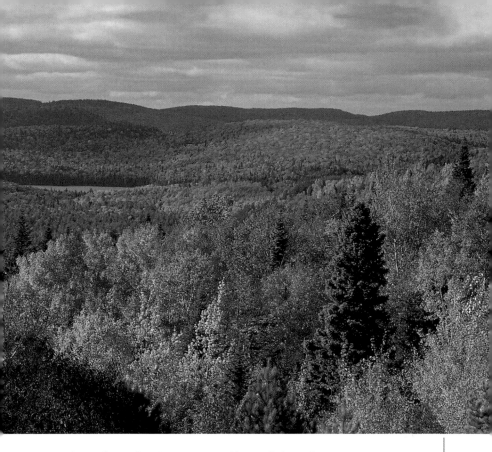

Accommodation. The *grande maison* that housed the offices and living quarters still stands, while imaginative symbolic structures evoke the outline of the other buildings of the complex. Excellent interpretive displays help bring to life this pioneering New World industrial site.

The atmosphere of religious devotion once so prevalent in Quebec is still very present at **Sanctuaire Notre-Dame du Cap.** This shrine stands at the confluence of the Saint-Maurice and the St. Lawrence, at what is the third most important place of pilgrimage in the province. A little, early 18th-century church still stands here, but it is the imposing octagonal basilica, completed in 1964 by a student of architect-monk Dom Bellot, that draws the crowds to celebrate the miracles

witnessed here in the late 19th century by Father Luc Désilets.

PARC NATIONAL DE LA MAURICIE

The Saint-Maurice River flows through one of Quebec's most industrial regions, with pulp mills, an aluminum smelter, and hydroelectric power stations. But industry is left far behind in this 210-square-mile national park, established in 1970 to protect a superb tract of Canadian Shield country of deep mixed forest and more than 150 lakes. Much of the park can only be explored by keen canoeists, but you can see some of its glorious landscape from the parkway connecting the two interpretive centers located at the park entrances at **Saint-Jean-des-Piles** and **Saint-Matthieu.** ∎

La Mauricie National Park is one of many parks protecting the landscape of the Canadian Shield.

Sanctuaire Notre-Dame du Cap
✉ 3 miles east of Trois-Rivières
☎ 819/374-2441

Parc National de la Mauricie
🅰 105C2
✉ 30 miles north of Trois Rivières, Hwy. 55
☎ 819/536-2638
💲 $

Quebec City

🅰 105C1

**Visitor
information**
✉ 60 Rue d'Auteuil
☎ 418/692-2471
✉ 835 Ave. Wilfred-
Laurier
☎ 418/651-2882

Château Frontenac
✉ 1 Rue des Carrières
☎ 418/692-3861
💲 $$$

**Basilique de
Notre-Dame-de-
Québec**
✉ 16 Rue Baude
☎ 418/692-2533

**Séminaire de
Québec and Musée
de l'Amérique
Française**
✉ 9 Rue de
l'Université
☎ 418/692-2843
🕐 Museum: closed Mon.
late Sept.–early
June
💲 $

QUEBEC'S PROVINCIAL CAPITAL HAS LONG OUTGROWN ITS
walls. Residential and commercial areas sprawl over the surrounding
countryside. The Assemblée Nationale (Provincial Parliament) dom-
inates the Grande Allée, the hub of the city's life today. Within the
walls of the Upper Town, all is enchantment: Old stone houses cozy
up to the great religious institutions built from the same gray stone.
Above it all rises Château Frontenac, the ultimate in romantic hotel
architecture. Below it, down the steps and stairways to the foot of the
cliff, are the even more romantic old streets of the Lower Town.

UPPER TOWN
(HAUTE-VILLE)

The sloping square of the Place
d'Armes is as good a place as any to
get your bearings in this city. The
dominant structure is the Canadian
Pacific's **Château Frontenac.**
With its outline of towers, steeply
pitched roofs, and dormer win-
dows, it is the archetype of the
château-style hotel and an unmis-
takable symbol of Quebec. Built
between 1893 and 1924, with a
wing added in the 1990s, it is
named after Louis de Baude,
Comte de Frontenac, a 17th-
century governor of New France.

Along the clifftop stretches
Terrasse Dufferin, a boardwalk
leading to the stairways of the
Promenade des Gouverneurs, cling-
ing to the cliffs beneath the Citadel
(see p. 140). Laid out in its present
form in the 1870s, Terrasse
Dufferin bears the name of the
governor-general of Canada at the
time, Lord Dufferin, who worked to
preserve the city's historic charac-
ter. With its little market stands and
other urban furniture, it has the
character of a resort, and for many
years was very fashionable.

After admiring the view down to
the Lower Town and across the St.
Lawrence to Lévis on the far bank,
visit one of several nearby estab-
lishments that stand ready to deliv-
er a painless history lesson. There is
a wax museum, the **Musée de**

Cire (22 *Rue Ste.-Anne, Tel
418/692-2289*) housed in a fine
18th-century dwelling; the **Musée
du Fort** features a model of the
city in 1750, (*10 Rue Ste.-Anne, Tel
418/692-1759*); and **Québec
Expérience** (*8 Rue du Trésor, Tel
418/694-4000*), the best of them all,
which explores the city's history
with inventive use of multimedia.

The forerunner of today's cathe-
dral was New France's first parish
church, built of stone in 1647, itself
a replacement for a timber church
erected by the Jesuits in 1633. In
1657 the church became a
cathedral. Badly damaged in the
course of the British bombardment
in 1759, the **Basilique de Notre-
Dame-de-Québec** was rebuilt
over a period of nearly two cen-
turies by the Baillairgé dynasty of
architects. Their work formed the
basis of reconstruction after a fire
in 1922. The best way to appreciate
the interior is to come to one of the
daily *son-et-lumière* shows. The
cathedral has been the scene of
many funeral masses for the great
and good of Quebec, from Samuel
de Champlain to Réné Lévesque.

The austere stone walls of the
Séminaire de Québec and
**Musée de l'Amérique
Française** sheltered the first edu-
cational institution in New France,
a training school for priests.
Founded in 1663 by Monsignor de
Laval (who became New France's

first bishop), it is now the home of the school of architecture. Look for the sundial on the wall of the late 17th-century Procure Wing; its inscription means "Our days pass like a shadow." The recently refurbished museum deals in a lively way both with its own history and with the stirring tale of the settlement and culture of New France.

Begun in 1800, **Holy Trinity Anglican Cathedral** (Cathédrale Anglicane de la Sainte-Trinité) was modeled on London's famous Church of St. Martin-in-the-Fields, and was the first Anglican cathedral to be built outside the British Isles. Its simplified classical architecture served as a model for many more churches across Canada. Hardly altered in 200 years, the interior features furniture, including a royal pew made from English oak.

Still caring for today's patients, the **Hôtel-Dieu Hospital** (*Rue Charlevoix, closed to public*) was founded by Augustinian nuns around 1640. Its church, begun in 1800, has a splendid interior with carvings by Thomas Baillairgé. A number of religious paintings confiscated by anticlerical zealots during the French Revolution eventually found a home here. There are more paintings, in this case from the early days of New France, in the **Musée des Augustines de l'Hôtel-Dieu de Québec.** They include portraits of Louis XIV and Cardinal Richelieu. An array of early medical instruments are among the museum's varied collections tracing the history of the monastery.

While the Augustinians cared for the sick, the Ursulines, who also landed in the new colony in 1639, concerned themselves with the education of girls, both French and native. The oldest institution of its kind in North America, the **Couvent des Ursulines** (*Rue Donnaconais*) is housed in buildings erected at various times during the monastery's three and a half centuries of existence. The **Chapelle des Ursulines**

A statue of Samuel de Champlain appears to salute the Château Frontenac.

Holy Trinity Anglican Cathedral
✉ 31 Rue des Jardins
☎ 418/692-2193

Musée des Augustines de l'Hôtel-Dieu de Québec
✉ 32 Rue Charlevoix
☎ 418/692-2492
🕐 Closed Mon.

Street life on Rue Champlain

(Tel 418/694-0413, closed Mon. & Nov.–April) dates from the beginning of the 20th century and incorporates the decorated interior of the 18th-century chapel it replaced. Much of the carving is the work of Quebec's master-sculptor Pierre-Noël Levasseur. The **Musée des Ursulines de Québec** contains many items evocative of early days in New France, including exquisite embroidery worked by the nuns.

Musée des Ursulines de Québec

✉ 12 Rue Donnaconais

☎ 418/694-0694

⊕ Closed Mon. & Dec.–Jan.

Place-Royale Information Centre

✉ 215 Rue du March-Finlay

☎ 418/643-6631

⊕ Closed Oct.–April

Église Notre-Dame-des-Victoires

✉ Place Royale

☎ 418/692-1650

⊕ Closed afternoons mid-Oct.–mid-May

LOWER TOWN (BASSE-VILLE)

Reached from the Upper Town via the steep and winding street called Côte de la Montagne and Escalier Casse-Cou (Breakneck Stairs), or by funicular from Terrasse Dufferin *(Tel 418/692-1132)*, the Lower Town is the nucleus from which Quebec grew. Here you will have a thrilling sense of New France's earliest days. The focal point is Place Royale, but be sure to stroll streets such as Rue du Petit-Champlain, Rue-Saint-Pierre, and Rue Saint-Paul, get a whiff of the sea from the boardwalks of the Old Port, and visit the Musée de la Civilisation.

Place Royale is lined with fine stone houses and dominated by the church of Notre-Dame-des-Victoires. It was laid out in 1688 on the site of the garden of Champlain's Habitation of 1608, and, as market square and public forum, was the epicenter of life in Quebec for many years. A reconstruction from the late 1960s forward has returned it to the appearance it had at the time of the conquest. As well as being the starting point for guided walks, the **Place-Royale Information Centre** gives a full account of the Lower Town's history.

Originally dedicated to the infant Jesus, Bishop Laval's chapel was rededicated in 1690 as **Église Notre-Dame-des-Victoires** when 34 British ships withdrew after a five-day siege of the city. "Victory" singular became "victories" plural in 1711 after a British naval attack was disrupted by a violent storm. When the British came a third time, in 1759, they stayed, and the church was almost completely destroyed by their bombardment. Rebuilt more than once since, it presents a steep gable to the square, topped by a spire. Inside, a large model ship is suspended in the nave, while the altarpiece symbolizes the fortified city of Quebec.

Housed in a superb modern building, the **Musée de la Civilisation** offers up to 12 exhibits at any one time. Wonderfully integrated into the urban fabric of the Lower Town, the museum incorporates the 18th-century **Maison Estebe.** In the spacious lobby, a striking, concrete sculpture evokes the springtime breakup of the ice on the St. Lawrence. One of the two permanent exhibits will be of great interest to anyone delving into just what it is that makes up the identity of Quebec. Entitled *Mémoires*, it houses some amazing objects, evoking four centuries of life and the emotions of people making their way in a new and difficult country. The other permanent exhibit, *Objets de civilisation,* encourages the visitor to look at the items shown with the eyes of those who made and used them. Among the vast array of objects, the outstanding exhibit is *La Barque*, a boat that was discovered on the museum's site by archaeologists.

Quebec boomed as a port city in the early 19th century, when raftsmen steered their long timber bundles down the St. Lawrence and St. Charles Rivers to be loaded aboard ships bound for Britain. In the other direction came migrants looking for a new life. Activity fell off toward the end of the century, but you can still see freighters from the observation deck of the **Old Port of Quebec Interpretation Centre.** Housed on the dockside of the Bassin Louise in what used to be a cement plant, the center brings to life the glory days of the port and the work of loggers, raftsmen, and shipbuilders. Beyond the lock connecting the Bassin Louise to the St. Lawrence, broad boardwalks give access to the riverside, whose performance area, Agora du Vieux Port, is popular in summer. ■

Musée de la Civilisation

- ✉ 85 Rue Dalhousie
- ☎ 418/643-2158
- 🕐 Closed Mon. & late Sept.–early June
- 💲 $$$

Old Port of Quebec Interpretation Centre

- ✉ 100 Rue St.-André
- ☎ 418/648-3300
- 🕐 Closed late Oct.–mid-May except by appt.
- 💲 $

A WALK AROUND OLD QUEBEC

A walk around Old Quebec

This walk explores both the Upper and Lower Towns, but leaves you with plenty more to discover. After a brief circuit of the Upper Town, capitalizing on its marvelous views over the great river, the walk goes downhill to meander through the streets and squares of the Lower Town.

Begin the walk in the **Place d'Armes ❶** by the Champlain memorial and the monument commemorating Quebec's UNESCO designation as a world heritage site. After admiring the view of the Lower Town and the St. Lawrence, go along the righthand side of the square and turn right down narrow Rue du Trésor and left along the flank of the **Notre-Dame basilique** (see pp. 134–5).

Go down Rue Sainte-Famille past the high walls of the Seminary, turn left along Rue Couillard, then right down Rue Saint-Flavien to the **ramparts ❷** and their view of the port. Rue Hamel and Rue Charlevoix lead to the **Musée des Augustines.** Come back uphill via Côte de la Fabrique and follow Rue des Jardins to the **Place de l'Hôtel de Ville,** dominated by the grandiose late 19th-century **Hôtel de Ville,** or City Hall. In its basement, the **Urban Life Interpretation Centre** (*43 Côte de la Fabrique, Tel 418/691-4606*) has displays on the development, past and present, of this uniquely fascinating city. To the left of City Hall is the Price Building, an art deco skyscraper that fits into the urban scene remarkably well. Nearby is the monument to Cardinal Taschereau, the first Canadian cardinal.

Follow Rue Donnacona to the Ursuline Monastery, and from there, walk back to your starting point, passing what may well be the city's oldest house, the **Maison Jacquet ❸** (*34 Rue Saint-Louis*), now a classy restaurant.

Descend the cliff separating the Upper and Lower Towns by flights of steps down Côte de la Montagne. At the foot of the precipitous second flight of steps (Casse-Cou or "Breakneck") is the charming **Rue du Petit-Champlain ❹**, lined with craft shops and cafés. At the end of Petit-Champlain, make a 180-degree turn and follow Boulevard Champlain, turning left past the imposing **Maison Chevalier** and its exhibits from the **Museé de la Civilisation** (see pp. 136–7). To the right, Rue Sous-le-Fort leads to the Batterie Royale, with its cannon trained on former foes approaching from the river. Walk along Rue Saint-Pierre, turn left, and end the walk in **Place Royale ❺.** ■

✚ See area map p. 137
▶ Place d'Armes
↔ 3 miles
◷ 2 hours
▶ Place Royale

NOT TO BE MISSED
- Notre-Dame basilique
- Urban Life Centre
- Maison Chevalier

Old Quebec's café life in full swing

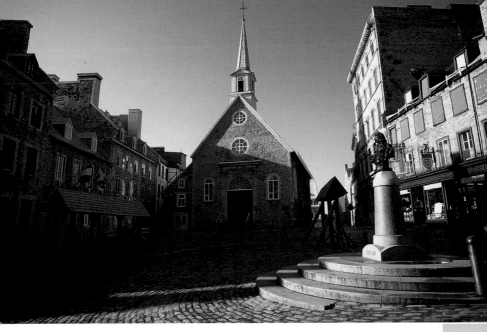

Église Notre-Dame-des-Victoire overlooks the Place Royale.

RUE ST.-ANDRÉ

RUE ST.-VALLIER EST

RUE ST.- PAUL

RUE DES REMPARTS

VIEUX-PORT

Hôtel-Dieu (Musée des Augustins) ❷

RUE HAMEL

RUE ST.-FLAVIEN

RUE DES REMPARTS

RUE HÉBERT

RUE ST.-PIERRE

RUE DALHOUSIE

RUE

Musée de la Civilisation

CÔTE DU PALAIS

RUE CHARLEVOIX

RUE COUILLARD

RUE ST.-FAMILLE

Musée de l'Amérique Française

RUE GARNEAU

Séminaire de Québec

BASSE-VILLE

RUE ST.-JEAN

CÔTE DE LA FABRIQUE

RUE CHAUVEAU

Hôtel de Ville

Basilique Notre-Dame-de-Québec

RUE PORT-DAUPHIN

CÔTE DE LA MONTAGNE

Gouvernement Provincial

RUE ST.-STANISLAS

RUE DES JARDINS

RUE BUADE

Musée du Fort

Place Royale

Batterie Royale

RUE COOK

RUE STE.-ANNE

Musée de Cire

ℹ

RUE DU FORT

START ❶

Place d'Armes

Couvent des Ursulines

Funiculaire

❺ **Notre-Dame-des-Victoires**

RUE DAUPHINE

RUE STE.-ANNE

Cathédrale Anglicane

RUE DU TRÉSOR

Maison Chevalier

❸

RUE ST.-LOUIS

Maison Jacquet

Château Frontenac

HAUTE-VILLE

RUE ST.-LOUIS

Parc Cavalier du Moulin

Parc des Gouverneurs

❹

Terrasse Dufferin

BOULEVARD CHAMPLAIN

RUE DU PETIT-CHAMPLAIN

St.-Laurent (St. Lawrence)

RUE D'AUTEUIL

0 | 300 meters
0 | 300 yards

Quebec's fortified defenses

Artillery Park NHS
- ✉ 2 Rue d'Auteuil
- ☎ 418/648-4205
- ⏲ Closed Nov.–April
- 💲 $

**Fortifications
Interpretation
Centre**
- ✉ 100 Rue St.-Louis
- ☎ 418/648-7016
- ⏲ Closed Nov.–March
- 💲 $

Citadel NHS
- ✉ Access from Rue
  St.-Louis via Côte de
  la Citadelle
- ☎ 418/694-2815
- ⏲ Closed Nov.–April
  except by
  appointment
- 💲 $$$

**National
Battlefields Park
Interpretation
Centre**
- ☎ 418/648-5641
- ⏲ Closed Mon., late
  Sept.–mid-May
- 💲 $

NEVER REALLY FREE FROM THE THREAT OF ATTACK BY THE Iroquois or the British, the capital of New France was constantly improving and adding to its defenses. Walls were built and strengthened, but the plan to construct a great citadel on the highest point of Cap Diamant failed to attract funds from a parsimonious Paris, and it was left to the British to build the great star-shaped stronghold that overlooks both the city and the St. Lawrence today.

It is a real thrill to walk around the fortifications of what is the only walled city in North America, one of the chief reasons for its designation by UNESCO as a world heritage site. There are interpretive panels along the nearly 3-mile circuit, while guided walking tours set off from the **Frontenac kiosk** (*Tel 418/648-7016*) on Dufferin Terrace. Each stretch of the circuit has its own interest, but be sure not to miss the giddy boardwalk called **Promenade des Gouverneurs** suspended from the cliff face below the Citadel.

Fascinating stops en route include **Artillery Park,** a complex of military installations that evolved over three centuries and is now a national historic site. There is a 500-foot-long, 18th-century barracks, a massive redoubt of the same period, and an old foundry housing a magnificent model of the city as it appeared at the beginning of the 19th century. Between here and the Citadel, the formidable walls are pierced by a number of gateways. Close to the St. Louis Gate, the **Fortifications Interpretation Centre** has displays on the development of the city's defenses.

THE CITADEL

After the conquest, the British inherited the much battered French defenses but only began work on a temporary stronghold following the American attack in 1775–76. The present 40-acre **Citadel** was only completed in 1831. Its design follows the classical star-shaped baroque pattern perfected in Europe, with projecting bastions commanding a field of fire over walls, ditches, and the exposed earthworks beyond.

The Citadel is the home of the Van Doos (*Vingt-deux*), the Royal 22nd Regiment, the prestigious French-speaking regiment of Canadian Forces. In summer, the Changing of the Guard (*June–Aug. 10 a.m.*) and the Beating of the Retreat (*Tues., Thurs., Sat., & Sun. July–Aug. 7 p.m.*) draw crowds.

The 250 acres of rolling parkland on the Plains of Abraham have been preserved as the **Parc des Champs-de-Bataille**—the site of the 15-minute battle that led to the end of the French regime in Quebec. It was here, in the early morning drizzle of September 13, 1759, that British General Wolfe's troops stood in line ready to resist the defending French under General Montcalm. Wolfe's men had made their way up from the St. Lawrence with great stealth, easily overcoming the sleeping Canadiens supposed to be on guard at the top of the cliff. Taken by surprise, Montcalm's mixed force of regulars and militiamen advanced in disorder and were cut to pieces by the redcoats' sustained fire. Wolfe perished on the field of battle; Montcalm died from his wounds the following day. The

**Military pride
on display at
Quebec's Citadel**

events of this most decisive day in Canadian history are recounted in the **National Battlefields Park Interpretation Centre,** housed in the **Musée du Québec** on the town edge of the park.

The comprehensive collections of Quebec art in the Musée du Québec were revitalized in 1991 when its original neoclassic building was dramatically linked to the former prison by a new Great Hall, a crystalline structure that allows the landscape of the battlefields park to flow over and around it.

The expanded museum now displays many more of its 22,000 works than before. There are sculptures, drawings, prints, photographs, and many items of decorative art, but it is the splendid painting collection that most captures the attention. It is a lesson in how artists have seen the Quebec landscape (look specially for pictures by Arthur Lismer and Clarence Gagnon) and the province's past (king-size history pictures by Henri Beau and Marc-Aurele Suzor-Côté). ■

The ramparts of Quebec's Citadel still loom over the city and the Plains of Abraham (top of picture).

Musée du Québec

✉ 1 Wolfe-Montcalm
☎ 418/643-2150
🕐 Closed Mon. late Sept.–May
💲 $$

Île d'Orléans & the Beaupré shore

This day drive takes you downstream from Quebec City to the tranquil Île d'Orléans (Orleans Island) and then along the Beaupré shore to one of North America's great centers of pilgrimage, the shrine of Sainte-Anne.

Jacques Cartier is supposed to have cried *"Quel beau pré!"* (What lovely meadows!) on sighting the lush grasslands along the shore of the St. Lawrence, downstream from where Quebec stands today.

Leave Quebec City heading north via Hwy. 440 and, after about 6 miles, cross the bridge over the northern arm of the St. Lawrence. At the junction, turn right toward **Sainte-Pétronille ❶**. It was here that farmers laid out the island's first settlement, and it was here that General Wolfe pondered his assault on the city which so splendidly fills the view upstream.

Continue your tour around the island in a counterclockwise direction. In the 19th century, **Saint-Laurent ❷** was a famous boatbuilding center, with 20 yards turning out *chaloupes* (longboats) in great numbers. The yard once known as the Chalouperie Godbout is now a museum, the **Parc Maritime de Saint-Laurent** (*Tel 418/828-9672*). The next parish, Saint-Jean, has one of the finest examples of an early manor house, the imposing **Manoir Mauvide-Genest** (*Tel 418/829-2630*), now a restaurant and museum. Climb up the viewing tower in the parish of **Saint-François ❸** at the downstream tip of the island and savor the superb views in all directions.

Competing for your attention in **Sainte-Famille ❹** are an old forge, the little visitor center in the **Maison Drouin,** and, above all, the twin-towered **Sainte Famille** parish church, consecrated in 1749. The north side of the island gives splendid views of the Beaupré shore. Just before the bridge, Saint-Pierre boasts the island's oldest church (St.-Pierre church).

Cross the bridge back to the mainland, and turn right along Hwy. 138. After about 18 miles turn into the parking lot for the great pilgrimage church of **Basilique Sainte-Anne-de-Beaupré ❺** (*Ave. Royale, Tel 418/827-3781*). This great basilica is dedicated to the patron saint of Quebec and attracts pilgrims from all over North America. Its

Military parade in Quebec City

Montmorency Falls

QUEBEC

Parc de la Chute-Montmorency ❻

Boischatel

L'Ange-Gardien

Petit-Pré

360

Montmorency

Petit-pré

Beauport

START

440

QUEBEC

Saint-Laurent

368

Saint-Pierre

Maheu

❶ Sainte-Pétronille

❷

Saint-Laurent

N

0   8 kilometers

0   4 miles

legendary origins go back to the mid-17th century, when storm-tossed sailors were delivered from disaster by praying to Saint Anne, mother of the Virgin Mary. Other miracles and healings followed, and successively greater shrines were built on the site. The present, magnificent building was completed in 1934 and rivals the great cathedrals of Europe in splendid proportions and opulent decor.

Unless you are in a hurry, go back in the direction of Quebec City along the Rte. 360, the **Avenue Royale,** laid out in the late 17th century by Bishop Laval as one of the first roads in Quebec and originally known as le Chemin du Roy (the King's Road). Close to the bridge to the Île d'Orléans lies the parking area for **Parc de la Chute-Montmorency** ❻ (*Tel 418/663-2877*)—where you will find one of the area's great natural attractions, the **Montmorency Falls.** These spectacular 272-foot waterfalls have long been a popular tourist site and have featured in many a painting. The elegant mansion known as the **Manoir Montmorency** (*Tel 418/663-3330*) houses a visitor center with displays on the falls and their history. ■

🅽 See area map pp. 104–105
▶ Quebec City
↔ 75 miles
🕐 Allow 1 day
▶ Quebec City

NOT TO BE MISSED
- Parc Maritime de Saint-Laurent
- Basilique Sainte-Anne-de-Beaupré
- Montmorency Falls

Art in the church of Ste.-Anne-de-Beaupré.

A harmonious
landscape of
forests, farms,
and country
cottages at Saint-
Siméon, near the
northern end of
the Charlevoix
Coast

Charlevoix

THE EVER BROADENING SWEEP OF THE ST. LAWRENCE
bordered by the plunging slopes of the Canadian Shield, deep forests,
old villages set in farmland—all this has given the Charlevoix coastline an irresistible appeal. Such landscapes, combined with a timeless way of life, inspired artists like Clarence Gagnon a century ago.
The region continues to work its charm, not only on artists but on
vacationers, who have been coming here even longer in search of
fresh air, abundant game, pristine scenery, and a warm welcome.

Baie-Saint-Paul

🗺 105C2

**Visitor
information**

✉ Centre d'Art,
4 Ambroise-Fafard,
Baie-St.-Paul

☎ 418/665-4454

Part of the seemingly unchanging
charm of Charlevoix can be traced
to an event that occurred around
350 million years ago. Traveling
at a speed of 6 miles a second, a
meteorite some 7,000 feet across hit
the Earth with unimaginable force.
In less than a minute, its 3-mile-
deep crater was formed, creating

the land forms that exist to this day.
The **Charlevoix crater** is one of
the biggest in the world; some 35
miles in diameter, it consists of a
central upland surrounded by a
deep trench and an outer escarpment. Half of this formation has
disappeared into the St. Lawrence;
the rest forms an exceptionally

varied habitat in which all the ecosystems of Quebec are present, from maple forest to tundra. This great diversity in a relatively small space led in 1988 to the designation of the Charlevoix area as a UNESCO world biosphere reserve.

BAIE-SAINT-PAUL

Before descending the steep hill into this artists' village, pause at the new **Centre d'Histoire Naturelle de Charlevoix** *(Tel 418/435-6275)* just off the highway. From the balcony there is a fine view of coast and uplands. Inside, displays recount the unique geology and natural history of the area, including the dramatic impact of the meteorite and its consequences.

Take time to stroll the streets of Baie-Saint-Paul. There are plenty of delightful dwellings dating from the 19th century, and it is easy to appreciate the appeal the village has always exercised on artists. A modern note is struck by the award-winning **Centre d'Exposition de Baie-Saint-Paul,** opened in 1992 as a setting for changing art shows. A number of other establishments draw on Baie-Saint-Paul's artistic traditions.

Traditional ways of life lasted longer on **Île-aux-coudres** (Hazel Island) than on the Baie-Saint-Paul mainland, and were memorably recorded by documentary filmmakers in the 1960s. The 7-mile-long island was particularly famous for building the schooners that, for many settlements along the St. Lawrence, were the only means of communication with the outside world. You can clamber aboard a *voiture d'eau* (water-wagon) at the museum devoted to these everyday runabouts, the **Musée les Voitures d'Eau.** Otherwise people come here for peace and quiet, and the best way to see the island is to pedal around slowly on a bicycle.

Between Baie-Saint-Paul and the resort of **La Malbaie-Pointe-au-Pic,** the scenic Rte. 362 follows a switchback course along the spectacular coastline, passing through delightful villages such as **Les Éboulements** and **Saint-Irénée. Saint-Joseph,** where the ferry leaves for the Île aux Coudres, once earned its living from boatbuilding, and you can see abandoned schooners lying around. This resort's glory days came in the early 20th century, when wealthy vacationers arrived by elegant steamship and either stayed in the château-style grand hotel called the **Manoir Richelieu,** or, like U.S. President William Howard Taft, in the fine vacation homes they built themselves on the upper slopes. The little **Musée de Charlevoix,** set in a striking modern building, puts on temporary exhibitions.

One of the most spectacular sights in eastern Canada is the gorge of the Malbaie River. Now forming Quebec's most extensive regional park, the **Parc Régional des Hautes-Gorges-de-la-Rivière-Malbaie** and reached by a 20-mile unpaved road, the gorge is an ideal place to appreciate the variety of vegetation in the Charlevoix area. Great elms grow in the sheltered valley, while above the 2,000-plus-foot sides of the gorge are plants of the arctic-alpine zone. ∎

Centre d'Exposition de Baie-Saint-Paul
- ✉ 23 rue Ambroise-Fafard
- ☎ 418/435-3681
- $ $

Musée les Voitures d'Eau
- ✉ 203 Chemin des Coudriers
- ☎ 418/438-2626
- 🕐 Closed winter
- $ $

Musée de Charlevoix
- ✉ 1 Chemin du Havre
- ☎ 418/665-4411
- 🕐 Closed Mon. Sept.–June

Parc Régional des Hautes-Gorges-de-la-Rivière-Malbaie
- ✉ Via Rte. 138 & Sainte-Aimée-des-Lacs

The grandest hotel along the Charlevoix Coast, the château-style Manoir Richelieu, now houses a casino.

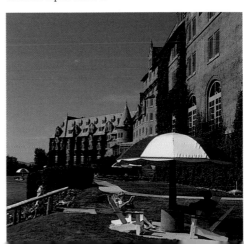

Saguenay Fjord & the Lac Saint-Jean region

Saguenay Fjord
🅰 105C2

Baie-Sainte-Catherine
🅰 105C2

Tadoussac
🅰 105C2

Marine Mammal Interpretation Centre
✉ 108 Rue de la Caie-Seche, Tadoussac
☎ 418/235-4701
🕐 Limited winter hours
💲 $$$

Sainte-Rose-du-Nord
🅰 105C2

Chicoutimi
🅰 105C2

THE SAGUENAY RIVER FINDS ITS WAY INTO THE St. Lawrence along a great crack in the Canadian Shield, a fault whose waters fill to a depth of 800 feet. Almost a mile wide in places, this 60-mile stretch of the river is bordered by superb forested cliffs rising to a height of 1,500 feet. The area around Lac Saint-Jean provides an altogether different experience—a restful oasis of fertile soil in the unforgiving Canadian Shield.

SAGUENAY FJORD

The occasional villages huddled in coves along the Saguenay Fjord can be reached by road, but the best way to experience this majestic waterway is to take one of the many boat cruises offered. A mini-cruise, a mere eight minutes long and costing nothing, crosses the mouth of the Saguenay 24 hours a day. It links the villages of **Baie-Sainte-Catherine** and **Tadoussac** and keeps traffic moving along Hwy. 138, the shoreline road. This meeting point of two great rivers is one of the most popular whale-watching spots in all of Canada. Five species of whale—fin, minke, beluga, humpback, and blue—frequent the area, drawn by the rich crop of krill and caplin that develops as a result of the mixing of icy cold salt water from the St. Lawrence with the freshwater of the Saguenay (see p. 147). If you can't take one of the highly recommended whale-watching trips (*Croisière Navimex Inc., Tel 418/237-4272*), you may well see some of these wonderful mammals from a number of lookouts; try the **Pointe-Noire Interpretation and Observation Centre** (*Tel 418/237-4383, closed Nov.–May*) on its clifftop site close to the southern terminal of the free ferry. The attractive little resort of Tadoussac has the excellent **Marine Mammal Interpretation**

Centre, with displays explaining why the Saguenay-St. Lawrence is being established as a marine park. Its strategic position made Tadoussac a focal point of trade among natives, leading Pierre Chauvin to establish Canada's very first fur-trading post here in 1600. Reconstructed, the steep-roofed timber building houses a little museum on these earliest days of native/European contact.

THE UPPER REACHES & LAC SAINT-JEAN

Rte. 172 from Tadoussac runs mostly out of sight of the river, so make sure you turn down the side road to the village of **Sainte-Rose-du-Nord** (*53 miles west of Tadoussac*).

Rte. 170 leaves the coastal highway at Saint-Siméon (*25 miles south of the mouth of the Saguenay*) and parallels the southern bank. For some of the finest views of the fjord, go down side roads, first to the tiny settlement of **L'Anse-Saint-Jean,** then, at Riviere-éternité, to **Cap Trinité,** where a 26-foot-tall statue of the Virgin Mary graces a ledge in the 1,700-foot-high headland.

CHICOUTIMI

Capital of the Saguenay/Lake Saint-Jean region, Chicoutimi makes its living from industry, and it is industry, in the form of the fine

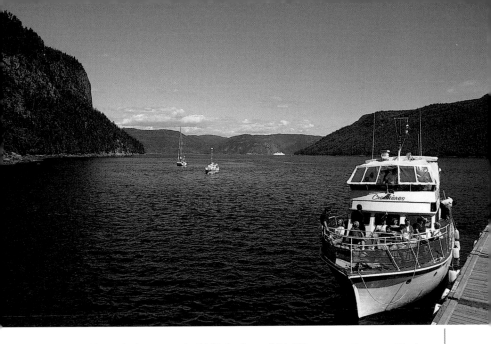

old granite buildings of a former **pulp mill,** that makes up the city's main visitor attraction. As well as housing displays of local interest and all kinds of cultural events, the mill tells the story of its past as the very first industrial enterprise founded by French-Canadians. Also here is the Arthur Villeneuve House, **La Pulperie,** gloriously decorated with the naive murals of this barber-turned-painter.

LAC SAINT-JEAN

An isolated pocket of reasonably fertile clay soil in the Canadian Shield, the shore of this 520-square-mile lake was settled from the mid-19th century by French-Canadian farmers unable to find land in the overcrowded valley of the St. Lawrence. It is a popular summer vacation spot for visitors from the rest of Quebec, with attractions that include the province's best zoo. At the **Jardin Zoologique de Saint-Félicien** it is the animals, many of them native Canadian species like bears, wolves and moose, that range freely, while visitors admire them from a sort of mobile cage. ∎

Saguenay Fjord can best be seen from the deck of a cruise boat.

Chicoutimi Pulp Mill
- ✉ 300 Rue Dubac
- ☎ 418/698-3100
- 🕐 Closed late Sept.–mid-June
- 💲 $

La Pulperie
- ✉ 300 Rue Dubuc
- ☎ 418/698-3158
- 🕐 Closed weekends mid-Oct.–Nov.
- 💲 $$$

Jardin Zoologique de Saint-Félicien
- ✉ Blvd. du Jardin, Chamouchouane Island
- ☎ 418/679-0543
- 🕐 Closed Oct.–early May
- 💲 $$$

Whales of the St. Lawrence

More than 30 species of whale live in or migrate through Canadian waters. Whale-watching, or whale-contact, has become popular ever since the 1972 moratorium on hunting. The little beluga or white whale (up to 16 feet long) has become one of the most cherished inhabitants of the St. Lawrence, though its numbers are down to about 500, from a former high of several thousand.

Other species encountered in the river include the minke whale (up to 35 feet long), the humpback (up to 50 feet), the fin whale (up to 65 feet), and occasionally the blue whale, the largest creature in the world, which can reach a length of 100 feet and weigh up to 150 tons. ∎

Côte Nord

UNTIL A 400-MILE HIGHWAY WAS BUILT AS FAR AS Havre-Saint-Pierre in the 1960s, any trip along the Côte Nord (North Shore) of the St. Lawrence beyond Tadoussac had to be undertaken by boat. Even now, if you wish to venture farther along the wild shoreline, you will have to board the weekly boat that takes two days to reach Blanc Sablon on the border with Labrador. Here, a short stretch of highway crosses the border, giving access to some of the remarkable sights along the Labrador coast. There is also a ferry connection with St. Barbe in Newfoundland.

The strange shapes of the Mingan Archipelago monoliths result from the weathering of limestone formed 500 million years ago.

FIRST SETTLERS

Now settled in a series of reserves scattered along the coast, the Montagnais have lived along the North Shore for more than 8,000 years and were among the first natives to have contact with Europeans. The Basque fishermen who set up their processing plants on the Labrador coast in the 1400s were active along this shore as well.

They were followed by a handful of French and English fishermen and traders, but it was only in the 20th century that large-scale developments took place, based first on pulp mills, then on the discovery of iron-ore inland and the harnessing of water resources for hydroelectric power.

The town of **Baie-Comeau** *(125 miles east of Tadoussac via Rte. 138)* was largely the creation of Colonel Robert McCormick, publisher of the *Chicago Tribune*, and the place is still dominated by a huge pulp mill.

On an even greater scale are the hydroelectric installations inland from the town, reached by virtually the only road to penetrate the wilderness that stretches out endlessly to the north of the St. Lawrence. Known collectively as the **Manic-Outardes Complex,** they consist of several dams and power stations along the Manicouagan and Outardes Rivers. **Manic 2,** 14 miles north of Baie-Comeau, can be visited. But the most spectacular feature of this gigantic undertaking is **Daniel Johnson Dam** of the Manic 5 generating complex, which is well worth the trip up the long and winding road. With a height of 702 feet and a length of 4,307 feet, the largest of its kind in the world, it bears the name of the prime minister of Quebec who unfortunately died here on the day it was to open in 1968. A breezy walk along the top of this titanic construction reveals something of the 770-square-mile reservoir, which, far upstream, has created a ring of water 40 miles across, outlining what is probably a gigantic meteorite crater.

The town of **Sept-Îles** *(142 miles east of Baie-Comeau)* has a fine deepwater port sheltered by the seven islands that give it its name. The railhead for the iron-ore line that reaches far inland to Shefferville and Labrador City, Sept-Îles has a couple of museums that between them show how a seemingly inhospitable land has been lived in, first by the native Montagnais **(Vieux-Poste),** then by Europeans **(Musée régional de la Côte-Nord).**

At the end of the highway, **Havre-Saint-Pierre** *(132 miles east of Sept-Îles via Rte. 138)* is not only the port for the weekly ferry service to Blanc Sablon, but also the point of departure for trips to the fascinating Mingan Archipelago and Anticosti Island (see p. 150).

MINGAN ARCHIPELAGO

Strung out along the Côte-Nord between Longue-Pointe and Aguanish, these 40 islands have formed a national park reserve since 1984. Their ecology is unique: The combination of the cold waters of the Labrador Current, harsh winters, and limestone soil means that an arctic-alpine flora flourishes here well to the south of its normal boundry. Some species, such as the Mingan thistle, are very rare, if not unique. Seabirds abound, notably that drollest of birds, the Atlantic puffin, and seals can be seen. But the most extraordinary natural features are the monoliths that have been weirdly sculpted in the limestone. Given fanciful names by local people, their endlessly fascinating shapes have been formed over millennia by the abrasive forces of wind and water.

The Mingan Archipelago can be reached by boat from Longue-Pointe and Havre-Saint-Pierre. Parks Canada operates two visitor centers. ∎

The Canadian Shield has an immense potential for hydropower.

Daniel Johnson Dam
- 133 miles north of Baie-Corneau via Rte. 389
- ☎ 418/294-3923

Vieux-Poste
- Blvd. des Montagnais
- ☎ 418/968-2070

Musée Régional de la Côte-Nord
- 500 Blvd. Laure
- ☎ 418/968-2070
- $ $

Mingan Archipelago visitor centers:
Longue-Pointe
- 625 Rue du Centre
- ☎ 418/949-2126 or 949-2845 winter; 418/538-3331 or 948-3669 summer

Havre-Saint-Pierre
- 975 Rue de l'Escale
- ☎ 418/538-3285

Île d'Anticosti

Île d'Anticosti
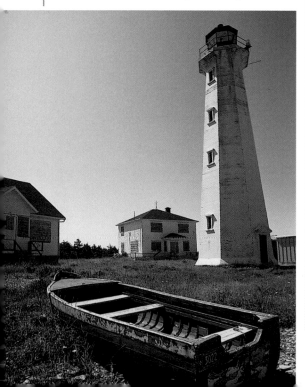 105E2

Port-Menier
105E2

LARGER THAN PRINCE EDWARD ISLAND, THE ISLAND OF Anticosti has a population of only a few hundred people. Extending for nearly 140 miles between the Straits of Jacques-Cartier and Honguedo in the Gulf of St. Lawrence, it has been known as the Graveyard of the Gulf because of the hundreds of vessels wrecked on its reefs. The fossil-rich limestone foundation of the island has been shaped into cliffs, canyons, and caverns. Coniferous forest covers much of the surface, while the eastern part of the island is marshy.

The lighthouse at Cap-du-Rabast is one of many erected in response to Anticosti Island's reputation as the Graveyard of the Gulf.

After many changes of ownership (for a while it was part of Newfoundland) and mostly fruitless efforts to develop Anticosti's economy, the island now belongs to the province of Quebec. The proprietor who had the most dramatic impact was the French chocolate tycoon, Henri Menier, who acquired it in 1895 and set about converting it into an immense private game park. The 220 white-tailed deer he introduced have multiplied to a herd of more than 100,000 animals, but Menier's fabulous hunting lodge at **Port-Menier,** the island's only village, was burned down in 1953. The foundations are a poignant reminder of his grandiose ambitions to make Anticosti a kind of feudal domain. Menier first rebuilt the village at Baie-Sainte-Claire (originally English Bay, but renamed in honor of his mother) close to the western tip of the island, but then moved to Port-Menier. Baie-Sainte-Claire now lies in ruins, but the **Pointe de l'Ouest lighthouse** is still here, as well as a cemetery.

In the graveyard of the ocean, the remains of the *Calou,* wrecked in 1982, are visible. With its deep-water harbor and shopping and other facilities, Port-Menier is the only settlement on the island, with a ferry link to Havre-Saint-Pierre or Sept-Îles.

People come here mainly to hunt the deer and fish in the island's many rivers, but if you're looking for a unique experience, and are well equipped, rent a four-wheel-drive and head off down the only road leading east from Port-Menier. As well as lonely beaches, dramatic cliffs, and the occasional shipwreck, you will find the phenomena characteristic of limestone country, including the **La Patate** cave system, only discovered in 1981, and the **Vauréal Canyon,** with its sheer limestone walls and 230-foot falls. ■

Îles de la Madeleine

IN THE MIDDLE OF THE GULF OF ST. LAWRENCE, CLOSER TO Prince Edward Island than to any part of Quebec, this intriguing archipelago consists of a crescent of islands, some linked by immensely long sandbars enclosing lagoons.

Everything contrives to make this a special place: trees cut by the wind into contorted shapes; red sandstone cliffs carved into arches, caves, and columns; emerald green grass contrasting with a brilliant blue sea and with the bright paintwork of the fishermen's houses.

Although some of the islands' population are English speakers, most are descendants of the Acadians who fled here from Nova Scotia or Saint-Pierre and Miquelon, preferring to live under the British Crown than submit to the rule of republican France.

Each of the islands has its own delights. **Cap aux Meules** *(Visitor information, Tel 418/986-2245)* is the most populated island. As well as having a fascinating fishing port, it is the terminal for the ferry *(Tel 418/986-6600)* from Souris on Prince Edward Island and the weekly freighter *(Tel 514/937-7656)* from Montreal. The best all-round view in the islands is from the summit of nearby **Butte-de-Vent** hill, and some of the most spectacular cliff formations are at **Cap Trou** and **L'Étang-du-Nord** on the west coast. **Notre-**

Dame-du-Rosaire, the church at the settlement of Fatima, is one of the most extraordinary modern buildings in Quebec. Every feature, from its shell-like outline to its interior decoration, speaks of the islanders' relationship with the sea. **Havre-Aubert** island, to the south, has gentler scenery, an aquarium, a maritime museum, and **La Grave,** a medley of old fishing installations. **Île d'Entrée** (Entry Island) has grassy hills culminating in **Big Hill** (571 feet), with splendid views of the archipelago. The island has an Anglican church serving its 200 or so inhabitants, most of whom are descended from Scottish settlers.

To the north, **Havre aux Maisons** island has perhaps the most harmonious landscapes of the archipelago, with old farm structures and characteristic houses as well as rugged rock formations. Reached via the long and narrow Dune du Nord, the **eastern islands** have sand dunes, superb beaches, and some of the best walking trails. The vast sandy beach of **Grand Échouerie** is the finest on the islands. ■

Above: White-tailed deer on Anticosti Island

Gaspésie

Gaspésie
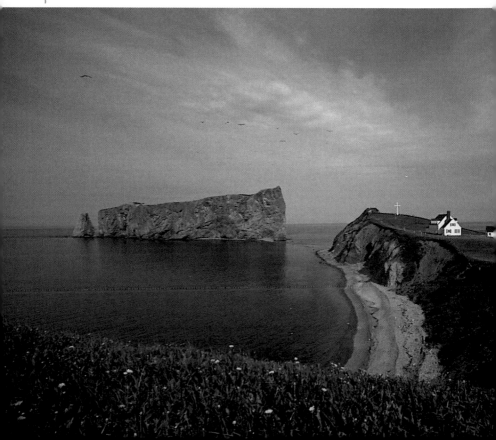
105D2

**Grosse-Île
& the Irish
Memorial National
Historic Site**
✉ 2 Rue d'Auteuil
☎ 418/248-8888
🕐 Closed Nov.–April
$ $$$

Musée de la mer
✉ 1034 Rue de la
Phare, 6 miles
east of Rimouski
☎ 418/724-6214
🕐 Closed mid-
Oct.–mid-June

GASPÉSIE (THE GASPÉ PENINSULA) CONSISTS OF A forested mountain backbone sweeping down to a rugged, sparsely inhabited coastline of cliffs and coves and the occasional fishing village. Its remoteness, natural grandeur, and the traditional ways of its inhabitants have long attracted visitors. Built in the 1920s, in a vain attempt to bring settlers to the area, the contour-hugging road along the north shore is one of the most splendidly scenic routes in Canada, especially as it nears the tip of the peninsula.

Gaspésie is approached from Quebec City by the highway to just beyond the town of Rivière-du-Loup, and then by Hwy. 132 along the shore. At **Montmagny,** about 35 miles from Quebec, boats take visitors to the old immigrant quarantine station on **Grosse-Île,** Canada's equivalent of Ellis Island, preserved as the **Grosse-Île and the Irish Memorial National**

Historic Site. It is a poignant spot, evoking the hopes and tribulations of more than four million migrants, many of them Irish. **Rivière-du-Loup** and **Trois-Pistoles,** 30 miles farther on, both have ferry services to the north shore of the St. Lawrence. Just beyond the industrial town of Rimouski, in village of Pointe-au-Père, the **Musée de la Mer,**

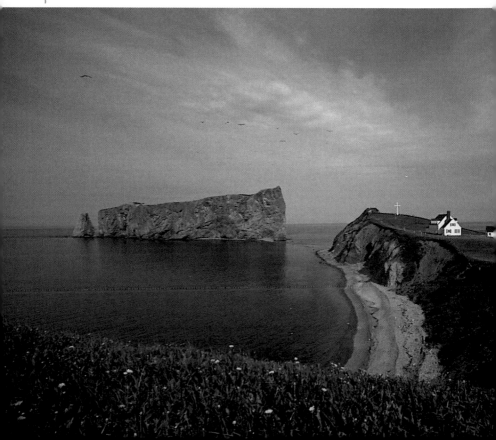

commemorates the 1914 sinking of the *Empress of Ireland*. When the fog-bound liner was rammed by a freighter in the St. Lawrence, 1,014 lives were lost. The disaster was comparable to that of the loss of the *Titanic* only two years earlier.

Six miles east of the resort of Sainte-Flavie on Rte. 132 are the **Jardins de Métis** *(Tel 418/775-2221, closed Nov.–May)*. The variety and luxuriance of these superb gardens owe much to the humid microclimate of the site at the mouth of the Mitis River, but much more to the enthusiasm and horticultural genius of Elsie Reford. Already well into middle age, she inherited what had been a fishing lodge from her uncle, George Stephen Redford, the first president of the Canadian Pacific Railway. From 1929 to 1954 she transformed

it into the gardeners' paradise that welcomes visitors today.

For a chance to see something of the bleak interior of the Gaspé Peninsula, make the short detour into the provincial park known as the **Parc de la Gaspésie.** This is the dramatic border where forest gives way to tundra on one of the highest points in eastern Canada, Mont Jacques-Cartier (4,159 feet). Uniquely, deer, moose, and caribou flourish here in close proximity.

THE OUTER PENINSULA

Designated a national park in 1970, the 93-square-mile **Parc National de Florillon** *(Tel 418/368-5505)* protects the rocky peninsula where the mountainous spine of the Gaspé finally meets the Gulf of St. Lawrence in sheer limestone cliffs. Seabirds are abundant, and a variety of land animals, including lynx and black bear, inhabit the densely forested interior of the park. The interpretation center near **Cap-des-Rosiers** has displays on the ecology and human history of the area.

To experience something of the traditional life of the area, be sure to stop by the old fishing community of **Grande-Grave National Historic Site,** founded by immigrants from the Channel Islands and now restored by Parks Canada. Reached by a spectacular footpath, one of Canada's tallest lighthouses perches on the clifftop at the very tip of the peninsula.

The deepwater port of **Gaspé** is worth a stop for its strikingly modern **Cathedral of Christ the King**, its excellent local museum, and for its historical associations, since it was here that Jacques Cartier landed in 1534 to claim the land for France by erecting a huge wooden cross in the name of his king, François I. An equally massive cross, this time in granite,

Parc de la Gaspésie
- ✉ Visitor center 24 miles south of Sainte-Anne-des-Monts on Rte. 299
- 🕒 Park open daily, visitor center daily early June–mid-Oct.
- ☎ 418/763-3301

Parc National de Florillon
- ▲ 105E2

Cap-des-Rosiers
- ▲ 105E2

Gaspé
- ▲ 105E2

Percé Rock was given its name in 1607 by Samuel de Champlain because of its pierced (*percé*) profile, though some of its original arches have since collapsed. The stack at the seaward end of the great rock is called the Obelisk.

**Musée
de la Gaspésie**
- ✉ 80 Blvd. Gaspé
- ☎ 418/368-1534
- 🕐 Closed Mon. mid-
  Oct.–late June

Percé
- 🅰 105D2

**Musée Acadien
du Québec**
- ✉ 95 Ave. Port-Royal,
  Bonaventure
- ☎ 418/534-4000
- 🕐 Limited hours
  in winter
- 💲 $

**Centre de
l'Heritage
Britannique
de la Gaspésie**
- 🅰 105D2
- ✉ 351 Blvd. Perron
  Ouest, New Richmond
- ☎ 418/392-5907
- 🕐 Closed late
  Sept.–May
- 💲 $

was installed near the cathedral 400 years later. A contemporary monument stands outside the **Musée de la Gaspésie.** The museum displays enlarge on the theme of *Un peuple de la mer* (people of the sea).

Percé

The long haul up the coast road is a reasonable price to pay for a sight of the great **Percé Rock** stretching its 1,500-foot-length just offshore. A compelling presence, altering its appearance as the light changes, the rock exercises a potent fascination on all who see it. It can be reached on foot at low tide, perhaps the best way to appreciate the grandeur of its cliffs, nearly 300 feet high in places. For a broader perspective of this geomorphological marvel, climb to the top of **Mont Sainte-Anne,** the 1,050-foot mountain that rises behind the town. Another way to experience the rock is from a boat *(Les Bateaux de Percé, Tel 418/782-2974)* that takes visitors around **Bonaventure Island** and its colony of tens of thousands of gannets, the largest in America.

Baie des Chaleurs

With a less severe climate and gentler landforms than the north shore of the peninsula, Baie des Chaleurs faces the coast of New Brunswick. It was named by Jacques Cartier for its (relatively) warm waters. While the population of the north shore is now almost entirely French-speaking, this coastline has many traces of its settlement by Scots, Irish, Channel Islanders, and Loyalists, as well as Acadians. Visit the **Musée Acadien du Québec** and the **Centre de l'Heritage Britannique de la Gaspésie,** with its restored traditional buildings.

Attractively located at the foot of the coastal hills is the resort of **Carleton,** which enjoys both Acadian and Loyalist heritage. Rising 1,830 feet above the town, **Mont Saint-Joseph** can be reached by road or on foot and has the best all-around view of the bay. The little **Miguasha Peninsula** is internationally famous for its fossils from the Upper Devonian period some 370 million years ago, many of which were removed by collectors before the area was protected as the provincial park, **Parc de Miguasha** *(11 miles west of Carleton, Tel 418/794-2475, closed mid-Oct.–May).* Spectacular fossil examples are displayed in a visitor center, and there are supervised tours of the site. At **Pointe-a-la-Croix** *(Rte. 132, Tel 418/788-5676)* the strikingly modern building overlooks the mouth of the Restigouche River. It was here in 1760, one year after the Battle of the Plains of Abraham, that the French fleet sent belatedly to the succor of Quebec was overcome by ships of the Royal Navy. Thus died the last hope of recovering New France from the British. Among the fascinating displays are recovered sections of the French vessel *Le Machault.* ∎

O ntario took its name
from the Iroquois
word meaning "shining waters,"
and here you can enjoy the
grandeur of lake and forest,
as well as Canada's greatest
metropolis and a crown of
smaller cities and towns.

Ontario

Hydro Place, Toronto

Ontario

ONTARIO COVERS AN AREA BIGGER THAN FRANCE and Spain combined. It stretches 1,000 miles from the barren coast of Hudson Bay in the north to the crowded cities of the south. Most of this vast province is part of the Canadian Shield, where two-billion-year-old rocks underlie a landscape of forest, muskeg, and countless lakes. Few people live here, although the rocks yield some of the most abundant mineral wealth on earth. The shield extends almost to the gates of Ottawa, once a rowdy logging town, now a true capital city with museums and other attractions to match.

To the south, a 500-mile strip of fertile land forms a peninsula bounded by three of the Great Lakes: Huron, Erie, and Lake Ontario itself. Clearance of the peninsula's dense forest and its conversion into farmland began only at the end of the 18th century, when Loyalists fled north from the newly formed United States. Known as Upper Canada until the mid-19th century, southern Ontario rapidly filled up with migrants, mostly from the British Isles. Railroad and canal construction laid the foundation for the modern commerce and industry that has since made Ontario the powerhouse of the Canadian economy, producing more goods than the other provinces and territories combined.

With 11 million inhabitants, Ontario is the most populous of Canada's provinces. More than 80 percent of Ontarians are town dwellers, nearly four million of them living in Toronto alone. Until quite recently, most were of British stock, ties to the old country were assiduously cultivated, and Ontarian life had a decidedly British "tone," though the Germanic character of the Kitchener area was reflected in its original name of Berlin. The province has a substantial minority of French speakers. Some descended from farmers who settled in the Windsor area long before British rule; others moved up the Ottawa River in search of farmland; others still helped provide the labor force for such mining towns as Sudbury. A late 20th-century wave of multiethnic immigration has transformed the character of many Ontarian cities. With the decline of anglophone Montreal, Toronto has become the focal point of English-speaking Canada, the capital of press and electronic media, with an array of office towers housing national and international headquarters. By contrast, time seems to have stood still in some of the province's smaller places, notably Niagara-on-the-Lake, apparently untouched since its rebuilding early in the 19th century.

There's a certain intimacy with the United States at Niagara Falls, where little Goat Island

Ontario's inhabitants live only a short distance from the pristine Algonquin Park.

separates the Horseshoe Falls in Canada from the American Falls. The falls are one of the world's great attractions, but if your stay in Ontario is limited to a day trip here from Toronto, you will miss out on most of what this province has to offer. Try to explore the woods and water of the shield country.

Some of Canada's most striking scenery can be enjoyed along the shores of the Great Lakes. Lake Erie has the jungle-like forest of Point Pelee, and there are fine beaches to be found on southern Lake Huron. Georgian Bay has beaches, too, but the main attractions here are clear waters, cliffscapes, and rocky wooded islands. The long shoreline of Lake Superior has an elemental grandeur all its own. ■

Upper Canada

By the middle of the 19th century, a million and a half people lived in the land bounded by Lakes Huron, Erie, and Ontario. Farms and towns had replaced the forest that once covered the landscape. They were linked by roads that included what was reputedly the longest street in the world, Yonge Street, running between Toronto and Lake Simcoe.

A century earlier, southern Ontario had been almost devoid of human habitation. Once numbering perhaps 25,000, the Hurons had disappeared in the middle of the 17th century, massacred or absorbed by the Iroquois League, who themselves then left the area. The Iroquois forced the retreat of the Jesuits from the mission now known as Sainte-Marie among the Hurons, established early in 1639 on the shores of Georgian Bay. Fur traders crisscrossed the area, but the only permanent population consisted of a few hundred French settlers, whose farmsteads were laid out along the Detroit River.

The transformation of an empty land began with the arrival of some 10,000 Loyalists fleeing the American Revolution and its aftermath. Among them were Iroquois, who had fought with the British under the leadership of the war-chief Joseph Brant. Many others of American origin came for the cheap land. By the time war broke out in 1812, the area had a population of some 80,000 people, more than three-quarters of them of American origin.

On his arrival in 1792, the first lieutenant governor, John Graves Simcoe (1752–1806) thought of establishing the capital of the newly created colony of Upper Canada at the appropriately named city of London. However, this was not to be. Upper Canada's first capital was Newark (Niagara-on-the-Lake), which turned out to be much too close to the United States for comfort, and the honor was given to York (Toronto).

During the War of 1812 between Great Britain and the United States, a majority of the new settlers remained loyal to the crown, and the warriors of Shawnee chief Tecumseh, whom the Americans had crushed at Tippecanoe a year earlier, rallied to the British cause. Upper Canada saw most of the fighting. Armies marched across the Niagara peninsula, and Canadian heroes were created like Laura Secord, who warned of an impending American attack (see p. 192). The British were driven out of York, and the town partly burned down. Newark suffered even more complete destruc-

The Battle of the Thames River, 1813, where the British ally Tecumseh (top left) was killed.

The Ontario wilderness witnessed many of the key moments in the War of 1812.

tion when the occupying force withdrew.

The defeat of the Royal Navy at the Battle of Lake Erie in 1813 gave the Americans naval control of the lake. Determined to maintain their hold on Lake Ontario, the British feverishly built ships at their naval yard at Kingston, but the war was over before the massive 112-gun man-of-war *St. Lawrence* could see action.

After the war, the British restricted immigration from the south, encouraging new migrants from the United Kingdom, and to a lesser extent from Germany. The policy was a success; in the 1840s up to 100,000 people a year crossed the Atlantic to Canada and while many moved on to the United States, many stayed. Only about a fifth were English. Most came from the western fringes of the British Isles—Highland and Lowland Scots as well as Catholic and Protestant Irish. The last were particularly

numerous and dominant in areas such as the Ottawa valley and western Ontario.

The British had been anxious to ensure that the developing colony did not fall prey to the democratic tendencies that had subverted their rule in the 13 Colonies. They attempted to create a social hierarchy whose status and privileges would encourage imperial loyalty. The layout of townships included blocks of land reserved for substantial landowners and the clergy. Town meetings were not permitted, and every effort was made, in the words of the first lieutenant governor, "to inculcate British Customs, Manners & Principles in the most trivial, as well as serious matters." The result was that for most of its existence, Upper Canada was a Tory society, ruled by a small group of interconnected families who came to be known as the Family Compact. ∎

Ottawa

"WESTMINSTER IN THE WILDERNESS" OR "WASHINGTON OF the North." Both epithets have been applied to Canada's capital city; the former is an accurate enough description of Ottawa's origins, while the latter is more of a goal to which it has aspired, often with impressive results. In the century and a half since it was declared capital of newly united Canada, Ottawa has changed from a brawling timber town to a city of some refinement, with a full array of national institutions that include not just the famous buildings on Parliament Hill but a number of excellent museums.

▲ 157E2

Capital Infocenter
✉ 90 Wellington St.
☎ 800/465-1867

It was not Ottawa but Hull, on the Quebec bank of the Ottawa River, that saw the beginnings of urban settlement in the area at the very start of the 19th century. Then, the first rafts of timber were floated downstream and the important Ottawa Valley timber industry got under way. Not long after, the War of 1812 made Britain nervous about the proximity of the strategic route along the St. Lawrence to the U.S. border. The need for a more secure link between Upper and Lower Canada led to the construction between 1826 and 1832 of the Rideau Canal. The waterway used existing rivers as well as new construction between the Royal Navy's Lake Ontario base at Kingston and the head of navigation near Hull. In charge of this engineering wonder was a Colonel By, whose splendid run of locks connecting the canal to the river were in effect Ottawa's foundation stone. On either side of the canal, the colonel laid out a township. Named Bytown, the new settlement soon overtook Hull in size, though with a population of laborers, lumbermen, and river rats, its character remained resolutely rough. When the time came for a capital of the new United Province of Canada to be chosen, both Toronto and Quebec City were disgusted with Queen Victoria's seemingly willful choice of Ottawa. In retrospect, however, the Empress's hatpin could be said to

Like the federal flag, Ontario's coat of arms includes the maple leaf.

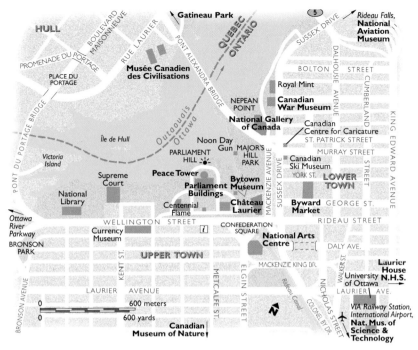

HULL

Gatineau Park

QUEBEC
ONTARIO

Rideau Falls,
**National
Aviation
Museum**

BOULEVARD MAISONNEUVE
RUE LAURIER
PROMENADE DU PORTAGE
PLACE DU PORTAGE
PONT ALEXANDRA BRIDGE
SUSSEX DRIVE

BOLTON STREET

**Musée Canadien
des Civilisations**

Royal Mint

DALHOUSIE AVENUE
CUMBERLAND

NEPEAN
POINT

**Canadian
War Museum**

KING EDWARD AVENUE

**National Gallery
of Canada**

Canadian
Centre for Caricature

ST. PATRICK STREET

PONT DU PORTAGE BRIDGE

Île de Hull

Outaouais
Ottawa

Noon Day
Gun

PARLIAMENT
HILL

MAJOR'S
HILL
PARK

MURRAY STREET

Canadian
Ski Museum

Victoria
Island

Peace Tower

YORK ST.

**LOWER
TOWN**

Supreme
Court

**Parliament
Buildings**

**Bytown
Museum**

MACKENZIE AVENUE
SUSSEX DRIVE

National
Library

Centennial
Flame

**Château
Laurier**

**Byward
Market**

GEORGE ST.

Ottawa
River
Parkway

WELLINGTON STREET

RIDEAU STREET

BRONSON
PARK

Currency
Museum

CONFEDERATION
SQUARE

**National Arts
Centre**

DALY AVE.

UPPER TOWN

MACKENZIE KING BR.

WALKER ST.
NICHOLAS STREET

**Laurier
House
N.H.S.**

KENT ST.
ELGIN STREET
METCALFE ST.

University
of Ottawa

LAURIER AVE.

BRONSON AVENUE

LAURIER AVENUE

0   600 meters
0   600 yards

Rideau Canal
COLONEL BY DR.

VIA Railway Station,
International Airport,
**Nat. Mus. of
Science &
Technology**

**Canadian
Museum of Nature**

have landed in the right place, safe both from American incursions and, on the border between Ontario and Quebec, safe from excessive Anglo-French rivalry.

The wilderness can still be sensed, not least in the broad waters of the Ottawa River flowing down from the Canadian Shield. The forest seems to close in from all around. A longstanding National Capital Commission has protected Ottawa with a green belt, torn up the railroad tracks, and laid out parks and parkways along canals and rivers. The magnificent location of the parliament buildings overlooking the river is hardly matched anywhere else in the world. There's a splendid route (*Rte. 17*) along the river to the east, where the clifftop road runs past the famous Rideau Falls and the prime minister's residence to Rockcliffe Park. In winter, civil servants skate to work along the frozen canal through the heart of the city.

For many years Ottawa had the reputation of being a dull, provincial town. The place closed down early in the evening, and night owls would take flight across the river to Hull, where Quebec laws allowed bars and nightspots to stay open an hour or two longer. As the city has grown a certain liveliness has crept in. There's lots of entertainment, interesting shops, and plenty of eating places, especially around the city's colorful Byward Market. Today Ottawa and Hull have taken on something of each other's coloring; government buildings have partly replaced the timber yards and mills that dominated Hull's townscape, and Ottawa is a place where bilingualism seems to thrive. In the old days, visitors came here mainly to see red-coated guardsmen and Mounties in front of the Houses of Parliament. This is still a great attractions, but Ottawa has become a city to be savored in its own right. ■

**Left: The Rideau
Canal penetrates
to the very heart
of Canada's
capital, leading
past one of the
city's landmarks,
the Château
Laurier.**

Parliament Hill

Parliament Hill
Visitor
information
✉ 14 Metcalf St.
☎ 613/239-5000

Information office
✉ East Block
☎ 613/992-4793

THE LIMESTONE BLUFF OVERLOOKING THE BROAD REACHES
of the Ottawa River is crowned by an extraordinary group of neo-
Gothic buildings, an expression in stone of Canada's aspirations to
nationhood. Almost every visitor to the country's capital climbs the
gentle slope up to "The Hill," which offers not only the richly decorated interior of the Houses of Parliament but also an array of statu-
ary and, in summer, a colorful display of pageantry with watchful
Mounties and a ceremonial Changing of the Guard.

Parliament Hill rises gently from
Confederation Square, the centerpiece of which is the **National
War Memorial,** a 70-foot granite arch topped by bronze figures of
Peace and Freedom and with
sculpted figures of World War I
combatants and auxiliaries. The
memorial was dedicated by King
George VI just before the outbreak
of World War II; it is the focus of
Remembrance Day observations
every November 11. Around the
square are a number of buildings
with some national significance.
The most remarkable of them is an
institution in its own right: The
Château Laurier Hotel
(1 Rideau St., Tel 613/241-1414) was
built by the Grand Trunk Railway
in 1912 and, with its towers, turrets,
steep pitched roofs, and dormer
windows, is a fine example of the
Canadian château style. The first
person to sign the guest register was
the hotel's namesake, Prime

Minister Sir Wilfred Laurier, and
the interior of the great building is
said to have seen as much politick-
ing as parliament itself, probably
because many politicians lived here.
The Grand Trunk complemented
its castle hotel with a palatial railroad terminus, but Ottawa's trains
have been banished to the distant
suburbs, and the neoclassic Union
Station is now the **Government
Conference Centre** (*2 Rideau
St., Tel 514/990-6700*). Next to it is
the **National Arts Centre** (*53
Elgin St., Tel 818/755-1111*), which
dates from 1967.

The parliamentary buildings
form three sides of a great open
forecourt some 650 feet square. The
dominant feature is the slim **Peace
Tower,** 300 feet high, offering an
unrivaled view of Ottawa from its
viewing gallery. The tower rises
from the **Centre Block,** rebuilt in
the 1920s after a disastrous fire had
destroyed the original 1866 building. Housing both the Commons
and Senate, the Centre Block is
flanked by the East and West Blocks,
once capable of accommodating the
whole apparatus of government and
civil service, but today providing
office space for members of parliament and senators, committee
rooms, and the like. A number of
rooms in the East Block have been
restored to their 19th-century
appearance. Linked to the far side of
the Centre Block is the great
Library, which, with its flying but-

*Red carpets,
murals, and a
gilded ceiling
make a dignified
setting for the
deliberations of
the nation's
Senate.*

tresses and conical cap, is perhaps the most extraordinary of all these great Gothic Revival structures.

Choice of the Gothic style seems to have been influenced by two great building complexes nearing completion at the time—Britain's Houses of Parliament and Washington's neoclassic Capitol. Given that Canada's parliamentary structures were to be closely modeled on those of the mother country and that the new Palace of Westminster was the supreme example of Gothic Revival, there could have been little doubt about the outcome of the architectural competition, though the designs submitted included styles ranging from Norman to Venetian. The buildings are as rich in intriguing detail as they are in grandiose spaces for the rituals of rule. Carvings includes humorously grotesque gargoyles and other figures, while interior decorations endeavor to express the character and history of the nation. Thus stained-glass windows in the House of Commons display the floral emblems of the country's provinces and territories, while the Senate has a frieze carved with Canadian plants and animals, as well as large-scale murals with scenes from World War I. The white pine paneling of the library matches the magnificence of its exterior; a pale statue of Queen Victoria seems to admonish readers to silence.

Victoria appears again outside, her statue gracing the grounds to the left of the Centre Building, while her great-great-granddaughter, Elizabeth II, can be seen astride her mount, Centennial, in a similar location to the right. There's equal symmetry in the statues of two of the Fathers of Confederation, Sir John A. Macdonald (to the right) and Sir George-Etienne Cartier (to the left). Many other statues on the grounds commemorate Canada's leading figures. ■

A forest of flagpoles on Ottawa's Parliament Hill

Museums of the capital

AS BEFITS A CAPITAL CITY, THE OTTAWA AREA HAS MORE museum space per capita than any other Canadian city. Superbly housed in impressive modern buildings, the Museum of Civilization and the National Gallery of Canada attract visitors from all over the world, but there are many other collections of interest too.

National Gallery of Canada

✉ 380 Sussex Drive

☎ 613/990-1985

NATIONAL GALLERY OF CANADA

Since 1988 the country's national art collections have been magnificently housed in this monumental modern building of granite, glass, and concrete, a masterpiece by Israel-born Moshe Safdie, the architect who first strode onto the Canadian scene with Expo 67's Habitat. Looking across an inlet of the river towards Parliament Hill, the gallery stands on what is probably the capital's second most prominent site. The glittering prisms of Safdie's Great Hall pay homage to the forms of the parliamentary library opposite, while the immensely long, sloping corridor leading to it was inspired by the Scala Regia in the Vatican.

The gallery has fine collections of photographs, prints, and drawings, and of contemporary Inuit art, and mounts an ambitious program of temporary exhibits. There is an Asian Gallery with mostly Indian artworks spanning the period from the third century A.D. to modern times, while the extensive contemporary art collection focuses on American as well as Canadian art of the last few decades. The European and American Galleries house a fine collection representing many aspects of the evolution of Western art from medieval times to the present. There are paintings by Simone Martini, Hans Memling, Cranach, Rembrandt, and El Greco, and a superb bust by Bernini. The original of one the most famous Canadian history pictures is here,

"The Death of General Wolfe," painted by American artist Benjamin West in 1770. Constable and Turner are represented, as are many 19th-century French painters, among them Corot, Cezanne, Monet, Pissarro, and Dégas, as well as Van Gogh ("Iris"). The 20th-century art extends from a decorative Klimt ("Hope I") to a dynamic Jackson Pollock ("No. 29").

Inevitably and rightly, the heart of the gallery is its vast and comprehensive Canadian collections. The paintings and other works benefit enormously from the sophistication of the surroundings in which they are displayed. Highlights from early days include a sumptuous mid-18th-century tabernacle from Quebec, charming portraits by William Bercy (1744–1813) and Antoine Plamondon (1804–1895), and immensely appealing naive wall paintings, which once decorated the living room of a Nova Scotia shipowner. Perhaps the most extraordinary single exhibit in the whole gallery is the **Rideau Street Convent Chapel** of 1888, a glorious neo-Gothic fantasy of slim columns and fan vaults saved from demolition and reerected here.

Plenty of space is given to innovative artists like Montreal's Paul-Emile Borduas (1905–1960), pioneer of Automatisme, but many visitors will be drawn again and again to the rooms containing works by those most Canadian of all painters, the Group of Seven and their associates (see pp. 186–7).

Right: Artist Paul Kane (1810–1871) made many trips across a Canada still largely unknown, recording people and landscapes. His majestic portrayal of Blackfoot Chief Big Snake was painted in 1856.

Facing Parliament Hill on the far bank of the Ottawa River, the superb Musée Canadien des Civilisations has helped to link the city of Hull to the capital.

Musée Canadien des Civilisations

- ✉ 100 Rue Laurier, Hull
- ☎ 819/776-7000
- ◷ Closed Mon. mid-Oct.–May
- 💲 $$$

They are all here, represented by some of their finest and most famous works ("The Jack Pine" by Tom Thomson, "Red Maple" by A.Y. Jackson, "North Shore, Lake Superior" by Lawren S. Harris, "Tangled Garden" by J.E.H. MacDonald). Sketches painted on wood shingles are a special treat, as are the panels painted to decorate the summer cottage of the group's patron, Dr. James MacCullum.

MUSÉE CANADIEN DES CIVILISATIONS

In contrast to the rational, crystalline character of the National Gallery of Art, this distinctive building complex takes its inspiration from flowing sculptural forms that resemble rock outcrops molded by the action of wind, rain, and ice. Designed by the Métis architect Douglas Cardinal, it was inaugurated in 1989 to house almost four million pieces explaining Canadian history and, to a lesser extent, world history and ethnology.

Framing a classic view of the parliament buildings atop the bluff on the far bank of the Ottawa River, the museum consists of two main parts linked by a basement: To the north, the serpentine terraces of the six-story Canadian Shield Wing housing administration, conservation, and storage functions, and to

the south the columns, high glazed walls, sinuous roofline, and copper domes of the Glacier Wing: This makes a dramatic setting for the museum's extensive displays, as well as housing a conventional auditorium, an IMAX theater, the **Canadian Postal Museum,** and the always lively **Children's Museum.**

The foyer, entered at street level, commands a view down into the curvilinear Grand Hall, its tall columns matched by a splendid line of totem poles. The hall is devoted to the art and culture of the native peoples of British Columbia's northwest coast, and also features copies of several chieftains' houses. While other galleries have both temporary and permanent exhibitions, the museum's other main display space is the third-floor Canada Hall, which takes visitors on a highly enjoyable trip through a thousand years of the country's history. The elaborately staged scenes feature both reconstructed buildings and a host of authentic artifacts. They include a Viking encampment, a Basque whaling station, a town square in New France, a voyageurs' camp, British officers' quarters, an early Ontario street, and a prairie settlement with railroad station, Ukrainian church, and grain elevators. ■

More places to visit around Ottawa

BYTOWN MUSEUM

Colonel By's canal descends to the level of the Ottawa River down a stately flight of eight locks, massively built out of limestone hewed from the adjacent bluff. The three-story stone structure that served as his commissariat is now the Bytown Museum, the oldest remaining building in the capital, with displays on the canal and those who constructed it.
☎ 613/234-4570 ⏰ Closed weekends mid-Oct.–mid-May 💲 $

CANADIAN WAR MUSEUM

The hundred-year-old building housing the national war museum has a forbidding air about it, very much in contrast to its welcoming neighbor, the National Gallery. The fascinating collection includes arms and uniforms, vehicles, and models, ingenious dioramas, and works of art. There are reminders of the blood spilled 1,000 years ago, when Vikings and Skraelings (Innu Indians) came to blows, and of many subsequent warlike episodes, including the War of 1812.
✉ 330 Sussex Dr. ☎ 800/555-5621 or 819/776-8600 ⏰ Closed Mon. in winter 💲 $

CANADIAN MUSEUM OF NATURE

Following the departure of the Museum of Civilization to its new building in Hull, the displays of the Museum of Nature have the whole of this splendid early 20th-century building to themselves. The exhibits tell the story of the earth and its creatures in an often fascinating way. The dinosaur displays are outstanding, and there is a very full account of Canada's wonderfully varied wildlife. A new gallery takes visitors into the frozen, but far from lifeless northland.
✉ Corner of Metcalfe St. & McLeod Ave. ☎ 613/566-4700 💲 $

GATINEAU PARK

One of the great attractions of life in the Ottawa area is this splendid 135-square-mile forest park on the Quebec side of the Ottawa River. Prime Minister Mackenzie King was largely responsible for its preservation, and his estate at Moorside (*Tel 613/239-5000, closed Oct.–late-May*) has an odd collection of ruins on the grounds. The name of the government retreat at Meech Lake entered the language after the accord reached here in 1979 failed to solve the country's perennial constitutional crisis regarding Quebec.

LAURIER HOUSE
NATIONAL HISTORIC SITE

This villa of 1878, with its charming verandas, became the home of Prime Minister Sir Wilfred Laurier in 1897 and passed to his successor William Mackenzie King in 1921. Now a national historic site, it contains many mementos of these two great prime ministers, among them the famous crystal ball used by Mackenzie King, a noted spiritualist.
✉ 335 Laurier Ave. East ☎ 613/992-8142 ⏰ Closed Mon. 💲 $

NATIONAL AVIATION MUSEUM

Beneath the roof of this huge, triangular hanger is a superb array of aircraft that gives a very complete picture of how aviation has evolved in the 20th century. A copy of the *Silver Dart* that flew over Nova Scotia's Baddeck Bay in 1909 evokes the early days of heavier-than-air flight in Canada. There are aircraft from both world wars, as well as the commercial planes that opened up the north. The greatest bush plane of them all, the De Havilland Beaver, has a prominent place. By contrast, there are only fragments of the Avro Arrow, the supersonic interceptor, whose cancellation on Black Friday (February 20, 1959) ended Canada's aspirations as an air superpower.
✉ Rockcliffe Airport, 3 miles NE of downtown off Rockcliffe Parkway ☎ 613/993-2010 ⏰ Closed Mon. 💲 $

NATIONAL MUSEUM OF SCIENCE
& TECHNOLOGY

A lighthouse moved from Nova Scotia signals the site of this museum, whose exhibits include many hands-on attractions as well as vintage vehicles, magnificent steam locomotives, shipping exhibits, and much more.
✉ 1867 St. Laurent Blvd., 3 miles east from downtown ☎ 613/991-3044 ⏰ Closed Mon. Sept.–April 💲 $$$ ■

Kingston & the St. Lawrence

Kingston
 157E2

**Visitor
information**

✉ 209 Ontario St.
☎ 613/548-4415
🕐 Closed Sat.–Sun.
   fall–spring

SITED AT THE POINT WHERE THE ST. LAWRENCE FLOWS out of Lake Ontario and at the terminus of the Rideau Canal, this old harbor town enjoyed a brief moment of glory between 1841 and 1843, when it served as the capital of the Province of Canada.

KINGSTON

The Loyalist settlement founded as "King's Town" in 1784 had been preceded by a French fur-trading post established in 1673, which, as Fort Frontenac, fell to the British in 1758. During the War of 1812, Kingston became an important military and naval base. The Royal Navy sailed away in 1852, but there is still a strong military presence in the shape of defense colleges and a nearby Canadian Forces base.

Early Kingston was built of timber, but by the 19th century masons were fashioning the local blue-gray limestone into fine houses and public buildings. Enough remain today to justify the town's appellation as the "Limestone City." Dominating the waterfront parkland, the massive neoclassic **City Hall** (*216 Brock St.*) begun in 1842 embodies Kingston's aspirations as a capital city. Built later in the century and almost matching City Hall in grandeur is nearby **St. George's Cathedral,** while

the earlier **Court House** of 1826 is a model of Georgian restraint. Architectural restraint had flown out of the window by the time **Bellevue House** (*35 Centre St., Tel 613/545-8666*) was built for a wealthy local grocer in 1841. In 1848–49 this extravagantly picturesque Italianate residence was let to future Prime Minister John A. Macdonald, who called it his "Eyetalian Willa." The house has been refurbished in the style of his time there.

A stroll along Kingston's waterfront is full of interest. There is a busy marina, the ferry terminal to Wolfe Island, and a clutch of museums. The **Marine Museum of the Great Lakes** (*B55 Ontario St., Tel 613/542-2261, closed weekends Jan.–March*) tells the fascinating story of hundreds of years of navigation on the lakes, and close by is the **Pump House Steam Museum** (*23 Ontario St., Tel 613/546-4696, closed late Sept.–May*), where pride of place is occupied by massive stationary steam engines. The museum in the **Murney Tower** (*Tel 613/ 544-9925, closed late Sept.–early May*) explains the military significance of this martello tower, one of several built in 1846–48 at a time of border tensions with the United States.

But Kingston's most imposing stronghold is on the far side of the harbor, beyond the Royal Military College on the promontory. Formidable **Fort Henry** (*Tel 613/542-7388, closed Oct.–mid-May*) was built overlooking Navy Bay in 1832–36 to protect the naval

The sharp marching precision of the military parades at Fort Henry keep the province in step with its past.

shipyard there. No shot was ever fired in anger at Fort Henry, but you wouldn't know that to judge from the gunfire accompanying the summertime military parades and maneuvers staged here, much to the delight of younger tourists.

THE THOUSAND ISLANDS
The first 35 miles of the St. Lawrence downstream from Kingston was known to the French as *le lac des mille îles*, the Lake of the Thousand Islands, and most visitors agree that a four-figure total can be justified. American raiders lurking among the islands harassed British convoys as they made their way up and down the St. Lawrence during the War of 1812. After the war the frontier was settled in an amicable way; the boundary line follows the main channel, and no island is divided between the two countries.

The prettily wooded islands have been a playground for a century and a half. The wealthy got here first, staying in luxury hotels or building extravagant residences, of which none was more extravagant than **Boldt Castle,** built by the Austrian owner of New York's Waldorf-Astoria, whose chef, it is said, was inspired by sojourns here

to invent Thousand Island salad dressing. Nowadays it's mostly weekenders who throng the islands, arriving here by cruiser or canoe. Other visitors wanting to get onto the water can take water taxis or join a cruise from Kingston *(Kingston 1,000 Island Cruises, Tel 613/549-5544).* Landlubbers can enjoy this wonderful watery landscape from the **Thousand Islands Parkway** and from the viewing tower close to the Thousand Islands International Bridge connecting Ontario and New York State.

UPPER CANADA VILLAGE
The area along today's Thousand Islands Parkway was settled by Loyalists in the late 18th century. Upper Canada Village is one of the most entertaining restorations of its kind in Canada. Consisting of some three dozen buildings rescued from flooding by the St. Lawrence Seaway project, as well as dwellings ranging from the primitive structures of early days to fine houses in brick and stone, it has mills, schools, stores, churches, a forge, printing press and tavern, all staffed by convincingly clad 19th-century folk engaged in appropriate activities. ■

Cruising on the St. Lawrence River among the Thousand Islands

Upper Canada Village
- ⓜ 157F2
- ✉ 7 miles east of Morrisburg on Hwy. 2
- ☎ 613/543-3704
- 🕐 Closed mid-Oct.–mid-May
- 💲 $$$

Toronto

◪ 157E2

**Visitor
information**
✉ 207 Queens
     Quay West
☎ 416/203-2500
     or 800-363-1990

OTTAWA MAY BE THE NATION'S CAPITAL, BUT TORONTO IS the epicenter of Canada's financial and commercial life, and, as far as Anglo-Canada is concerned, its cultural life, too. Following its latest (1997) amalgamation with outlying municipalities, Toronto has become North America's fourth largest city, its dynamism proclaimed by its splendid cluster of downtown skyscrapers, its aspirations indicated by the immensely tall CN tower. Despite its great size, it's a livable city, with clean and relatively safe public spaces, cohesive neighborhoods, every imaginable kind of shopping and entertainment opportunity, lakeside amenities, and other green spaces. Some of the country's finest museums and galleries are here, too, most notably the Art Gallery of Ontario and the magnificent Royal Ontario Museum.

Apart from the lakeside, there seem to be few natural features to compete with the dominance of man-made structures: To the north of downtown, the ancient shoreline of the prehistoric ancestor of Lake Ontario is marked by a ridge that makes a site for prestige houses, but otherwise Toronto is flat. However, threading through the built-up area is a network of wooded ravines carved out by streams, such as the Don, that flow south into the lake, an asset described as equivalent to Venice's canals and San Francisco's hills.

The first European to visit the site of present-day Toronto seems to have been the Frenchman Étienne Brulé, who came here in 1615 along an old native trail from Lake Huron, later used by English and Dutch fur traders from New York. In the early 18th century, the French built a fort to interfere with this trade, but it was abandoned in 1759. In the late 18th century, British interest in the area was boosted by the arrival of Loyalists who settled along the shore of Lake Ontario; in 1794 the choice of a capital of newly created Upper Canada finally fell on Toronto, renamed York in honor of George

Toronto's contemporary skyline, seen from the islands sheltering the harbor

The once dominant bulk of the Royal York Hotel (1929) is now dwarfed by Toronto's downtown towers.

Lester B. Pearson International Airport

Summerville

Casa Loma
Spadina House
Corso Italia

VERMONT SQUARE
VERMONT STREET
SPADINA ROAD
BATHURST STREET
AVENUE ROAD
YONGE STREET
MOUNT PLEASANT ROAD

Dupont
RAMSDEN PARK
Rosedale

SIBELIUS SQUARE
Spadina
Museum of the History of Medicine
KETCHUM PARK
YORKVILLE
Metro Toronto Library
Ontario Science Centre

Spadina
Bathurst
St. George
Bay
Bloor Yonge

BLOOR STREET WEST
BLOOR STREET EAST

Royal Ontario Museum
Bata Shoe Museum
Gardiner Museum of Ceramic Art
St. Paul's Church

McLaughlin Planetarium
Museum
QUEEN'S PARK

University of Toronto
QUEENS PARK CRES. W.
QUEENS PARK CRES. E.
Ontario Parliament Buildings
Wellesley
JARVIS STREET

Ontario Hydro
Queen's Park
Maple Leaf Gardens

COLLEGE STREET
COLLEGE STREET
CARLTON STREET
College
ALLAN GARDENS

Kensington Market
CHINATOWN
UNIVERSITY AVENUE

The Craft Gallery
St. Patrick
Eaton Centre

DUNDAS STREET WEST
ALEXANDRA PARK
Art Gallery of Ontario
The Grange
Museum for Textiles
Dundas
DUNDAS ST. E.
Mackenzie House

GRANGE PARK
Toronto City Hall
NATHAN PHILLIPS SQUARE
Campbell House
Osgoode
Queen
QUEEN ST. EAST

QUEEN STREET WEST
Royal Alexandra Theatre
Old City Hall
Thomson Gallery
ST. JAMES' PARK

KING STREET WEST
St. Andrew
KING ST. EAST
King

VICTORIA MEMORIAL SQUARE
SPADINA AVENUE
CLARENCE SQUARE
Roy Thomson Hall
Royal Bank Plaza
T.D. Centre
FRONT ST. EAST
St. Lawrence Market

FRONT STREET WEST
Union

Fort York
GARDINER EXPRESSWAY
CN Tower
Union Station
GARDINER EXPRESSWAY

SkyDome
QUEENS QUAY E.

Ontario Place
QUEENS QUAY W.
HARBOURFRONT
York Quay Centre
Queen's Quay Terminal
Island Ferry Docks

Toronto Harbour
Toronto Islands

0   600 meters
0   600 yards

N

III's second son (the native name Toronto was reinstated in 1834, when it was incorporated as a city).

Well into the 19th century, growth was slow, and the little frontier settlement seems to have deserved the derisive epithet of "Muddy York." But it was as if the inhabitants were aware of the place's destiny; the sacking of the town by the Americans during the War of 1812 was soon made good, and the attempt by Kingston to usurp York's capital city status was beaten off. For many years, a tightly knit group of mostly British merchants (collectively known as the Family Compact) dominated government and social life as well as commerce, and made quite sure that the bulk of Upper Canada's trade passed through their hands.

When the Erie Canal was completed in 1825, Toronto no longer had to rely on Montreal as a port of entry but could use New York, the beginnings of an American tie which has remained important ever since. As Ontario developed throughout the 19th century, Toronto became the natural focus for its agricultural products, its industry, and its commerce. The violence and disorder of the Mackenzie Rebellion of 1837 (see p. 36) was seen as a disgraceful interruption of the city's stately progress, based on virtue as much as effort. Muddy York metamorphosed into "Toronto the Good," a sternly Protestant town of moral rectitude and the strictest Sunday observance.

Only in the mid-20th century was its utterly Anglo-Saxon ethos diluted, as immigrants arrived, first from northern, then from southern Europe, then from all around the world. Today's Toronto has a population of striking diversity, visible over the city as a whole, and not just in the lively neighborhoods with their distinctive Greek, Italian, Portuguese, Indian, and Chinese communities.

No visit to Toronto is complete if just the center and the lakefront are explored. Among the inner suburbs, choose from **Yorkville** (once hippy, now just hip), **Corso Italia** on St. Clair Street, **Chinatown** between the University of Toronto and Spadina Avenue, or **Kensington Market,** the arrival point for many of the successive waves of migrants, once Jewish, then Portuguese, now predominantly Caribbean. The inner city is served by excellent public transportation (*Visitor information, Tel 416/393-4636*), but to reach some of the many attractions in the outer suburbs or beyond, it may pay to rent a car. ■

One of the many vessels that dock at Toronto's Queen's Wharf

Toronto's lakefront & islands

OVER THE YEARS TORONTO HAS STEADILY EXTENDED itself southward into the lake, leaving Front Street (once lapped by water) high and dry and creating a long sliver of man-made land up to 1,800 feet across. Mainly a working area, with docks, commercial buildings, and railroad tracks, it was also the embarkation point for the pleasure steamers that used to ply the lake. As the St. Lawrence Seaway neared completion in 1959, plans were made to extend docking facilities, but the expected boom in harbor traffic never came. From the 1970s on, the waterfront has been colonized by hotels, offices, apartments, and a mixture of marinas, cafés, restaurants, shops, places of entertainment, and a thriving antiques market. New paving, landscaping, and placing of public sculpture has added to the area's attractiveness, and what is now called the Harbourfront is an essential part of any tour of Toronto. As well as a stroll along the waterfront, there are two other unmissable experiences: a dizzy trip up the CN Tower for a vertiginous view of the city, and a ride on one of the ferries to the miniature Toronto Islands archipelago, with the shining towers of the downtown as a magnificent backdrop.

CN Tower
- ⊠ 301 Front St.
- ☎ 416/868-6937
- Ⓜ Subway: Union, then CN Skywalk
- $ $$$

SkyDome
- ⊠ 1 Blue Jays Way
- ☎ 416/341-3663
- Ⓜ Subway: Union, then CN Skywalk
- $ $$$

Toronto Islands
- ☎ 416/392-8193
- ⊠ Island Ferry Docks, Queens Quay East
- $ $$$

CN TOWER
Toronto's unmistakable urban icon shoots an extraordinary 1,815 feet into the air, a fluted concrete column contrasting with the bulbous SkyDome crouching nearby. It is still the tallest freestanding structure in the world, high enough for the Skypod and its minaretlike spike to pierce low cloud cover, or for visitors to look down on aircraft heading for the city's international airport. The tower was built in 1976, not only as a telecommunications facility but as the centerpiece for a vast urban redevelopment project that never took place. In any event, it has more than earned its keep as a visitor attraction.

The view is the thing, of course, both from the observation decks of the Skypod (1,136 feet up) or the even higher Space Deck (1,465 feet). For those unscathed by vertigo on the ride up the outside elevator, there is the additional challenge of the glass floor, with only space between your feet and the SkyDome's infield far below.

Left: The sleek steel-and-glass towers of Toronto's financial district frame a view of the CN Tower.

There's a revolving restaurant, and, at the base of the tower, more thrills such as laser games.

SKYDOME

The SkyDome bills itself as the World's Greatest Entertainment Centre, but everyone knows it as the shrine where up to 53,000 of the faithful can express their devotion to the Blue Jays, World Series champions in 1992 and 1993. The Toronto Argonauts (Canadian football) also play here, as does the Blizzard soccer team; other entertainment ranges from circuses to pop concerts and ice shows. The SkyDome is an attraction in itself, with guided tours taking in a video show and explanations of how the world's largest retractable roof is made to open and close.

The roof of the SkyDome weighs 12,100 tons and rises to a height of 300 feet.

TORONTO ISLANDS

The 18 verdant islands sheltering the broad waters of Toronto's fin natural harbor have long been a valuable refuge from the pressures of city life. The ramshackle but charming residences on **Ward's Island** and **Algonquin Island** at the eastern extremity of the archipelago are the remains of a more extensive settled area that the Parks Department is converting to public open space over a period of years. The ferries terminate at Ward's Island, at Hanlan's Point near the busy Island Airport, and at the Centre Island Dock, close to the popular amusement park. With no competition from cars, the best way of exploring the nearly 4-mile-long crescent of islands is by renting a bicycle. ■

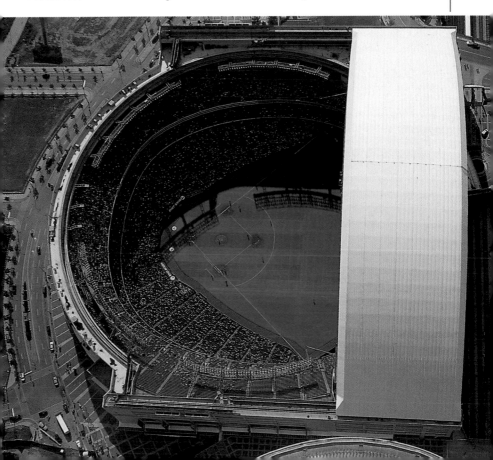

Toronto walk: Union Station to City Hall

The streets in Toronto's heart are lined with buildings that provide ample evidence of Canada's architectural heritage. Between Union Station and the Eaton Centre are treasured landmarks, innovative skyscrapers, and fine examples of modern architecture.

Linked by underground passageway, both the **Royal York Hotel** and **Union Station ❶** recall the great days of train travel and tourism. The station—the third Union Station to stand on this site—was begun in 1913 and took 17 years to complete. Behind its long facade with its central colonnade is an imposing ticket hall 88 feet high and lit from each end by tall arched windows.

Built in 1929, the dignified art deco giant of a hotel makes a fine partner for the station, and is one of several buildings in Canada that for a while could boast of being the largest in the British Empire. The Canadian Pacific later added the steep roof to harmonize with its other château-style hotels. From the level beneath the hotel's sumptuous lobby, the city's downtown walkway (called PATH) leads through the Royal Bank Plaza, then, on the far side of Bay Street, up into **BCE Place.** This development of 1993 with its stunningly elegant galleria incorporates one of the oldest surviving stone buildings in Toronto, the Commercial Bank of the Midland District, which had to be dismantled and moved south 20 yards to fit into the new scheme.

At the corner of Front and Yonge Streets, another old bank building, the ornate Bank of Montreal, houses the **Hockey Hall of Fame** (*Tel 416/360-7765*). Walk east along Front Street past the **St. Lawrence Centre for the Arts.** The south side of the street has a number of 19th-century warehouses and former chandlers' stores, reminders of the one-time proximity of the lakeside. There's now an intriguing mix of shops and cafés. The rear of the 1892 Flatiron or **Gooderham Building** has a wonderful mural, with its turret making an appealing composition when seen against the background of the office towers to the west.

Toronto's Flatiron Building of 1892 predates its namesake in New York by 11 years.

Follow Front Street East for another 400 yards to the corner of Jarvis Street and find **St. Lawrence Market ❷** (*92 Front St. E., Tel 416/392-7219, closed Sun.-Mon.*). This cornucopia of tempting comestibles is at its liveliest on Saturdays, when people come from all over town to pick and choose from the marvelous fresh produce in the North Building's farmers market. The South Building incorporates parts of the 1845 City Hall, and the old council chamber is now the **Market Gallery** with exhibits on historical themes.

Just a few paces north of the St. Lawrence Market is the corner of Jarvis Street and King Street East, featuring the richly decorated **St. Lawrence Hall ❸.** Splendidly restored for the 1967 Centennial, the hall was the city's mid-19th century social and cultural center. The little oasis of **St. James' Park,** behind it, is an excellent place to pause and take stock. To the west, the spire of **St. James'**

Old City Hall, one of the landmark structures of late 19th-century Toronto

See city map p. 172

Union Station (Subway: Union)

1.8 miles

Allow 1 day

Nathan Phillips Square
(Subway: Dundass or Queen)

NOT TO BE MISSED

- Hockey Hall of Fame
- St. Lawrence Market

Cathedral *(65 Church St., Tel 416/364-7865)* rises more than 300 feet and for many years was Toronto's principal landmark.

Continue west along King Street West, where the early evolution of the skyscraper can be traced. The 18-story **Canadian Pacific Building,** 400 yards along at the corner of Yonge Street, was one of the tallest buildings outside New York when completed in 1915. It was outdone in 1931 by the **Bank of Commerce** at No. 25 King Street West, a stylish tiered tower of 34 stories with a wealth of Canadian symbolism in its fascinating decoration. This really was the tallest building in the British Empire, not only at the time of its completion but for 35 years thereafter. Continue along King Street West for another hundred yards; on the south side, beyond the intersection with Bay Street, is the group of classic modernist towers in black metal and bronze glass that make up the **Toronto**

Dominion Centre. The first two towers to be built, between 1963 and 1969, were the work of Mies van der Rohe, famous for his minimalist approach to architecture. The shopping concourse beneath the plaza marks the beginning of the PATH system.

Continue a half mile north along Bay Street to **Old City Hall** ❹. With its beckoning tower, this center of municipal government was ceremonially opened in 1899, after taking ten years to build and going more than ten times over the original budget. It's a splendid example of the late 19th-century Richardson Romanesque style, built in textured two-toned sandstone. The extravagantly ornate interior now serves as law courts.

Public protests saved Old City Hall from demolition as part of the site clearance for the construction of the Eaton Centre, its immediate neighbor to the east. The multilevel **Eaton Centre** *(Yonge St., Tel 416/598-8700)* itself, spreading 900 feet along Yonge Street, is worth more than a casual glance. Beneath its glazed roof is one of the finest—and most popular—shopping centers in the world, with more than 300 stores as well as a famous flight of sculpted Canada geese.

At the Eaton Centre follow Queen Street West 200 yards west to **Nathan Phillips Square,** the plaza fronting **City Hall,** to end the walk (see p. 182). ■

The Great Lakes

The massed towers of Toronto's downtown look southward over oceanlike Lake Ontario toward the shore of New York State, 35 miles away. Vast though the lake is, it is the second smallest in area of the five Great Lakes, which collectively make up the largest body of freshwater in the world. Connected by waterways and discharging into the mighty St. Lawrence River, the lakes formed a natural route, tempting European explorers into the heart of the continent. Today, the basin in which they lie is the home of no less than half of the population of Canada and one-fifth of that of the United States, a focus of commerce, industry, communications, tourism, and of cross-border cooperation.

The shape of the lakes reflects the underlying geological structure. While Lakes Huron and Michigan arc around the Michigan basin, Erie and Ontario share the southwest-northeast axis of the Appalachian Mountains. The outline of austere Lake Superior is influenced by the structure of the ancient Precambrian rock of the Canadian Shield (see p. 20). The largest (31,700 square miles) and deepest (average 483 feet) of the lakes, Superior is also the most elemental, a true inland sea where waves can reach 50 feet in height, and whose chill waters are reputed never to give up the bodies of the drowned. Michigan (22,300 square miles) is the only lake with no Canadian shore. The main body of Lake Huron (23,000 square

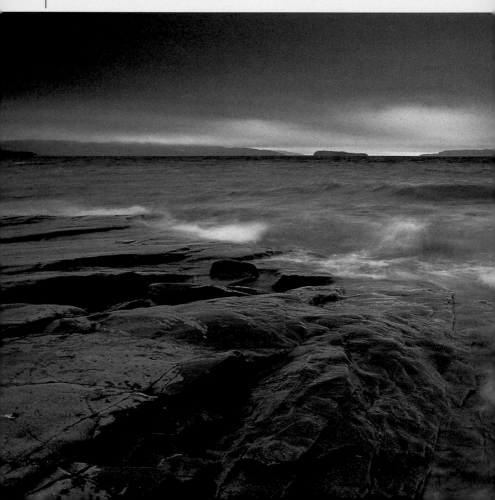

miles) is almost separated from the North Channel and Georgian Bay by the line of the Niagara Escarpment that forms the Bruce Peninsula and Manitoulin Island. Bigger than Lake Ontario in area, Erie is shallow (average depth 62 feet), and contains by far the smallest quantity of water of all the lakes (116 cubic miles compared with Superior's 2,900 cubic miles). So it regularly freezes over in winter.

The change in level from Lake Superior (about 600 feet above sea level) to Lake Ontario (about 243 feet above sea level) is taken up by rapids at Sault Ste. Marie between Lakes Superior and Huron, and along the Niagara River between Lakes Erie and Ontario. But the most dramatic change of level is the 160-foot drop of the world-famous Niagara Falls. Natives and early explorers overcame these obstacles to navigation by

laborious portages. Canals were built at an early stage—1798 at Sault Ste. Marie, the first Welland Canal (see p. 192) bypassing Niagara in 1829. They steadily improved, enabling increasingly larger ships to travel not only from lake to lake, but, via the St. Lawrence River, to and from the Atlantic. The final, triumphant stage in improvement of the waterway was the completion of the St. Lawrence Seaway in 1959. This monumental joint Canada-U.S. venture involving the construction of new canals, locks, and channels between Montreal and Lake Ontario allowed oceangoing vessels ("salties") to make the 2,355-mile journey inland from Anticosti at the river's mouth to Duluth, Minnesota, at the far western end of Lake Superior. It was hailed at the time, not only as a stupendous engineering achievement but also as a symbol of goodwill and cooperation; both Queen Elizabeth II and President Dwight D. Eisenhower attended the opening ceremony, on June 26, 1959. Much was made of the effective addition of 8,300 miles of coastline to the two countries and of the galvanizing effect the seaway would have on their economies. But time has shown that the seaway has its limits. Ice impedes navigation for part of the year, and salties are limited to about 30,000 tons, thus excluding the largest ocean vessels.

The seaway was a symbol of 1950s and 1960s optimism about economic growth. In the 1970s, 1980s, and 1990s, the Great Lakes were seen more as an object lesson in the dire environmental effects of that growth. Eutrophication, the reduction in fish numbers, and the identification of more than 300 potentially harmful chemical compounds and of 42 "hot spots" of concentrated pollution all contributed to public concern. The Great Lakes Water Quality Agreement, signed by Canada and the United States in 1972, has led to the expenditure of billions of dollars to improve water quality, with sometimes dramatic results. But there is still a long way to go before the Lakes are once more the "sweetwater seas," about which French Jesuit missionaries rhapsodized. ■

A view from the north shore of Ontario's inland sea—Lake Superior

Royal Ontario Museum

✉ 100 Queen's Park
☎ 416/586-8000
🚇 Subway: Museum
💲 $$$

SIX MILLION OBJECTS AND MORE THAN 40 GALLERIES make the largest museum in Canada a place for repeated visits. You approach the galleries through a superb octagonal rotunda, its domed ceiling sumptuously decorated with mosaics representing the world cultures. Four great cedarwood totem poles, carved by craftspeople of the Haida and Nisga'a nations of the Northwest, reach up through the museum's stairwells.

On the ground floor, exhibits of the outstanding Chinese collections include a wonderful array of decorative, ceremonial, and functional objects of many kinds. The centerpiece of the T.T. Tsui Galleries is a Ming Tomb, the only complete example in the Western world. Probably conceived as the last resting place of a 17th-century warrior, it consists of a processional way leading past archways and monumental figures of animals and people to the tumulus, or burial mound. The design of the Bishop White Gallery of Temple Art evokes all the atmosphere of a 14th-century temple, and features life-size representations of Buddhist figures as well as large-scale mural paintings.

Among the natural history displays on the second floor, the perennially popular dinosaurs draw crowds of old and young. More than a dozen skeletons are artfully posed in settings resembling the Jurassic and Cretaceous landscapes in which these doomed giants roamed. If you venture into the Bat Cave, you'll be treated to an unnervingly realistic encounter with thousands of bats and other denizens, while closer to home stuffed Canadian birds and an elaborate diorama show the life of Ontario wetlands.

The ancient world of the Mediterranean can be thoroughly explored on the third floor, thanks to the museum's exceptionally wide-ranging collection of Egyptian antiquities and Greek and Roman artifacts. There are masks and mummies of outstanding quality, as well as casts of wall reliefs from the famous temple of Queen Hatshepsut. Greek sculptures are arranged to superb effect in a court. The evolution of European decorative arts from the Middle Ages onward is traced in the Samuel European Galleries, where exhibits include arms and armor, selections from Canada's largest costume collection, and a series of elaborately re-created period rooms.

On the museum's lower level, there are more re-created interiors: The Sigmund Samuel Canadiana Gallery is devoted to the culture and decorative arts of both French and British Canada from the 17th to the early 19th centuries. ∎

As well as being a popular visitor attraction, the ROM is an important research center.

Art Gallery of Ontario

✉ 317 Dundas St. West

☎ 416/979-6648

🚇 Subway: St. Patrick

💲 Donation $

TORONTO'S GREAT GALLERY OF ART IS STRONG IN European and Canadian art, but its collection of Henry Moore sculpture is unrivaled. The museum has been enriched and extended many times since the early 20th century, when it inherited The Grange, the splendid Georgian mansion that served as the principal stronghold of Toronto's 19th-century Family Compact.

The European collections include many old masters, among them Brueghel the Younger, Tintoretto, Rembrandt, Frans Hals, de la Tour, and Poussin. Most of the late 19th- and early 20th-century movements in painting are represented; among the pictures by the French Impressionists are canvases by Monet, Gauguin, Dégas, and Renoir, and there are works by Chagall, Picasso, Dufy, and Modigliani. The evolution of Canadian art can be followed, both in Quebec, with fine pictures by artists such as Joseph Legare and James Morrice, and most comprehensively of all, in English Canada, where there is a splendid selection of works by the Group of Seven (see pp.186–7) and their associates. A real attraction is an innovative installation where you are taken through an intimate encounter with one of Canada's modern masterpieces.

The setting for the magnificent collection of Henry Moore sculptures dates from the 1974 and was designed by the artist himself. The recent 55-million-dollar extensions to the gallery have left plenty of room for contemporary works. One superb feature is the Tannenbaum Sculpture Atrium, whose glass south wall has wonderfully reintegrated The Grange with the modern museum building. ∎

The gallery's collection of Henry Moore's works contains several "Reclining Figures," one of the sculptor's favorite themes.

More places to visit in Toronto

BATA SHOE MUSEUM

From modest beginnings in what is now the Czech Republic, the Bata firm became the world's largest shoe manufacturer. With more than 10,000 items in the witty shoebox building designed by Raymond Moriyama, the museum tells the story of footwear in an informative and highly entertaining way.

✉ 327 Bloor St. West ☎ 416/979-7799
🕐 Closed Mon. 🚇 Subway: St. George
💲 $$$

CASA LOMA

Casa Loma, the "house on the ridge," was built in 1914 to satisfy the architectural fantasies of Sir Henry Pellatt and show off the vast fortune he accumulated in developing hydroelectricity in Ontario. The mammoth edifice is a sort of souvenir of Sir Henry's trips around the monuments of Europe. It was designed by E.J. Lennox, previously employed by Pellatt to build the even more monumental (but perhaps more tasteful) hydropower station at Niagara Falls. There are 98 lavishly furnished rooms, a 70-foot-high ceiling in the Great Hall, and all the latest conveniences. Poor Sir Henry came to grief in the early 1920s when the province took public ownership of the power supply, and Casa Loma was repossessed for unpaid debts.

✉ 1 Austin Terrace ☎ 416/923-1171
🚇 Subway: Dupont 💲 $$$

CITY HALL

In 1957 the architectural competition for a new headquarters for city government attracted an astonishing 510 entries from all around the world. The winner was a Finn, Viljo Revell; despite inviting epithets like "two boomerangs over half a grapefruit," his astonishingly original design has long been accepted as one of the city's great civic symbols. It's an exercise in sculptural concrete, with a saucer-shaped Council Chamber embraced by two curving towers of unequal height. It's worth going inside, perhaps taking the elevator to the amphitheater-like Council Chamber, or just admiring the great mushroom-shaped column that supports it. In front is **Nathan Phillips Square,** named for the mayor who insisted

the city have a building worthy of a modern metropolis. In winter, it becomes a skating rink. The sculpture that adorns the square, the bronze "Archer" by Henry Moore, stirred up as much controversy as the building itself.

✉ Queen St. West ☎ 416/392-7341
🚇 Subway: Osgoode or Queen

FORT YORK

Squashed between railroad tracks and dominated by the multilane Gardiner Expressway, Fort York appears even less menacing today than it did to the well-armed American troops who stormed ashore in the early morning of April 27, 1813, easily overcoming its feeble defenses and putting the raggle-taggle Canadian force of regulars, militiamen, and natives to flight. Before retreating across the Don River and abandoning the town to its fate, the American-born commander of the Canadian troops ordered the fort's 500 gunpowder barrels to be blown up.

What is on view today is Fort York as it was subsequently rebuilt and improved. There are ramparts, blockhouses, and magazines, and the officers' barracks have been refurbished in the style of the period. The Blue Barracks contain exhibits on early days in Toronto and on military history, and in summer there are soldierly drills and displays.

✉ Garrison Rd. & Fleet St. ☎ 416/ 392-6907
🕐 Closed Mon. Sept.–June 💲 $$$

GARDINER MUSEUM OF CERAMIC ART

Once associated with the Royal Ontario Museum, this specialized institution has a stunning collection of more than 2,000 ceramic items, ranging from pre-Columbian pottery through Italian Renaissance majolica and delftware to the classic porcelain of Meiéen, Sèvres, Chelsea, and Bow.

✉ 111 Queen's Park ☎ 416/586-8080
🚇 Subway: Museum 💲 Donation

THE GRANGE

Revealed in all its pedimented Georgian splendor from the fragment of its once extensive grounds, the Grange was built in 1818 by D'Arcy Boulton, a member of what a political

Military history is brought to life in Fort York by its authentically costumed militia.

rival described as "one of the most unprincipled families of the Tory compact." One of the oldest and finest of the city's historic buildings, it has been furnished in the style of the 1840s, when the power and prestige of the Family Compact was at its zenith and much of what happened in Toronto decided in its elegant rooms.

✉ 317 Dundas St. West, entry via Art Gallery of Ontario ☎ 416/979-6608 🚇 Subway: St. Patrick 💲 $$$$$

ONTARIO PARLIAMENT

This massive sandstone structure dominating Queen's Park and the University quarter to the west is the seat of a legislature that governs a province of some 11 million inhabitants, more than the population of many European countries. Originally Ontario was to be ruled from a Gothic edifice modeled on the British Houses of Parliament, but the U.S.-based architect Richard Waite succeeded in pushing through his more up-to-date Romanesque Revival design of 1893, overcoming the united opposition of the province's architects. The somber, exterior belies the opulence of the interior with its rich and, in places, playful decoration.

✉ Queen's Park ☎ 416/325-7500
🕐 Closed weekends in winter 🚇 Subway: Queen's Park

ONTARIO PLACE

Toronto's riposte to Montreal's 1967 Expo, this amusement park is laid out on a series of islands offshore from the somewhat rundown Canadian National Exhibition Centre. With its array of structures in steel and glass, Ontario Place was truly innovative when built in the early 1970s by Eberhard Zeidler, architect of the Eaton Centre. Since then it has strived to keep abreast of the trends. There are restaurants, a large amphitheater for outdoor performances, and a six-story-high IMAX cinema.

✉ 955 Lake Shore Blvd. ☎ 416/314-9900
🕐 Closed Sept.–mid-May

SPADINA HOUSE

A grocer-turned-banker, James Austin acquired the Spadina estate in 1866 on the ridge overlooking the city. Extended by his heirs, the original house is opulent enough, but contrasts with nearby Casa Loma in the refinement of its decorative objects, furnishings and architecture.

✉ 285 Spadina Rd. ☎ 416/392-6827
🚇 Subway: Dupont 💲 $$$

THOMSON GALLERY

Lovingly assembled by press magnate Lord Thomson of Fleet and hung in a series of rooms atop a department store, this is the finest private collection of Canadian art on public display. Relatively little visited, it offers the chance to make the acquaintance of 19th-century artists such as the ubiquitous genre painter Cornelius Krieghoff (1815–1872) and the meticulous recorder of native life and landscape Paul Kane (see pp. 186–7). There are beautifully lit winter scenes by the Quebec artist Clarence Gagnon and a number of Emily Carr's vigorous depictions of the Northwest's totems and forests (see p. 280). But the collection's great strength lies in the fine array of paintings by members of the Group of Seven and their allies. Particularly striking is Arthur Lismer's evocation of what has been described as the "Canadian Jungle," the violently colored forest, in the fall, while nothing could be more tranquil than the snow-blanketed roofs depicted in A.J. Casson's "House Tops in the Ward."

✉ The Bay, 176 Yonge St. ☎ 416/861-4571
🕐 Closed Sun. 🚇 Subway: Queen 💲 $ ■

Outer Toronto excursions

The Dominion Carriage Works is one of a number of industrial and commercial buildings rebuilt at Black Creek Pioneer Village.

BLACK CREEK PIONEER VILLAGE

This open-air museum of Ontarian rural life centers around the original farmstead of a Pennsylvania Dutch family that erected a log house here in 1816. In addition to their second house, smokehouse, and barn, another 30 or so mid 19th-century buildings—including a substantial mill building, a printshop, and the Half Way House, a tavern which once stood midway between York and Scarborough—have been brought here from other sites. Gardens, fences, and boardwalks complete the rustic scene, and the village is given added authenticity by the presence of old breeds of farm animals.

✉ 1000 Murray Ross Parkway, Downsview, 18 miles northwest of downtown ☎ 416/736-1733 🕐 Closed Jan.–May 💲 $$$

McMICHAEL CANADIAN ART COLLECTION

In 1954 Bob and Signe McMichael bought their first painting—"Montreal River" by Lawren Harris. The $250 it cost them was paid off on the installment plan. Over the years, they collected further works by the Canadian artists known as the Group of Seven (see pp. 186–7) and in 1965 donated this unique collection to the province of Ontario. What eventually became the country's largest collection of paintings by this renowned group is housed in several timber and fieldstone structures clustered around the McMichael's original 1951 cabin. Plenty of windows look out over the densely wooded Humber Valley, a landscape quite similar to the wilderness that inspired the artists. Now in provincial care, the collection consists of nearly 6,000 works, most of them donated by private collectors.

In addition to the paintings by the Group of Seven, there is an extensive collection of works by First Nations and Inuit artists and exhibitions of works by modern and living Canadian artists. But it is the evocations of the Canadian landscape by group members Tom Thomson, Lawren Harris, A.Y. Jackson, J.E.H. MacDonald, Franklin Carmichael, Arthur Lismer, Frederick Varley, and Frank Johnston that compel the greatest attention, together with work by those they influenced, like Emily Carr.

✉ Islington Ave., Kleinburg, 25 miles northwest ☎ 905/893-1121 🕐 Closed Mon. mid-Oct.–mid-May 🚇 Subway: Yorkdale 💲 $$$

METRO TORONTO ZOO

This magnificent zoo occupies over a square mile of parkland, within which superbly designed pavilions and external spaces house more than 4,000 animals in natural habitats. Thus the luxuriant vegetation of the Africa pavilion provides a home to monkeys, gorillas, pygmy hippos, and pythons, while outside roam zebras, lions, cheetahs, and elephants. Other pavilions are devoted to the wildlife of Eurasia, the Americas, the Indo-Malayan Peninsula, and Australia.

361A Old Finch Ave., Meadowvale Road, Scarborough, about 24 miles northeast of downtown ☎ 416/392-5900 $ $$$

ONTARIO SCIENCE CENTRE

One of the first of its kind, the lavishly equipped Ontario Science Centre makes science and technology not just fascinating, but fun. Opened in 1969, it is housed in an early masterpiece by architect Raymond Moriyama, a series of glass-walled pavilions that respects the natural forms and vegetation of the ravine in which it is set. Inside are more than 800 interactive exhibits, embracing every aspect of the human relationship with the physical world. You can land on the moon, keep a hot-air balloon in flight, instigate an earthquake, and enjoy a hair-raising electrical charge. There is also a newly opened OMNIMAX theater.

770 Don Mills Rd., Don Mills, 14 miles northeast of downtown via Don Valley Parkway ☎ 416/429-4100 $ $$$

OSHAWA

Oshawa began as a port, but owes its fortune to the automobile works created by Robert S. McLaughlin (1871–1972). Responsible for shifting the emphasis of the family firm from carriages to cars, McLaughlin sold the business to General Motors in 1918, becoming G.M.'s vice president. His opulent estate and luxurious gardens at **Parkwood** (270 Simcoe St. North, Tel. 905/433-4311), attest to his wealth and fine taste. The products that he helped to found are on display at the **Canadian Automotive Museum** (99 Simcoe St. South, Tel. 905/576-1222), which traces the evolution of the car in Canada. ■

Sure to shock—the Van der Graaf Generator at the Ontario Science Centre

Canadian painting & the Group of Seven

Until the early 20th century, Canadian art was strongly tied to European models. Canadian artists were trained in the traditions and techniques of the Old Masters and of contemporary art movements on the far side of the Atlantic. This did not, however, inhibit an open-hearted response to the special character of the Canadian landscape or its inhabitants. Between them the country's major art galleries give a comprehensive and fascinating account of the changing ways in which artists have seen this vast country.

Of German ancestry, the highly accomplished Cornelius Krieghoff (1815–1872) painted countless picturesque scenes—especially snowscapes—of life in Quebec, in a style owing much to Dutch genre paintings. Krieghoff's contemporary Paul Kane, who was born in Ireland in 1810, accompanied fur traders across the prairies and over the Rockies to the Pacific coast, sketching all he saw en route (including the last great bison hunt). Still in the genre mode, his works constitute a wonderful record of the West as it stood on the brink of change. At the end of the 19th century, painters from Quebec were strongly influenced by the French Impressionists, whose techniques they applied to the landscapes and cityscapes of eastern Canada. The way Montrealers look at their winter city will probably always be influenced by the urban snowscapes of Maurice Cullen (1866–1934), while Quebec City and its surroundings received a similar treatment from James Wilson Morrice (1865–1924).

A later generation of artists, based in Toronto, deliberately set out to create a school of painting that would not only record the Canadian scene, but would reinforce a distinctive Canadian identity. Calling themselves the Group of Seven, they proclaimed in their exhibition catalog of 1920 that they were "imbued with the idea that an Art must grow and flower in the land before the country will be a real home for its people."

The group's origins date back to the 1911 showing in Toronto of "At the Edge of the

Maple Wood" by the Montreal painter A.Y. Jackson. Its vibrant color and texture made a deep impression on local artists, who persuaded Jackson to come to Toronto. Here he shared studio space with his admirers, and began to accompany the self-taught Tom Thomson on sketching trips to Algonquin Park to the north of the city. Thomson was a countryman, an expert with rod, gun, and canoe paddle; his crude style was refined thanks to the influence of Jackson and the other painters, who in turn were inspired by Thomson's understanding of land and landscape and by his bold technique.

A prosperous patron, Dr. James MacCallum, lent the group his summer residence on Georgian Bay. Together with the wealthy artist Lawren Harris (1885–1970), who was connected with the agricultural machinery firm of Massey-Harris, MacCallum provided the painters with the famous Studio Building overlooking Toronto's Rosedale Ravine. Holed up in a shack on the studio's grounds, Thomson worked up some of his finest paintings from oil sketches made in the wild; among them were some of the nation's most loved pictures, including "The West Wind" and "The Jack Pine." Thomson's death by drowning in 1917 was a terrible shock to his friends, who nevertheless came together in 1920 to formally found the Group of Seven. In addition to Jackson and Harris, they included Frederick Varley, Frank Johnston, Arthur Lismer, Franklin Carmichael, and J.E.H. MacDonald. They devoted themselves to the wild Canadian Shield, often depicting it in a way that owed much to his vigorous handling of color and texture. But each member of the group had his own distinctive vision and his own technique. Macdonald's painting was perhaps the closest to Thomson's, while Lismer's depictions of the "Canadian Jungle" have an intensity all their own. Varley excelled at portraiture, while Carmichael was as much at home among farmsteads and mining towns as in nature. Harris developed even more elemental landscapes of the far north before turning to complete abstraction. ■

Left: The Group of Seven at Toronto's Arts and Letters Club
Below: "Afternoon, Algonquin Park" (ca 1914) by Tom Thomson

Niagara Falls

157E1

Niagara Falls Visitor & Convention Bureau
Victoria Ave.
905/335-6061
or 800/563-2557

Maid of the Mist
Access by elevator from River Rd.
905/358-5781
Operates daily late April–Oct., weather permitting
$$$

"TO SAY ANYTHING ABOUT THIS WONDROUS PLACE would be sheer nonsense," exclaimed Charles Dickens upon visiting Niagara Falls in 1842. In fact, the great Victorian wordsmith did go on to remark that "it would be harder for a man to stand nearer to God than he does here." Few people fail to be deeply stirred by this awesome manifestation of elemental forces, though they might share Dickens' modesty in putting it into adequate words.

Although the days of tightrope-walking and barrel-riding are long since past, the falls can be experienced in a number of ways. Since 1876 the sturdy little **Maid of the Mist** boats have nudged their way through the spray, past the **American Falls** to the very foot of the **Horseshoe Falls.** An elevator decants its passengers onto an outdoor observation platform or into tunnels that lead to miraculous views from behind the Horseshoe Falls. Rising from the top of the steep slope marking the edge of the town of Niagara Falls are observation towers that give spectacular panoramas of the falls. Finally, a promenade and parkway accompany the Niagara River as it accelerates toward the falls, crashes into the depths, then reconstitutes itself as a river and foams down the

American Falls illuminated

gorge toward its outlet into Lake Ontario. The most crowded spot is **Table Rock,** where the promenade directly overlooks the very lip of the cataract.

Niagara Falls are the result of dynamic geological processes that continue to this day. As the glaciers retreated at the end of the last ice age, about 12,000 years ago, the waters of Lake Erie, which had previously drained southward, found an outlet over the Niagara Escarpment into Lake Ontario. Since then the softer underlying shales and sandstones of the escarpment have been continuously eroded by the action of falling water, causing the harder upper layer of limestone to collapse. The vertical face of the falls is maintained, but the falls themselves slowly move back upstream, leaving behind a steadily lengthening gorge, now some 7 miles from **Queenston,** the original point of entry to the then much higher Lake Ontario.

The abstraction of water to generate hydroelectricity has slowed the rate of erosion, originally about 3 feet a year, to about one foot every ten years. Nevertheless, the southward retreat of the falls is destined to continue. At some point in the distant future, **Goat Island,** which at present separates the American Falls (1,000 feet long) from the Horseshoe Falls (2,600 feet long) will disappear, and

the falls will eventually meet Lake Erie and probably become a series of rapids.

Originally the home of the Neutral Indians, who were largely wiped out by the Iroquois, the Niagara area had a mild climate, fertile soils, and a strategic location between two of the Great Lakes. Early explorers had been intrigued by local tales of a great cataract somewhere in the heart of the continent. Explorer Jean Louis Hennepin wrote in 1678 about "Waters which fall from a horrible Precipice…making an outrageous Noise, more terrible than that of

Canadians take pride in noting that "their" falls are more dramatic than those on the U.S. side.

Thunder." Hennepin's fellow Frenchmen founded a trading post at Lewiston in 1721, then built Fort Niagara (now on the U.S. side) to guard the river's outlet into Lake Ontario. In 1759 the British took control of the Niagara area from the French; during the Revolutionary War and later, during the War of 1812, the area was the scene of much conflict between the combatants. The peace established in 1814 allowed both Canadians and Americans to concentrate on the problems and opportunities presented by the falls. The barrier they presented to navigation was overcome, first by the construction of the Erie Canal in 1825 (see p. 192), which linked the upper Niagara River to the Hudson, then by the Welland Canal (1829), which connected Lakes Erie and Ontario across the Niagara Peninsula.

Sightseers have visited the falls ever since they were first discovered. A crude inn was built at Table Rock at the end of the 18th century, but the real commercialization began in the early 19th century.

By the 1870s, squalid shacks and tawdry booths aimed at exploiting visitors had reached such proportions that a commission (predecessor of today's Niagara Parks Commission) was founded to regulate the needs of ever increasing numbers of visitors (currently about 12 million a year).

The viewing areas and manicured **Niagara Parkway** showcases the commission's efforts; meanwhile, the showmen and hucksters have retreated to the city of Niagara Falls, where the attractions range from honeymoon hotels to Dracula's Castle and the Believe It Or Not Museum.

The doughty *Maid of the Mist* is an enduring symbol of Niagara Falls.

WELLAND CANAL

Completed in 1932, the present canal, the fourth to link Lakes Erie and Ontario, runs 28 miles from Port Colbourne, Ontario, to Port Weller, Ontario. Part of the St. Lawrence Seaway, its eight locks overcome a height difference between the two lakes of 326 feet and accept "salties" (oceangoing ships) of more than 33,000 tons. You can view some of the 3,000-plus vessels that pass through every year from the visitor center at Lock No. 3, near the city of St. Catherines. ∎

Maj. Gen. Sir Isaac Brock, the fearless British commander who fell at the Battle of Queenston Heights

ALONG THE NIAGARA PARKWAY

The 35-mile parkway along the Niagara River between Lakes Erie and Ontario completed in 1923, was enjoyed by Winston Churchill, who described it as "the prettiest Sunday afternoon drive in the world."

Restored **Fort Erie** *(Tel 905/871-0540)* marks the southern limit of the drive, 20 miles south of the falls. First built by the British in 1764, the fort was twice destroyed by masses of ice driven ashore from the lake. U.S. forces captured the third fort in 1814, and demolished it before their withdrawal.

Just upstream from the falls stands the enormous neoclassic **Toronto Power Generating Station,** completed in 1913. Its generators shutdown in 1974, but it remains an imposing relic of the numerous schemes on both sides of the border to harness the power of the falls to generate electricity. In order to maintain the flow of water over the falls and give visitors the spectacle they have come here for, the amount of water diverted is strictly regulated by international treaty, with greater quantities drawn off at night and outside the main visitor season. Downstream from the falls, the river narrows and foams over rapids. The elevator of the **Great Gorge Adventure** *(Tel 905/374-1221)* descends to a boardwalk with a close-up view of the angry-looking waters. At a bend a half mile farther north, cables slung across the gorge carry the charming old **Spanish Aero Car** *(Tel 905/356-2241)* high above the Whirlpool Rapids, where the agitated river swirls in a spiral before resuming its course downstream.

At the **Niagara Glen Nature**

Reserve, it is possible to escape the crowds by hiking into the gorge and wandering through a landscape of fallen boulders and luxuriant deciduous forest. More trees, as well as immaculately maintained flowers and shrubs, are on show at the delightful botanical gardens of the **Niagara Parks Commission's School of Horticulture** *(Tel 905/356-7944).*

The original location of the falls was at **Queenston Heights** on the Niagara Escarpment, now an attractive and popular park *(8 miles north of falls, Tel 905/262-4857).* The heights were fiercely contested in the War of 1812, and it was here that Maj. Gen. Sir Isaac Brock fell while leading a Canadian counterattack against the Americans. Narrow stairs lead to Brock's statue atop the 184-foot column commemorating him. Another heroic figure is remembered by a memorial on the heights, as well as at the **Laura Secord Homestead** *(Partition St., Tel 905/262-4851)* in the pretty village of Queenston itself. In 1813, having overheard American officers discussing their plans, Laura Secord rushed 20 miles through difficult terrain to warn the British of the impending attack, enabling them to ambush and defeat their opponents at the Battle of Beaver Dams.

NIAGARA-ON-THE-LAKE

Elegant, early 19th-century brick and clapboard houses line tree-shaded streets, making this little town at the outlet of the Niagara River into Lake Ontario one of the most charming in North America. Originally called Newark, it was the first capital of Upper Canada in 1792, but within two years fears about its proximity to the American frontier had ceded that role to York (later renamed Toronto). The fears were very well grounded; in 1813 the Americans burned the town to the ground and consequently destroyed some of the finest Georgian mansions in Canada. Rebuilding took place almost immediately, in the best possible taste, and the look of the town has hardly changed since. This is partly thanks to the fact that, from the late 1820s on, commerce no longer flowed this way, but along the new Welland Canal. Among the refined shops on broad Queen Street—with its central clock tower—is the delightful **Apothecary,** dating

from 1866 (*Tel 905/468-3845, closed Sept.–June*). **St. Andrew's Church** is a particularly impressive example of a Georgian church building.

Just outside the town is **Fort George National Historic Site** (*River Rd., Tel 905/468-4257, closed Oct.–April*). Burned during the War of 1812, its earthworks survived and in the 1930s its palisade and most of the structures within it, including barracks, artificer's shop, and powder magazine, were rebuilt. ■

Early 19th-century elegance at Niagara-on-the-Lake

Niagara-on-the-Lake
🅰 157E1
Visitor information
✉ 153 Kings St.
☎ 905/468-4263
🕐 Closed weekends Jan.–Feb.

Canadian wines

To the surprise of many visitors, this northern land not only produces wine of fine quality (and in some quantity, too), but also has vineyards and wineries that are attractive places to visit. Vineyard tours and tastings enhance a stay in the two main production areas, southern Ontario and southern British Columbia.

Connoisseurs can be surprised by the fine wines of these northern latitudes.

With vineyards covering about 18,000 acres, southern Ontario is the heartland of Canadian wine. Most of the vines are concentrated on the Niagara Peninsula, but there are also vineyards on the north shore of Lake Erie near Windsor and on Pelee Island. The success of viticulture in the area is not surprising, given its location at the same latitude as Spain's Rioja and France's Languedoc-Roussillon. The difference, of course, is the climate. But the harsh Canadian winter is tempered by the presence of Lakes Erie and Ontario, which absorb heat in the summer and slowly release it as the land cools down in winter. The lakes also produce refreshing breezes to mitigate the effects of the fierce summer sun.

The first vines were planted in the area more than 150 years ago. But for a long time Canadians' favorite tipples were beer and whisky; wine was only drunk in tiny quantities, and Canadian grapes were mostly turned into fortified sherry or port-type beverages that wine connoisseurs would hardly recognize. All this has changed in recent decades; palates have become more sophisticated and local growers, stimulated by the increased import of American wine thanks to the Canada-U.S. Free Trade Agreement, have looked for ways to satisfy them.

Some wineries got clever, abandoning the reliable but boring labrusca grape for hybrid or European grape varieties adapted to the particular soil and microclimatic conditions of individual vineyards. The results were dramatic. Since the early 1990s, Ontario wines have been winning prizes at international events and have been gaining the approval of seasoned wine drinkers. The cellars of Canadian Pacific's prestigious Royal York Hotel may still be full of fine Burgundy and Bordeaux, but the establishment is also proud to offer the wines from its own three-acre Niagara vineyard.

The well-marked **Wine Route** *(for information contact Niagara-on-the-Lake visitor center. See p. 193)* around the Niagara peninsula is an excellent way of getting to know this fascinating area, with its rich mixture of vineyards and wineries, orchards, natural attractions, historic places, and numerous festivals. The wineries are open to the public, offering tastings and vineyard tours, as well as bistros, restaurants, events and entertainment, and even bed-and-breakfasts.

Most Niagara wines are whites, Chardonnays, Pinot Blancs, Rieslings, and Vidals, but there are fine reds, too: Cabernets, Gamay Noirs, and Merlots. Icewine has become a specialty. In Germany, its country of origin, Eiswein can only be made when winter sets in early. As a result, it is incredibly expensive. Canadian icewine is more affordable, thanks to the reliable frostiness of the Canadian winter. The grapes are left on the vine until December or even January, picked (by freezing hands!) and pressed while still frozen. With most of the water in the grape

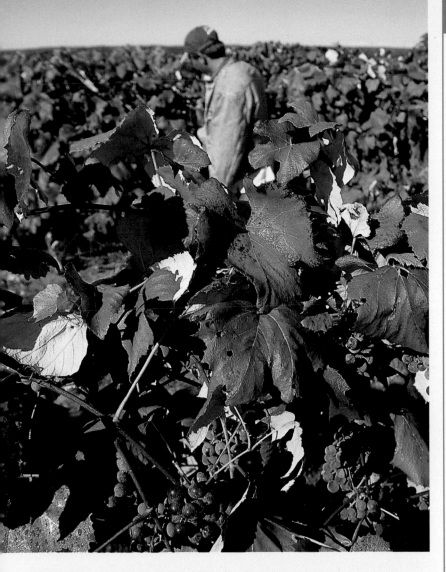

Predictable summer sun and an abundance of moisture help mature the grapes in the vineyards of southern Ontario.

locked up in crystals, the resulting syrupy liquid is rich and luscious. But there's not much of it, and the delicious wine (usually presented in 375 ml half-bottles) is best reserved for an extra special occasion.

Far to the west of Ontario, British Columbia's vineyards are concentrated in the Okanagan area, close to the U.S. border, though vines also grow in the lower Fraser Valley and on Vancouver Island. If southern Ontario corresponds with Bordeaux, the more northerly Okanagan is close to the latitude of France's Champagne and the Rhine Valley in Germany. As in Ontario, a great lake tempers winter cold, while irrigation helps to overcome the dearth of rain, which in the south sometimes amounts to only six inches a year. Most of the province's wines are whites, but there is an increasing number of rather light but sophisticated reds. ■

Huron-Erie Peninsula

**Kitchener
& Waterloo**

157D1

**Visitor
information**

✉ 2848 King St. E.

☎ 519/748-0800
or 800/265-6959

🕐 Closed weekends
Sept.—June

**A place for quiet
contemplation as
well as serious
horticultural
study and
research—
Hamilton's
immaculate Royal
Botanical
Gardens**

JUTTING SOUTHWEST FROM METROPOLITAN TORONTO
toward the U.S. border with Michigan, the Huron-Erie Peninsula
divides two Great Lakes and contains the southernmost point on
Canada's mainland. The character of the peninsula changes along the
way, beginning with the commercial centers of Kitchener, Waterloo,
and Hamilton, and becoming increasingly more rural.

KITCHENER & WATERLOO

Until the outbreak of World War I,
when the city patriotically adopted
the name of a British field marshal,
Kitchener was known as Berlin, a
reflection of its predominantly
German character. The first
German speakers, Mennonites from
Pennsylvania, came to this area in
1805, their pacifism having made
them unwelcome in the United
States. They were joined by German
immigrants who farmed or, as
skilled workers and entrepreneurs,
built the city's commercial and
industrial reputation. Today, people
of German descent make up
roughly half of the population of
Kitchener and its twin, Waterloo.
The dark-clad and plain-living
Mennonites have mostly retreated
to the countryside; their little black,
horse-drawn buggies can
sometimes be seen on back roads,
perhaps heading to the market
town of **St. Jacobs,** where many
of their crafts are displayed for sale.

Kitchener is at its most
Germanic on Thursdays and
Saturdays, when the sausage stalls
of the **Farmers' Market** (*Market
Sq. at Frederick & Duke Sts.*) present
a tempting array of wurst. Every
fall, wurst is consumed in quantity

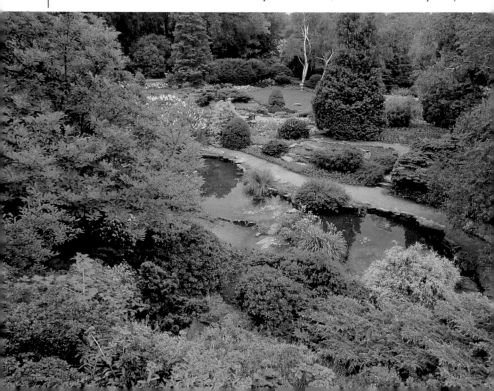

with the limitless flow of beer at the Oktoberfest, second only to Munich's famous festival for general enjoyment and *Gemütlichkeit* (amiability).

The oldest building in town was the home of the first sausage king, Joseph Schneider. His attractive frame farmhouse, built around 1816, is now a museum with German-Canadian memorabilia *(Joseph Schneider Haus, 466 Queen St. South, Tel 519/742-7752).* Another residence open to the public is **Woodside National Historic Site** *(528 Wellington St., Tel 519/571-5684),* the completely rebuilt boyhood home of long-serving Prime Minister William Lyon Mackenzie King. In old age, King was consulted about the restoration and furnishing of the brick-built house, which among other items includes some belongings of his equally eminent grandfather, William Lyon Mackenzie, leader of the ill-fated Rebellion of 1837 (see p. 36).

HAMILTON

At the western end of Lake Ontario, the steel town of Hamilton claims two outstanding attractions in addition to the **Art Gallery of Hamilton** *(123 King St. West, Tel 905/527-6610, closed Mon.-Tues.),* which showcases a fine collection of Canadian and international art.

The splendid porticoed neo-classic villa known as **Dundurn Castle** *(York Blvd., Tel 905/527-2872, closed a.m. Sept.–May)* was built in 1835 for Sir Allen Napier MacNab, one of the most powerful members of Upper Canada's oli-garchy, the Family Compact. MacNab rose from humble begin-nings to great wealth, to a knight-hood conferred for his part in crushing the Mackenzie Rebellion, and finally to high office as prime minister of what by then had become the Province of Canada.

The great blue heron thrives in the wetlands of southern Ontario.

The park around his castle provides fine views over Hamilton Harbour and the city where he made his for-tune in land dealings.

On the far side of the isthmus linking Hamilton with Burlington are the **Royal Botanical Gardens** *(Plains Rd., Tel 905/527-1158).* Extending along the shoreline of the harbor and covering a total area of 2,700 acres, this is a vast and exceptionally fine collection of trees, shrubs, and flowers, impossible to take in on a single visit. Features of special interest include a lilac garden with more than 800 varieties, a lav-ish rock garden in a former quarry, a two-acre rose garden, and a terraced Mediterranean garden, that enjoys southern Ontario's Mediterranean light but is protected from its winter by a great conservatory.

STRATFORD

At one time a railroad town, Stratford has acquired an interna-tional reputation for its annual Shakespeare Festival *(Box office, Stratford Festival, P.O. Box 520, Tel 519/273-1600).* The festival was first staged in 1953, when Sir (then Mr.) Alec Guinness starred in *Richard III,*

Hamilton
🅰 157D1
Visitor information
✉ 127 King St. E.
☎ 905/546-2666

Stratford
🅰 157D1
Visitor information
✉ York St.
☎ 519/273-3352

✉ 88 Wellington St.
☎ 519/271-5140
🕐 Closed weekends

Mohawk chief Joseph Brant, Brantford

Brantford
🏛 157D1
Visitor information
☎ 519/751-9900

Point Pelee National Park
🏛 157D1
Visitor information
☎ 519/322-2365

Point Pelee National Park

beneath a huge tent. In 1957 a permanent building was completed, inspired by the layout of the Elizabethan theater, with the audience sitting around three sides of the stage. The festival has gone from strength to strength, and can claim to be one of the foremost classical theater festivals in North America, with an annual attendance of about a half million.

BRANTFORD

This country town owes its name to Mohawk war chief Joseph Brant, who fought on the British side in the American Revolution. Forced to leave the United States after the war, he and his followers resettled here on land granted by the British government. King George III paid for **Her Majesty's Chapel of the Mohawks** (*291 Mohawk St., Tel 519/445-4528*), a modest clapboard structure built in 1785 and the oldest place of worship in Ontario.

Brantford was also the home of the inventor of the telephone, Alexander Graham Bell (1847–1922), who moved here from Scotland in 1870. The **Bell Homestead** (*94 Tutela Heights Rd., Tel 519 756-6220, closed Mon.*) chronicles the inventiveness of this extraordinary man, as well as showcasing his family's comfortable lifestyle. The world's first long-distance telephone call was made from here to Paris, Ontario, 7 miles away, in 1876.

POINT PELEE NATIONAL PARK

Point Pelee, the southernmost point in mainland Canada, is a sand spit extending 10 miles into Lake Erie. Designated a national park in 1918, the southern part of the peninsula claims a greater variety of flora and fauna than that found anywhere else in Canada. In some places, luxuriant near-jungle growth tangled with vine-draped trees resemble the southern United States more than Canada. Even more compelling is its overlapping position on the Mississippi and Atlantic flyways, making it a stopover for vast numbers of migrating birds in spring and fall. Bird-watchers from all over North America and from as far away as Europe crowd the park to observe at least some of the 350 species that have been recorded here. The spring migration, in May, is the more colorful, with the birds decked out in their mating plumage; the fall scene is equally impressive and lasts longer, usually through September and October. Another fall migrant, the monarch butterfly, congregates on the hackberries near the tip of the peninsula before setting off on the long flight to Mexico's Sierra Madre.

Stopping points along the road fringing the western shore of the peninsula give access to trails into the different habitats, which include shifting shorelines and extensive wetlands. From the visitor center, a shuttle takes visitors to the tip of Point Pelee. ∎

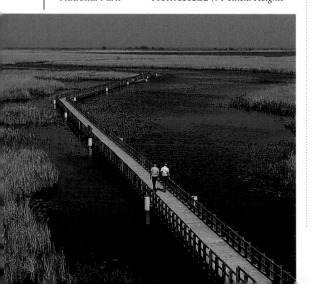

More places to visit on the Huron-Erie Peninsula

FORT MALDEN

Forced by Jay's Treaty of 1794 to abandon their base at Detroit, the British withdrew to this splendid site overlooking the Detroit River as it flows into Lake Erie. As well as constructing a fort, they established a naval dockyard that turned out vessels of up to 400 tons to secure British interests on the Great Lakes. The fort saw action both in the War of 1812, when it was occupied by U.S. forces, and during the Mackenzie Rebellion of 1837 (see pp. 36 & 173). The remains include barracks as well as substantial earthworks.
157D1 ⊠ 100 Laird Ave., Amherstburg
☎ 519/736-5416 $ $

GODERICH

This port and resort town on the shore of Lake Huron was the terminus of the famous Huron Road, cut through the primeval forest of western Ontario in the 1820s to encourage pioneer settlement. The town has kept its planned layout, with leafy streets radiating from a central octagonal square. The splendid stone-built 1842 **Huron Historic Gaol** *(181 Victoria St. North, Tel. 519/524-6971, closed Sept.–May)* combined cells and courtroom. The country's last public hanging took place here in 1865. The displays in the local **Huron Country Museum** *(110 North St.,*

Tel 519/524-2686, closed Sat. Sept.–April) bring home the immense effort that went into the conversion of the forest into today's neat pattern of fields and farmsteads.
157D1 ⊠ Visitor information booth at Nelson & Hamilton Sts. ☎ 519/524-6600

WINDSOR

Looking north across the Detroit River to its far larger neighbor on the American shore, Windsor is Canada's southernmost city. The town's origins go back to the early 18th century, when French settlers established themselves on the southern bank of the river.

Vehicle manufacture began in Windsor in 1904, when the Ford Motor Company of Canada joined the town's previous largest employer, the famous distillery, which now houses the **Hiram Walker Historical Museum** *(2072 Riverside Dr. East, Tel 519/736-5433, closed Mon.)*. By the 1920s, Windsor called itself the Auto Capital of the British Empire, and had dozens of car plants and component producers.

The town is connected to Detroit by rail, by the Ambassador road bridge, and by the only international road tunnel in the world.
157D1 ⊠ Visitor information, 333 Riverside Dr. W. ☎ 519/255-6530
Closed weekends ∎

The Windsor Community Museum is housed in this attractive early 19th-century brick house built by François Baby.

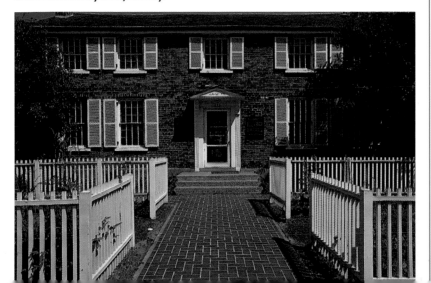

Southern Ontario's weekend paradise

Peterborough

157E2

Visitor information

175 George St.

705/742-2201

Closed weekends mid-Sept.–mid-May

Petroglyphs Provincial Park

Northeast of Peterborough via Hwy. 28

705/877-2552

Closed mid-Oct.–mid-May

$$$

VISITORS MAY MAKE THE LAKESHORE DRIVE TO NIAGARA a priority, but come the weekend, the inhabitants of urban Ontario head north to the fringe of the Canadian Shield, where cottage country gives way to real wilderness only two to three hours' drive from the metropolis.

PETERBOROUGH

Growing up as a logging center, Peterborough became the largest town along the 240-mile **Trent-Severn Canal,** which linked Trenton on Lake Ontario to the eastern shore of Georgian Bay. The Peterborough canoe, a particularly efficient example of that archetypal Canadian craft, was developed here. The town is now best known as the urban center for the **Kawartha Lakes,** the popular recreation and weekend cottage region that stretches westward to **Lake Simcoe.**

The freight once carried on the canal has long since transferred to road and rail, and the waterway is now used instead by leisure craft making the week-long trip between Lakes Ontario and Huron. The most impressive structure in Peterborough is the canal's **Lock No. 21,** at 65 feet the highest hydraulic elevator in the world at the time of its construction in 1904 and the first of its kind in North America. Boats are raised and lowered simultaneously in twin chambers, each of which holds 1,700 tons of water. A modern visitor center (*Tel 705/750-4950, closed Nov.–April*) has displays on this century-old engineering marvel.

In the forest close to **Stony Lake,** 34 miles northeast of Peterborough, is Canada's biggest concentration of native stone carvings. Now protected in **Petroglyphs Provincial Park,**

more than 800 petroglyphs were carved in the bedrock of this southernmost extension of the Canadian Shield up to one thousand years ago, probably by Algonkian-speaking people. For the contemporary Ojibwa people, this is a sacred place, its symbolic shapes and figures full of significance.

Muskoka Lakes is cottage country par excellence, a gorgeous chunk of Canadian Shield whose lakes and forests are a mere two-hour drive north of Toronto.

The area's rise to recreational paradise began in the late 19th century, when luxury hotels attracted wealthy guests in search of wilderness plus comfort from as far afield as Europe. Changing lifestyles, combined with the destruction by fire of many of the original hotels, has altered the character of the area; some 20,000 weekend and vacation houses now occupy the wooded shorelines of Lakes Joseph, Rosseau, and Muskoka. The towns of **Bracebridge, Gravenhurst,** and **Huntsville** help cater to the needs of up to a million and a half visitors a year. In summer, it is still possible to board the pleasure steamer *Segwun (Tel 705/687-*

6667) for an old-fashioned trundle among the myriad wooded islands.

GEORGIAN BAY

Virtually separated from Lake Huron by the Bruce Peninsula and Manitoulin Island, this vast stretch of water is sometimes referred to as the sixth Great Lake. Its rugged eastern shore and myriad islands are extremely popular with vacationers; their landscape of shining water, bare rock, and wind-blasted pines were favorite subjects of the Group of Seven painters.

Midland

A popular launch for boat trips around the Georgian Bay islands, this port and manufacturing town makes the most of its location in former Huronia, where the Huron

Georgian Bay
◪ 157D2

You can easily find solitude in the woods and waterways of southern Ontario.

Midland
🗺 157D2

**Visitor
information**
✉ King St.
☎ 705/526-7884
🕐 Closed weekends
    Oct.–May

**Sainte-Marie
among the Hurons**
🗺 157D2
✉ 3 miles east of
    Midland on Hwy. 12
☎ 705/526-7838
🕐 Closed mid-
    Oct.–mid-May
💲 $$$

Penetanguishene
🗺 157D2

**Georgian Bay
Islands National
Park**
🗺 157D2

**Visitor
information**
✉ P.O. Box 28,
    Honey Harbour
☎ 705/756-2415

or Wendat people lived during the period of French contact. There is a **Huronia Museum** and a reconstructed **Huron Indian Village** (both in Little Lake Park), but the best place to become acquainted with the area's troubled past is the reconstructed Jesuit mission known as Sainte-Marie among the Hurons.

Sainte-Marie among the Hurons

In the early 17th century, the Huron people of the Huron-Erie Peninsula led a settled life, practicing agriculture around their palisaded villages and acting as middlemen in the European fur trade (see pp. 220–21). Their social cohesion was undermined by the French missionaries' attack on ancestral beliefs as well as by a panoply of European diseases. These factors made them easy prey for the invading Iroquois from the south, who either killed them or absorbed them into their own society. By the 18th century, the area was almost completely depopulated.

These events and the context in which they took place are brilliantly evoked at Sainte-Marie among the Hurons, a reconstruction of the mission established in 1639 by Jesuits on the banks of the Wye River near present-day Midland. An enthralling audiovisual presentation precedes a visit to the settlement, which has some 20 rebuilt structures within its timber palisade. There were separate quarters for missionaries and their helpers and for the natives, who lived in tepees and longhouses that some Jesuits only entered with reluctance.

Increasingly harassed by the Iroquois, the Jesuits and many of their Huron protégés abandoned the mission in 1649, first setting it on fire. The failure of the mission

and the savagery of the Iroquois attack made a lasting impression on the European mind. The torturing to death of several of the Jesuit missionaries was depicted by Goya, and in 1930 several of them were canonized by Pope Pius XI. They are also commemorated at the nearby Martyrs' Shrine, a twin-towered church erected in 1926.

Penetanguishene

This bilingual little town on an inlet of Georgian Bay began as a community of French fur traders and voyageurs. In 1817 they were joined by the soldiers and sailors of the Royal Navy base established to keep a watchful eye on American activities on the Upper Lakes at **Discovery Harbour** *(93 Jury Dr., Tel 705/549-8064)*. More than a dozen buildings at the base have been rebuilt, and a number of vessels are moored at the dock. Among them are authentically rigged reproductions of the supply schooners that once sailed the lake. Today, the schooners are available for pleasure tours conducted by equally authentic-looking jolly Jack Tars.

GEORGIAN BAY ISLANDS NATIONAL PARK

The starting point for a boat ride to this string of some 60 islands along the east coast of Georgian Bay is little Honey Harbour, at the end of Rte. 3 off Hwy. 69. The biggest island is **Beausoleil,** where walking trails lead through two distinct landscapes. To the south, a mixed forest of conifer and hardwood grows on deep soil deposited by retreating glaciers, while to the north the same glaciers scoured the granite, gneiss, and quartz bedrock, creating the elemental shield landscape that the Group of Seven painters (see pp. 186–7) found so inspiring.

BRUCE PENINSULA

Partly separating Georgian Bay from the main body of Lake Huron, the tip of the 50-mile-long Bruce Peninsula holds two of Ontario's most fascinating national parks. The main feature of "The Bruce" is the Niagara Escarpment, which here forms 200-foot cliffs along the eastern shore of the peninsula, their bleached limestone contrasting with the intense blues of the clear water and with the dark greens of the trees. Along the escarpment runs Canada's first long-distance hiking path, the **Bruce Trail** *(Tel 416/529-6821)*. Beginning at Queenstown more than 400 miles away, the trail reaches a scenic climax here before terminating at **Tobermory,** the ferry port for the crossing to Manitoulin Island *(Tel 519/376-6601)*. The final, spectacular section of the trail can be reached from **Cyprus Lake** in **Bruce Peninsula National Park** *(P.O. Box 189, Tobermory, Tel 519/596-2263)*, 55 square miles of forest and wetland, where more than 40 species of orchid flourish.

The peninsula's other protected area, **Fathom Five National Marine Park** *(Tel 519/596-2233)* is Canada's first park of its kind, set up in 1987 to preserve the pristine lake environment. In addition to underwater caves and other submerged features of the Niagara Escarpment, there are dramatically sculpted freestanding limestone columns known as "flowerpots" because of their topping of scraggy tree growth. Scuba divers come here to enjoy the exceptionally clear water and to admire the many shipwrecks, some of which can also be seen from glass-bottomed boats.

ALGONQUIN PROVINCIAL PARK

Covering an area greater than Prince Edward Island, this 2,934-

square-mile park on the edge of the Canadian Shield marks the transition between northern coniferous forest and the southern forest of maple, beech, and birch. Its wildlife is accordingly rich and varied, with some 250 species of birds as well as moose, deer, beavers, bears, and wolves. More than 2,500 lakes stud its surface, many linked along 1,000 miles of canoe trails.

Its designation in 1893 was intended not just to conserve nature, but also to satisfy timber interests; logging continues today, though careful management ensures minimal impact on the most visited places.

Algonquin celebrated the 100th anniversary of its designation with the opening of a lavish new **visitor center.** It is located on the Parkway Corridor, the sliver of land along Hwy. 60 in the southwestern corner of the park where most facilities are concentrated. ∎

Camping by the Barron River in Algonquin Provincial Park

Bruce Peninsula
157D2

Algonquin Provincial Park
157E2

Algonquin visitor center
✉ 30 miles from West Gate (Hwy. 60)
☎ 705/633-5538

Minerals & mining towns

When incredibly hot magma flows welled up from the earth's interior and forced apart the hard and ancient rocks of the Canadian Shield, they created ideal conditions for the formation of mineral veins. Indeed, in the 19th and 20th centuries, rich veins of gold and silver, nickel, cobalt, zinc, copper, and iron lured prospectors to northern Ontario's shield country, an otherwise inhospitable region. Many mines have long since been worked out and abandoned; some have disappeared, reclaimed by the ubiquitous forest, others have been turned into visitor attractions. Elsewhere, the shield continues to give up its riches, in places such as Sudbury (see p. 206), with its billion-dollar nickel production, transforming the landscape on a truly gigantic scale.

Measuring 35 miles long and 16 miles across, the Sudbury Basin may have been created by volcanic processes or by the devastating impact millions of years ago of a meteorite. Interestingly, it was here that NASA astronauts Neil Armstrong and Buzz Aldrin familiarized themselves with North America's closest approximation to a lunar environment before their epoch-making trip to the moon in 1969. Sudbury has made amends for a century of reckless mineral exploitation, and much of the scraped and polluted surface of the surrounding country is green once more. The city also brings five billion years of the region's geological history alive with Science North's 3-D film and laser show (see p. 208).

GOLD & SILVER

Next to nickel in terms of production, and far ahead in glamour, is Ontario's gold, the search for which led to the establishment of mining camps across the whole of northern Canada from the Quebec border to Manitoba.

Nowadays you are unlikely to meet more than a handful of other vehicles on the road running north from Ignace (150 miles north of Thunder Bay) to Pickle Lake, but in the early 1900s it was packed with people heading to Ontario's Gold Belt, whose mines produced more of the precious metal than all the other

Molten gold, glowing symbol of Canada's mineral wealth

mines in the province combined. The largest camps sprang into existence when the South Porcupine strike of 1909 unearthed an exceptionally rich deposit, and mines were sunk to a depth of 5,000 feet. The scattered mining settlements in the area were amalgamated in 1971 to form Timmins, which, covering 1,240 square miles, is the second largest city in North America, though its population amounts to fewer than 50,000 people.

Timmins is named for one Noah Timmins, who settled there after making his fortune in the Cobalt silver rush a few years earlier. The silver had been discovered in 1903 by workmen building the Ontario Northland Railway close to the Quebec border. Within months dozens of shafts had been sunk, and by 1910 Cobalt was one of the largest silver producers in the world. The price paid was a ruined landscape stripped of trees, covered in slag, and undermined by abandoned pits and shafts. Those who could kept their distance from the workings, preferring to live in Haileybury and New Liskeard on the nearby shore of Lake Temiskaming.

The town's fortunes swung with the

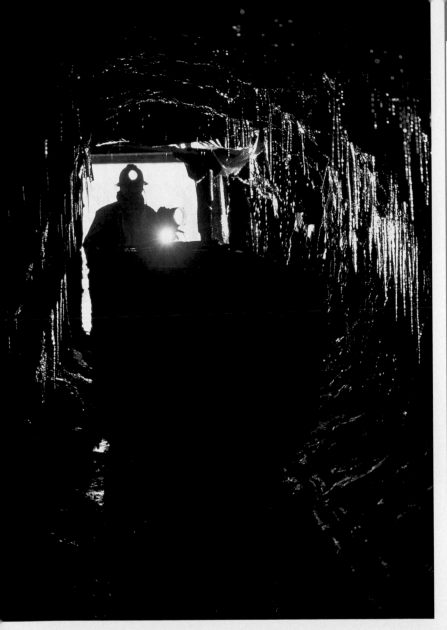

Entering the tunnel of an Ontario gold mine

changing value of silver on the world market; it once supported a population of 7,000, but today only a thousand or so live here, despite a recent upturn that permitted a limited reopening of the works. Visitors can tour the Silver Heritage Trail, a 4-mile drive around abandoned headframes and mine shafts. After donning miner's overalls and boots, lamp and helmet, you can go down into the old Hollinger Mine *(James Reid Rd., Tel 705/267-6222)*, walk through low-ceilinged tunnels, watch machinery at work, brace yourself for underground explosions, and perhaps even take some gold away as a souvenir. ■

North by Northwest in Ontario

WHILE MUCH OF NORTHERN ONTARIO IS INACCESSIBLE TO visitors, transcontinental roads and railroads access a scattering of towns of distinct character, national and provincial parks, and other areas where the magnificent Canadian Shield country can be easily enjoyed. Motorists heading westward can make for North Bay or Sudbury, or alternatively take the ferry from Tobermory on the Bruce Peninsula to 100-mile-long Manitoulin Island, which the Ojibwa called Island of the Great Spirit. The country's biggest powwow is held here every July and August, at the Wikwemikong Reserve.

On the mainland, facing the north shore of Georgian Bay and reached from Sudbury, sprawls **Killarney Provincial Park** (*Tel 705/287-2900*). Promoted as the crown jewel of Ontario's parks, its delights—including the many lakes and spectacular quartzite ridges—are really accessible only on foot or by canoe.

The 350-mile stretch of Lake Superior shorelines between Sault Ste. Marie and Thunder Bay is one of the most spectacular in Canada. The lake, however, is not a hospitable environment. Blowing winds over it can be fierce—whipping waves up to 50 feet in height. Some of the finest stretches of shore are protected in **Lake Superior Provincial Park** (*Tel 705/856-2284*), which lies about 70 miles northwest of Sault Ste. Marie and is crossed by Trans-Canada 17. Here is Agawa Rock, a fearsome cliff rising 100 feet from the water, and painted with pictographs, one of which represents Mishipizjhiw, the "god of troubled waters." At **Pukaskwa National Park** (*P.O. Box 39, Heron Bay, Tel 807/229-0801*), the granite of the shield meets the lake in massive headlands and boulder beaches, while **Sleeping Giant Provincial Park** (*Tel 807/977-2526*) consists of a tableland jutting 25 miles into the lake

and shielding Thunder Bay from some of its storms.

NORTH BAY

Located on Lake Nipissing, North Bay's road and rail links underpin its claim to being the gateway to Ontario's "Near North." Vacationers enjoy the lake, and the rivers that flow from it, once used by the traders who came this way on the fur route between the Ottawa River and Georgian Bay. The town is famous as the birthplace of the Dionne quintuplets (see p. 209), born here on May 28, 1934. Their home is now the **Dionne Homestead Museum** (*1375 Seymour St., Tel 705/472-8480*)

SUDBURY

Built on the ruthless exploitation of mineral resources (see p. 204) and the relentless destruction of the environment, Sudbury has metamorphosed into a regional capital with a wide range of amenities.

The Sudbury Basin's mineral wealth was discovered during the construction of the Canadian Pacific Railway, and has since been worked for its nickel, cobalt, gold, lead, platinum, selenium, silver, tellurium, and zinc. By the early 20th century, Sudbury was producing more than three-quarters of the world's nickel, while the impact of

North Bay
🅰 157D3

Visitor information
✉ Seymour St.
☎ 705/472-8480

Sudbury
🅰 157D2

Visitor information
✉ Welcome Centre, South of Sudbury on Hwy. 69
☎ 705/522-0104 or 800/465-6655

Right: The loneliness of a long-distance driver...the Trans-Canada Highway threads its way through northern Ontario.

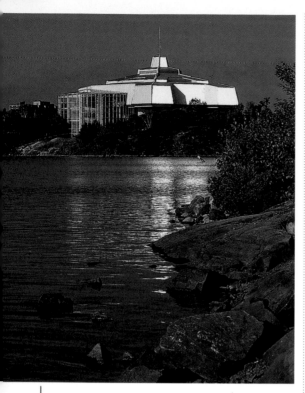

the entrance to the **Big Nickel Mine** *(Tel 705/522-3701)*. At the mine, visitors can go 70 feet underground in a miners' cage and watch demonstrations of the noisy processes involved in mineral extraction.

A far greater range of processes, one expressly intended for visitor participation, can be enjoyed at **Science North** *(Romsey Lake Rd., Tel 705/522-3701)*. On the shore of Lake Ramsey, this ambitious science center is housed in two structures: an extraordinary snowflake-shaped structure designed by Toronto architect Raymond Moriyama and in a chamber hewn into the lakeside rock outcrop. Inside, all kinds of "-ologies" are brought to life by means of vivid hands-on displays. A fascinating 3-D show takes you back through billions of years of geological time to the formation of Sudbury's mineral resources.

SAULT STE. MARIE

Known affectionately as The Soo, Sault Ste. Marie stands on the north bank of the St. Mary's River, which flows from Lake Superior into Lake Huron and forms the boundary with Michigan. The river's rapids had long attracted native fishermen before French explorers came here and called the place Sault ("falls" in French). To make navigation easier, the first lock was constructed by the North West Company in 1798. It was destroyed by U.S. forces during the War of 1812. It became clear a new Canadian lock was needed when, in 1870, Canadian troops on their way west to crush the Red River Rebellion (see p. 228–9) were refused passage through the lock in U.S. territory. Construction began in 1887. With a mile-long channel cut through solid rock, the largest lock chamber in the world, and

The striking building of Science North and its array of attractions has put workaday Sudbury firmly on the tourist map.

Sault Ste. Marie
◩ 157C3

Sault Ste. Marie visitor information
✉ 261 Queen St. W.
☎ 705/949-7152

huge open-cast mines—severe air pollution from the ore roasting processes, and unchecked urban sprawl—devastated the surrounding land forms, lakes, and vegetation. Beginning in the 1970s, the city began to clean itself up, restoring thousands of acres of degraded land and, in the process, gaining an international reputation for the environmental technology involved. Even many lakes within the city limits have lost much of their acidity, thanks in part to the construction of the city's most prominent landmark, the world's tallest smokestack, which rises to an astonishing 1,250 feet above International Nickel's huge plant.

Sudbury's other nickel landmark, also a giant of its kind, is the 30-foot-high five-cent coin overlooking the Trans-Canada 17 near machinery operated by electricity, the lock was a contemporary engineering wonder that functioned for nearly a century before a structural fault closed it down. It is now the **Sault Canal National Historic Site** *(1 Canal Dr., Tel 705/941-6205)*, with original buildings constructed from the red sandstone excavated from the channel.

The Soo is far from being a backwater. More ships pass through the four American locks than through the Suez or Panama Canal, and upstream there is a huge steelworks, now employee owned. Overlooking the river, the stately, five-bay **Ermatinger House** was built in 1814 by a Swiss director of the North West Company and his Ojibwa wife, Charlotte. It is the oldest stone house in Canada west of Toronto and has been restored to its original appearance.

Sault Ste. Marie is the starting point for a rail tour that repeats trips taken by the Group of Seven painters. Between 1918 and 1923 Lawren Harris, A.Y. Jackson, Frank Johnston, J.E.H. MacDonald, and Arthur Lismer hired a boxcar that they used as a mobile studio on sketching expeditions to the Algoma wilderness, to the north.

The **Algoma Central Railway** still exists, and, although no boxcars are rented, passenger excursions head out on one- or two-day trips to explore the rocks, ravines, and primeval forests of this pristine part of Ontario.

THUNDER BAY

Poised at the geographical center of Canada, and at the Canadian head of navigation on Lake Superior, Thunder Bay could hardly avoid becoming a transshipment center between the eastern and western halves of the country. During the first decades of the 19th century, the North West Company post built here and known as Fort William was the summer rendezvous point between voyageurs bringing up supplies from Montreal and traders

Ermatinger House
- ✉ 831 Queen St. East
- ☎ 705/759-5443
- 🕐 Closed Sat.–Sun. Oct.–May & daily Jan.–Mar.
- 💲 $

Algoma Central Railway
- ✉ 129 Bay St.
- ☎ 705/946-7300
- 💲 $$$$$

Thunder Bay
- 🅰 154B3

Visitor information
- ✉ Terry Fox Centre, east of town on Hwy. 11
- ☎ 807/625-2149

Canada's Quints

Annette, Emilie, Yvonne, Cecile, and Marie were five little rays of sunshine in Depression-era Canada when they were born on May 28, 1934, to Ontario francophons Elzire and Oliva Dionne. Not only Canadians but many people around the world were fascinated by the quintuplets, a rare phenomenon at the time. Fearful of commercial exploitation, the Ontario government moved the little girls to a specially built hospital, where hundreds of thousands of people could view them. All seemed for the best, or so it was thought. Accusations of childhood abuse have since been made, and funds set aside for the girls' welfare were woefully mismanaged. Emilie died in

1954, Marie in 1970. After an attempt at reparation was bungled, Ontario Premier Mike Harris traveled to Montreal in 1998 to make a public apology to the three remaining sisters for the government's part in blighting lives that had started so brightly. ∎

No hint here of the less than happy fate that awaited the Dionne quints

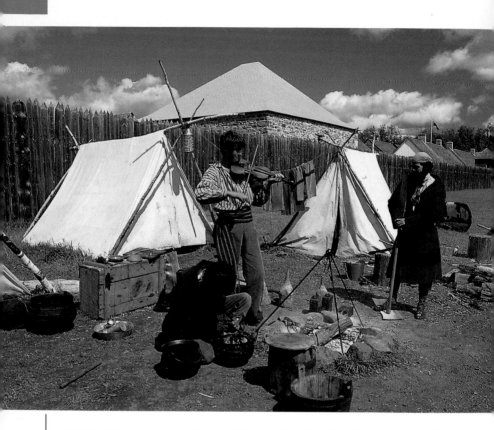

Outside Old Fort William, where every July the rambunctious rendezvous of fur traders and voyageurs is enthusiastically reenacted

Old Fort William

✉ 10 miles southwest of Thunder Bay on Hwy. 61

☎ 807/577-6645

🕐 Closed mid-Oct.–April

$ $$$

returning from the wilderness with their year's supply of furs (see p. 220–21). In 1870 the force heading west to counter the Red River Rebellion (see pp. 228–9) disembarked 4 miles north, at a place subsequently named Port Arthur. Fierce competition broke out between fort and port, which intensified when the former was chosen as the starting point for the construction of the Canadian Pacific Railway to the west. The railroad brought grain from the prairies to Thunder Bay's developing harbor facilities, which by the early 20th century included the massive grain elevators that still dominate the townscape. Their contents are discharged into ships that then head down the seaway to Great Lakes harbors and the ocean.

Forced into union under the name of Thunder Bay by an insistent provincial government, Fort William and Port Arthur have given up their old rivalry, together offering visitors a number of attractions. Thunder Bay promotes itself as the Sports Capital of Canada, with an impressive array of sports facilities. There is also a fine new auditorium where the city's symphony orchestra performs, and a public gallery devoted to First Nations art. But the great attraction is **Old Fort William.** Within its palisade, this lavish rebuilding of the North West Company's trading post has more than 40 structures, seemingly staffed by the traders of old, their servants, and native helpers (who are actually convincingly clad actors and students). ∎

Its endless grasslands replaced a century ago by wheat fields and cattle ranches, the stretch of country between the Canadian Shield and the Rockies forms Canada's heartland, prefiguring in its ethnic variety the multicultural nation of today.

The Prairies

Prairie agriculture near Calgary

The Prairies

SOMETIMES PASSED OVER BY VISITORS CAPTIVATED BY THE OBVIOUS charms of the Rocky Mountains or eastern cities, Canada's Prairie Provinces—Manitoba, Saskatchewan, and eastern Alberta—offer landscapes far more varied than commonly supposed, as well as a human heritage of exceptional interest.

Flatness, the overwhelming characteristic of the prairie landscape, presents a world in which any vertical element takes on a special significance—be it a grain elevator, an onion-domed church, or the surprise of a city skyline seen from far away. Skies are magnificent, with what writer Wallace Stegner called "whole navies of clouds" moving across them.

But flatness is not the whole story, nor is prairie the only landscape of this part of Canada. From sea level on Hudson Bay, the terrain rises in a succession of steps, first to the Manitoba Escarpment, then to the Missouri Coteau, and finally to the Rockies' foothills.

Along the way rivers have carved deep valleys, and isolated upland blocks, such as the Cypress Hills, are shared between Saskatchewan and Alberta. A mantle of boreal forest covers the greater part of the surface of the three provinces, stretching southward from a thin strip of tundra vegetation along the shore of Hudson Bay. This largely uninhabited land of rivers, countless lakes, rock outcrops, and muskeg, is crossed in Manitoba by a solitary railroad line to the Hudson Bay port of Churchill, famous for its polar bears (see p. 219).

To the southwest the spruce, pine, and tamarack of the boreal forest give way to a crescent-shaped zone of aspen parkland roughly 100 miles across, most of which is now given over to farming or urban development. The true prairie lies southwest, or rather, what is left of it, since virtually the whole of what was once a sea of grass and wildflowers extending from Manitoba to the Rockies has been turned over to cultivation. A few fragments of native grassland remain, in Grasslands National Park in southwestern Saskatchewan, for example. But the development of hardy varieties of grain and the irrigation of the drier areas has made cereal farming here some of the most profitable in the world, while other areas, notably around the Cypress Hills, provide extensive grounds for cattle.

Grain and cattle have taken the place of the bison that once roamed the prairies by the millions. The bison formed an invaluable resource for the nomadic tribespeople, providing food, clothing, and the material for cladding tepees. Techniques of hunting included the use of jumps, cliffs over which the herds were driven to their death as at the famous Head-Smashed-In Jump in southeastern Alberta. In Mesozoic times, between 225 and 63 million years ago, Alberta was a landscape of warm seas and swamps, the home of many different species of dinosaur. Today the terrain of the Alberta badlands has some of the richest fossil beds in the world. Current excavations can be seen at Dinosaur Provincial Park, while the spectacular displays of the Royal Tyrell museum at Drumheller bring to life not only the world of the dinosaurs but the whole story of evolution of life on Earth.

The prairies were the fulcrum of the modern Canadian nation and their history is fascinating. The North West Mounted Police (see p. 225) were established to control this vast territory; many of their forts can still be seen, either in their original isolation or re-created in the cities where they were the nucleus. The Métis' resistance to settlement can be traced at

Batoche, site of the battle that ended their 1885 rebellion. Also evocative is the annual reenactment of Louis Riel's trial in Regina.

Today most people travel across the prairies by airplane or highway. Linking Winnipeg and Calgary, the Trans-Canada 1 follows a southerly alignment, while farther north the Yellowhead Highway passes through Saskatoon and gives access to two outstanding national parks, Riding Mountain in Manitoba and Prince Albert in Saskatchewan. ■

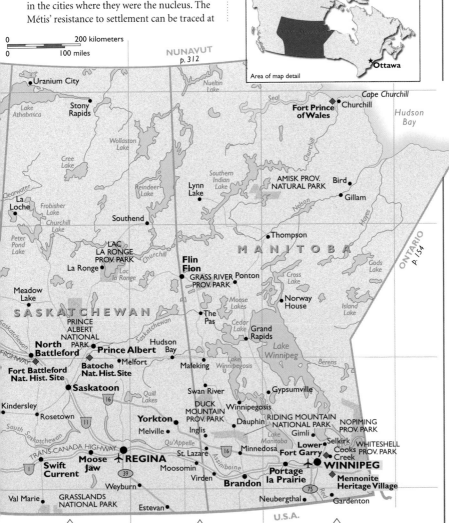

Area of map detail

Ottawa

Populating the Prairies: Métis to the Human Mosaic

Conventional maps of the southern Prairie Provinces are painted with a broad brush, showing great swathes of grassland and parkland stretching for hundreds of miles. The ethnic map, by contrast, is a kaleidoscope of colors, the outcome of Canada's call to land-hungry farmers from Europe to colonize the sparsely populated land.

The Métis, the offspring of European fur traders and native women, had long developed their unique way of life, and a small number of settlers had established themselves in the Red River Colony. But when seen from Ottawa in the 1870s, the prairies remained an "Empty Quarter." Strenuous efforts were made to encourage settlers: A land survey divided the terrain along the American checkerboard model, and potential farmers were offered 160 acres of land—provided they brought it into cultivation within a specified period and built a dwelling. A trickle of anglophone migrants moved in to Manitoba from Ontario, Britain, and the United States, joined by French speakers, Mennonites from Russia, Scandinavians, Belgians, Germans, and even Icelanders, who established the Republic of New Iceland at Gimli on the shore of Lake Winnipeg.

In the last years of the 19th century, an economic upturn combined with the work of Clifford Sifton, the energetic minister of the interior, to boost immigration. Though preferring settlers of Canadian or American stock, Sifton encouraged migrants from the Slav lands of east-central Europe: "A stalwart peasant in a sheepskin's coat, born on the soil, whose forefathers have been farmers for ten generations, with a stout wife and half a dozen children, is good quality."

Most settlers had to build a farm out of whatever materials came to hand: timber in the wooded areas; sod, mud, and thatch in the grasslands. Later, more permanent structures drew on vernacular building traditions in the migrant's country of origin until the availability of standardized materials and even complete prefabricated buildings encouraged, in the words of writer Harold Kalman, the "Bodnarchuks, Tatasoffs, and Silbersteins…to keep up with the Joneses." A few examples can be seen outside museum villages.

In the 1870s the first non-French or non-English people to arrive were the Mennonites, members of a German-speaking cultural-religious group from Russia and central Europe. Their settlements in the East and West Reserves south of Winnipeg are street villages, with farmsteads in sociable proximity, rather than scattered over the landscape. A characteristic example with typical Mennonite house barns has been preserved at New Bergthal, Manitoba. Toward the end of the century, the Doukhobors, an egalitarian and pacifist sect from southern Russia, were also allowed to establish communal settlements; in early photographs, their village at Khristianovka in Saskatchewan looks as if it belongs on the shores of the Black Sea, with more than 40

Cathedrals of the Prairies

Impacting the landscape on an even greater scale than that of the Ukrainian churches was a very different building type, the grain elevator. These superb timber structures, nicknamed the "Cathedrals of the Prairies," built at intervals along the railroad tracks, usually within horse-drawn carting distance of local farms. They were brightly painted, and carried company names and sometimes the name of the railroad station. Some rose to a height of 100 feet, although 65 feet was more typical. Their simple, unmistakable outline concealed quite elaborate machinery to weigh, hoist, store, and discharge the grain. There were some 6,000 by the 1930s; they have since decreased to about 1,500, many made obsolete by motor transportation, closure of branch lines, and advances in agriculture. To prevent this symbol of the Canadian prairies from disappearing altogether, a row of five of them have been designated the Inglis Elevators National Historic Site *(Tel 204/564-2243)*. ■

thatched-roof houses and newly planted trees lining a tidy main street. Together with other migrants, the Doukhobors arrived in such numbers that in the 20 years between the completion of the main railroad network and the outbreak of war in 1914, the population of the prairies had increased almost five-fold, from about 150,000 to 1.5 million.

Equally exotic, and now an integral part of the prairie image, are the Ukrainian churches that raise their onion domes toward the huge vault of the prairie sky. Built from the earliest days of the massive Ukrainian influx that began toward the end of the 19th century, they house congregations of both the Roman Catholic and Russian Orthodox faiths. A well-conserved early example with a richly decorated interior is St. Michael's at Gardenton, Manitoba, completed in 1899. Many Ukrainian churches are the work of one man, the extraordinary Father Ruh. This self-taught architect and tireless laborer built places of worship all across the Prairie Provinces during his 50-year ministry. ■

Winnipeg

 213E2

Tourism Winnipeg
✉ Johnston Terminal, The Forks
☎ 204/943-1970 or 800/665-0204

STILL THE "GATEWAY TO THE PRAIRIES" DESPITE THE growth of great cities farther west, Winnipeg, Manitoba, is strategically located at the crucial point where the Canadian Shield meets the Canadian frontier. This is also the junction of some of North America's coldest winds, and the city has come up with an imaginative way of sheltering itself—by moving much of its business underground.

The confluence of the Assiniboine and Red Rivers had long served as a meeting place for aboriginal people. Later it was the site of forts built by both the Hudson's Bay Company and the North West Company. Today this historic core is known as **The Forks,** a cheerful gathering ground for townsfolk and visitors, with a covered market, boutiques, restaurants, and cafés, as well as riverside open spaces that include a national historic site.

To the west, off Broadway, a 19th-century gateway is all that remains of the Hudson's Bay Company's Upper Fort Garry, but the real nucleus of the modern metropolis is about a mile to the north; here, at the intersection of Portage Avenue and Main Street, is the site of Henry McKenney's Royal Hotel, built in 1862 when the Red River Colony was evolving from an isolated frontier settlement into a modern commercial city.

Winnipeggers take a perverse pride in the fact that the **Portage and Main** intersection is reputed to be the windiest corner in North America. Pedestrians can now escape into the city's extensive underground walkway system.

In addition to modern office towers, Winnipeg holds a fascinating array of older buildings. Many date from the late 19th- and early 20th-century boomtown days, when settlement of the prairies led to an insatiable demand for goods and services of all types. Grand banks and ornate warehouses reflect the dynamism of these pioneering times, particularly in the Exchange District area just north of Portage and Main. Beyond downtown spread several distinctive neighborhoods: Only incorporated into Winnipeg since 1971, French-speaking **St. Boniface** traces its heritage from the mission founded in 1818. In contrast, the **North End** received its decisive imprint from the stream of Scandinavian and Slavic immigrants in the early 20th century.

Winnipeg's cultural dynamism is reflected in its **Folklorama festival** every August, and in its array of institutions—theater, opera, symphony orchestra, and above all, the Royal Winnipeg Ballet (*Tel 204/956-2792*). ■

Each of the Prairie Provinces boasts a splendid neoclassic edifice built to house its parliament. Completed in 1920, Manitoba's Legislative Building was the last to be finished.

Manitoba Museum
of Man and Nature

THIS MODERN MUSEUM, OPENED TO COMMEMORATE Winnipeg's 1974 centennial, succeeds magnificently in its aim of interpreting the complex relationship between humankind and the natural environment of this part of Canada.

190 Rupert St.
204/956-2830
or 204/943-3139
Closed Mon. mid-Sept.–mid-May
$$$

Vivid dioramas enliven many of the galleries, though few surpass the impact of the Red River Buffalo Hunt, with a Métis horseman closing in on his charging prey. Others depict an ice cave in the Arctic with a polar bear settling down to a meal of ringed seal, or caribou migrating through the subarctic landscape of the Wolverine River, among other scenes. Visitors walk past a waterfall in the boreal forest and enter a scene populated by moose and by a Cree band, some of whom are engaged in pictograph painting. But even more striking than these dioramas is the extraordinary full-size reproduction of the *Nonsuch*. Built in Devon, England, to mark the 300th anniversary of the voyage that opened up Hudson Bay and its vast hinterland to the fur trade, the 50-foot ketch sailed the English Channel in the summer of 1969, was shipped across the Atlantic, and came to rest here, deep in the interior of the continent, on the artificial mud of a meticulously re-created English harbor complete with dockside Boar's Head tavern. The efforts paid off and the vessel seems quite at home.

These are the highlights, but the museum holds much more. A strangely man-shaped inukshuk, an Inuit marker built of stone, guards the entrance to the Arctic/Sub-Arctic Gallery. The haunting cry of the loon evokes the loneliness of the northern wilderness, while other displays bring home the nature as well as the nastiness of the biting flies that infest it—punkies, gnats, sandflies and no-see-ums, in addition to mosquitoes, blackflies, and horseflies. A section on the winter landscape shows how snow and frozen soil shelter an amazing variety of life, while other exhibits demonstrate the extraordinary root depth of prairie grasses. There's an example of the famous Red River cart, the region's primary mode of transportation before the coming of the railroad. Poignant pamphlets proclaiming "Canada, Deine Neue Heimat" or "Canada, your new homeland" recall the Europe-wide appeal for hardy settlers to populate and cultivate the hitherto untouched Prairie Provinces. ■

Visitors to the Manitoba Museum of Man and Nature are greeted by its dramatic diorama of stampeding buffalo.

More places to visit around Winnipeg

THE FORKS
NATIONAL HISTORIC SITE

Winnipeg's **Union Station** is one of the grandest in Canada, built in beaux arts style in 1911 by architects also involved in the design of New York's Grand Central. Once occupied by countless boxcars and grain wagons, the vast tract of land between the station and the Red and Assiniboine Rivers has been renamed The Forks and reclaimed for public use. Archaeologically the richest part of the riverside is the Forks National Historic Site, complete with an amphitheater, a striking "Path of Time" sculpture, and landing stages for river trips. Old railroad storage buildings now house a market, specialty shops, and cafés, as well as the elaborate displays of the Manitoba Travel Ideas Centre and a children's museum. The Forks are frequented all year, but are at their best when thronged with lively performers and spectators at the many events that take place in summer.
✉ Off Main St. at Water Ave. ☎ Events Hotline: 204/957-7618

MANITOBA
LEGISLATIVE BUILDING

Rising over a 30-acre parkland that extends to the banks of the Assiniboine, the home to Manitoba's parliament is built on a truly imperial scale. It was completed in 1920, and is one of a number of beaux arts structures intended to express civic pride and consolidate urban civilization in the prairies. Richly decorated with allegorical sculpture, it has a tall dome capped by the famous "Golden Boy," a spirited, gilded youth bearing a torch (representing economic progress) and a wheat sheaf (agriculture). Beyond the classical portico is a triumphal stairway guarded by a brace of bronze bison cast in New York.
✉ 405 Broadway Ave. ☎ 204/945-5813

RIEL HOUSE
NATIONAL HISTORIC SITE

The modest home of the Riel family (see pp. 228–9) has been restored and refurbished to its original appearance. Built in 1881, mostly of timber from the family's previous dwelling, the house was never actually lived in by Louis Riel, though he came here briefly in the summer of 1883, and it was here that he lay in state after his execution in 1885.
✉ 330 River Rd., St. Vital ☎ 204/257-1783 🕐 Closed Sept.–mid-May 💲 Donation

ST. BONIFACE MUSEUM

The former Convent of the Gray Nuns was completed in 1851. Winnipeg's oldest building, and a fine example of Red River frame construction, it now houses a museum that tells the story of the frontier past of Western Canada through the eyes of the Métis and of Manitoba's francophone community. They now form some ten percent of the province's population, mostly resident in St. Boniface and other districts of Winnipeg. Close by looms the modern St. Boniface Cathedral, the sixth place of worship to stand on this site. Built in 1972, it incorporates the imposing twin-towered facade in pale stone of the old cathedral, gutted by fire in 1969.
✉ 494 Ave. Taché, St. Boniface ☎ 204/237-4500 🕐 Closed weekends late Sept.–mid-May 💲 $

WINNIPEG ART GALLERY

This major gallery is as notable for its architecture as for its excellent specialist art collections. An assertive triangular structure terminating in a knife-edge, its design was hailed at the time of its implementation in 1971 as a "brilliant symbolization of contemporary Winnipeg." Thanks to the enthusiasm of its Viennese curator in the early 1950s, the gallery has an unequaled collection of Inuit art, some 10,000 sculptures, prints, drawings, textiles, and paintings. Selections from this treasure store are exhibited in rotation. There's also a fine collection of other Canadian paintings, but the gallery's second great strength, hardly paralleled in Canada, is the Gort Collection of Gothic and Renaissance paintings. Still glowing with vitality these mostly German and Flemish masterworks include paintings by Cranach and an outstanding "Adoration of the Magi" by the group of artists called the Master of the Heilige Sippe.
✉ 300 Memorial Blvd. ☎ 204/942-5483 or 204/786-6641 💲 $

Churchill

△ 213E4

THIS URBAN OUTPOST, CLINGING TO THE BLEAK southwestern shore of Hudson Bay, has a long history as a trading post, fort, and harbor and, more recently, as a major vacation center. Links by rail and air make its extraordinary arctic and subarctic wildlife and landscape accessible to a growing number of visitors eager to see the "Polar Bear Capital of the World."

Visitor information

⊠ Bayport Plaza
☎ 204/675-8863
🕐 Closed a.m. mid-May—mid-Nov.

The Danish explorer Jens Munck first visited the site at the mouth of the Churchill River in 1619, but no permanent European settlement was established until the Hudson's Bay Company built a post here in 1717. Anglo-French competition for control of the bay led to construction of the huge star shaped Prince of Wales Fort—a task which took more than 40 years. It still broods over the tundra and the entrance to the harbor. Despite the fort's 40-foot thick walls , it meekly surrendered to the French on the only occasion it was ever attacked, in 1782.

In the late 19th century, the prairies buzzed with talk of a rail and harbor link to free them from control by eastern Canadian interests and give them an outlet to the sea and to Europe. After several false starts, resources were made available and the problem of laying track on the permafrost was overcome. The Hudson Bay Railroad opened to

Churchill in 1929, and the first cargo of prairie wheat reached England two years later.

The port has never enjoyed the expected success, not least because it is icebound for eight months of the year. But the trains making the journey from Winnipeg (*VIA Rail, Tel 204/944-8780*) bring visitors eager to see the abundant bird life (more than 200 species), the seals, the beluga whales, which play in the (relatively) warm water of the estuary in the summer, and above all, the polar bears. A short boat trip across the river mouth gives access to the **Prince of Wales Fort National Park** (*Tel 204/675-8863*) as well as the riches of the **Eskimo Museum** (*242 La Vérendrye Ave., Tel 204/675-2030, closed Sun.*). The **Parks Canada Visitor Reception Centre** (*Tel 204/675-8863*) is the best place to begin a visit to what is, for most people, an unfamiliar environment. ∎

Above: Winter displays of aurora borealis are a highlight of Churchill.

Below: Polar bear

Churchill's bears

Polar bears are big as well as beautiful. A female weighs an average of 660 pounds, a male more than 1,300 pounds. From September to early November, bears returning from their summer ranges to the south of Churchill congregate along the shore of the bay, waiting for the water to freeze and give them access to their favorite food, the seal.

Contemporary environmental impact studies would probably have ruled out Churchill as a suitable site for a town, as it lies directly on the bears' route to the shore. Locals are wary of these large and fearless carnivores, and visitors need to heed advice before attempting to get close to them. The tundra buggy tours (*Tel 204/675-8863*) run by a number of operators are the best way to enjoy a unique experience of bear contact. ∎

The Hudson's Bay Company & the fur trade

Fish brought Europeans to the coasts of Canada, fur to the interior. Far from empty, the vast land proved to be teeming with animals whose pelts commanded high prices in Europe, where the most desirable of all furbearing animals, the beaver, was on the point of extinction. Beaver pelts were particularly valuable because, once subjected to expert processing by natives, they could be made into a durable, malleable felt—the ideal material for the styles of hats worn by European gentlemen throughout the 18th and 19th centuries.

The French dominated the fur trade at first, establishing good relations with the natives, whose expertise in hunting, trapping, and processing was an absolute prerequisite for success. Trade routes led west far into the interior from just above the famous rapids at Lachine near Montreal. The trade reached Lakes Michigan and Superior, and, in the middle of the 18th century, even farther, across the prairies and into the far northwest. Here waited a formidable adversary—the Hudson's Bay Company (HBC).

The English quest for the elusive Northwest Passage leading from the Atlantic to the Pacific Ocean brought their sailors through the long strait and into the great bay named for Henry Hudson, who explored its shores in 1610. But it was left to a pair of Frenchmen to point out the bay's significance as a doorway to the riches of the fur trade. Médart Chouart, sieur des Groseilliers, and Pierre Esprit Radisson had learned of the existence of the bay from the Cree, but could not obtain backing for its exploration from the French authorities. A more enthusiastic reception awaited them at the English court, and, backed by a consortium of businessmen and nobles, the pair set off from London in 1668 aboard the *Nonsuch* and the *Eaglet*. Only the *Nonsuch* made it to

Hudson Bay; it returned laden with furs of such quality and in such quantity as to delight the backers. Formed in 1670, the Hudson's Bay Company was granted far-reaching powers and a trading monopoly over the whole of the drainage basin of the bay, a vast area now given the name of Rupert's Land.

A style of trading developed, quite distinct from that of the questing, adventurous French, with their intimate contact with natives and willingness to learn their ways. The Hudson's Bay officials tended to remain in the forts built at the mouths of the rivers running into the bay, content to await the arrival of the natives with their annual consignment of furs. Transactions were often carried out through a hatch in the wall of the fort, rather than with the elaborate ceremony preferred by the natives and enthusiastically taken up by the French. Company employees were forbidden to cohabit with native women.

This ponderous approach proved inadequate as the French extended their sphere of operations into the northwest, and the company began to move out from its bayside bases to establish trading posts far inland. Rivalry failed to diminish when Quebec fell to the British; the Montreal base of the trade might now be dominated by Scottish fur barons, but business was business, and conflict continued—the HBC on one side and the newly formed North West Company on the other.

The half century after the conquest by the British marked the final, glorious years of the

Above: Fort Garry in the 19th century
Right: Fur trappers had a solitary existence in the 18th and 19th centuries.

Montreal-based fur trade. French voyageurs with their unparalleled skills still formed the elite of the traders. Great prestige attached to those who had wintered at least once in the far northwest, the *pays d'en haut*, while a lower status was enjoyed by the *mangeurs de lard* (pork-eaters) who returned in the fall to the comforts of civilization. The Beaver Club was founded in Montreal, with membership limited to those who had experienced the hardships of the northwest. They celebrated their distinction with annual dinners of roast beaver and pemmican. The arduous route between Montreal and Fort William on Lake Superior was improved with roads around portages and with locks at Sault Ste.-Marie. By the first decade of the 19th century, North West Company men had traced routes through the mountains to the Pacific, 3,000 miles from Montreal, opening up the last untapped reserves of furbearing animals to the trade.

Company rivalries came to an end in 1821, when the Hudson's Bay Company absorbed the Nor' Westers. For a while the HBC continued to exercise its near-dictatorial powers over its huge domain. By mid-century, however, as it became ever more clear that the future of the prairies belonged to the farmer rather than the bison hunter or fur trader, this role had become an anachronism. In 1870 the HBC sold Rupert's Land to the Canadian government.

Thanks largely to the prime lands it was allowed to retain, the company remained prosperous. Shortened to The Bay (or *La Baie*), its name still dominates many a shopping district. The records kept by its army of administrators and employees form a huge archive, perhaps the most important single source for Canadian history. And in Winnipeg's Museum of Man and Nature (see p. 217), a full-size copy of the 50-foot ketch that began it all, the *Nonsuch*, sails on forever. ■

Lower Fort Garry
National Historic Site

🏛 213E2
✉ 20 miles north of Winnipeg on Hwy. 9
☎ 204/785-6050 or 204/785-6071
🕐 Closed Oct.–mid-May
💲 $$$

In 1826 one of the Red River's periodic floods caused severe damage to Fort Garry at the confluence of the Red and the Assiniboine Rivers. Already concerned at the effect raw frontier society was having on his young wife, Governor George Simpson decided to move his headquarters downstream to a less vulnerable site, one that could be developed not just as a fort and trading post, but also as the center of a refined country estate.

Construction began on what came to be called Lower Fort Garry in 1831; restored by Parks Canada, the complex of buildings is today inhabited by 19th-century folk who role-play and help interpret life as lived here before railroads and steamships displaced the Red River cart and York boat.

The heart of the complex is the Big House, a substantial one-and-a-half story stone structure with high roof and veranda. Elegantly furnished, it nevertheless failed to become the sophisticated social center Simpson planned, and, disappointed with his endeavors, he sailed home to England in 1833. Around it stand the more workaday buildings in which the functions of the trading post were carried out: warehouses, a granary, and a well-stocked fur loft. ∎

🏛 213E2
✉ Just north of Steinbach on Hwy. 12
☎ 204/326-9661
🕐 Buildings closed Oct.–April
💲 $

Traditional farm buildings rebuilt at the Mennonite Heritage Village

Mennonite Heritage Village

Beyond the modern visitor center that tells the often troubled story of the Mennonites from 1500 onward sprawls a 40-acre site. Here one of their prairie villages has been reconstructed in its original form, using reproductions as well as buildings saved from other sites. There are opportunities to sample typical Mennonite fare, hear the German Mennonite dialect spoken, and enjoy a range of special events.

Houses, churches, schools, shops, workshops, and farm buildings are primarily arranged in typical fashion along a street, very different from the isolated farmsteads dictated by the surveyors' plans in most parts of the prairies. The first building encountered is a copy of a semlin, one of the sod houses hastily built as temporary shelters when the pioneers first arrived in their new environment. These were quickly replaced by more permanent structures such as the substantial combination house and barn known as the Hochfeld House, with its characteristic central brick heater system. This type of building can be traced back to medieval Frisia on the North Sea coast. Dominating the village is an exact reconstruction of the Steinbach windmill, the only one of its kind in Canada. ∎

Riding Mountain National Park

THIS NATIONAL PARK WEST OF LAKE MANITOBA INCLUDES some of the highest land in the province—part of the upland known as the Manitoba Escarpment, which runs 1,000 miles from North Dakota to Saskatchewan. Here the escarpment rises 1,500 feet above the flat farmland of the adjoining prairie, forming a dramatic contrast to the tamed landscape.

- 211D2
- Wasagaming
- 204/848-7275 or 800/707-8480
- $

The park's 1,150 square miles have been protected since 1906, when it was designated as a forest reserve. National park status followed in 1930, when the Wasagaming town site was laid out and a number of buildings, including the Interpretive Centre, were designed in a distinctively Canadian rustic style. The park, long a favorite recreation and vacation area locally, has made the town at its entrance a busy summer resort, with sunbathers and swimmers crowding the beach at **Clear Lake.** In winter, **Agassiz Ski Hill** offers downhill skiing with a modest 500-foot vertical drop.

But Riding Mountain's real fascination lies in its juxtaposition of three very different ecosystems. On its eastern edge, at the foot of the escarpment, a tract of deciduous woodland thrives far to the west of its normal occurrence. Elm, oak, and maple shelter a rich lower level of vines, shrubs, and ferns—a habitat that has virtually disappeared from the prairie. West of the escarpment the plateau has been scraped by glaciers, leaving rock outcrops, countless prairie potholes, and a mantle of boreal forest. Farther west still are stands of aspen intermixed with grassland.

Riding Mountain has partly recovered from the trapping that threatened to eliminate much of its wildlife in the 19th century. There are bears, moose, elk, lynx,

beaver, and wolves, as well as a bison herd in a large enclosure at **Lake Audy.** Some 250 miles of trails offer hiking in summer, and some are groomed in winter for cross-country skiing or snowshoeing. The pathways enable visitors to explore the park and even visit the cabin at **Beaver Lodge Lake** built by the early conservationist Grey Owl (1888–1938) during his brief stay as park warden. ■

Largest of the bodies of water in Riding Mountain National Park, Clear Lake is fringed with glorious conifer forest.

Regina

M 213 C2

Regina Visitor information
✉ East of town on Hwy. 1
☎ 306/784-5099

Saskatchewan Legislative Building
✉ Wascana Centre
☎ 306/787-5357

Royal Saskatchewan Museum
✉ Wascana Centre, College Ave. & Albert St.
☎ 306/787-2815 or 306/787-2810

R.C.M.P. Training Academy
✉ Dewdney Ave. W.
☎ 306/780-5838

Wheat sheaves grace Saskatchewan's coat of arms.

"THE CITY THAT DID THE MOST WITH THE LEAST" WAS Pierre Berton's tribute to the capital of Saskatchewan, a city founded in the middle of a treeless plain, virtually without water, on soil that turned to mud after rain and to dust when the sun shone. Just over a century after the Canadian Pacific Railway arrived in this desolate spot, Regina prides itself on fine civic buildings and facilities, nearly as much parkland as Ottawa, and an urban forest of 350,000 trees. The regional center for the wheat producers of southern Saskatchewan, Regina is the home of many government institutions.

The town began life in 1883 as the capital of the Northwest Territories, on a spot by the Wascana Creek named Pile O'Bones for the bison remains left by Cree hunters. At first growth was as sluggish as the muddy waters of the creek, but Regina boomed at the turn of the century as settlers flooded to the plains. In 1905 it became capital of the new province of Saskatchewan.

Regina's distinctiveness lies less in the grid of streets that make up its commercial core than in the 2,300-acre park known as the **Wascana Centre.** Partly in order to solve the problem of water supply, the creek was dammed to form a large serpentine lake. The surrounding parkland was the subject of a typically ambitious beaux arts landscaping scheme by Thomas Mawson in the course of his trans-Canada journey, of which the much admired formal gardens around the legislative building survive. The park provides a green setting for many of the city's foremost attractions.

LEGISLATIVE BUILDING
Completed in 1912, the home of the Saskatchewan legislature is a splendidly self-confident structure in classical style, its long wings firmly anchored by a great portico and high dome. In addition to visiting the Legislative Chamber, the guided tour reveals some of the building's rich collection of artwork.

ROYAL SASKATCHEWAN MUSEUM
Excellent displays in the museum's Earth Sciences Gallery reveal the region's extraordinary geological past, with particular attention paid to Saskatchewan's unusually rich fossil deposits. Visitors can even design their own dinosaur. Nearby, the acclaimed First Nations Gallery tells the story of the province's aboriginal heritage in a comprehensive and accessible way, with lifelike dioramas and an array of other exhibits. The outstanding Life Sciences Gallery is currently under renovation.

ROYAL CANADIAN MOUNTED POLICE TRAINING ACADEMY
An inspection of the place where future Mounties get their training has to be a highlight of any stay in Regina. There's a daily Sergeant Major's Drill at 12:45 on the Parade Ground and on Tuesdays in summer the splendid spectacle of the Sunset Retreat as the flag is lowered. The **R.C.M.P. Centennial Museum** gives a thorough account of the force's history, with emphasis on such episodes as the 1885 Riel Rebellion and the Klondike Gold Rush. ∎

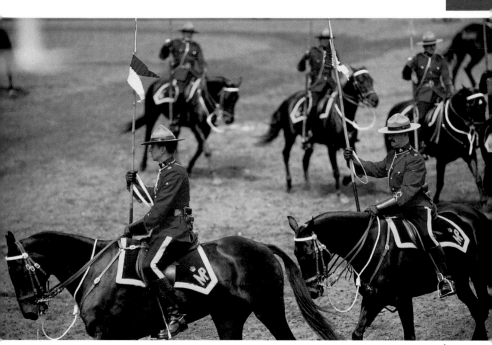

Horses and riders perform at the Sergeant Major's Drill.

The Mounties

Few figures symbolize a country so effectively as the Mountie in his (or her, nowadays) red tunic and stiff-brimmed scout's hat. Originally called the North West Mounted Police, the force was hurriedly organized to deal with the aftermath of the Cypress Hills Massacre in the 1870s and to bring law and order to the west generally. The color of the uniform was calculated to carry with it a potent whiff of British imperial authority. The Mounties' network of forts brought a skeletal settlement pattern to the west (Fort Edmonton, Fort Calgary, Fort Macleod), while the men themselves acquired a reputation for fearlessness and evenhanded meting out of justice.

A Blackfoot chieftain declared: "The police have protected us as the feathers of a bird protect it from the frosts of winter" and the fact that the settlement of the west proceeded so peacefully has been attributed to the respect all parties felt for these near-legendary figures. Surprisingly, the NWMP was almost disbanded on more than one occasion, but survived to acquire its "Royal" title in 1920 and play the role of a federal force. It has survived being mythologized (by comic books, novels, films, and even TV sitcoms) and more recent spying and phone-tapping scandals to retain a place in most Canadian hearts. ■

Reconstruction of an NWMP office at Fort Calgary

Saskatoon

213C2

Tourism Saskatoon
✉ 6–305 Idylwyld Dr. N.
☎ 306/242-1206

STILL SMARTING SOMEWHAT AT REGINA'S CAPITAL CITY status, and larger than its southern Saskatchewan competitor, Saskatoon nevertheless prides itself on its fine setting on both banks of the South Saskatchewan River, on its elegant university campus, and on a longstanding tradition of civic improvement and urban landscaping. The city was founded in 1882 by sober-minded Ontarians as the center of a temperance colony. Growth was slow; by the turn of the century there were only 100 or so inhabitants. But boom time came suddenly; lines of all three Canadian railroad companies met here and settlers flocked in to farm the surrounding prairie. By the outbreak of World War I, the population numbered nearly 20,000. Recently, the city has taken on a vital role in the development of the province's potash reserves and uranium deposits.

Saskatoon's popular Farmers' Market

The winding South Saskatchewan River, crossed by seven bridges, is accompanied by the **Meewasin Trail,** an 11-mile hiking and biking route that links many of the city's attractions. The **Meewasin Valley Centre** (*3rd Ave. S., Tel 306/665-6888*) on the west bank introduces visitors to the city and its surroundings. On the same side of the river is one of Saskatoon's Ukrainian museums, the **Ukrainian Museum of Canada** (*910 Spadina Cres. E., Tel 306/244-3800*), with traditional artifacts and displays on the evolution of the sizable Canadian-Ukrainian community and its culture. Farther north the **Mendel Art Gallery** (*950 Spadina Cres. E., Tel 306/975-7610*) offers a luxuriantly planted conservatory as well as the exceptionally rich collection of Canadian art assembled by Fred Mendel, a public-spirited local millionaire. On the grounds of the University of Saskatchewan on the far bank of the river, the **Diefenbaker Canada Centre** (*101 Diefenbaker Pl., Tel 306/966-8384*) commemorates "The Chief," politician John

Dicfenbaker from the prairies who was Canada's prime minister between 1957 and 1963.

Away from the river, Saskatoon's other sights include the **Western Development Museum** *(2610 Lorne Ave. S., Tel 306/931-1910)* and **Wanuskewin Heritage Park** *(405 3rd Ave. S., Tel 306/931-6767).* The former celebrates the European settlement of the prairies through its collections of agricultural equipment and its Boomtown, a copy of an early 20th-century street. The latter explores the far older heritage of the Plains Indians.

BATOCHE NATIONAL HISTORIC SITE

Overlooking the South Saskatchewan River, the village of Batoche was a center of Métis settlement and the short-lived capital of Louis Riel's "provisional government of the Saskatchewan." It was here in 1885 that his followers made their last stand under the command of the skilled guerrilla leader Gabriel Dumont against the force led by Maj. Gen. Frederick Middleton. The outnumbered Métis held up Middleton's advance on Batoche, but after four days inferior weaponry and lack of ammunition made their defeat inevitable (see pp. 228–9).

Visitor center displays and audiovisual presentations provide an excellent introduction to this evocative national historic park. Although most of the village of Batoche has disappeared, the church and rectory that served as Riel's headquarters are intact, along with traces of the defenders' rifle pits and a poignant cemetery.

FORT BATTLEFORD NATIONAL HISTORIC SITE

For a brief period following the construction of the North West Mounted Police post at this site on the North Saskatchewan River in 1876, Battleford became the capital of the Northwest Territories; an honor it lost to Regina when the Canadian Pacific Railway decided to build its line far to the south. During the Northwest Rebellion of 1885, the Cree sacked the town while its inhabitants huddled in the shelter of the fort. Within the reconstructed stockade several of the fort's original structures have been refurbished, and the barrack building outside the perimeter houses a visitor center. ∎

The modern facade and gardens of City Hall

Batoche National Historic Site
- 213C2
- 27 miles southwest of Prince Albert on east bank of South Saskatchewan River
- 306/423-6227
- Closed mid-Oct.–mid-May
- $

Fort Battleford National Historic Site
- 213C2
- Off Trans-Canada 16, 95 miles northwest of Saskatoon
- 306/937-2621
- Closed mid-Oct.–mid-May.
- $

Louis Riel & rebellion

A controversial figure well over a century after his death, Louis Riel (1844–1885) led not one but two rebellions against the Canadian advance into the prairies. A sorry sequence of misunderstanding and poor communications, combined with Riel's own erratic behavior, led to his tragic trial and execution.

Seven-eighths French and one-eighth Indian, Riel trained in Montreal for the Catholic priesthood, but found his vocation in politics when called upon in 1869 by Métis anxious about the activities of Canadian surveyors on their traditional lands. Though there was no intention on the part of Ottawa to dispossess the Métis, fears had been fanned—Riel's National Committee prevented the lieutenant governor of Rupert's Land from entering the territory, then seized Fort Garry at the confluence of the Red and Assiniboine Rivers. While Riel issued proclamations and Ottawa made soothing statements, a number of free-booting Ontarians made what seemed to be threatening noises from nearby Portage La Prairie. Captured by Métis, they were imprisoned in Fort Garry and one, a troublesome Orangeman named Scott, was executed. This was Riel's undoing in the eyes of Anglo-Canada, and he was never forgiven. Although the Manitoba that came into existence in 1870 may have owed much to his successful negotiations with the Canadian government, unrelenting Ontarian animosity left him unable to take the seat he had won in Parliament, and he was forced into American exile.

By the mid-1880s, history was about to repeat itself. Many Métis had moved northward from the Red River area, where they had been cheated by speculators out of the lands granted them by the government, to the banks of the South Saskatchewan River, where they hoped to continue living their traditional way of life undisturbed by the western march of progress. The hope was a vain one. Once more, survey parties invaded the area, the advance guard of land speculators and settlers. Riel, by now a U.S. citizen and long since amnestied for his part in the Red River

Above: Louis Riel, who was executed after leading not one, but two rebellions against insensitive central authority
Top right: Native Canadian and Métis rebels were forced to yield to the overwhelming force of the 3,000 troops sent from Ontario.
Bottom right: Louis Riel was laid to rest outside St. Boniface Basilica, Winnipeg.

Rebellion, was called from his Montana exile to help in the defense of land rights. In 1884 he arrived in Batoche on the North Saskatchewan River, investigated the situation, and sent a petition to Ottawa.

Irritated by apparent government inaction, and taunted by some of his followers for his seeming ineffectiveness, Riel appeared to lose the balance he had recovered following a nervous breakdown ten years earlier. Declaring himself the "Prophet of the New World," he set up a military headquarters at the parish church of Batoche and ordered the North West Mounted Police to leave the area or face extermination. Ottawa, not inclined to leave this threat unanswered, now had the means of rapid reinforcement, since the rails of the Canadian Pacific were being swiftly laid across shield and prairies. A force of 3,000 men rushed from Ontario and despite a skilled, guerrilla-type defense conducted by Riel's military commander, Gabriel Dumont, the rebellion was doomed.

As the four-day battle ended, Dumont fled to the United States and Riel, who had encouraged his followers with cries of "Fire in the name of the Father! Fire in the name of the Son! Fire in the name of the Holy Ghost!," was captured and brought to trial in Regina.

Inevitably, the charge against him was that of treason. Though he had never fired a shot himself, he had raised a rebellion, in the course of which perhaps a hundred people had lost their lives. Sympathy for his cause, particularly in Quebec, contrasted with Ontario's implacable hostility. Riel's lawyers pleaded insanity, but the defendant himself spoke so eloquently that the plea failed. Despite the jury's recommendation of mercy, Riel was hanged on November 16, 1885. ■

A rider surveys the empty acres of Saskatchewan's Grasslands National Park.

Saskatchewan parks

PRINCE ALBERT NATIONAL PARK

The particular fascination of this 1,500-square-mile national park, established in the very heart of Saskatchewan in 1927, lies in its juxtaposition of two of Canada's major ecosystems.

In the south, aspen parkland intermixes with swaths of prairie grasslands, habitat of creatures from ground squirrels to an introduced herd of plains bison. (The wood bison is more at home in this habitat.) To the north, parkland gives way to a boreal forest of spruce, tamarack, and jack pine—the domain of mink, otters, foxes, black bears, and wolves. The once rare beaver is common again, not least thanks to the pioneering conservation work of Grey Owl, whose cabin stands at the end of one of the park's many trails. Myriad lakes, rivers, and other bodies of water attract numerous vacationers and pleasure-seekers, particularly around the **Waskesiu Lake** town site. **Lavallée Lake,** however, is out of bounds, since it is the home of a flock of white pelicans.

🅰 213C3 ✉ 50 miles north of Prince Albert via Hwy. 2 ☎ 306/633-5322 💲 $

GRASSLANDS NATIONAL PARK

Still early in its evolution, this national park's mandate is to conserve significant remnants of the once extensive mixed-grass prairie. Visitor facilities are limited to a small information center in **Val Marie,** but the park provides an insight into this quintessential prairie landscape, with its wildflowers and 40-plus species of grasses forming the tough cover known as "prairie wool." Fauna includes gophers, pronghorn, mule deer, and Canada's only colony of black-tailed prairie dogs.

🅰 213C1 ✉ Between Val Marie and Kildeer south of Hwy. 18 ☎ 306/298-2257

CYPRESS HILLS INTERPROVINCIAL PARK

Shared by Saskatchewan and Alberta, the Cypress Hills are the highest land between Labrador and the Rockies, rising to more than 4,800 feet. With a moister climate, richer vegetation, and a delightfully varied relief, they seemed "a perfect oasis in the desert" to the surveyor John Palliser in 1859.

🅰 212B1 ✉ 17 miles south of Maple Creek on Hwy. 21 ☎ 306/662-4411

Edmonton

"A CITY YOU COME FROM, NOT A PLACE TO VISIT," WAS Montrealer Mordecai Richler's grumpy dismissal of the capital of Alberta, one of the northernmost big cities in the world, with a ferocious winter climate to match. Yet Edmonton has much going for it: The checklist of the usual metropolitan amenities is full enough, with museums, a symphony orchestra, a year-long round of festivals, and a wonderful network of green spaces based on the valley of the North Saskatchewan River that bisects the built-up area. In addition to a light rail rapid transit line, the first of its kind in North America, a citywide system of "ped-ways" offers refuge from the rigors of winter.

◪ 212B3

Visitor information

✉ Shaw Conference Centre, Ped-way level

☎ 780/426-4715

The valley of the North Saskatchewan attracted early human occupation for thousands of years, with its relatively abundant resources of water, wood, and wildlife. Trading posts arrived late in the 18th century, and were rebuilt several times before Fort Edmonton was consolidated on the site now occupied by the provincial legislative building (*97th Ave. & 107th St.*). Always the Gateway to the North, Edmonton lost out when the Canadian Pacific routed its tracks on the southern alignment through Calgary in 1883. The arrival of the other transcontinental railroads in the early 20th century was some compensation, as was the city's selection as provincial capital (1905) and site of the University of Alberta. During World War II Edmonton was the operations base for the construction of the Alaska Highway and the Canol oil pipeline. In 1947 the first of several oil fields was discovered—dictating the city's fortunes ever since.

The core of the city is formed by **Churchill Square,** dominated by modern structures including the acclaimed City Hall (1993), the five-auditorium **Citadel Theatre** (*9828–101A Ave., Tel, 780/426-4811*), the Court House, and the **Art Gallery** (*2 Churchill Sq., Tel 780/422-6223*), with its changing

exhibits of mainly Canadian art. Stepping down the 200-foot-deep valley of the North Saskatchewan River is the unusual Convention Centre, greeted from the far bank by the equally striking glass pyramids of the **Muttart Conservatory** (*9626–96 A St., Tel 780/496-8755*), which contain the exotic plant communities of desert, jungle, and "temprete forrest" (sic). From here there is a striking panorama of the bulky building blocks of the city center. Upstream, around the bend in the river, stands the massive beaux arts **Alberta Legislative Building.** Completed in 1913, its grandiose portico and dome made it perhaps the most imposing of all the prairie parliaments—a far cry from the crude fort that once occupied the site. ∎

Referred to by some as "Giza on the Saskatchewan," the glass pyramids of Muttart Conservatory (1977) make a dramatic addition to the Edmonton townscape.

More places to visit around Edmonton

FORT EDMONTON PARK

What is claimed to be Canada's largest living history park is a thorough attempt to re-create Edmonton's past by means of authentic-looking reproductions of buildings and authentically costumed and scripted townsfolk. The trip in time is based on four periods: the 1846 fur-trading post of Fort Edmonton with the Big House of the chief factor; Jasper Avenue of 1885 with its stores and NWMP post; a 1905 Street with its tramway; and 1920 Street.
✉ Off Whitemud Dr., 5 miles southwest of downtown ☎ 780/496-8787 🕐 Closed Sept.–May 💲 $$$

PROVINCIAL MUSEUM OF ALBERTA

This museum offers a fine introduction to the human and natural history of the province. A highlight, the recently refurbished Aboriginal Peoples Gallery, features all aspects of the lives of the original inhabitants of the western plains. Other galleries explain the major ecosystems of the province, its exceptional wealth of natural resources, its prehistory, and the story of European settlement.
✉ 12845–102nd Ave. ☎ 780/453-9100 💲 $

WEST EDMONTON MALL

More than 800 stores, 100 or more eating places, late night spots, the biggest covered amusement park and largest indoor water park in the world, the world's largest indoor lake (which, some would jest, has more submarines afloat on it than the Canadian Navy owns)…the list of superlatives goes on. The 5.2 million-square-foot mall may be architecturally undistinguished, but its sheer size and popularity (more than six million visitors a year) make a visit almost an obligation.
✉ 170th St. & 87th Ave., 5 miles west of downtown ☎ 780/444-5200

Thriving West Edmonton Mall has defied critics who said that the sparsely populated provinces would never support such a massive commercial venture.

Alberta badlands

FOR MANY MILES ALONG THE VALLEY CARVED BY THE RED
River, gullies, buttes, flat-topped mesas, and the mushroom-shaped pinnacles known as hoodoos form a weird moonscape known as the Alberta badlands. One of the world's richest sources of dinosaur remains, the area includes the world heritage site of Dinosaur Provincial Park as well as the Royal Tyrrell Museum of Palaeontology, one of the finest of its kind.

In complete contrast to the featureless prairie all around, the deep channel carved by the glacial ancestor of today's Red River is full of strange, even uncanny forms, made all the more stark in appearance by the lack of vegetation and the somber coloring of the exposed rocks. The hoodoos are the most spectacular, their caps of resistant red ironstone protecting softer layers of sandstone or siltstone beneath—at least temporarily, since this whole landscape is in a constant state of transformation.

The rate of erosion here is rapid, up to one-fifth of an inch a year, 2,000 times more than the far harder rocks of the mountains to the west. There is also human interference in the form of trampling and tampering, and visitors are asked to respect these strange and beautiful—but ultimately, delicate—features.

The badlands extend along creeks and gullies some distance from the main valley. An impressive introduction to the area can be seen on the approach from Calgary, at the lookout giving a panoramic view over **Horseshoe Canyon** (Hwy. 9). Northwest of where the old mining town of **Drumheller** spreads out along the valley floor is the **Dinosaur Trail** (*Tel 403/823-7566*), a 32-mile circular driving route offering an overview of the changing landscapes of the valley and a ferry ride across the river. The best hoodoos are 10 miles southeast of Drumheller, just off Hwy. 10. And an essential stop along the Dinosaur Trail is the magnificent Royal Tyrrell Museum.

Formed from sediments deposited in an ancient inland sea, Alberta's badlands have been eroded into their present strange forms by the action of water and weather.

Most terrible of
all the dinosaurs,
Tyrannosaurus rex
evokes awe even
as a skeleton.

ROYAL TYRRELL MUSEUM OF PALAEONTOLOGY

Guarded by sprinting sculptures of dinosaurs, this long and low museum building echoes the shapes and colors of its setting.

Visitors can admire the colorful denizens of a Devonian reef, wander among the primeval plants of the Paleo-conservatory, plunge their hands deep into a pile of simulated *Triceratops* dung to identify its diet, enjoy audiovisual shows, work at computer stations, and even watch laboratory experts preparing fossils for preservation. But the heart of the museum is the superb array of skeletons in the Dinosaur Hall. Thirty-five in all, they constitute the largest display of its kind in the world. Here is *Albertosaurus* with its daggerlike fangs and clawed hind feet, and the weak-toothed but well-armored *Edmontia*, as well as *Quetzacoatlus*, the largest flying creature ever, and, of course, *Tyrannosaurus rex*.

The museum is still evolving, in conjunction with its field station in Dinosaur Provincial Park, which contributes to its 150,000-item fossil collection. More dioramas are planned, including one devoted to the unique underwater environment of the Burgess Shale, another Canadian world heritage site.

DINOSAUR PROVINCIAL PARK

Established in 1955, the 18,000-acre park was given world heritage status in 1979 in recognition of its extraordinary wealth of dinosaur remains, unequaled except in the Nemegt Valley of Mongolia. The park's badland scenery includes stately stands of plains cottonwoods, a valuable habitat for the area's rich bird life.

There are campsites and other services, but the focal point of the park is the **Field Station** of the Royal Tyrrell Museum. A base for continuing scientific work, it also displays skeletons and other material in an exhibit building. There are self-guided trails, conducted hikes, and, most interesting of all, bus tours to areas under excavation not otherwise accessible to the public *(reservations needed)*. ■

Royal Tyrrell Museum of Palaeontology
- 212B2
- 4 miles northwest of Drumheller in Midland Provincial Park
- 403/823-7707
- Closed Mon. Oct.–April
- $$$

Dinosaur Provincial Park
- 212B2
- 30 miles northeast of Trans-Canada 1 from Brooks
- 403/378-4342
- Closed mid-Oct.–mid-May weekends
- $$$

Calgary

CALGARY IS SET 3,000 FEET UP AMID THE COWBOY country of the Alberta ranch lands, with the eastern range of the Rockies as an incomparable backdrop. Its strong identity has in recent years been enhanced by a cluster of handsome office towers. Despite the city's historic reliance on vulnerable, resource-based industries—first agriculture, then oil—it survived sometimes violent fluctuations in prosperity to maintain its cheerful, very Western spirit, best experienced during its world-famous Calgary Stampede. Even the climate is friendly: The sun shines here more than in the rest of Canada, and the winter cold is often relieved by the warm wind from the west known as the Chinook.

212B2

Tourist information

Calgary Tower Centre, 101 9th Ave. S.

403/263-8510

The city's beginnings go back to 1875 and the construction of the North West Mounted Police fort at the confluence of the Bow and Elbow Rivers. When the tracks of the Canadian Pacific reached Fort Calgary in 1883 the railroad craftily built its station on its own land, across the Elbow and opposite the settlement that had grown up around the fort. Residents soon migrated to what was obviously going to be a boomtown, roping up their dwellings and dragging them across the frozen river.

Spectators at the Calgary Stampede

Calgary's distinctive skyline rises above a simple wooden wagon recalling the city's pioneering days.

Calgary prospered because of its strategic position on the transcontinental railroad and, as the western prairies filled up with ranchers and other settlers, became a great agricultural center. Oil, the region's other major source of wealth, was tapped in the Turner Valley southwest of the city as early as 1914. But the real oil boom came after World War II, boosting population growth and fueling construction of glamorous corporate buildings as well as urban expressways and an efficient public transportation system based on light rail rapid transit.

DOWNTOWN

The city's closely spaced high-rise buildings give it an instantly recognizable profile, whether seen from far across the prairie or close up, from the high rim of the valley carved by the Bow River. A number of older structures remain from the late 19th century, many built from excellent local sandstone. Several stand along **Stephen Avenue Mall,** one of the main east-west streets, now open only to pedestrians. East beyond **Olympic Plaza,** built for the ceremonies of the Winter Games hosted here in 1988, the rugged sandstone of the old **City Hall** makes a fascinating contrast with the sleek blue glass of its new annex. To the west, the most distinguished of the towers gracing the townscape are probably those of the Petro-Canada complex, chisel-topped and completed in 1984.

As in several other Canadian cities, Calgary has a weather-proof circulation system for pedestrians, known here as Plus-15, since its 40 or so bridges and 7 miles of walkways are built 15 feet above street level. Offering access to most shops and offices is **Devonian Gardens,** a 2.5-acre paradise of water features and luxuriant plant growth above the streets. ∎

More places to visit in Calgary

CALGARY TOWER

Its impact somewhat diminished by the office towers, the Calgary Tower nevertheless offers the best all-around view of the city and its setting. Completed in 1968, its 626 feet are topped by a revolving restaurant.

🖂 9th Ave. & Centre St. S. ☎ 403/266-7171
💲 $$$

CALGARY ZOO, BOTANIC GARDEN & PREHISTORIC PARK

Well located on an island in the Bow River, Calgary's zoo hosts animals from all over the world. But its originality lies in a bold re-creation of characteristic western habitats, featuring not just the animals but the landscapes in which they live. So far the Aspen Woodlands and the Rocky Mountains have been reproduced in a convincing way, and a Northern Plains Habitat is under construction. Also popular is Prehistoric Park, although the artificial dinosaurs seem incongruous in an institution otherwise populated by live animals.

🖂 1300 Zoo Rd., Whitehorn C-Train to Zoo Station ☎ 403/232-9300 💲 $$$

FORT CALGARY

The stockade surrounding the NWMP fort was torn down as early as 1882 and the fort itself rebuilt after destruction by fire in 1887. It finally disappeared under the installations of the Grand Trunk Railroad in 1914. This historic site, the nucleus of today's city, was turned into parkland as part of Calgary's centennial celebrations in 1975. While the structure is being reconstructed, the interpretive center gives a good account of the city's evolution from simple stockade to world-class metropolis.

🖂 750 9th Ave. S.E. ☎ 403/290-1875
🕐 Closed mid-Oct.–mid-May
💲 Interpretive Centre $

GLENBOW MUSEUM

A giant, icicle-like sculpture representing the aurora borealis rises up through all floors of this modern building named for the ranch of the oil tycoon who assembled many of the varied collections of this fine museum.

Calgary Zoo specializes in re-creating convincing western habitats.

Here, a wonderful array of artifacts illustrate the lives of the varied human groups that have made an impact on the Canadian West. The First Nations Gallery features objects of rare beauty and interest such as a superb Stony Indian headdress of 96 eagle feathers, and a big tepee, its flaps east-facing to welcome the sun and the Creator. The ethnic and cultural diversity of European settlers is effectively communicated in the domestic objects piled high in "Homage to the Homeland," while the golden age of ranching in the 1880s is evoked, as are the sodbusters, homesteaders who followed the cattlemen and plowed up the prairie after fencing it off with barbed wire.

Among other interestingly arranged and interpreted displays is a celebration of West African cultural achievements, and "Warriors," a fascinating cross-cultural account of combat.

🖂 130 9th Ave. S.E. ☎ 403/268-4100
🕐 Closed Mon. Oct.–May 💲 $$$

HERITAGE PARK HISTORICAL VILLAGE

Claiming to be the largest of its kind in Canada, this site is a thorough attempt to re-create the atmosphere of the pre-1914 Canadian West—more than 150 buildings and exhibits, plus stagecoaches, trams, a steam train, and an antique fairground, attended by people in period garb.

🖂 1900 Heritage Dr. S.W. ☎ 403/259-1900
🕐 Closed Nov.–April & Mon.–Fri. Sept.–Oct.
💲 $$$

Calgary Stampede

Every July the sleek skyscrapers of Calgary look down on a colorfully chaotic scene as business suits give way to western outfits—Stetsons, blue jeans, bolo ties, and hand-heeled boots—and citizens join genuine cowboys in a ten-day celebration of the city's cowtown heritage. Billed as the greatest outdoor show on earth, the Calgary Stampede offers thrills galore: bronco busting, bull riding, steer wrestling, calf roping, and, most heart-stopping of all, chuck-wagon racing.

Organized by American rodeo cowboy Guy Weadick, the very first stampede opened on September 2, 1912, with a spectacular parade of 1,000 cowboys and 3,000 Indians in full ceremonial dress, as well as veterans of the early days of the North West Mounted Police and even survivors of the Riel Rebellion. Rodeo stars flocked in from all over Canada and the United States. Skeptics had prophesied a flop, saying that the great days of ranching and cowboys were over, and that the future belonged to the sodbusters and their wheat crop. "All the more reason to stage a show," was Weadick's retort. In fact, ranching survived while many homesteaders failed in the dry years of the Dirty Thirties. This first stampede was a great success, with an estimated 40,000 spectators at a time when Calgary counted only 60,000 inhabitants. A special thrill was the subjugation of the legendary black bronco Cyclone by the little-known rodeo rider Tom Three Persons, who outperformed established stars to win a purse of one thousand dollars.

World War I stopped the shows, but the stampede was revived and, in 1923, linked with the big annual agricultural fair to become the Calgary Exhibition and Stampede. Today prize money amounts to some $600,000, and visitor numbers reach the million mark. They fill Stampede Park just south of downtown not just for the thrills and spills of the rodeo and chuck-wagon races, but also to enjoy the livestock shows, the fairground, and a myriad of other attractions. In the evening the Stampede Grandstand features precision kicking dancers and other spectacular entertainment. Down-town streets come alive with revelers and country music as bars, restaurants, and night spots do a roaring trade. Strict vegetarians wrestle with their principles at the sight of beef-dominated menus.

By morning it's time to begin all over again, fortified with a free breakfast of

Chuck-wagon racing: The wagon's original role was to carry food and other supplies to the men on the range.

pancakes and coffee.

First featured in the 1923 stampede, chuck-wagon races evolved from what was originally a stagecoach race. Each team consists of a driver, four horses, and four outriders. Before setting off, the wagon is loaded with tent poles and a stove, all of which must remain well stowed during the contest. The wagon is then steered around a figure-eight course marked by barrels before tearing around the half-mile-long main track. Casualties among riders and horses are not uncommon, despite a tightening-up of rules. Animal-rights activists have intervened on behalf of the horses, but the human participants pursue the race with a passion that defies the risk of broken bones.

Ranching legacy

Beef came in quantity to the Calgary area in the 1880s, when cattle were driven up from Montana to satisfy the healthy appetites of the newly arrived Mounties and provide an alternative source of protein to the once-plentiful

Staying on a bronco for eight seconds or more is achievement enough for even an ambitious rider.

bison. Great ranches were established, many by wealthy landowners from Britain as well as eastern Canada. Early difficulties and the arrival of homesteaders intent on crop farming seemed to spell ranching's demise. But it survived to play an important role in the economic life of the province, and an even more pervasive cultural role, as any visitor to the stampede will realize.

Several of the most famous ranches are open to the public. The site of the 100,000-acre Cochrane Ranche on the Bow River just to the west of Calgary is now the Western Heritage Centre, with lavish displays on the history of the rodeo and livestock farming, while the equally prestigious Bar U Ranch is now run by Parks Canada as a national historic site *(Western Heritage Centre, Tel 403/932-3514; Bar U Ranch National Historic Site, Tel 403/396-4996 or 800/568-4996).* ■

Calgary excursions

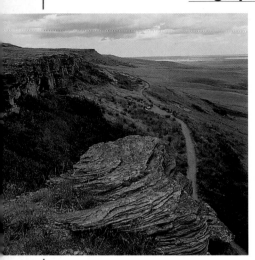

Head-Smashed-In Buffalo Jump was exploited masterfully by early hunters.

HEAD-SMASHED-IN BUFFALO JUMP

The bison jump in the Porcupine Hills of southwestern Alberta is one of the most evocative Plains Indian sites in Canada, its importance recognized in the granting of UNESCO world heritage status in 1981. An interpretive center, inserted into the escarpment with consummate skill, tells the story of the site's use as a bison-killing ground for several millennia.

The long period of use beginning some 5,700 years ago left 35-foot-thick bone beds at the base of the cliffs over which the bison were driven. This invaluable resource for archaeological investigation is especially intriguing for the light shed on the evolution of tool making and use. Inside the center's seven-tiered building superb displays give a comprehensive account of the techniques of the jump and of its material and spiritual significance. A path leads from the building's uppermost terrace along the top of the cliff, offering wonderful views of the prairies to the east and, to the west, of the terrain so expertly used to drive the bison herds to their doom.
📍 212B2 ✉ 11 miles northwest of Fort Macleod via Rte. 785 ☎ 403/553-2731 💲 $$$

FORT MACLEOD

The kernel of the Canadian presence in the West, the fort was named in honor of NWMP Assistant Commissioner Macleod, who helped lead the epic expedition of 1874. Its timber stockade, together with a number of fascinating reproduction buildings, has been reconstructed to make a setting for rides and other events.
📍 212B2 ✉ Fort Macleod ☎ 403/553-4703 🕐 Closed weekends mid-Oct.–May and Jan.–Feb.

FRANK SLIDE INTERPRETIVE CENTRE

The road to the **Crowsnest Pass,** part of the southernmost route through the Canadian Rockies, links a number of poignant reminders of the coal industry that briefly thrived here in the early 20th century. As you approach the fine old powerhouse building of the **Leitch Collieries,** a great mass of rock appears to block the way ahead. This is the Frank Slide, more than a billion cubic feet of limestone which in April 1903 detached itself from Turtle Mountain and crashed into the valley, instantly burying 70 people in their homes. The story of this horrific event, together with other aspects of the area's history, is told in the modern interpretive center built high on a bluff overlooking the valley.
📍 212B2 ✉ Crowsnest Pass on Hwy. 3 ☎ 403/562-7388 💲 $

REMINGTON-ALBERTA CARRIAGE CENTRE

Founded in 1887 by Mormons who arrived in one of the very last covered wagon treks, the little town of **Cardston** is an appropriate home for this magnificent array of horse-drawn vehicles, the largest in North America. More than 250 strong and displayed in a modern building with state-of-the-art techniques, the collection ranges from crude carts to elaborate vehicles such as park drags and sumptuous hearses, many shown in carefully re-created settings.
✉ 623 Main St., Cardston ☎ 403/653-5139 💲 $$$

The gleam of snowcapped peaks and the glitter of ice fields is reflected in the aboriginal name for the Canadian Rockies, the "Shining Mountains." Today, these same glories attract thousands of visitors from all over the world.

The Rockies

**Maligne Lake,
Jasper National Park**

The Rockies

IT IS NOT HARD TO SEE WHY THE CANADIAN ROCKY MOUNTAINS have become one of the country's most mesmerizing attractions, even drawing visitors from other mountainous countries to marvel at their untamed splendor. Most come to the mountain core formed by the national parks of Banff, Jasper, Yoho, and Kootenay, whose global significance (together with the provincial parks of Mounts Robson and Assiniboine) was designated in 1985 as a world heritage area. Rising from the rolling prairies in the east, the Rockies are bounded to the west by the great rift valley known as the Rocky Mountain Trench. Beyond are the Columbia Mountains, embracing Glacier and Revelstoke National Parks, which, together with Alberta's Waterton Lakes National Park, are described here because of their strong links with the Rocky Mountains.

The natural wonders of the Rockies combine to form a pristine landscape that was the birthplace in Canada of what elsewhere seem incompatible twins, tourism and conservation. In the late 19th century and early 20th century, as the railroads approached the Rockies from the east, government and business capital joined forces both to attract visitors and protect the environment. Clever publicity encouraged the leisured classes of Europe and North America to visit what was billed as a mountain wilderness while staying in the luxury of château-style hotels. At the same time, reserves were established that were later expanded to become forest parks, then national parks; Banff was among the very first of the world's great landscapes to be so protected.

A century of conservation means that today's visitors can come into easy contact with superlative scenery still in its near-natural state. A network of roads such as the Icefields Parkway not only leads along the river valleys but crosses high passes and even gives access to the awesome Athabasca Glacier. The Canadian Pacific still threads its way through some of the harshest terrain ever penetrated by a railroad, though the only passenger trains to use its track these days are visitor specials. Few experiences could be more sublime than watching the peaks roll past from the comfort of the panorama car attached to such a train, though a leisurely drive along the incomparable Icefields Parkway comes close.

Road and rail are not the only ways to see the Rockies; at Banff and Jasper gondolas float above it, while the Snocoaches at the Columbia Icefield grind over it. But in order to be really "in" the landscape there is no alternative to

The sublime beauty of Moraine Lake in Banff National Park

walking. This does not necessarily mean hiking into the backcountry with a tent and several days' supply of food, though some of the finest wilderness trails in North America can be explored here, and for even more adventurous spirits there are both summer and winter mountaineering. The majority of visitors are more than satisfied with the superb network of footpaths, which range from lakeside strolls with full wheelchair access to half- and whole-day hikes. Bicycling is becoming an increasingly popular way of getting around—the Icefields Parkway is recognized as one of the best routes in the world. For those attracted to water, there is everything from paddling a canoe on a tranquil lake to braving the fiercest white water.

Banff's Sunshine Village downhill ski area has the longest season of anywhere in Canada. As well as many cross-country ski trails, there are three other downhill areas within the national parks, and two more in Kananaskis

Country. This is the name of the 1,550-square-mile area of provincial parkland southeast of Banff. It has the same superlative landscape as the national parks, but encourages controlled development of recreational facilities, thereby relieving more vulnerable areas. Kananaskis Country (*Tel 403/297-3362*) is where to look for accommodations when Banff and Jasper are booked solid, as they often are in summer. ∎

Banff National Park

A 243D3

**Banff
Visitor Centre**

📧 224 Banff Ave.

☎ Park information:
403/762-1550
Town information:
403/762-8421

💲 Day pass for park
$$$

CANADA'S FIRST AND MOST FAMOUS NATIONAL PARK combines some of the most spectacular scenery in the Rockies with ease of access and a long tradition of catering to visitors.

The park's origins go back to 1883. Construction of the Canadian Pacific Railway up the valley of the Bow River had stopped for the winter, and a pair of workers occupied themselves with prospecting for minerals around the recently completed Siding No. 29. Instead of precious metals, they came upon an equally valuable resource, the hot sulfurous springs noted by an earlier explorer. The men's attempt to stake a claim came to nothing: Within two years the area around

OUTDOOR ACTIVITIES

For those looking for a break from the pampered luxury of the Banff Springs Hotel—or who simply want to make the most of the magnificent surroundings—Banff offers a wide choice of exhilarating pastimes. The Banff Visitor Centre provides information on these activities, with white-water rafting and heli-hiking topping the list for many thrill-seekers. There are also a number of recommended climbs and hikes in the surrounding mountains. Horseback riding and mountain biking are also popular around Banff. Less strenuous, but no less enjoyable, are glacier ice-field tours aboard Snocoaches and boat trips on Lake Minnewanka. ■

the springs was designated as the Banff Hot Springs Reserve, and then, in 1887, renamed the Rocky Mountains Park. After Yellowstone and Australia's Royal, it was only the third area in the world to be protected as a national park. It was extended to its present size, 2,563 square miles, in 1902.

By 1887, the Canadian Pacific's energetic general manager, Van Horne, had already commissioned his architect to design a 250-bed spa hotel, part of his plan to lure the rich and famous to the "Mountain Playground of the World," by CPR train, of course. The trek from Siding No. 29 up to the **Banff Springs Hotel** proved inconvenient and the station was soon moved to its present location, though it no longer has regular passenger train service. The hotel, by contrast, has gone from strength to strength; successive extensions have made it a supreme example of what has been termed the Canadian château style, and it is as dominant

Banff Springs Hotel

✉ Spray Ave.

☎ 403/762-2211

💲 $$$ Tours of the complex

A solitary hiker admires Banff National Park's incredible panoramas.

Banff townsite
 243D2

**Archetypal
château-style
architecture—
the Banff Springs
Hotel**

a feature in the landscape of Banff township as the surrounding mountains.

BANFF TOWNSITE

The vast majority of visitors arrive in the resort of Banff by road, most of them along Trans-Canada 1, as it climbs away from the prairie up the valley of the Bow River. The town's permanent population of about 5,000 swells to more than 30,000 in summer. Most of the national park's nearly four million annual visitors spend at least some time here.

The town has a fair number of man-made attractions, and it is perfectly possible to spend a stay here strolling the streets, shopping, seeing and being seen, all against the backdrop of fabulous mountain scenery. But Banff's main role is as a starting point for the excellent drives and trails that bring visitors into immediate contact with the mountains. Not surprisingly, Parks Canada runs a very full interpretive program, and a visit to the Banff Visitor Centre makes a worthwhile start to any stay in the national park. ∎

Around Banff townsite

BANFF PARK MUSEUM
NATIONAL HISTORIC SITE
This is western Canada's oldest natural history museum, founded in 1903. The array of stuffed native animals is evidence of a now-outdated approach to wildlife interpretation, but the museum has lots of character.
✉ 93 Banff Ave. ☎ 403/762-1558 ⊕ Closed a.m. mid-Sept.–mid-June 🅢 $

BOW FALLS
Just before it joins the Spray River at the foot of the Banff Springs Hotel, the Bow River has cut these falls into an outcrop of Sulphur

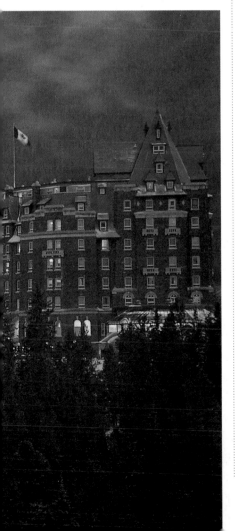

Mountain siltstone. Trails along both sides of the Bow River provide easy access to overlooks and superb views of the Banff Springs Hotel.

CAVE AND BASIN
NATIONAL HISTORIC SITE
The first facilities to take advantage of Banff's hot springs were bath houses built in 1887. These were replaced in 1914 by a more elaborate structure and swimming pool, which eventually became unsafe due to the weakness of the tufa deposits on which it was built. A rebuilding project has restored the site to its glamorous 1914 appearance—although you may not swim. Displays tell the story of the site, the starting point of Banff and the whole Canadian parks movement.
✉ End of Cave Ave. ☎ 403/762-1557 🅢 $

LUXTON MUSEUM
Norman Luxton settled here in 1901 and devoted most of his life to promoting Banff as a resort. On good terms with the First Nations people of the area, he organized the town's Indian Days and dedicated a museum to their heritage. For a while after his death, Luxton's collections were managed by Calgary's Glenbow Museum, but they are now cared for by descendants of his friends.
✉ 1 Birch Ave. ☎ 403/762-2388 ⊕ Closed Mon.–Tues., mid-Oct.–mid-May 🅢 $$$

WHYTE MUSEUM
OF THE CANADIAN ROCKIES
Born in Banff, Peter Whyte and his American wife, Catherine, both of them artists, devoted their lives to portraying local people and landscape and collecting documents and artifacts relating to the region. Their collection forms the basis of the Archives of the Canadian Rockies, an important research resource. Displays give an overview of how the Rockies were conquered and how Banff developed as a resort. Together with the library of the Alpine Club of Canada and galleries for temporary exhibitions on local themes, the archives are housed in a fine modern building.
✉ 111 Bear St. ☎ 403/762-2291 ⊕ Closed Mon. mid-Oct.–mid-May 🅢 $ ∎

Short excursions from Banff townsite

BOW VALLEY PARKWAY

The original road built in 1920 to link Banff and Lake Louise, 30 miles away, has become a relaxed alternative to the more recent Trans-Canada 1, a busy road used by heavy trucks. Numerous turnoffs offer views of the valley and its dramatic mountain backdrop, and there is a chance of encountering wildlife such as caribou, deer, or moose.

At **Johnston Canyon,** 16 miles from Banff, Johnston Creek has eroded a deep cleft in the limestone, which is made accessible by a carefully constructed catwalk. Waterfalls occur where the flow of water encounters layers of harder dolomite, as at the 50-foot high **Lower Falls** (just over 0.5 mile from the parking lot) and at the 100-foot **Upper Falls** (just over 1 mile). Farther still (3.5 miles from the parking lot) are the **Ink Pots,** a series of cold-water springs, normally clear blue in color, but sometimes changing to an inky black.

Continuing along the walkway as far as **Castle Junction,** the serrated mountains to the northeast belong to the distinctive Sawback Range, which make up part of the front ranges of the Rocky Mountains. At Castle Junction, the fault line is crossed, separating the front ranges from the eastern main ranges to the west. Part of the eastern main range, the great landmark of Castle Mountain (9,075 feet), 21 miles northwest of Banff, is a supreme example of a castellated mountain, with its typical layer cake appearance produced by a series of cliffs and ledges.

THE HOODOOS

A short interpretive trail along the Bow River leads to a viewpoint overlooking these strange columns, a geological freak sculpted in debris-flow deposits.

[A] 243D2 [✉] 2.5 miles from Banff townsite on Tunnel Mountain Drive

LAKE MINNEWANKA LOOP DRIVE

The largest water body in the national park is a reservoir, used to generate hydroelectric power and a popular venue for boating and fishing.

[A] 243D2 [✉] 15-mile round-trip from Banff townsite

MOUNT NORQUAY

A well-engineered road with a series of hairpin bends climbs steeply up the northern flank of the Bow Valley to give ever wider views of the mountain landscape. The Mount Norquay Ski Area saw the beginnings of the sport here in the early 20th century. A network of trails leads into the mountains from the parking lot, and Mount Norquay itself can be ascended by chairlift.

[A] 243D2 [✉] 5 miles from Banff townsite on Norquay Rd. [☎] 403/762-4421 [$] $$$$$

SULPHUR MOUNTAIN

The 7,497-foot-high crest of Sulphur Mountain, reached by an eight-minute gondola ride, offers those who are not up to a challenging walk a superb high-level panorama of Banff townsite in its mountain setting. There is a restaurant, the highest in Canada, and the mountaintop is a favorite spot for bighorn sheep to hang around and look for a handout. A 0.6-mile trail leads to the restored weather station of 1903.

[A] 243D2 [✉] 2 miles from Banff townsite [☎] 403/762-2523 [$] Gondola: $$$$$

UPPER HOT SPRINGS

The Upper Hot Springs have been exploited as a visitor attraction since the turn of the century. The water in this large outdoor pool, which was built when the springs were redeveloped in the 1930s, stays at an average temperature of 38ºC. A steamroom, massage, and plunge pool complement your swim. There is also a poolside restaurant.

[A] 243D2 [✉] 2 miles from Banff townsite on Mountain Ave. [☎] 403/762-1515 [$] $$$

VERMILION LAKES DRIVE

This 2.5-mile drive leads past a series of shallow lakes in the broad floodplain of the Bow River and gives fine views toward Mount Rundle. The lakes are frequented by beavers (responsible for damming two of them), moose, deer, bighorn sheep, and wolves, and they are an excellent spot for bird-watching, particularly in the early morning or at dusk.

[A] 243D2 [✉] 2 miles west of Banff townsite off Norquay Rd. ■

The unmistakable peak of Mount Assiniboine stands well clear of its neighbors.

Mount Assiniboine

Part of the world heritage area and a paradise of glacial lakes and alpine meadows, Mount Assiniboine Provincial Park in British Columbia guards its secrets from all but those prepared to backpack. No roads lead to the park, which is named for the Assiniboine, members of the Sioux Confederation. The park has a score of peaks exceeding 8,000 feet. The mightiest of them all is Mount Assiniboine itself (11,870 feet), whose distinctive horn profile recalls that of Switzerland's famous Matterhorn. *(Visitor information, BC Parks 250/422-4200)* ■

Lake Louise

🏔 243D3

Parks Canada visitor center
✉ Next to Samson Mall
☎ 403/522-3833

Château Lake Louise
✉ Lake Louise Dr.
☎ 403/522-3511

Black bear

FEW SCENES CAN BE MORE PHOTOGENIC THAN THE ONE revealed from the lawns in front of Château Lake Louise. In their frame of dark green forest, the emerald lake and its backdrop of white-capped mountains combine to make an irresistible composition for the cameras of the million or so visitors who come here every year.

The lake, which owes its summer color to the rock flour suspended in its waters, was first seen by a European in 1882, when Tom Wilson, a packhorse owner working for the Canadian Pacific, was brought here by his Stoney guide, Edwin Hunter. The Stoney called it the Lake of Little Fishes, but Wilson could find no better name for it than Emerald Lake. Two years later, the lake was officially renamed after Princess Louise Caroline Alberta, one of Queen Victoria's daughters and the wife of the then governor-general.

The CPR was quick to see the potential of what Wilson had called "a matchless scene;" its first accommodations were built in the form of a log cabin in 1890. This was succeeded by the **Château Lake Louise,** which, like its counterpart at Banff Springs, was progressively

extended, housing 200 guests by 1900, 400 by 1913, and 1,100 by the 1990s.

The château-style hotel stands in splendid isolation on the moraine at the eastern end of the lake. The township of Lake Louise, with its motels and other facilities, is 2.5 miles away. In the town there is an excellent **Parks Canada visitor center** with displays and an audiovisual show on the natural and human history of the area. The tramline that operated between 1912 and 1930, linking the townsite to the lake, is now an attractive bicycle and walking trail. On the east side of Trans-Canada 1 is the **Lake Louise Ski Area** (*Skiing Lake Louise, P.O. Box 5, Lake Louise, Tel 403/522-3555*), the largest in Canada. The **Mount Whitehorn gondola** (*Tel 403/522-3555*) operates in summer,

Bear safety

Black bears are still quite common in most of Canada's national parks, whereas grizzlies now only live in western and northern mountain parks. Both species are attracted to the aromatic refuse strewn around by careless campers. When camping, keep everything in secure containers or hoist it out of reach, and eat all you cook. Avoid pitching your tent on a trail and do your hiking in groups to announce your presence.

If you do come face to face

with a bear, stop walking and stay calm; sudden movements or noises may provoke an attack. Then move quietly and slowly away, avoiding all eye contact. Make absolutely certain that you don't come between a mother and her cubs. Leaving your pack on the ground could distract the bear. If worst comes to worst, and it is a black bear that's approaching, fight back! You've nothing to lose! If it is a grizzly, play dead; your adversary may accept your submission and leave you alone. ■

Vast though it is, the Château Lake Louise hotel is dwarfed by its surroundings.

taking visitors to a fine viewpoint above Lake Louise.

It is tempting to try to walk around the lake, but there is no recognized path on the south shore. The following day walks are within the capacity of most visitors.

PLAIN OF SIX GLACIERS

The trail along the north shore of Lake Louise flanks 300-foot cliffs near the far end of the lake, then climbs through forest and across avalanche slopes to moraines, from which there are views of six glaciers. The prominent **Victoria Glacier,** which once stretched to the lip of the lake, has receded about half a mile in the last 150 years. The path continues to climb, eventually reaching a teahouse built in 1924.

✉ 7 miles round-trip, 1,200-foot ascent

LAKE AGNES

The most popular summer walk in the Rockies leads up through the forest. The trail gives ever more spectacular views, passing little **Mirror Lake** and the **Bridal Falls** before reaching Lake Agnes in its lovely mountain setting. Here, too, is a teahouse, successor to the CPR chalet built in 1901. From here it is possible to take short strolls to the distinctive features known as the

Big and **Little Beehives,** or a more arduous walk to link up with the Plain of Six Glaciers teahouse.

✉ 4 miles round-trip, 1,300-foot ascent

MORAINE LAKE

Half the size of Lake Louise, Moraine Lake has water of an even more intense blue-green hue. Its setting is equally splendid, if not more so, with great fans of scree at the foot of the 3,000-foot walls of the Wenkchemna Peaks. "No scene has given me an equal impression of inspiring solitude and rugged grandeur," commented explorer Walter Wilcox in 1899. It was he who gave the lake its misleading name: Its waters are held back, not by a moraine, but by a rock slide. The view from the top of the slide once featured on the back of Canada's $20 bill. A lodge and chalets designed by the Vancouver architect Arthur Erickson blend with the surroundings.

Moraine Lake is the starting point for a number of trails. You can take a short stroll along the western shore of the lake, or a 2-mile walk that leads along **Consolation Valley,** past the pinnacle called the **Tower of Babel** to the little Consolation Lakes. A more demanding but popular excursion is the climb through **Larch Valley** and **Sentinel Pass,** 2,362 feet above the surface of the lake. ■

Icefields Parkway drive

To travel this 143-mile route between Lake Louise and Jasper is to experience one of the world's great scenic highways. The careful engineering of the road, and the generous provision of stopping places, viewpoints, and interpretive information allow the sublime scale and wonderful variety of mountain scenery to be fully appreciated.

Linking the valleys of the Bow, Mistaya, North Saskatchewan, Sunwapta, and Athabasca Rivers, the road introduces visitors to the highest mountains in the Canadian Rockies, to glaciers and ice fields, to pristine forests, lakes, waterfalls, and wild rivers.

Begun in the early 1930s as an unemployment relief scheme, the road was opened in 1940 and improved in the 1960s. It is a generously dimensioned two-lane highway with relatively easy grades and paved shoulders, popular with bicycle riders as well as with motorists, a million of whom travel it every year. There is no special advantage in driving from southeast to northwest or vice versa, although if you are bicycling, you may benefit from tailwinds by starting out from Jasper. The description below starts from Lake Louise, and the mileages given are from there. Stopping places are well marked.

Note that between Lake Louise and Jasper the only services are at Saskatchewan Crossing and the Columbia Icefield.

Ten miles along the Icefields Parkway from Lake Louise is **Hector Lake ❶**. Set at the foot of the Waputik Range and ice field, the lake is the second largest in Banff National Park. Some 10 miles farther, the parkway rounds the isolated mountain of Bow Peak to reach a viewpoint from which **Crowfoot Glacier,** the first of a series of superb glaciers, can be seen. It originally had three lobes that made it resemble a crow's foot, but the glacier has retreated and no longer resembles its name.

Continue for another 3 miles to reach beautiful **Bow Lake,** which is fed by water from the Bow Glacier, one of the eight glaciers descending from the **Waputik Icefield.** The red roof of the little Num-ti-jah Lodge contrasts strikingly with the blue of the lake, the green of the forest, and the minerals in the rocks. The building is the successor to a cabin built in the early 1920s by a famous trapper and guide, Jimmy Simpson. **Bow Summit,** at 6,850 feet, is the highest point along the route, as well as the watershed between the Bow and Mistaya Rivers. A short trail leads to a viewpoint overlooking Peyto Lake with its startlingly blue-green glacier-fed waters.

The road now starts to drop down a long incline into the **Mistaya Valley,** passing a series of lakes for 12 miles before reaching **Upper Waterfowl Lake ❷**. Take advantage of the lakeside viewpoint to marvel at the awe-inspiring mountains of the Continental Divide, including a 6-mile ridge—whose highest points are the majestic **Howse Peak** (10,794 feet) and the splendid pyramid-like peak of **Mount Chephren** (10,850 feet).

As it drops from its hanging valley into the basin of the North Saskatchewan River, the Mistaya is hard at work, and 10 miles along it carves itself back into the limestone as the **Mistaya Canyon ❸**. A short footpath leads into the cleft with its vertical walls, potholes and a natural bridge. **Saskatchewan River Crossing** is 3 miles ahead. Some 2,000 feet below Bow Summit, the valley of the North Saskatchewan River belongs to the montane zone of the Rockies, with a mixed forest cover and a less severe climate.

Designated a Canadian heritage river in 1989, the North Saskatchewan runs 760 miles from its source toward Lake Winnipeg and Hudson Bay. Early travelers experienced great difficulty in crossing

the braided stream, especially when it was flooding, and even in the 1930s, highway engineers had trouble finding a suitable spot to construct a bridge. Gas, food, and lodging are available here. Just before the crossing is the junction with Hwy. 11, the David Thompson Highway, named for the great explorer and mapmaker and connecting with the town of **Red Deer,** 159 miles to the east. To the north of the crossing you can see massive **Mount Wilson** (11,880 feet), with its cliffs of yellowish quartzite.

- See area map p. 243
- Lake Louise
- 143 miles
- Allow 1-2 days
- Jasper

NOT TO BE MISSED
- Hector Lake
- Mistaya Valley
- Columbia Icefield
- Sunwapta Falls
- Athabasca Falls

Hector Lake

Sunwapta Falls

The Bow River

By the time it reaches **Weeping Wall ④**, 17 miles ahead, the valley is much narrower, defined on its eastern flank by 2,000-foot cliffs streaked with waterfalls fed by melting snow high up on Cirrus Mountain. The road climbs the hairpin known as the **Big Bend** to two further viewpoints. The first, the **Cirrus Mountain viewpoint,** commands a splendid panorama of the North Saskatchewan Valley, while the second overlooks **Bridal Veil Falls** and gives access to **Panther Falls** down a roughly constructed path.

Parker Ridge is another 8 miles along. A steep but very rewarding trail (1.5-mile round trip) rises about 900 feet through subalpine forest and tundra to an unforgettable view of the Saskatchewan Glacier, at 6 miles the longest of the glaciers descending from the Columbia Icefield.

At 6,637 feet, **Sunwapta Pass** marks the boundary between Banff and Jasper National Parks and the divide between the North Saskatchewan River and the Sunwapta ("turbulent one"), which drains to the Arctic.

Early travelers found the Sunwapta Valley blocked by the Athabasca Glacier and had to climb up and around it. By the time the parkway was built, the glacier had receded, and a detour was no longer necessary.

A 6-mile drive past Parker Ridge leads to the **Columbia Icefield** and **Athabasca Glacier ⑤**. Covering an area of about 125 square miles with an estimated maximum depth of more than 1,000 feet, the Columbia Icefield is the most extensive of its kind in the Rockies. Take time to appreciate this awe-inspiring relic of the Ice Age. The ice field gives rise to a whole series of glaciers, some of them unnamed. Visible from the parkway are the Athabasca, **Dome, Kitchener,** and **Stutfield,** while the longest, the **Saskatchewan,** can be viewed from Parker Ridge. Meltwater from the glaciers eventually arrives in three oceans, the Arctic via the Athabasca and Mackenzie Rivers, the Atlantic via the North Saskatchewan, and the Pacific via the Columbia.

To service the constant stream of visitors, a new **Icefield Centre** (*Tel 780/852-6560*) with a full range of interpretive displays was opened in 1996.

Take a ride in one of the chunky, 56-passenger Snocoaches to experience the glacier; the vehicle makes a thrillingly steep descent from the lateral moraine to travel some distance along the surface of the glacier,

Snocoach tours offer an easy means of viewing the wonders of the Columbia Icefield's Athabasca Glacier.

allowing passengers a brief walk on the ice before returning. For a more intimate look you can take a three-hour conducted walk; it is also quite possible to make your own way to the toe of the glacier from the parking lot at the glacial tarn known as **Sunwapta Lake.** A series of marker posts shows the extent to which the ice has retreated in recent years.

Continue along the parkway for 30 miles to

Superbly engineered, the Icefields Parkway ranks among the world's finest scenic highways.

Sunwapta Falls 6. Here the waters of the Sunwapta River crash into a limestone gorge threaded by a trail, which leads to a series of smaller falls and rapids.

To the north of the falls, the parkway enters the superb **Athabasca Valley,** the longest and widest in the Rockies. Some 764 miles long (its national park section is designated a heritage river), the Athabasca River discharges into **Lake Athabasca** in northwestern Alberta through a delta that gives it its Cree name—"place of reeds."

The **Goats and Glaciers Viewpoint,** 11 miles beyond Sunwapta Falls, provides a magnificent panorama over the valley, its floor covered in a superb forest of lodgepole pine.

A left turn along the Athabasca Parkway, 3 miles beyond Goats and Glaciers Viewpoint, leads a few hundred yards to the parking lot for **Athabasca Falls 7**. The Athabasca carries the most water of any Rocky Mountain river, and the 70-foot falls present a spectacle of roaring water, spray, and mist.

As you approach Jasper townsite, the dominant feature you see to the north is the mighty outline of Pyramid Mountain. ∎

Rock, ice, & water

The building blocks of the Canadian Rockies are the sediments deposited on the bed of ancient seas by rivers that scoured the surface of the precursor of the Canadian Shield. For about a billion years sands, silts, clays, and lime muds accumulated on the ocean floor, in places reaching a thickness of 12 miles and eventually hardening into sandstones, siltstones, shales, and limestones.

Around 175 million years ago, the continental plate beneath North America came into collision with offshore land masses, setting in motion a series of moving shocks that buckled the sedimentary layers, uplifting them to form first the Columbia Mountains, then the main ranges of the Rockies. A further collision around 120 million years ago led to more crumpling and folding; the main ranges were uplifted further and the Front Range and foothills created. In places, the force behind these processes was so great that huge sheets of rock were forced over the top of much younger strata. Such overthrusts, like the Lewis Overthrust in Waterton Lakes National Park (see p. 270), moved eastward as much as 60 miles.

Once built, the mountains began to be worn down by the processes of erosion that continue today. Their present outline is the result of the sculpturing that took place during a succession of ice ages that began about a quarter of a million years ago. The final shaping was carried out during the most recent ice age, which ended some 11,000 years ago. The remorseless grinding action of great glaciers widened valleys like that of the Bow, Athabasca, and Kicking

Moraine Lake is a superb example of a glacier-fed body of water.

Horse to their characteristic U-shape. Higher up, smaller glaciers worked on tributary valleys left hanging above the main valley; today, streams and rivers escape many of these hanging valleys in spectacular waterfalls like Takakkaw Falls in Yoho National Park (see p. 264). Alternatively, when softer rocks were present, the rivers cut gorges like Maligne Canyon.

Niche glaciers scooped out the sides of mountains, forming the natural amphitheaters called cirques. Some mountains were attacked in this way on several sides, giving them a distinctive pinnacle shape. Known as horn mountains, these great landmarks include Mount Chephren and Mount Assiniboine (see p. 249).

Other characteristic mountain types

While the glaciers we see in the Rockies today are undoubtedly impressive, they are only the remnants of the vast sheets of ice that sculptured the range millions of years ago.

include the "writing desk" shapes formed by overthrusts, where a southwest-facing slope contrasts with a near-vertical wall facing northeast; a well-known example is Mount Rundle above Banff. Where the once horizontal layers of rock were tilted into a vertical position, the erosion of weaker strata has left more resistant rocks in the shape of pinnacles and spires. Mount Edith Cavell in Japser National Park is a fine example of such a "dogtooth" mountain. But of all the mountain types that occur in the Canadian Rockies the "castellated" is the most renowned. These natural fortresses are made up of layers of soft shales alternating with harder bands of limestone, dolomite, and quartzite. The shales erode rapidly to form ledges, while the more resistant rocks remain as cliffs, giving a typical "layer-cake" appearance. Few travelers fail to marvel at aptly named

Castle Mountain standing guard over Bow Valley north of Banff.

The severe climate, with its high rain and snowfall, continues the work of erosion. But the Rockies are not ripe for leveling; it is estimated that the mountains are being reduced in height by an average of three feet every 17,000 years. What becomes of the peaks can be seen along rivers like the Sunwapta and Athabasca. These typical glacier-fed watercourses carry mountain debris that fills the valley floor and diverts the river into multiple channels. Water color in the upper reaches of these rivers is gray. But the smallest particles, known as rock flour, metamorphose in the lakes, absorbing all colors in the spectrum except the blue-green that in summer gives them their enchanting emerald sheen. ■

7 Tributary glacier

1 New snow converts into glacial ice in the accumulation zone

2 The glacial ice melts into water in the ablation zone

3 Ice at the surface of the glacier is under greater pressure than that underneath (which moves against solid bedrock). Surface ice therefore descends over drops at a greater speed and consequently becomes heavily fissured. These fissures are called crevasses.

4 Bedrock

5 The toe

6 Meltwater stream

Jasper National Park

243C4

**Parks Canada
Information
Centre**
- 500 Connaught Dr.
- 780/852-6176
- Park permits: $$$

**Townsite visitor
information**
- 632 Connaught Dr.
- 780/852-4919

**Yellowhead
Museum &
Archives**
- 400 Pyramid
  Lake Rd.
- 780/CPR-3013
- $

WITH SOME OF THE FINEST AND WILDEST SCENERY IN THE
Rockies, Jasper is the largest (4,199 square miles) of the Rocky
Mountain national parks, less frequented by visitors than Banff, but
with equally spectacular displays of mountain, lakes, and forest.

Jasper National Park was founded
(originally as a forest park) in 1907.
The successful establishment of
Banff National Park several years
earlier had demonstrated the
winning combination of railroad
construction, tourism, and conser-
vation, and served as a model
when the Grand Trunk Pacific
Railway began to lay the tracks of a
second transcontinental line
through the mountains. The rail-
road's alignment, previously sur-
veyed, then rejected by the CPR,
followed the old route used by fur
traders and gold seekers along the
Athabasca River and its tributary,
the Miette. The route crossed the
Continental Divide at the lowest
pass along its entire length, the
Yellowhead Pass.

Both the national park and the
townsite, the only settlement within
its boundary, were named for
Jasper House, a North West
Company depot on Brule Lake.

JASPER TOWNSITE
Jasper townsite is the focal point.
It was founded as a railroad town,
and its station is still a stopping
place for scheduled services linking
eastern Canada with Vancouver
and Prince Rupert. The equivalent
of the CPR's Banff Springs Hotel,
the famous Jasper Park Lodge hotel,
built in 1922 by the Canadian
National Railway just outside
town, expresses something of the
difference in spirit between the
two places: While Banff Springs is
an assertive citadel of luxury
rearing up above the town, Jasper
Park Lodge lies low, spreading its

timber structures with great subtle-
ty around the lakeside.

Another building that fits in
well with its mountain setting is the
**Parks Canada Information
Centre,** built in stone and timber
in 1914 and now a national historic
site in its own right. An excellent
source of all kinds of local informa-
tion, it is complemented for
historical background by the
**Yellowhead Museum and
Archives.** ∎

**Canoeists wonder
at the landscape
of Maligne Lake,
14 miles long, up
to 315 feet deep,
and fed by
meltwater from
the glaciers at its
southern end.**

Excursions around Jasper

The valley of the Athabasca around Jasper townsite is much broader than that of the Bow around Banff, so the mountains form a relatively distant backdrop. The best excursions require a vehicle, though some of the lakes studding the valley floor are within easy reach of the townsite and have trails along their shores. Among the most popular are **Patricia** and **Pyramid Lakes** (about 3 miles northwest) and **Lakes Edith** and **Annette** (about 4 miles northeast).

JASPER TRAMWAY
Canada's longest cable car ride lifts passengers 3,074 feet in seven minutes to a ridgetop chalet beneath the summit of **Whistler Mountain** (named for the warning call of the local marmots). You can enjoy the all-around view of Jasper in its superb setting, or if you are feeling energetic—and have good hiking shoes—you can make the 600-foot climb up a rocky pathway to the top of the mountain (1.5 hours round-trip—8,084 feet).
🗻 243C4 ✉ 4 miles south on Whistler Mountain Rd. ☎ 780/852-3093 🕐 Closed Nov.–early March 💲 $$$$$

MOUNT EDITH CAVELL
This drive brings visitors into close contact with the austere north face of this mountain, named for a British nurse executed during World War I and at 11,047 feet the highest near Jasper. The route takes in part of the old alignment of the Icefields Parkway, renamed the Athabasca Parkway, then climbs up a narrow twisting road, not suitable for RVs, above the course of the Astoria River. You can get a fine view of the mountain from a point close to the

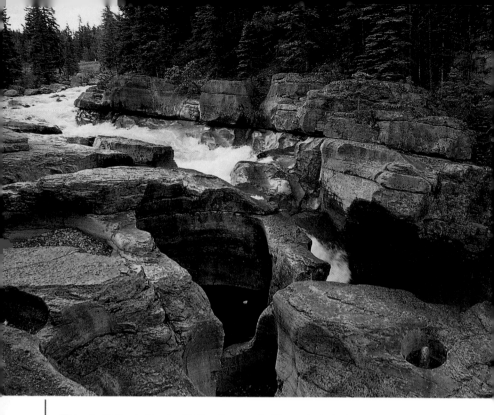

Tonquin Valley trailhead, with **Cavell Lake** in the foreground. From the end of the road there is a magnificent close-up view of the mountain, its cliffs a challenge even for experienced mountaineers. The Mount Edith Cavell trail, which follows the former course of the Angel Glacier, is an object lesson in the effects of ice retreat.

243C4 ✉ 18 miles south off Hwy. 93A
🕐 Closed in winter

MALIGNE VALLEY

One of the most popular excursions in the Rockies, Maligne Valley belies the name (meaning "nasty") given to it by a French missionary, who got into difficulties crossing the river at its confluence with the Athabasca.

Maligne Canyon is up to 180 feet deep, the most spectacular of the accessible canyons in the Rockies, carved into the Palliser limestone by the Maligne River as it drops from its hanging valley to join the Athabasca. Shaded by lush, damp forest, the canyon is so narrow in places that squirrels jump across. If you are hiking, you should not follow their example but keep to the bridges on the 2-mile interpretive trail.

The rocky bed of the Maligne River winds its way through Maligne Canyon in Jasper National Park.

Lovely **Medicine Lake** is remarkable for the fluctuations in its water level. The lake is drained by a series of holes in its bed, a not uncommon feature in limestone country. In periods of high runoff, the capacity of the sinkholes is exceeded and the level rises, sometimes spilling over the lakeside; when there is little flow, the lake almost empties. The sinkholes feed an underground river system, which has so far defeated all attempts to explore it and may well be one of the most extensive in the world.

Nestled in a ring of snowcapped mountains, **Maligne Lake** is impossibly beautiful. It measures 14 miles from end to end—the longest natural lake in the Rockies. Its waters, which originate from the Brazeau Icefield, are held back by a massive landslide. Their color changes southward from green to turquoise as the amount of suspended rock flour increases. Carefully protected from unsuitable development, the lake can only be fully explored on foot or by boat. Beyond **Samson Narrows,** where the lake is constricted by an alluvial fan, lies dreamlike **Spirit Island,** its grassy surface a level platform for a clump of skyward-straining conifers.

M 243C4 ✉ 55 miles round-trip from Jasper ☎ Maligne Tours 780/852-3370, for boat tours and equipment rental

MIETTE HOT SPRINGS

Tucked away in a gorge running east from the Athabasca Valley, these are the hottest springs in the Canadian Rockies; their waters emerge at a temperature averaging 129°F. The springs had long been known to locals, and in 1910 miners from the Pocahontas Coal Mine built a track to reach them. A projected luxury resort came to nothing when the president of the Grand Trunk Railway perished aboard the *Titanic*, taking the plans with him. Today the springs feed a hot pool kept at 104°F as well as a pool kept at a cool temperature in which you can swim.

The route to the springs takes the Yellowhead Highway eastward along the braided course of the Athabasca in its superb mountain setting, past **Jasper Lake** and a cairn commemorating the old trading post of Jasper House on the far bank of the river. By **Disaster Point** you can see mineral licks

For many daring visitors to Jasper National Park, white-water rafting on the Maligne River is a must.

frequented by bighorn sheep. The isolated limestone peak of **Roche Miette** (7,599 feet) is a prominent landmark. The winding 11-mile side road to the hot springs leaves the Yellowhead Highway close to the old Pocahontas mine, closed in 1921.

M 243C4 ✉ 38 miles east of Jasper via Yellowhead Hwy. ☎ 780/866-3939 🕐 Closed mid-Oct.–mid-May 💲 $

Mount Robson Provincial Park

At 12,972 feet, Mount Robson is the highest peak in the Canadian Rockies, and was first climbed only in 1913. It is a formidable presence, dominating the British Columbia provincial park that bears its name. The summit is often obscured by clouds, and its ascent is still considered exceptionally difficult. The visual impact of this magnificent mountain is all the more impressive since, for a considerable time it is hidden from view on the approach from the east.

The Yellowhead Highway follows the valley of the Miette River and the Canadian National railroad to **Yellowhead Pass,** the lowest on the Continental Divide and the border between Alberta and British Columbia. To the west of the pass, the road

crosses the **Fraser River** just beyond **Yellowhead Lake,** then reaches 8-mile-long **Moose Lake.** A trail (half-hour round-trip) leads to **Overlander Falls,** where the Fraser River plunges into a deep canyon. From the visitor center, a short distance along the highway, there is a fine view of Mount Robson, though more intimate contact with the great peak is reserved for serious backpackers. The **Berg Lake Trail** is 14 miles long and climbs 2,600 feet. Your reward is an unforgettable prospect of the mountain's great ramparts, rising a full 8,000 feet from the lake. Two glaciers descend the mountain's flanks, one of them feeding the lake with icebergs.

M 243C4 ✉ 55 miles west of Jasper via Yellowhead Hwy. ■

Routes through the Rockies

"All I can say is that the work has been well done in every way" were the sober words with which William Cornelius Van Horne concluded the simple ceremony on November 7, 1885, which marked the completion of the Canadian Pacific Railway. His colleague on the board of the CPR, Donald Smith, had just succeeded in his second attempt at securing the last spike (of iron, not gold) on the Eagle Pass in British Columbia. This significant occasion was marked with all due solemnity by Smith, a number of other eminent men, and surrounded by a small crowd of railroad workers, one of whom had suddenly cried "All aboard for the Pacific!"

Perhaps even the normally exuberant Van Horne was overawed by his achievement—a 3,000-mile railroad built across the continent in far less than the allotted time.

Van Horne was famous for his "can-do" qualities when hired by the CPR in 1882 to complete the transcontinental railroad linking the Atlantic to the Pacific. Drawing on experience gained in the American Civil War, he organized construction along military lines, with impressive results: The iron road advanced across the prairies at rates some-times exceeding 6 miles a day. But the prairies were easy terrain compared to the mighty mountain barrier to the west, much of which remained unknown. In 1872, surveyor Sandford Fleming had recommended a westward rail route to run from Edmonton over the relatively low Yellowhead Pass. Fearful of possible U.S. encroachment on the Northwest, the Canadian government ordered the railroad to be aligned much farther south, regardless of the engineering difficulties.

By 1883 rails were reaching up the Bow Valley toward Kicking Horse Pass. The next year saw the conquest of the pass and the building of the line down the canyon of the Kicking Horse River. Common caution, to say nothing of the railroad rule book, dictated the construction of tunnels on the descent toward the town of Field in order to reduce the steep grade. Van Horne would have none of it; the CPR needed to earn revenue as soon as possible, and building tunnels would delay the opening of the line by at least a year.

The tracks were run directly down to Field at the horrendous grade of 4.5

One of the most famous photographs in Canadian history shows CPR director Donald Smith hammering home the last spike at Craigellachie, high up on the Eagle Pass, in 1885.

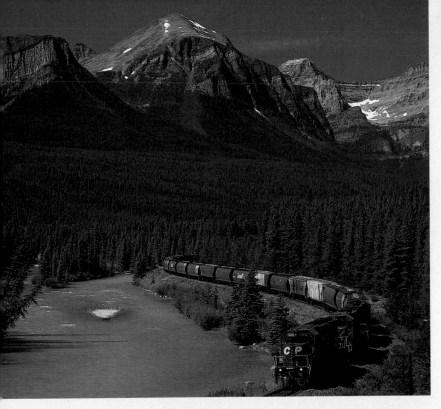

Locomotives winding through the Rockies have been a common sight since the 1880s.

percent. The 4-mile long "Big Hill," as it came to be known, was a nightmare; the first construction train to venture onto it plunged into the canyon, killing three workmen. Trains using the completed line had to be limited in weight and length. Eastbound trains required several locomotives to shove them uphill, while westbound trains were restricted to not much more than a walking pace.

By the early 20th century, the CPR could afford to bypass the Big Hill by building one of the railroad wonders of the world: The famous Spiral Tunnels were completed in 1909, a great figure eight of track built into the flanks of Mount Ogden and Cathedral Mountain. They reduced the grade to a manageable 2.2 percent and offered the spectacle of a freight train locomotive leaving a tunnel while the last car has still to enter.

Farther west, in 1881, surveyor Albert B. Rogers had found a way through a seemingly impenetrable mountain fastness of ice, snow, and avalanche, now known as Glacier National Park. For 35 years the railroad followed the pass named after him, shielding itself from the elements with a series of tunnels and snowsheds. This old route is now a visitor attraction, accessible from Trans-Canada 1. Now safe from avalanches, the railroad has buried itself deep underground in the 5-mile-long Connaught Tunnel, completed in 1916.

Though it was the railroad that opened up the Rocky Mountains, alternatives had previously been discussed, including a colonization roadway for wagon traffic and even a "perpetual sleigh road," which would whisk passengers along at speeds of up to 100 mph. The first automobile arrived in Banff along the railroad track, provoking a ban on motor traffic that was only lifted in 1915. The forerunner of the Trans-Canada Highway reached Lake Louise in 1921 and crossed the Continental Divide to Field in 1926. On entering very British B.C., drivers needed to be reminded to drive on the left. The modern Trans-Canada was built in the 1950s and early 1960s, paralleling the route, as well as the achievement, of the CPR. ∎

Yoho National Park

243D3

Park visitor
information,
1 mile east of Field

250/343-6783

Park permits
$$$–$$$$$

BRITISH COLUMBIA'S YOHO NATIONAL PARK LIES AT EITHER
side of the valley of the Kicking Horse River, a major route for both
road—Trans-Canada 1—and rail—the main line of the CPR. With
some of the most spectacular lakes, waterfalls, and mountain scenery,
the park more than deserves its name, derived from a Cree word
meaning "awe." Road, rail, and a well-developed network of hiking
trails give easy access to some of the park's finest features.

As with Banff, the designation of
Yoho as a protected landscape was
closely linked to the activities of the
Canadian Pacific Railway. The rail-
road's conquest of the Continental
Divide was the most heroic episode
in its construction, and even today
its route over **Kicking Horse
Pass** is an object of wonder and
admiration. As elsewhere in the
mountains, the CPR immediately
saw the potential for attracting
visitors along its tracks. Stunningly
located at the foot of magnificent
Mount Stephen, the depot town
of **Field** (*Visitor information: Tel
250/343-6324, closed weekends*) was
given a dining room that turned
into a hotel. Named Mount Stephen
House, this very first of the CPR's

Rocky Mountain hotels soon
became a venue for alpinists, artists,
and wealthy visitors. Around it, the
original 6-square-mile preservation
area was extended in 1911 to
become the country's second
national park.

Trans-Canada 1 climbs parallel
to the railroad from Alberta to the
B.C. boundary at Kicking Horse
Pass, 5,330 feet above sea level and
the highest point along its route.
The pass and the valley to the west
both owe their name to the blow
administered to Scotsman James
Hector by a horse's hoof, as he and
his party explored the area in 1858.

The first of several side valleys
leading off the highway from the
east is that of the **Cataract**

**Yoho National
Park has more
than 30 "three
thousanders"—
peaks of more
than 9,800 feet
(3,000 m).**

Brook, which descends from **Lake O'Hara.** The lake is cradled in an incomparable setting, which includes the mountains of the Continental Divide to the north. In contrast to bustling Lake Louise, on the far side of the ridge, Lake O'Hara is secluded. The fragility of the alpine ecosystem has led to restriction of access; cars (and even bicycles) are banned, and the chalet hotel and campsite can only be reached by a bus service (three per day) up the 8-mile road (*Reserve in advance: Tel 250/343-6433*). A network of trails enables walkers to enjoy the small lakes and flower-rich alpine meadows.

Crowds gather at the **Spiral Tunnel viewpoint** (*6 miles from eastern entrance*), the most popular in any Canadian national park, for the spectacle of immensely long freight trains snaking through the Canadian Pacific's spiral tunnels (see pp. 262–3).

A narrow, winding 8-mile road with hairpin bends runs up **Yoho Valley** (*7 miles from eastern entrance*) to the **Takakkaw Falls.** Fed by meltwaters from the Waputik Icefield, the falls are among the highest in North America, dropping a spectacular 1,247 feet in a series of magnificent cascades.

EMERALD LAKE & WAPTA FALLS

Dating from the Middle Cambrian period, more than 500 million years ago, the extraordinarily rich fossil beds on the mountains above **Emerald Lake** have yielded—and are still yielding—important evidence about the evolution of life on earth. Their palaeontological significance led to their being designated a UNESCO world heritage site in 1981 (*Visitor information, 800/343-3006*). Specimens are on display at the visitor center at Field.

The 5-mile road to Emerald Lake (*2 miles west of Field*) leads past a stopping place with a view of a natural bridge, where the Kicking Horse River has cut away soft deposits of shale, leaving an arch of harder limestone. Of stunning beauty, its blue-green waters set among high mountains and surrounded by lush forest, Emerald Lake is the biggest of Yoho's water bodies and is a popular destination.

Farther along the road, look for the trail head to **Wapta Falls** (*3 miles round-trip*). Most of the precipitation falling on Yoho National Park eventually passes over these falls, whose relative lack of height (100 feet) is more than made up by their sheer volume. ■

Yoho's Emerald Lake

Kootenay National Park

243D2

West Gate Information Centre

✉ Off Hwy. 93

☎ 250/347-9615

TO THE WEST OF THE CONTINENTAL DIVIDE OFF Hwy. 93, the 543-square-mile Kootenay National Park links the high mountains to the milder environment of the Rocky Mountain Trench.

The range of habitats in Kootenay National Park is astonishing. Upland meadows and moist coniferous forest in the valley of the Kootenay River contrast with cactus and prickly pear in the warm environment of the Rocky Mountain Trench.

Whereas railroads were the reason for the designation of Banff, Jasper, and Yoho National Parks, Kootenay owes its existence to a road. The Kootenay Parkway was originally conceived before World War I as a route for orchard produce from the Columbia Valley to be trucked northeastward. When private promoters and the B.C. provincial government ran out of money, the federal government completed the road, on condition that a strip of land 5 miles wide on either side become a national park. Kootenay National Park was designated in 1920, and the 58-mile parkway opened in 1923.

The road rises out of the Bow Valley from **Castle Junction,** giving fine views back to Castle Mountain. Five miles from Castle Junction, Vermilion Pass (5,412 feet) marks the B.C./Alberta boundary and the border between Banff and Kootenay National Parks. The

short **Fireweed Trail,** through an area devastated by a forest fire in 1968, demonstrates how a burn can enhance wildlife diversity and how controlled burns are essential to the mountain environment.

Rushing down from its hanging valley, the **Tokkum Creek** has eroded the 2,000-foot-long **Marble Canyon** (*11 miles from Castle Junction*) in the dolomite and Cathedral limestone, which has been so polished by the silt-rich stream as to resemble marble. The short interpretive trail criss-crosses the canyon and passes a natural bridge.

Twelve miles west of Castle Junction off Hwy. 93 a 0.5-mile trail crosses a suspension bridge over the **Vermilion River** to this mysterious place, where mineral-rich springs seeping upward have created the Ochre Beds, colorful deposits of clay. The **Paint Pots** themselves are a series of pools formed by the accumulation of minerals around their rim. An active trade was developed by the Kutenai Indians (after whom the park is named), who processed what they called the "red earth" of this sacred place into pigments for rock-, body-, or tepee-painting. In the early 20th century a short-lived effort was made to mine the deposits on an industrial basis.

After the Paint Pots, Hwy. 93 runs southeast down the valley of the Vermilion River. To the west, one of the most popular backpacking routes in the Rockies follows the foot of the **Rockwall,** a spectacular 3,000-foot cliff of Ottertail limestone.

Vermilion Crossing has services and a new **visitor center** (*just inside entrance, Tel 250/347-3505*), and offers fine views of one of the park's most spectacular peaks, Mount Verendrye (10,125 feet). At the foot of **Mount Wardle** it is sometimes possible to see moose, deer, or mountain goats—the symbol of the park—taking advantage of the roadside mineral licks. **Kootenay Crossing** marks the start of a run along the **Kootenay Valley,** in the course of which the damp subalpine forest gives way to the drier, more fragmented woodland of the B.C. interior, characterized by Douglas-fir. As the road leaves the river and climbs southwestward, there is a fine panorama.

Sinclair Pass and **Sinclair Valley** are named after the leader of a group of settlers sent this way by the Hudson's Bay Company, in an (unsuccessful) attempt to forestall the colonization of Oregon by the United States.

RADIUM HOT SPRINGS

Emerging via a fault in the earth's crust at a temperature of 104°F, the waters were known to local residents, who regarded their outlet as a sacred place. Mineral content is minimal, and consequently the waters are virtually odorless. They are, however, mildly radioactive, a property once considered highly beneficial.

Around the turn of the century, the springs were developed by private interests in a rather fitful way until the government took them over in 1922 as part of the national park. Today there are two popular open-air pools, one hot, one cool. ■

Radium Hot Springs

243D2

2 miles east of the town of Radium, off Kootenay Parkway

250/347-9485

$$$

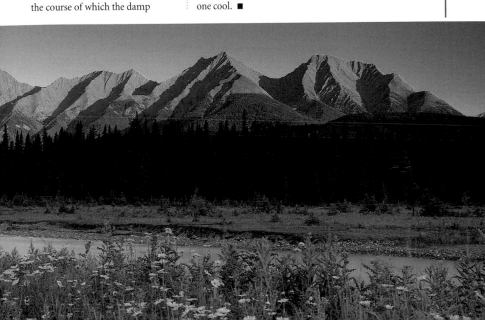

Glacier & Mount Revelstoke National Parks

🅰 243C3

Glacier National Park

✉ Rogers Pass Visitor Centre, 0.75 mile west of Rogers Pass

☎ 250/837-6274

Mount Revelstoke

✉ Park admin. office, 301 Campbell Ave.

☎ 250/837-7500

A plaque commemorates engineer Walter Moberley's feat in forging a route through the seemingly impenetrable Monashee Range.

CANADA'S ADJOINING NATIONAL PARKS WERE DESIGNATED to conserve the jagged Selkirk Mountains, part of the Columbia range just to the west of the Rocky Mountain Trench. The peaks are at least as formidable as those to the east; the highest point, Mount Dawson, reaches 11,122 feet. The climate here is exceptionally harsh—Glacier's 400-plus glaciers are fed by a snowfall averaging 370 inches a year. The steep valleys are regularly swept by avalanches capable of burying the Trans-Canada Highway under 30 feet of snow.

GLACIER

Glacier National Park shares railroad origins with Yoho and Banff. Its designation as a park in 1886 coincided with the opening of the CPR's line through the pass heroically discovered by surveyor Albert Rogers a few years earlier. A visitor boom developed, based on the long-since demolished Glacier House hotel, conceived as a railroad restaurant to save locomotives the burden of pulling dining cars up the severe grades. Climbers flocked here from Europe, and today alpinists consider Glacier to be the birthplace of mountaineering in North America. The area's heyday came to an end in 1916 when the CPR, tired of the wear and tear on its rolling stock and the cost of constantly repairing avalanche damage, abandoned Rogers Pass in favor of a 5-mile tunnel through Mount Macdonald. After decades of isolation, the construction of the Trans-Canada Highway across the pass in 1962 once more brought visitors into the area. The avalanche problem is kept within bounds by the presence of snowsheds along the road and by the use of artillery; the buildup of snow formations is carefully monitored, and army howitzers are fired to dislodge them in a controlled way.

Much of Glacier is inaccessible except to climbers and serious walkers, but a road or rail journey through the park is a memorable experience, to say the least. A number of short trails starting at or near the highway introduce the park's landscapes and history. Among them is the **Abandoned Rails Trail** (0.75 mile one way), which follows the old route of the CPR through Rogers Pass. The pass itself is a national historic site, with displays in the visitor center. The **Illecillewaet campground** (2.5 miles west of visitor center) is the starting point for trails of varying length, while **Bear Falls Trail** and the **Hemlock Grove Trail** lead through surprisingly lush forest produced by the abundant precipitation.

MOUNT REVELSTOKE

Revelstoke National Park also offers the experience of luxuriant woodland. Not far from the eastern entrance to the park on Trans-Canada 1, the boardwalk of the **Giant Cedars Trail** leads through a majestic stand of 600-year old western red cedar and hemlock, a fine example of British Columbia's interior rain forest. But the main attraction of this tiny national park (100 square miles) is the ease with which visitors can enjoy the floral wealth of its alpine

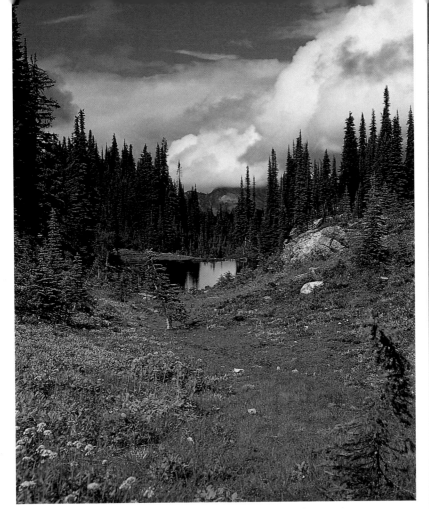

meadows, the chief reason for the park's creation in 1914.

The 16-mile **Meadows in the Sky Parkway** climbs from the park's western entrance toward the 6,358 feet summit of Mount Revelstoke. The zigzag route offers magnificent views of the great sweep of the **Columbia River Valley** and the **Monashee Mountains** to the west, but the real treat comes at the summit, where the 0.75-mile **Meadows in the Sky Trail** leads through a glorious display of mountain flowers, at their showiest in high summer. Other, longer, trails give access to a number of delightful alpine lakes.

Revelstoke townsite stands at the point where the Illecillewaet River flowing westward from Glacier National Park discharges into the Columbia River. A service center for travelers, the town is named for the man who in the 1880s financed the Canadian Pacific Railway in its most difficult hour, Lord Revelstoke of Barings Bank of London. Just to the north of the town, the waters of the Columbia are held back by the huge 574-foot dam. The dam's visitor center (*Tel 604/837-6211*) has displays on the construction of this awe-inspiring piece of engineering and on the management of the Columbia River system. ∎

One of Mount Revelstoke's many alpine meadows

Waterton Lakes National Park

⛰ 24ID1

Visitor information
✉ Entrance Rd.
☎ 403/859-2445
🕐 Closed winter

Park Admin. Office
✉ 215 Mount View Rd.
☎ 403/859-2477

RISING WITH DRAMATIC SUDDENNESS DIRECTLY OUT OF the prairies of southwestern Alberta, the mountains of Waterton Lakes National Park are unique among the Rocky Mountain parks and are a world heritage area in their own right. Between 175 million and 125 million years ago, a 100-mile-long by 4-mile-thick slab of ancient rock was violently uplifted and pushed 60 miles northeastward atop the much younger rocks of the prairies. Known as the Lewis Thrust, this extraordinary event reversed the usual geologic sequence—young rocks overlying older rocks—and explains the surprising lack of transition between prairie and mountain; in places the elevation changes 4,000 feet only a half mile from the prairie floor.

The park is small (202 square miles) and, unlike the other parks, has no through roads. Visitors can relax by the shores of the lakes **(Maskinonge Lake** and **Lower, Middle,** and **Upper Waterton Lakes)** and above all make use of the superb 150-mile trail network. The park came into being in 1895 (to preserve it from encroaching settlement); in 1932 it was linked with Montana's **Glacier National Park** to become the world's first International Peace Park.

The most prominent man-made feature in the park is the splendid timber structure of the **Prince of Wales Hotel** (*Waterton Lake, Tel 403/859-2231),* built by the U.S. Great Northern Railway in 1926 as a base for Rocky Mountain bus tours. The hotel overlooks Upper Waterton Lake and **Waterton townsite,** the focal point of the park. This is the starting point for a number of trails and for boat trips (*Tel 403/859-2362)* on the Upper Lake. The boats cross the international border and give access to the spectacular trail leading via a tunnel to **Crypt Lake,** high up in a superb glacial amphitheater *(11-mile round-trip, 2,100-foot ascent).* This is an excursion for determined hikers, but there are plenty of easy walks in the park, including the **Red Rock Canyon trail,** which leads through a 65-foot-deep cleft with rocks of purple, green, yellow, and red. ∎

Waterton Lakes National Park juxtaposes alpine landscapes with the aspen groves and grasslands of the prairie.

Lying beyond the barrier of the Rocky Mountains, British Columbia, Canada's westernmost and third largest province, is almost a separate country, proud of its 5,000 miles of magnificent coastline.

West Coast

Fall in British Columbia

West Coast

BRITISH COLUMBIA (B.C.) OFFERS A BEWILDERING VARIETY OF CLIMATES and landscapes. Eternal snows cloak the peaks of the ranges that parallel the Rocky Mountains, while along the U.S. border scarce water makes irrigation necessary in the orchards and vineyards. Primeval rain forest spreads inland from the fjord-cut littoral, while in the interior, deprived of the rain that falls on the Coast Mountains, patches of near-desert coexist with fine ranch lands. The bleak northern half of the province is hardly inhabited: More than half the population is crowded into the Lower Fraser Valley around Vancouver, with another half million in Victoria and the southeastern tip of Vancouver Island.

It is to this metropolitan region based on the balmy shores of the Strait of Georgia that most of the province's visitors come. Many arrive from the nearby states of the Pacific Northwest, others from the far side of the ocean, others still by the east-west road and rail routes through the mountains that have become classic journeys in their own right.

With all the allure of a great and growing city, vibrant Vancouver also enjoys an unrivaled setting of water and mountains. On the opposite shore of the strait, and much smaller, is Victoria—hardly less enticing, pleased to be the provincial capital, and coyly playing on its British heritage. Both cities have outstanding museums: In Vancouver, the University of British Columbia Museum of Anthropology houses an unrivaled collection of Northwestern native art and artifacts; in Victoria, the lavish displays of the Royal British Columbia Museum deal with the same themes, as well as introducing the province's history and its richly diverse landscapes.

Neither city is far from wilderness. Most of the population of Vancouver Island clings to the east-facing shore of the strait, sheltered by the island's mountain spine from the rain and storms of its western coast. Here, Pacific Rim National Park Reserve protects a savage, surf-battered shore and its rain forest-clad heights. Vancouver's urban sprawl threatens the productive farmlands won with much effort from the swampy levels of the Lower Fraser Valley, but immediately to the north a whole series of parks, among them Garibaldi Provincial Park, enables hikers to escape into the forests and alpine meadows of the Coast Mountains.

Well-trod visitor routes lead away from the province's urban heartland. Vancouver Island's principal highway terminates at Port Hardy, terminus for the spectacular ferry trip through the Inside Passage, the easiest way for visitors to experience something of the magnificence of the islands and inlets of the lonely northwestern coast. To the east of Vancouver, two rail-

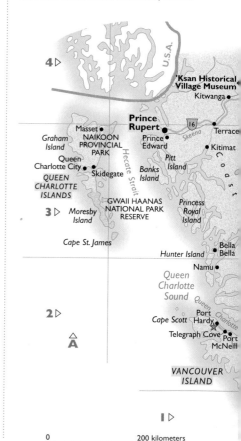

roads as well as the Trans-Canada Highway follow the Fraser River upstream, leaving the lush pastures of the lower valley to make their way through the canyons that early explorers and prospectors found so formidable. At Kamloops, the Canadian National turns north to break through the barrier of the Rockies at Yellowhead Pass, while the Canadian Pacific, accompanied by the Trans-Canada, penetrates increasingly dramatic mountain country on its way to Kicking Horse Pass. Originally a fur-trading post, Kamloops thrived as a supply center for the gold rushes that opened up the interior of the province in the mid-to-late 19th century. Most prospectors followed the famous Cariboo Road, striking north from the Fraser's tributary, the Thompson River.

An alternative route into the Cariboo country follows the magnificent ocean inlet of Howe Sound inland, passing the world-famous ski resort of Whistler. Besides a highway, the route is followed by the regular passenger service of B.C. Rail, which terminates at the province's largest inland city, Prince George. From here, rail and road accompany each other on the long journey westward to Prince Rupert. The final stretch along the Skeena River passes villages where a revival of Gitksan culture has added new totems to those already there. The Port Hardy ferry docks at Prince Rupert, as does the boat to and from the far-off Queen Charlotte Islands, stronghold of the once fierce Haida people, whose deserted coastal villages are among the country's most evocative sites.

Along the U.S. frontier in the far south of the province, the north-south river valleys, with their chains of beautiful lakes, made natural routes for the first white settlers. Laid out against the grain of the country, the modern Crowsnest Highway, successor to the Dewdney Trail of the 1860s, is a fascinating alternative to the Trans-Canada between Pacific coast and prairie interior. Overcoming a series of high passes, it gives access to the orchard-patterned lowlands of the Okanagan, with its lakeside resorts, or to fascinating heritage towns such as Nelson, on the shore of Lake Kootenay. ■

Super-natural British Columbia

Superabundant natural resources in ocean, rivers, and forests helped Northwestern natives achieve an unusually high standard of material culture long before the arrival of Europeans, drawn here by this same natural bounty. The fur traders were the first to come, followed by mineral prospectors, fishermen, ranchers, and lumbermen. Today's provincial economy still depends largely on the exploitation of what were once seen as almost limitless resources.

Organized mostly in huge conglomerates, forestry still occupies first place among the province's resource-based industries. At the same time, the highly mineralized rocks of the province are mined according to the fluctuating demands of the world market for an A to Z of metals—from antimony to zinc. The rain from Pacific clouds on uplands and mountains feeds lakes and rivers, many of which have been tapped for hydropower, in sufficient quantity for export to the United States. The stars of the province's fishery are its five species of salmon, once so abundant that at places such as Salmon Arm they were hauled from the water in armfuls and spread on the land as fertilizer. The damming of rivers for hydroelectricity and the consequent barring of the salmons' way upstream to their spawning grounds is one of many factors contributing to a dismaying decrease in their number. Drastic restrictions have been placed on the catch and disputes between U.S. and Canadian fishermen over who is entitled to fish have led to many unpleasant incidents such as the blockade of an Alaska ferry by B.C. fishing boats.

Forestry resources

But it is B.C.'s forestry industry that has been the focus of most controversy. Almost 60 percent of the province is mantled in trees, but the temperate rain forest of the coast, with its red cedar, western hemlock, Douglas-fir, and Sitka spruce, attracts most attention. Here, where the soggy conditions inhibit fires, trees grow to immense size, sometimes reaching a height of 300 feet. Luxuriant undergrowth and the presence of slowly decaying fallen trees act as a filter, ensuring the purity of the runoff feeding streams and lakes. The cedar's aromatic and lightweight wood was a staple of Northwestern First Nations culture—its trunk used for canoes and totem poles; its timber split into planks for house construction, carved into masks, or steam-bent into storage boxes. But lumbermen have found a use for most trees: The straight trunk of the Douglas-fir has always made it ideal for construction, while even the once-despised soft wood of the hemlock can be converted into excellent pulp for paper and synthetics. The attack on the forest began in early colonial days on the coast or along rivers, where trees were easily accessible, and the felled timber could be transported by water. Railroads extended the scope of operation immensely, and nowadays roads and modern machinery mean that virtually no forest is inaccessible, and areas once thought to be remote can be easily reached and exploited.

The environmental effects of logging can be devastating. The removal of tree cover through clear-cutting leads to soil erosion and landslides (often long after the clearing has taken place), the silting of streams, and their destruction as salmon spawning grounds. The loss of wildlife habitat can be particularly serious in the case of large mammals such as grizzlies or mountain lions, which require extensive ranges. The efforts of timber companies to replant require many years, and in any case it is impossible to replicate the ecological or aesthetic value of old-growth forest.

Throughout the 1980s and early 1990s, resistance grew to what was seen by environmental activists as the destruction of British Columbia's greatest natural resource. Government concern was tempered by the need to sustain an industry that employed over a quarter-million people, many of them living in communities where there were no alternative jobs. Matters came to a head in 1993. The hitherto untouched valleys of Clayoquot

For better or worse, logging remains a staple of the British Columbian (and Canadian) economy, though it no longer requires the dash and daring of "white-water men" to break up log jams.

Sound on Vancouver Island's west coast had for several years been the scene of protests as local First Nations people as well as environmentalists protested against clear-cutting proposals. The B.C. government's announcement in April 1993 of a policy that would allow clear-cutting to continue over much of the area enraged activists. Citizens came from all over Canada to support a blockade of logging oper-

ations by the massive MacMillan Bloedel Company; more than 900 people were arrested in one of Canada's biggest ever civil disobedience campaigns. While the deforestation continues the event has become a symbol for environmental awareness, not just in British Columbia, but all over Canada and even worldwide. ■

Vancouver

⚐ 273C1

Visitor information
✉ 200 Burrard St.
☎ 604/683-2000 or 800/663-6000

CANADA'S WESTERNMOST GREAT CITY REVELS IN ITS glorious setting of sea and mountains, offering its inhabitants a tempting lifestyle in which leisure and pleasure are underpinned by the prosperity engendered by Vancouver's position on the Pacific Rim. The reason for the city's existence, the splendid deepwater harbor formed by fjordlike Burrard Inlet, is backed by the often snowcapped Coast Mountains. To the west, the peaks of Vancouver Island rise over the waters of the Strait of Georgia, while to the south Mount Baker, the giant of the U.S. Cascade Range, can often be seen.

Residents never tire of telling of the wonders of swimming, sailing, or skiing at whim, or of being able to disappear into the wilderness just a few minutes' drive from a city with all the cultural delights of a multicultural metropolis. Despite the frequent sight of snow on the mountaintops, Vancouver enjoys a mild climate, though mist is common and rainfall heavy (about 60 inches annually—50 percent more than New York City).

The city is built on a peninsula defined by the **Burrard Inlet** on the north and the delta of the **Fraser River** to the south. From the compact downtown core, less than a mile square, the densely built-up and now fashionable West End soon gives way westward to one of the world's great green spaces, Stanley Park, the forested tract occupying the tip of the peninsula. To the east is attractively renovated Gastown, where Vancouver began; it was here in 1867 that garrulous John Deighton opened the doors of his saloon to workmen from the recently established sawmills nearby. His nickname, "Gassy Jack," is supposed to have influenced the present-day name of the settlement that grew up around his bar. Otherwise the slowly growing town was called Granville, a name discarded in favor of Vancouver on the initiative of William Van Horne, general

manager of the Canadian Pacific Railway in the 19th century.

The CPR arrived here in 1886 (see pp. 262–3), much to the chagrin of the speculators who had bought up land around the original terminus at Port Moody a few miles upstream. Van Horne's choice of name stuck, despite resentful rumblings from Vancouver Island on the far shore of the strait. Though its timber buildings were devastated in a great fire in 1886, Vancouver flourished, rebuilding in stone and brick and soon surpassing

Downtown Vancouver, as seen from its harbor

Victoria in size and importance.

By the 1920s it had become Canada's third largest city. Very British at first, Vancouver has inevitably attracted migrants not only from Europe but from the far shores of the ocean on which it is set; its longstanding Chinese community is now one of the largest in North America. Today, with a metropolitan population approaching two million, it has become an excellent location for many kinds of economic activity, including corporate headquarters. You can see evidence of this in the high-rise structures that dominate the downtown skyline. Some of these, like the chisel-capped Cathedral Place, are fine examples of postmodern elegance, worthy successors to the extravagantly ornamented art deco **Marine Building** of 1930.

Vancouver is a pleasure to explore. Downtown is compact, easy to get around on foot, and the shore of Burrard Inlet is becoming increasingly accessible as

redevelopment of old port installations proceeds. Protruding into the waters of the harbor, Canada Place, with its superb views of the city's setting, is one of a number of assets added for Expo '86. No visit is complete without some sort of trip on the water, perhaps an inexpensive ferry ride across to North Vancouver aboard the Seabus, part of a developed public transportation system (*B.C. Transit, Tel 604/521-0410*) that includes Skytrain, a futuristic driverless train linking downtown with some suburbs.

Beyond the center, some attractions such as the thriving market quarter of Granville Island and the museums in Vanier Park can be reached by bus, but it is far more fun to take the little ferries that ply the waters of False Creek. Farther afield still, but not to be missed for its marvelous collection of Northwest First Nations artifacts, is the campus of the University of British Columbia and its superb

STAGE FOR ALL THE WORLD

Vancouver is one of the most popular film settings in the world, doubling not only as near-neighbor Seattle, but also as New York, Beverly Hills, and countless other places even more exotic. But one of its staunchest customers, the long-running TV series *X-Files*, finally gave up and returned to Los Angeles, when series star David Duchovny complained about the city's 400 inches of rain a day, an act that earned him derision throughout the province. ∎

Museum of Anthropology.

Anchored to the shore by a luxury hotel, **Canada Place** resembles a great sailing vessel about to cast off from the dockside. With superlative views of the harbor from its boardwalks, it is perhaps the best place to begin an exploration of the city center, whose clustered towers rise just inland. Designed by Eberhard Zeidler, architect of Toronto's Eaton Centre, as the Canadian pavilion for Expo '86, it now houses a trade and convention center and an IMAX cinema beneath its five great sails of fiberglass fabric. True to the past—it is built on the site of Harbour Pier B-C, where the famous ships of the White Empress Line once docked—Canada Place welcomes cruise liners as well as the occasional naval vessel.

Granville Square, which is graced with an enigmatic modern sculpture, overlooks the embarkation point for the Seabus linking downtown to North Vancouver. Though no longer the terminus for transcontinental trains, the grandiose Canadian Pacific Railroad station of 1914 (*Tel 604/669-3050*) is still a transport hub, serving not only Seabus but also Skytrain and the regional West Coast Express. Its great halls are decorated with Canadian travel scenes and have earned it a well-merited heritage award.

No city worth its salt lacks a revolving restaurant and observation deck, and here in Vancouver it is called the Lookout, an awesome 548 feet above the street via a vertiginous outside elevator. It is the crowning glory of the **Harbour Centre.**

Gastown

Threatened by total redevelopment in the early 1960s, Vancouver's late

Today's British Columbians are increasingly aware of the First Nations heritage of the West Coast. These totems stand in Vancouver's Stanley Park.

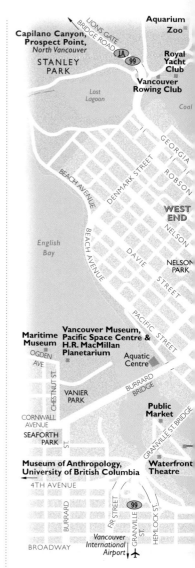

19th-century urban nucleus was saved by the efforts of local people and developers, who restored and refurbished old buildings and ensured that most new structures fitted in with the established townscape. Today, Gastown is a busy and rather self-conscious heritage area with trendy boutiques, souvenir shops, bars,

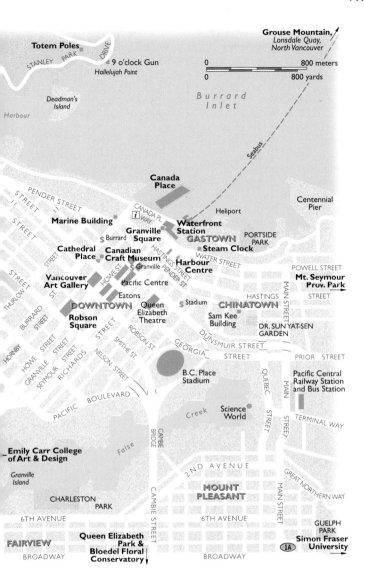

and restaurants, saved from smugness by its proximity to the city's east end and its numerous skid row residents.

The basic grid of Gastown's streets is angled to accommodate the outline of the waterfront, and the odd angles of some of the junctions are occupied by flatiron buildings like the **Europe Hotel.**

Tidewater once lapped the very edge of **Water Street,** now the main thoroughfare. At the corner with Cambie Street stands the **Steam Clock,** a favorite spot for photographs. Inaugurated in 1977, the clock powers its old paddle-steamer whistle with steam from the district heating system. The improbable founder of the area,

Harbour Centre

✉ 555 W. Hastings St.

☎ 604/689-0421

$ $$$

Dr. Sun Yat-Sen Garden
- ⊠ 578 Carrall St.
- ☎ 604/689-7133
- ⑤ $$$

Canadian Craft Museum
- ⊠ 639 Hornby St.
- ☎ 604/687-8266
- ⊕ Closed Tues. in winter
- ⑤ $

Art Gallery
- ⊠ 750 Hornby St.
- ☎ 604/662-4719
- ⊕ Closed Mon.–Tues. mid-Oct.–April
- ⑤ $$$

loquacious saloon owner "Gassy Jack," is commemorated in **Maple Tree Square** by a statue atop a whiskey barrel.

Chinatown

Just to the east of Gastown is North America's third largest Chinatown, the focal point of a 100,000-plus community whose origins go back to the gold rush and the construction of the Canadian Pacific Railway. Behind high white walls is the **Dr. Sun Yat-Sen Garden,** an exquisite reproduction of a Ming Dynasty landscape, constructed for the Expo '86 by an expert team of horticulturalists from the People's Republic of China.

Cathedral Place

Completed in 1991, this elegant office tower with its chiseled copper cap has become a city landmark. It exemplifies postmodernist concern for context by incorporating details from the much-loved art deco structure it replaced and with its sensitivity to its long-established neighbors, **Christ Church Cathedral** and the **Hotel Vancouver.** Approached by an attractive courtyard is the similar but much smaller structure housing

the **Canadian Craft Museum.** It houses an unequaled selection of fine objects by international as well as Canadian craftspeople.

Vancouver's public art collection, known simply as the **Art Gallery,** is housed in the former city courthouse, a neoclassic structure designed by Francis Rattenbury and carefully converted into an elegant setting for art by local architect Arthur Erickson. Most of the usual Canadian figures are represented, as are a number of European and American artists, but the greatest attraction for visitors is the extensive collection of the works of Emily Carr (see below).

A tour-de-force of progressive architect and landscape designer Arthur Erickson, **Robson Square** comprises a 7-story law court building and extensive and attractive outdoor spaces on several levels. With its lush planting and extensive use of water, the complex occupies two whole city blocks and leads under Robson Street via a skating rink and convention center to the Art Gallery, making a fascinating sequence of urban spaces.

Stanley Park

The 1,000-acre Stanley Park,

Emily Carr

Born of English parents in Victoria, Emily Carr (1871–1945) was one of the most fascinating figures in Canadian art. It was only in middle life that her utterly original talent was recognized. Up to then, she had followed a lonely path, recording the villages and the art of the First Nations of the Northwest and supporting herself by running a lodging house. On meeting members of the Group of Seven (see pp. 186–7) in 1927 and seeing their work she exclaimed,

"Oh, God, what have I seen? Where have I been?" Encouraged by Lawren Harris, a member of the group, she returned to her earlier themes, painting monumental pictures of the totems that are her best known works and that "throb and sway with the vital energy of conviction." Her later works apply the same intensity to the depiction of the deep forests of British Columbia and capture the transcendental qualities of the open sky. ∎

which covers an area as large as Vancouver's downtown, is a wonderful asset for a city already bountifully blessed with natural landscape. Mostly forested, the park extends to the very tip of the peninsula at the **Narrows,** the entrance to Burrard Inlet. The peninsula was a military zone that would have no doubt been clear-cut, but it was saved by the foresight of the city fathers, who petitioned to preserve it within a month of Vancouver's founding in 1886. Facilities and attractions abound, but the main function of Stanley Park is as a vast open space, directly accessible from the city, in which people can do as they want—jog, walk, Rollerblade, cycle, swim, or just laze. A ride along the 6-mile scenic road that runs one-way counterclockwise around the shore is an essential experience for all visitors, best undertaken by rented bicycle with frequent stops to savor the ever changing views of city, sea, and mountain.

As the road curves around **Coal Harbour** with its Royal Yacht Club and Rowing Club, bird-rich **Lost Lagoon** is to the left, a former inlet that almost dries up at low tide. Among the trees just short of **Hallelujah Point** is a brightly painted group of totem poles. Near **Prospect Point,** the path crosses over the approach to the 5,000-foot-long **Lions Gate Bridge** over First Narrows, built in 1938 to link the city with the exclusive residential area of West Vancouver. There is a fine view of ships passing in and out of Burrard Inlet from Prospect Point. Between here and west-facing Ferguson Point, the forest of cedar, hemlock, and Douglas-fir gives a good idea of what the site of Vancouver must have looked like before clearance began in the 1880s.

Within Stanley Park are two of Vancouver's most popular attractions, the **Children's Zoo** and the internationally renowned **Vancouver Aquarium** (*Tel 604/268-9900*). Emphasis is on the marine life of the Northwest and Arctic, with sea otter, octopus, and beluga whale, but this magnificent institution has much else besides, including a convincingly steamy re-creation of the Amazon rain forest with its abundant bird, fish, and reptilian life, as well as a reproduction of an Indonesian coral reef. ■

A cruise ship ties up alongside Canada Place, a dramatic addition to Vancouver's waterfront.

Children's Zoo
☎ 604/257-8531
🕐 Closed Mon.-Fri. Sept.–May
💲 $$$

More places to visit in Vancouver

GRANVILLE ISLAND

Granville Island, a 20-acre landfill site in **False Creek** created in 1915 for industrial purposes, is now a vibrant meeting place, which has admirably fulfilled the Granville Island Trust's aim of making it a place of "randomness, curiosity, delight and surprise." The remains of industry coexist happily with a whole array of other activities, including shops, studios, restaurants, galleries, theaters, a marina, brewery, and large indoor market. On fine weekends, everyone who's not on the beach seems to head here, and the island becomes almost impossibly crowded, but no one complains. Hardly heritage material, the old industrial buildings have been brightly reclad and repainted to house their new uses; the market, with its array of tempting comestibles and other articles, still has pulleys

and derricks hanging from the ceiling. There are no sidewalks, but people and cars mingle in friendly proximity in the spaces between the buildings, where railroad tracks still run. In the middle of it all and setting the tone is the **Emily Carr College of Art and Design.**

VANCOUVER MUSEUM

Fronted by a glittering giant sculpture of the crab that, in First Nations legend, is the guardian of the harbor, the museum presents a dutiful account of the history of Vancouver from the earliest European incursions onward, as well as rotating displays from its splendid collection of First Nations art and artifacts. There are reconstructions of a fur-trading post, the steerage quarters in an immigrant ship, the interior of a railroad "colonist car," all

Visitors are invited to "boldly go" and enjoy such sensational delights as a virtual voyage to Mars. On it they brave a close shave with the sun and a brush with a meteor shower to bring relief to the inhabitants of a late 21st-century colony on the surface of the red planet.

✉ 1100 Chestnut St., Vanier Park
☎ 604/736-5417 🕐 Closed Mon. 💲 $$$

MARITIME MUSEUM

This relatively small museum in a striking A-frame building has as its superb centerpiece the RCMP vessel *St. Roch*. In 1940, concerned enough to emphasize its presence in the far north, Canada dispatched this large supply and patrol boat from Vancouver on the first west–east voyage through the Northwest Passage. The epic trip took 27 months to reach Halifax, but, undaunted, the *St. Roch* returned to Vancouver, the first vessel ever to sail the passage in both directions. The return journey lasted a mere 86 days. The *St. Roch* has been fully restored to its appearance in 1944, down to a team of huskies on deck.

The museum's other exhibits are minor compared with the *St. Roch*, but there is plenty of maritime memorabilia (including items from Canada's worst shipping disaster, the sinking of the *Empress of Ireland* in the St. Lawrence in 1914), lots of fascinating ship models (and a glimpse into the modelmakers'

Outdoor performers make the most of a sunny day to entertain the weekend crowd on Granville Island.

in great contrast to opulent urban interiors from the turn of the century. A thought-provoking model of the site of Vancouver shows what is now a great metropolis when it was nothing more than a thickly forested peninsula with a solitary trail leading to a tiny harbor.

Attached to the museum is the recently opened and lavishly equipped **Pacific Space Centre,** which incorporates the long-established **Macmillan Planetarium.**

Bill Reid's "Raven" at the U.B.C. Museum of Anthropology. The sculptor, of Haida descent, devoted his working life to reviving and reinterpreting the First Nations' artistic tradition.

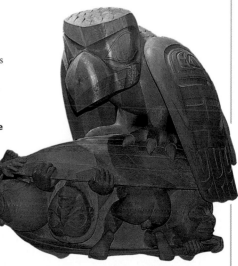

workshop), and a chance to skipper a tugboat as it noses out of False Creek.

A dock on English Bay has a number of small vessels, most of them in working order.

✉ 1905 Ogden Ave., Vanier Park
☎ 604/257-8300 🕐 Closed Mon.,
Sept.–early May 💲 $$$

UNIVERSITY OF BRITISH COLUMBIA

Almost a city in its own right, the vast campus of the University of British Columbia, with nearly 500 buildings, is located on Point Grey overlooking the Georgia Strait and the mountains of Vancouver Island. From early days, agriculture and forestry played an important role in the life of the university, and 70 acres of the campus are given over to the marvelous trees and shrubs of the **University of British Columbia Botanical Garden** (*Tel 604/822-3928*). In addition, there is the exquisite **Niobe Japanese garden** (*Tel 604/822-9666*), but most visitors come to the campus for the unrivaled collections of First Nations art in the **Museum of Anthropology** (*6393 Northwest Marine Dr., Tel 604/822-2974, closed Mon.*).

Embedded in woodland with a prospect of sea and mountains, the museum building is a superb showcase for a fascinating array of sculptures, carvings, totem poles, and other art and craft objects. The building was designed by Arthur Erickson and completed in 1976. It's inspiration was the traditional post-and-beam structures of the Kwakwaka'wakw people; the concrete posts of the glass-walled and top-lit Great Hall are up to 50 feet high, matching in scale the imposing totems assembled within and allowing their full grandeur to be appreciated. The totems are complemented by other large carvings, but there are objects of all sizes, some, in precious metals, argillite, or bone, of great intricacy and delicacy. Although the emphasis is on peoples of the Northwest, the collections include items from the Arctic and from all around the world. In addition, the magnificent European ceramics of the Koerner Collection, their centerpiece a huge and elaborate 16th-century Central European tiled stove, are housed in a recently completed side gallery. The Visible Storage Galleries allow visitors access to more than 15,000 objects that might otherwise be hidden.

At the very heart of the building, in a rotunda lit dramatically from above, is the powerful presence of Bill Reid's "Raven and the First Men." Sculpted in cedar and weighing 4.5 tons, the piece is dominated by the massive figure of Raven atop a clam shell from which human figures struggle to emerge, an allegory of creation by this world-famous contemporary artist, many of whose other works are on display.

Outside the Great Hall, on top of the low cliffs dropping to the water, are more totems as well as two Haida houses.

QUEEN ELIZABETH PARK

Running south from the Vancouver city center, ruler-straight Cambie Street curves round in obeisance to this superb hilltop park. Competing for attention are the magnificent views of the city, the richly planted sunken gardens, and the geodesic dome of the **Bloedel Floral Conservatory** (*West 33rd Ave. & Cambie St., Tel 604/257-8570*) with its luxuriant vegetation.

SIMON FRASER UNIVERSITY

Few contrasts could be greater than between the campuses of the University of British Columbia and Simon Fraser, Vancouver's "other" university. Begun in 1914, the former is laid out along beaux arts lines, with long vistas and sweeping avenues. The latter, a product of the 1960s, is based on a concrete spine of interconnected structures crowning the ridge of Burnaby Mountain. An "Acropolis for our time," Simon Fraser pioneered not just architectural but also academic structures and enjoys a reputation as a progressive institution.

☎ 604/291-3210

THE NORTH SHORE

The mountains of the North Shore are not simply there to be looked at, but can be easily explored due to their proximity to the city and accessibility by road. The excursion to the top of **Grouse Mountain** (*8 miles from Lions*

Right: A short bus and ferry ride from downtown, Grouse Mountain can be climbed via this high-capacity cable car.

Gate Bridge or Seabus from Lonsdale Quay, Tel 604/984-0661) is popular in both summer and winter thanks to the aerial tram that whisks passengers up to the summit station (3,700 feet). At the top, visitors can enjoy wining and dining, "Theatre in the Sky," helicopter tours, logging shows, and floodlit skiing, but the view's the thing, a wonderful panorama extending on clear days as far as Vancouver Island. A network of walking trails leads into the mountains.

With fine stands of fir and cedar, **Capilano Canyon** (6 miles from Lions Gate Bridge on Capilano Rd., Tel 604/985-7474) is also accessible on foot from Grouse Mountain, and has a number of fascinating features including a salmon hatchery. But the feature that attracts most visitors is the spectacular

suspension footbridge, at 450 feet the longest of its kind in the world. An almost constant stream of daring individuals pays a not inconsiderable sum to defy vertigo and walk across the bridge as it sways 250 feet above the floor of the canyon. Lookouts along the winding Mount Seymour Parkway in **Mount Seymour Provincial Park** (10 miles via Second Narrows Bridge off Mount Seymour Parkway, Tel 604/924-2200) give splendid views of the city and Indian Arm, the prolongation of Burrard Inlet. The parkway climbs to a height of more than 3,300 feet before terminating at the base of a chairlift, much used by skiers in season. There is an excellent choice of day and half-day hikes, including one to the summit of Mount Seymour (4,767 feet). ■

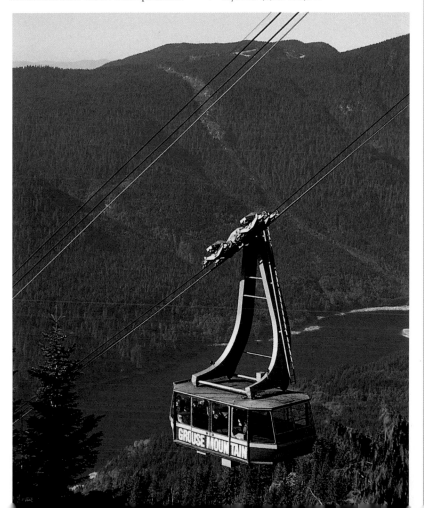

Excursions from Vancouver

Vancouver is also a good base for a number of longer excursions. Some merit an overnight stop, although most can be treated as day trips, or possibly combined as a tour.

HOWE SOUND & THE SEA TO SKY HIGHWAY

An excursion up the fjordlike Howe Sound to the logging town of Squamish and the internationally renowned ski resort of Whistler encompasses many of the attractions that make West Coast life so enjoyable.

Grandly named the Sea to Sky Highway, Hwy. 99 is not the only way to make this trip, at least as far as Squamish. In the 1950s, the Pacific Great Eastern Railway finally completed its line along the shore of the sound to North Vancouver. Its track is now used by B.C. Rail (*Tel 604/984-5236*) as well as by tour trains pulled by the Royal Hudson steam locomotive No. 2860 (*Tel 604/688-7246*). Travelers can take the train one way to Squamish and sail back aboard the M.V. *Britannia*, the entry into

Burrard Inlet making an unforgettable end to the excursion.

North of Horseshoe Bay, a ferry port for boats to Vancouver Island, road and rail squeeze together between cliff and shoreline with spectacular views of Howe Sound in its mountain setting.

BRITANNIA BEACH

In its heyday in the 1920s and '30s, the Britannia Copper Mine was the most productive in the British Empire. Altogether some 56 million tons of copper were extracted before prices fell and the ore dwindled. Closed in 1974, it is now the **British Columbia Museum of Mining** (*Brittania Beach, Tel 604/688-8735 or 604/896-2233, closed Nov.–April*), a national historic site offering a fascinating account of its often troubled history (accidents, rock slides, fire and floods) as well as underground tours.

SQUAMISH

In a splendid setting beneath snow-tipped Mount Garibaldi (8,786 feet), Squamish is the terminus for the steam-hauled tour train and has a developing railroad museum at the **West Coast Railway Heritage Park** (*39645 Government Rd., Tel 604/898-9336, closed Nov.–April*). Squamish means "Mother of the Wind" in Coast Salish, and windsurfers make use of the stiff breezes of the sound to achieve speeds of nearly 40 mph.
🚠 273C1 ✉ Visitor Information, Cleveland Ave. ☎ 604/932-3434

GARIBALDI PROVINCIAL PARK

This vast (750-square-mile) park has typically glorious B.C. landscapes in abundance, from lush river valleys to glaciers and high peaks such as **Wedge Mountain** (9,482 feet). Most of the park is quite unspoiled, with access off the highway to a limited number of trails of varying length and difficulty.
🚠 273D2 ☎ 604/898-3678

WHISTLER

This world-famous ski resort promotes itself with an array of well-founded superlatives reflected in its consistently high ranking in

Unbeatable snow cover and superlative scenery draw many to Whistler Mountain. Opposite: One of the many excursion trains that run to Squamish

international skiing surveys. Forgetting jet lag, people fly here from Europe as well as from all over North America to enjoy the superb quality of the skiing. Overlooked by the two great peaks of **Whistler Mountain** (7,160 feet) and **Blackcomb Mountain** (7,494 feet), the resort boasts the largest ski area on the North American continent, a long season, an astounding 30-foot snowfall, high speed lifts, and amazing downhill runs (Mount Blackcomb is 5,280 feet—nearly a vertical mile). There is skiing in summer, too. It is the only place in North America offering the chance to ski or snowboard on a glacier. 🅰 273D2 ✉ Visitor information, Whistler Conference Center ☎ 604/932-2394

FORT LANGLEY NATIONAL HISTORIC SITE

In 1858 this Hudson's Bay Company fort on the Fraser River only just failed to become the capital of newly created British Columbia. This focal point of the HBC's supply opera-

tions for the whole of the Columbia District, was originally built in 1827, 2.5 miles downstream from its present location. As the fur trade flagged, the importance of the fort's farm and its salmon-packing business grew; provisions from here were exported to Hawaii and Australia as well as to San Francisco and the Russian outposts in North America.

Within the stockade, now a national historic site, the only original building is the storehouse dating from 1840. It has the distinction of being the oldest nonnative structure in British Columbia, and served for a while as a cooperage, barrel production being crucial for the successful export of fish. The other buildings, including the factor's Big House, have been carefully rebuilt, and are peopled by a variety of costumed characters who give a lively impression of the life that went on in the mid-19th century in this mainland nucleus of Canada's westernmost province. 🅰 273D1 ✉ 23433 Mavis St. ☎ 604/888-4424 ∎

Vancouver Island & Victoria

SOME 300 MILES IN LENGTH AND WITH A TOTAL AREA OF about 12,000 square miles, Vancouver Island is the largest of the islands off the western coast of North America. Mountains of volcanic origin form the island's spine, part of a mostly submerged formation that includes the Queen Charlotte Islands and the Wrangell Mountains of Alaska. Luxuriant rain forest thrives in the generally damp and mild climate, and though much of it has been logged, fine stands of fir, cedar, and hemlock still thrive.

The population is overwhelmingly concentrated in Victoria and in the lowlands along the Strait of Georgia. Few people live very far from the highway linking Victoria at the southern tip of the island to Port Hardy in the north, embarkation point for the Inside Passage ferry.

Virtually every visitor to Vancouver Island is drawn to Victoria, which assiduously cultivates the Britishness of its heritage. Others head for the breakers and beaches of the spectacular coastline of Pacific Rim National Park or the wilderness of Strathcona Provincial Park, which has the island's highest peak, Golden Hinde (7,218 feet).

Abundant marine and forest resources helped the First Nations people here reach a high level of cultural and economic development and there are a number of places on the island where their heritage is readily accessible.

VICTORIA

Long since left behind in metropolitan ambition by Vancouver, sedate Victoria remains the capital of British Columbia, quite content to polish its image as a welcoming haven for the retired and its many visitors from all over the world. The image is based on realities: A wonderful site on a splendid natural harbor, a climate classed as Mediterranean, a gentlemanly pace of life, and a carefully tended downtown where high-rises are few

 273 C1

Visitor information

✉ Victoria Infocentre, 812 Wharf St.

☎ 250/953-2053

Victoria's Parliament building overlooks the city's inner harbor.

and flowers many. An array of other attractions includes the Royal British Columbia Museum, held by many to be the country's finest institution of its kind.

Victoria's much vaunted Britishness has some foundation in fact as well as in double-decker buses and afternoon tea and crumpets at the Empress Hotel. "Cheltenham with sea air" was one American's epithet, and Victoria's clement weather is not unlike (though definitely superior to) that of the famous English spa town and retirement spot and is equally kind to old bones. After working lives spent battling with the rigors of other Canadian climates, many Anglo-Canadians were more than happy to settle here and spend their declining years in a neo-Tudor mansion or reproduction Cotswold villa, perhaps cultivating one of the English-style gardens for which this southeastern part of Vancouver Island is famous. The tone of the place had been set at the beginning in the mid-1800s: Charged with producing as much food as possible from the company's farms, Hudson's Bay Company chief bailiff Kenneth McKenzie found that his colleagues were more inclined to

Forests, mountains, and coastlines similar to Half Moon Bay in Pacific Rim National Park Reserve are much more characteristic of Vancouver Island than the refined townscapes of Victoria.

**Fort Rodd Hill
National Historic
Site**

✉ 501 Belmon Rd.

☎ 250/380-4662

"introduce the outlook, the pleasures, and the customs of the
English gentry, and with complete
indifference to profit-making, live a
life of comparative ease."

Bastion Square and Fort Street
recall Victoria's origin as a fortified
post of the Hudson's Bay Company
(see pp. 220–21), moved here in
1843 from Fort Vancouver in what
is now Washington State as the
company's Pacific coast base. Long
since demolished, the fort was the
nucleus from which the town developed from the early 1850s on;
Government Street, laid out in
1851, was the very first street in
British North America west of the
Rockies. The 1858 Gold Rush, with
the sudden arrival of between
20,000 and 30,000 feverish prospectors on their way to the Fraser
River, gave the town's development
a kick start, and also led to the
establishment of Victoria's substantial Chinatown. The insubstantial
one- and two-story buildings of

this era with their flat-topped
boomtown fronts rising over the
raised boardwalks gave the town a
very un-British look.

The rambunctious behavior of
the mostly American prospectors
was considered by the authorities to
be very un-British, too; it was primarily to maintain law and order
that the government took over control of Vancouver Island from the
Hudson's Bay Company and
created the new colony of British
Columbia. Victoria's vocation was
henceforth that of a government
town; a first set of colonial administration buildings was replaced in
1897 by the enormously imposing
Parliament Buildings that still
dominate the harbor today. **Fort
Rodd Hill,** now a national historic
site and still a magnificent vantage
point, was developed as a part of a
system of defenses, and the Royal
Navy made its Pacific base on the
southwestern orner of the harbor
at Esquimault.

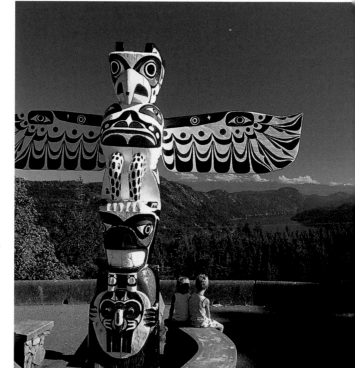

**First Nations
traditions abound
throughout
Vancouver Island.
Here, a totem
pole overlooks
Saanich Inlet.**

ROYAL BRITISH COLUMBIA MUSEUM

Built on a grand scale in the late 1960s, the museum hosts temporary exhibitions of international importance as well as a permanent collection. The permanent displays include the superb natural history dioramas and models, as well as galleries covering the modern history of the province and, above all, the **First Peoples Gallery,** a comprehensive and thrilling account of early Pacific coast life and heritage. The light and airy entrance hall of the museum has space enough for tall, 19th-century totems, whose fascinating detail can be examined close-up from the upper floor.

In the **Open Ocean,** visitors are invited in small groups (timed ticketing) to embark on an underwater voyage and experience the life of the seas. This is a state-of-the-art walk-through experience, involving all kinds of special effects, and is not for the nervous.

With its huge tusks pointing ominously at the visitor, a woolly mammoth makes an impressive guardian to the **Living Land, Living Sea Gallery.** Here are the great dioramas, with their impeccable attention to detail, sound effects, and lighting. They make a marvelous introduction to the extraordinary array of natural environments in this huge province, which boasts Canada's wettest mountains, driest valleys, deepest snows, and warmest coast. The dominant features of the dioramas are the great trees of the various types of forest—coastal, Columbia, subalpine, boreal—which cloak much of the province, making it all the more thrilling to emerge on the simulated shore of Vancouver Island, with its guano-streaked headland, playful seals, and triumphant bull sea lion atop his rock.

The **Modern History Gallery** deals with the province's relatively short but colorful history in reverse, from modern times backward. The most striking exhibit is perhaps the reconstruction of a turn-of-the-century street, with shops, offices, dimly lit Chinatown, and plush interior of the Grand Hotel. The telegraph taps away in the railroad station until drowned out by the noisy arrival and departure of a train.

Other displays convincingly re-create the ambience of the Tremblay Farmstead in the Peace River District, the inhospitable landscape of the Stikine Country that was the scene of Anglo–Russian rivalry, and a fish-canning plant complete with seagull scavengers and slimy fish-gutting bench. The gallery ends at the beginning of B.C.'s European history, aboard the three-master sloop *Discovery*, in which Captain Vancouver's quarters served as charthouse and botanical laboratory as well as cabin.

The dimly lit spaces of the First Peoples Gallery heighten the impact of the superbly presented exhibits. Divided into two main sections, the gallery shows the art and culture of the nations of the Northwest before and after the arrival of the Europeans, their technology, and their diseases. It is the best possible introduction to the subject, with an array of objects that demonstrates the richness and diversity of the material culture of the different groupings and gives some insight into magic, ritual, and the spiritual life. The centerpiece is the reconstructed full-size plankhouse of Chief Kwakwabalasami with its glowing fire. Don't miss the audiovisual presentation on cosmology, myth, and image, where the supernatural is evoked by song, dance, costume, and eerily illuminated masks. ∎

Royal British Columbia Museum
✉ 5 Belleville St.
☎ 250/387-3701
   or 800/661-5411
💲 $$$

A walk around Victoria

This short walk introduces the staid downtown of this miniature provincial capital, its fascinating harbor, and the clutch of grandiose buildings dominating the waterfront. With comfortable walking shoes you should have no trouble completing this tour in just over an hour, having worked up enough appetite for afternoon tea at the Empress Hotel, one of this pleasant city's defining experiences.

See area map pp. 272–3
► Parliament Buildings
◐ 1.5 miles
⊕ Allow 1 hour
► Empress Hotel

NOT TO BE MISSED

- Parliament Buildings
- Thunderbird Park
- Crystal Garden
- Empress Hotel
- Maritime Museum

Begin at the **Parliament Buildings ❶** *(South side of James Bay, Tel 250/387-3046)*, completed in 1898 by a young English architect, Francis Mawson Rattenbury, who used local granite, slate, and andesite for his ambitious scheme—three wings beneath a central dome topped by a gilded statue of Captain Vancouver. The building launched Rattenbury's career as Victoria's civic architect.

To the east, along Belleville Street and beyond the archives building with its belfry is **Thunderbird Park ❷** *(Front of Royal British Columbia Museum, Tel 250/953-2033)*. Around the reproduction Bighouse is a fine collection of totems, some of them superb copies from the hand of Kwakwaka'wakw master carver Mungo Martin. Close by are Victoria's two oldest buildings, the cabinlike **St. Anne's Schoolhouse** and a modest dwelling built by pioneer doctor John Sebastian Helmcken in 1852.

Walk north on Douglas Street. The great days of the **Crystal Garden ❸** *(731 Douglas St., Tel 250/381-1213)* on the right were between the wars, when it was enlivened with tea dances and swimmers frolicking in the country's biggest indoor pool. The renovated garden now houses a restaurant, stores, and a tropical conservatory. Go up the steps into the 1989 **Victoria Conference Center,** which has been sensitively integrated into the venerable **Empress Hotel** *(721 Government St., Tel 250/384-8111)*, and walk through the palatial ground floor spaces of this great Edwardian institution. Leave by the front doors and head up **Government Street,** with its clipped and disciplined trees and harmonious heritage buildings. Even Eaton's extensive new mall is discreetly hidden behind the original 19th-century facades. Turn left into **Bastion Square ❹,** named for the Hudson's Bay Company's fort, whose northeast bastion was sited where the square meets

Adding to Victoria's atmosphere of Britishness, double-decker buses await sightseers outside the stately Empress Hotel.

Empress of Victoria

Architect Francis Rattenbury followed the completion of Victoria's legislative buildings with a monumental château-style design for the Canadian Pacific Railway's Empress Hotel. Begun in 1904, the hotel was was seen as a "fitting companion to the historic pile on the heights of Quebec," that is, Château Frontenac, completed a decade earli-

er. It was built on piles sunk 125 feet into what was then a tidal swamp, and has always been as much a civic institution as a hotel. No visit to Victoria is complete without a stroll through its halls and lobbies, or, better still, a drink in the Bengal Lounge with its memories of an empire whose way of life lingered longer here than almost anywhere else. ■

Government Street. The square has a number of attractive old edifices, including the former courthouse, now the home of the **Maritime Museum** *(Tel 250/385-4222)*.

Walk along Wharf Street with its renovated warehouses. To the east, both Yates and Johnson Streets have fine examples of late 19th-century commercial buildings. Cross Wharf Street and descend past rock outcrops to the **waterfront boardwalk.** The **Johnson Street Bridge** carries the single

track of Vancouver Island's only railroad. Walk south along the waterfront and enjoy the varied activity of the **harbor** ❺—training sloops, the Seattle catamaran, and floatplanes taking off and landing. Climb the steps by the art deco tower of the **Tourist Information Centre** *(Tel 250/953-2053)* and finish the walk by the statue of Captain Cook opposite the Empress Hotel. If your timing is right, this could be the moment to indulge in afternoon tea in the hotel's sumptuous surroundings. ■

Excursions from Victoria

CRAIGDARROCH CASTLE

Scottish-born Robert Dunsmuir commissioned this hilltop castle in 1887, but died before it was completed in 1890. Dunsmuir's story seems to encapsulate much of B.C.'s early social history. A penniless arrival in the province was soon overcome when he made a fortune from Nanaimo coal. He and his son James built the Nanaimo and Esquimault Railway to export the coal, receiving a huge land grant amounting to about a quarter of the area of Victoria in the process. Ownership of an iron foundry, a fleet of merchant ships, and a newspaper followed, as did James's appointment as provincial lieutenant governor. The house, has been described as an exercise in Richardsonian Romanesque, but its exaggerated proportions speak more of arriviste pretensions than architectural taste.

🅐 273C1 ✉ 1050 Joan Crescent
☎ 250/592-5323 💲 $$$

ART GALLERY OF GREATER VICTORIA

This substantial clapboard house of about 1890 was built by a banker and served for a few years as Government House. In 1958 it was extended to house the city's art gallery, which has a small collection of European art as well has two great strengths: A fine collection of Asian art and works by Emily Carr, born in Victoria in 1871 (see p. 280). The paintings, sketches, and other memorabilia here remind visitors of her passion for the Northwest and its First Nations heritage and of how she "clung to earth and her dear shapes."

🅐 273C1 ✉ 1040 Moss St. ☎ 250/384-4101
💲 $$$

BUTCHART GARDENS

The mild, damp climate of southeastern Vancouver Island is particularly favorable to plant growth, and English-style gardening began as soon as the first settlers had established themselves. **Government House** in Victoria marries a degree of formality with informal use of native plants, while the city's **Beacon Hill Park** has showpiece gardens as well as wildflower meadows. The **University of Victoria** boasts a superb rhododendron

Butchart Garden's ever popular centerpiece—the Sunken Garden

Early locomotive's run through Duncan's Forest Museum Park

collection, and the Royal British Columbia Museum has an array of native plants.

The greatest of all island gardens is a private venture, the wonderful displays of Butchart Gardens on the Saanich Peninsula to the north of Victoria. The gardens had a strictly utilitarian origin in the limestone quarry of Robert Pim Butchart, who had established a Portland cement plant at Tod Inlet. In 1904 the worked-out quarry, a ready-made sheltered habitat for a variety of plants, inspired his wife, Jenny Butchart, to start creating the gardens that have become one of western Canada's foremost visitor attractions.

The gardens' centerpiece is the splendid **Sunken Garden** laid out on the floor and sides of the original quarry. Sumptuous floral displays are set off by immaculate lawns and tree growth. An imposing rock garden recalls the site's industrial beginnings. But the 50-acre grounds include much more, from the aromatic rose garden where the perfume of the blooms assails the senses, to exquisitely planned Japanese and Italian gardens.

The huge popularity of Butchart Gardens means that visitors are unlikely to be able to savor them in solitary peace. In summer, the owners recommend a late afternoon visit.
273C1 13 miles north of Victoria off Hwy. 17A 250/652-4422 $$$

DUNCAN

The town of Duncan pays tribute to the

Cowichan on whose land it stands by calling itself "the town of totems" and by displaying an array of poles, many of them along the Trans-Canada 1. The **Native Heritage Centre** (*200 Cowichan Way, Tel 604/746-8119*) is one of the best places to get the flavor of First Nations life today, watch totem carving and other crafts being practiced, take part in events, or visit Vancouver Island's largest native arts and crafts shops. Also close to the town, the **British Columbia Forest Museum Park** (*1 mile north of Duncan on Trans-Canada 1, closed Oct.–April*) tells visitors everything they are ever likely to want to know about forestry. A narrow-gauge railroad runs around the 100-acre site, past the working sawmill and a host of other logging installations and demonstrations.
273C1 Visitor information: 381 Trans-Canada Hwy. 250/746-4636

CHEMAINUS

Claiming to be the oldest deepwater port in British Columbia, this small town came to depend on its huge sawmill, and faced disaster when it closed in 1983. A concerted campaign to put the place back on the map involved covering as much wallspace as possible with murals. The results are impressive, as well as entertaining, and have helped bring some new life to the town.
273C1 Visitor information, 9758 Chemainus Rd. 250/246-3944 ■

Western and Northern Vancouver Island

PACIFIC RIM NATIONAL PARK RESERVE

Some of the finest stretches of Vancouver Island's wild western coast are protected by this reserve, which consists of three distinct units. In the north, great waves beat on the sands and rocky headlands of **Long Beach;** to the south an archipelago, the **Broken Group Islands,** adorns the waters of **Barkley Sound;** farther south still, the **West Coast Trail** created for shipwrecked sailors threads its way through the wilderness. The narrow coastal strip has cliffs, caves, rain forest, and waterfalls, while inland rise snow-covered mountaintops. The park is reached via Hwy. 4 from **Parksville** on the east coast. The route cuts across the grain of Vancouver Island and introduces some of its most characteristic landscapes.

🅰 273C1 ✉ Park visitor center at Long Beach, off Hwy. 4. ☎ 250/726-4212 🕐 Visitor center closed mid-Oct.–mid-Mar. 💲 $$$

ENGLISHMAN RIVER & FALLS PROVINCIAL PARK

The name of the river recalls the anonymous Englishman who perished in its waters, which tumble over the upper and lower falls set among the luxuriant trees, shrubs, and ferns of the rain forest of this park.

✉ 5 miles along side road 2.5 miles west of Parksville

LITTLE QUALICUM FALLS PROVINCIAL PARK

Between its upper and lower falls, the Little Qualicum River foams through a canyon, visible from a trail though the forest. The falls themselves add a note of noisy grandeur within this primeval setting.

✉ 16 miles west of Parksville via Hwy. 4

CATHEDRAL GROVE

Just beyond the western end of Cameron Lake, a short trail gives access to this famous stand of Douglas-fir. Perhaps as much as a thousand years old, these forest giants induce in most visitors the reverence that is suggested by the grove's name.

✉ 22 miles west of Parksville via Hwy. 4

PORT ALBERINI

On a long inlet connecting it to Barkley Sound stands workaday Port Alberni. It is famous for its salmon fishing, but its role as a logging center is equally important. One of the easiest ways of seeing something of the sound and its scattering of islands is to travel aboard

The perfect calm at Chesterman's Beach, a short distance from the fishing village and resort of Tofino, contrasts with the exhilarating days of storm and surf, more common on the west coast of Vancouver Island.

M.V. *Mary Rose* (*Tel 250/723-8313*), which makes a daily trip from Port Alberini to **Bamfield** or **Ucluelet** and back. Local lumber mills offer tours and an old logging locomotive can be seen chugging along the dockside in summer. Outside the town is **McLean Mill NHS** (*5 miles northwest via Beaver Creek Rd. & Smith Rd., Tel 250/723-2181, closed weekends*), Canada's last steam-powered sawmill. Since it was a recently declared a national historic site, it has been undergoing restoration.

🅜 273C1 ✉ Visitor information, 2533 Redfod St. ☎ 250/724-6535

LONG BEACH

On its way to Tofino, the fishing village just beyond the northern boundary of the national park reserve, the highway passes a number of short trails leading to the pristine shore of Long Beach, stretching some 10 miles northward, from Ucluelet. One of the best overall views of coast and mountain is from the World War II military site at **Radar Hill.** Excellent displays at the **Wickanninish Interpretive Centre** explain the complex and fascinating ecology of the area; from it, a trail leads to a superb pebble beach among rocky bluffs, where the waves surge in through a natural arch. En route is **Lismer Beach,** named for painter and Group of Seven member, Arthur Lismer, who came here often. Up to 20,000 gray whales swim past between February and May in the course of their annual migration from Baja California to Alaska. Other whales can be seen, too, including killer whales, or orcas, in pursuit of the sea lions, whose favorite spot is **Sea Lion Rocks.**

   Tofino (*Visitor information: 380 Campbell St., Tel 250/725-3414*) itself stands on a narrow neck of land at the end of Hwy. 4, looking out over **Clayoquot Sound.** Crowded in summer, the village is the point of departure for explorations, not only of the national park reserve's shoreline, but also of the superb and still intact rain forest of Clayoquot Sound, subject of much recent controversy over the conflicting claims of loggers and conservationists. Some of the finest old-growth forest can be seen on **Meares Island,** just offshore from Tofino.
🏔 273C1

BROKEN GROUP ISLANDS

The Broken Group Islands are most easily visited in the course of a day trip aboard the M.V. *Mary Rose*, though their special delights are reserved for kayakers and scuba divers. With many wrecks to be explored, the name Graveyard of the Pacific was well deserved.

WEST COAST TRAIL

After the *Valencia* disaster of 1906 when all hands perished, the predecessor of today's 45-mile **West Coast Trail** between **Bamfield** and **Port Renfrew** was equipped with cabins with emergency supplies for shipwrecked survivors and with telephones for them to contact the outside world. As rescue services improved, the trail fell out of use. Restored today, it tempts experienced hikers prepared to rough it for a week or so.

CAMPBELL RIVER

The southern Kwakwaka'wakw people had fished for salmon here for many years before the first white visitor landed a 66 pounder here in 1891. A ferry service links the town with **Quadra Island,** a First Nations village site for more than 2,000 years; the seashell-shaped **Kwagiulth Museum** (*Cape Mudge Village, Tel 604/285-3733, closed Sun. in winter*) has potlach regalia (see pp. 306–7) and other fascinating objects confiscated by the government in 1922 but subsequently returned.
🏔 273C2

STRATHCONA PROVINCIAL PARK

Designated in 1911, British Columbia's oldest provincial park protects some of Vancouver Island's grandest scenery. Numerous peaks rise from the forest and alpine meadows, among them the island's summit, Golden Hinde (7,216 feet). Wildlife includes deer, elk, wolf, and even the elusive mountain lion. Many of the park's trails are for experienced backpackers only, but shorter walks include those around popular **Buttle Lake.**
🏔 273C1   ✉ Visitor information, jct. of Hwy. 28 & Buttle Lake Rd. ☎ 604/286-3122

PORT MCNEILL

A modern logging town, Port McNeill has a ferry to the fishing village of **Alert Bay** on Cormorant Island. The **U'Mista Cultural Centre** (*Front St., Tel 250/974-5403, closed weekends off-season*) derives its name from a native word meaning "those returned from slavery." Local people were at the center of the events that resulted in the Kwakwaka'wakw being deprived of their potlatch artifacts in 1922; the returned objects are displayed in the center, which also hosts events and courses.

   Also near Port McNeill is the delightful village of **Telegraph Cove,** dating from the early years of the 20th century and still with its boardwalk and many of its stilt buildings intact.
✉ 112 miles north of Campbell River ■

The Inside Passage

Although discovering the Northwest Passage proved an unattainable goal for European explorers in North America, finding the Inside Passage along Canada's Pacific coast proved to be an achievable—and scenic—aim. Today it is one of the most dramatic voyages in the world, tracing a route north from the tip of Vancouver Island to Canada's border with Alaska.

The waters of Hecate Strait, which separates the Queen Charlotte Islands from the host of small islands that line Canada's Pacific shore, and of Queen Charlotte Sound, which separates Vancouver Island from the same small islands, are treacherous. Despite the fact that the Haida (closely related to the Tlingit), who settled the Queen Charlotte Islands, are known to have traveled these waters, and later explorers such as the Russians and Captain Cook also sailed them, a calmer, less dangerous route along the Pacific coast was needed. The Haida had, in fact, established it before Europeans settled the area, showing those early settlers the Route of the Haidas, as it was known for many years. The Inside Passage is a less romantic but more descriptive name for a sea route that threads a way between the islands and mainland of Canada's Pacific coast.

NORTH TO ALASKA

The Inside Passage can be followed from Vancouver all the way to the Lynn Canal in Alaska, the canal being a dead-end fjord that ends at Skagway. For many travelers, the Canadian passage starts with a boarding of the *Queen of the North*, the ship that travels the route from **Port Hardy** ❶ on Vancouver Island's northern coast, to Prince Rupert at the mouth of the Skeena River. The 15-hour trip—all of it in daylight during the summer months—takes in beautiful scenery rich in both human and natural history.

Port Hardy was named for Thomas Masterman Hardy, the captain of H.M.S. *Victory* at the Battle of Trafalgar in 1805. Today the town is a center for mining, logging, and fishing.

From the port the ship crosses **Queen Charlotte Strait,** an exposed piece of water

Passengers continuing their journey along the Inside Passage into Alaska admire the spectacular sights of Glacier Bay National Park.

Chatham Sound

Prince Rupert

16

Skeena River

BRITISH COLUMBIA

PORCHER ISLAND

Kitimat

QUEEN CHARLOTTE ISLANDS

Hecate Strait

Grenville Channel

BANKS ISLAND

HAWKESBURY ISLAND

PITT ISLAND

4

GRIBBELL ISLAND

GILL ISLAND

PRINCESS ROYAL ISLAND

C O A S T

Fishing vessel at Prince Rupert.

ARISTAZABEL ISLAND

SWINDLE ISLAND

Finlayson Channel

PRICE ISLAND

3

M O U N T A I N S

Milbanke Sound

CAMPBELL ISLAND

Bella Bella

Dean Channel

KING ISLAND

Burke Channel

HUNTER ISLAND

Namu

2

Queen Charlotte Sound

Fitzhugh Sound

CALVERT ISLAND

Cape Scott

Pacific Ocean

N

0   80 kilometers

0   40 miles

Queen Charlotte Strait

Port Hardy

1

START

19

VANCOUVER ISLAND

> ⓜ See area map pp. 272–3
> ▶ Port Hardy
> ⬌ 310 miles
> 🕐 Allow 15 hours
> ▶ Prince Rupert
>
> **INFORMATION**
>
> Information on all British Columbia
> Ferries is available from:
> ✉ B.C. Ferries, 1112 Fort St.,
>   Victoria, B.C.
> ☎ 250-386-3431 or 604-669-1211

that occasionally tests the sea legs of travelers. Here the ship is plying the Pacific Ocean: To the west, there is only water until the eastern coast of Russia is reached. At the far side of the sound is the highly exposed lighthouse on **Egg Island.** In 1948 a storm blew the lighthouse away, fortunately just after it had been abandoned by the keeper and his wife.

The lighthouse marks the approach to **Fitzhugh Sound** ❷ and the true entrance to the Inside Passage. Toward the northern end of Fitzhugh, to the right, is **Namu.** The First Nations' name of the town, meaning "whirlwind," reflects the sound's famous winds. The locals refer to them as *williwaws*. The ship now rounds the northern end of **Hunter Island:** Ahead here, the waterway leads to the **Dean Channel** where, Alexander Mackenzie reached the Pacific at the end of the first land crossing of the North American continent on July 22, 1793.

You now turn north, passing **Bella Bella** village, then rounding **Campbell Island** to reach **Milbanke Sound** ❸. Here, again, the ship is exposed to the Pacific, another trial in poor weather. But on a good day, the sound is a wonderful place. When Pacific salmon—the chinook, sockeye, pink, coho, and chum—are making their spawning run, fishing boats compete for the fish with nature's predators. If you are lucky, you will see orca (the correct name for the usually, and inappropriately, named killer whale), Steller sea lion, and northern fur seal. The orca, in particular, is a magnificent sight—25 feet long and patterned in black and white, its high dorsal fin scything the sea. You may also see bald eagles fishing.

The sound's famous herring shoals attract humpback whales that can often be seen breaching—hurling themselves out of the water. The energy required to lift a 50-foot, 40-ton whale out of the water is colossal, and no one knows exactly why they do it. All these animals can be seen at various points along the passage—the humpbacks infrequently in the narrower channels.

Northward, you follow the Finlayson Channel to reach the **Boat Bluff lighthouse** on the southern tip of Sarah Islands. Boat Bluff is the most picturesque of all the passage's lighthouses. To the left, **Princess Royal Island** is the home of white black bears and black gray wolves. Beyond the island, the ship crosses the **Whale Channel** to reach the **Grenville Channel** ❹, named by Capt. George Vancouver for William Grenville (1759–1834), briefly a British prime minister. Grenville Channel is 11 hours' sailing from Port Hardy and just a couple of hours from Prince Rupert, but travelers are well rewarded for the wait. The channel has the most spectacular scenery on the entire passage, with mountains up to around 3,500 feet high on each side, their flanks covered in pine and cedar forests. The channel is remarkably deep (about 1,600 feet) and sharp-sided, so the ship can travel extremely close to the shore. At the narrowest point, the channel is only 600 yards wide. Beyond the Grenville Channel, the scenery is no less breathtaking, but set farther back: It is just a few minutes now to the terminus at **Prince Rupert.**

Prince Rupert is the end of the true Inside Passage, but it is possible to continue on another vessel along an inner channel, crossing Chatham Sound to reach the Canada-U.S. border and continuing to **Ketchikan,** the first town in Alaska. Northward, the Clarence Strait is followed to Wrangell, from where island-hopping reaches **Petersburg.** The Alaskan passage now splits into two, an outer route visiting **Baranof Island** before reaching the **Lynn Canal,** an inner route reaching **Juneau,** Alaska's capital. The Lynn Canal to **Skagway** is the last stretch of the inner passage, but as a fine alternative many will want to the spectacular sights in the magnificent **Glacier Bay National Park** *(Tel 250/837-7500).* ■

Prince Rupert, Skeena Valley, & Queen Charlotte Islands

Prince Rupert
🅰 27023

Museum of Northern British Columbia
✉ 1st Ave. & McBride St.
☎ 250/624-3207
🕐 Closed Sun. in winter
💲 $

North Pacific Cannery Village Museum
✉ 1889 Skeena Dr. Port Edward
☎ 250/628-3538
💲 $$$

'Ksan Historical Village Museum
✉ Northwest of New Hazleton on Rte. 62
☎ 250/842-5544
💲 $$$

PRINCE RUPERT IS A PORT THAT JUST MISSED ITS APPOINT-ment with destiny when it lost out to Vancouver as the Pacific end of the transcontinental rail line. However, it remains a vital link to the less explored extremities of British Columbia. The valley of the mighty Skeena River has been a corridor for trade for many centuries, with a long history of skillful native transportation along its rushing waters. Offshore lie the rain-soaked and geologically fascinating Queen Charlotte Islands, where traces of the original temperate rain forest are still host to a number of species that are extinct elsewhere.

PRINCE RUPERT

Superbly located among mountains on an island at the mouth of the Skeena River, Prince Rupert owes its existence as a modern city to the Grand Trunk Railway's hope that the western terminus of its transcontinental line would rival Vancouver's port and metropolis. But in 1912 the railroad's visionary president, Charles M. Hays, went down with the *Titanic*. The town's layout followed the bold plan he commissioned, but the port has never quite achieved the potential he envisaged. Its population is barely a hundredth of that of Vancouver, 500 miles farther from Japan. Nevertheless, Prince Rupert is a significant communications hub; the Yellowhead Highway terminates here, as does VIA Rail's remaining transcontinental service, exchanging passengers with the ferries to and from Vancouver Island, Alaska, and the Queen Charlotte Islands.

For centuries before the arrival of Europeans, the site of the town had been a meeting place for the Tsimshian and Haida peoples. The recently renovated **Museum of Northern British Columbia** has excellent First Nations collections that bring alive 10,000 years of settlement history along this northwestern coast. The museum has a carving shed where craftspeople can be seen at work, and also runs tours to some of the many archaeological sites in the area.

Fish-canning was one of British Columbia's staple industries, and in its late 19th-century heyday, more than 200 canneries operated along the coast. Near **Port Edward,** 13 miles southeast of Prince Rupert, one of the last canneries is now a national historic site known as the **North Pacific Cannery Village Museum.**

SKEENA VALLEY

The second longest river (after the Fraser) to run entirely within British Columbia, the turbulent and beautiful **Skeena River** has long been a corridor for trade and travel. The often mist-shrouded stream was named "water of the clouds" by the Tsimshian. It was navigated by 60-foot-long native canoes long before the 1870s, when stern-wheelers brought prospectors upstream en route to the goldfields at Omineca. Today it is followed through the 6,000-foot **Coast Mountains** by VIA rail, the Canadian National Railway, and the Yellowhead Highway.

The valley has a strong First Nations presence. The national historic site at **Fort Kitwanga** was a stronghold built atop a glacial mound by the Gitwangak people, who devised ingenious ways of crushing any attackers by releasing stacked up logs on to them. But the real fascination of the Skeena lies in its concentration of totem poles, some modern, some dating back to the mid-19th century. There are poles at Kitwanga itself, and at Kitwancool, Kitseguecla, and Kispiox. The reconstructed traditional village of **'Ksan** lies at the confluence of the Skeena and Bulkley Rivers. It has poles and a series of stately longhouses sheltering a carving school, as well as an extensive collection of artifacts.

QUEEN CHARLOTTE ISLANDS

Separated from the mainland by the broad waters (up to 80 miles across) of Hecate Strait, this remote and rain-soaked archipelago of some 150 islands remained largely untouched by glaciers, leaving it with an exceptionally rich ecology with many relict species such as deer mouse, Lairly woodpecker, and black bear. The homeland of the ethnically distinct Haida people, who call it Haida Gwaii ("islands of the people"), the islands bear witness to their past and present creativity. Logging has diminished some of the glory of the islands' rain forest, but much remains, particularly in the **Gwaii Haanas National Park Reserve** *(Tel 250/559-8818),* which covers a large part of **Moresby Island.**

The ferry *(B.C. Ferries, Tel 250/386-3431)* from Prince Rupert to **Graham Island,** the largest and most populous in the archipelago, terminates at Skidegate landing. To the west, **Queen Charlotte City,** a community of a thousand or so inhabitants, serves as the non-First Nations administrative center of the islands. At Skidegate itself, the exhibits in the **Haida Gwaii Museum** *(Tel 250/559-4643)* include a collection of carvings in argillite and make a fine introduction to Haida culture. ∎

Decimated by disease, many Haida abandoned their coastal villages at the end of the 19th century, leaving remains like this mortuary pole on the fringe of the encroaching forest.

Queen Charlotte Islands
⛰ 272A3

Visitor information
✉ Infocentre, 3220 Wharf St.
☎ 250/386-8818

First Nations peoples of western British Columbia

The First Nations residents of western British Columbia are geographically and culturally unique. The province's collection of First Nations historical sites makes it ideal for the visitor interested in this aspect of Canadian history.

In the northern interior were the Athapaskan, who occupied a vast area of forest and plains. The Athapaskan were a seminomadic people who are usually credited with having introduced the potlatch—a ritual ceremony involving feasting and dancing. The European settlers, fearing the potential for inciting rebellion, banned the potlatch between the 1880s and the 1950s. Recently, many of the ceremonial objects for the potlatch, confiscated and placed in museums, have been returned. One collection can still be seen in the Kwagiulth Museum on Quadra Island (see p. 298) at the north end of the strait of Georgia, between Vancouver Island and the mainland.

Another famous coastal First Nations people are the Tlingit, who inhabited the area north of (and including) the Queen Charlotte Islands. Though the coast was a rugged one, and a harsh place in winter, it was also an area well stocked with food. Of the shoreline it was said that "when the tide goes out, the table is set," so abundant were the shellfish. These Tlingit are famous for weaving Chilkat blankets from the wool of the mountain goat (three goats for one blanket). The blankets are still produced in the traditional way: Panels are woven on a primitive loom and then stitched together.

Even more famous are the Tlingit's totem poles. There are several misconceptions about totem poles, many claiming that all First Nations peoples carved them, and that they were a religious object. In fact, totem-carving was almost exclusively a North American west

Left: Historic Edward S. Curtis photo of
a Kwakiuti bridal group. The bride is
pictured between two dancers, hired
especially for the celebration.
Right: A typical west coast totem

coast tradition. Totems represented a family's
pride in its ancestry, rather than performing
ritual or religious functions. The various
carvings on an individual pole represented
supernatural creatures (humans and animals),
and the form was specific to a family and
group. Totem pole carving, like potlatch, was
banned for many years, and as a result few
older poles exist. One place where they can
be seen in this original setting is in Hazleton
near the 'Ksan Historical Village Museum (see
p. 303), close to New Hazleton in the Skeena
River Valley. The site also has traditional
Tlingit longhouses. Totems can also bee seen
at the Native Heritage Centre (see p. 295) near
Duncan on Vancouver Island.

At both 'Ksan and Duncan you'll also find
examples of the beautiful wood carvings of
the coastal peoples. Also notable are those at
the Kwagiulth Museum. Many of these are of
monsters and supernatural creatures, the most
famous being the Thunderbird, the lord of the
sky, the most powerful spirit of the spirit
world. Though the Thunderbird is the most
famous of the carvings, the most exotic is the
raven of the Kwakwaka'wakw peoples who
inhabited the coast to the south of the Tlingit
(to whom they were related). The raven mask
is a five-foot-long head and beak in black, red,
and white, with "feathers" of shredded cedar
bark that fell to the shoulders of the dancer
who wore it. During the dance, the wearer
would "clack" the hinged beak.

But to feel more of the spirit of Haida
Gwaii, it is necessary to venture farther afield.
Close to the town of Masset, at the far end
of Graham Island, is the largest Haida community in the Queen Charlottes. Once known
as Old Masset, it is now usually called Haida.
Its people not only produce souvenirs for
visitors, but have added an array of fine new
totems. To the south, Moresby Island in the
Queen Charlotte Islands has poignant
testimony to the high level of development
reached by the Haida in the late 19th century,
before death and disease forced them from

their villages. With their ruined houses and
well-weathered totem poles, these villages are
extraordinarily evocative sites. Some, guarded
by the Haida Gwaii Watchmen, are accessible
by sea and air to visitors, but in restricted
numbers only. Skedans, is one such village,
while another, Ninstints, is protected as a
world heritage site. ■

Historic photo of performers re-creating
the legend of the mythological birds
Kotsuis and Hohhuq, by Edward S. Curtis

The Cariboo

🅰 273D3

THE CARIBOO IS THE NAME GIVEN TO THE ROLLING uplands of the interior plateau, bounded on the west by the Coast Mountains and on the east by the Cariboo range. Threaded by the Fraser River, this is gold rush, forestry, and ranching country, with many traces still of the days when prospectors flocked northward by the tens of thousands in search of fortune.

Barkerville's gold deposits provided 19th-century prospectors with a good living for only ten years, but the town still stands, an intriguing relic of B.C.'s gold rush days.

The key to the area was the **Cariboo Road,** surveyed and built in part by the Royal Engineers. By 1863 it extended from Yale as far as **Soda Creek,** where passengers boarded the steamship for Quesnel in the heart of the goldfields. Along the highway, roadhouses were built at more or less regular intervals to serve as rough hotels and livery stables. The pioneers had to make their own way to the area. The first gold strike had been made in 1860, and the biggest find of all came two years later, when Billy Barker, a Cornishman after whom the archetypal gold rush town of Barkerville was named, struck a rich deposit at a depth of more than 50 feet. As gold rush settlements sprang up, cattle ranchers moved north

to supply the prospectors with beef, the origin of the area's still flourishing ranching activity.

The original single-story cabin known as **Hat Creek House** (*7 miles north of Cache Creek off Hwy. 99, Tel 250/457-9732*) was built as a rough-hewn roadhouse by Donald McLean, but is now embedded in an elegant two-story building with a double veranda. It has been restored, and with its outbuildings now forms a visitor ranch run by the B.C. Heritage Trust. Marking the beginning of the real Cariboo, the little town of **Clinton** began life as the 47 Mile House, and acquired the name of a British duke as it grew.

The Cariboo Road bypassed the site of the workaday town of **Williams Lake,** serving a wide ranching and lumbering area; Williams Lake only developed once the Pacific Great Eastern Railway arrived in 1920. The town is the starting point for the 285-mile, partly paved road that crosses the plateau and the Coast Mountains to the remote fishing village of **Bella Coola,** on the north arm of Burke Channel on the Pacific shore.

Prospectors disembarked in **Quesnel** *(Visitor information, La Bourdais, 703 Carson Ave., Tel 250/992-8716)* from the stern-wheelers that had brought them up the Fraser River into the heart of gold rush country. Quesnel still has its 1867 Hudson's Bay Company depot, but is otherwise dominated by the logging industry, whose activities can be watched from an observation tower 2 miles north of the town.

On its way from Quesnel to Barkerville, Rte. 26 passes relics of gold-mining activity, as well as the restored **Cottonwood House.** Built in 1864, Cottonwood House began as a roadhouse and served many purposes before being restored as a provincial historic site.

Barkerville *(Visitor information, Pooley St., Tel 250/994-3237, closed in winter),* too, has been undergoing restoration since the 1950s, and is now British Columbia's finest example of a town of its time. Not long after Billy Barker's gold find, the town had more than 10,000 inhabitants and trumpeted itself as the biggest city west of Chicago and north of San Francisco. Nevertheless, it was a makeshift place, with irregular boardwalks high above a narrow street barely wide enough for two carts to pass. In 1868 it burned down, but was substantially rebuilt. By the 1930s, it had almost faded away, but recent restoration has added many reconstructed buildings to these surviving originals. Visitors can attend school, go to the theater, ride a stagecoach, or watch mining demonstrations. ■

The simply furnished interior of one of Barkerville's many preserved buildings evokes the town's glory days of the 1860s and '70s.

Hope to Kamloops drive

On its way from Vancouver into the dry interior of British Columbia, the Trans-Canada Highway follows the route taken by 19th-century travelers, who used every conceivable means of transportation to overcome the formidable obstacle of these river canyons. This tour, which calls for none of that 19th-century endurance, follows Fraser and Thompson Canyons.

Today's smooth, four-lane highway belies the difficulties faced by these pioneers. "We had to pass where no human being should venture" was Simon Fraser's comment after completing his epic journey down the river to which he gave his name. His party only descended the Fraser River Canyon with the help of native guides, who made their way along the seemingly impassable cliffs on fragile structures of poles and twigs far above the deadly foaming waters. Below Yale, the Fraser was navigable, and in the 1858 Gold Rush prospectors could get this far by steamboat. From here, a rough mule track northward was constructed by the miners themselves. This precarious trail was replaced, from 1863 onward, by the famous Cariboo Road (see p. 304). Traces of this narrow and vertiginous road can still be seen today.

Construction of the CPR through the canyons posed massive problems. The difficulties were confronted head-on by the contractor, New Yorker Andrew Onderdonk, helped by an army of Canadian, Chinese, local, and Norwegian laborers, who dangled from ropes to blast out tunnels and the narrow ledge on which the railroad runs. Onderdonk completed his epic of construction in 1885. In 1914 the line through the Fraser Canyon was joined by the Great Northern Railway, predecessor of the CNR, and today the two lines, together with the Trans-Canada Highway, make light of this once daunting obstacle.

The drive begins at **Hope ❶**, 93 miles east of Vancouver. Founded as a Hudson's Bay Company post in 1848, this small town is located among mountains at the point where the valley of the Fraser River narrows and turns northward.

From Hope follow Trans-Canada 1 north along the Fraser River for 13 miles until you reach **Yale ❷** (*Visitor information, Douglas St., Tel 604/863-9277*). Minuscule today, the town swarmed with "gamblers, ruffians, drinkers, turncoats, highwaymen, thieves, murderers, and painted women" at the height of the 1858 Gold Rush. Mementos of gold rush and railroad building days, include the **Historic Yale Museum.**

Leave Yale and keep north, crossing the river on the bridge at Spuzzum. Follow the Fraser Canyon Highway, along the wooded east bank of the river. Here you will find the most spectacular section of the Fraser. The 600-foot-deep chasm of **Hells Gate ❸** forces the river into what seems an impossibly narrow channel, through which it seethes at great speed. It is worthwhile descending by **Airtram** (*Tel 604/867-9277, closed mid-Oct.–mid-April*) into the gorge, where there is a suspension footbridge.

Then continue north, passing into the dry interior. After about 30 miles, sited at the confluence of the skyblue Thompson River and the muddy waters of the Fraser is **Lytton ❹**—on record as the hottest place in Canada. Dozens of rapids make it the proclaimed "white-water rafting capital of Canada."

Follow the highway northeast from Lytton, through the often barren landscape along the Thompson River. Cross to the west bank at Spences Bridge and continue through the countryside around **Cache Creek**—often referred to as the Arizona of Canada because

---

✚ See area map pp. 272–3
► Hope
⟷ 200 miles
🕐 Allow 2 days
► Kamloops

NOT TO BE MISSED
- Hells Gate
- Rapids at Lytton
- Cache Creek

of its desertlike ecology, with prickly pear, and even rattlesnakes.

Pick up Rte. 97 at Cache Creek and follow it east to busy **Kamloops** ⑤. Its name derived from the Shuswap word Cumloops, meaning the "meeting of the waters," it stands at the confluence of the North and South Thompson Rivers, which flow into the 25-mile-long **Kamloops Lake.** From there the Canadian National Railway heads north to Jasper and Edmonton, east to Revelstoke, Banff, and Calgary. ∎

Cache Creek

Fraser River

Jasper
Edmonton

97

Cache Creek

Kamloops
Lake

Walhatchin Savona

Ashcroft

1920m

Kamloops

⑤

Revelstoke
Banff
Calgary

North Thompson

South Thompson

COQUIHALLA HWY.

Thompson

Spences
Bridge

Fraser

④

Lytton

LILLOOET

2944m
Skihist Mt.

Falls Creek

2282m
Stoyoma Mt.

Merritt

Nahatlatch

FRASER CANYON HWY.

RANGE

Boston Bar

*Hells Gate
Canyon*

③

Spuzzum

②

Yale

5

COQUIHALLA HWY.

| 0 | | 40 kilometers |
| 0 | | 40 miles |

Fraser Canyon

Choate

①

Fraser

Hope
START

3

Fraser

Chilliwack

Vancouver

U.S.A.

The Kootenays

A 273E1

Castlegar visitor information
A 273E1
✉ 1995 6th Ave.
☎ 250/365-6313

Doukhobor Heritage Museum
✉ Off Hwy. 3 near Castlegar Airport
☎ 250/365-6622
🕐 Closed Oct.–April
💲 $

Nelson visitor information
A 273E1
✉ 225 Hall St.
☎ 250/352-3433

Balfour
A 273E1

Ainsworth Hot Springs
A 273E2

Kaslo
A 273E2

IN THE FAR SOUTHEASTERN CORNER OF BRITISH COLUMBIA, the Kootenay River almost joins the Columbia River at Canal Flats before flowing south in a great bend that takes in part of the United States, finally making its junction at Castlegar. In most of what is loosely called Kootenay Country, the roughly north-south valleys are defined by mountains and receive heavy rain and snow, while to the south, a strip of land along the U.S. border enjoys a mild and sunny climate like that of the neighboring Okanagan Valley.

After David Thompson had mapped the region in 1808, it was ignored by Europeans until the mid-1860s, when the Dewdney Trail was built from Hope to the Rockies. Then, in the 1880s, a series of mineral finds began: Many of the towns that sprang up as a result of this boom have disappeared; others, like pretty little Nelson, have survived, though logging and tourism have replaced mining almost everywhere.

On its plateau at the confluence of the Columbia and Kootenay Rivers, the site of **Castlegar** lay at the division between Interior Salish and Kutenai territory, and both groups came here to fish for the rivers' abundant salmon. The modern settlement grew up as a communications center, when stern-wheelers ferried passengers up the Columbia and Arrow Lakes (now dammed) to Revelstoke. Many Doukhobors settled in the area, and the **Doukhobor Heritage Museum** introduces visitors to the sect's spartan way of life. Reached by a little suspension bridge, wooded **Zuckerberg Island** still has the delightful church built by a Russian mystic who came here in the 1930s to teach Doukhobor children.

Attractively located at the point where the Kootenay River flows out of the western arm of Kootenay Lake, **Nelson** sprang up when a silver deposit was discovered on

nearby **Toad Mountain** in 1886. The town flourished as a service center for this and other mineral workings and hence survived their demise. Today it is justifiably proud of the sustained restoration program that has given new life to its late 19th-century townscape, comprising no fewer than 350 heritage buildings. Among them, a sign of turn-of-the-century civic pride, is the **Courthouse,** the work of British Columbia's premier architect, Francis Rattenbury, designer of the province's Parliament Buildings in Victoria.

The road running north from Nelson along the lakeshore passes **Balfour,** the terminus for the free ferry to Kootenay Lake. This is part of an optional east-west route to Hwy. 3 over the Kootenay Pass, which, at 5,820 feet, is Canada's highest paved roadway and is subject to frequent closures. Nine miles beyond Balfour is **Ainsworth Hot Springs,** a little settlement that began as a mining town and continued as a spa (*Ainsworth Hot Springs Resort, Tel 250/229-4212*). The waters have a higher mineral content than any other hot springs in Canada. Farther north is **Kaslo** (*Visitor information, 324 Front St., Tel 250/353-2525*), a miniature version of Nelson with a similar charm, despite having only a tenth of the population of its heyday as a center for the silver mines to the west. A reminder of the glory days floats on the lake: The S.S. *Moyie (Visitor information, Kaslo visitor center)* is a fine example of the stern-wheelers that once plied the lake. Launched in 1898, it is the oldest surviving craft of its kind in Canada.

In a superb setting at the foot of the Rockies, **Fort Steele Heritage Town** originated as a ferry crossing over the Kootenay River and gained its name when famous Superintendent Sam Steele came this way in 1887 to settle a dispute between settlers and Kutenai people. In 1898 the Canadian Pacific Railway's

decision to bypass the town in favor of running its line through nearby Cranbrook sounded Fort Steele's death knell. Today its collection of early buildings is in the care of the province, which has supplemented them with other structures to make the splendid provincial heritage park, with costumed inhabitants, stagecoach rides, and a steam train. There are other trains in **Cranbrook,** where the developing **Canadian Museum of Rail Travel** features a tour through a complete set of luxury passenger coaches of the early 1900s. ■

Some B.C. landscapes are best experienced on horseback. Riders from the Top of the World Ranch near Fort Steele pause in awe at the snow-capped Rockies.

Cranbrook & Fort Steele
🅰 273E1

Fort Steele Heritage Town
✉ 10 miles northeast of Cranbrook via Hwy. 95
☎ 250/439-3351

Canadian Museum of Rail Travel
✉ Hwy. 3/95 in Cranbrook
☎ 250/489-3918
⑤ $

The Doukhobors

Some 7,500 members of this pacifist sect, dissenters from the Russian Orthodox Church, were helped by Russian author Leo Tolstoy and American and British Quakers to resettle in Saskatchewan at the end of the 19th century. When their exemption from the oath of allegiance was revoked, many moved to southern British Columbia

under the leadership of Peter Vasilevitch Verigin, who established an initially successful self-contained community of some 6,000 people. But when Verigin was killed in a train explosion, the community was split by internal rifts that included protests by naked members of a fanatical subsect. In 1939 Doukhobors' land was confiscated by the provincial government. ■

Okanagan Valley

273D1/D2

Penticton
273D1

Kelowna
273D2

Vernon
273D2

Historic O'Keefe Ranch
✉ 7 miles north of Vernon off Hwy. 97
☎ 250/542-7868
🕐 Closed mid-Oct.–mid-May
💲 $$$

The Blue Mountain Vineyard and other Okanagan wines are popular in Vancouver restaurants .

THE SUNNY CORRIDOR OF THE OKANAGAN VALLEY, WITH its river and chain of lakes, leads northward from the U.S. border through a smiling countryside of irrigated orchards and vineyards. The mild climate, delightful landscape, and easy access from north and south draw vacationers as well as retired people. There are attractions and recreational activities aplenty, from water sports to zoo parks. One of the best ways to explore the Okanagan is to follow the signed Okanagan Wine Route, which takes in 25 of the region's wineries, now enjoying a renaissance after the introduction of new vines and advanced winemaking techniques.

Known to the Salish as Pen-Tak-Ton meaning a "place to live in forever" (because its favorable climate was conducive to year-round living), **Penticton** is built between two lakes, **Skaha Lake** and the much larger **Okanagan Lake.** Originally a center for the surrounding ranching and orchard country, it has developed rapidly as a summer resort, with marinas and miles of sandy beaches. The visitor center shares a stylish modern building with the **British Columbia Wine Centre** (*Visitor information, Tel 250/860-5999),* offering a full range of information on winer-

ies, wine tours, and events. At one end of the poplar-lined lakefront is the beached stern-wheeler S.S. *Sicamous (Tel 250/492-0403).* Dating from 1914, the 500-passenger vessel is undergoing restoration.

Rapidly expanding **Kelowna,** approached from the west bank of Lake Okanagan by an unusual floating bridge, was where the valley's modern history began. In 1859 a mission founded near here by members of the Oblate Order was the first European settlement established in British Columbia independently of the Hudson's Bay Company. Oblate Father Charles Pandosy is credited with planting the first vines and fruit trees. Then in the 1890s, Canada's governor general, Lord Aberdeen, together with his energetic wife, Isabel, bought a ranch here and promoted orchards on a large scale.

The resort town of **Vernon** *(Visitor information: 6326 Hwy. 97 N., Tel 250/542-1415),* north of Kelowna, was founded in the 1860s by the Vernon brothers, miners-turned-ranchers. The O'Keefe Ranch also goes back to the 1860s and remained family owned for 100 years. It is now open to the public as the **Historic O'Keefe Ranch,** and is a great place to enjoy the atmosphere of early ranching days. A dozen original buildings include the family mansion, a forge, general store, and St. Anne's Church. ■

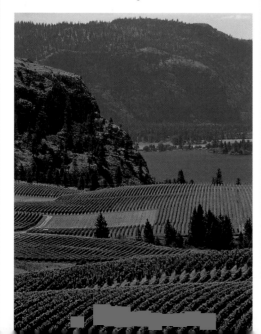

The northern territories are a complete contrast to the south's orderly cities and the fertile plains that separate them, but their harsh beauty make them equally alluring. Adventurous visitors will be well rewarded.

The North

Snow *inukshuk,*
Northwest Territories

The North

THE NORTHERN TERRITORIES OF THE YUKON AND THE Northwest Territories (N.W.T.), and the new Nunavut make up around 40 percent of Canada's land area. Yet apart from a few cities, the subarctic region is an empty land, where miles of unspoiled landscape separate small communities still imbued with the pioneering spirit. North of the Arctic Circle there are even fewer settlements, mostly belonging to the Inuit. Canada's Arctic islands are largely uninhabited, a wilderness where animals have had to battle and evolve to survive the savage environment.

On April 1, 1999, the Northwest Territories split to become two new territories—the new territory of Nunavut and the remaining western portion of the N.W.T. A caucus of "western" members of the territorial legislature voted in 1998 to continue using the name Northwest Territories. Nunavut, which means "our land" in the Inuit language, was the result of negotiations between the Inuit and the Canadian

Axel Heiberg
Island
Ellesmere
Island
ELIZABETH ISLANDS
Bathurst
Island
ISLANDS
Cornwallis
Island
Devon Island
Qausuittuc
(Resolute)
Lancaster Sound
Bylot
Island
Somerset
Island
Brodeur
Peninsula
Nanisivik
Ikpiarjuk
(Arctic Bay)
Baffin Bay
Kangiqlugaapik
(Clyde River)
Prince
of Wales
Island
Gulf of Boothia
McClintock Channel
Baffin Island
Davis Strait
Broughton
Island
Boothia
Peninsula
Igloolik
2591m
Mt Asgard
AUYUITTUQ
NATIONAL
PARK
King
William
Island
Ursuqtuq
(Gjoa Haven)
Melville
Peninsula
Prince
Charles
Island
Nettilling
Lake
Pangnirtung
Kekerton Island
Historic Park
Queen Maud
Gulf
Cumberland Sound
Foxe
Basin
Amadjuak
Lake
NUNAVUT
Naujat
(Repulse Bay)
Quammaarviit
Historic Park
Iqaluit
Arctic Circle
Garry
Lake
Back
Mallikjuaq
Historic
Park
Kingait
(Cape Dorset)
Frobisher Bay
Lake Harbour
Southampton
Island
Hudson Strait
Dubawnt
Lake
Qamanittuaq
(Baker Lake)
Fisher Strait
Kangiqliniq
(Rankin Inlet)
Coats
Island
Mansel
Island
QUEBEC
p. 102
Ennadai
Lake
Arviat
(Eskimo Point)
Hudson Bay
Nueltin Lake
0   400 kilometers
0   200 miles
G
MANITOBA
p. 210
E   F

government to return to Inuit control a land first peopled by them thousands of years ago.

YUKON

The Yukon will remain as it has always been. When people think of the Yukon, its association with the Klondike Gold Rush springs to mind. It is true that the gold rush built some of the territory's roads and it is likewise true that Dawson still has the feel of a gold rush town, many of its buildings dating from those romantic times.

But there is much more to the Yukon. The highways that traverse it allow visitors to explore its subarctic wilderness more easily than any other part of the Canadian north. Travelers can go from the Kluane National Park, where wild sheep roam a land close to Canada's highest mountains, to the Arctic Circle. This is a harsh land, home to the migrating herds of barren-ground caribou, whose territory stretches all the way to the shores of the Arctic Ocean. The Dempster Highway traverses this land to reach Inuvik, N.W.T., a town on the Mackenzie Delta.

NORTHWEST TERRITORIES

The N.W.T. is crossed by the Mackenzie River system which, at 2,600 miles, is longer than either the Mississippi or Missouri Rivers. At the headwaters of the Mackenzie, on the Great Slave Lake, lies Yellowknife, the territorial capital. Viewed from the lake shore Yellowknife's log cabins and skyscrap-ers characterize the N.W.T.—a mix of the pioneering spirit of the region's early settlers, and the modern world of Canadian commerce. The N.W.T. is less accessible to the visitor than its Yukon neighbor: Fewer roads mean that the traveler has to be more adventurous in exploring. The Mackenzie River can be followed in the comfort of modern transportation—a wonderful journey—but to enjoy the awesome beauty of the Nahanni National Park you must simply use a canoe or walk.

During the summer caribou migrate en masse over the Arctic tundra.

NUNAVUT

Although the Inuit settled the shoreline of the Arctic Ocean several thousand years ago, the present inhabitants are descended from Thule peoples who crossed the Bering Strait about 4,500 years ago. These people were given the name Eskimo by Cree Indians, a name meaning "those who eat their meat raw." The Cree used it to express their distaste and over the years it became a term of abuse. As such its use is rightly decried today, and it has been replaced by "Inuit," which means "the people" in their Inuktitut language. The creation of Nunavut is a landmark for the Inuit: At last they will control the evolution of the land their ancestors settled so long ago. And a magnificent land it is, a rugged wilderness of incomparable beauty studded with settlements in which Inuit arts and crafts flourish. ■

Arctic animals

Of the more than 4,000 species of animal that exist on the earth, fewer than 50 live all or part of their lives in the Arctic. Of these, 31 inhabit the Canadian Arctic. This small fraction indicates how harsh the Arctic environment is—plant-eating animals have to exist on a few scattered plants, while the carnivores find little to prey on. The animals have adapted remarkably to the environment.

Most of Canada's Arctic animals are rodents that are found close to tree line or in the tundra. But for most people, it is the big animals of the high Arctic that define the region.

Polar bears

The polar bear evolved from the same ancestor as the brown bear but is now quite distinct from its land-based cousin. To survive the Arctic cold, the bear has a layer of blubber below its skin and a thick coat of hair which covers its entire body apart from the nose and pads of the feet. The bear's skin is black, a good color for absorbing heat from the sun, and the coat has some hollow hairs that

Adult male polar bears engage in a bit of recreational wrestling.

transport sunlight to the skin. The coat is white—though it can appear cream or even pale yellow as the light changes—an adaptation for camouflage on the Arctic ice rather than insulation. As with all Arctic animals, evolution has reduced the size of the bears' extremities—small ears and short tails help to reduce heat loss. An exception to this rule are the bears' enormous feet, which spread their considerable weight on thin ice and also act as paddles when the bears are swimming. The polar bear is so much at home in water that some naturalists classify it as a sea mammal. The polar bears' diet has also been subject to adaptation—it is the world's only wholly carnivorous bear, consuming the seals that it hunts on the sea ice.

On land, polar bears are often followed by arctic foxes, who scavenge on the bears' leftover kills. While bears spend almost their entire lives on the ice, the fox is a land mammal. Consequently its coat changes color season by season, dark in summer for camouflage against the earth, changing to a denser (and much warmer) white coat when the winter snows fall.

The ragged coats of musk-oxen may look scruffy, but they are vital to the creatures' survival in the harsh climate.

Musk-oxen

Another typically Arctic animal is the musk ox. Musk-oxen have a permanently dark brown coat. This coat is made up of an inner layer of fine hair protected by long, silky "guard" hairs. The outer coat extends almost to the ground, giving the animal an almost comical appearance. The undercoat molts annually; the hair falls away in huge tufts, leaving the animal looking decidedly unkempt.

Musk-oxen have huge horns whose weight is concentrated across the forehead. The males use these during the rut, when two animals crash against each other in a fierce and noisy trial of strength. The females use theirs to protect the young. To combat the threat occasionally offered by wolves, adult musk-oxen form circles facing outward with their young safe in the center—the attackers are confronted by a barrier of heavy, pointed horns. Only if the wolves can spook the musk-oxen into fleeing will they be able to grab a sick or young animal. This circle formation is very effective against wolves, but useless against a man armed with a rifle. Consequently, musk-oxen were exterminated in much of their former range. Today, with active protection, numbers are on the increase.

Arctic birds

Birds differ greatly from land-based mammals in their ability to migrate easily from the Arctic at the onset of winter—a strategy adapted by all but a very few species. Of the resident species, both the rock and willow ptarmigan turn white in winter; they also increase their feather volume and lower their metabolic rate. The snowy owl is white at all times: Its feathers have the highest insulation quality of any bird species' plumage. The owl's feathers extend right down the bird's legs to the claws. The bill is also very short and almost hidden by the dense plumage covering the face. Despite these adaptations to the Arctic cold, snowy owls head south in winter, where they are sure to find enough lemmings, their major prey, to sustain them through the Arctic night. ■

The Alaska Highway

After the heady days of the gold rush, mining and the Yukon declined. For 40 years the area was left alone. Then, in the wake of the attack on Pearl Harbor, the fear that the Japanese might invade the continent via Alaska prompted President Franklin D. Roosevelt to order the construction of a highway linking Dawson Creek, British Columbia (which was already linked by road and railroad to Washington state), to Fairbanks, Alaska.

The highway was a massive project, involving the building of more than 100 bridges and the creation of more than 1,500 miles of road. Astonishingly, in only eight months the road was fit for military traffic, and it was officially opened in November 1942 at a ceremony on **Soldiers' Summit** (*Mile 1061*) above Kluane Lake; it was another year before the road was

Elk warning

Kluane National Park

NOT TO BE MISSED
- Stone Mountain Provincial Park
- Liard Hot Springs
- Kluane National Park

✚ See area map p. 314
➤ Dawson Creek
🔄 1,450 miles
🕐 Allow 7 days
➤ Fairbanks

finally completed. The road opened the Yukon, although not until the 1970s was it fully paved. Then in 1996, the highway was granted the status of International Historic Civil Engineering Landmark, one of only 16 projects to be so recognized to date.

The highway is marked with historical mileposts (distances in Canada are given in kilometers) that, while they allow travelers to locate historic sites and provide information, do not accurately reflect current distances.

The logical place to begin an exploration of the highway is Mile 0, located on Tenth Street in the the heart of **Dawson Creek** ❶ *(Visitor information, 250/782-9595)* in British Columbia. Follow the road northwest from the town. At Mile 21 stop and admire the elegantly carved **Kiskatinaw Bridge**—the only surviving original bridge. A few miles further north at Mile 35 cross the **Peace River Bridge.** The First Nations named the Peace River for a treaty that identified the wide river as a frontier between two

Crowds gather for the Yukon's Sourdough Rendezvous.

tribes. The stretch of road halfway between Dawson Creek and Suicide Hill is marked by reminders of the road's military importance. The **Beatton River airstrips** ❷ *(Mile 73)* were for emergency use by the U.S. military and **Blueberry Control Station** *(Mile 101)* was a manned checkpoint maintained 24 hours a day throughout World War II.

Continue northwest, through Wonowon toward Suicide Hill. From here follow the long mountainous section of the highway: A major rerouting in 1992 eliminated many of the curves, but did not spoil the views, which are superb all the way to **Fort Nelson** ❸ *(Visitor information, 250/774-2541)* at Mile 300. Follow the highway west of the town— where you find that the vistas before were just a prelude. The scenery improves even more on the approach to **Stone Mountain**

NORTH WEST TERRITORIES

The Alaska Highway

Block

ALASKA HWY.

Watson Lake

Coal River

❺ **Liard Hot Springs** ❹

Liard River

Liard

Swift River

37

Muncho Lake

Muncho Lake
Muncho Lake Provincial Park

BRITISH COLUMBIA

77

Fort Nelson ❸

Summit Lake
Stone Mt. Provincial Park
2972m ▲

R O C K Y   M O U N T A I N S

Prophet

ALASKA HWY.

Sikanni Chief

Pink Mountain

Suicide Hill
Wonowon
❷ Beatton River

ALBERTA

Peace

0 ____ 150 kilometers
0 ____ 150 miles

97

Fort St. John

97

START

2

❶ **Kiskatinaw Bridge**
Dawson Creek

Beautiful panoramas are commonplace in Kluane National Park.
Right: Whitehorse's famous Anglican log cathedral

Provincial Park (*Mile 392*), which represents the high point of the road, at 4,250 feet. The views on this section of the highway are among the most magnificent along its length. Keep west as the road threads through **Muncho Lake Provincial Park,** cross the Liard River and you will reach **Liard Hot Springs** ④ at Mile 496. During the highway's construction the soldiers used these springs as a natural bath on six days of the week, the seventh day being reserved for female staff.

From Liard Hot Springs, remain on the highway as it follows the north bank of the Liard River. Though the highway crosses the British Columbia-Yukon border seven times between Miles 588 and 627, 627 represents the official crossing. From here it is only a short drive to **Watson Lake** ⑤ (*Mile 635*), the Yukon's first town. Leaving westward you will find that the highway actually dips back into British Columbia again before reaching **Teslin** (*Mile 804*), a lake taking its name from the First Nations' description—"long, narrow lake." After rounding the lake, the highway heads west to **Whitehorse** ⑥ at Mile 918 (see p. 323).

From Whitehorse, some travelers switch to the Klondike Highway, a more romantic road (see pp. 324–5). But, if you remain on the Alaska Highway, you will also be rewarded as it enters one of its most majestic sections.

At **Haines Junction** ⑦ (*Mile 1016*), the highway meets the Haines Highway (from the south and the Lynn Canal) and turns north along the border of **Kluane National Park** ⑧ (*Visitor information, 867/634-7250*). Together with Wrangell-St. Elias National Park, just across the border, this breathtaking park preserves one of the world's most pristine wilderness areas.

Follow the highway along the park's edge to Kluane Lake. **Destruction Bay** (*Mile 1083*), by the lake, is so named because a winter storm all but destroyed the camp and machinery of the highway's builders.

Farther on, at **Beaver Creek** ⑨ (*Mile 1202*), the construction crews pushing the road northward met those working their way south from Fairbanks. The Alaskan border is just a short distance away now (*Mile 1221*), but the highway continues for another 220 miles or so to Fairbanks. ■

Whitehorse

THE FORTUNE-SEEKING HORDES WHO BRAVED THE Chilkoot Trail on their way to Dawson spent the early spring camped by Lake Bennett, waiting for the Yukon River to thaw and for rafts to be built to run it. The river journey was fraught with danger, one of the biggest hazards being Miles Canyon near the lake. The canyon held the Yukon's roughest waters and was christened White Horse Rapids because rafters likened them to the white manes of horses.

314B2

Visitor information

✉ Second Ave.
☎ 867/667-2915
🕐 Closed mid-Sept.–mid-May

The rapids ended many expeditions, some of them tragically. The Mounties tried to control rafters, discouraging the foolhardy and encouraging experienced boatmen: Jack London is said to have earned $3,000 as a boatman in 1898. Then an enterprising group laid a 5-mile tramway around the canyon, reaching the river again at a site where a town rapidly grew up. The town's founders called it Whitehorse as a reminder of the rapids.

While the best place to begin a visit to Whitehorse is at the **Tourist Information Centre,** many visitors go straight to the **S.S. Klondike** (*Waterfront, Tel 867/667-3910, closed Sept.–May*), a stern-wheeler built in 1937 to travel the river between Whitehorse and Dawson. The downriver trip took one and a half days and burned 40 cords of wood; the upriver return took three times longer and required 120 cords. Visitors can join a free tour around the boat.

Back toward the center of town and close to the river, the **MacBride Museum** (*1st Ave., Tel 867/667-2709, closed Sept.–May*) has a wonderful collection of gold rush photographs and some remarkable items—Sam McGee's cabin, an engine from the White Pass & Yukon Railroad, and a fine (mounted) collection of Yukon wildlife. Whitehorse's **log "skyscraper"** stands on the corner of Lambert and Second. Just before the skyscraper, a right turn on Elliott reaches the town's **Log Church** (*3rd Ave., Tel 867/668-2555, closed late Sept.–May*). Built in 1900, this beautiful church is now a religious museum. ∎

Above: Once a main supply ship for Dawson, the S.S. *Klondike* is now a dockside museum to the old days.

The Klondike Highway

For 24-hour information on the road:
☎ 867/667-8215

TECHNICALLY, THE KLONDIKE HIGHWAY STARTS AT Skagway, Alaska. But for most people the real Klondike Highway is the road between Whitehorse and Dawson, a route that closely follows the trail of the gold rush hopefuls of the late 1890s.

The Klondike Highway branches off the Alaska Highway a little north of Whitehorse, soon reaching the shore of lovely **Lake Laberge;** in gold rush times the lake's trout were transported to Dawson in bargeloads. Laberge is also famous as the actual scene of the cremation of Sam McGee, the event immortalized in Robert Service's famous poem. Beyond the lake, a side road at the Fox Lane campground leads up to picturesque **Little Fox Lake.**

The highway now follows the Nordenski River, which flows into the Yukon at **Carmacks,** 118 miles from Whitehorse. **Five Fingers Rapids,** 16 miles farther north, is the halfway point between Whitehorse and Dawson, and a section of the Yukon feared by rafters. Here the river forms five parallel channels of dangerous rapids.

The highway now follows the majestic river through unspoiled country, passing **Minto** and **Pelly Crossing,** each little more than a provision stop, before reaching **Stewart Crossing.** Adventuring American author Jack London's only Yukon winter was spent in Stewart Crossing; his cabin has since been

This mountain goat appears to be blissfully unaware of the disruption it is causing.

Above: Dall's sheep are found in abundance throughout the Yukon.

Left: In Dawson, the cabin of Robert Service, poet, adventurer, and author of "The Cremation of Sam McGee," remains exactly as he left it.

dismantled and reassembled in **Dawson** (see p 328). Stewart is named for the discoverer of the Stewart River. The next town, **McQuesten,** also remembers a Yukon pioneer, Leroy (Jack) McQuesten, who discovered gold in the Stewart River. Beyond McQuesten the highway reaches the Klondike River. The river's name derives from a mispronunciation of its native name, thron diuck—hammer water—so called because the First Nations hammered stakes into its waters to catch salmon. The same people also named the Yukon: To them it was yuckoo—clear water. In just a few miles now, the hammer water will reach the clear water at Dawson. ■

The Gold Rush

Many legends surround the discovery of gold in the Canadian north, so many that the whole truth concerning this fascinating moment in the region's history will never be revealed. A likely story began in 1895 when Robert Henderson, a Nova Scotia-born prospector, arrived near what is now Dawson and began to pan the local creeks for gold. He had little success in his first summer, but the following spring he climbed King Solomon Dome, a 4,048-foot peak to the east of the junction of the Klondike and Yukon Rivers. From the peak a series of creeks ran off in all directions. Henderson chose one and began to pan. In his first wash he found more gold than he had ever seen before in a single pan.

In those early days, with few prospectors in the area, it was an unwritten rule among pioneers that such news was shared. Henderson immediately told his fellow prospectors, and they worked the creek until the next August. Henderson then journeyed south to pick up fresh supplies. While returning to his creek, he met George Washington Carmack, who was traveling with his Athapaskan wife and two of her native relatives, Tagish Charlie and Skookum Jim. Henderson told them about the new find and returned to his creek.

Carmack and his companions headed for the peak, but instead of following Henderson they chose a creek on the west side of the mountain—soon known as Bonanza Creek, for the three men's first pan revealed more gold than even Henderson had found. This find consequently helped spark the Klondike Gold Rush. Ironically, the only person who did not benefit from the new find was Henderson. Carmack and his partners staked three claims and headed south to file them. They revealed all to those in the supply villages—who promptly deserted their houses and shops and headed north—but they neglected to cross King Solomon Dome to tell Henderson.

The outside world did not know about the find until the summer of 1897, when the first prospectors, carrying vast quantities of gold, arrived by steamer in Seattle and other ports along the U.S. West Coast. Within days those hopeful of getting rich quickly had set off northward. It is estimated that at least 100,000 people began the trek to Dawson. So many of them moved so fast that they resembled a cattle stampede, earning the nickname Klondike Stampeders. Some went via Edmonton, others via Anchorage, but those anxious to be first to arrive went by ship to Skagway and then walked over the Chilkoot or White Pass to reach Lake Bennett and the Yukon River.

Many arrived in late summer and reached the passes in early winter. With little sustenance available near the Klondike River, they carried huge quantities of supplies. Many were unprepared for the snow and bitter cold of winter. On the passes and the frozen shores of Lake Bennett and the Yukon River, many froze to death, died of disease, or committed suicide to escape the appalling conditions. Others simply turned back. And even those who survived until the ice on the Yukon thawed were not saved. Having built rafts, they ran the river to Dawson, but most had no idea of raft design and even less about navigating a river. The White Horse Rapids of Miles Canyon and the Five Fingers Rapids farther north smashed boats and drowned men. Not until the Mounties arrived to regulate the Stampeders, turning back those with inadequate clothing and supplies and setting up a team of qualified boatmen, did the death toll fall.

Many found their fortune in gold. In 1896 some 14,000 ounces were extracted from the streams and frozen ground around Dawson. By 1897 this rose to more than 120,000 ounces; by 1900 it was more than a million ounces. In Dawson the gambling halls and good-time girls did their best to relieve the wealthy of their gold, often successfully. Fortunes were sometimes made on the turn of a card—but just as often lost.

By 1901 the amount of gold extracted from the Klondike decreased, and three years later all the Stampeders had gone as large companies with steam-powered dredging machines took over. The Klondike Gold Rush was short lived, but it remains one of the most colorful episodes in North American history. ∎

The early gold-seekers panned the streams, but the search soon became more intensive, with huge spoil heaps created by digging machines.

Dawson

314B3

Visitor information

✉ Front St.
☎ 867/993-5566
🕐 Closed mid-Sept.–mid-May

DAWSON'S GOLD BOOM LASTED JUST A COUPLE OF YEARS, during which time the town was built and burned three times. After the third fire there were barely enough people left to do the rebuilding: News of a new gold strike at Nome in Alaska had taken them all west. Dawson's population fell to a few hundred, although recent hikes in the price of gold have increased it to around 2,000.

Set where the Klondike River joins the Yukon River, Dawson is built on permafrost. From October to April or May temperatures in the town are below freezing, while in summer temperatures rise to 60°F, making the ground boggy. Dawson's roads are unpaved, and its houses rest on wooden pads, to prevent sinking and to block heat from the houses thawing the ground surface more than once.

The town is laid out on a grid between the two rivers. The ferry crossing the Yukon to reach the Top of the World Highway leaves from Front Street, where the **Tourist Information Office** stands opposite the **Han National Cultural Centre** (*Tel 867/993-5735*). Here the history of the area's first inhabitants is explored. On King Street is the **Palace Grand Theatre**, built in 1899 by Arizona

Charlie Meadows, Dawson's most famous bartender (and gunfighter). The original palace was demolished in 1959, but the present one is an exact copy. Ahead is **Diamond Tooth Gerties** (*Corner of 4th & 8th Ave.s, Tel 867/993-5575*), Canada's first casino. It was named for Gertie Lovejoy, who had a diamond wedged between her front teeth. Closer to the Klondike River is the **Dawson City Museum** (*Tel 867/993-5291*) by **Minto Park,** on the other side of which is **Robert Service's Cabin** (*8th Ave.*), looking just as the famous poet/adventurer (author of "The Cremation of Sam McGee") left it. Close by is **Jack London's Cabin** (*8th Ave., Tel 867/993-5575, closed mid-Sept.–mid-May*), brought from Stewart Crossing; daily readings are given here from works of the Yukon's most famous writer. ∎

You can get a magnificent view of Dawson from the Midnight Dome Road.

Inuvik

FOR 700 YEARS, THE GWICH'IN DENE INUIT, COASTAL AND tundra hunting people, left their settlements on the Peel River and the delta of the Mackenzie River (a river the Inuit called Deh Cho) and drove their dogsleds to the Yukon River to trade furs. One of their principal settlements, now Inuvik in the Northwest Territories, has enjoyed a recent resurgence as a base for exploring the vast Arctic region with its delicate ecosystems.

Some years ago Inuvik was a rather disappointing place, the Inuit occupying poor housing with very inadequate facilities at one end of town, and the more prosperous white population residing in better places at the other end. But recent and increasingly progressive changes of policy and attitude have ended this anomaly: Today Inuvik is a much more lively town, its buildings a cheerful splash of color in the barren wilderness. Look on Mackenzie Road for the circular **Our Lady of Victory** "igloo" church, with its roof of domes and cupolas, just as innovative a design as can be found anywhere below the circle. Its Stations of the Cross, by local Inuit artist Mona Thresher, are masterpieces.

ARCTIC BASE
As the visitor center for the western Arctic, Inuvik has excellent accommodations and offers many opportunities for day or longer trips to the several surrounding national parks that have been set up to preserve the region's fragile Arctic ecosystem. **Aulavik National Park,** with its brief growing season, supports grasses, sedges, heathers, and the dwarf willows that become food for the population of several thousand musk-oxen. Located on the Bank's Island across the Amundsen Gulf, the park is the breeding ground for numerous arctic birds. There is also an excellent bird reserve at **Cape**

Parry, east of Inuvik, close to the **Tuktut Nogait National Park,** the newest of the Arctic reserves. In the park's southern region, between the Peel and Arctic Red Rivers, roam Dall's sheep, caribou, grizzly bear, and the elusive gyrfalcon. On the Beaufort coast, close to the Inuit settlement of **Tuktoyaktuk,** is a famous collection of pingos—cones of gravel or soil forced up by the pressure of underlying ice. The pingos of the Mackenzie Delta, some of which reach 130 feet in height and measure almost 1,000 feet across the base, are among the most impressive in the whole Arctic. ■

314B3

Visitor information
✉ Parks Canada, Western Arctic District, P.O. Box 1840 EG, Inuvik
☎ 867/777-3248

Western Arctic Tourism Association
✉ P.O. Box 2600, Inuvik
☎ 867/777-2434

Inuit art is an evocative integration of myth and reality, prey animals sometimes merging with imagined events.

The Inuit people

The Arctic's unforgiving environment ensured that northern Canada was one of the last places on earth in which humans settled permanently. It also meant that those who settled did so in very small numbers in comparison to the vastness of the land. Other continents' populations expanded as they filled the landscape, but in the Arctic the population never rose beyond the scattered handful of settlements and nomadic groups who first occupied the area.

As the ice sheets of the last ice age retreated small groups of Paleo-eskimo peoples arrived in Arctic Canada. The settlers had come from Alaska, having earlier crossed the Bering Sea from Siberia.

The earliest inhabitants probably lived in tents year-round, using animal skins stretched over a framework of lashed-together bones. In winter they would have used double skins with an insulating layer of heather or other vegetation between them. These people crafted tools from ivory, bone, antler, and stones; they hunted land and sea mammals and took freshwater fish as they migrated up or down rivers. They were a nomadic people, traveling mostly on foot, although they did use a one-person boat called a qajaq (kayak) for fishing. Then, about 2,800 years ago, a people now known as "Dorset" (named after Cape Dorset on Baffin Island) gradually emerged, probably as a result of a cooling in the local climate that induced a change in lifestyle. People of the Dorset constructed the first igloos, the most well-known feature of the Inuit to outsiders, using them as winter quarters. They did not use the bow and arrow, perhaps because the change in climate meant there were fewer land animals to hunt. Instead they harpooned sea mammals from ice floe edges or at breathing holes. The Dorset people also produced exquisite ritualistic art work—carving bone, ivory, and antler.

The Dorset culture existed for about 2,000 years. Then, with the warming climatic trend, Neo-eskimo peoples migrated from the west bringing larger boats (called umiat—skin-covered vessels capable of ferrying an entire

family) and sleds pulled by dogs. Excavations at Thule on Greenland's west coast led to this people being named the Thule. Like people of the Dorset culture, the Thule also hunted sea mammals, but instead of limiting their catch to walrus, seal, beluga, and narwhal they were technologically advanced enough to hunt the huge bowhead whale. The Thule people were also nomadic, dwelling in stone or sod dwellings and igloos (in winter) and skin tents (in summer). Their campsites have been excavated in a number of locations like Ellesmere Island—the untouched stone circles used to anchor the bottom of the skins can still be seen, together with the weathered bones of slaughtered whales. A surprising aspect of Thule culture is how little artwork they created, however, they were capable of producing marvelous carvings in bone, ivory, and wood. This aspect of Thule culture is still apparent in the Inuit population today, who produce wonderful works of art in ivory, soapstone, and serpentine. Many of the works illustrate aspects of the rich Inuit culture, featuring men or women in ritual dances or dressed in ritual masks. They also portray the Inuit myths about the creation of the arctic animals, or of the spirits of those animals.

The Thule Inuit settled in Arctic Canada about 1,000 years ago but within 600 years their way of life received a shock from which it could never recover—the first meeting with Europeans. In seeking a passage between the Atlantic and the Pacific explorers like Martin Frobisher inevitably encountered the Inuit, although these early Europeans had little effect on Inuit life and culture. The pace of change was accelerated in the early 19th century when British whalers began exploiting the west coast of Baffin Island. While Europeans brought improved weapons for hunting, they also brought new diseases that the Inuit were unable to tolerate.

In the 20th century the changes were almost overwhelming, as the Inuit way of life was increasingly threatened by industrial mineral extraction and, more importantly, continued whaling—the wholesale slaughter of these creatures by Europeans brought them to the

An important lesson Inuit children must learn is how to recognize the safe forms of sea ice.

brink of extinction. For the Inuit, whose reliance on hunting whales was incalcuable, the effects were devastating. Communities were uprooted, moved, and resettled. Employment within the mining industry forced young men into the new economy and consequently many traditions were lost. More recently, conservationists have threatened the hunting and trapping lifestyle.

Today, the creation of Nunavut, the new Canadian territory which came into existence on April 1, 1999, will return much of the Arctic lands to their Inuit owners. It is hoped that Nunavut will provide a more positive future for the Inuit peoples, one in which they will be able to control their own destiny. ■

Mackenzie River

314C3

✉ N.W.T. Arctic
Tourism, P.O. Box
1320, Yellowknife

☎ 867/873-7200

ONE OF NORTH AMERICA'S GREAT RIVERS, THE MACKENZIE traces its way from Great Slave Lake northwestward for 1,068 miles before emptying into the Beaufort Sea. It takes its name from the Scottish-born explorer Alexander Mackenzie, whose 18th-century voyage along the river rivaled Meriwether Lewis and William Clark's 1804-1806 exploration of the Pacific Northwest for scientific inquiry. The Mackenzie remains an untamed and majestic feature of Canada's north.

As a young employee of a fur-trading company, Mackenzie led an expedition from **Lake Athabasca** (on the Alberta–Saskatchewan border) to continue the exploration of the Canadian north. Between June 3 and September 12, 1783, the expedition traveled the length of the river, following it for over 1,000 miles all the way to the Arctic Ocean. Mackenzie's diary details the birds and fish caught for food each day, as well as the weather.

The Mackenzie has been canoed many times since, but an easier way to enjoy this massive river system is aboard the **M.S. Norweta** (*17 England Cres., Yellowknife, Tel 867/873-2489*), which makes round-trips each summer between **Yellowknife** and **Inuvik.** The downriver journey takes 10 days, the upriver 12.

From the town of **Norman Wells,** real adventurers can follow the **Canol Heritage Trail** (*"A Hikers Guide" available from 867/587-2054*), which follows a roadbed built during World War II and abandoned in 1945. The trail heads southwest to the **MacMillan Pass** (the border with the Yukon). Few will have the time or energy to walk its entire 230-mile length, but airstrips allow sections to be walked; the lucky walker sees moose, wolf, black bear, woodland caribou, and perhaps even a grizzly. ■

On its way to Inuvik, the Dempster highway crosses the Mackenzie River at the tiny village of Arctic Red River.

Nahanni National Park

314C2

**Nahanni
National Park**

✉ P.O. Box 348,
Fort Simpson

☎ 867/695-2310

$ $

NORTHERN CANADA IS A LAND OF SUPERLATIVES: IT IS EASY to think that the panorama you are currently viewing is the finest in the country, only to discover another, better, farther along. While many of the landscapes are breathtaking, the South Nahanni River, much of which is protected by the Nahanni National Park, capitalizes on the repeated discovery of magnificent scenery. ■

The park is best viewed from the river, and there are many opportunities for canoe trips lasting from a single day to several weeks. **Virginia Falls** is the most famous of the park's attractions. Here the river drops in two mighty falls, the upper one 295 feet high, the lower 171 feet, the two separated by a vast pillar of rock known (locally) as Mason Rock. The total height of the falls is twice that of Niagara. Upriver of the falls are the **Rabbitkettle Hotsprings,** volcanic springs that gush water at a temperature of 70°F. In winter Virginia Falls freezes almost solid—a wonderful sight—while the hot springs continue nonstop. The hot water is rich in calcium carbonate, which is deposited around the vents, creating tufa in weird shapes.

The park also has an area of karst landforms: As water dissolves the limestone, it produces vast canyons and gorges with steep cliffs; sinkholes into which rivers disappear and where they then carve huge caves; and unusual rock formations such as the double arch near Raven Lake.

As a complete contrast, just outside the national park stands one of the world's most impressive series of rock walls, the hard granite cliffs of the **Cirque of the Unclimbables.** These vast walls, many hundreds of feet high, were so intimidating to those who first saw them that they assumed no one would be skilled (or mad) enough to climb them. History has proved them wrong. Add the beautiful canyons through which the Nahanni River flows and the glaciers from the high peaks at the river's head, and the landscape is seen to be one of the most comprehensive in the world. ■

The sheer power of Virginia Falls has carved a narrow canyon (Fourth Canyon) for the Nahinni River.

The Northwest Passage

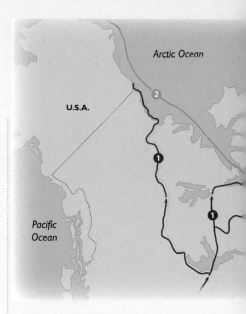

In the 15th century, faced with hostile kingdoms to the east, the countries of western Europe sought an alternative route to the fabulous wealth of China and Japan. Spurred by this, rather than by the idea of a New World, Christopher Columbus set out on the journey that ended on the northern shore of Cuba. Many other Europeans followed Columbus in the search for the western route to the east, but it soon became clear that America was a solid barrier to progress westward, and the search began for a way around the continent. The route around the Cape of Good Hope was long, that around Cape Horn dangerous. Was there a route linking the Atlantic to the Pacific around the northern edge of Canada? The search for the Northwest Passage had begun.

Throughout the 16th century the Spanish, French, and Portuguese all sent expeditions to explore the northern Atlantic shores of what is now Canada. These were all driven back by the ice, as were those of the English, whose first attempts to reach China, involved exploring the northern coast of Norway and Russia in the hope of finding a northeast passage.

Spanish successes in Latin America ensured that if England was to retain its position as an important European (and therefore world) power, it had to control trade routes to the East. So by the late 16th century they, too, were seeking the Northwest Passage. The early English explorers gave their names to the places they discovered—Frobisher (Bay), Davis (Strait), Baffin (Island) and, most famous of all, Hudson (Bay).

In 1607 Henry Hudson began his exploration of the Canadian Arctic, returning again in 1609 and 1610. On the final voyage he discovered the bay to become known as Hudson Bay, but it ended in tragedy when his crew mutinied. Hudson's ship was inadequately stocked with food and his men were poorly clothed. When, after a winter locked in ice, his ship was freed, Hudson declared his intention of continuing the search for the passage rather than returning home. Appalled by this prospect, the crew put him, his 14-year-old son, and seven other men into an open boat and set them adrift on the bay with just one musket and a kettle. They were never seen again.

In 1631, with Charles I's backing, the rival ports of London and Bristol sent ships (Luke Fox in the *Charles* and Thomas James in the *Henrietta Marie*, named for Charles's Queen) on a race for the passage. Each captain carried a letter of greeting to the Japanese Emperor, signed by the king. The letters were in English, since it was assumed that the Emperor, being a noble, cultured man, would speak the language. Captain James also has the dubious distinction of almost roasting his men to death (on an island in what is now James Bay). When they were half frozen in the grip of an Arctic winter, James started a fire that went out of control, burning down the island's forest and forcing the men to flee the flames.

Just when the English realized that even if there was a passage it would not be a practical trade route is not clear. The problem was, and is, that the line of the passage is dictated by the ice. This may force ships to travel one side of an island one year, but on the other side the

GREENLAND

Baffin
Bay

Baffin
Island

CANADA

Atlantic
Ocean

Hudson
Bay

1 John Franklin

2 Roald Amundsen

3 Henry Hudson

4 Martin Frobisher

Left: Over the course of several voyages in the 1850s, Francis Leopold McClintock (1819–1907) investigated the fate of Sir John Franklin's expedition. The tragic story unfolded through conversations with the region's Inuit population.

next. In the following year it may stop them altogether. The passage is also tortuous, weaving a route through the maze of islands that lie off Canada's northern coast.

By the time of Sir John Franklin's famous 1845 expedition, the purpose was scientific research and national prestige. Unfortunately, Franklin, his ships *Erebus* and *Terror*, and all his men disappeared, leading to a search for survivors that included such experiments as the sending of dozens of messages to the expedition in small balloons. The truth emerged— that the expedition succumbed to the Arctic

winter and scurvy, and, in a desperate overland trek, had been forced into cannibalism.

But the search for Franklin had one significant outcome. By approaching the northern waters from the Pacific end, the Bering Strait, Robert McClure discovered the final leg of the passage, although it was not until 1903-06 that Roald Amundsen, the Norwegian who was the first to the South Pole, completed the journey. Today, icebreakers can follow the passage with ease, but to try it without such modern devices still requires great courage and endurance. ∎

Yellowknife

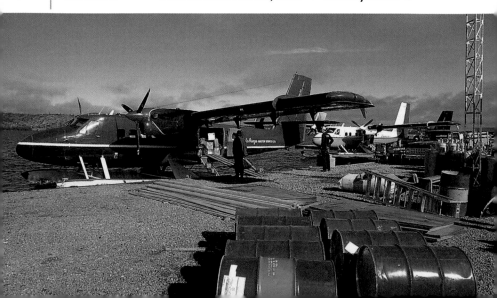

314C2

Visitor information

✉ N.W.T. Arctic Tourism, P.O. Box 1320, Yellowknife

☎ 867/873-7200

City of Yellowknife

✉ P.O. Box 580, Yellowknife

☎ 867/920-5600

VISITORS TO YELLOWKNIFE ARE GREETED BY A LARGE *inuksuit*—a "man" built of stone blocks. Such statues are ancient markers erected to guide travelers across a landscape devoid of distinguishing features. In contrast, the skyscrapers of Canada's most northerly city rise beyond.

Yellowknife, the capital of the Northwest Territories, is a hub for exploring the north; the excellent **Prince of Wales Northern Heritage Centre** (*Off Ingraham Trail, Tel 867/873-7551*) is a good place to start. More than that, though, it is a lively place, especially during one of its numerous festivals. In March, a three-day, 150-mile dogsled race, offering the largest purse in Canada, begins and ends here. At the same time, the **Caribou Carnival** enlivens the city with ice sculpting, waiter/waitress races, dancing and feasting, and much more. In July, the **Festival of the Midnight Sun** is a weeklong festival that celebrates the culture of the north.

From Yellowknife, scheduled flights allow visitors to reach places that are as different from each other as is imaginable. A short flight south reaches **Fort Smith**, where

visitors can drive through subarctic **Wood Buffalo National Park** (*P.O. Box 750 EG, Fort Smith, Tel 867/872-7900*). Here Canada's largest herd of bison roams—and is hunted by wolves. A flight north, via Cambridge Bay to **Resolute**, brings you to the real Arctic. Situated on **Cornwallis Island,** less than 200 miles from the North Magnetic Pole, Resolute is an Inuit settlement where residents follow the old ways, hunting and trapping on the tundra and sea ice. Although it has no luxury hotels, there are comfortable accommodations at Resolute for those wanting to use it as a center for trips of a lifetime— to see belugas and polar bears on the north coast of **Somerset Island,** narwhals near **Devon Island,** or the graves of members of Franklin's ill-fated expedition (see pp. 334–5) on nearby **Beechey Island.** ∎

To explore the area around Yellowknife, visitors might use floatplanes and canoes.

Baffin Island

BAFFIN IS THE LARGEST ISLAND OF THE CANADIAN ARCTIC. Indeed, at over 190,000 square miles, it is the fifth largest on earth. Yet for all its vast size, it has only a scattering of settlements, some on the north coast, twice as many on the south, and only one main settlement in its center. That central region settlement is also coastal: A place of majestic beauty, with a wild, rugged terrain, inland Baffin supports little life, offering few hopes for the hunter or trapper.

315F4

Visitor information

✉ Regional Visitor Centre, Iqualit
☎ 876/979-4636

Northern Baffin has no national park as yet, although a bird sanctuary on **Bylot Island** has been set up to protect the nesting cliffs of 300,000 thick-billed murres and 80,000 black legged kittiwakes. In the waters of Pond Inlet, between Bylot Island and the mainland, and in **Lancaster Sound,** to the north of Bylot, there are walruses, beluga and bowhead whales, narwhals and orcas, and several species of seals, on which polar bear prey. Trips to Bylot to see the birds and to watch whales can be organized in the village of **Pond Inlet** (*Hamlet*

Office, Tel 867/899-8935). The village has limited accommodations, but there is a good restaurant. Regular flights from Iqaluit in southern Baffin and from Resolute serve Pond Inlet. The other two settlements in the north may also be reached by regular flights. Each year **Nanisivik** hosts the world's most northerly marathon.

Central Baffin is a remote, isolated wilderness, although the area to the north of **Cumberland Sound** is becoming increasingly popular, with hikers and climbers visiting the **Auyuittuq National**

The remote village of Pond Inlet is a good starting point for trips to study arctic wildlife.

**Auyuittiq
National Park**
✉ P.O. Box 353,
Pangnirtung
☎ 867/473-8828

Park. Auyuittuq means "the land that never melts" and it was the first Arctic national park in Canada, set up in 1972. The most popular hiking trail traverses the park from **Broughton Island** to **Pangnirtung,** but many walkers prefer to follow a shorter route,

(Tel 867/979-5537, closed Nov.–May), housed in an old Hudson's Bay Company trading post, is worth a visit for its collection on the history of southern Baffin. In addition to Pangnirtung and Auyuittuq, Iqaluit is also the starting point for trips to several other parks. At **Qaummaarviit Historic Park** (*Unikkaarvik Visitor Centre, Iqaluit, Tel 867/979-4636*)—about 7 miles by boat from the town— are the remains of Inuit turf houses dating from the Thule period, perhaps 1,000 years ago. About a half-hour's walk north from Iqaluit leads to the **Sylvia Grinnell Territorial Park** (*Unikkaarvik Visitor Centre, Iqaluit, Tel 867/979-4636*), a quiet spot renowned for its fishing, and populations of caribou and arctic fox.

**Babysitting
on Baffin Island**

heading north from Pangnirtung to **Summit Lake,** where the huge, vertical walls of Mount Asgard can be seen. **Mount Thor** has the highest uninterrupted rock face in the world.

Pangnirtung, a small village reached by regular flights from Iqaluit, is the starting point for visiting **Kekerton Island Historic Park** (*Angmarlik Interpretative Centre, Pangnirtung, Tel 867/473-8737*). Here the ruins of a whaling station can still be seen. Between the late 1850s and early 1860s, whalers virtually exterminated the bowhead whale from habitats such as the one on Kekerton.

Lying at the head of Frobisher Bay, **Iqaluit,** the main settlement on Baffin, is the capital of Nunavut, the new territory as of April 1, 1999. It is a lovely place with a population of more than 4,400, more than 60 percent of them Inuit. It has a range of good hotels and restaurants, and the **Nunatta Sunakkutaangit Museum**

To the south of Iqaluit is **Lake Harbour,** a beautiful village at the edge of the **Katannilik Territorial Park** (*Park Interpretive Centre, Kimmirut, Tel 867/939-2084*). The name means "place of waterfalls," and the falls add to the beauty of a surprisingly fertile area. Arctic fox and hare, caribou, peregrine and gyrfalcons, and rough-legged hawk can all be seen here.

Finally, to the west of Iqaluit is **Cape Dorset,** the famous center for Inuit artists. Museums throughout Canada display the works of these artists, who work in antler, bone, ivory, and stone. The artists' studios can (and should) be visited. To the northwest of the village—about 45 minutes on foot—is **Mallikjuaq Historic Park** (*Hamlet of Cape Dorset Community Development Office, Cape Dorset, Tel 867/897-8996*), where the 1,000-year-old remains of a Thule settlement have been carefully preserved. ■

Travelwise

Floatplane

TRAVELWISE INFORMATION

PLANNING YOUR TRIP

WHEN TO GO

Any time is a good time to visit Canada, depending on your interests. Cold winter weather produces some spectacular skiing, and the warmth of summer gives rise to a myriad of outdoor festivals and activities.

As a general rule, the climate is mildest on the country's coasts, especially on Vancouver Island. However, what the East and West Coasts don't get in snow is made up for in rain and fog. The landlocked prairies have bitterly cold and drawn-out winters but beautiful warm summers. Ontario and Quebec can be a little humid in mid-summer and their winters are cold, but these are punctuated by short crisp springs and brilliant mild falls with stupendous colors. In the north of the country, summers are short and warm with 24 hours of daylight, winters are long and Siberianlike.

With the huge size of some provinces and territories, there is considerable variation within their borders. Quebec, for example, stretches from the temperate south to the Arctic, and the weather varies accordingly.

The vast majority of tourists visit Canada between mid-May and mid-October. Outside these months, facilities might be reduced, unless you are going to a ski area or major city. Thus, it is advisable to check in advance that hotels and sights are open during the off-peak season.

WHAT TO TAKE

Most of southern Canada has a climate similar to the northern U.S., so you should dress accordingly. Expect hot summer days with cooler evenings. If you are staying in the Rockies or beside a lake or the ocean, evenings tend to be cool even in mid-summer. A sweater or light jacket is recommended.

On the coasts, rain is frequent and a raincoat is essential, plus an umbrella if you are in a city. In Vancouver natives never seem to use umbrellas. So be forewarned that if you buy an umbrella there, it is likely to say "visitor to Vancouver" inside.

In May or June in the north, or in lake country, you will need insect repellent, especially if you are camping or planning a wilderness excursion. Sometimes, depending on the rainfall, biting insects can be so ferocious near lakes or streams that a hat with mosquito netting attached is a good idea.

Sunglasses are important, not only in the south as you would expect, but the light of the north is surprisingly bright, and it lasts for 24 hours a day in summer. Sunscreen is also a good idea if you are going to spend lengthy periods outside.

For winter visits, your car should be winterized. Snow tires are essential except in the major cities. You should have warm mittens, a hat, a scarf, a warm coat, boots, and long johns, to save your legs from freezing.

BEFORE YOU GO

PASSPORTS

U.S. citizens do not need a passport or a visa to visit Canada. However, proof of citizenship and photo identification are essential. Identifying papers such as a passport or birth, baptismal, or voter's certificate should be carried. U.S. residents who are not U.S. citizens should carry their Alien Registration cards.

Any person under 19 traveling alone or in a group requires a letter from a parent or guardian giving permission to visit Canada, in addition to proof of identity. Such a letter should state the traveler's name and the duration of the trip. Canadian officials are very cautious when it comes to children traveling across the border.

CUSTOMS

Certain restrictions apply to goods that you bring into Canada. Smokers can bring in a maximum of 200 cigarettes, 50 cigars, or 14 ounces of tobacco. The limit on alcoholic beverages and wine is a one-liter bottle; for beer it is 24 regular-size cans or bottles.

There are very strict regulations concerning the importation of plants, flowers, and other vegetation. It is not advisable to bring anything of this sort into Canada. Likewise check with customs before bringing firearms into Canada.

Obtain details on restrictions or regulations from: Revenue Canada, Customs and Excise, Ottawa, ON K1A 0L5.

VACCINATIONS

No vaccinations are required before entering Canada from the United States.

PETS

Americans may bring their dogs and cats with them on a visit to Canada as long as they have a health certificate (issued by a veterinarian) and a valid vaccination certificate against rabies. Such a vaccination has to have been administered at least 30 days before departure and should not be more than a year old.

Restrictions on animals vary from province to province. In Quebec, for example, dogs are not allowed in national or provincial parks at all, even on leashes. However, they are allowed in parks on leashes in Ontario. Pets are not allowed in restaurants with the exception of guide dogs. Some hotel chains permit pets—often for an extra charge. It is advisable to check when making your reservation.

HOW TO GET TO CANADA

AIR

Since Canada is such a huge country (the second largest in the world), air travel is generally the fastest and most practical means of transportation. For some northern communities, it is the only means of visiting.

The major international airports in Canada are:
Dorval International Airport, Tel 514/633-3105, Montreal, Que.
Lester B. Pearson International Airport, Tel 416/247-7678, Toronto, Ont.
Vancouver International Airport, Tel 604/276-6101, Vancouver, B.C.

In addition, major cities like Halifax, N.S., Edmonton, Alta., Calgary, Alta., and Winnipeg, Man. have important airports, which are connected to each other and to neighboring U.S. cities.

There are two national air carriers in Canada: Air Canada, Tel 800/361-3000 (Canada), Tel 800/776-3000 (United States); and Canadian Airlines International, Tel 800/426-7000.

Regional air carriers in Canada are nearly all aligned with one of the two major carriers, sometimes as subsidiaries, sometimes as partners. For example, for details of flights with Air Atlantic and Canadian Regional, contact Canadian Airlines International; for Air Nova, Air BC, and Air Ontario, contact Air Canada.

Air Canada and Canadian Airlines both have networks of non-stop routes serving more than 125 destinations, many of them in the U.S.

In northern Canada, the major carriers are Canadian North, Tel 867/873-5533 and NWT Air, Tel 867/920-2500, serving the Yukon, Northwest Territories, and Nunavut. In addition, there are many charter companies providing air service to remote areas; the provincial tourist offices are the best places to obtain further information about these.

In addition, many U.S. airlines offer regular flights between the United States and Canada. American Airlines, Continental Airlines, Delta Air Lines, Northwest Airlines, United Airlines, and US Airways all serve Canada's major airports. Connecting flights within Canada serve some 75 additional places.

It is worthwhile shopping around to get the best price for international connections on the busy U.S. to Canada routes; there are many special offers that require you to fly at certain times or on particular dates. In addition, domestic flights within Canada generally cost less than flying from U.S. cities. Thus, in certain cases, you may find it cheaper to drive across the border and then pick up a flight.

DRIVING YOUR OWN CAR

Driving across the border into Canada from the United States is no problem. There are more than a dozen major entry points, and numerous others are open limited hours.

Driving in Canada is always done on the right with passing on the left. Speed limits are posted in kilometers (see conversion chart p. 343).

Speed limits vary slightly between provinces, but the uniform top speed on expressways is 100 kph (about 90 mph); 90 kph (55 mph) on the Trans-Canada and Yellowhead highways; 80 kph (50 mph) on most rural roads; and between 40 and 60 kph (25 to 35 mph) in urban areas. Speed limits are rigidly enforced, with spot-fines for violations.

Fuel or gas is sold by the liter in three grades of octane levels, as well as in unleaded.

Drivers and passengers are required by law to wear seat belts in every province. Drivers must also carry proper vehicle registration and proof of insurance. Right-hand turns are allowed on red lights, except in the province of Quebec.

RENTING A CAR

Renting a car in Canada can be quick and easy. You must be over 21 years of age and produce identification and a valid driver's license (a U.S. license is acceptable), which has been held for at least one year.

Car rental companies will expect you to have a credit card; if you don't have one, you may have to leave a hefty deposit. Look out for additional charges, notably GST, provincial taxes, and "drop-off" charges, often equivalent to a week's rental, when you rent the car in one town and leave it in another.

For an additional charge, collision or "Loss Damage Waiver," an insurance against accident or damage, is worth considering. Check with your credit card company or insurance agent about automatic coverage. Also check to see whether the rental includes unlimited mileage, or whether you incur an additional charge after reaching a set mileage.

Car rental rates vary widely across the country, ranging from a starting rate of about $14 a day in Montreal to $23 a day in Vancouver.

All the major car rental companies are represented in Canada, along with Tilden, a major Canadian company. They can be reached at the following numbers:
Tilden: Tel 800/361-5334
Dollar: Tel 800/421-6868
Hertz: Tel 800/620-9620 (Toronto), Tel 800/263-0600 (elsewhere)
Budget: Tel 800/268-8970 (Quebec), Tel 800/268-8900 (elsewhere)
Thrifty: Tel 800/367-2277
Avis: Tel 800/387-7600 (Ontario

and Quebec), Tel 800/268-2310 (elsewhere)

In case of a car breakdown, contact the Canadian Automobile Association (Tel 613/247-0117) or its local affiliate. AAA members are entitled to full service with the CAA.

RAIL

Train travel is a pleasant alternative to driving and is usually cheaper than flying. It is often slower and more expensive than the equivalent journey by bus, but it can be a pleasant and scenic way to view the country, especially when using the "Silver and Blue" first-class service on trans-Canada trains, which offers exclusive use of the famous domed cars that allow an uninterrupted rooftop view of the countryside.

AMTRAK

From the U.S., Amtrak, Tel 800/872-7245 has regular train service to both Montreal and Toronto from New York, also to Toronto from Chicago and to Vancouver from Seattle.

VIA RAIL

Once in Canada, most passenger services are operated by VIA Rail Canada, Tel 888-VIA-RAIL (Canada), Tel 800/561-3949 (U.S.), which offers a good standard of comfort and service. Reserve seats whenever possible, certainly for the trans-Canada service (Toronto–Vancouver).

VIA regional offices in Canada:
Newfoundland: Tel 800/561-3926
Prince Edward Island, Nova Scotia, and New Brunswick: Tel 800-561-3952
Quebec: Tel 800/361-5390
Ontario: Tel 800/361-1235 (area codes 519, 613, 705, 905), Tel 800/561-8630 (area code 807), or Tel 416/366-8411 (Toronto)
Manitoba, Saskatchewan, Alberta, British Columbia, Yukon, Northwest Territories, and Nunavut: Tel 800/561-8630

FERRIES

Ferries form part of the highway system in much of Canada, providing vital links in the country's road network. They also offer connections to islands off both the East and West Coasts.

WEST COAST

Several ferry companies operate between Washington State and Victoria, the capital of British Columbia. Black Ball Transport, Tel 250/386-2202 runs between Port Angeles, Wash. and Victoria; Washington State Ferries, Tel 250/656-1831 between Anacortes, Wash. and Victoria; Victoria Clipper between Seattle, Wash. and Victoria, Tel 250/382-8100.

Once in Canada, the main West Coast company, with some 42 ports of call, is the British Columbia Ferry Corporation, 1112 Fort Street, Victoria, BC V8V 4V2, Tel 604/656-0757. Its key services operate between the British Columbia mainland and Vancouver Island (Horseshoe Bay, North Vancouver, to Nanaimo and Tsawwassen to Swartz Bay); between Vancouver Island and Prince Rupert (the Inside Passage); and between Prince Rupert and the Queen Charlotte Islands.

EAST COAST

Two services link Nova Scotia and the state of Maine. Prince of Fundy Cruises, P.O. Box 609, Yarmouth, NS, B5A 4B6 or P.O. Box 4216, Station A, Portland, ME, 04101, Tel 800/341-7540 operates between Portland, Me. and Yarmouth, N.S.

Bay Ferries, 94 Water St., P.O. Box 634, Charlottetown, PE, C1A 7L3, Tel 888-249-7245 operates between Bar Harbor, Me., and Yarmouth, N.S., and between Digby, N.S., and Saint John, N.B.

Once in Canada, there are ferries to the province of Newfoundland from Nova Scotia operated by Marine Atlantic, Box 250, North Sydney, NS, B2A

3M3, Tel 902/794-5700 or 800/341-7981. These ferries run between North Sydney, N.S., and either Port-aux-Basques or Argentia, Nfld.

Despite the construction of the Confederation Bridge, the province of Prince Edward Island is still accessible by ferry. Northumberland Ferries, 94 Water St., P.O. Box 634, Charlottetown, PE, C1A 7L3, Tel 902/566-3838, operates the only remaining ferry service between Caribou, N.S., and Wood Islands, P.E.I.

BUSES

Travel by long-distance bus is relatively cheap and provides access to most of Canada. There is no national transportation company. Instead many private coach companies share the road. The major companies are Greyhound, Tel 800/661-8747, which covers most of Western Canada, Yukon, and Ontario; Voyageur, Tel 514/842-2281, which serves Quebec and the Maritimes; and Brewster Transportation, Tel 800/661-1152, which serves the Rocky Mountain area.

If you are planning to cover a lot of ground, you might want to consider purchasing a long distance bus pass. Greyhound offers a 15-day Canada Pass, which covers all of the west, north, and Ontario (for about $385). Voyageur offers a 14-day pass for travel within Quebec and Ontario for about $250. Certain restrictions apply, so it is best to contact them before doing detailed planning for a trip. There are also considerable savings if tickets are purchased in advance.

PRACTICAL ADVICE

BEER, WINE, & ALCOHOL

Across Canada, provincial governments are responsible for regulating alcohol. It is sold in special liquor stores across the country. Beer and wine can be purchased in grocery stores in Quebec and in special government beer and wine stores in other provinces.

The legal drinking age in Canada is 19, except in Quebec where it is 18. Certain northern communities are "dry" towns, where the sale or consumption of alcohol is strictly forbidden.

COMMUNICATIONS

POST OFFICES

It costs a minimum of 46 cents to mail a regular letter within the country, about 55 cents to send it across the border to the U.S., and 95 cents to send it abroad. Priority Post is a fast and rather expensive service which promises "next day delivery" within Canada. It is available 24 hours a day, seven days a week. Otherwise, there is one mail delivery per day, Monday through Friday.

Post offices are generally open Monday to Friday 8:30 a.m. to 5:30 p.m. Some larger branches in the major cities are open Saturday, Sunday, and holidays. Stamps can also be purchased at designated retailers often found in hotel lobbies, airports, and news stands. Certain small stores are licensed to sell stamps, and post offices are often found inside larger stores and railway stations, so be on the lookout for the Canada Post sign.

TELEPHONES

Public phones work the same as they do in the U.S. and are widely available and relatively cheap. Pay phones accept American coins and U.S. telephone credit cards. There are no problems dialing direct to the United States. If you have any problems placing an international call (outside Canada and the U.S.), dial "0" and ask for the international operator.

For directory assistance, dial 1, the area code, and 555-1212.

Provincial telephone area codes: Alberta—Calgary area 403; Edmonton and northern Alberta 780
British Columbia—Vancouver 604; rest of BC 250
Manitoba 204
New Brunswick 506
Newfoundland and Labrador 709
Northwest Territories 867
Nova Scotia 902
Nunavut 867
Ontario—Toronto 416; region 905; Central and North 705; SW peninsula 519; Ottawa and St. Régis, Que. region 613; northwest Ont. 807
Prince Edward Island 902
Quebec—Montreal 514; metro region 450, Central and North 819; East 418
Saskatchewan 306
Yukon 867

CONVERSIONS

All across Canada today, the metric system is used for measuring distances, weights, and temperatures.

On the roads, speed limits are given in kilometers per hour; gasoline is sold in liters; and things are weighed in kilograms.
1 kilometer = 1.62 miles
100 kilometers = a little more than 60 miles
1 meter = 3.28 feet or 39.37 inches
1000 meters = a little more than 3000 feet
1 liter = 0.264 U.S. gallons
10 liters = a little more than 2.5 gallons
1 kilogram = 2.20 pounds
2 kilograms = nearly 4.5 pounds

Weather forecasts and reports in Canada are given in Celsius. The freezing point is 0° Celsius so for an approximate conversion from Fahrenheit to Celsius, subtract 30 and divide by 2. To convert Celsius to Fahrenheit multiply by 2 and add 30.

$0°C = 32°F$; $100°C = 212°F$
$10°C = 50°F$
$20°C = 68°F$
$30°C = 86°F$

ETIQUETTE & CUSTOMS

Canadian culture and manners are similar in many ways to those of Americans and British, but you should be sensitive to the more traditional ways of life encountered in many rural areas. It is also important to respect the customs of the First Nations and Inuit—native Canadians—who are increasingly asserting their rights and distinct cultural identities. It is an insult, for example, to address an Inuit as an Eskimo, or First Nations as Indians.

In the French-speaking parts of Canada, notably Quebec, you should be prepared to acknowledge French as the first, and sometimes only, language. French is the official language of the province, and all road signs and other indications are given in this language. Outside the main tourist areas (Montreal, Quebec City) and major resort hotels, you may have difficulty being understood in English. Visitors are advised to learn a few phrases to help them in these situations. Most restaurants, certainly in the tourist areas, will have English versions of the menus, but you may have to ask for them.

FESTIVALS

A list of the major festivals in each region is included in the Entertainments section (see pp. 380-89).

HUNTING AND FISHING

Hunting is regulated by federal, provincial, and territorial laws. You must obtain a permit from the province or territory in which you plan to hunt. Hunting of certain species is severely restricted, and, in some cases, only a few permits are given every year. For information about this, contact the appropriate provincial or territorial tourist office, which can tell you how to obtain your permit.

Fishing is regulated by law, and again you must obtain a non-resident permit for the province or territory in which you want to fish. In most cases, permits are on sale at sports stores and local outfitters. The tourist office can help you choose the most convenient place to obtain your permit.

MEDIA

NEWSPAPERS

Canada has two national newspapers, *The Globe & Mail* and *The National Post*. They are both on sale at newsstands and newspaper and magazine stores across the country. In addition, the Sun chain of newspapers reaches most of the country.

All large cities boast their own newspapers, often with a circulation as large as that of the nationals. Examples include the *Toronto Star*, the *Calgary Herald*, the *Edmonton Journal*, the *Winnipeg Free Press*, the *Ottawa Citizen*, the *Vancouver Sun*, *The Gazette* in Montreal, and the *Chronicle Record Mail Star* in Halifax. In Montreal, the major French newspapers are *Le Devoir*, *Le Journal de Montréal*, and *La Presse*.

Again in the major cities, English and French-language newspapers are often supplemented by a wide variety of ethnic publications.

The major U.S. newspapers (*New York Times*, *Wall Street Journal*, etc.) are available in the large cities as well as the publications of neighboring cities (*Detroit Free Press–Detroit News* in Windsor, etc.).

TELEVISION & RADIO

Today, television reaches everyone in Canada even in the extreme north where service is assured by satellite. There are a wide variety of channels. In the major cities, attachment to a cable service offers an average of 12 to 15 different alternatives.

The Canadian Broadcasting Corporation, a publicly funded television and radio network, has channels throughout the country broadcasting in both English and French. Their radio stations broadcast hourly news updates, general information programs, and commercial-free music.

Some of the other national television channels are Global, CTV, Baton Broadcasting Systems, and MuchMusic. In recent years, homegrown specialty cable channels such as the Women's Television Network, The Life Channel, and History Television have gained popularity.

In addition, the four major U.S. television networks are widely available throughout Canada, supplemented by local American stations broadcasting near the border.

MONEY MATTERS

U.S. currency is widely accepted in Canada. At the present time (early 1999) the Canadian dollar is worth about $0.66 U.S. Exchange rates are notoriously variable, so it is wise to check the current rate just before leaving on a trip.

Canadian currency has almost the same denominations as American money, with the exception of the paper $1 and $2 notes which no longer exist in Canada. Single Canadian dollars come in the form of a gold-colored coin bearing a picture of a loon (thus their nickname "loonie"), two-dollar coins have gold centers and silver rims.

Outside the major cities and resort areas, there are relatively few places devoted just to currency exchange in Canada. Exchange facilities can usually be found in large hotels, airports, and railway stations, but rates are often poor and commission fees high. In addition, most banks offer exchange facilities, and many charge a fee.

A good way to carry money is in the form of travelers' checks, which, if made out in Canadian dollars, can be used as cash in most shops, restaurants, and service stations across the country (change is given in cash). American Express and Visa checks are the most common. There is no limit to the amount of Canadian or foreign currency that can be exchanged or brought into or taken out of the country.

Automated Teller Machines
The simplest method of obtaining money is by using an automated banking machine. This avoids hassles with currency exchange rates and service charges, since your own bank does the exchange. Nonetheless, there is usually a charge for their use.

To be able to use your bank or credit card at an ATM in Canada, it needs to have been programmed with a personal identification number, or PIN. This enables you to withdraw money directly from your account or get cash advances on a credit-card account. Before leaving home, it is wise to check for restrictions such as how much money you can withdraw at any one time or on any one day.

NATIONAL HOLIDAYS

There are seven national holidays celebrated in every province and territory of Canada:

New Year's Day (January 1)
Good Friday
Victoria Day (Third Monday in May)
Canada Day (July 1)
Labour Day (First Monday in September)
Thanksgiving Day (Second Monday in October) Please note this is not at the same as American Thanksgiving.
Christmas Day (December 25)

Some provinces also celebrate the following days as holidays:
Easter Monday

Remembrance Day (November 11)
Boxing Day (December 26)
January 2

In addition, there are also holidays specific to certain provinces or cities:
John the Baptist Day (June 24): Quebec
Natal Day (First Monday in August): Halifax and Dartmouth, Nova Scotia
Civic Holiday (First Monday in August): Ontario

On these holidays, you are likely to find banks and government offices closed, but increasingly stores, tourist sights, and other services are staying open.

OPENING TIMES

In general across Canada, stores are open between 9 a.m. and 6 p.m. Monday through Saturday, with later hours on Thursday and Friday evenings. If open on Sunday, store hours are usually noon to 5 p.m.

Shopping malls tend to have longer hours than downtown shops, and often close between 7:30 and 9 p.m. In some suburban areas of big cities, supermarkets stay open until 10 or 11 p.m. nightly. In addition, most towns have all-night pharmacies and stores.

Bank hours are generally Monday to Friday 10 a.m.–3 p.m. although this can vary by branch (some open 9 a.m.–4 p.m.). There are often extended hours (10 a.m.–5 or 6 p.m.) on certain days, usually Thursday or Friday.

PLACES OF WORSHIP

Major hotels in all Canadian cities list the places of worship close to them. If this is not the case, the local Tourist Office can always supply a list. There will normally be a Roman Catholic Church, an Episcopal Church (Anglican), a United Church (Methodists and Presbyterians), and sometimes a Baptist Church.

In addition, the major cities have synagogues and most of them mosques, and Buddhist and Hindi temples, too.

SMOKING

Many Canadians still smoke, but smoking in public places is increasingly frowned upon or forbidden. It is prohibited in most shopping centers, in government offices, banks, and hospitals, and on buses and subway systems.

Some provinces, notably British Columbia, are experimenting with a no-smoking policy for all restaurants and bars. Elsewhere, it is generally the law that public places (including restaurants, bars, and cafés) have both smoking and non-smoking sections.

Cigarettes are for sale in grocery stores, bars, newspaper and magazine stores, and most corner stores.

TAXES

A 7 percent Goods and Services Tax (GST) is added to everything you buy in Canada except food from the grocery store. It is applicable on all hotel and restaurant bills, all transportation tickets, and on admissions to tourist sights. In addition, most provinces add their own sales tax. So you may find yourself paying a surcharge of anything between 7 percent (GST) in Alberta, where there is no sales tax, to 19 percent in Newfoundland where the sales tax is 12 percent plus 7 percent GST.

These are not hidden taxes. They are added to the bill and explained as such on the sales slip. In some cases, the GST is refundable to visitors taking goods out of the country. Certain conditions apply (type of product, minimum purchase, etc.) so it is best to obtain the sales slip at the time of making a purchase. All major hotels and tourist offices have a supply of refund forms. The provincial

sales tax (PST) is also refundable in Quebec and Manitoba.

For more information on refunds, contact Revenue Canada, Visitor Rebate Program, Ottawa, ON K1A 1J5, Tel 800/668-4748 (Canada) or 902/432-5608.

TIME ZONES

Canada is divided into six time zones. The list below shows each zone with its time relationship to Eastern Standard Time (EST).

Atlantic Standard Time: The Maritime Provinces, Labrador, and the most easterly part of Quebec (EST +1 hour)
Newfoundland Standard Time: The Island of Newfoundland has its own time zone half an hour ahead of the Maritimes. (EST +1.5 hours)
Eastern Standard Time: Most of Quebec and Ontario east of Thunder Bay (EST)
Central Standard Time: The extreme northwest of Ontario, Manitoba and Nunavut (EST −1 hour)
Mountain Standard Time: Saskatchewan, Alberta, the southeast corner of British Columbia and the Northwest Territories (EST −2 hours)
Pacific Standard Time: The rest of British Columbia and the Yukon (EST −3 hours)

Daylight Saving Time: All provinces except Saskatchewan put clocks forward from the first Sunday of April to the last Sunday of October.

TIPPING

As in the rest of North America, tipping is a fact of life in Canada, and many people in service jobs depend on it to make ends meet. That being said, tipping is an acknowledgment of good service. If the service is not satisfactory, don't tip.

Service charges are not automatically added to restaurant bills except in a few rare cases. It is customary to leave a tip of about 15 percent (of the bill before taxes) for waiters and waitresses.

As a general rule, hotel porters should be given about $1 a bag, room service staff 10 percent of the bill before taxes, and cab drivers 15 percent of the total. Tour guides should be given a little something also; in general, if you are satisfied with the service, $1 per person is adequate.

TRAVELERS WITH DISABILITIES

Canada has become increasingly sensitive to the needs of visitors with disabilities. Today, all public buildings must have wheelchair accessibility and provide special toilets. Curbs in most cities and large towns are dropped at corners to meet the needs of wheelchair users. Difficulties may still be encountered on public transportation, although buses are increasingly being adapted to accommodate wheelchairs. VIA Rail trains can accommodate wheelchairs up to 250 pounds in weight, and measuring no more than 2.6 feet by 6 feet. However, 48 hours notice is required on all routes.

Some of the main hotel chains have wheelchair access and some even provide special suites for guests with disabilities. However, visitors may find barriers in older accommodations and restaurants. For new properties, there are now strict compliance codes in effect. Details of suitable hotels can usually be obtained from Provincial tourist offices.

The following agencies in Canada and the U.S. provide information on tour operators, special guides, and other aspects of traveling abroad for visitors with disabilities:

Canadian Paraplegic Association National Office, 520 Sutherland Dr., Toronto, ON M4G 3U9, Tel 416/422-5644—provides information about touring in Canada.

Canadian Rehabilitation Council for the Disabled, 1 Yonge St., Ste. 2110, Toronto, ON M5E 1E5, Tel 416/250-7490

Information Center for Individuals with Disabilities, Fort Point Place, 27–43 Wormwood Street, Boston, MA 02210, Tel 617/727-5540

Society for the Advancement of Travel for the Handicapped, 347 5th Ave., Ste. 610, New York, NY 10016, Tel 212/447-7284, Fax 212/725-8253

Travelin' Talk, P.O. Box 3534, Clarksville, TN 37043, Tel 615/552-6670, Fax 616/552-1182

VISITOR INFORMATION

All the Canadian provinces and territories have government operated tourism bureaus, which welcome American calls. They also all have internet web sites. However, the amount of information on the latter varies tremendously across the country. Some provinces have full lists of accommodations and sights and are user-friendly; others offer just a few pages of photographs and general text.

Alberta: Travel Alberta, 10155–102nd St., Edmonton, AB T5J 4L6, Tel 800/661-8888; www.discoveralberta.com
British Columbia: Tourism British Columbia, Parliament Buildings, Victoria, BC V8V 1XA, Tel 800/663-6000; www.tbc.gov.bc.ca/tourism/touri smhome.html
Manitoba: Travel Manitoba, 7th Floor, 155 Carlton St., Winnipeg, MB R3C 3H8, Tel 800/665-0040; www.travelmanitoba.com/
New Brunswick: Tourism New Brunswick, P.O. Box 12345, Fredericton, NB E3B 5C3, Tel 800/561-0123; www.gov.nb.ca/tourism
Newfoundland and Labrador: Newfoundland and Labrador Department of Tourism, Recreation and

Culture, P.O. Box 8730, St. John's, NF A1B 4K2, Tel 800/563-6353; http://public.gov.nf.ca/tourism
Northwest Territories: Northwest Territories Tourism, P.O. Box 1320, Yellowknife, NWT X1A 2L9, Tel 800/661-0788; www.nwttravel.nt.ca
Nova Scotia: Nova Scotia Tourism, 1800 Argyle St., Ste. 515, Halifax, NS B3J 3N8, Tel 800/565-0000; explore.gov.ns.ca/virtualns
Nunavut: Nunavut Tourism, P.O. Box 1450, Iqaluit, NT X0A 0H0, Tel 800/491-7910; www.nunatour.nt.ca
Ontario: Travelinx Ontario, Queen's Park, Toronto, ON M7A 2R9, Tel 800/668-2746; www.travelinx.com
Prince Edward Island: Prince Edward Island Department of Tourism, Parks and Recreation, P.O. Box 940, Charlottetown, PE C1A 7M5, Tel 800/463-4734; www.peiplay.com
Quebec: Tourisme Quebec, P.O. Box 979, Montreal, QC H3C 2W3, Tel 800/363-7777; www.gouv.qc.ca/tourisme/indexa .htm
Saskatchewan: Tourism Saskatchewan, 500-1900 Albert St., Regina, SK S4P 4I9, Tel 877/237-2273; www.sasktourism.com
Yukon: Tourism Yukon, P.O. Box 2703, Whitehorse, YT Y1A 2C6, Tel 867/667-5340; www.touryukon.com

EMERGENCIES

CONSULATES

U.S. Embassy Ottawa 490 Sussex Dr., Ottawa, ON, Tel 613/238-5335, Fax 613/238-5720; www.usembassycanada.gov

In addition to its embassy in Ottawa, the United States maintains consulates in the following cities:
Montreal, 1155 rue St.-Alexandre, Tel 514/398-9695; Quebec City, 2 Pl. Terrasse

Dufferin, Tel. 418/692-2095; Toronto, 360 University Ave., Tel 416/595-1700; Vancouver, 1075 W. Pender St., Tel 604/685-4311.

CRIME & POLICE

For the most part, Canada is a remarkably crime-free country. The streets of the larger cities are considerably safer than those of most American cities. However, reasonable caution should be exercised. It is wise to avoid parks, back streets, and unlit areas after dark. In all large cities, where there is always a danger of pickpockets, visitors need to be aware in crowded areas and on the subway. Avoid leaving luggage or valuables in cars, do not carry large quantities of cash or wear expensive-looking jewelry, and keep passports and credit cards out of sight. If you do have anything stolen, report it immediately to the police and/or your hotel.

For fast access to police, fire department, and ambulance services, call 911 in most parts of Canada. On Vancouver Island and Prince Edward Island, and in Nova Scotia, the Yukon, and the Northwest Territories, dial 0 for the operator. This is the best way to report an emergency situation and saves you hunting for a police station or hospital.

The Royal Canadian Mounted Police are Canada's federal police force. The "Mounties" also act as the regular police in all provinces except Ontario and Quebec, which have their own provincial forces. On duty, RCMP officers look just like any other police officers and drive cars. The red jackets, Stetsons, and horses are only used on ceremonial occasions.

HEALTH & HEALTH INSURANCE

The health service in Canada is government-supported and free for Canadian citizens. It is generally of a very high standard, but foreigners requiring treatment on vacation will not get it for free, so it is advisable to take out full travel insurance before a visit. If you become ill on vacation and are hospitalized, you will be treated and charged later; in some provinces, there is a surcharge of as much as 30 percent for the treatment of non-residents.

Traveler health insurance should be as complete as possible. Make sure it covers all types of medical costs—hospitalization, nursing services, doctors' fees, etc. A medical transportation clause is also important in case sufficient care is not available on site and you need to return home.

If you require medical help in Canada, the best thing to do is to consult your hotel. Most hotels keep a list of doctors and medical centers, which can save considerable time. Otherwise, consult the Yellow Pages of the telephone book. You should also keep any receipts or paperwork for future insurance claims.

Another wise precaution to take in case of emergency is to make a note of the generic name of any prescription medications you take before you leave home. They may be sold by a different trade name in Canada.

Canada's main health hazards are associated with the outdoors. *Giardi lamblia* (beaver fever) is a parasite which thrives in warm water so any small stream or shallow lake can be a breeding ground in summer. Check tap water at campsites and boil water when camping in the backcountry to guard against it. Medical help should be sought if the fever persists.

Lyme's disease is also increasingly common in the woods of the south. It is caused by bites from woodland ticks. Signs of infection include a rash and flu-like symptoms. Tick repellents are available, and you can reduce the risk of bites by wearing thick socks, long pants, and long-sleeved shirts. Again, medical help should be sought if the fever persists.

In the wooded areas of southern Ontario and Quebec, clumps of poison ivy can cause rashes, blisters, and sores. Creams and ointments are widely available to help ease discomfort. Rashes will clear up after about 10 days, so it is not essential to seek medical attention unless the irritation persists.

Less unpleasant, but equally irritating, are the hordes of blackflies and mosquitoes that are common in the north any time after April, but especially in May and June. All kinds of insect repellents are available for purchase.

HOTELS & RESTAURANTS

Accommodations in Canada are varied, reasonably priced, and normally of a high standard. But there are differences between the types of facilities available, and it will help you to understand these differences when deciding where to stay. Remember that large areas of the country are remote, so the available accomodations may fill quickly during the busy summer months. Therefore it is always best to check the availability of rooms before setting off.

Eating out can be a great pleasure, with most major cities offering a wide variety and range of eating possibilities. Menu prices are usually reasonable, and there are often appetizing regional specialities available.

PRICES

HOTELS
An indication of the cost of a double room without breakfast is given by $ signs

$$$$$	Over $280
$$$$	$200– $280
$$$	$120–$200
$$	$80–$120
$	Under $80

RESTAURANTS
An indication of the cost of a three-course dinner without drinks is given by $ signs

$$$$$	Over $80
$$$$	$50–$80
$$$	$35–$50
$$	$20–$35
$	Under $20

Accommodations

There are three general types of accommodations: First there are the low cost, basic rooms usually found in less desirable locations, frequently sought by students. Next, mid-range hotels and motels are widely available, easy to find and to contact, and offer a consistent format and quality. Finally, there are the large, top-of-the-range city and resort hotels offering high international standards of quality and service. Listed below are some of the up-market and reliable mid-priced hotel chains with toll-free telephone numbers:

Best Western International, Tel 800/528-1234; 0181/541-0033 (U.K.)

Canadian Pacific Hotels and Resorts, Tel 800/441-1414; 0800/898852 (U.K.)

Choice Hotels International, Tel 800/424-6423; 0800/444-4444 (U.K.)

Days Inn, Tel 800/329-7466; 01483/440470 (U.K.)

Delta Hotels, Tel 800/877-1133; 0171/937-8033 (U.K.)

Four Seasons Hotels, Tel 800/332-3442; 0800/526648 (U.K.)

Hilton Hotels, Tel 800/445-8667

Holiday Inns, Tel 800/465-4329; 0800/897121 (U.K.)

Hyatt Hotels, Tel 800/223-1234; 0717/580-8197 (U.K.)

Marriott Hotels and Resorts, Tel 800/228-9290; 0800/282811 (U.K.)

Novotel Hotels, Tel 800/668-6835

Radisson Hotels, Tel 800/333-3333; 0800/891999 (U.K.)

Ramada, Tel 800/228-2828; 0181/688-1418 (U.K.)

Relais & Châteaux Tel 800/743-8033

Sheraton, Tel 800/325-3535; 0800-353535 (U.K.)

Travelodge, Tel 800/225-3050; 0345-404040 (U.K.)

Westin Hotels, Tel 800/228-3000; 0171/408-0636 (U.K.)

Bed and breakfast lodgings are numerous and available in most Canadian towns, cities, and rural backwaters. When reserving, remember to inquire about details that will affect your stay, such as whether smoking is permitted, whether credit cards are accepted, and the rates. For help in booking these, you can contact the relevant tourist board, which may be able to provide you with a listing of B&Bs or refer you elsewhere for information on availability and reservations. Also, there are associations you can contact directly, the telephone numbers for these associations are listed under the regional headings. Please note that **unless otherwise stated:**
1. All hotel rooms have dining rooms and private bathrooms.
2. Hotels are open 365 days a year.

Restaurants

Except for fast-food establishments, reservations are recommended for lunch during the week and for dinner on Friday and Saturday evenings. Most restaurants open from noon–11 p.m., longer on weekends; dinner-type establishments in small towns and villages may close earlier (8–9:30 p.m.). The following listings contain a selection of good quality restaurants throughout the country. Wherever possible we have chosen establishments that are both individual and typical, perhaps with notable local associations.

Tipping

Tipping is widely prevalent in Canada. Service charges are rarely added to the check, and even in the most humble diners and restaurants—where waitresses rely heavily on tips—it is usual to leave around 15 percent of the total bill. The tip should reflect the standard of service, so there is no need to tip at all if the service is substandard. In bars drinks are often brought to the table and here, as well, bar staff should always be tipped.

Credit cards

It is virtually essential to have at least one credit card when traveling in Canada. Giving a card number is usually the only way to reserve hotels rooms. The most commonly accepted cards are Visa, Mastercard, Diners Club, and American Express.

MARITIMES

Maritime hospitality eschews formality in favor of a warm and friendly atmosphere. The local seafood and fish—lobster, mussels, salmon, scallops, oysters—is outstanding. Be careful not to mistake St. John's, Nfld. for Saint John, N.B.

B&B Association for P.E.I., c/o Bed and Breakfast Country Inn, P. O. Box 2551, Charlottetown, PE CIA 8C2

FREDERICTON, N.B.

🏨 SHERATON FREDERICTON
$$$
225 WOODSTOCK RD.
TEL 506/457-7000 or 800/325-3535, FAX 506/457-4000
Award-winning property bordering the majestic Saint John River and featuring elegant French country decor, just five minutes from the city core.
🛏 223 🅿 🔄 🔅 ⚊
🍽 🆑 All major cards

🏨 CARRIAGE HOUSE INN
$
230 UNIVERSITY AVE.
TEL 506/452-9924,
FAX 506/458-0799
A Victorian mansion refitted in 1987 and furnished with antiques. Delicious made-from-scratch breakfasts served in the glassed-in solarium.
🛏 10 🅿 🔅 🆑 All major cards

🍽 LUNA PIZZA
$
168 DUNDONALD ST.
TEL 506/455-4020
Enormous portions of Caesar salad, pizza, pasta, steak, and seafood. Outdoor terrace for fine-weather dining.
🍴 110 🅿 🔅 🆑 All major cards

MONCTON, N.B.

🏨 BEST WESTERN CRYSTAL PALACE
$$
499 PAUL ST.
TEL 506/858-8584,
FAX 506/858-5486
Downtown property with regular guest rooms and a dozen elaborate theme rooms; the Victorian fantasy is the most popular.
🛏 115 🅿 🔄 🔅 ⚊ 🆑 AE, MC, V

🏨 HOTEL BEAUSÉJOUR
$$
750 MAIN ST., MONCTON
TEL 506/854-4344 or 800/441-1414, FAX 506/858-0957
Downtown, contemporary property with country touches and river views. Award-winning Windjammer Restaurant serves contemporary French cooking.
🛏 310 🅿 🔄 🔅 ⚊ 🍽 🆑 All major cards

🍽 CHEZ FRANÇOISE
$$
93 MAIN ST., SHEDIAC
TEL 506/532-4233
Twenty minutes northeast of Moncton in Shediac, this converted Victorian mansion serves continental seafood preparations rich in butterfat. Fixed-price menu available. Fifteen guest rooms available.
🍴 60 🅿 🕐 Closed L, & Jan.–May 🆑 All major cards

🍽 CY'S SEAFOOD RESTAURANT
$$
170 MAIN ST.
TEL 506/857-0032
Seafood and steaks in a cozy room overlooking the Tidal Bore. Live lobster year round, plus homemade baked goods, including the occasional sugar pie.
🍴 200 🅿 🕐 Closed L 🔅 🆑 All major cards

ST. ANDREWS, N.B.

🏨 ALGONQUIN RESORT HOTEL
$$$$
184 ADOLPHUS ST.
TEL 506/529-8823 or 800/268-9411 (CANADA), 800/828-7447 (U.S.), FAX 506/529-7162
Canadian Pacific's "castle-by-the-sea," this famous hotel in neo-Tudor style was built in 1889 and rebuilt after a fire in 1914. Fully renovated with a modern wing, it dominates this charming and tranquil New Brunswick community. Golf course, tennis courts, and whale watching. Full restaurant facilities.
🛏 240 rooms and suites 🅿 🕐 Closed Oct.–May (main hotel) 🔄 ⚊ 🆑 All major cards

🏨 SEASIDE BEACH RESORT
$$
339 WATER ST.
TEL 506/529-3846 or 800/506-8677, FAX 506/529-4479
Charming rustic housekeeping chalets beside Passamaquoddy Bay with waterfront boardwalk and barbecue pits. Magnificent views and sunsets. Freshly caught fish for sale nearby. Note—no swimming.
🛏 24 🅿 🕐 Closed Oct.–April 🆑 MC, V

SAINT JOHN, N.B.

🏨 SAINT JOHN HILTON
$$$
1 MARKET SQ.
TEL 506/693-8484 or 800/561-8282, FAX 506/657-6610
Newly renovated from top-to-bottom in warm, charming decor. Majority of rooms overlook harbor. The Turn of the Tide restaurant specializes in steak.
🛏 197 🅿 🔄 🔅 ⚊ 🍽 🆑 All major cards

🏨 SHADOW LAWN COUNTRY INN
$
3180 ROTHESAY RD.

TEL 506/847-7539 or 800/561-4166, FAX 506/849-9238
Old Victorian home located in a genteel suburb 15 minutes from downtown. Elegant dining room specializes in seafood dishes such as salmon en croûte. ❶ 9 🅿 🅢 2 rooms 🅢 All major cards

🍴 INCREDIBLE EDIBLES
$
42 PRINCESS ST.
TEL 506/633-7554
Home-style dishes such as freshly baked biscuits, pasta salads, and fruit pies are served in cozy rooms or on the outdoor terrace. ❏ 50–80 🕒 Closed Sun. 🅢 All major cards

🍴 MEXICALI ROSA'S
$
88 PRINCE WILLIAM ST.
TEL 506/652-5252
California-Mexican dishes such as chimichangas are served up with flair in an adobe room straight out of New Mexico. Fixed-price menu. ❏ 92 🅿 🅢 All major cards

BRACKLEY BEACH, P.E.I.

🍴 DUNES CAFE
$$
RTE. 15
TEL 902/672-2586
Dine on local produce, seafood, and lamb while overlooking the dunes of Covehead Bay outside Prince Edward Island National Park. ❏ 53 to 75 🅿 🕒 Closed D weekdays June, Sept., & Oct., & Nov.–May 🅢 AE, MC, V

CHARLOTTETOWN, P.E.I.

🏨 THE CHARLOTTETOWN
$$$
75 KENT ST.
TEL 902/894-7371 or 800/565-7633, FAX 902/368-2178

Centrally located and oozing old-fashioned charm. Victorian furnishings include crystal chandeliers and plenty of wood. ❶ 110 🅿 🖨 🅢 🏊 🍸 🅢 All major cards

🏨 DUNDEE ARMS
$$
200 POWNAL ST.
TEL 902/892-2496, FAX 902/368-8532
Two contrasting styles of accommodation under one management; choose from a cozy Victorian inn or 1956 drive-up motel. ❶ 18 🅿 🅢 🅢 AE, MC, V

🏨 PRINCE EDWARD HOTEL
$$
18 QUEEN ST.
TEL 902/566-2222 or 800/441-1414, FAX 902/566-1745
A modern property right on the waterfront, with a spectacular lobby complete with towering waterfall. The majority of rooms have harbor views. ❶ 211 🅿 🖨 🅢 🏊 🍸 🅢 All major cards

🍴 OFF BROADWAY RESTAURANT
$$
125 SYDNEY ST.
TEL 902/566-4620
Yuppie favorite offering private booths and well-priced continental cooking featuring Black Angus steak, seafood, crêpes, and excellent homemade desserts. ❏ 50 🅿 🅢 🅢 All major cards

🍴 THE SELKIRK
$$
PRINCE EDWARD HOTEL
18 QUEEN ST.
TEL 902/984-1208
Sophisticated menu highlights regional produce and seafood. Live piano music and comfortable wing chairs. Fixed-price dinner. ❏ 126 🅿 🅢 🅢 All major cards

TYNE VALLEY, P.E.I.

🍴 SEASONS IN THYME
$$
RTE. 178
TEL 902/888-3463
The island's famous potatoes are well represented in 27 different preparations, many are available each day along with excellent local game birds, organic produce, and the renowned Malpeque oysters. ❏ 60 🅿 🕒 ☎ Closed D Sun., & Mon. in winter 🅢 1 room 🅢 AE, MC, V

CHESTER, N.S.

🍴 THE GALLEY
$
115 MARINA RD.
TEL 902/275-4700
Live lobster from its own pond and seafood chowder are menu highlights at this nautical-themed eatery on Mahone Bay popular with sailors and yachters. Reservations strongly recommended. ❏ 100 🅿 🕒 Closed Nov.–Mar. 🅢 🅢 All major cards

DIGBY, N.S.

🏨 PINES RESORT HOTEL
$$$$
SHORE RD.
TEL 902/245-2511 or 800/667-4637, FAX 902/245-6133
Elegant hotel and attractive cottages on wooded site overlooking Digby Gut. Walking trails, golf, and tennis courts. Close to ferry to Saint John, N.B. Annapolis Dining Room—see below. ❶ 83 (lodge), 30 cottages (61 rooms) 🅿 🕒 Closed mid-Oct.–mid-May 🅢 All major cards

🍴 THE ANNAPOLIS DINING ROOM
$$$
PINES RESORT HOTEL
SHORE RD.
TEL 902/245-2511 or 800/667-4637, FAX 902/245-6133

KEY 🏨 Hotel 🍴 Restaurant ❶ No. of bedrooms ❏ No. of restaurant places 🚇 Metro 🕒 Closed 🖨 Elevator

Local seafood specialities, such as the prized Digby scallop, prepared in the French style. Fixed-price menu available. Reservations required for dinner and Sunday brunch.
🛏 180 🅿 🕐 Closed mid-Oct.–mid-May 🚫 All major cards

HALIFAX, N.S.

🏨 HOTEL HALIFAX
$$$
1990 BARRINGTON ST.
TEL 902/425-6700 or 800/441-1414, FAX 902/425-6214
Large rooms with stunning harbor views distinguish this well-located property.
🛏 299 🅿 ⬌ 🚫 ♨
📺 🚫 All major cards

🏨 SHERATON HALIFAX
$$$
1919 UPPER WATER ST.
TEL 902/421-1700 or 800/325-3535, FAX 902/422-5805
Waterfront hotel with the city's only casino in the lobby. Historic location, but modern amenities.
🛏 350 🅿 ⬌ 🚫 ♨
📺 🚫 All major cards

🏨 HALIBURTON HOUSE INN
$$
5184 MORRIS ST.
TEL 902/420-0658, FAX 902/423-2324
Three 19th-century townhouses seamlessly renovated. Two blocks from the water.
🛏 25 🅿 🚫 🚫 All major cards

🍴 GEORGIO'S RESTAURANT
$$
PRINCE GEORGE HOTEL
1725 MARKET ST.
TEL 902/492-7822
Contemporary California cuisine in a casually elegant room. Specialties include gourmet pizza, bouillabaisse, and a daily changing crème brûlée. Fixed-price dinner.
🛏 78 🅿 🚫 🚫 All major cards

🍴 MACASKILL'S RESTAURANT
$$
88 ALDERNEY DR.
DARTMOUTH FERRY TERMINAL BUILDING
TEL 902/466-3100
Romantic dining room overlooking Halifax Harbor. Local ingredients go into seafood, chicken, beef, and pasta dishes.
🛏 150 🅿 🕐 Closed L Sat. & Sun. 🚫 🚫 All major cards

🍴 SALTY'S ON THE WATERFRONT
$$
1869 UPPER WATER ST.
TEL 902/423-6818
Floor-to-ceiling windows overlooking Privateer's Wharf compete for attention with skillfully prepared fish, pasta, and steak. The premier dessert—Belgian chocolate mousse over white chocolate praline crust—is justifiably famous.
🛏 120 🅿 🚫 🚫 All major cards

INGONISH, N.S.

🏨 KELTIC LODGE
$$$
MIDDLE HEAD PENINSULA, INGONISH BEACH
TEL 902/285-2880 or 800/565-0444, FAX 902/285-2859
Spectacular location on a peninsula with views of mountains and sea in all directions. On the scenic Cabot Trail and part of Cape Breton Highlands National Park. Hiking trails to view sea birds, famous golf course, whale watching, and ski center in winter.
🛏 32 (lodge), 9 cottages (26 rooms) 🅿 🕐 Closed Oct.–Nov. & March–June ⬌ ♨ 🚫 All major cards

🍴 PURPLE THISTLE ROOM
$$$
KELTIC LODGE
INGONISH BEACH
TEL 902/285-2880 or

800/565-0444
Seafood stars on the menu of this eatery perched on the cliffs at the terminus of the Cabot Trail in Cape Breton Highlands National Park.
🛏 160 🅿 🕐 Closed Nov.–April 🚫 🚫 AE, D, DC

LISCOMB MILLS, N.S.

🏨 LISCOMB LODGE
$$$
LISCOMB MILLS, GUYSBOROUGH COUNTY
TEL 902/779-2307 or 800/665-6343, FAX 902/779-2700
On the Liscomb River near Chedabucto Bay, this modern lodge is a perfect retreat for nature lovers. Marina, canoe and bicycle rentals, tennis.
🛏 65 units (lodge and cottages) 🅿 🕐 Closed mid-Oct.–mid-May ♨ 🚫 All major cards

NEWFOUNDLAND

Fellow Canadians like to tease Newfoundlanders about eating cod's tongues and seal flipper pie, but the commitment to freshly harvested, seasonal food, is no laughing matter. Sadly, cod is no longer widely available.

BAY FORTUNE

🏨 INN AT BAY FORTUNE
$$
RTE. 10
TEL 902/687-3745 or 860/633-4930 (OFF SEASON)
Fresh ingredients prepared in a contemporary style compete only with the views of Fortune Harbor and the Northumberland Straight. Eleven-room inn was once home to Broadway playwright Elmer Harris and later to Canadian actress Colleen Dewhurst. Dinner only. Fixed-price menu available.
🛏 70 🕐 Closed late-Oct.–mid-May 🚫 MC, V

CAPE ONION

⊞ TICKLE INN
$$
R.R. I
TEL 709/452-4321 (JUNE–SEPT.)
or 709/739-5503
Inexpensive dishes served in
the dining room of this
renovated fisherman's house,
just a 25-minute drive from
the L'Anse aux Meadows
National Historic Site.
🔌 🅿 🕒 Closed Oct.–
May 💲 MC, V

CORNER BROOK

🍴 THE CARRIAGE ROOM & THE WINE CELLAR
$$
GLYNMILL INN, RTE. I
TEL 709/634-5181 or 800/563-
4400, FAX 709/634-5106
Newfoundland specialties
such as baked cod and
Partridgeberry pie are served
in one of the hotel's upstairs
dining rooms (The Carriage
House); the downstairs
restaurant (The Wine Cellar)
specializes in steak. Reservations recommended. Fixed-
price menu.
🍴 80 🅿 🕒 Closed Sun.,
& Dec. 25 💲 AE, MC, V

GROS MORNE NATIONAL PARK

⊞ SUGAR HILL INN
$$
115–119 SEXTONS' RD.
NORRIS POINT
TEL/FAX 709/458-2147
An enchanting inn with
cathedral ceilings and modern
conveniences; the dining room,
for guests only, specializes in
health-conscious gourmet
meals. Sea kayaking and guided
wilderness hikes available.
🛏7 🅿 🕒 Closed mid-
Oct.–mid-Jan. 💲 AE,
MC, V

ST. JOHN'S

⊞ DELTA ST. JOHN'S
$$$
120 NEW GOWER ST.
TEL 709/739-6404 or 800/563-
3838, FAX 709/570-1622
Close to the business and
entertainment districts, this
convention hotel has special
amenities in newly-renovated
guest rooms.
🛏276 🅿 🛗 💲 🏊
📺 All major cards

⊞ HOTEL NEWFOUNDLAND
$$$
CAVENDISH SQ.
TEL 709/726-4980 or 800/441-
1414, FAX 709/726-2025
Comfortable, modern rooms
overlooking the harbor. Fine
dining in the award-winning
Cabot Club; Sunday brunch at
the Outport Restaurant is a
local tradition.
🛏301 🅿 🛗 💲 🏊
📺 All major cards

⊞ COMPTON HOUSE BED & BREAKFAST
$
26 WATERFORD BRIDGE RD.
TEL 709/739-5789,
FAX 709/738-1770
Charming property within
walking distance of down-
town; rooms are uniquely
furnished and can include
whirlpool, fireplace, kitchen
facilities, or sunroom.
🛏12 🅿 All major
cards

🍴 THE CELLAR RESTAURANT
$$
BAIRD'S COVE AT WATER ST.
TEL 709/579-8900
Continental fine dining with
Asian and local influences. A
cigar den and a 125-label
wine list are bonuses. Reservations essential.
🍴100 🅿 🕒 Closed L Sat.
& Sun. 💲 All major
cards

PRICES

HOTELS
An indication of the cost of a
double room without
breakfast is given by $ signs

$$$$$	Over $280
$$$$	$200–$280
$$$	$120–$200
$$	$80–$120
$	Under $80

RESTAURANTS
An indication of the cost of a
three-course dinner without
drinks is given by $ signs

$$$$$	Over $80
$$$$	$50–$80
$$$	$35–$50
$$	$20–$35
$	Under $20

🍴 THE HUNGRY FISHERMEN
$$
MURRAY PREMISES,
5 BECK'S COVE
TEL 709/726-5790
Delights of the deep as well
as lamb, chicken, veal, and
steak. Seafood pot in tomato
sauce with filo pastry is a
best-seller, as is the home-
made chocolate-rum
"screech" pie.
🍴75 🅿 🕒 Closed
Sat.–Sun. 💲 All major
cards

🍴 THE STONE HOUSE
$$
8 KENNA'S HILL
TEL 709/753-2380
Historic property with oodles
of atmosphere. Inventive
selections such as roast
pheasant with pecans, red
currants, and Tia Maria sauce
highlight local ingredients.
🍴96 🅿 🕒 Closed L Sat.
& Sun. AE, DC, V

QUEBEC

Gracious, European-style hospitality abounds in La Belle Province. English is widely spoken in Montreal and Quebec; you may have to brush up on your high school French to help smooth things over outside the major cities. But what could be more *charmant* than ordering a *tartine de jambon,* even if it is simply a ham sandwich?

AYER'S CLIFF

🏨 **RIPPLECOVE INN**
$$$
700 RIPPLECOVE RD.
TEL 819/838-4296 or 800/668-4296, FAX 819/838-5541
Attractive inn at south end of Lake Massawippi set in lovely gardens. Finely furnished interior, dining room, summer terrace.
🛏25 🅿 ⬜ 🌊 ⬜AE, MC, V

BAIE-ST.-PAUL

🏨 **AUBERGE LA MAISON OTIS**
$
23 RUE ST.-JEAN-BAPTISTE
TEL 418/435-2255,
FAX 418/435-2464
Quiet, romantic hostelry offering rooms with verandas and/or fireplaces. The dining room serves traditional French fare with local touches.
🛏40 ⬜ 🌊 ⬜MC, V

KNOWLTON

🏨 **AUBERGE LAKEVIEW INN**
$$$
50 RUE VICTORIA
TEL 450/243-6183 or 800/661-6183, FAX 450/243-0602
Splendid example of Victorian architecture built in 1874, this hotel offers attractively renovated rooms within walking distance of the boutiques and antique stores. Dining room, pub, garden terrace in summer. Despite its name, trees totally block the view of Brome Lake.
🛏28 🅿 ⬜ 🌊 ⬜All major cards

LAURENTIANS

🏨 **LE CHANTECLER**
$$
1474 CHEMIN CHANTECLER, STE.-ADÈLE
TEL 450/229-3555 or 800/363-2420, FAX 450/229-5593
Twenty-two downhill ski runs begin right at the door of this comfortable hotel. In summer, there are golf and tennis plus a private beach and boating on Lac Ste.-Adèle.
🛏295 🅿 ⬜ ⬜130 rooms 🌊 ⬜

🏨 **CHÂTEAU MONT-TREMBLANT**
$$
3045 CHEMIN PRINCIPAL, MONT TREMBLANT
TEL 819/681-7000,
FAX 819/681-7099
Modern hotel decorated with old-fashioned wood paneling and stained glass. Resort activities available year round. Heated whirlpools.
🛏316 🅿 ⬜ ⬜ 🌊 🌊 ⬜ ⬜All major cards

🏨 **AUBERGE DU COQ DE MONTAGNE**
$
2151 CHEMIN PRINCIPALE
TEL 819/425-3380 or 800/895-3380, FAX 819/425-7846
Cozy inn on Lac Moore with modern amenities and year-round activities; Nino & Kay's Restaurant offers five-course Italian feasts for under $30 per person.
🛏16 🅿 ⬜Closed mid-Oct.–mid-Nov. ⬜ ⬜All major cards

🍴 **BISTRO À CHAMPLAIN**
$$$$
75 CHEMIN MASSON, STE-MARGUERITE-DU-LAC-MASSON
TEL 450/228-4988
French restaurant particularly famous for the wines available by the glass and art work by Jean-Claude Riopelle. Wine cellar tours. Reservations recommended.
🍽125 🅿 ⬜Closed Mon., & Tues.–Wed. in winter ⬜ ⬜All major cards

🍴 **L'EAU À LA BOUCHE**
$$$
3003 BLVD. STE.-ADÈLE, STE.-ADÈLE
TEL 450/229 2991
Top-rated dining room showcases innovative seasonal cuisine and updated traditional Quebec dishes; 25 guest rooms available. Fixed-price dinner available.
🍽75 🅿 ⬜Closed L ⬜ ⬜All major cards

🍴 **LA CLEF DES CHAMPS**
$$
875 CHEMIN STE.-MARGUERITE, STE.-ADÈLE
TEL 450/229-2857
Romantic countryside eatery offering elegant French cuisine. Focus on wild game and locally produced foie gras. Reservations essential.
🍽60 🅿 ⬜Closed L & off-season ⬜ ⬜All major cards

MONTEBELLO

🏨 **CHÂTEAU MONTEBELLO**
$$$$
392 NOTRE-DAME ST.
TEL 819/423-6341 or 800/268-9411, FAX 819/423-5283
This extraordinary star-shape wooden structure was built in the 1930s from 10,000 red cedar logs, as a private club. Today, a Canadian Pacific resort, it stands on secluded grounds beside the Ottawa River. Golf course, tennis courts, walking trails, and cross-country ski trails. Renowned cuisine.
🛏211 🅿 ⬜ ⬜ 🌊 🌊 ⬜ ⬜All major cards

MONTREAL

🏨 BONAVENTURE HILTON

$$$$

1 PLACE BONAVENTURE

TEL 514/878-2332 or 800/267-2575 (CANADA), 800/HILTONS (U.S.), FAX 514/878-1442

Built on the upper floors of the huge Place Bonaventure retail and wholesale center, this downtown hotel has extensive roof gardens, an exterior heated pool used even in mid-winter, and views of the surrounding city.

🛏 395   🅿   🚇 Place Bonaventure   🛗   🕐   🏊   🆑 All major cards

🏨 DELTA MONTRÉAL

$$$$

475 AVE. DU PRÉSIDENT-KENNEDY

TEL 514/286-1986 or 800/268-1133 (CANADA), 800/877-1133 (U.S.), FAX 514/284-4306

Centrally located modern hotel with spacious rooms, most with balconies. Children's creativity and activity center.

🛏 453 + 6 suites   🅿   🚇 Place des Arts   🛗   🕐   🏊   🏊   🕐   🆑 All major cards

🏨 HÔTEL INTER-CONTINENTAL MONTREAL

$$$$

360 RUE ST.-ANTOINE OUEST

TEL 514/987-9900 or 800/361-3600, FAX 514/847-8730

A luxury property close to Old Montreal offering spacious guest rooms overlooking either the downtown or the waterfront.

🛏 357   🅿   🚇 Square Victoria   🛗   🕐   🏊   🕐   🆑 All major cards

🏨 LE WESTIN MONT-ROYAL

$$$$

1050 RUE SHERBROOKE OUEST

TEL 514/284-1110 or 800/228-3000, FAX 514/845-3025

English furniture and chintz mark the guest rooms of this property, favored by corporate types during the week. The downstairs Zen restaurant serves excellent Chinese cooking.

🛏 300   🅿   🚇 Peel   🛗   🕐   🏊   🕐   🆑 All major cards

🏨 LE CENTRE SHERATON

$$$

1201 BLVD. RENÉ-LÉVESQUE OUEST

TEL 514/878-2053 or 800/325-3535, FAX 514/878-3958

Business types and tourists alike appreciate the downtown location and little extras provided by this chain property, such as coffeemakers in the rooms.

🛏 825   🅿   🚇 Peel   🛗   🕐   🏊   🕐   🆑 All major cards

🏨 LOEWS HÔTEL VOGUE

$$$

1425 RUE DE LA MONTAGNE

TEL 514/285-5555 or 800/465-6654, FAX 514/849-8903

Chic and central, this hostelry features pristine duvets in the guest rooms and decadently furnished bathrooms.

🛏 142   🅿   🚇 Guy   🛗   🕐   🆑 All major cards

🍴 MAISON PIERRE DU CALVET

$$$

405 RUE BONSECOURS

TEL 514/282-1725, FAX 514/282-0456

Romantic European-style auberge in the heart of Old Montreal, partially located in a French-regime house built in 1725. Rooms furnished with antiques and heirlooms. Breakfast served in Victorian conservatory. Cossetted comfort. Pierre du Calvet Restaurant—see p. 356.

🛏 10   🅿   🚇 Champ de Mars   🕐   🆑 All major cards

🏨 QUEEN ELIZABETH HOTEL

$$$

900 BLVD. RENÉ-LÉVESQUE OUEST

TEL 514/861-3511 or 800/441-1414, FAX 514/954-2256

Archetypal downtown railway hotel built over the Central Station and belonging to the Canadian Pacific chain, connected into the maze of Montreal's underground city. Although some rooms have been renovated, facilities in others are rather tight. The hotel is excellently located for shopping and restaurants.

🛏 963 + 57 suites   🅿   🚇 Place Bonaventure   🛗   🕐   🏊   🕐   🆑 All major cards

🏨 RITZ-CARLTON KEMPINSKI

$$$

1228 RUE SHERBROOKE OUEST

TEL 514/842-4212 or 800/363-0366, 800/241-3333, FAX 514/842-3383

Personal attention is the hallmark of this European-style hostelry. Rooms mix old-world style with modern touches.

🛏 229   🅿   🚇 Peel   🛗   🕐   🆑 All major cards

🏨 AUBERGE DE LA FONTAINE

$$

1301 RUE RACHEL EST

TEL 514/597-0166 or 800/597-0597, FAX 514/597-0496

Charming small hotel in renovated Victorian house beside La Fontaine Park in city's east end. Tranquil yet close to vibrant rue Saint-Denis. Breakfast, no restaurant, access to kitchen for snacks.

🛏 21   🅿   🚇 Mont-Royal   🕐   🆑 All major cards

🏨 AUBERGE DU VIEUX-PORT

$$

97 RUE DE LA COMMUNE EST

TEL 514/876-0081 or 888/660-7678, FAX 514/876-8923

Beautifully renovated warehouse in Old Montreal offers interesting rooms with stone and brick walls and massive wooden beams. Fine dining at

Les Remparts Restaurant.
[i] 27 ☒ Place d'Armes ☒
☒ ☒ All major cards

🏨 L'APPARTEMENT-IN-MONTRÉAL
$$
455 RUE SHERBROOKE OUEST
TEL 514/284-3634 or 800/363-3010, FAX 514/287-1431
Well-priced studios with kitchenette, television, and telephone. Maid service available and 24-hour staff.
[i] 126 P ☒ Place des Arts or McGill ☒ ☒ ☒
☒ All major cards

🏨 CHÂTEAU AND TOUR VERSAILLES
$$
1659 (TOUR)/1808 (CHÂTEAU) RUE SHERBROOKE OUEST
TEL 514/933-3611 or 800/361-3664, FAX 514/933-7102 or 514/933-8401
Choose between rooms in a modern tower or in an Edwardian townhouse; either way, the service is impeccable. Limited access for handicapped.
[i] 177 P ☒ Guy-Concordia ☒ ☒ ☒
☒ All major cards

🏨 HÔTEL WYNDHAM
$$
4 COMPLEXE DESJARDINS
TEL 514/285-1450 or 800/361-8234, FAX 514/285-1243
Built atop the boutiques of the Complexe Desjardins, this ultramodern property boasts smart guest rooms with sleek designer furniture.
[i] 600 P ☒ Place des Arts ☒ ☒ ☒ ☒ All major cards

🏨 HÔTEL DE LA MONTAGNE
$$
1430 RUE DE LA MONTAGNE
TEL 514/288-5656 or 800/361-6262, FAX 514/288-9658
Rococo meets art nouveau in this quirky downtown hostelry. Guest rooms are large and comfortable, their decor much tamer than that

of the flamboyant lobby.
[i] 134 P ☒ Peel ☒
☒ ☒ ☒ All major cards

🏨 HÔTEL AMÉRICAIN
$
1042 RUE ST.-DENIS
TEL 514/849-0616
Clean, eccentric downtown hotel close to the Old Port and the Latin Quarter. A choice of rooms in an older "historic" wing or newer annex with kitchenette apartments.
[i] 54 P ☒ Berri-UQAM
☒ All major cards

🏨 HÔTEL LE SAINT-ANDRÉ
$
1285 RUE ST.-ANDRÉ
TEL 514/849-7070 or 800/265-7071, FAX 514/849-8167
Award-winning hotel located conveniently close to historic Old Montreal and the Latin Quarter.
[i] 61 P ☒ Berri-UQAM
☒ ☒ ☒ All major cards

🍴 LE JARDIN DU RITZ
$$$$
1228 RUE SHERBROOKE WEST
IN RITZ-CARLTON HOTEL
TEL 514/842-4212
Exquisite setting, excellent food, impeccable service, high prices—the ultimate in dining out for that special occasion. An added attraction is the cute ducklings on the pond in the center of the garden. Reservations essential. Also open for breakfast.
🍴 125 P ☒ Closed Oct.–mid-May ☒ Peel
☒ All major cards

🍴 CLAUDE POSTEL
$$$
443 RUE ST.-VINCENT
TEL 514/875-5067
Superior French Provençal restaurant hidden away in Old Montreal. Refined and elegant service, excellent cuisine. Reservations recommended. Summer terrace.
🍴 100 ☒ Champ de Mars
☒ ☒ All major cards

🍴 GIBBYS
$$$
298 PLACE D'YOUVILLE
TEL 514/282-1837
This restaurant occupies part of the historic d'Youville Stables built in 1800. Stone walls line the dining rooms on several levels. Famous as a steak house, Gibbys also serves seafood and offers home made desserts. Outdoor bar in summer months. Reservations recommended.
🍴 450 P ☒ Closed L ☒ Place Victoria ☒ ☒ All major cards

🍴 LA MARÉE
$$$
404 PLACE JACQUES CARTIER
TEL 514/861-9794
In the heart of Old Montreal on busy Place Jacques Cartier, this well-known Montreal establishment offers a touch of class in an area of otherwise touristy attractions. Formal service in Louis XIII-style dining room, and attractive terrace outside in summer months. Wonderful fresh seafood. Reservations recommended.
🍴 90 P ☒ Closed L Sat.-Sun. winter ☒ Champ de Mars ☒ ☒ All major cards

---

SOMETHING SPECIAL

🍴 LE CAFÉ DE PARIS
Formal room serving time-tested French cuisine; ample space between the tables allows the sumptuous dessert cart room to maneuver. Jacket required. Reservations essential. Fixed-price menus available.
$$$
RITZ-CARLTON KEMPINSKI HOTEL, 1228 RUE SHERBROOKE OUEST
TEL 514/842-4212
🍴 110 P ☒ Peel ☒
☒ All major cards

🍽 MILOS
$$$
5357 AVE. DU PARC
TEL 514/272-3522
High-end Greek cooking featuring fresh fish and seafood modestly seasoned and grilled to perfection. Meat-eaters are also well treated in the relaxed setting.
🛏 180 🅿 🕒 Closed L Sat.-Sun. 🚇 Laurier 🛗
♿ AE, MC, V

🍽 PIERRE DU CALVET
$$$
405 RUE BONSECOURS
TEL 514/282-1725
Good French food with elegant Victorian decor and huge fireplace (winter) in Old Montreal. Sunday brunch. Reservations recommended.
🛏 100 🅿 🚇 Champ de Mars 🕒 Closed L 🛗
♿ All major cards

🍽 TOQUÉ
$$$
3842 RUE ST.-DENIS
TEL 514/499-2084
Innovative cooking that combines solid techniques with fresh, regional ingredients for dazzling results. Fresh foie gras a highlight. Fixed-price menu available.
🛏 65 🕒 Closed L
🚇 Sherbrooke 🛗 ♿ AE, MC, V

🍽 BEAVER CLUB
$$
HÔTEL REINE ELIZABETH, 900 BLVD. RENÉ LÉVESQUE OUEST
TEL 514/861-3511
Classic dishes such as roast beef au jus and duck à l'orange are served in this former social club; the old boys' ambience lives on with the jacket and tie recommendation for men. Fixed-price dinner available.
🛏 200 🅿 🕒 Closed L Sat., Sun., & July 🚇 Bonaventure 🛗 ♿ All major cards

🍽 BONAPARTE
$$
443 RUE ST.-FRANÇOIS-XAVIER

TEL 514/844-4368
Exposed brick walls create a warm atmosphere for enjoying contemporary French cuisine in the heart of Old Montreal. Escargot with pesto and lobster with vanilla sauce are favorites. Fixed-price dinner available.
🛏 120 🅿 🚇 La Place d'Armes 🛗 ♿ All major cards

🍽 CHEZ LA MÈRE MICHEL
$$
1209 RUE GUY
TEL 514/934-0473
Excellent French cooking served in a converted mansion; the enclosed garden has spectacular art nouveau tiled walls. Specialties include lobster soufflé, bison in pepper sauce, and strawberry Napoleon. Fixed-price dinner available.
🛏 90 🅿 🕒 Closed L Sat. & Mon., & all day Sun. 🚇 Guy 🛗 ♿ All major cards

🍽 L'EXPRESS
$$
3927 RUE ST.-DENIS
TEL 514/845-5333
Good, simple food arrives quickly in this Parisian-style bistro, complete with tiled floors, mirrored walls, and stamped tin ceiling. Beware, there is no sign out front.
🛏 85 🅿 🚇 Sherbrooke 🛗 ♿ All major cards

🍽 LE PASSE-PARTOUT
$$
3857 BLVD. DÉCARIE
TEL 514/487-7750
Fresh market cooking done with discipline and flair. The homemade alderwood smoked salmon, excellent breads, and divine pâtés are available as carry out next door. Fixed-price dinner available.
🛏 34 🅿 🕒 Closed L Tues.–Fri., D Thurs.–Sat., & first 2 weeks Aug. 🚇 Villa-Maria 🛗 ♿ All major cards

PRICES

HOTELS
An indication of the cost of a double room without breakfast is given by $ signs

$$$$$	Over $280
$$$$	$200– $280
$$$	$120–$200
$$	$80–$120
$	Under $80

RESTAURANTS
An indication of the cost of a three-course dinner without drinks is given by $ signs

$$$$$	Over $80
$$$$	$50–$80
$$$	$35–$50
$$	$20–$35
$	Under $20

🍽 LES CAPRICES DE NICHOLAS
$$
2072 RUE DRUMMOND
TEL 514/282-9790
Incredibly romantic interior garden and an extensive wine list enhance such dishes as fresh foie gras over a salmon-potato crêpe.
🛏 65 🅿 🕒 Closed L Mon., & Sun. 🚇 Peel 🛗 ♿ All major cards

🍽 LES HALLES
$$
1450 RUE CRESCENT
TEL 514/844-2328
Classic and nouvelle cuisine served in bright surroundings; save room for the decadent pastries and desserts. Fixed-price dinner available.
🛏 135 🕒 Closed L Sat. & Mon., & all day Sun. 🚇 Peel 🛗 ♿ All major cards

🍽 MEDITERRANEO GRILL & WINE BAR
$$
3500 BLVD. ST.-LAURENT
TEL 514/844-0027
Note the absence of traditional pasta dishes at this nouvelle Mediterranean boîte. Partake instead of seared tuna and unusual side dishes such

as spicy frites. Generous portions. Reservations esssential in this eatery.
🔲 150 P ⏱ Closed D 🚇 St.-Laurent ⬤ AE, MC, V

🍴 MOISHE'S STEAKHOUSE
$$
3961 BLVD. ST.-LAURENT
TEL 514/845-3509
Aged, marbled hunks of beef share table space with complimentary pickles and coleslaw in this family steakhouse with enormous portions. Extensive wine list recognized by *Wine Spectator.*
🔲 200 P 🚇 St.-Laurent ⬤ All major cards

🍴 WITLOOF
$$
3619 RUE ST.-DENIS (NEAR RUE CHERRIER)
TEL 514/281-0100
Belgian restaurant on busy rue Saint-Denis known for excellent mussels, steaks, and frites, also for appetizers and desserts. Terrace open in summer.
🔲 65 🚇 Sherbrooke ⬤ All major cards

🍴 BENS
$
990 BLVD. DE MAISONNEUVE OUEST
TEL 514/844-1000
Hand-cut smoked meat sandwiches, crunchy potato pancakes, and tangy coleslaw dished out in fifties-style cafeteria; check out those who've come before you on the wall-of-fame photo gallery.
🔲 211 🚇 Peel ⬤ MC, V

🍴 SCHWARTZ'S DELICATESSEN
$
3895 BLVD. ST.-LAURENT
TEL 514/842-4813
Officially, this venerable eatery is named Montreal Hebrew Delicatessen, but everybody calls it Schwartz's. Brusque waiters and long lines do little

to diminish the pleasures of smoked meat sandwiches, grilled rib-eye steaks, and velvety chicken livers. Cash only, no reservations.
🔲 68 P 🚇 St.-Laurent ⬤

NORTH HATLEY

🏨 MANOIR HOVEY
$$$
575 CHEMIN HOVEY
TEL 819/842-2421 or 800/661-2421, FAX 819/842-2248
Antique-and-lace furnished rooms, some with fireplaces, overlooking Lac Massawippi. Restaurant, open to all, serves excellent French cuisine.
ℹ 40 P ⬤ 38 rooms 🌊 🍴 ⬤ All major cards

🍴 AUBERGE HATLEY
$$
325 CHEMIN VIRGIN
TEL 819/842-2451
Award-winning meals served in an elegant country inn with 25 guest rooms; extensive wine cellar. Specialties include foie gras, barbary duck, fallow deer, rabbit with black truffles, and heavenly chocolate desserts. Reservations essential. Fixed-price dinner.
🔲 90 P ⏱ Closed last 2 weeks Nov. ⬤ AE, MC, V

QUEBEC CITY

🏨 AUBERGE SAINT-ANTOINE
$$$
10 RUE ST.-ANTOINE
TEL 418/692-2211 or 888/692-2211, FAX 418/692-1177
Charming inn located in an ancient shipping warehouse; modern furnishings mix with antiques in rooms that offer river views or terraces.
ℹ 31 P ⬆ ⬤ All major cards

🏨 CHÂTEAU FRONTENAC
$$$
1 RUE DES CARRIÈRES
TEL 418/692-3861 or 800/441-

1414, FAX 418/692-1751
This landmark hotel offers extensive amenities and excellent views. Sunday brunches are famous, and Le Champlain, the fine dining room, serves classic French cuisine.
ℹ 613 P ⬆ ⬤ 🌊 🍴 ⬤ All major cards

🏨 HÔTEL LOEWS LE CONCORDE
$$$
1225 PLACE MONTCALM
TEL 418/647-2222 or 800/463-5256 (CANADA), FAX 418/647-1773
Contemporary decor and a great location near the lively Grande Allée make this hotel popular among tourists and business types alike.
ℹ 409 P ⬆ ⬤ 🌊 🍴 ⬤ All major cards

🏨 QUEBEC HILTON
$$$
1100 BLVD. RENÉ LÉVESQUE OUEST
TEL 418/647-2411, 800/HILTONS (U.S.), 800/447-2411 (CANADA), FAX 418/647-6488/2986
Located just outside of the walled city, this property has ultramodern rooms with standard furnishings.
ℹ 565 P ⬆ ⬤ 🌊 🍴 ⬤ All major cards

🏨 HÔTEL CHÂTEAU BELLEVUE
$$
16 RUE LAPORTE
TEL 418/692-2573 or 800/463-2617, FAX 418/692-4876
Comfortable accommodations in an excellent location just behind the Château Frontenac. Modern rooms vary considerably in size.
ℹ 57 P ⬆ ⬤ ⬤ All major cards

🏨 HOTEL CLARENDON
$$
57 RUE STE.-ANNE
TEL 418/692-2480 or 800/463-5250, FAX 418/692-4652
Centrally located hotel. Some of the rooms have been

beautifully renovated.
(i) 151 **P** **⬌** **(S)**
(S) All major cards

🏨 LE CHÂTEAU DE PIERRE
$$
17 AVE. STE.-GENVIÈVE
TEL 418/694-0429,
FAX 418/694-0153
A renovated 1853 manor with ornate chandeliers and Victorian rooms, some with either a balcony, fireplace, or vanity room. Front rooms overlook Governors' Park.
(i) 15 **P** **(S)** 3 rooms
(S) AE, MC, V

🏨 L'HÔTEL DU THÉÂTRE
$$
972 RUE ST.-JEAN
TEL 418/694-4040 or 800/363-4040, FAX 418/694-1916
Stars—the decorative kind—abound at this choice hostelry, built within the shell of an abandoned theater.
(i) 40 **P** **⬌** **(S)** **(S)** All major cards

🏨 MANOIR D'AUTEUIL
$$
49 RUE D'AUTEUIL
TEL 418/694-1173,
FAX 418/694-0081
Stunning art deco and art nouveau details make this newly restored inn one of the most lavish in town.
(i) 16 **P** **(S)** 9 rooms
(S) All major cards

🏨 MANOIR STE-GENVIÈVE
$$
13 AVE. STE.-GENVIÈVE
TEL/FAX 418/694-1666
Elaborate Victorian furnishings and genteel service create a country inn atmosphere in this 1880 building.
(i) 9 **P** **(S)** 8 rooms
(S) No credit cards

🏨 L'AUBERGE DU QUARTIER
$$
170 GRANDE ALLÉE OUEST
TEL 418/525-9726
Housed in an 1852 building

outside the city walls, this inn offers cheerful rooms.
(i) 15 **P** **(S)** 1 room
(S) All major cards

🏨 L'AUBERGE ST-LOUIS
$$
48 RUE ST-LOUIS
TEL 418/692-2424,
FAX 418/692-3797
A central location with small guest rooms, minimalist furniture, and friendly service.
(i) 27, 14 with bath **P**
(S) MC, V

🍴 LA MAISON GASTRONOMIQUE SERGE BRUYÈRE
$$$$$ and $$
1200 RUE ST.-JEAN
TEL 418/694-0618
Internationally acclaimed French dining at the Grande Table de Serge Bruyère, considered by some among the best restaurants of North America; others find the service just too slow. Plan to spend the entire evening there. Reservations recommended.
🍴 120 **P** **(L)** Closed L
(S) **(S)** All major cards

🍴 LE CHARLES BAILLAIRGÉ
$$$
57 RUE STE.-ANNE
TEL 418/692-2480
Refined cuisine in rich wood-paneled decor, with piano and chamber music accompaniment.
🍴 125 **(S)** **(S)** All major cards

🍴 AUX ANCIENS CANADIENS
$$
34 RUE ST.-LOUIS
TEL 418/692-1627
Traditional French-Canadian favorites such as *tourtière* and *fèves au lard* are showcased in an ancient stone house in the Upper Town.
🍴 115 **(S)** **(S)** All major cards

🍴 L'ECHAUDÉ
$$
73 SAULT-AU-MATELOT
TEL 418/692-1299
A chic Lower Town bistro that draws both locals and tourists with its well-crafted dishes of game and fish and its modern decor.
🍴 70 **(L)** Closed L Sat., & D Sun. in winter **(S)** All major cards

🍴 LAURIE RAPHAËL
$$
117 RUE DALHOUSIE
TEL 418/692-4555
Classical haute cuisine tweaked with international flavors. A toned-down room sets off the bold flavors of such dishes as shrimp and yellow beets served with foie gras in sauternes sauce. Reservations essential.
🍴 90 **P** **(L)** Closed L Sat.
(S) **(S)** All major cards

🍴 LE MARIE CLARISSE
$$
12 RUE DU PETIT-CHAMPLAIN
TEL 418/692-0857
Singular seafood dishes, such as halibut with nuts and honey, star in this cozy restaurant located in an ancient building in the Lower Town; both lunch and dinner fixed-price menus are real bargains.
🍴 48 **(L)** Closed L Sat. & Sun. in winter **(S)** **(S)** All major cards

🍴 LE PARIS BREST
$$
TEL 418/529-2243
Well-executed French dishes of beef, veal, fish, and seafood served to a lively crowd seated amid yellow walls and halogen lighting. Fixed-price menus available.
🍴 130 **P** **(L)** Closed L Sat. & Sun. **(S)** **(S)** All major cards

🍴 LE SAINT-AMOUR
$$
48 RUE STE.-URSULE
TEL 418/694-0667

Haute cuisine in a welcoming atmosphere. Specialties include seafood, fish, game, and luscious chocolate desserts. Fixed-price dinner available.
🎫 150 🅿 ⏲ Closed L Sat.–Mon. 🚭 All major cards

QUEBEC CITY REGION

🍴 MANOIR MONTMORENCY
$$$
2490 AVE. ROYALE, BEAUPORT
TEL 418/663-3330
With a spectacular location overlooking Montmorency Falls, this restaurant offers fine Quebec cuisine. Terrace available in summer.
🎫 130 🅿 ⏲ Closed Jan.–Feb. 🚭 All major cards

🍴 AUBERGE BAKER
$$
8790 AVE. ROYALE, CHÂTEAU-RICHER
TEL 418/824-4478 or 418/666-5509
Occupying a lovely old Quebec house, this restaurant offers traditional Quebec cuisine as well as some contemporary dishes. Terrace available in summer.
🎫 200 🅿 ⏲ Closed L in winter 🚭 All major cards

SAINT-GEORGES-DE-MALBAIE (GASPÉSIE)

🏨 FORT PRÉVEL
$$
2053 BLVD. DOUGLAS, PRÉVEL
TEL 418/368-2281 or 888/377-3835, FAX 418/368-1364
Located at the tip of the Gaspé Peninsula between Gaspé and Percé, this resort motel occupies a former World War II military installation where heavy artillery faced the Atlantic to guard against German attack. Golf course, fine dining.
🛏 72 🅿 ⏲ Closed Dec. 24–Jan. 5 🚭 All major cards

ST.-MARC SUR RICHELIEU

🍴 LES TROIS TILLEULS
$$$
290 RUE RICHELIEU
TEL 450/856-7787 or 800/263-2230
Traditional French preparations served at a 24-room inn overlooking the Richelieu River, about an hour from Montreal. Cream of onion soup, salmon in red wine sauce, and *marquise au chocolate* are among the specialties. Reservations essential for dinner. Fixed-price dinner available. Limited access.
🎫 250 🅿 🚭 🚭 All major cards

ONTARIO

Ontario is one of the country's two wine regions (British Columbia is the other). The vineyards in the province's southern corner consistently produce excellent wines, some of which have won medals in world competition.

Federation of Ontario Bed and Breakfast Accomodations, P.O. Box 437, 253 College St., Toronto, ON M5T IR5, Tel 416/515-1273; www.fobba.com Ontario Farm Vacation Assoc., RR 2, Box 7766, Alma, ON N0B IA0, Tel 519-846-9788

ALLISTON

🏨 NOTTAWASAGA INN
$$$$
1110 HWY. 89, ALLISTON
TEL 705/435-5501, FAX 705/435-5840
Large and luxurious resort hotel on 475 acres. Golf course, cross-country skiing, and sports.
🛏 164 🅿 🚭 🚭 🚭 All major cards

ALTON

🏨 MILLCROFT INN
$$$
55 JOHN ST.
TEL 519/941-8111
FAX 519/941-0192
Fine hostel made up in part of a converted knitting mill; the Mennonite villages of St. Jacobs and Elmira are 30 minutes away.
🛏 30 🅿 🚭 🚭 🚭 🚭 All major cards

CAMBRIDGE

🏨 LANGDON HALL COUNTRY HOUSE
$$$–$$$$
R.R. 33
TEL 519/740-2100 or 800/268-1898, FAX 519/740-8161
Magnificent Federal Revival mansion with top-notch amenities, close to Kitchener, Waterloo, and Stratford. The award-winning restaurant uses produce right from the kitchen garden.
🛏 43 🅿 ⏲ Closed 1st week Jan. 🚭 🚭 🚭 🚭 All major cards

COLLINGWOOD

🏨 BLUE MOUNTAIN INN
$$
R.R. 3
TEL 705/445-0231 or 416/869-3799, FAX 705/444-1751
The largest ski resort in Ontario offers outstanding golf in the summer, with pared-down guest rooms.
🛏 97 🅿 🚭 🚭 🚭 🚭 🚭 All major cards

ELORA

🏨 ELORA MILL
$$
77 MILL ST., ELORA
TEL 519/846-5356
FAX 519/846-9180
Converted mill with luxury accommodations and superb dining. Restaurant specialties include chateaubriand and Caesar salad prepared tableside.

ⓘ 32 🅿 🕒 Closed 2nd
week Jan. ⬌ Main building
🅢 🅰 All major cards

HUNTSVILLE

🏨 DEERHURST RESORT
$$
1235 DEERHURST DR.
TEL 705/789-6411
FAX 705/789-2431
Ultra-deluxe resort on 800
acres offer modern accom-
modations and year-round
activities.
ⓘ 120 🅿 ⬌ 🅢 🐾
🐾 🅰 All major cards

INGERSOLL

🏨 ELM HURST INN
$$$
ON RTE. 19 AT HWY. 401
TEL 519/485-5321 or 800/561-
5321, FAX 519/485-6579
A short drive south of
Stratford, Victorian country
inn with charming rooms.
Golf course, walking trails.
ⓘ 49 🅿 🅢 🐾 🅰 All
major cards

MCKELLAR

🏨 THE INN AT
MANITOU
Luxurious resort on the
shores of Lake
Manitouwabing offering
gourmet dining, top-notch
tennis instruction, spa
services, and a summer music
festival. Meals included.
$$$$
CENTER RD.
TEL 705/389-2171 (MAY–
OCT.) or 416/245-5606,
FAX 705/389-3818 or
800/571-8818
ⓘ 33 🅿 🕒 Closed mid-
Oct.–early May 🅢 🐾
🐾 🅰 All major cards

KINGSTON

🏨 HOLIDAY INN
KINGSTON
WATERFRONT
$$$
1 PRINCESS ST.
TEL 613/549-8400 or 800/465-
4329, FAX 613/549-3508
Great location right on the
waterfront with views of Lake
Ontario activities.
ⓘ 195 🅿 ⬌ 🅢 🐾
🅰 All major cards

NIAGARA FALLS

🏨 SHERATON
FALLSVIEW HOTEL
$$$$
6755 OAKES DR.
TEL 905/374-1077 or 800/267-
8439, FAX 905/374-6224
Oversize guest rooms, many
with breathtaking views of the
Canadian and American Falls,
in a modern, high-rise hotel.
ⓘ 295 🅿 ⬌ 🅢 🐾
🐾 🅰 All major cards

🍴 CASA MIA
$
3518 PORTAGE RD.
TEL 905/356-5410
Pink stucco Italian restaurant
off the tourist track specializ-
ing in homemade pasta. Live
music Friday and Saturday
nights.
🍽 80 🅿 🕒 Closed L Sat.
& Sun. 🅢 🅰 AE, MC, V

NIAGARA-ON-THE-LAKE

🏨 OBAN INN
$$$
160 FRONT ST.
TEL 905/468-2165,
FAX 905/468-4165
Broad verandas and mani-
cured gardens surround this
historic country inn, with lake
views and antique-filled
rooms. The restaurant serves
prime rib, salmon, and lamb at
reasonable prices.
ⓘ 22 🅿 ⬌ 🅢 🅰 All
major cards

HOTELS
An indication of the cost of a
double room without
breakfast is given by $ signs
$$$$$ Over $280
$$$$ $200– $280
$$$ $120–$200
$$ $80–$120
$ Under $80

RESTAURANTS
An indication of the cost of a
three-course dinner without
drinks is given by $ signs
$$$$$ Over $80
$$$$ $50–$80
$$$ $35–$50
$$ $20–$35
$ Under $20

🏨 QUEEN'S LANDING
$$$
155 BYRON ST.
TEL 905/468-2195 or 800/361-
6645, FAX 905/468-2227
Knockout views and antique
canopy beds. Innovative
cuisine and area wines shine
in the award-winning dining
room.
ⓘ 138 🅿 ⬌ 🅢 🐾
🐾 🅰 All major cards

🏨 THE PRINCE OF
WALES
$$
6 PICTON ST.
TEL 905/468-3246 or 800/263-
2452, FAX 905/468-1310
Modern annex has less charm
than the original 1864
building, but the bright rooms
and excellent downtown
location can't be beat.
ⓘ 101 🅿 ⬌ 🅢 🐾
🐾 🅰 All major cards

OTTAWA

🏨 CHÂTEAU LAURIER
$$$
1 RIDEAU ST.
TEL 613/241-1414 or 800/441-
1414, FAX 613/562-7030
One of the country's great
railroad hotels, this venerable
property offers great service

and comfortable rooms at the foot of Parliament Hill. Sunday brunch, served in the conservatory, is truly sumptuous.

🚪 425 + 40 suites 🅿 🔄 🕭 🏊 🐴 🛅 📳 All major cards

🏨 WESTIN HOTEL
$$$
11 COLONEL BY DR.
TEL 613/560-7000, 800/228-3000, or 800/WESTIN1,
FAX 613/234-5396
High-rise hotel attached to the Rideau Centre. Modern rooms, done up in pastels, have floor-to-ceiling windows.
🚪 484 🅿 🔄 🕭 🏊 🛅 📳 All major cards

🏨 LORD ELGIN HOTEL
$$
100 ELGIN ST.
TEL 613/235-3333 or 800/267-4298, FAX 613/235-3223
Good value for its central location within walking distance of major sights. Dining room.
🚪 310 🅿 🔄 🕭 📳 All major cards

🍴 LES MUSES
$$$
100 RUE LAURIER IN CANADIAN MUSEUM OF CIVILIZATION, HULL, QUE.
TEL 819/776-7009
Elegant French restaurant with stunning views across the Ottawa River to the Canadian Parliament, particularly lovely for summer evenings on the terrace. Reservations recommended.
🚻 100 🅿 🕭 Closed Mon. winter months, L only Tues.–Fri. & Sun. 📳 All major cards

🍴 CAFÉ HENRY BURGER
$$
69 RUE LAURIER, HULL, QUE.
TEL 819/777-5646
Converted home serving well-prepared continental dishes in an intimate setting, just across the river from Ottawa. The spacious summer patio overlooks Parliament

and the Canadian Museum of Civilization.
🚻 90 🅿 🕭 Closed L Sat. & Sun. 🕭 📳 All major cards

🍴 COURTYARD RESTAURANT
$$
21 GEORGE ST.
TEL 613/241-1516
Fine continental cuisine is the star at this venerable stone restaurant just off the Byward Market. More contemporary dishes include scallops and shrimp with a tomato and basil sauce.
🚻 150 🅿 🕭 📳 All major cards

🍴 FRESCO
$$
354 ELGIN ST.
TEL 613/235-7541
Italian dishes, done in the Tuscan style, include seafood and veal in a choice of 10 different sauces.
🚻 50 🕭 📳 All major cards

PICTON

🏨 ISAIAH TUBBS RESORT
$$$
WEST LAKE RD., PICTON, QUINTE'S ISLE
TEL 613/393-2090 or 800/724-2393, FAX 613/393-1291
Picton on Quinte's Isle was founded by Loyalists in 1786. Set among the pine trees beside West Lake, this resort occupies an 18th-century inn and contemporary housekeeping cottages. Tennis and cross-country skiing.
🚪 63, 30 cottages 🅿 🕭 🏊 🛅 📳 All major cards

PORT CARLING

🏨 SHERWOOD INN
$$$
P.O. BOX 400
TEL 705/765-3131 or 800/461-4233, FAX 705/765-6668
Beside Lake Joseph in the Muskoka Lakes region of Ontario, this is a lovely and

very private resort hotel with lakeside cottages. Countryhouse cuisine and fine wines complete the experience.
🚪 39 🅿 🕭 📳 All major cards

ST. JACOBS

🏨 JACOBSTETTEL GUEST HOUSE
$$$
16 ISABELA AVE.
TEL 519/664-2208,
FAX 519/664-1326
Located on 5 acres of pleasant grounds, this Victorian guest house is really a large bed and breakfast with charming rooms, all with their own bath.
🚪 12 🅿 🕭 🏊 📳 AE, MC, V

ST. MARYS

🏨 WESTOVER INN
$$$
300 THOMAS ST.
TEL 519/284-2977 or 800/268-8243, FAX 519/284-4043
Built in Confederation year 1867, this limestone mansion has wonderful carved gingerbread decoration outside, attractive guest rooms, and two dining rooms.
🚪 22 🅿 🕭 🏊 📳 All major cards

STRATFORD

🏨 QUEEN'S INN AT STRATFORD
$$
161 ONTARIO ST.
TEL 519/271-1400,
FAX 519/271-7373
Country inn in downtown Stratford, which offers good value and easy access to the world-renowned Stratford Festival.
🚪 32 🅿 🔄 🕭 🛅 📳 All major cards

HOTELS & RESTAURANTS

TORONTO

SOMETHING SPECIAL

🏨 FOUR SEASONS TORONTO

This downtown property sets new standards of luxury and service, with beautifully appointed rooms and staff happy to fulfill any request.

$$$$
21 AVENUE RD.
TEL 416/964-0411 or
800/332-3442,
FAX 416/964-2301
🛈 210 🅿 🚇 Museum,
Bay 🔁 🌀 🎇 🛳
🎦 🅰 All major cards

🏨 INTER-CONTINENTAL
$$$$
220 BLOOR ST. W.
TEL 416/960-5200 or 800/327-0200, FAX 416/960-8269
Step outside and you are just one block from the excellent Royal Ontario Museum and world class shopping. Inside: well-furnished guest rooms with pampered service.
🛈 198 🅿 🚇 St. George
🔁 🌀 🎇 🛳 🅰 All major cards

🏨 WESTIN HARBOUR CASTLE
$$$$
1 HARBOUR SQ.
TEL 416/869-1600,
FAX 416/869-0573
Although large and host to numerous conventions, this hotel's lakefront location and facilities are superb. Each of its rooms has a view of the lake. Revolving restaurant and Grand Yatt (Chinese).
🛈 981 🅿 🚇 Union 🔁
🌀 🎇 🅰 All major cards

🏨 DELTA CHELSEA
$$$
33 GERRARD ST. W.
TEL 416/595-1975 or 800/268-9070, FAX 416/585-4302
A large, efficiently run hotel. Excellent facilities for children

include a supervised creative center for 3- to 8-year-olds.
🛈 1,590 🅿 🚇 College
🔁 🌀 🎇2 🅰 All major cards

🏨 LE ROYAL MERIDIEN KING EDWARD
$$$
37 KING ST. E.
TEL 416/863-9700, 800/225-5843, or 800/311-4393,
FAX 416/367-5515
Understated elegance defines this distinguished hotel, built in 1903. Take tea in the palm-dotted lobby, or dine on well-prepared continental dishes at Chiaro's.
🛈 298 🅿 🚇 King 🔁
🌀 🎇 🅰 All major cards

🏨 METROPOLITAN
$$$
108 CHESTNUT ST.
TEL 416/977-5000,
FAX 416/597-6351
A reasonably-priced new hotel challenging the Four Seasons in the luxury market.
🛈 467 🅿 🚇 St. Patrick
🔁 🌀 🅰 All major cards

🏨 SUTTON PLACE HOTEL
$$$
955 BAY ST.
TEL 416/924-9221 or 800/268-3790, FAX 416/924-1778
Modern highrise with antiques-filled guest rooms close to Queen's Park, the University of Toronto, and the upscale shops of Yorkville and Bloor Street West.
🛈 220 🅿 🚇 Wellesley
🔁 🌀 🎇 🛳 🅰 All major cards

🏨 PARK PLAZA (GRAND BAY TORONTO)
$$$
4 AVENUE RD.
TEL 416/924-5471 or 800/977-4197, FAX 416/924-4933
Formerly known as the Park Plaza. Recently completed renovations to the north tower include larger guest rooms and the opening of a Morton's Steak House.

🛈 264 🅿 🚇 Museum 🔁
🌀 🎇 🛳 🅰 All major cards

🏨 HOLIDAY INN ON KING
$$
370 KING ST. W.
TEL 416/599-4000 or 800/465-4329, FAX 416/599-7394
Good value conveniently located near famous attractions such as the SkyDome, CN Tower, and the entertainment district.
🛈 425 🅿 🚇 St. Andrew
🔁 🌀 🎇 🛳 🅰 All major cards

🏨 RADISSON PLAZA HOTEL ADMIRAL
$$
249 QUEENS QUAY W.
TEL 416/203-3333 or 800/333-3333, FAX 416/203-3100
Harborfront hotel with rooftop pool, bar, and terrace. Rooms are well furnished and equipped. Squash court, two restaurants, and bar.
🛈 157 🅿 🚇 Union 🔁
🌀 🎇 🅰 All major cards

🏨 ROYAL YORK HOTEL
$$
100 FRONT ST. W.
TEL 416/368-2511 or 800/441-1414, FAX 416/860-5008
Beautifully refurbished to its original 1929 decor, direct access to the shops and businesses of the underground PATH walkway.
🛈 1,365 🅿 🚇 Union 🔁
🌀 🎇 🛳 🅰 All major cards

🏨 SHERATON
$$
123 QUEEN ST. W.
TEL 416/361-1000,
FAX 416/947-4854
Although it's the city's largest hotel, the Sheraton still provides efficient service. Six restaurants and bars, and two cinemas on the premises.
🛈 1,382 🅿 🚇 Osgoode
🔁 🌀 🎇 🛳 🅰 All major cards

🏨 WESTIN PRINCE
$$
900 DON MILLS RD.,
DON MILLS
TEL 416/444-2511,
FAX 416/444-9597
Set on 15 acres of land, this Japanese-owned hotel is a 20-minute drive from downtown Toronto in the Don Valley. The Katsura restaurant offers sushi and robata bars, a tempura counter, and teppanyaki-style cuisine. Tennis courts and putting green.
🛏 363 + 18 suites 🅿
🚇 York Mills 🚻 🕃 🏊
🕃 All major cards

🏨 HOTEL SELBY
$
592 SHERBOURNE
TEL 416/921-3142,
FAX 416/923-3177
Located in a handsome heritage Victorian building, this midtown hotel is one of the city's best bargains. High-ceilinged rooms are individually decorated and furnished. All have televisions and telephones.
🛏 68 🅿 🚇 Sherbourne
🚻 🕃 📺 🕃 All major cards

🏨 HOTEL VICTORIA
$
56 YONGE ST.
TEL 416/363-1666,
FAX 416/363-7327
Steps away from the heart of the financial district, this intimate hostelry offers clean rooms at affordable prices.
🛏 48 🚇 Union, King 🚻
🕃 🕃 All major cards

🍴 360 REVOLVING RESTAURANT
$$$
CN TOWER, 301 FRONT ST. W.
TEL 416/362-5411
The food is expensive but tasty, the view is simply stunning at lunch and even better at night, and well worth the price. Reservations essential.
🍴 500 🅿 🚇 Union 🚻
🕃 🕃 All major cards

🍴 AUBERGE DU POMMIER
$$$
4150 YONGE ST.
TEL 416/222-2220
Modern French dining in a romantic cottage in the city's northern end. Menu changes every three months. Fixed-price dinner available.
🍴 160 🅿 🕐 Closed L Sat. & all day Sun. 🚇 York Mills 🕃 🕃 All major cards

🍴 AVALON
$$$
270 ADELAIDE ST. W.
TEL 416/979-9918
Top-notch ingredients prepared with European techniques and breathtaking creativity. The serene location is around the corner from the SkyDome and theater district.
🍴 65 🅿 🕐 Closed L Wed.–Fri. & all day Sun. 🚇 St. Andrew 🕃 🕃 All major cards

🍴 CENTRO GRILL AND WINE BAR
$$$
2472 YONGE ST.
TEL 416/483-2211
Ground-breaking restaurant seamlessly melding Canadian ingredients with world flair. The funky, high-ceilinged room remains a local gathering spot.
🍴 220 🅿 🕐 Closed L 🚇 Eglinton 🕃 🕃 All major cards

🍴 NORTH 44°
$$$
2537 YONGE ST.
TEL 416/487-4897
Creative continental cuisine in a sophisticated setting with 50 wines available by the glass. House specialty is roast duck with sherry-hoisin marinade.
🍴 202 🅿 🕐 Closed L & all day Sun. 🚇 Eglinton 🕃 🕃 All major cards

🍴 OPUS RESTAURANT
$$$
37 PRINCE ARTHUR AVE.
TEL 416/921-3105
Converted brownstone

around the corner from Yorkville serving California cuisine. Wine connoisseurs appreciate the thoroughness of the high-quality cellar.
🍴 60 🅿 🕐 Closed L 🚇 St. George 🕃 🕃 All major cards

🍴 PAN RESTAURANT
$$$
516 DANFORTH AVE.
TEL 416/466-8158
Nouveau Greek cooking served in a funky nightclub that has little in common with its souvlaki house neighbors. Specialties include grilled loin lamb with fig-orange glaze.
🍴 72 🅿 🕐 Closed L 🚇 Pape, Chester 🕃 🕃 All major cards

🍴 SCARAMOUCHE RESTAURANT
$$$
1 BENVENUTO PL.
TEL 416/961-8011
Sparkling cuisine and an outstanding view take precedence over dated decor and rushed service in what some consider Toronto's best restaurant. A pasta bar downstairs serves lighter meals in a more casual setting.
🍴 100 🅿 🕐 Closed L & all day Sun. 🕃 🕃 All major cards

🍴 SPLENDIDO BAR & GRILL
$$$
88 HARBORD ST.
TEL 416/929-7788
Cal-Ital cooking in a sleek contemporary room around the corner from the University of Toronto. Try such house specialties as lemon-ricotta gnocchi with cracked pepper.
🍴 100 🅿 🕐 Closed L & all day Sun. 🚇 Spadina 🕃 🕃 All major cards

🍴 TRUFFLES
$$$
FOUR SEASONS HOTEL
21 AVENUE RD.
TEL 416/928-7331

A temple of gastronomy with flawless service. Couples sit side-by-side in the sedate and luxurious room, dining on masterful dishes beautifully presented. Reservations essential. Fixed-price available.
🎫 80 🅿 🕐 Closed L & all day Sun. 🚇 Bay 🔧
🅰 All major cards

🍴 AGORA
$$
ART GALLERY OF ONTARIO
317 DUNDAS ST. W.
TEL 979-6612
Bold, inventive cuisine served in the art gallery's stunning sculpture gallery. Specialties include an upscale pierogi plate, braised rabbit, and sophisticated desserts.
🎫 100 🅿 🕐 Closed L Mon., Wed., Fri. 🚇 St. Patrick 🔧 🅰 All major cards

🍴 ALICE FAZOOLI'S
$$
294 ADELAIDE ST. W.
TEL 416/979-1910
The patio with its fountain and gardenias is warmed by a fire in winter, and often features dancing to a DJ. Inside, the main draws are crab, gourmet pizza, pasta, and raw bar specialties, plus 50 wines by the glass. Reservations recommended. Open until 2 a.m.
🎫 400 🚇 St. Andrew 🔧 🅰 All major cards

🍴 ARLEQUIN
$$
134 AVENUE RD.
TEL 416/928-9521
Comfy booths and simple, well-prepared dishes with an international twist. A take-out counter up front is perfect for grabbing a bite while shopping at nearby Hazleton Lanes. Fixed-price dinner available.
🎫 46 🕐 Closed Sun. 🚇 Museum 🔧 🅰 All major cards

🍴 CAFÉ BRUSSEL
$$
786 BROADVIEW AVE.
416/465-7363
Crowded space on edge of Greektown that dishes up 28 kinds of steamed mussels, and bistro favorites steak and duck. Extensive beer selection.
🎫 30 🅿 🕐 Closed L Tues.–Sat. & D Sun. 🚇 Broadview 🔧 🅰 AE, MC, V

🍴 HOUSTON'S STEAKHOUSE & SEAFOOD BAR
$$
257 ADELAIDE ST. W.
TEL 416/351-1601
Gorgeous hunks of red meat paired with creative side dishes. Cigar lounge and huge wine list add to the fun. Fixed-price menus available.
🎫 150 🅿 🕐 Closed L Sat. & all day Sun. 🔧 🅰 All major cards

🍴 JAMIE KENNEDY AT THE R.O.M.
$$
ROYAL ONTARIO MUSEUM
100 QUEEN'S PARK
TEL 416/586-5578
The focus is on organic ingredients imaginatively prepared, with wines matched to every dish. Sunlight streams into the room, making it cheery even in winter. Fixed-price Sunday lunch.
🎫 120 🚇 Museum 🕐 Closed D 🔧 🅰 All major cards

🍴 LA MAQUETTE
$$
111 KING ST. E.
TEL 416/366-8191
Pasta and risotto offerings in addition to such classic French dishes as roast duck and grilled beef tenderloin. Elegant room overlooks small sculpture garden; close to theaters. Fixed-price dinners available.
🎫 150 🅿 🕐 Closed L Sat. & all day Sun. 🚇 King 🔧 🅰 All major cards

---

PRICES

HOTELS
An indication of the cost of a double room without breakfast is given by $ signs
$$$$$ Over $280
$$$$ $200– $280
$$$ $120–$200
$$ $80–$120
$ Under $80

RESTAURANTS
An indication of the cost of a three-course dinner without drinks is given by $ signs
$$$$$ Over $80
$$$$ $50–$80
$$$ $35–$50
$$ $20–$35
$ Under $20

🍴 MERCER STREET GRILL
$$
36 MERCER ST.
TEL 416/599-3399
Fresh-market cuisine with southeast Asian flavors. The Japanese garden patio is an exotic and popular hangout for locals.
🎫 45 🅿 🕐 Closed L Oct.–April 🚇 St. Andrew 🔧 🅰 AE, MC, V

🍴 ORO
$$
45 ELM ST.
TEL 416/597-0155
La nuova cucina Italiana in a sophisticated setting just steps from the Eaton Centre. House specialties include tea smoked sea bass and barley risotto with beets.
🎫 120 🅿 🕐 Closed L Sat. & all day Sun. 🚇 Dundas 🔧 🅰 All major cards

🍴 PANGAEA
$$
1221 BAY ST.
TEL 416/920-2323
High ceilings and mission-style furniture form the backdrop for well-executed fresh market cuisine, and the afternoon tea is a great pick-me-up following an afternoon

---

of shopping along Bloor Street.

🛏 160 🕐 Closed Sun. 🚇 Bay 🅂 🅂 All major cards

🍴 THE HOST
$$
1121 BAY ST.
TEL 416/962-4678
Fine northern Indian cuisine in a rococo setting (courtesy of the previous tenant). Tandoor-baked chicken, fish, and breads are moist and flavorful, as is the spicy Goan-style shrimp curry. Fixed-price lunch available.

🛏 300 🅿 🚇 Bay 🅂 🅂 All major cards

🍴 BLOOR STREET DINER
$
55 BLOOR ST. W.
TEL 416/928-3105
Serving shoppers and late-nighters, this restaurant combines an espresso bar, rotisserie where meats, poultry, and fish are prepared in Provencal style, and a café-terrace that is a great place to relax in summer.

🛏 100 (50 on terrace) 🅿 🚇 Bay or Bloor-Yonge 🅂 🅂 All major cards

🍴 LEE GARDEN RESTAURANT
$
331 SPADINA AVE.
TEL 416/593-9524
Greaseless Cantonese favorites such as grandfather smoked chicken and sizzling beef platter. Plastic tablecloths belie the caring service in this popular Chinatown restaurant. Reservations not accepted.

🛏 90 🅿 🚇 St. Patrick 🕐 Closed L 🅂 🅂 AE, MC, V

🍴 THE ELEPHANT AND CASTLE
$
212 KING ST. W.
TEL 416/598-4455
British pub with traditional restaurant fare located

opposite Roy Thomson Hall, which makes it handy before or after a concert. Very popular.

🛏 390 in two bars 🅿 🅂 All major cards

PRAIRIES

Waves of settlers have left their culinary mark on the Prairie provinces. Ukrainian pierogi, Mennonite pre-serves, and Chinese fried rice are prevalent, as is locally raised beef. Hotels maintain the standards of their bigger city counter-parts.

Bed & Breakfast of Manitoba, 434 Roberta Ave., Winnipeg, MB R2K 0K6; www.bedandbreakfast.mb.ca
Manitoba Country Vacations, Tel 204/633-3326
Saskatchewan Country Vacations, Tel 306/936-3353
Alberta Country Vacations, Tel 403/785-3700

CHURCHILL, MAN.

🏨 AURORA INN
$$
P.O. BOX 1030
TEL 204/675-2071 or 800/265-2563, FAX 204/675-2850
Dedicated to hospitality, provides opportunity to experience aurora borealis, whales, polar bears, and caribou in season.

🛈 18 🅂 MC, V

WINNIPEG, MAN.

🏨 HOTEL FORT GARRY
$$
222 BROADWAY
TEL 204/942-8251 or 800/665-8088, FAX 204/956-2351
Historic railroad hotel with large guest rooms decorated in dark wood and florals. The downtown location makes it a popular gathering place.

🛈 243 🅿 🔁 🅂 🏊 🍸 🅂 All major cards

🏨 THE LOMBARD
$$
2 LOMBARD PL.
TEL 204/957-1350, 800/228-3000, 800/441-1414, FAX 204/956-1791
Skywalk access to office buildings and retail shops is the payoff for staying at this Canadian Pacific luxury hotel in the city's core.

🛈 350 🅿 🔁 🅂 🏊 🍸 🅂 All major cards

🏨 SHERATON WINNIPEG
$$
161 DONALD ST.
TEL 204/942-5300 or 800/463-6400, FAX 204/943-7975
Inexpensive option right in the heart of the city within walking distance of major attractions. Restaurant.

🛈 271 🅿 🅂 🏊 🅂 All major cards

🍴 LE BEAUJOLAIS
$$$
131 PROVENCHER BLVD., ST. BONIFACE
TEL 204/237-6306
Classic French with a light touch at this suave St. Boniface favorite. Signature dishes are roasted ostrich filet with balsamic vinaigrette and cappuccino mousse in a chocolate cup.

🛏 120 🅿 🕐 Closed L Sat. & all day Sun. 🅂 🅂 All major cards

🍴 AMICI
$$
326 BROADWAY
TEL 204/943-4997
Sophisticated spot serving northern Italian nouvelle cuisine. The Bombolini Wine Bar downstairs serves simpler dishes at lower prices.

🛏 86 🅿 🕐 Closed Sat. L & all day Sun. 🅂 🅂 All major cards

🍴 PI WIISIININ
$$
208 EDMONTON ST.
TEL 204/943-6111
Winnipeg's only Amerindian restaurant, Pi Wiisiinin means "come and eat." Menu

HOTELS & RESTAURANTS

features modern twists on traditional Native fare: bannock appetizers, grilled salmon, venison, buffalo burgers, roast elk, Métis meat pie, wild rice salad, etc.
🍴56 🅿 🕐 Closed Sun. 🗺V

REGINA, SASK.

🏨 DELTA REGINA
$$$
1919 SASKATCHEWAN DR.
TEL 306/525-5255 or 800/209-3555, FAX 306/781-7188
Convenient downtown location with the Saskatchewan Trade and Convention Centre across the street from the Cornwall Centre Shopping Mall.
ⓘ55 🅿 🗺 🖂 🗺All major cards

🏨 SANDS HOTEL AND RESORT
$$
1818 VICTORIA AVE.
TEL 306/569-1666 or 800/667-6500, FAX 306/525-3550
Modern downtown property with airy guest rooms and a dramatic lobby.
ⓘ251 🅿 🔁 🗺 🖂 🖂 🗺 🗺All major cards

🍴 THE DIPLOMAT
$$
2302 BROAD ST.
TEL 306/359-3366
Upscale setting for an extensive selection of steaks, seafood, and a superb rack of lamb; extensive wine list.
🍴120 🅿 🕐 Closed L Sat. & all day Sun. 🗺 🗺All major cards

SASKATOON, SASK.

🏨 DELTA BESSBOROUGH
$$$
601 SPADINA CRES. E.
TEL 306/244-5521 or 800/268-1133, FAX 306/653-2458
Castle-like, landmark hotel on the South Saskatchewan River with traditionally-furnished guest rooms and modern amenities.

ⓘ225 🅿 🔁 🗺 🖂 🖂 🗺All major cards

🏨 RADISSON HOTEL SASKATOON
$$
405 20TH ST. E.
TEL 306/665-3322 or 800/333-3333, FAX 306/665-5531
Eighteen-story tower in downtown core on the banks of the South Saskatchewan River. Recreational complex with water slides.
ⓘ291 luxury suites 🅿 🗺 🖂 🗺All major cards

🍴 ST. TROPEZ BISTRO
$
243 3RD AVE. S.
TEL 306/652-1250
Sophisticated international cooking in an intimate setting. Homemade breads and pastas are outstanding; theme nights liven up an already imaginative menu. Fixed-price dinner available.
🍴82 🅿 🕐 Closed Sat., Sun., Mon. L 🗺 🗺AE, MC, V

CALGARY, ALTA.

🏨 THE PALLISER
$$$$
133 9TH AVE S.W.
TEL 403/262-1234, 800/268-9411, 800/441-1414, FAX 403/260-1260
Grand, historic railroad hotel offering guest rooms with traditional furniture, high ceilings, and ornate moldings.
ⓘ405 🅿 🔁 🗺 🖂 🗺All major cards

🏨 WESTIN HOTEL
$$$
320 4TH AVE. S.W.
TEL 403/266-1611 or 800/WESTIN-1, FAX 403/233-7471
Luxury downtown high-rise offering large rooms with contemporary decor.
ⓘ525 🅿 🔁 🗺 🖂 🗺All major cards

🏨 PRINCE ROYAL SUITES HOTEL
$
618 5TH AVE. S.W.

TEL 403/263-0520 or 800/661-1592, FAX 403/262-9991
Rooms at this downtown hotel come with fully equipped kitchens.
ⓘ301 🅿 🔁 🗺 🗺All major cards

🏨 HOLIDAY INN AIRPORT
$
1250 MCKINNON DR.
TEL 403/230-1999 or 800/465-4329, FAX 403/277-2623
Convenient and comfortable airport location with bright rooms tastefully decorated.
ⓘ170 🅿 🔁 🖂 🗺 🗺All major cards

🍴 HY'S STEAK HOUSE
$$$
316 4TH AVE. S.W.
TEL 403/263-2222
Charcoal-broiled steak is king at Calgary's most popular chop house, a franchise eatery done up in dark velvet fabrics and Victorian wood panelling.
🍴150 🅿 🕐 Closed L Sat. & Sun. 🗺 🗺All major cards

🍴 OWL'S NEST DINING ROOM
$$
WESTIN HOTEL
320 4TH AVE. S.W.
TEL 403/266-1611
Quality continental dining enhanced by a sweeping wine list and top-notch service. Specialties include roasted lamb, pan-seared sea bass, and curried breast of chicken.
🍴175 🅿 🕐 Closed L Sat. & all day Sun. 🗺 🗺All major cards

DRUMHELLER, ALTA.

🏨 DRUMHELLER INN
$
100 S. RAILWAY AVE.
TEL 403/823-8400, FAX 403/823-5020
The Alberta Badlands are not blessed with great hotels, but the Drumheller Inn is very satisfactory, with a view overlooking the town and its

spectacular natural setting.
Restaurant.
🛈 100 🅿 🔄 🏊 🚿 All
major cards

EDMONTON, ALTA.

🏨 FANTASYLAND HOTEL
$$
17700 87TH AVE.
TEL 780/444-3000 or 800/661-6454, FAX 780/444-3294
Part of the West Edmonton Mall shopping complex. Theme rooms cater to Roman, Victorian, Polynesian, or automotive fantasies.
🛈 354 🅿 🔄 🚿 🚿
All major cards

🏨 HOTEL MACDONALD
$$
10065 100TH ST.
TEL 780/424-5181 or 800/441-1414, FAX 780/424-8017
Landmark hotel with traditionally furnished guest rooms and stunning views of the Saskatchewan River.
🛈 198 🅿 🔄 🔄 🏊
🚿 All major cards

🏨 WEST HARVEST INN
$
17803 STONY PLAIN RD.
TEL 780/484-8000 or 800/661-6993, FAX 780/486-6060
Five minutes from the West Edmonton Mall, this hotel offers clean, modern accommodations. Rooms in the new wing are slightly larger and more expensive.
🛈 161 🅿 🔄 🚿 All
major cards

🍴 FRANK'S PLACE
$$
10020 101 A AVE.
TEL 780/422-0282
Seafood lovers in this landlocked city come here for the fresh catch flown in daily. Nautical decor doesn't detract from excellent mesquite-grilled dishes and Italian offerings. Reservations essential for lunch.
🪑 150 🅿 🕐 Closed L Sat. & all day Sun. 🔄 🚿 All major cards

🍴 UNHEARD OF DINING LOUNGE
$$
9602 82ND AVE.
TEL 780/432-0480
Imaginative cooking in an antique-filled setting. The menu changes with the seasons, but Mongolian-style bison medallions and Alberta beef remain perennial favorites. Reservations essential. Fixed-price dinner available.
🪑 118 🅿 🕐 Closed Mon.
🔄 🚿 All major cards

🍴 BISTRO PRAHA
$
10168 100 A ST.
TEL 780/424-4218
Trendy café serving such Central European favorites as steak tartare, wiener schnitzel, and goulash. Pastries are perfect for ending the meal or as a snack with coffee.
🪑 82 🅿 🔄 🚿 All major cards

THE ROCKIES

Boasting spectacular skiing and dramatic golf courses, the Rockies attract visitors year round. Casual dining is the rule, and hotel rooms are generally booked well in advance for summer months.

BANFF TOWNSITE, ALTA.

Rooms are scarce in the summer in Banff and Lake Louise. For assistance in locating a room contact:
Banff-Lake Louise Central Reservations, Tel 800/661-1676 ext. 9; Canadian Rockies Reservations, Tel 888-678-0801; Room Finders, Tel 800-392-1996

🏨 RIMROCK RESORT HOTEL
$$$$
MOUNTAIN AVE.
TEL 403/762-3356 or 800/661-

1587, FAX 403/762-4132
Modern property on Sulphur Mountain offering Bow Valley views and leather and velvet furnishings in guest rooms.
🛈 345 🅿 🔄 🚿 🚿
🚿 All major cards

🏨 TUNNEL MOUNTAIN CHALETS
$$$$
TUNNEL MOUNTAIN RD.
TEL 403/762-4515 or 800/661-1859, FAX 403/762-5183
Attractive wooden chalets featuring kitchenettes and fireplaces are arranged among the trees.
🛈 75 🅿 🏊 🚿 All major cards

🏨 BANFF SPRINGS HOTEL
$$$
SPRAY AVE.
TEL 403/762-2211 or 800/441-1414, FAX 403/762-5755
Majestic building offering more than 80 styles of guest rooms, all with high ceilings and antique furniture.
🛈 770 🅿 🔄 🏊 🚿
🚿 All major cards

🏨 RED CARPET INN
$-$$
425 BANFF AVE.
TEL 403/762-4184 or 800/563-4609, FAX 403-762-4894
These no-frills motel rooms are a rare lodging bargain in downtown Banff. Front rooms, facing onto Banff Avenue, can be noisy.
🛈 52 🅿 🔄 🚿 AE, MC, V

🏨 STORM MOUNTAIN LODGE
$-$$
HWY. 93
TEL/FAX 403/762-4155
Just east of Vermilion Pass, this former Canadian Pacific Railway lodge now offers cabin accommodations with fireplaces and down comforters.
🛈 12 🕐 Closed late Sept.–early June 🚿 AE, MC, V

HOTELS & RESTAURANTS

🍴 LE BEAUJOLAIS
$$$
212 BUFFALO ST.
TEL 403/762-2712
Neoclassic setting for rich French cooking. Tableside preparations include chateaubriand, filet mignon au poivre, and crêpes suzettes..
🍽 100 🅿 🕐 Closed Nov.
◈ MC, V

🍴 RISTORANTE CLASSICO
$$$
RIMROCK RESORT HOTEL MOUNTAIN AVE.
TEL 403/762-3356
Northern Italian cuisine framed by stunning views of the Bow Valley. Grilled veal chops, salmon roulades, and fresh fruit desserts fill out the menu.
🍽 64 🅿 🕐 Closed L ◈
◈ All major cards

🍴 BARBARY COAST
$$
119 BANFF AVE.
TEL 403 762 4616
Certified Black Angus steak, pizza, and pasta anchor the Californian menu. Live jazz and blues Thursday through Saturday nights in the bar; no cover charge.
🍽 100 🅿 ◈ ◈ AE, MC, V

ICEFIELDS PARKWAY, ALTA.

🏨 COLUMBIA ICEFIELD CHALET
$$$
ICEFIELDS PARKWAY, BORDER BANFF/JASPER NATIONAL PARKS
TEL 780/852-6550,
FAX 780/852-6568
Spectacular site overlooking the Athabaska Glacier as it plunges down the valley from the Columbia Icefields.
🛏 32 (17 with glacier view)
🅿 🕐 Closed mid-Oct.–mid-May ◈ MC, V

🏨 NUM-TI-JAH LODGE
$$
ICEFIELDS PARKWAY, BANFF NATIONAL PARK
TEL 403/522-2167,
FAX 403/522-2425
Simple rustic accommodation beside beautiful Bow Lake (25 miles north of Lake Louise) overlooking glaciers and peaks. The name refers to the marten, a fast-moving animal. It was the nickname of outfitter Jimmy Simpson who founded the lodge. Good location for hiking neighboring terrain.
🛏 21 🅿 🕐 Closed mid-Oct.–mid-Dec. ◈ All major cards

JASPER, ALTA.

🏨 JASPER PARK LODGE
$$$$
OLD LODGE RD.
TEL 780/852-3301 or 800/441-1414, FAX 780/852-5107
A village unto itself. Rooms are modern or rustic in style. Summer activities include golf, horseback riding, and boating on Lac Beauvaire.
🛏 447 🅿 ◈ ◈ ◈
◈ All major cards

🍴 LE BEAUVALLON
$$
CHÂTEAU JASPER, 96 GIEKIE ST.
TEL 780/852-5644
Crimson walls and live harp music provide an elegant backdrop to a continental menu specializing in game. Kids are welcome. Reservations essential.
🍽 120 🅿 ◈ ◈ All major cards

KANANASKIS, ALTA.

🏨 BREWSTER KANANASKIS GUEST RANCH
$$
P.O. BOX 964
TEL 403/762-5454 or 800/265-7094, FAX 403/762-3953
This ranch resort 30 minutes east of Banff offers cabins and chalets, antique furniture, and

horseback riding. Some guest rooms with whirlpool. Dining room.
🛏 33 🅿 🕐 Closed Nov.–April ◈ ◈ MC, V

LAKE LOUISE, ALTA.

🏨 POST HOTEL
$$-$$$
200 PIPESTONE RD.
TEL 403/522-3989 or 800/661-1586, FAX 403/522-3966
Choose from 16 types of rooms at this elegant Relais & Châteaux property. All rooms have wood and leather furniture, and decadent bathrooms attached.
🛏 99 🅿 🕐 Closed Nov. ◈ ◈ ◈ AE, MC, V

🍴 THE STATION
$$
200 SENTINEL RD.
TEL 403/522-2600
Local beef and lamb anchor the expertly prepared menu. Casual dining in the restored log railway station; formal atmosphere in the two heritage dining cars.
🍽 166 🅿 ◈ MC, V

KEY 🏨 Hotel 🍴 Restaurant 🛏 No. of bedrooms 🍽 No. of restaurant places 🚇 Metro 🕐 Closed 🛗 Elevator

SOMETHING SPECIAL

🏨 CHÂTEAU LAKE LOUISE

Dramatic location facing the Victoria Glacier. Guest rooms, some with terraces, have reproduction antique furniture; all meals and activities included in rates.

$$$$$
LAKE LOUISE DR.
TEL 403/522-3511 or 800/441-1414,
FAX 403/522-3834
🛈 1100 🅿 🔄 🏊
🍽 🍴 All major cards

LAKE LOUISE AREA, ALTA.

🏨 MORAINE LAKE LODGE
$$$$$
8 MILES FROM LAKE LOUISE ON MORAINE LAKE
TEL 403/522-3733
FAX 403/522-3719
Spectacular site beside what many consider to be the most dramatic lake of the Rocky Mountains in the valley of the Ten Peaks. Casually elegant cabins with fireplaces; outstanding food, complimentary afternoon tea, and pre-dinner sherry. Canoes, hiking. No one under 16 allowed.
🛈 18 cabins, 6 other units, 8 rooms in lodge, & 1 suite
🅿 🕐 Closed Sept.–June
🍴 All major cards

YOHO NATIONAL PARK, B.C.

🏨 CATHEDRAL MOUNTAIN LODGE AND CHALETS
$$$
YOHO VALLEY RD.,
2 MILES E OF FIELD
TEL 250/343-6442 (OFF-SEASON 403/762-0514)
On wooded site beside Kicking Horse River with magnificent views of Cathedral Mountain, this lodge has simple log cabins with fireplaces, and more rustic units with cooking facilities. Restaurant. No pets.
🛈 20 🕐 Closed mid-Oct.–mid-May 🍴 All major cards

🏨 EMERALD LAKE LODGE
$$$
EMERALD LAKE RD.
TEL 250/343-6321 or 800/663-6336, FAX 250/343-6724
No cars allowed on the grounds of this enchanting resort 20 minutes from Lake Louise. Cabins have fireplaces and balconies. Excellent cuisine in dining room.
🛈 85 🅿 🍽 🍴 All major cards

🏨 LAKE O'HARA LODGE
$$$
7 MILES S OF TRANS-CANADA HWY., E OF FIELD
TEL 250/343-6418
(OFF-SEASON 403/678-4110)
Only accessible by foot, on skis, or by daily reserved bus in summer, this is a real mountain hideaway beside lovely Lake O'Hara. The lakefront cottages and lodge units are perfect base for hiking, climbing, or back country skiing. Meals included. No pets permitted. Reservations essential well in advance.
🛈 23 🕐 Closed Oct.–Jan. & mid-April–mid-June 🍴 All major cards 🍴

THE WEST

Cosmopolitan restaurants and intimate lodgings abound along Canada's West Coast. Vancouver boasts world-class dining in addition to vibrant ethnic eateries. The region's wines are featured on many menus, along with local seafood and game.
British Columbia Bed and Breakfast Association,
Tel 604/276-8616
Western Canada Bed & Breakfast Innkeepers Association,
Tel 804/255-9199

KELOWAN

🏨 LAKE OKANAGAN RESORT
$$
2751 WESTSIDE RD.
TEL 250/769-3511 or 800/663-3273, FAX 250/769-6665
Located on 300 acres with lodging choices from one- to three-bedroom chalets.
🛈 150 🅿 🍴 All major cards

NANAIMO

🏨 BEST WESTERN DORCHESTER HOTEL
$$
70 CHURCH ST.
TEL 250/754-6835, 800/528-1234, 800/661-2449, FAX 250/754-2638
Converted opera house in the city center with harbor views. Elegant decor, winding hallways, and comfortable guest rooms.
🛈 65 🅿 🔄 ❄ 🍽
🍴 All major cards

🍴 MAHLE HOUSE
$
CEDAR AND HEEMER RDS.
TEL 250/722-3621
Innovative Northwest coast cuisine served in an intimate, country-style setting.
🪑 65 🕐 Closed L & Mon. & Tues. ❄ Access 🍴 All major cards

PRINCE RUPERT

🏨 THE INN ON THE HARBOUR
$–$$
720 1ST ST.
TEL 250/624-9107,
FAX 250/627-8232
Terrific views of the harbor make this a good base for train and ferry travelers.
🪑 49 🅿 ❄ 🍴 MC, V

🏨 EAGLE BLUFF BED & BREAKFAST
$
201 COW BAY RD.

TEL 250/627-4955,
FAX 250/627-7945
Next to Cow Bay, rooms look
out on the yachts only 10 feet
away.
🍴6 🅂 MC, V

SOOKE

🍴 SOOKE HARBOUR HOUSE
$$$
1528 WHIFFEN SPIT RD.
TEL 250/642-3421,
FAX 250/642-6988
One of British Columbia's
finest restaurants, featuring
fresh-caught fish and herbs
and vegetables from the
kitchen garden.
🍴75 🅿 🅂 🅂All major
cards

TOFINO

🏨 THE WICKANINNISH INN
$$$$
OSPREY LANE
CHESTERMAN BEACH
TEL 250/725-3100 or 800/333-
4604, FAX 250/725-3110
Country inn surrounded by
ocean and trees. Spacious
rooms have balconies and
fireplaces. Excellent dining
room serves West Coast
wines exclusively.
🛈46 🅿 🕓Closed mid-
Oct.–mid-Dec. 🅂All major
cards

VANCOUVER

🏨 FOUR SEASONS
$$$$$
791 W. GEORGIA ST.
TEL 604/689-9333 or 800/332-
3442 (U.S.), FAX 604/844-6744
Central location with
luxurious service; even pets
are pampered, with mineral
water in silver bowls.
🛈385 🅿 🔄 🅂 🏊
🏊 🗋 🅂All major cards

🏨 METROPOLITAN HOTEL
$$$$$
645 HOWE ST.
TEL 604/687-1122 or 800/667-

2300, FAX 604/602-7846
Intimate luxury hotel in the
heart of downtown Van-
couver. Spacious guest rooms
with mahogany furnishings.
🛈197 🅿 🔄 🅂 🏊
🗋 🅂All major cards

🏨 PAN PACIFIC HOTEL
$$$$$
999 CANADA PL.
TEL 604/662-8111, 800/937-1515
(U.S.), or 800/663-1515
(CANADA), FAX 604/685-8690
Relative quiet amid the sprawl
of a convention center and
cruise ship terminal.
Elegantly understated rooms.
🛈506 🅿 🔄 🅂 🏊
🗋 🅂All major cards

🏨 RENAISSANCE VANCOUVER
$$$$$
113 WEST HASTINGS ST.
TEL 604/689-9211 or 800/468-
3571, FAX 604/689-4358
Overlooking the North Shore
Mountains and one of the
busiest harbors on the
continent, this hotel is right on
the waterfront near the cruise
ship terminal. Rooftop
revolving restaurant and
casino.
🛈425 🅿 🔄 🗋 🏊2
🅂All major cards

🏨 WATERFRONT CENTRE HOTEL
Elegant, dramatic glass
tower offers calming
views of Burrard Inlet from
the majority of guest rooms.
Contemporary art in every
room.
$$$$$
900 CANADA PLACE WAY
TEL 604/691-1991 or
800/441-1414,
FAX 604/691-1999
🛈489 🅿 🔄 🅂 🏊
🗋 🅂All major cards

🏨 WESTIN BAYSHORE
$$$$$
1601 W. GEORGIA ST.
TEL 604/682-3377 OR 800/228-
3000, FAX 604/687-3102
Good location right on the
water overlooking North
Shore Mountains and
downtown skyline, near
Stanley Park. Marina, fishing
and cruising charters.
Restaurant facilities.
🛈517 🅿 🏊 🗋 🅂All
major cards

🏨 HOTEL VANCOUVER
$$$
900 W. GEORGIA ST.
TEL 604/684-3131 or 800/441-
1414, FAX 604/662-1901
Regal property with
mahogany furniture and deep
bathtubs in guest rooms.
Lobby lounge offers afternoon tea daily, followed by live
jazz throughout the evening.
🛈555 🅿 🔄 🅂 🏊
🗋 🅂All major cards

🏨 SUTTON PLACE
$$$
845 BURRARD ST.
TEL 604/682-5511 or 800/961-
7555, FAX 604/682-5513
Intimate and aristocratic
despite its large size. Rooms
are richly decorated with dark
woods. Apartment suites
available for extended stays.
🛈397 🅿 🔄 🅂 🏊
🗋 🅂All major cards

🏨 WEDGEWOOD HOTEL
$$$
845 HORNBY ST.
TEL 604/689-7777 or 800/663-
0666, FAX 604/608-5348
Small, exquisite property run
by devoted staff. Extra
touches, such as turndown
service and morning news-
paper, make it popular.
🛈89 🅿 🔄 🅂 🗋
🅂All major cards

🏨 PARK ROYAL
$$
440 CLYDE AVE.,
W. VANCOUVER
TEL 604/926-5511
A romantic mock-Tudor

building on the west bank of the Capilano River. Dining room and pub overlook an old English garden. Rooms are elegant rooms with king-size beds in brass frames and rich wood furnishings. Complimentary coffee or tea in the morning and newspaper.
🛏 30 🅿 🚭 All major cards

🏨 SYLVIA HOTEL
$$
1154 GILFORD ST.
TEL 604/681-9321
Very popular hotel overlooking English Bay near Stanley Park. Housekeeping suites; restaurant.
🛏 118 🅿 ⬍ 🚭 All major cards

🍴 BISHOP'S
$$$
2183 W. 4TH AVE.
TEL 604/738-2025
Pioneering restaurant still serving cutting-edge West Coast dishes featuring local ingredients. Specialties of the house include seared sea scallops over a potato pancake with lemongrass-lobster sauce.
🍴 48 ❄ 🚭 All major cards

🍴 FIVE SAILS
$$$
PAN PACIFIC HOTEL,
999 CANADA PL.
TEL 604/891-2892
Pacific Rim cooking with a panoramic view of Lions Gate Bridge and the North Shore. Favorites include Thai-style lobster ragout.
🍴 120 🅿 ⊕ Closed L ❄ 🚭 All major cards

🍴 IL GIARDINO DI UMBERTO
$$$
1382 HORNBY ST.
TEL 604/669-2422
Contemporary and classic northern Italian cooking in a country villa with garden. Specialties include florentine grilled steak.

🍴 250 🅿 ⊕ Closed L Sat. & Sun. 🚭 All major cards

🍴 LUMIÈRE
$$$
2551 W. BROADWAY
TEL 604/739-8185
Modern French cuisine using reduced stocks instead of butterfat to boost flavor. Specialties include goat cheese and potato ravioli and herb-crusted beef tenderloin. Fixed-price available.
🍴 45 🅿 ⊕ Closed L & all day Mon. ❄ 🚭 AE, MC, V

🍴 THE TEAHOUSE RESTAURANT
$$$
FERGUSON POINT,
STANLEY PARK
TEL 604/669-3281,
FAX 604/687-5662
Elegant location for a leisurely lunch or relaxed dinner, with views of English Bay stunning at sunset. Fine cuisine specializing in fish and seafood. Reservations recommended.
🍴 150 🅿 🚭 All major cards

🍴 TOJO'S
$$$
777 W. BROADWAY
TEL 604/872-8050
Legendary sushi and seasonal hot preparations; in spring, try scallops on cherry blossoms. "Up-to-Chef" fixed menu the runaway favorite. Fixed-price available.
🍴 95 🅿 ⊕ Closed L & all day Sun. ❄ 🚭 All major cards

🍴 BEACH SIDE CAFÉ
$$
1362 MARINE DR.
TEL 604/925-1945
Contemporary West Coast cooking and an extensive summer patio. Year-round delights include Thai rock shrimp cakes and Parmesan-herb crusted rack of lamb.
🍴 75 🅿 🚭 AE, MC, V

🍴 DIVA AT THE MET
$$
METROPOLITAN HOTEL
645 HOWE ST.
TEL 604/602-7788
Nouvelle cooking using regional ingredients with a heavy Asian influence. Dazzling presentation matches knockout room. Fixed-price dinner available.
🍴 108 🅿 ❄ 🚭 All major cards

🍴 IMPERIAL CHINESE SEAFOOD
$$
355 BURRARD ST.
TEL 604/688-8191
Tanks of live seafood and fish guarantee impeccably fresh-tasting dishes at this Cantonese restaurant with stunning views across Coal Harbour.
🍴 280 🅿 ❄ 🚭 All major cards

🍴 LE CROCODILE
$$
909 BURRARD ST.
TEL 604/669-4298
Roomy location serving simple, well-cooked French food at reasonable prices. Specialties include creamy Alsatian onion tart and duck à l'orange. Fixed-price dinner available.
🍴 85 🅿 ⊕ Closed L Sat., & all day Sun. ❄ 🚭 All major cards

🍴 LILIGET FEAST HOUSE
$$
1724 DAVIE ST.
TEL 604/681-7044
The only authentic Amerindian restaurant in Vancouver and a great dining experience. Dinners, including such things as oolichans, seaweed, and barbecued salmon or caribou, are served in a cedar-lined room which resembles a traditional longhouse.
🍴 50 🅿 ⊕ Closed L 🚭 AE, MC, V

HOTELS & RESTAURANTS

🍴 MESCALERO CANTINA GRILL
$$

1215 BIDWELL ST.

TEL 604/669-2399

Cajun-Mexican tapas and entrées are the stars here, with such specialties as chipotle-steamed mussels and oven-roasted rack of lamb with brie-mashed potatoes.

🍴 100 🅿 🌀 🏨 AE, MC, V

🍴 PINK PEARL
$$

1132 E. HASTINGS ST.

TEL 604/253-4316

Cantonese seafood restaurant serving such specialties as clams in black bean sauce, sauteed crab with seasoned salt, and dim sum on weekends.

🍴 680 🅿 🌀 🏨 All major cards

🍴 STAR ANISE
$$

1485 W. 12TH AVE.

TEL 604/737-1485

Superior Pacific Rim cuisine and great service. Specialties include garlic lobster sausage served with pickled ginger chutney, and venison wellington stuffed with enoki mushrooms.

🍴 41 🕐 Closed L Sat. & Sun. 🌀 🏨 All major cards

🍴 VIJ'S
$$

1480 11TH AVE. W.

TEL 604/736-6664

Innovative Indian cooking in a contemporary setting. Short menu changes bi-weekly. Favorites include squash dumplings in tomato-curry-cream sauce and garlic-grilled pork chops. No reservations.

🍴 50 🕐 Closed L 🌀 🏨 AE, MC, V

🍴 VILLA DEL LUPO
$$

869 HAMILTON ST.

TEL 604/688-7436

Romantic setting for top-notch Italian dishes, such as roasted sea bass in tomato-olive-lemon sauce served with potato cannelloni and pheasant breast stuffed with Parmesan.

🍴 77 🕐 Closed L 🅿 🌀 🏨 All major cards

🍴 A KETTLE OF FISH
$

900 PACIFIC BLVD.

TEL 604/682-6661

Family-run restaurant on the north end of the Burrard Bridge serving more than a dozen varieties of quality fish and seafood.

🍴 240 🕐 Closed L Sat. & Sun. 🌀 🏨 All major cards

🍴 PHNOM PENH RESTAURANT
$

955 W. BROADWAY

TEL 604/734-8988

This establishment's helpful staff serves Vietnamese and Cambodian fare, including warm beef salad and garlic-pepper shrimp fried in the shell.

🍴 120 🅿 🕐 Closed Tues. 🌀 🏨 All major cards

🍴 SEOUL HOUSE GARDEN KOREAN RESTAURANT
$

36 E. BROADWAY

TEL 604/687-0655

Korean and Japanese specialties, including do-it-yourself Korean barbecue cooked on a table-mounted grill; barbecue dinners include six side dishes, soup, and rice.

🍴 160 🅿 🕐 Closed L Sun. 🌀 🏨 MC, V

🍴 ZEFFERELLI'S SPAGHETTI HOUSE
$

1136 ROBSON ST.

TEL 604/687-0655

Spaghetti, yes, of course, but grilled seafood and chicken in Marsala sauce, too. Pasta sauces range from traditionals such as bolognese to moderns, including roasted garlic-broccoli.

PRICES

HOTELS

An indication of the cost of a double room without breakfast is given by $ signs

$$$$$	Over $280
$$$$	$200– $280
$$$	$120–$200
$$	$80–$120
$	Under $80

RESTAURANTS

An indication of the cost of a three-course dinner without drinks is given by $ signs

$$$$$	Over $80
$$$$	$50–$80
$$$	$35–$50
$$	$20–$35
$	Under $20

🍴 75 🕐 Closed L Sat. & Sun. 🌀 🏨 All major cards

VICTORIA

🏨 ABIGAIL'S HOTEL
$$$

906 MCCLURE ST.

TEL 250/388-5363 or 800/561-6565, FAX 250/388-7787

Charming Tudor-style inn close to downtown. Guest rooms feature down comforters; some rooms have spa tubs and fireplaces.

🛏 22 🅿 🏨 AE, MC, V

🏨 CLARION HOTEL GRAND PACIFIC
$$$

450 QUEBEC ST.

TEL 250/386-0450 or 800/485-6262, FAX 250/385-6579

Comfort, convenience, and wonderful views of Victoria Harbour or the Olympic Mountains mark this elegant property.

🛏 130 🅿 🔁 🌀 🏊 🔽 🏨 All major cards

🏨 COAST VICTORIA HARBOURSIDE
$$$

146 KINGSTON ST.

TEL 250/360-1211 or 800/663-1144, FAX 250/360-1418

Serene relaxation and modern comfort next to Fisherman's Wharf.

① 132 **P** **⬧** **⬧** **⬧**
⬧ **⬧** **⬧**All major cards

🏨 EMPRESS HOTEL
$$$
721 GOVERNMENT ST.
TEL 250/384-8111 or 800/441-1414, FAX 250/381-4334
This grand old Canadian Pacific hotel overlooks the inner harbor. Designed by Francis Rattenbury and built in 1905, the turreted ivy-covered structure typifies Victoria for many people. Afternoon tea at the Empress is a fine tradition and so popular in mid-summer that you must reserve. Dinner in the Empress Room is also a treat—see right.

① 475 **P** **⬧** **⬧** **⬧**All major cards

🏨 OCEAN POINTE RESORT
$$$
45 SONGHEES RD.
TEL 250/360-2999 or 800/667-4677, FAX 250/360-1041
Modern hotel with spectacular views of the Parliament buildings from spacious guest rooms. European spa on site.

① 250 **P** **⬧** **⬧** **⬧**
⬧ **⬧**All major cards

🏨 CHERRY BANK HOTEL
$$
825 BURDETT AVE.
TEL 250/385-5380,
FAX 250/383-0949
Popular old-style hotel with breakfast included. A few minutes from the harbor in a nice residential location. Some family units with kitchen. No telephones, no television. Restaurant.

① 26 **P** **⬧**AE, MC, V

🍽 CAMILLES
$$$
45 BASTION SQ.
TEL 250/381-3433
Intimate room showcasing creative West Coast cooking

in generous portions. Dijon-mint lamb, served with blackberry port glaze and gorgonzola whipped potatoes, is a perennial favorite.

⬧ 50 **P** **⬧** Closed L & late Dec.–early Jan. **⬧**AE, MC, V

🍽 THE EMPRESS ROOM
$$$
EMPRESS HOTEL
721 GOVERNMENT ST.
TEL 250/384-8111
Every meal is a special occasion in this sophisticated room serving innovative Pacific Northwest cooking. Fresh local salmon, char, and venison are featured. Reservations essential.

⬧ 125 **P** **⬧** Closed L
⬧ **⬧**All major cards

🍽 MARINA RESTAURANT
$$
1327 BEACH DR.
TEL 250/598-8555
Extremely popular spot serving such favorites as warm salmon salad and whole crab with drawn butter.

⬧ 130 **P** **⬧** **⬧**All major cards

🍽 PESCATORE'S FISH HOUSE AND OYSTER BAR
$$
614 HUMBOLDT ST.
TEL 250/385-4512
The downtown business crowd gathers here for exuberant dining where freshly caught ingredients star in Pacific Northwest preparations.

⬧ 115 **⬧** Closed L **⬧**
⬧All major cards

🍽 CAFÉ MEXICO
$
1425 STORE ST.
TEL 250/386-5454
Mexican classics such as grilled chipotle chicken served in hearty portions in renovated eatery just off waterfront. Fixed-price menu available.

⬧ 100 **P** **⬧** Closed L
⬧ **⬧**All major cards

🍽 IL TERRAZZO
$
555 JOHNSON ST.
TEL 250/361-0028
This romantic outdoor eatery is tucked off an alley. Modern northern Italian dishes include such specialties as wood-fired pizzas and salmon.

⬧ 90–150 (with patio)
⬧ Closed L Sat. & Sun. **⬧**
⬧All major cards

🍽 PAGLIACCI'S
$
1011 BROAD ST.
TEL 250/386-1662
Fine Italian bistro serving dozens of homemade pasta dishes, chicken, and veal in a room lined with photos of Hollywood movie stars. Justifiably famous cheesecake. Reservations not accepted.

⬧ 65 **⬧**AE, MC, V

WHISTLER

🏨 CHÂTEAU WHISTLER
$$$
4599 CHÂTEAU BLVD.
TEL 604/938-8000 or 800/441-1414, FAX 604/938-2055
Imposing-looking fortress at the foot of Blackcomb Mountain with year-round outdoor activities.

① 563 **P** **⬧** **⬧**
⬧ **⬧** **⬧** **⬧**All major cards

🍽 TRATTORIA DI UMBERTO
$$$
MOUNTAINSIDE LODGE
4417 SUNDIAL PL.
TEL 604/932-5858
Home-style Italian cooking. Tuscan grilled meats and fish compliment design-your-own pasta dishes. Reservations essential. Fixed-price dinner available.

⬧ 130 **P** **⬧** **⬧**All major cards

🍽 LES DEUX GROS
$$
1200 ALTA LAKE RD.
TEL 604/932-4611
Simply enormous portions of

HOTELS & RESTAURANTS

HOTELS & RESTAURANTS

well-prepared rustic French cuisine. Favorites include Alsatian onion tarte, rack of lamb, and salmon wellington.
🍴 100 🅿 🕒 Closed L 💳 All major cards

THE NORTH

In the far north, the sparsity of the population is echoed in the number of dining and lodging choices. Hotels are generally comfortable, though with fewer amenities than those in the south. Restaurants are casual, with well-prepared, traditional items occasionally enlivened by ethnic influences.

DAWSON, YUKON

🏨 DOWNTOWN HOTEL
$$
2ND AVE. AND QUEEN ST.
TEL 867/993-5346,
FAX 867/993-5076
This hotel still retains its gold rush era look, but it has been refurbished since 1898. It stands out among the colorful seasonal places to stay in this community, affected every year by permafrost.
🛏 60 🅿 🕒 Closed Christmas–mid-Jan. 🛗 💳 All major cards

🍴 JACK LONDON GRILL
$$
DOWNTOWN HOTEL
2ND AVE. AND QUEEN ST.
TEL 867/993-5346
Old-fashioned, clubby room specializing in steaks, which come in three sizes.
🍴 72 🅿 💳 All major cards

🍴 KLONDIKE KATE'S
$
3RD AVE. AND KING ST.
TEL 867/993-6527
Extremely good, ethnic-influenced dishes served in an atmosphere that is both friendly and casual. Large summertime patio and

vegetarian selections are added draws.
🍴 100 🅿 🕒 Closed Dec.–Mar. 💳 MC, V

WHITEHORSE, YUKON

🏨 EDGEWATER HOTEL
$$
101 MAIN ST.
TEL 867/667-2572,
FAX 867/668-3014
Large rooms with modern furnishings in a quiet environment. The Cellar dining room serves such high-end fare as Alaska king crab.
🛏 30 🅿 💳 All major cards

🏨 WESTMARK WHITEHORSE HOTEL
$$
201 WOOD ST.
TEL 867/668-4700 or 800/544-0970, FAX 867/668-2789
Attractive rooms with wood furniture and coffeemakers. Frequent tour groups sometimes make for crowded hallways.
🛏 181 🅿 💳 All major cards

🍴 ANTONIO'S VINEYARD
$$
202 STRICKLAND ST.
TEL 867/668-6266
Greek and Italian favorites along with local seafood, steak, and game. Wonderful views and polished service.
🍴 123 🕒 Closed L 🅿 💳 💳 MC, V

INUVIK, N.W.T.

🏨 THE MACKENZIE HOTEL
$$$
P.O. BOX 1618, INUVIK
TEL 867/777-2861
FAX 867/777-3317
There is really little to choose between this place and the Eskimo Inn, but the Mackenzie wins by a hair because the eating facilities are better.
🛏 33 🅿 💳 All major cards

YELLOWKNIFE, N.W.T.

🏨 EXPLORER HOTEL
$$$
4825 49TH AVE.
TEL 867/873-3531 or 800/661-0892, FAX 867/873-2789
Modern 8-story block in downtown Yellowknife, with all "southern" conveniences and gold mine executives thrown in for good measure. The Factors Club is considered by some the best place to eat in the Northwest Territories.
🛏 128 🅿 🛗 💳 💳 All major cards

🏨 DISCOVERY INN
$$$
4701 FRANKLIN AVE.
TEL 867/873-4151,
FAX 867/920-7948
Newly renovated rooms with kitchenettes right in downtown Yellowknife. Popular for long-term stays.
🛏 41 🅿 💳 💳 All major cards

IQALUIT, NUNAVUT

🏨 REGENCY FROBISHER INN
$$$
P.O. BOX 610, IQALUIT
TEL 867/979-2222,
FAX 867/979-0427
This centrally-located hotel is connected to government offices and stores. Unparalleled views of Frobisher Bay.
🛏 49 (some suites) 💳 All major cards

SHOPPING IN CANADA

Browsing in shops and malls has become an acceptable pastime for both Canadian residents and visitors to the country. Sales are advertised in nearly every shop window; closing sales, year-end sales, back-to-school sales, you name it and someone has thought of it. Apart from the shopping malls there are also plenty of smaller specialized shops. In the Prairie Provinces and the North you will find Inuit and First Nations crafts that are always a good souvenir idea.

SALES TAX

Canada is riddled with federal and provincial taxes on goods and services. A general sales tax (GST) of 7 percent is levied on most transactions. Visitors are eligible for a GST rebate on most goods taken out of Canada within 60 days. Claim forms are available at airports, shops, and hotels, and from any Canadian embassy. All receipts must be enclosed with the forms, which should be returned within 60 days of leaving Canada.

In addition to GST a 5–12 percent tax is levied on goods bought in many provinces.

OPENING HOURS

Stores are generally open Monday through Saturday, 10 a.m. to 6 p.m., unless otherwise noted. Many retail stores stay open late on Thursday and Friday evenings. Shopping malls have longer hours than most stores, usually about 7:30–9 p.m., and most towns have 24-hour pharmacies and stores, e.g., Mac's or 7-Eleven. The so-called "blue laws" for shops regarding Sunday opening are enforced in much of Canada, although some provinces are increasingly allowing limited 12–5 p.m. openings.

MARITIMES

AREAS TO SHOP
Market Square
St. John, N.B.
Some fascinating small boutiques are housed in the warehouses surrounding the Market Slip in Old Saint John.
St. Andrews, N.B.
This gracious community on the Fundy shore of New Brunswick

has an interesting collection of boutiques along Water Street.
Historic Properties
1868 Upper Water St.
Halifax, N.S.
This collection of waterfront warehouses is home to a wide selection of interesting shops, cafés, and pubs.
Spring Garden Road
Halifax, N.S.
A fascinating street for wandering and browsing in boutiques and art galleries.

ARTS & ANTIQUES
Gallery 78
796 Queen St.
Fredericton, N.B.
Tel 506/454-5192
Works by local artists are sold in this gallery.
Micmac Heritage Gallery
1903 Barrington St.
Halifax, N.S.
Tel 902/422-9509
This cooperative gallery features Mi'kmaq and Maliseet art and crafts.

CRAFTS & JEWELRY
Aitkens Pewter
65 Regent St.
Fredericton, N.B.
Tel 506/453-9474
Hand-crafted pewter goblets, accessories, and jewelry.
Jennifer of Nova Scotia
5635 Spring Garden Rd.
Halifax, N.B.
Tel 902/425-3119
Locally made jewelry, pottery, wool sweaters, and soaps.
Confederation Centre Gift Shop
145 Richmond St.
Charlottetown, P.E.I.
Tel 902/628-6149
Specializes in quality handcrafts from Prince Edward Island and across Canada, as well as an

extensive assortment of books.
Nova Scotia Crystal
Lower Water St.
Historic Properties
Halifax, N.S.
Tel 902/492-0416
Canada's only crystal manufacturer producing hand-crafted pieces in the time-honored way. Visitors can watch craftspeople at work and view their products in the showroom.
The Plaid Place
1903 Barrington St.
Halifax, N.S.
Tel 902/429-6872
This "New Scotland" store specializes in tartans, kilts, highland dress, sweaters, and other accessories, especially the Nova Scotia variety.

MARKETS
Boyce Farmers' Market
Bounded by Regent, Brunswick, and George Sts.
Fredericton, N.B.
A great source of local meats and produce, baked goods, crafts, and such seasonal items as holiday wreaths and maple syrup, on Saturday mornings.
Brewery Market
1496 Lower Water St.
Halifax, N.S.
An active and attractive farmers' market on Saturdays.
Old City Market
47 Charlotte St.
St. John, N.B.
Tel 506/658-2820
One city block's worth of foods and hand-crafted souvenirs. But don't visit on Sunday because it is closed then.

NEWFOUNDLAND

AREAS TO SHOP
Murray Premises
Harbour Dr.
St. John's
These restored mercantile premises house an interesting collection of boutiques.

ARTS & ANTIQUES
Christina Parker Fine Art
7 Plank Rd.

St. John's
Tel 709/753-0580
Paintings, sculptures, and
drawings by local artists.
Murray's Antiques
414 Blackmarsh Rd.
St. John's
Tel 709/579-7344
Top-notch selection of silver,
china, and wooden furniture.

CLOTHES & ACCESSORIES
Nonia
286 Water St.
St. John's
Tel 709/753-8062
Homespun woollen clothing
crafted in outlying regions.
The Cod Jigger
245 Duckworth St.
St. John's
Tel 709/726-7422
Newfoundland's own Grenfell
coats are sold here.

CRAFTS & JEWELRY
The Devon House Craft Gallery
59 Duckworth St.
St. John's
Tel 709/753-2749
Only juried crafts are carried in
this gallery, owned by the
Newfoundland and Labrador
Crafts Development
Association.

GIFTS & MISCELLANEOUS
Newfoundland Bookstore
100 Water St.
St. John's
Tel 709/722-8220
This store offers a full selection
of Newfoundland books as well
as other fine souvenirs.

QUEBEC

AREAS TO SHOP
Quartier Petit-Champlain
Lower Town
Quebec City
Along this charming old street is
a fine collection of artisan-
owned boutiques, galleries, and
cafés specializing in Quebec
crafts and designs.

Knowlton (Ville du Lac-Brome)
This small community in
Quebec's Eastern Townships has
a fine collection of antique
stores and other interesting
boutiques housed in original
Victorian houses on English Hill,
its main street.

ARTS & ANTIQUES
L'Antiquaire Joyal
1475 rue Amherst
Montreal
Tel 514/524-0057
Two stories of religious antiques
and art in addition to Victorian
furniture.
Antiques Row
Rue Notre-Dame Ouest
between Guy and Atwater
Montreal
This run-down section of Notre-
Dame Street houses a large
number of antique and second-
hand stores. It is not a glamorous and glitzy district, but can
be paradise for the person
intent on seeking out a bargain.
Most stores open about 11 a.m.,
some not before noon, and they
close by 5 or 6 p.m.
Rue du Trésor
Between rue Ste.-Anne and
rue Buade
Quebec City
Along this narrow street in Old
Quebec, 36 artists display their
works—watercolors, prints,
etchings, silkscreens, reproductions, etc.

CLOTHES & ACCESSORIES
McComber
402 blvd. de Maisonneuve Ouest
Montreal
Tel 514/842-9005
Stylish house designs for mink
and other furs at a century-old
business.
Robitaille Fourrures
1500 des Taneurs
Quebec City
Tel 418/681-7297
High-quality furs since 1894.

CRAFTS & JEWELRY
Bonsecours Market
350 St.-Paul E.
Old Montreal

This former wholesale market
now houses a fascinating
collection of craft and design
stores on its main floor, and food
outlets are planned for the
lower level.
Canadian Guild of Crafts
2025 Peel
Montreal
Tel 514/849-6091
Wonderful store run by the
non-profit institution that
promotes Canadian art and
crafts. Superb Inuit art gallery,
too.
Joaillier Louis Perrier
48 rue du Petit-Champlain
Quebec City
Tel 418/692-4633
Locally designed gold and silver
jewelry.
Les Trois Colombes Inc.
46 rue St.-Louis
Quebec City
Tel 418/694-1114
First Nations and Inuit carvings,
jewelry, pottery, paintings, and
handwoven fabrics.

GIFTS & MISCELLANEOUS
Papeterie St.-Gilles
304 rue F.A. Savard
St.-Joseph-de-la-rive
Tel 418/635-2430
Wondrous handcrafted
stationery, made on antique
machines.
Paragraphe
2220 McGill College Ave.
Montreal
Tel 514/845-5811
Large and well-stocked English
bookstore for anyone interested
in books on Canadian or general
subjects.
Ulysse Travel Bookshop
4176 Saint-Denis
Montreal
Tel 514/843-9447
Bookstore that specializes in
travel books to every part of the
globe. There is also a branch in
the downtown Infotouriste
Centre (1001 Dorchester Sq.),
which carries local travel guides.

MARKETS
Faubourg Sainte-Catherine
1616 Ste.-Catherine W.
Montreal

Not a true market in the strict sense of the word but a wonderful collection of food outlets and restaurants.

Les Halles de la Gare
Central Station
895 rue de la
Gauchetière Ouest
Montreal
A fine collection of restaurants and take-out food. Just the place for lunch or to pick up a gourmet picnic. Access from Queen Elizabeth Hotel or Place Ville-Marie.

Marché Atwater
138 Atwater at
rue Notre-Dame Ouest
Montreal
The market building houses an amazing collection of traditional butchers and cheese stores. In season, the exterior is alive with flowers and a wide variety of fruit and vegetables.

Marché Jean-Talon
7075 Casgrain
Montreal
In the center of the city's Italian quarter, this market really comes to life in the late summer and fall when farmers from far and wide bring their produce to sell. It is surrounded by small Italian meat and pasta shops.

ONTARIO

AREAS TO SHOP
Queen's Quay Terminal
207 Queen's Quay W.
Toronto
This building at the foot of York Street on the waterfront houses over 100 specialty shops, galleries, and restaurants.

Queen Street West
Between University Ave. and Bathurst
Toronto
Known for its eclectic and eccentric stores selling a wide variety of antiques, books, hip fashions, and other bric-a-brac.

Toronto Eaton Centre
220 Yonge St.
Toronto
The Toronto Eaton Centre is like no other shopping complex.

The architecture is fabulous. You can sit and admire it or venture into some of the over 300 stores.

ARTS & ANTIQUES
Isaacs Inuit Gallery
9 Prince Arthur St.
Toronto
Tel 416/921-9985
This gallery has an international reputation for its wonderful Inuit sculpture, prints, and drawings.

The Guild Shop
118 Cumberland St.
Toronto
Tel 416/921-1721
Aboriginal painters and sculptors are among the many Canadian artists represented.

BOOKS
Albert Britnell Book Shop
765 Yonge St.
Toronto
Tel 416/924-3321
Great British ambience and a fine stock of literature and coffee-table books.

GIFTS & MISCELLANEOUS
Amethyst Gift Centre
400 Victoria Ave. E.
Thunder Bay
Tel 807/622-6908
Wonderful selection of pieces of precious purple amethyst. The area north of Lake Superior is one of the very few places in the world where the stone is found.

Arts-on-King
169 King St. E.
Toronto
Tel 416/777-9617
Funky home decor store with unique glass, ceramic, papier mâché, and wood offerings.

Honest Ed's Department Store
581 Bloor St.
Toronto
Tel 416/537-1574
This is a massive and quite amazing bargain shopping center run by Toronto personality, Ed Mirvish. Worth a visit even if you don't buy anything.

Jane Corkin Gallery
179 John St., Ste. 302
Toronto
Tel 416/979-1980

World-renowned names in photography are found here.

National Gallery of Canada Gift Store
380 Sussex Dr.
Ottawa
Tel 613/990-1985
This world-class art gallery has a magnificent gift store where you can purchase wonderful Canadian souvenirs as well as art books and other collectibles.

William Ashley China
55 Bloor St.
Toronto
Tel 416/964-2900
Considered North America's largest shop devoted to tableware, this store stocks fine china, crystal, silver, and many other items.

MARKETS
Byward Market
Between George and York Sts. just E of Sussex Dr.
Ottawa
This colorful market with its fruit and flowers in season has existed since 1846. The main building houses craft stores, and it is surrounded by a myriad of restaurants.

Harbourfront Antique Market
390 Queen's Quay W.
Toronto
Tel 416/260-2626
Up to 200 dealers displaying their wares and inviting you to bargain.

Kensington Market
NW of Dundas St. and Spadina Ave.
Toronto
Open-air food market serving the city's newest immigrants from Asia and Africa.

Kitchener Market
Frederick and Duke Sts.
Kitchener
Tel 519/741-2287
Hundreds of farmers come each week to sell their produce and crafts.

St. Lawrence Market
Front and Jarvis Sts.
Toronto
Covered food hall with two levels of butchers, cheese shops, and bakeries. Market is set up

every Saturday in a building on the north side of Front Street.

PRAIRIES

AREAS TO SHOP
Osborne Village
Osborne St. near Corydon Ave.
S of the Assiniboine River
Winnipeg, Man.
Along five blocks of Osborne Street, you can shop for unique pieces by local artisans, jewelry, and clothing. Also offers cafés.

ARTS & ANTIQUES
Antique Exchange and Warehouse
370 Donald and 41 Princess St.
Winnipeg, Man.
Tel 204/943-1315
These two warehouses located kitty-corner from each other in the Exchange District offer antique furniture and other items on several floors.
Northern Images
216 Portage Place Mall
393 Portage Ave.
Winnipeg, Man.
Tel 204/942-5501
Inuit and Déné artists belonging to the North Territories Co-operative showcase their work.

CLOTHES & ACCESSORIES
Winnipeg Fur Exchange
250 McPhillips St.
Winnipeg, Man.
Tel 204/775-9653
Extensive selection of Western wear for men and women, as well as Amerindian handicrafts, and items in polar bear, black bear, timberwolf, musk ox, and sheepskin. Gear for extremely cold weather is their specialty.
Smithbilt Hats
1235 10th Ave. S.W.
Calgary, Alta.
Tel 403/244-9131
You can buy Western gear all over Calgary, but this is the place to purchase that white Stetson hat that everyone wears during the Stampede.
Alberta Boot Manufacturing
614 10th Ave. S.W.
Calgary, Alta.

Tel 403/263-4605
You've bought your hat, now for the cowboy boots. This company sells thousands of pairs every year, but they're not cheap—expect to pay up to $250.

CRAFTS & JEWELRY
Trading Post Ltd.
226 2nd Ave. S.
Saskatoon, Sask.
Tel 306/653-1769
Vast selection of aboriginal crafts and Saskatoonberry products.
Crafts Guild of Manitoba
183 Kennedy St.
Winnipeg, Man.
Tel 204/943-1190
Carvings, weavings, and jewelry by local artisans.

GIFTS & MISCELLANEOUS
Heartland Century Store
940 2nd Ave. N.W.
Calgary, Alta.
Tel 403/270-4542
Country store atmosphere, enhanced by smells from bakery.

MALLS & DEPARTMENT STORES
West Edmonton Mall
8770 170th St. at 87th Ave.
Edmonton, Alta.
Tel 403/444-5300
The world's biggest mall, with 800 stores, two amusement parks, a hotel, submarine, reproduction renaissance ship, casino, bingo parlor, and chapel.

MARKETS
Forks Market
Winnipeg, Alta.
Offers fresh produce including meat, fish, and bread, as well as taste sensations from all over the world reflecting the ethnic origins of Winnipeg's population.

THE ROCKIES

AREAS TO SHOP
Banff Avenue
Banff
The main street of this mountain community in the heart of Banff National Park is lined with tempting stores selling arts,

crafts, and souvenirs of every description for almost any pocket.

GIFTS & MISCELLANEOUS
Banff Book and Art Den
110 Banff Ave.
Banff
Tel 403/762-3919
Extensive collection of guidebooks, maps, and general information.
Banff Indian Trading Post
Cave Ave.
Banff
Large selection of Amerindian arts and crafts, jewelry, moccasins, and other clothing.

LEISURE
Mountain Magic
224 Bear St.
Banff
Tel 403/762-2591
Three floors of hiking, skiing, running, and biking equipment, as well as a 30-foot climbing wall to test some of it.

THE WEST

AREAS TO SHOP
Fan Tan Alley
Chinatown
Victoria
These former opium dens and gambling parlors house neat little stores selling bric-a-brac of every description.
Gastown
Water St.
Vancouver
In this attractive area of restored 19th-century buildings, there is a wide range of art galleries, craft stores, and other boutiques.
Government Street
N of Empress Hotel between Humboldt and Johnson
Victoria
Victoria's main shopping street (closed to traffic) is lined with stores selling English bone china, Scottish woollens, Irish linen, and no doubt something Welsh. These imports from the "Olde Country" are very good values.

Pender Street
Between Richards and Hamilton
Vancouver
Large concentration of second-hand book stores.
Robsonstrasse
Robson St. between Hornby and Thurlow Sts.
Vancouver
Vancouver's main shopping street with its trendy boutiques and sidewalk cafés is always lively. Its name comes from the original German occupants of the area.

ARTS & ANTIQUES
Antique Row
Fort St. between Blanshard and Cook
Victoria
This strip of Fort Street boasts over two dozen antique shops.
The Inuit Gallery of Vancouver
345 Water St.
Vancouver
Tel 604/688-7323
Coastal native art.

CLOTHES & ACCESSORIES
Hills Indian Crafts
Hwy. I
Duncan
Tel 250/746-6731
Large selection of Cowichan wool sweaters.
Dorothy Grant
757 W. Hastings St.
Vancouver
Tel 604/681-0201
Unique clothing incorporating traditional Haida designs.

CRAFTS & JEWELRY
Cowichan Trading Co. Ltd.
1328 Government St.
Victoria
Tel 250/383-0321
Jewelry, moccasins, and sweaters produced by the eponymous native tribe.

FOOD & DRINK
Roger's Chocolates
913 Government St.
Victoria
Tel 250/384-7021
Hand-crafted chocolates made without preservatives.

GIFTS & MISCELLANEOUS
Vancouver Aquarium Gift Store
Stanley Park
Vancouver
Tel 604/631-2529
The famous aquarium has a splendid gift store featuring items with a fishy flavor, local crafts, and Amerindian art.
Bollums Bookstore
650 W. Georgia St.
Vancouver
Tel 604/687-0083
This huge bookstore is open late every night and stocks nearly 100,000 titles, as well as newspapers from all over the world.

MALLS & DEPARTMENT STORES
Market Square
560 Johnson St.
Victoria
Tel 250/386-2441
Three levels of funky boutiques and specialty stores selling everything from comic books to incense.

MARKETS
Granville Island Public Market
1669 Johnson St.
Vancouver
Tel 604/666-6477
Unique boutiques and a dazzling selection of produce, including smoked salmon packaged for travel.
Lonsdale Quay Market
Seabus Terminus
North Vancouver
Food counters, coffee bars, and bookstores as well as fresh fruit and vegetables in season.

THE NORTH

GIFTS & MISCELLANEOUS
Mac's Firewood
203 Main St.
Whitehorse, Yukon
Tel 867/668-2434
Features books and maps about Alaska, the Yukon, and the Klondike Gold Rush.

Midnight Sun Gallery and Gifts
205C Main St.
Whitehorse, Yukon
Tel 867/668-4350
Specializes in Yukon-made products, local art, posters, pottery, jewelry, and other souvenirs.
Murdoch's Gem Shop
207 Main St.
Whitehorse, Yukon
Tel 867/668-7867
Fax 867/667-7403
Gold nuggets from the world's biggest manufacturer.
Nunavut
Almost every community in the Arctic has its own cooperative to sell local arts and crafts. For a complete list, contact:
Nunavut Tourism
P.O. Box 1450
Iqaluit, Nunavut X0A 0H0
Tel 800/491-7910
Tgit Geomatics Ltd.
Yellowknife, N.W.T.
Tel 867/873-8448
The place to buy maps of the north as well as aeronautical and hydrographic charts. Agents for the Geological Survey of Canada and the National Air Photo Library.
The Yellowknife Book Cellar
Yellowknife, N.W.T.
Tel 867/920-2220
Good selection of northern and native studies books as well as current titles in hardcover and paperback.
Wolverine Sports Shop
Centre Square Mall
Yellowknife, N.W.T.
Tel 867/873-4350
Specializes in mountain outdoor wear and camping, fishing, and hunting supplies. In downtown Yellowknife.

ENTERTAINMENT & ACTIVITIES

Canada is a vast and varied country with an amazing array of possibilities for entertainment. The variety of different activities across the country is staggering so only the major and most typical ones are mentioned here. Every city has its own cultural, sporting, and social life often reflecting the origins of its inhabitants. In addition, cultural centers and nightlife vary enormously from coast to coast.

MARITIMES

FESTIVALS
Scotia Festival of Music
Halifax, N.S.
Tel 902/429-9467
May and June
Master classes and concerts by internationally recognized classical musicians.
Nova Scotia International Tattoo
Metro Centre
Halifax, N.S.
Tel 902/420-1114
First week of July
Every day for a week, two-hour spectacles featuring over 2,000 Canadian and international, military and civilian performers with pipes, drums, military bands, singing, dancing, acrobatics, etc.
Antigonish Highland Games
Antigonish, N.S.
Tel 902/863-4275
Mid-July
Staged annually since 1861, these games highlight the best in Scottish music, dance, and sports. The saber toss is one of the more popular features.
Loyalist Days
St. John, N.B.
Tel 506/634-8123
July
The origins of this oh-so-Loyalist city are celebrated every year with a re-enactment of the arrival of the first settlers. Everyone dresses up in 18th-century garb for a large parade, street dances, and general merrymaking.
Natal Day
Halifax & Dartmouth, N.S.
First Monday in August
The Halifax and Dartmouth area celebrates the anniversary of its foundation in grand style with parades in both communities,

and lots of other activities capped by a massive concert on the slopes of Citadel Hill.
Gaelic Mod
South Gut St. Ann's
Cape Breton Island, N.S.
First full week of August
Seven-day festival of Celtic culture at the Nova Scotia Gaelic College of Arts and Culture—the only Gaelic College in North America. Bagpipe playing, Highland dancing, and other activities.
Festival Acadien
Caraquet, N.B.
August
Celebration of Acadian culture with lots of joie de vivre. Also the official Blessing of the Fishing Fleet.
Atlantic Film Festival
Halifax, N.S.
Tel 902/422-3456
Regional feature films, TV movies, and documentaries are screened at half-a-dozen venues over nine days in September; call for tickets, times, and places.

CULTURAL CENTERS
Confederation Centre for the Arts
145 Richmond St.
Charlottetown, P.E.I.
Tel 902/566-1267
The musical version of *Anne of Green Gables* plays here during the Charlottetown Festival, which runs from June through September. The building houses three theaters, a gift shop, art gallery, museum, public library, and restaurant.
Imperial Theatre
King Square
St. John, N.B.
Tel 506/674-4100
Beautifully restored vaudeville theater is the year-round venue for both local and touring

theater, opera, ballet, and symphony companies.
The Playhouse
686 Queen St.
Fredericton, N.B.
Tel 506/458-8344
Venue for Theatre New Brunswick and Symphony New Brunswick.
Neptune Theatre
1593 Argyle St.
Halifax, N.S.
Tel 902/429-7300
Year-round performances of drama classics and contemporary Canadian works.

NIGHTLIFE
Benevolent Irish Society Hall
582 North River Rd.
Charlottetown, P.E.I.
Tel 902/892-2367
Traditional Celtic ceilidhs, a combination of music, dancing, and comedy, take place here Friday nights from mid-May through October.
Dolan's Pub
Pipers Lane
Fredericton, N.B.
Tel 506/454-7474
Celtic bands play Thursday, Friday, and Saturday nights.
The Lunar Rogue
625 King St.
Fredericton, N.B.
Tel 506/450-2065
Old-fashioned pub with acoustic folk, rock, and Celtic music on Fridays and Saturdays.
Club Cosmopolitan
700 Main St.
Moncton, N.B.
Tel 506/857-9117
Open Wed.–Sun.
A mature crowd gathers from 3 p.m. to 8 p.m. on Fridays and Saturdays for live jazz and blues; at other times rock and dance music draws a twentysomething crowd.
O'Leary's Pub
46 Princess St.
St. John, N.B.
Tel 506/634-7135
Wednesday is audience participation night at this folksy Maritime pub; bands play Thursday through Sunday evenings.

OTHER ACTIVITIES
Reversing Falls Jet Boat Ride
55 Fallsview Dr.
St. John, N.B.
Tel 506/634-8987
A close-up view of this natural phenomenon, which takes place twice daily, from late May through September.
Small Craft Aquatic Center
Behind Victoria Health Centre off Brunswick St.
Fredericton, N.B.
Tel 506/462-6021
Late May–Labor Day
Rent canoes and kayaks here to explore the Saint John River on your own or with a guide.
Tea with the Mayor
Halifax City Hall, Grand Parade
Halifax, N.S.
July–Aug., Mon.–Thurs.,
3:30–4:30 p.m.
All visitors are invited to join the Mayor for tea, lemonade, and cookies in the gracious Victorian reception room of City Hall.
Whale-Watching Cruises
Cape Breton Island, N.S.
Tel 902/285-2714 (Ingonish Harbour), 902/224-1088 (Chéticamp)
Explore the rugged coast of Cape Breton and search for pilot, minke, fin, and humpback whales as well as seals, bald eagles, cormorants, and other sea birds.
St. Andrews, N.B.
Tel 506/529-3000
Several companies offer whale-watching trips into the wild waters of the Bay of Fundy where whales go up and down with the 50-foot tides.
Lobster Suppers
St. Ann's Church, P.E.I.
Tel 902/621-0635
Mon.–Sat. 4–9 p.m.
There are many places in P.E.I. to enjoy this tradition, which began as an activity to raise money for the church. Today, the lobster supper in the church hall at St. Ann is one of the few which remains a charitable affair. Home-cooked food: salads, rolls, seafood, desserts, and, of course, lobster.

NEWFOUNDLAND

FESTIVALS
Newfoundland and Labrador Folk Festival
St. John's
Tel 709/576-8508
Second weekend in August
Three days of traditional music at Bannerman Park draws 30,000 listeners.

CULTURAL CENTERS
Resource Centre for the Arts
LSPU Hall
3 Victoria St.
St. John's
Tel 709/753-4531
Open year-round, experimental theater in the fall and winter, cabarets and outdoor concerts in the summer.

NIGHTLIFE
Trapper John's
George St.
St. John's
Tel 709/579-9630
Good place to undergo that famous (or infamous) Newfoundland activity, the "screech-in."

OTHER ACTIVITIES
Signal Hill Tattoo
St. John's
Tel 709/772-5367
July and August
Military exercises of the 19th century performed high above the city on Signal Hill. A great pageant on a fine day, cancelled in bad weather. Call for exact days and times.
Birds, Whales, and Icebergs
These boat trips offer magnificent experiences, but rough seas and wild weather can lead to cancellations on few hours' notice.
St. John's
Tel 709/726-5000
May–October
Watch icebergs and whales from a two-masted schooner.
Trinity
Tel 709/464-3738
May–September
Whales up close in summer

months, seals and sea birds, too.
Twillingate
Tel 709/884-2242
May–September
Exciting trips to see icebergs, whales, birds, dolphins, and seals.
Witless Bay
Tel 709/334-2002
May–October
The largest puffin colony in North America is located just off this community 20 miles south of St. John's. Murres, whales, and icebergs also abound.

QUEBEC

FESTIVALS
Carnaval d'Hiver (Winter Carnival)
Quebec City
Tel 418/626-3716
February
A great winter celebration for the whole family—art, culture, sports, and entertainment, presided over by a huge snowball called Bonhomme Carnival.
International Pyrotechnical Competition
La Ronde, Île Notre-Dame
Montreal
Tel 514/872-4537
June and July
Amazing firework displays in a popular competition with about 10 competing countries. The shows take place at La Ronde amusement park, but it is possible to view them for free along the waterfront. Extremely popular, so streets and bridges are closed to vehicles.
International Jazz Festival
Montreal
Tel 514/871-1881
or 888/515-0515
July
One of the continent's great jazz festivals with many free shows on outdoor stages, in addition to the big-name ticketed events.
Juste pour Rire (Just for Laughs)
Montreal
Tel 514/845-3155
July
One of the world's few comedy

festivals, with 600 artists from 14 countries in over 1,000 shows.

Festival d'été international (Summer Festival)
Quebec City
Tel 418/692-5200
July
The largest Francophone cultural event in North America. Activities take over the streets and squares of the Old City.

Montreal World Film Festival
Montreal
Tel 514/848-3883
August
Competitive festival and great popular event drawing 350,000 viewers.

Fêtes gourmandes internationales
Montreal
Tel 514/861-8241
August
Held on Île Nôtre-Dame, this is a huge gourmet feast with food from five continents for sale.

Festival de Montgolfières (Hot Air Balloon Festival)
Saint-Jean-sur-Richelieu
Tel 450/346-6000
August
More than 100 brightly colored balloons, some with unusual shapes, fly every evening.

Les Mediévales du Québec
Quebec City
Tel 418/692-1993
August, odd-numbered years
Quebec turns the clocks back five centuries for a few days. Medieval celebrations include a Grand Cavalcade with costumed horseback riders, jousting tournaments with knights in armor watched by ladies in wimples, and troubadours singing and playing medieval ditties.

CULTURAL CENTERS
Place des Arts
Corner rue Ste.-Catherine Ouest and Jeanne Mance
Montreal
Tel 541/285-4200 (information)
514/842-2112 (box office)
Montreal's showcase for the performing arts comprises five multifaceted halls including the prestigious Salle Wilfrid Pelletier

concert hall with nearly 3,000 seats. Home to the symphony orchestra, the Opéra de Montréal, the city's principal ballet company, Les Grands Ballets Canadiens, and several theater companies. There is also an informal Sunday brunch series.

Saidye Bronfman Centre
5170 chemin de la Côte Ste.-Catherine
Montreal
Tel 514/739-2301
or 514/739-7944
English- and Yiddish-language dramas are staged here, along with many free lectures and concerts.

Grand Théâtre de Quebec
269 blvd. René Lévesque Ouest
Quebec City
Tel 418/643-8131
Plays (in French), dance, and symphony performances are staged September through April.

Palais Montcalm
995 Place d'Youville
Quebec City
Tel 418/670-9011
Municipal theater just outside the St. Jean gate presents a broad range of productions. In summer, there are open-air concerts.

Théâtre Lac Brome
267 rue Knowlton
Knowlton
Tel 450/242-2270
Broadway and West End hits come to life in English-language productions running during summer months.

The Piggery
Rte. 108
North Hatley
Tel 819/842-2431
A converted pig barn offering new Canadian plays and bilingual productions from June through August.

NIGHTLIFE
Le Cheval Blanc
809 rue Ontario Est
Montreal
Tel 514/522-0211
Traditional pub with beer brewed on the premises. Cultural chat at the communal tables sometimes drowns out

the music.

Les Foues
87 rue Ste.-Catherine Est
Montreal
Tel 514/844-5539
Les Foues considers itself Montreal's cultural and musical mosaic. Eccentric interior decor attracts a diverse range of customers to this bar and music venue.

Angels
3604 blvd. St.-Laurent
Montreal
Tel 514/282-9944
Nightly 8 p.m.–3 a.m.
The two floors of this popular nightspot cater to large-screen sports fans as well as high-energy clubbers.

Aux Deux Pierrots
104 rue St.-Paul Ouest
at rue St.-Sulpice
Montreal
Tel 514/861-1270
Traditional Québecois folk music (outdoor terrace performances in summer). Crowded but convivial.

Café Campus
57 rue Prince-Arthur Est
Montreal
Tel 514/844-1010
Alternative music from live bands and DJ's in this small venue. Popular with many young Montrealers.

L'Air du Temps
191 rue St.-Paul Ouest
Montreal
Tel 514/842-2003
Old city jazz club showcasing local talent.

Biddles
2060 rue Aylmer
Montreal
Tel 514/842-8656
Montreal's premier jazz club known for its nightly live music and excellent barbecued ribs.

Hurley's Irish Pub
1225 rue Crescent
Montreal
Tel 514/861-4111
Celtic music and dancing every night of the week, Guinness for sale, too.

L'Emprise at Hôtel Clarendon
57 rue Ste.-Anne
Quebec City

Tel 418/692-2480
Art deco jazz bar with live performances Thursday, Friday, and Saturday nights.
Casino de Montreal
1 ave. du Casino
Montreal
Tel 514/392-2746
or 800/665-2274
One of the 10 largest casinos in the world, with a strict dress code.

OTHER ACTIVITIES
Glissades de la Terrasse (Dufferin Terrace Slides)
Quebec City
Mid-December–mid-March
In a toboggan, slide down the ice onto the wide terrace beside the Château Frontenac. Also skating.
Mont-Sainte-Anne Ski Centre
25 miles E of Quebec
Tel 418/827-4561
54 slopes, a vertical drop of over 2,000 feet, and stunning views of the St. Lawrence and the capital. Also snowboarding, cross-country skiing, and snowshoeing.
Owl's Head Ski Area
Rte. 243 S.
Magog
Tel 450/292-3342
or 800/363-3342
December–mid-April
Quiet slopes with 27 trails and the area's longest runs.
Mont-Tremblant Ski Hill
Mont-Tremblant
Tel 819/681-2000
or 800/461-8711
Late November–mid-April
More than 70 downhill ski trails and 56 miles of cross-country trails at this resort, a two-hour drive northwest of Montreal.
Ice Hockey at Molson Centre
1260 rue de la Gauchetière Ouest
Montreal
Tel 514/932-2582
Canada's unofficial national sport fires the passions of most Canadians, but in Montreal hockey is not a sport—it's a religion. The Montreal Canadiens, known as Les Habs (short for les Habitants), have won the

National Hockey League's Stanley Cup a record 24 times, twice as many times as any other team.
Canadian Grand Prix
Circuit Gilles Villeneuve
Île Notre-Dame
Montreal
Tel 514/871-1421
Every year, the Canadian Grand Prix is run in Montreal. For a week in June, the pace reaches fever pitch as Formula One racing takes over the city. Reserve accommodations far in advance.
Harness Racing
Hippodrome Blue Bonnets
7440 blvd. Décarie
Montreal
Tel 514/739-2741
Two-wheel trotting races are held at this hippodrome in northern Montreal.
Cirque du Soleil
Montreal
Tel 514/522-2324
Montreal's circus has achieved international fame with its blend of daredevil acts and state-of-the-art presentation. No animals are used. Trapeze artists, acrobats, jugglers, clowns, and contortionists perform innovative acts to the accompaniment of stunning light shows and original music. It can only be seen in Montreal every two years.
Saute Moutons Jet-boating (Lachine Rapids Tours)
Old Port, Quai de l'Horloge
Montreal
Tel 514/284-9607
Shoot the Lachine Rapids aboard open hydrofoil-type boats. Wild, wet, and wonderful. Reservations required. No children under 6.
Jacques Cartier Excursions
978 ave. Jacques Cartier Nord
Tewkesbury
Tel 418/848-7238
Half-day rafting trips on the Jacques Cartier River leaving from Tewkesbury, about 30 minutes northwest of Quebec City.
Whitewater Rafting
Calumet, Rivière Rouge
Tel 819/242-7238
or 800/361-5033

Thrilling expeditions down this wild river and through its swirling rapids. Not for the faint of heart.
Lachine Rapids Tours Ltd.
105 rue de la Commune
Clock Tower Pier
Montreal
Tel 514/284-9607
White-water rafting on nearby Class V rapids.
Whale-Watching Cruises
Tadoussac and other places on the North Shore of the St. Lawrence
Tel 800/463-5250
The junction of the St. Lawrence and Saguenay Rivers is a rich summer feeding place for whales. Small craft sail far out into this deep water to offer close-up views of these huge sea mammals that could easily overturn your boat (or so it seems).
Hull/Chelsea/Wakefield Steam Train
Hull
Tel 800/871-7246
Summer months
Reservations are essential for excursions aboard one of the last steam trains in operation in Canada.
Snow Geese Migration
Cap-Tourmente
October
During their annual migration south, thousands of snow geese stop in the bulrushes beside the St. Lawrence below Cap-Tourmente. It's amazing to see these huge birds rise off the water like a cloud.

ONTARIO

FESTIVALS
Tulip Festival
Ottawa
Mid-May
Since the Dutch Royal family took refuge in Ottawa during World War II, the city has received annual gifts of tulips from Dutch bulb growers. The result is millions of tulips of every shape and color decorating the city, especially the

Rideau Canal and the area around Dow's Lake.

Winterlude
Ottawa
Tel 613/239-5000
Mid-February
In winter, 6 miles of the Rideau Canal are cleared to make a wonderful long skating rink with great views and numerous events.

Metro International Caravan
Toronto
June
Tel 416/977-0466
Nearly one hundred ethnic groups offer dance demonstrations, craft shows, regional cuisine, and other manifestations of their cultures.

Caribana
Toronto
July
Tel 416/465-4884
The city takes on the appearance of a Caribbean Island for two weeks with traditional foods and activities of the Caribbean and Latin America.

International Freedom Festival
Windsor (and Detroit)
July
Together, these twin cities in Canada and the U.S. celebrate July 1st (Canada Day) and July 4th (Independence Day). Activities take place on both sides of the river and culminate in a fireworks display.

Wikwemikong Powwow
Manitoulin Island
August
A major powwow is held on this island in Lake Huron where about 2,500 Ojibwa live as well as people of Odawa and Potawotami descent.

Canadian National Exhibition
CNE Grounds
Toronto
August
Tel 416/393-6000
An enormous extravaganza with display pavilions, grandstand performances, and an air show.

Toronto International Film Festival
Tel 416/967-7371

Ten days of top-notch cinema in September.

Oktoberfest
Kitchener-Waterloo
Tel 519/570-4267
October
The distinctly Germanic origin of these twin cities is celebrated in their Bavarian festivities with a grand pageant and parade, lederhosen, schnitzel, sauerkraut, strudel, and, of course, beer.

CULTURAL CENTERS
National Arts Centre
Ottawa
This cultural complex on the banks of the Rideau Canal offers a wide range of concerts, plays, musicals, and other activities.

Shaw Festival
Niagara-on-the-Lake
Tel 905/468-2172
or 800/511-7429
April–mid-October
Almost a dozen plays by G.B. Shaw and contemporaries mounted in three theaters.

Stratford Festival
55 Queen St.
Stratford
Tel 519/273-1600
or 800/567-1600
Early May–late October
The works of the Bard, along with contemporary dramas and musicals, play to packed houses.

Hummingbird Centre for the Performing Arts
1 Front St. E.
Toronto
Tel 416/872-2262
Home to the Canadian Opera Company, which also performs free outdoor summer concerts at Harbourfront.

Roy Thomson Hall
60 Simcoe St.
Toronto
Tel 416/872-4255
This is home to the Toronto Symphony Orchestra and the Toronto Mendelssohn Choir. Modern design and outstanding acoustics make it the city's preeminent concert hall.

Premiere Dance Theatre
Queen's Quay
Toronto
Tel 416/973-4000
Many major dance companies

perform at this venue including the Toronto Dance Theatre, a leading contemporary dance company.

Theater in Toronto
Toronto has a very active theater scene and is considered by many to be the world's third great center of English-language production (after London and New York).

Royal Alexandra Theatre
260 King St. W.
Toronto
Tel 416/872-1212
Broadway shows in an amazing 1906-7 beaux arts building, which is worth seeing in its own right.

Princess of Wales Theatre
300 King St. W.
Toronto
Tel 416/872-1212
A spectacular state-of-the-art theater opened by the late Princess. Popular for large productions such as *Miss Saigon*.

Pantages Theatre
244 Victoria St.
Toronto
Tel 416/872-2222
Magnificent theater hosting Broadway shows such as *The Phantom of the Opera*.

Buddies in Bad Times
12 Alexander St.
Toronto
Tel 416/975-8555
Not only is this the premier gay theater company in Canada, but it has also nurtured many contemporary straight writers. It is always cutting edge, delivering productions that challenge social boundaries. Also home to Tallulah's Cabaret, which is very popular on Friday and Saturday nights.

Young People's Theatre
165 Front St.
Toronto
Tel 416/862-2222
Productions from October through May offering adaptations of Dickens, C.S. Lewis, and other popular children's authors.

NIGHTLIFE
Top O' The Senator
249 Victoria St.
Toronto

Tel 416/364-7517
Intimate jazz club on the third
floor of the Senator restaurant.
Supper packages available.
Chick 'N' Deli
744 Mount Pleasant Rd.
Toronto
Tel 416/489-3363
Busy and youthful club serving
up contemporary pop for the
energetic dancer and barbecue
dishes for the hungry.
Industry
901 King St. W.
Toronto
Tel 416/260-2660
Exciting strobe-ridden hot spot
catering to Toronto's nocturnal
inhabitants. The fun doesn't really
begin until 2 a.m. and goes on
until dawn.
Bar Italia
582 College St.
Toronto
Tel 416/535-3621
Young and trendy spot in Little
Italy. Italian specialties plus a
smart pool area upstairs.
Wayne Gretzky's
99 Blue Jays Way
Toronto
Tel 416/979-7825
A shrine to the Canadians'
premier ice hockey player. Not
necessarily the best place to eat,
but great views from the rooftop
patio.
Yukyuk's
2335 Yonge St.
Toronto
Tel 416/967-6425
Inspired by the comedy theaters
of New York and Los Angeles,
this venue was begun in the
1960s and has subsequently
nurtured Canadian comedy stars
like Jim Carrey.
Second City
110 Lombard St.
Toronto
Tel 416/863-1111
Canadian comics like John Candy
and Bill Murray performed at
this venue before achieving fame
south of the border.
Horseshoe Tavern
370 Queen St.
Toronto
Tel 416/598-4753
A magnet for rock fans from
Thursday through Saturday.

Previous performances by The
Police and The Band have
enhanced this venue's reputation. Country music Monday
through Wednesday.
El Mocambo
464 Spading Ave.
Toronto
Tel 416/968-2001
Grungy rock spot whose stage
was once graced by The Rolling
Stones. Showcases local talent
on Monday evenings.

OTHER ACTIVITIES
Maple Leafs Ice Hockey
Toronto
Tel 416/977-1641
Witness Canadians succumbing
to unbridled passion as they
support their local hockey team.
Tickets are expensive and
difficult to obtain.
Glen Abbey
1333 Dorval Dr.
Oakville
Toronto
Tel 905/844-1800
Top-notch, 18-hole golf course
about 45 minutes from Toronto.
The Canadian Open Champion-
ship is played here.
Premier Tour and Reception
St. Catherine's
Tel 905/641-3097
or 888/881-5558
Tours of the region's wineries.
Baseball at the Sky Dome
1 Blue Jays Way
Toronto
Tel 416/341-2770 (information)
or 416/341-1234 (tickets)
The Toronto Blue Jays attract 4
million fans every season. Their
stadium with its retractable roof
is so revolutionary in design that
people tour it in its own right.
Changing of the Guard
Parliament Hill
Ottawa
July–August, 10 a.m. daily
A colorful and popular cere-
mony held on the lawns in front
of the Canadian Parliament, with
over a hundred soldiers parading
in busbies and scarlet tunics.
Agawa Canyon Train Tours
Sault Ste. Marie
Tel 800/242-9287
June–October
Scenic day trips into the rugged

wilderness north of Lake
Superior. Summer stop-over in
Agawa Canyon or the awesome
beauty of the fall colors. Reservations essential.
Polar Bear Express
Cochrane, Northern Ontario
Tel 705/472-4500
or 416/314-3750 (Toronto)
Mid-June–mid-September
All-day train trip to the Arctic
watershed, Moosonee, on the
shores of James Bay. Frontier life,
muskeg, and scrub bush. A
naturalist's delight. Reservations
essential.
Playdium
99 Rathburn Rd.
Mississauga
Tel 416/273-9000
Interactive games, simulators,
rock-climbing walls, go-carts, and
an IMAX theater make this a
paradise for kids.
Casino Niagara
5705 Falls Ave.
Niagara
Tel 888/946-3255
or 905/374-3598
All the usual gambling
distractions, plus entertaining
variations on poker.

PRAIRIES

FESTIVALS
**Calgary Exhibition and
Stampede**
Calgary, Alta.
Tel 800/661-1678
July
One of the biggest cowboy
events of them all and it's fun. A
wonderful spirit overtakes the
city and wearing Western gear
becomes de rigueur. Even oil
company executives, who've
never been near a horse in their
lives, don white Stetsons and
cowboy boots. Offering a huge
parade, chuckwagon races,
rodeo events such as riding
bucking broncos, roping calves,
and wrestling steers, a stock
show, and much more. The city
is packed. Hotel reservations
must be made months in
advance.

Folklorama
Winnipeg, Man.
Tel 204/982-6210
Multicultural pavilions through-
out the city offer entertainment,
exotic foods, and cultural
displays.
**Shakespeare on the
Saskatchewan**
Saskatoon, Sask.
Tel 306/653-2300
July and August
Award-winning theater with
innovative interpretations of the
classics held in two brightly
colored festival tents on the
riverbank.
Klondike Days
Edmonton, Alta.
July
For ten days, Edmonton re-
creates the era of the 1890s
with a King of the Klondike
parade, sourdough raft races,
and other gold rush activities.
The Trial of Louis Riel
Mackenzie Art Gallery
Regina, Sask.
Tel 306/525-1185
August
This play is an historically
accurate account of the trial of
this figure who still raises
controversy a hundred years
after his death.

CULTURAL CENTERS
Globe Theatre
1801 Scarth St.
Regina, Sask.
Tel 306/525-9553
Local dramatic works performed
on a round stage inside the old
Regina City Hall.
**Twenty Fifth Street Theatre
Centre**
616 10th St.
Saskatoon, Sask.
Tel 306/664-2239
Mounts works by Sasketchewan
playwrights, and hosts a summer
Fringe Festival.
MTC Warehouse Theatre
140 Rupert Ave.
Winnipeg, Man.
Tel 204/942-6537
Experimental theater produc-
tions from the Manitoba Theatre
Centre.
Citadel Theatre
9828 101A Ave.

Edmonton, Alta.
Tel 780/426-4811
or 780/425-1820 (box office)
One of the largest and busiest
theater complexes in Canada
today. There are five auditoriums
adapted to different types of
productions and audiences, as
well as workshops and
classrooms.
**Calgary Centre for
Performing Arts**
205 8th Ave. SE
Calgary, Alta.
Tel 403/294-7455
Home to the Calgary Philhar-
monic Orchestra and Theatre
Calgary.
Rainbow Stage
2021 Main St. (in Kildonan Park)
Winnipeg, Man.
Tel 204/784-1281
July and August
Outdoor summer theater on
the banks of the Red River
under the stars.

NIGHTLIFE
Rose & Crown
Sheraton Grande
10235 101st St.
Edmonton, Alta.
Tel 780/428-7111
English-style pub with darts and
an extensive selection of beers.
The Bassment
245 3rd Ave.
Saskatoon, Sask.
Tel 306/668-2277
Home to the Saskatchewan Jazz
Society with year-round
performances.
Crazy Horse
1315 1st St. S.W.
Calgary, Alta.
Tel 403/266-3339
Stampede all year long. This
immensely popular club is open
Thursday through Saturday.
Casino Regina
1880 Saskatchewan Dr.
Regina, Sask.
Tel 800/555-3189
or 306/565-3000
Newly renovated train station
with slot machines and table
games.

OTHER ACTIVITIES
Canadian Olympic Plaza
88 Canada Olympic Rd. SW
Calgary, Alta.
Tel 403/291-5208
Site of several venues for XV
Olympic Winter Games. Open
for tours, bobsleigh bullet, and
luge rides.
Nakiska
Kananaskis Village, Alta.
Just west of Calgary, Nakiska
was the location for the
downhill ski events during the
Calgary Winter Olympic Games
of 1988.
**RCMP Sergeant Major's
Parade**
RCMP Training Academy
Regina, Sask.
Tel 306/780-5900
Drill parade demonstration daily,
all year, weather permitting. Also,
Sunset Retreat Ceremonies,
centered around the lowering of
the flag (Tuesdays in July and
August).
Prairie Dog Central
Winnipeg, Man.
Tel 204/832-5259
Weekends June–Sept.
Two-hour excursions north of
Winnipeg in a 1900 steam train
offer vistas of prairie landscape
as it was when the first settlers
arrived.

ROCKIES

CULTURAL CENTERS
Banff Centre
St. Julien Rd.
Banff, Alta.
Tel 403/762-6281
Music, theater, and dance
performances year-round,
culminating in the three-month
Banff Festival of the Arts each
summer. The Walter Philips
Gallery displays contemporary
works by Canadian and
international artists.

NIGHTLIFE
Barbary Coast
119 Banff Ave.
Banff, Alta.
Tel 403/762-4616
No cover charge for live jazz

and blues Thursday through Saturday nights in this eatery.
Athabasca Hotel
510 Patricia St.
Jasper
Tel 403/852-3386
Dancing to Top 40 music and live bands.

OTHER ACTIVITIES
Numerous outfitters provide help for visitors looking to enjoy the natural parks of the Rockies. Several are listed below. Many provide more than one service so ask about other areas of interest.
Biking
Trailmasters Mountain Bike Guides
Canmore, Alta.
Tel 403/678-0384
Cycling the Rockies
Lake Louise, Alta.
Tel 403/522-2211
Fishing
Monod Sports
Banff, Alta.
Tel 403/762-4571
Maline Tours
Jasper, Alta.
Tel 780/852-5650
Helihiking
Canadian Mountain Holidays
Banff, Alta.
Tel. 403/762-7100
Alpine Helicopters
Canmore, Alta.
Tel 403/678-4802
Horseback Riding
Warner Guiding and Outfitting
Banff, Alta.
Tel 403/762-4551
Brewster Lake Louise Stables
Lake Louise, Alta.
Tel 403/762-5454
Emerald Lake Lodge
Yoho National Park, B.C.
Tel 250/343-6321
Rail Trips through the Rockies
From Vancouver, Jasper, or Calgary
Tel 800-665-7245
The *Rocky Mountaineer* makes two-day excursions through Banff National Park or Jasper National Park. From the comfort of the train, you can experience the grandeur of these mountains. Both trips either

start or finish in Vancouver and overnight in Kamloops.
River Adventures
White Water Rafting
Jasper, Alta.
Tel 780/852-7238
Jasper Raft Tours
Jasper, Alta.
Tel 780/852-2665
Ski Centers
Ski Banff/Lake Louise
Tel 403/762-4561; Marmot Basin
Tel 403/852-3816
Mount Norquay and Sunshine Village near Banff, the Lake Louise Ski Centre, and Marmot Basin at Jasper offer wonderful downhill skiing.

For additional recommendations contact the individual national parks:
Banff (Tel 403/762-1550)
Jasper (Tel 780/852-3858)
Yoho (Tel 250/343-6324)
Kootenay (Tel 250/347-9505)

THE WEST

FESTIVALS
Polar Bear Swim
English Bay
Vancouver
Tel 604/605-2304
New Year's Day
Thousands of hardy Vancouverites rush into the icy cold waters of English Bay to celebrate the new year. Visitors can join them or just watch.
Flower Count Week
Victoria
Tel 250/384-3211
February
To emphasize the mildness of its winter when most of the rest of Canada is deep under snow, the British Columbia capital organizes a count of the thousands of flowers that bloom in February.
Nanaimo to Vancouver Bathtub Race
Finishes at Kits Beach
Vancouver
Tel 250/753-7223
July
This famous race is part of Vancouver's Seafest Festival

every year. Participants really do use bathtubs, but they are powered by outboard motors today rather than muscles as in the past. There are also barbecues, concerts, fireworks, and a parade.
Squamish Days Logger Sports Festival
Squamish
Tel 604/892-9244
Late July–early August
Demonstrations of all aspects of logging and the lumberjack's life.
International Air Show
Abbotsford, Fraser Valley
Tel 604/852-8511
August
One of Canada's major air shows.
Pacific National Exhibition
PNE Grounds
Vancouver
Tel 604/253-2311
August
One of the great agricultural and industrial shows of the Pacific Northwest. Livestock shows and all kinds of other entertainment. The lumberjack competitions are a highlight.
Christmas Carol Ship Parade
English Bay
Vancouver
Tel 604/878-9988
December
Onboard ship, young carollers parade around the harbor as they sing, followed by dozens of other craft covered with lights.

CULTURAL CENTERS
Ford Centre for Performing Arts
777 Homer St.
Vancouver
Tel 604/844-2808
Newly built facility for traveling Broadway shows.
Orpheum Theatre
801 Granville St.
Vancouver
Tel 604/665-3035
Many musical events are held in this gracious and elegant venue, built as a vaudeville hall in 1927 and now the official home of the Vancouver Symphony.
Waterfront Theatre
Granville Island

ENTERTAINMENT & ACTIVITIES

Vancouver
Tel 604/685-6217
Local theater with performances varying from Shakespeare to popular drama and works by local playwrights.
Theatre under the Stars
Stanley Park
Vancouver
Tel 604/687-0174
Popular plays and musicals at the Malkin Bowl bandstand in Stanley Park from June through August, weather permitting. Especially good with a picnic under a full moon.
Bard on the Beach
Vanier Park
Vancouver
Tel 604/737-0625
Summer months
Shakespeare on the sands to the sounds of the ocean with mountains as a backdrop.
University Centre Auditorium
Finnerty Rd.
Tel 250/721-8480
Year-round classical music concerts.
McPherson Playhouse
3 Centennial Square
Victoria
Tel 250/386-6121
Baroque Edwardian concert hall restored in 1962, home to the Victoria Symphony Orchestra, the Pacific Opera Victoria, and many other musical and theatrical groups.
Royal Theatre
805 Broughton St. at Blanshard
Victoria
Tel 250/383-9711
or 250/386-6121 (box office)
A variety of theatrical presentations including summer "Pops" concerts by the Victoria Symphony Orchestra.
BC Place Stadium
Vancouver
Major Canadian and international music groups entertain in this huge stadium, which seats 60,000 people.

NIGHTLIFE
Hotel Vancouver
900 W. Georgia St.
Vancouver
Tel 604/684-3131

Live jazz trio in the lounge Thursday, Friday, and Saturday.
Rattlesnake Grill
2340 W. 4th St.
Vancouver
Tel 604/733-2911
Jazz and blues every night, along with dining on such delicacies as smoked rattlesnake in a comfortable southwestern adobe setting. Reservations recommended.
The Yale
1300 Granville St.
Vancouver
Tel 604/681-9253
Funky rhythm and blues any evening. Sunday blues jam: bring your instrument and join in.
Graceland
1250 Richards
Vancouver
Tel 604/688-2648
A warehouse-style dance club. The great sound and light system, big dance floor, pool tables, video games, music—sometimes live, sometimes canned—and cordial staff attract many enthusiastic patrons.

OTHER ACTIVITIES
Skiing at Whistler
75 miles N of Vancouver
Whistler Visitor Info Centre
Tel 604/932-5528
World-famous, the Whistler-Blackcomb complex is the largest and most popular ski resort in North America. Mile-high vertical drops, hundreds of marked runs, opportunities for snowboarding and helicopter skiing, glacier skiing in the summer months, and a full range of other activities attract crowds of people.
The Royal Hudson
From North Vancouver
Tel 604/984-5246
June–mid-Sept.
Spectacular whole-day trips by steam train along the shores of Howe Sound and into the Coast Mountains to Squamish. Return can be made by boat.
Bayshore Bicycles
745 Denman St.
Vancouver
Tel 604/688-2453
Bicycle rentals for Stanley Park.

Pacific Spirit Park
4915 W. 16th Ave. on campus of University of British Columbia
Vancouver
Tel 604/224-5739
Almost 40 miles of hiking trails located only 15 minutes from downtown.
Whale-Watching Cruises
Great Pacific Adventures
Victoria
Tel 250/386-2277
Whale-watching tours all year round.
For a list of companies in Tofino and other places on Vancouver Island
Tel 250/953-2033
March–October
It is a magnificent experience to take one of these cruises to see gray whales, porpoises, orcas, seals, sea lions, and sea birds.
Hiking the West Coast Trail
Pacific Rim National Park
Vancouver Island
Tel 800/663-6000 (Discover BC) for info and reservations.
Considered an adventure of a lifetime by hikers and backpackers and one of the world's most challenging treks. It can take 10 days to complete the entire 45 miles of this rugged trail.
Swan Lake Christmas Hill Nature Sanctuary
3873 Swan Lake Rd.
Victoria
Tel 250/479-0211
Nature walks and bird watching just minutes from downtown.

THE NORTH

FESTIVALS
Only major festivals are listed below but every small Inuit or Dene community in the North has celebrations or festivities of its own, generally in the summer. For details, contact the tourism departments of Yukon, the Northwest Territories, and Nunavut (addresses on page 341).
Yukon Quest Sled Dog Race
Whitehorse, Yukon
Tel 867/668-4711
February

International 1,000-mile race between the Yukon capital and Fairbanks, Alaska. Considered the toughest dogteam race in the world.

Arctic Winter Games
Yellowknife, N.W.T.
Tel 867/669-2850
March
International sporting competition and cultural gala. Harpoon throwing, dog mushing, ice fishing, drum dancing, etc. Wear your long johns!

Discovery Days Festival
Dawson, Yukon
Tel 867/993-1996
Mid-August
The anniversary of the first great gold find, which sparked the Klondike Gold Rush, is celebrated in style with a jamboree.

Midnight Sun Golf Tournament
Yellowknife, N.W.T.
Tel 867/873-4326
Summer solstice
Famous golf tournament with teeing off at midnight. The greens are artificial grass and the fairways are sand, but this is a tournament much enjoyed by everyone—including Yellowknife's huge black ravens, which have an unfortunate habit of making off with the golf balls.

Yukon Gold Panning Championships
Dawson, Yukon
Tel 867/993-5575
July 1st
In this annual event, prospectors, amateur and professional, compete against each other to see who can find gold first. There are timed trials and then finals. And yes, there still is gold to be found in the Yukon.

Great Canadian Yukon River Rubber Duck Race
Whitehorse, Yukon
July 1st
There is something about living in the North that sometimes makes people slightly silly. As poet Robert Service wrote: "you wouldn't believe the things done by the Midnight Sun...." Yes, they really do race rubber ducks on this wild and turbulent river.

NIGHTLIFE
Diamond Tooth Gertie's Gambling Hall
4th Ave. and Queen St.
Dawson, Yukon
Tel 867/993-5575 (Klondike Visitors' Association)
Glimpse of the Gold Rush with cancan dancers and gambling. No minors allowed.

Gaslight Follies
Palace Grand Theatre
Dawson, Yukon
Tel 867/993-5575
Two-hour musical comedy reflecting the lavish and exciting times of the Klondike Gold Rush era. Summer months only.

Frantic Follies Vaudeville Revue
Westmark Whitehorse Hotel
Whitehorse, Yukon
Tel 867/668-2042
Zany and popular show recreating the halcyon days of the Gold Rush.

OTHER ACTIVITIES
The Canadian North is a paradise for adventurous people seeking the ultimate outdoors experience. Possibilities are endless for white-water canoe trips, fishing remote lakes, hiking the wilderness, seeing wildlife up close, etc. Outdoor service providers are abundant in the North. Some outfitters that might assist you with planning and transportation are:
National Tours of Yukon
Watson Lake, Yukon
Tel 867/667-2028
    Provides assistance with
    backpacking, canoeing, and
    dogsledding.
Wild Woods Expedition
Whitehorse, Yukon
Tel 867/668-6909
    Completely supported
    winter and summer trips by
    canoe and dogsled.
Oldsquaw Lodge
Whitehorse, Yukon
Tel 867/668-6732
    Naturalist-led outdoor
    activities from a base lodge
    located on the Canol
    Heritage Trail.
Great Canadian Ecoventures
Fort Smith, N.W.T.

Tel 867/920-7110
    Guides lead trips focused on
    the native habitat and the
    creatures that inhabit it.

Arctic Tour Company
Tuktoyaktuk, N.W.T.
Tel 867/977-2230
    Specializes in activities on
    Banks and Herschel Islands.
Enodah Wilderness Travel
Yellowknife, N.W.T.
Tel 867/873-4334
    Boat trips for bird-watching
    and visits to historical and
    cultural sites.
Sah Naji Kwe Wilderness Spa
Rae-edzo, N.W.T.
Tel 867/371-3144
    Traditional outdoor
    experience and cross-cultural
    programs.

Note, exploring the North frequently requires charter flight services. A few of the commercially licensed operations are:
Alkan Air
Whitehorse, Yukon
Tel 867/668-2102
Trans North Helicopters
Whitehorse, Yukon
Tel 867/668-2177
North-Wright Air
Norman Wells, Yukon
Tel 867/587-2333
Aero Arctic Helicopters
Yellowknife, N.W.T.
Tel 867/873-5230
Air Tindi
Yellowknife, N.W.T.
Tel 867/669-8200
Great Slave Helicopters
Yellowknife, N.W.T.
Tel 867/873-2081
Simpson Air
Fort Simpson, N.W.T.
Tel 867/695-2505

As always, the tourism departments of the Yukon, the Northwest Territories, and Nunavut, as well as the national parks of the region, can supply you with longer lists of registered outfitters, suppliers, and other companies specializing in northern travel (addresses on page 346).

CREDITS

ILLUSTRATIONS CREDITS

Cover: (tl), Photographers Library. (tr), Image Bank. (bl), Tony Stone Images. (br), Tony Stone Images

9, AA Photo Library. 11, G Wallace. 13, Gerd Ludwig. 14, Telegraph Colour Library. 15, Rex/Sipa. 16/17, Maggie Steber. 18/19, Brian and Cherry Alexander. 21, Telegraph Colour Library. 22/23, Telegraph Colour Library. 24, G Wallace. 26/27 Bridgeman Art Library. 30, Corbis. 31, Giraudon. 32/33, E T Archive. 34, Hulton Getty. 35,Winston Fraser. 36/37, Maggie Steber. 38, J Allan Cash. 39, Ivy Images. 40/41, Gerd Ludwig. 42, AA Photo Library/Chris Coe. 43, Masterfile. 44/45, Telegraph Colour Library 46/47, Winston Fraser. 48a, Winston Fraser. 48b, Rex. 49a, Associated Press. 49b, Rex/Sipa. 50/51, Chris Noble. 52, Telegraph Colour Library. 53, Masterfile. 56, Colorific! 57, Hulton Getty. 58, Winston Fraser. 58/59, Winston Fraser. 60, Ivy Images. 61,Telegraph Colour Library/Masterfile. 62(t), Winston Fraser. 62(b), Ivy Images. 63, Winston Fraser. 66, AA Photo Library/Chris Coe. 67, Ivy Images. 68, Masterfile. 69, Colorific! 70, Masterfile. 71, Telegraph Colour Library. 72, Pix. 73, Telegraph Colour Library/Masterfile. 74, Telegraph Colour Library/Masterfile. 75, Telegraph Colour Library/Masterfile. 78(t), Winston Fraser. 78(b), AA Photo Library/Jean Francois Pin. 79, Winston Fraser. 80, Masterfile. 81(t), Masterfile. 81(b), Winston Fraser. 82, Masterfile. 84, Telegraph Colour Library. 85, Telegraph Colour Library/Masterfile. 86, Masterfile. 88/89, AA Photo Library/Jean Francois Pin. 91, Zefa. 92, AA Photo Library/Jean Francois Pin. 93a, Ann Ronan. 93(b), J Allan Cash. 94, Pix/Masterfile. 95, AA Photo Library/Jean Francois Pin. 96, Hulton Getty. 97, J Allan Cash. 98, Winston Fraser. 99(t), Winston Fraser. 99(b), AA Photo Library/Jean Francois Pin. 100, AA Photo Library/Jean Francois Pin. 101(t), Ivy Images. 101(b), AA Photo Library/Jean Francois Pin. 102, Colorific! 103, Jean François Pin. 106, Image Select. 107(t), Bridgeman Art Library. 107(b), Image Select. 108, Masterfile. 109, Masterfile. 110, (no copy) FPG. 111, Masterfile. 113, FPG. 114, Colorific! 115,Winston Fraser. 116, Ivy Images. 117, Winston Fraser. 119, Telegraph Colour Library. 120, Winston Fraser. 121, Pix/Masterfile. 122, AA Photo Library/Jean Francois

Pin. 123,Winston Fraser. 124, Winston Fraser. 125, AA Photo Library/Jean Francois Pin. 127, J Allan Cash. 128, Winston Fraser. 129, Winston Fraser. 130, Pix. 131, Masterfile. 133, Pix/Masterfile. 135, Telegraph Colour Library/Masterfile. 136 (no copy) AA Photo Library/Jean Francois Pin. 138, Pix. 139, Pix. 140, Ivy Images. 141, Masterfile. 144, Masterfile. 145,Winston Fraser. 147,Winston Fraser. 148, Ivy Images. 149, Winston Fraser. 150, Winston Fraser. 151, Winston Fraser. 152/3, Zefa. 154, Pix. 155,The Photo Source. 156, Planet Earth. 158(t), Mary Evans. 158(b), Mary Evans. 159, Masterfile. 160(t), AA Photo Library/Chris Coe. 160(b), Masterfile. 162, J Allan Cash. 163, Telegraph Colour Library. 165, AA Photo Library/Jean Francois Pin. 166, Telegraph Colour Library/Masterfile. 168, Ivy Images. 169, Zefa. 170/1, FPG. 172, Masterfile. 173, AA Photo Library/Jon Davison. 174, Chris Fairclough Colour Library. 175, AA Photo Library/Jean Francois Pin. 176, Telegraph Colour Library. 177, Telegraph Colour Library. 178/9, Telegraph Colour Library/Masterfile. 180, AA Photo Library/Jon Davison. 181, AA Photo Library/Jean Francois Pin. 183, AA Photo Library/Jon Davison. 184, Ivy Images. 185, AA Photo Library. 186, McMichael Canadian Art Collection. 187, McMichael Canadian Art Collection. 188, J Allan Cash. 189, J Allan Cash. 190/1, Pix. 192, Hulton Getty. 193, Masterfile. 194, Ivy Images. 195, Ivy Images. 196, Masterfile. 197, Ivy Images. 198(t), Winston Fraser/National Archives of Canada. 198(b), NigelTucker. 199, Masterfile. 200/1, Telegraph Colour Library/Masterfile. 203, Winston Fraser. 204, Pix/Masterfile. 205, Masterfile. 207, Masterfile. 208, Ivy Images. 209, Ivy Images. 210, Ivy Images. 211, Pix. 214/5, Winston Fraser. 216, Telegraph Colour Library/Masterfile. 217, Winston Fraser. 219(t), Brian &Cherry Alexander. 219(b), Masterfile. 220, Ann Ronan. 221(t), AA Photo Library/Chris Coe. 221(b), Bridgeman Art Library. 222, Masterfile. 223, Masterfile. 224, AA Photo Library/Chris Coe. 225(t), Telegraph Colour Library. 225(b), Winston Fraser. 226, Winston Fraser. 227, Winston Fraser. 228, National Archives of Canada. 229(a), Mary Evans. 229(b), Winston Fraser. 230, Pix/Masterfile. 231, Telegraph Colour Library/Masterfile. 232, AA Photo Library/Chris Coe. 233, Pix/Planet Earth. 234, Colorific! 235, Winston

Fraser. 236, Pix. 237, Ivy Images. 238, Telegraph Colour Library. 239, Telegraph Colour Library/Masterfile. 240, Winston Fraser. 241, Telegraph Colour Library/Masterfile. 242, G Wallace. 244/5, Masterfile. 246/7, G Wallace. 249, G Wallace. 250, J Allan Cash. 251, Telegraph Colour Library/Masterfile. 252, G Wallace. 254, G. Wallace. 255, FPG. 256, G Wallace. 256/7, Maltings. 258/9, TCL/Masterfile. 260, Chris Fairclough Colour Library. 261, Chris Coe. 262(t), AA Photo Library/Chris Coe. 262(b), National Archives of Canada. 263, J Allan Cash. 264, Pix/Masterfile. 265, AA Photo Library/Chris Coe. 266/7, Telegraph Colour Library. 268, Ivy Images. 269, AA Photo Library/Chris Coe. 270, FPG. 271, Chris Fairclough Colour Library. 275a, Telegraph Colour Library. 275b, Ann Ronan. 276/7, Zefa. 278, AA Photo Library/Michael Diggin. 280, Winston Fraser. 281, Pix. 282/3, AA Photo Library/Chris Coe. 283, AA Photo Library/Chris Coe. 285, AA Photo Library/Harold Harris. 286, Ivy Images. 287, J Allan Cash. 288, Telegraph Colour Library/Masterfile. 288/9, Telegraph Colour Library. 290, AA Photo Library. 293, Pix. 294, Pix. 295, AA Photo Library/Peter Timmermons. 296/7, Pix/Masterfile. 299, J Allan Cash. 303, Masterfile. 304, Telegraph Colour Library. 305, Spectrum. 306, Ivy Images. 307a, AA Photo Library/Chris Coe. 307(b), Bridgeman Art Library. 311, J Allan Cash. 312, Masterfile. 313, Pix. 316/7, Brian & Cherry Alexander. 318, Brian & Cherry Alexander. 318/9, Brian & Cherry Alexander. 321, Winston Fraser. 322(t), AA Photo Library/Chris Coe 322(b), Winston Fraser. 323, Winston Fraser. 324, AA Photo Library/Chris Coe. 325(t), J Allan Cash. 325(b), AA Photo Library/Chris Coe. 327(t), AA Photo Library/Chris Coe. 327(b), Ann Ronan. 327(br), Brian & Cherry Alexander. 328, Brian & Cherry Alexander. 329, AA Photo Library/Chris Coe. 332,Winston Fraser. 333, Ivy Images. 335(t), Ann Ronan. 335(b), Brian & Cherry Alexander. 336, Winston Fraser. 337, J Allan Cash. 338, Eric Hayes. 339, Colorific!